Meletij Smotryc'kyj

Meletij Smotryc'kyj

David A. Frick

Distributed by Harvard University Press
for the
Harvard Ukrainian Research Institute

Publication of this volume has been made possible through the support of Sonia Mykytka, outstanding benefactor of the Ukrainian Studies Fund, and a publications grant from the National Endowment for the Humanities, an independent federal agency.

ISBN 0-916458-55-5 (cl.)
ISBN 0-916458-60-1 (pb.)

∞ *This book has been printed on acid-free paper and bound to meet ANSI standard Z39.48.*

The Harvard Ukrainian Research Institute was established in 1973 as an integral part of Harvard University. It supports research associates and visiting scholars who are engaged in projects concerned with all aspects of Ukrainian studies. The Institute also works in close cooperation with the Committee on Ukrainian Studies, which supervises and coordinates the teaching of Ukrainian history, language, and literature at Harvard University.

Editorial Statement

The Harvard Series in Ukrainian Studies publishes original scholarship, archival research, and conference proceedings for the Harvard Ukrainian Research Institute, which was established in 1973 as an integral part of Harvard University.

Within the Series, we endeavor to use place-names in a form which reflects the language of the current political jurisdiction of the place, for example, L'viv instead of Lwów or L'vov, and Mahilëŭ instead of Mohyliv or Mogilev. When a place-name refers to a historical province or region that does not have an exact equivalent among contemporary states, then the historical form is preferred, for example, Podolia when referring to the palatinate of the Polish-Lithuanian Commonwealth, but Podillja when referring to the geographic region in contemporary Ukraine. Throughout, preference is given to English-language forms of long standing, for example, Kiev, Odessa, Warsaw, Moscow, Vienna, Munich.

The presentation of personal names defies such an easy formula. Many of those mentioned within the present volume were of Ruthenian ethnic origin, but were born into, and spent their active lives in, a Polish-speaking milieu within the Polish-Lithuanian Commonwealth. As a series dedicated to the encouragement and dissemination of Ukrainian studies, it is our mandate to promote a recognition of the Ruthenian element in the history of the Commonwealth. The term "Ruthenian" itself has varying meanings. At present, it often means simply "Ukrainian"; however, in the early-modern period it referred to a shared social, intellectual, and religious sphere that gave rise to modern Ukrainian and Belarusian culture, language, and identity. Since the Series is dedicated primarily to the Ukrainian part of this sphere, the names of all those considered Ruthenian are rendered in Ukrainian form, even though they may have been equally important to Belarusian history and culture.

Belarusian, Polish, Russian, and Ukrainian variants of place-names and personal names are given in the index as necessary.

Contents

List of Maps and Illustrations

A textual critic engaged upon his business is not at all like Newton investigating the motions of the planets: he is much more like a dog hunting for fleas. If a dog hunted for fleas on mathematical principles, basing his researches on statistics of area and population, he would never catch a flea except by accident. They require to be treated as individuals; and every problem which presents itself to the textual critic must be regarded as possibly unique.

A.E. Housman, "The Application of Thought to Textual Criticism," in his *Selected Prose*, John Carter, ed., pp. 132–33 (Cambridge, 1961).

Preface

Who? This is a question I have been asking myself since sometime in the 1978–1979 academic year, when Riccardo Picchio, then professor at Yale University, suggested I might write a dissertation on Meletij Smotryc'kyj. Since I had never heard the name before, I mentally reserved my question on this first occasion, in the hope of saving face with Professor Picchio. I went directly to the main reading room of Sterling Library and looked Smotryc'kyj up in the Brokgauz-Efron encyclopedia. There—as I would later find in other Slavic reference works and scholarly studies—I came upon one variant of the standard wisdom on this enigmatic and controversial figure.

The son of Herasym Danyjilovyč, who was himself one of the leading literary figures in Rus' in the late sixteenth century, and grandson of a certain "deacon Danyjil," also apparently a man of letters, Meletij Smotryc'kyj was born into one of Ukraine's first documented literary families sometime toward the end of a century marked by confessional controversy, probably circa 1577. Danyjil left only an anti-Hussite tract copied in his hand as testimony to his literary efforts. Herasym had been one of the editors of the Ostroh Bible of 1580–1581, the first printing of Holy Scripture in Church Slavonic, the sacral language of the Orthodox Slavs. Traditionally, he also is considered to have been the first rector of the Orthodox school established late in the century on the holdings in Ostroh of Prince Konstantyn Ostroz'kyj, where Meletij may have received his first schooling. Herasym was the author of confessional polemical pamphlets in defense of Orthodoxy and may have been one of Ukraine's earliest versifiers.

Meletij Smotryc'kyj was himself one of the outstanding figures in the great flourishing of Orthodox spirituality that occurred in the late sixteenth and early seventeenth century in response to the challenge posed first by the Polish heterodox (especially the more radical sects, who were most active in the eastern lands of the Polish-Lithuanian Commonwealth), and later, especially during the reign of King Sigismund III Vasa, by the Polish Counter-Reformation led by the Society of Jesus. His life reflected the tensions and contradictions that characterized his "nation," Rus', the so-called Ruthenian nation—by which was meant the Orthodox Christians of the Polish-Lithuanian Commonwealth, who inhabited roughly the territory of present-day Ukraine and Belarus. Ruthenian patriots—and let us assume for the moment that Smotryc'kyj was one—were torn between allegiance to their nation, Church, and traditions on the one hand, and a desire for personal or collective advancement, or both, in the increasingly hostile environment of the Commonwealth on the other hand. They further had to choose among allegiance to Orthodoxy, the allure of heterodox sects as a means for protecting their rights and privileges and for rebuffing the Catholics, and the appeal of Catholicism as a means for social advancement within the Commonwealth. Finally, after the Union of Brest in 1596, a Ruthenian could choose to swear allegiance to the Roman Catholic Church, to the Uniate version of Orthodoxy, which acknowledged the primacy of the pope, or to the traditional version of Orthodoxy, which did not.

In Smotryc'kyj's life, and in the life of his nation, we can observe one of the later acts in the drama of the European Age of Reform, all the more fascinating and important here because for the first time—at the eastern edge of the Western European cultural sphere—the Reformation and Counter-Reformation came into direct daily contact with the Byzantine world of Orthodox Slavdom. As in the Jesuit missions to India, China, Japan, and the New World (and this was a comparison Smotryc'kyj himself drew), we can examine here the ways in which more or less altered versions of established cultures resulted from the cross-cultural understandings and misunderstandings that arose when two or more highly developed cultures entered into a relationship of competition and of mutual forming and deforming.

Smotryc'kyj was among those best prepared to play this game. His world had encompassed much of Christendom—East and West, Protestant, Catholic, and Orthodox. His schooling had taken him from the Orthodox school of Ostroh, to the Jesuit Academy of Vilnius, to the Protestant universities of Leipzig and Wittenberg. He could use at least five languages: Greek, Latin, Church Slavonic, Polish, and Ruthenian. His career as archbishop of Polack brought him in person to Palestine and to Constantinople for talks with his former teacher, Patriarch Cyril Lukaris (who had, by that time, been trumpeted by Rome to all of Europe as a crypto-Calvinist). He was in frequent epistolary contact with the Vatican, particularly with the Holy Congregation for the Propagation of the Faith, concerning both his own career and the Roman "Eastern Question."

Smotryc'kyj's writings as a layman in the 1610s included a grammar of Church Slavonic that remained the standard until the early nineteenth century and a collection of sermons for the use of Orthodox preachers. This made him one of the leading men of letters in his nation. His consecration to the archiepiscopal see of Polack in 1620, and his subsequent appointment as archimandrite of the influential Vilnius Brotherhood Monastery of the Church of the Descent of the Holy Spirit made him second only to Metropolitan Jov Borec'kyj in the Orthodox Church hierarchy. At a practical level, due to his ready pen in the writing of polemical tracts and petitions to the king, he was perhaps the outstanding defender of the Orthodox Church in the period after the "illegal" reestablishment of the hierarchy in 1620.

However, after his return to Rus' from Constantinople, Smotryc'kyj converted—covertly in 1627, overtly in 1628—to the Uniate Church and spent the rest of his life writing pamphlets against his former coreligionists (he died at the end of 1633). His conversion has been portrayed as a betrayal by some and as a tardy recognition of the truth by others, and has made of him an object of abiding competition and controversy. It is readily apparent that, with the exception of studies devoted to the grammar alone, the historiographic debate has made the conversion the central episode in Smotryc'kyj's biography and has interpreted his entire life's work in the light of that act; thus, there are few studies that do not belong to what might be termed either Orthodox or Uniate and Roman Catholic interpretative traditions.

In the course of my dissertation research I became convinced that these interpretations were wrong, and that it might prove more fruitful to shift my attention from the "change" to the "constants," and specifically to a reevaluation of the contextual meaning Smotryc'kyj assigned to such concepts as Ruthenian language, Ruthenian faith, Ruthenian nation. This, I felt, might lead to a better, fuller ("more objective," I thought then) understanding of the ways Smotryc'kyj sought to shape himself, his language, his nation, his religion, his Church, and his culture in response to the various challenges he experienced at that time.

My investigation of Smotryc'kyj's language led me to consider one of his specific tasks in these terms: faced with two basic, confessionally marked versions of the Bible in Polish—one Protestant and the other Catholic—how did an Orthodox polemicist (who wrote primarily in Polish) cite Polish Scripture? This, I discovered, was not simply a matter of idle philological curiosity, but went to questions of authority at the center of the new Ruthenian national culture. The results of my investigation were written up for publication over a decade ago; I have on occasion referred to this research under the title "Meletij Smotryc'kyj's Critical Use of Biblical Citations." I have now incorporated some of the materials and the results of this research in parts of chapter 11 and in appendix B.

My interest in Smotryc'kyj's critical use of Polish Bibles led to a lengthy deviation into the realm of Polish sacred philology in the Reformation and the Counter-Reformation (Frick 1989), which in turn has led to a longer study of my favorite among the Polish biblical philologists of that age, the radical Antitrinitarian Szymon Budny (forthcoming as an introduction to a facsimile edition of Budny's translation of 1572 in the series *Biblia Slavica*). I have come to realize that there were some connections between Budny and Smotryc'kyj— and not limited to the direct borrowings of the latter from the former (Frick 1988). What I have come to find most interesting about both men are the ways in which they exploited the fact—of which they were both well aware—that they stood at the line of intersection between the Latin West and the Byzantine East and were thus able to shape themselves and their worlds by drawing to varying degrees on the resources of both cultures. In spite of his "radicalness," Budny was still more firmly a part of the dominant culture of his world than was Smotryc'kyj, and his position on the boundary was something over which he was (at least in his own mind) master: he could take and leave whatever suited him without considering how and to whom he might be required to render account. For Smotryc'kyj, too, this position was a source of great spiritual nourishment; but, as a representative of a self-consciously subordinate culture in a period of growing intolerance, it was also a source of the internal conflicts that moved him, tormented him, caused him to act, and caused him ultimately to fail in his attempts to realize his goals.

Although I have continued to investigate the constants in Smotryc'kyj's program for what might be termed (as a response to the Reformation and the Counter-Reformation or Catholic Reform) an Orthodox Slavic Reform, and to draw on some of my earlier studies in the process, I have shifted much of my attention in this book from the continuities back to the discontinuities, especially in the first half of my discussion. Nonetheless, here too I write in reaction to the two standard historiographic traditions that have emplotted Smotryc'kyj's life either as a tragedy or a romance, either as a story of betrayal and personal demise, motivated by greed and pride, or as a story of the pilgrim's progress to responsibility and salvation, driven by humility and an overriding respect for the truth.

Both of these views are totalizing: they tend to present all the events in a life as components of a harmonious whole. In my biography of Smotryc'kyj, I have chosen to emphasize precisely the fragmentariness, the disjointedness, the inharmoniousness of this "life." I do this for a number of reasons. Probably not least (but certainly not the most) important among them is the fact that I am comfortable with this ironic view of the world: I have attempted to understand who Smotryc'kyj was, and in the process I have, at least in part, found a Smotryc'kyj I am capable of understanding. But there are other important motivations for this mode of presentation and argumentation. The nature of the primary sources is one of them. A more honest and a more useful way of dealing with an extremely fragmentary documentation is to document the fragmentariness of our picture of this man and his culture. I am drawn to this mode of presentation, however, not only by the quantity of the sources, but also by their qualities: the documents at our disposal for a biography of Meletij Smotryc'kyj reflect, most of them, an attempt to impose a particular vision of events for particular goals in particular contexts. To phrase the problem in extreme terms, the sources seek to distort the "historical truth" about Smotryc'kyj for goals that were sometimes quite short-term, rather than to reflect that truth.

It has been the rather clear portrayals of Smotryc'kyj's allegiances and motivations that have reigned in the secondary literature. These are drawn, ultimately, from often uncritical readings of only one portion of the primary sources. In opposition to this interpretive tradition, I have chosen to focus upon what the primary sources sometimes obscured (only sometimes, because it also served the interests of Smotryc'kyj's opponents to portray him as a man of inconstancy): the lack of clarity in Smotryc'kyj's allegiances and the shadowy periods of his indecision. I seek, especially in the first half of my book, to offer as unclear a picture of his allegiances as possible. This, I have come to realize, is *one* key to *one* truth about who Smotryc'kyj was.

Working with Smotryc'kyj has made me attuned to some of the peculiarities of cultural borderlands. I have come to realize the importance of the fact that Smotryc'kyj himself saw his world as that place where the various authorities that defined Western European culture began to lose their hold over the allegiances of even the elites, and that Smotryc'kyj exploited this situation in his public postures—in different ways, perhaps, from the Orthodox and the Uniate sides of the fence, but quite definitely throughout his career. In the second half of this book I have sought supplementary information about who Meletij Smotryc'kyj was in the ways he exploited the areas of lessening authority in the various cultures to which he belonged in order to give shape to his vision of a personal and a Ruthenian national identity.

The approach I have developed in response to the witnesses in the Smotryc'kyj affair has certain affinities with some of the "new histories," and especially with the emphasis that "microhistory" places upon "individuals making choices and developing strategies within the constraints of their own time and place" (Muir 1991, viii), upon the contextual nature of historical truth, and upon the ways "misunderstandings . . . offer clues to now-lost ways of thinking" (Muir 1991, x). I find Giovanni Levi's description of the microhistorians' work a useful assessment of the similar problems with which I have been struggling:

> Their work . . . [employs] an action and conflict model of man's behaviour in the world which recognizes his—relative—freedom beyond, though not outside, the constraints of prescriptive and oppressive normative systems. Thus all social action is seen to be the result of the individual's constant negotiation, manipulation, choices and decisions in the face of a normative reality which, though pervasive, nevertheless offers many possibilities for personal interpretations and freedoms. The question is, therefore, how to define the margins—however narrow they may be—of the freedom granted an individual by the interstices and contradictions of the normative systems which govern him. In other words, an enquiry into the extent and nature of free will within the general structure of human society. In this type of enquiry the historian is not simply concerned with the interpretation of meanings but rather with defining the ambiguities of the symbolic world, the plurality of possible interpretations of it and the struggle which takes place over symbolic as much as over material resources (1991, 94–95).

In spite of the suggestiveness of this statement, I have for the most part resisted the temptation to recast my discussion in terms of the reluctant theoretical statements of the "microhistorians." Nonetheless, I would make a few observations concerning these methodological affinities. Carlo Ginzburg, for one, came to his "microhistorical" approach partially because of the wealth of sources in Italian archives. I came to my methodology rather because of the poverty of my sources. There is an issue of relativity here. Most "microhistorians" have focused on "history from below" (see, for example, Ginzburg's studies of the *benandanti* and of the cosmology of the heretical Friulian miller Menocchio). I have written a study of a member of the elite. (For how many individuals or episodes from the social netherlands of early modern Rus' would the sources permit a "microhistorical" investigation?) Italian archives contain sources on the ways of thinking of the subordinate classes that are rich relative to similar testimonies from other nations. My sources are relatively stingy for such an important member of an elite. The point in common between my study and the approaches of the "microhistorians" is an interest in reconstructing the manners in which individuals made their ways in the world and a preoccupation with those aspects of testimonies in the source materials that reflect conflicts of individual world views with each other and with the various larger authorities. It probably is not coincidental that I became convinced of the usefulness of my approach after I discovered the importance of the *ars dissimulandi* in Smotryc'kyj's life. The point is that an elite can be dominant with respect to its own subordinate classes, but subordinate with respect to other elites within a larger political and cultural community. The Ruthenian elites of the old Polish-Lithuanian Commonwealth lend themselves well to a "microhistorical" investigation. Even the elites (as the "microhistorians" acknowledge: see, for example, Redondi's study of Galileo), and especially Ruthenian elites, who were caught in the middle between the Ruthenian burghers and Cossacks, on the one hand, and the Polish and Lithuanian authorities, on the other hand, had to negotiate their ways in their worlds. We can learn much about these members of the elite, about the culture they represented and shaped, and about the cultures to which they reacted (both above and below) by attempting to follow them as they choose their paths, step by step.

This work has been in progress for some time now, and I owe thanks to more people than I can mention here. My first word of gratitude goes to my dissertation adviser Riccardo Picchio and to the other members of that committee, Alexander Schenker and Harvey Goldblatt. They guided my first efforts in this field and have continued to offer valued advice and support. Thanks also go to Francis J. Whitfield, Hugh McLean, and to my department at the University of California, Berkeley for taking an interest in someone who works in such a rarely visited field.

I benefitted from two fellowships in the course of this project: a Doctoral Dissertation Fellowship from IREX and Fulbright-Hays to conduct the initial research in Poland during the memorable year 1980–1981, and a Research Fellowship from the Alexander von Humboldt-Stiftung, which gave me the time to write much of this book in Germany in the fall of 1991. I offer thanks to my host in Bonn, Professor Hans Rothe, as well as to Professor Helmut Keipert and Ioannis Kakridis, for making the Slavistisches Seminar of Bonn University feel like home. Thanks also to Professor Tadeusz Ulewicz, the sponsor of my first studies in Poland, and to Aleksander Naumow and Andrzej Borowski, all of whom continue to receive me so warmly in Cracow and to make the Jagiellonian University feel like home, too.

Many libraries and their staffs provided help in completing this book, but two were crucial: the Library of the Jagiellonian University in Cracow and the National Library in Warsaw. To both, many thanks.

Although he was not directly connected with any of these institutions, I would like to say a special word of gratitude to Roman Koropeckyj, who continues to offer much appreciated criticisms and encouragement.

And finally, I give my thanks to members of the Publications staff at the Harvard Ukrainian Research Institute: to Dzvinka Dobrianska and Joan Fusco for their help typesetting the text; to Jennie Bush for the jacket design; to Marius L. Cybulski for his assistance and advice on terminology in the page proofs and the index; and to the editor of this book, Robert De Lossa, for his enthusiastic and careful work.

All remaining errors, it goes without saying, are my own fault.

A Note on Usage

1. The Gregorian calendar replaced the Julian calendar in Catholic Europe in 1582. The primary and secondary sources for this study employed both old and new calendars for their dates. In general, documents that originated in Rome, or represented correspondence between Rome and the Polish-Lithuanian Commonwealth (whether authors or recipients were Catholic or Uniate, and in both directions) employed the new, Gregorian calendar. Both Uniates and Orthodox employed the old, Julian calendar, which was then ten days behind the Gregorian, in their correspondence and works addressed to audiences within Rus'. Some nineteenth-century Russian scholars working on this material used old style dates, others used new style. I have done my best to sort this out. Single dates in my text are new style. Old style dates are followed by their new style equivalents (for example, 28 October/7 November 1629). A few specific warnings: Jakiv Suša used new style dates in his *vita* of Smotryc'kyj published in Rome in 1666. Stefan Golubev used old style dates in his studies, P. Žukovič used new.

2. Double page references (for example, Smotryc'kyj 1621b, 49^v/374) mark passages first in original printings and then in more readily available reprints or facsimile editions. Bibliographic information for the reprint or facsimile edition can be found under the entry for the original. In most instances, I was able to consult, and I cite from, the original. In those cases where the original was unavailable to me, I have indicated in the bibliographic entry that I cited from the reprint. I have not modernized any spellings. I have also resisted the urge to correct any of the obvious and not-so-obvious errors in the originals and reprints.

3. In the polemical rhetoric of the period the first person was always orthodox and catholic, signifying children of the One Holy Christian Church; the second person was reserved for schismatics, heretics, apostates, etc. I have found it useful in places to speak in the voices of the participants in the debates, and from all sides. I trust that this will be evident. My use in such passages of terms like schismatic, heretic, heterodox, and so forth, should imply no sign of disrespect or disapproval on my part for any of these people or their allegiances.

Meletij Smotryc'kyj

Who Was Meletij Smotryc'kyj?

 We know at least two Smotryc'kyjs. One was the author of a grammar of Church Slavonic (1618–1619) that would retain some of its authority throughout the Orthodox Slavic world until the appearance of Josef Dobrovský's *Institutiones* in 1822.[1] The other was the learned archbishop of Polack and the famous convert from Orthodoxy to the Uniate Church, perhaps the most notorious figure of his generation. Actually, Smotryc'kyj appears to us even more fragmented than this. The body of scholarly literature on the second Smotryc'kyj, unanimous in seeing his conversion as the key to his life, has offered two different views that are diametrically opposed in their interpretation of that event. There are thus two larger bodies of interpretation here: one has viewed the conversion as a betrayal of previous loyalties, whereas the other has seen it as Smotryc'kyj's belated recognition of the values offered by the opposition. The characterization of the entire man has been framed in terms of the chosen interpretation of his conversion.[2]

The foundation of the present study is a reaction to a number of the underlying assumptions that have governed all these works. First a note of optimism: if we hope to understand anything about Smotryc'kyj, we should attempt to put him back together. Philology should not be separated from the entire gamut of questions in the early seventeenth century related to Church and culture. At the core of Smotryc'kyj's formation, as that of so many others of his age, was the field that can be described as sacred philology. Doctrinal concerns shaped his philology, and philological arguments informed his confessional and cultural polemics. A separation of the two spheres does violence to a unity that lay at the heart of the man. Bringing the two spheres back together offers at least one more source of information for understanding the way Smotryc'kyj viewed and sought to shape himself and his culture in response to the pressures exerted by the Churches and by the Polish-Lithuanian state.

But now a note of pessimism: we are far removed from detailed knowledge of the "historical Smotryc'kyj." In Smotryc'kyj's case, this statement is much more than a historiographic piety. Most of the literature on Smotryc'kyj and his times has been shaped by an overriding optimism that we already know what key concepts—Orthodoxy, Catholicism, Byzantine culture, Latin culture, the Slavonic, Polish, and Ruthenian languages, the Polish, Lithuanian, and Ruthenian nations—meant, or ought to have meant, to Smotryc'kyj, and that we can thus focus on what the sources tell us about Smotryc'kyj's defense or betrayal of one or the other of them. We should rather begin with the assumption that we know very little for certain. We must identify the key concepts underlying Smotryc'kyj's thoughts and actions and then attempt—through a contextual analysis of usage—to understand the ranges of their meanings. And we need to be most alert where Smotryc'kyj seems to have used terms that we know; it is precisely here that we may overlook crucial differences in thought. Are we really certain that these terms, familiar to us from the better established cultures of Western Europe, maintained their precise definition at the intersection of the Latin and the Byzantine worlds? Are we really certain that the basic assumptions of the culture that Smotryc'kyj reflected and sought to shape survived the upheavals of the middle of the seventeenth century? Are we really certain that these terms did not undergo subtle (or even not so subtle) changes in meaning from the context of one polemical argument to another (even within the corpus of works of one author)?

This, then, is the first step: there can be no talk of betrayals or defenses until we are certain that we know what is being betrayed or defended. But once we have identified the key concepts and come to some understanding of their contextual meanings, we should carry our critical questioning one step further. Do we really understand the nature of conversion or betrayal in this period? Do we really know which aspects of faith and culture were, for Smotryc'kyj, defined by authority—and thus subject to conversion from or to, defense or betrayal of—and which were relatively undefined, subject to innovation, shaping, etc? As Frank E. Sysyn has noted (1984, 169), the habit of creating "camps with completely opposed religious views, linguistic preferences, cultural sources, and literary styles does not correspond to the realities of seventeenth-century Ukraine, where the lines were neither so clearly nor so consistently drawn."[3] We see occasional fascinating hints of these attitudes in the sources: Smotryc'kyj described one of his predecessors in the archiepiscopal see of Polack (Herman Zahors'kyj) as a man "only somewhat in the Union."[4] For us who have come to think in terms of "either-or" definitions of Orthodoxy and Catholicism, this sounds like being "only slightly pregnant"; but apparently Smotryc'kyj, for one, could envisage—at least in this particular polemical context—an entire range of possibilities.

Perhaps the most critical hindrance to us in our quest for the historical Smotryc'kyj is the quantity and quality of the documents. I refer to the meager quantity of documents dealing with Smotryc'kyj and his age partially out of the frustration and envy I feel when I compare the corpus of materials in this area with that available to my colleagues who study the lives of figures occupying similar positions in other nations of Reformation and Counter-Reformation Europe. The sum of our sources for a study of the life of Meletij Smotryc'kyj is quite limited: the writer's own polemical, homiletical, grammatical, and epistolary work; the polemical works written in answer to him; and a handful of other isolated references in various contemporary legal, polemical, homiletic, and historiographical documents.[5] Major factual questions remain in a chronology of Smotryc'kyj's life that, from our vantage point, contains gaps of entire years in crucial periods.

And yet, Smotryc'kyj is certainly much more clearly delineated than many of his contemporaries—relatively important men, at that—who remain for us little more than names and titles. Aspects of Smotryc'kyj's biography appeared with some frequency in the sources. In fact, Smotryc'kyj himself, his views, his behavior, his allegiance, were significant aspects of the confessional polemic in which he took part throughout his life. The real difficulty in knowing the historical Smotryc'kyj lies more in the quality than in the quantity of the documents: most of our scanty primary sources for a biography of Meletij Smotryc'kyj—including "autobiographical" statements—stemmed from an often vicious campaign of rumor, innuendo, half-truth, and outright slander, at the heart of which was a struggle for control over the man's public persona, and thereby, it was hoped, over his realm of action.

We should further bear in mind that Smotryc'kyj lived at the height of what might be termed the age of "honest dissimulation." For a variety of reasons many figures of the Age of Reform (and this included the Orthodox Reform) often maintained a healthy silence on their "own" views, if they had such. The *ars dissimulandi* was a highly codified branch of knowledge in the sixteenth and seventeenth centuries.[6] As will become evident later on, Smotryc'kyj was well read in the theory of licit lying, and the primary sources clearly reflect his use of its techniques on at least two occasions. We should not, then, expect to find that he presented his beliefs on all issues *expressis verbis*.

We may not always find the historical truth about Smotryc'kyj near the surface of the primary sources. But we may find some other things: that all sides wished to control his allegiance; that his allegiance was often in question; that his allegiance was difficult to control; that certain aspects of his life—real or alleged—were useful in attempting to gain control over him or his posthumous fame; that at certain points in his life he felt a need to dissimulate. And if we listen to these testimonies with care and suspicion we may be able to learn something about the man Smotryc'kyj wished to seem, about the man his contemporaries wished him to be, and even, on occasion, about the man he was.

Let us consider just one example here. Suppose we wished to pose the following question: was Smotryc'kyj wordly or ascetic, arrogant or humble? Of course, these could be two separate questions: we can find plenty of examples of arrogant spirituality and modest epicureanism in the daily paper. But in Smotryc'kyj's case the debate has united them; and so, for the sake of argument, let us also consider the question in the terms in which it has come down to us: was the archbishop of Polack a haughty man concerned only with his own fame and temporal well-being, or did he lead a life of quiet asceticism in expectation of his future reward?

Two examples from the scholarly literature will suffice. One of the more valuable treatments of Smotryc'kyj's life was written by the nineteenth-century Russian Orthodox historian Stefan Golubev, whose monumental study of Peter Mohyla and his times remains an important source of information. How did Golubev explain Smotryc'kyj's conversion to the Uniate Church?

> Meletij Smotryc'kyj was faced with the following perspective: on the one hand, his faltering power as archbishop and archimandrite, inevitable reproaches and suspicion from his flock, insufficiency of material means, and, on the other hand (on the condition that he would go over to the side of the Uniates), archimandritehood of the wealthy Derman' monastery, an honorable place in the ranks of the Uniate

hierarchy, etc. In order to resist the temptation before him it would have been necessary to have sufficiently firm religious convictions, to have a sincere devotion to Orthodoxy and to place its interests above one's own personal interests. The absence of these traits along with a highly developed ambition were precisely—at least in our opinion—the main reason for Meletij Smotryc'kyj's switch to the Latin-Uniate camp (Golubev 1883, 145–46).

But in describing the same—that is, the post-conversion—period in Smotryc'kyj's life, the twentieth-century Ukrainian Catholic (Uniate) historiographer Father Meletij M. Solovij wrote:

> Meletij was content with a worn-out cassock, and none of the monks had a more wretched cassock than he. He gladly wore a hair shirt, and he girded himself with a leather strap. He did without an attendant, and he kept only church singers and a secretary (Solovij 1977, 262).

Which one is "historically accurate?"

We should note first that both of these pictures are offered in support of interpretations of Smotryc'kyj's conversion. Until we are certain that we understand the nature and significance of his conversion (was it really central?), we should mistrust all characterizations of Smotryc'kyj that stem from an attempt to explain that act. I am convinced that both scholars could have offered their characterizations of Smotryc'kyj without reading any of the primary sources. Golubev—by far the more thorough scholar of the two—began from the unexpressed point of departure that no one, in any age, could possibly have a serious, dignified reason for converting to the Uniate Church, therefore—and it was only at this point that his reasoning became explicit—Smotryc'kyj must have been drawn by desire for personal gain. This conviction led Golubev to misrepresent the facts; it is not at all clear from the information he offered that the convert's material condition and standing within the hierarchy was better in the Uniate Church. In fact, Smotryc'kyj was unable to obtain a regular bishopric in the Ruthenian Uniate Church, and it was only with some difficulty and delay that he managed to obtain from Pope Urban VIII an archbishopric *in partibus infidelium*. It is true that conversion was made a condition for obtaining the archimandritehood of Derman', but it does not necessarily follow that Smotryc'kyj converted in order to receive this position. Only a year before—a little-known document tells us—the Orthodox nobleman Bohdan Solomerec'kyj had given

Smotryc'kyj control over the Barkalabava Monastery (*Arxeografičeskij* 1867, 31–38). And conversely, Father Solovij could imagine nothing but altruistic reasons for converting to his own Church, even though it is not at all certain that Smotryc'kyj was as indifferent to the things of this world as he portrayed him.

Both these scholars, however, had read some of the primary sources, and Golubev had made a thorough study of them. It was precisely these documents that told them that the conversion was a central question; moreover, one portion of the sources—for each scholar it was a different portion—told each of them the "correct answer" to the question. In fact, the two critical opinions I have cited above are pale reflections of a rather more raucous exchange of charges and counter-charges preserved in the contemporary sources.

Let us examine those sources carefully. I begin at the end, with the posthumous Roman Catholic and Uniate views of Smotryc'kyj. In his funeral oration on the death of Meletij Smotryc'kyj, the Polish Jesuit Wojciech Kortycki, who was the recent convert's confessor in his last days at Derman' and head of the chapter in nearby Ostroh, used a dramatic flourish to bring Smotryc'kyj's asceticism to life before his audience:

> And here I ask my listeners, eagerly incline to me not only your ears, but also your eyes. Did you know, worthy listeners, His Grace, Father Meletij Smotryc'kyj, Archimandrite of Derman'? Did you know a man, most illustrious for his piety, wisdom, and dignity? Did you know a man who, ruined through constant labor and truly dried out through daily tribulations, barely kept his soul within him? Did you know these limbs, dried out through fastings, these bones truly dessicated in illnesses and tribulations? So you knew him? Then look here at what sort of weapon he used to discipline his body.[7]

At this point the printed version of the sermon switched from black letter to italics in describing Kortycki's performance at the funeral service, *"Here the people were shown from the pulpit [Smotryc'kyj's] scourge of hitherto unseen harshness, twisted into two straps of wire loops and tightly tied with hard knots."*[8]

This piece of funereal theatrics was to make its way into the official Uniate *vita* of Smotryc'kyj published some thirty years later. While he was in Rome in the mid-1660s pressing a campaign for Vatican support for the Uniate Church in the Ruthenian lands after the Xmel'nyc'kyj

Uprising, the archbishop of Chełm, Jakiv Suša, wrote lives of the two figures that had come to represent the aspirations of his flock: Josafat Kuncevyč, the Uniate Archbishop of Polack and Vicebsk, and Meletij Smotryc'kyj, Josafat's onetime Orthodox counterpart and nemesis. The first, who died a martyr's death at the hands of angry Orthodox citizens in Vicebsk on 12 November 1623, had been beatified in 1643, and Suša's mission in Rome, it is clear, was to accelerate the process of canonization, since the Uniate Ruthenian Church was in dire need of its patron saint. In the process that led to Josafat's beatification, Smotryc'kyj had been declared at least indirectly responsible for the mob's actions; and his conversion to the Uniate Church had been offered as evidence for Josafat's efficacy as intercessor. This formula, which was repeated with increasing frequency in the beatification process, became the title of Suša's *vita: The Saul and Paul of the Ruthenian Union Transformed by the Blood of Blessed Josafat, Or Meletij Smotryc'kyj* (Rome, 1666). To impress upon his readers the asceticism of the final years of Smotryc'kyj's monastic life as Archimandrite of the Uniate monastery at Derman' in Volhynia, Suša described the reaction of the audience to Kortycki's sermon.[9] He even thought it worth informing his readers that the scourge itself had found a suitable resting place in the treasury at Derman' Monastery where it could serve as a model for the faithful.[10]

In the works of both Kortycki and Suša, the account of the scourge was emblematic proof for a more general claim that Smotryc'kyj's very existence was characterized by humility and spirituality. According to Kortycki, Smotryc'kyj employed three weapons in his struggle with his earthly self: constant labor in discourse, meditation, and writing on behalf of the faith;[11] severe fasts, during which he would eat only a little morsel of fish and drink very little wine, even when Kortycki himself suggested to him that he make allowances for his weakened state;[12] and a coarse hair shirt that he removed only once a week, or whenever he needed to flagellate himself.[13]

Although Suša wrote thirty years later and drew much of his information from Kortycki, he often managed to add some details— whether from eyewitness reports or from his own invention, it is difficult to say. According to Suša, Smotryc'kyj not only drank no wine, but he also refrained from any of the other, more popular, local alcoholic drinks.[14] He added to the monastery building at Derman' and improved its library and collection of liturgical apparatus, drawing not only from the monastery's funds, but even (nota bene) from his own sources.[15]

Why did these two writers devote so much attention to Smotryc'kyj's humility and other-worldliness? The naive answer, which should not automatically be discounted, is that at some level this was simply how the man lived. Another answer is that they were writing encomia, the one a funeral oration, the other a *vita,* and these are among the traits that are expected of good Catholic bishops. Yet another, related answer is that in 1634 and in 1666 the Uniate side needed a saint, and both works bear the stamp of an organized attempt to further the campaign to attain one. (Here Smotryc'kyj's function may have been ancillary: if Smotryc'kyj was a saint, then how much more miraculous was Josafat's intercession?) All of these answers may be correct to some degree, but we need to be aware of another aspect: in stressing Smotryc'kyj's spirituality, both Kortycki and Suša were answering specific charges to the contrary. In fact, it was precisely the Uniate and Roman Catholic side that had helped only a few years earlier to establish quite a different view of Smotryc'kyj.

What were some of the Uniate and Roman Catholic views of Smotryc'kyj that were expressed before his conversion? (As will soon become clear, the crucial criterion in chronology in this study will be not whether the sources dealt with the pre- or post-conversion Smotryc'kyj, but whether they were themselves written before or after that event.) In response to Smotryc'kyj's *Verification of Innocence* of 1621, the *Letter* written that same year in the name of leading (Uniate) Ruthenian noblemen stressed the *superbia* of the recently elevated Orthodox archbishop of Polack:

> Possessed by disgusting ambition, you [i.e., the "illegally" consecrated Orthodox hierarchy] force your way, against God and the people, onto the thrones of the metropolitan and the bishops. But that of Polack entices you the most: Reverend Melentij already appropriates for himself the insignia and episcopal power of the archbishopric of Polack, in spite of the authority of His Majesty the King—a pitiful thing, since he [i.e., the king] did not submit or nominate him. He uses the titles, submits them in print, himself revering himself (truly a ludicrous thing), and he celebrates not only in episcopal, but perhaps even in metropolitan vestments. He has episcopal seals cut for himself, he has inscriptions made on chalices. He allows himself to be led by the hand of the nobility (*ne quid ambitioni et arrogantiae desit* [lest there be anything lacking in ambition and arrogance]), being himself of the condition which he is, and he flaunts this.[16]

Smotryc̆kyj himself, for all practical purposes the sole spokesman for the Orthodox side in this period, responded by focusing upon Father Smotryc̆kyj's love of learning and long-standing desire to enter the monastery (he wrote anonymously and referred to himself in the third person):

> Father Smotryc̆kyj, who spent his young years up to manhood honorably on liberal arts, both here in the fatherland and in foreign countries, when, after a few years spent on courtly amusements as a sort of rest from the dust of the school, it came time for him to order his life and to employ, for his own benefit and that of his neighbors, the tool of the studies that he had gathered for so many years, had always intended not to enter the monastic order (for which he had an eager soul almost since the days of his childhood) until he had obtained certain knowledge of the intended goal of both sides within the confounded brethren (for that had always bothered him).[17]

After 1628 the positions on this question would be reversed. If the Uniate Church now needed Smotryc̆kyj to be a saint, the Orthodox side could not afford to lose their most talented defender without mounting a campaign to tarnish his reputation. Thus when Smotryc̆kyj converted to the Uniate Church, charges of greed and arrogance surfaced once again, but this time in Orthodox works. In the *Synopsis* of 1632—a brief work of historiography put out by the Orthodox Brotherhood of Vilnius, which aimed at influencing the policy of the new king toward the Orthodox after the death of Sigismund III Vasa—the entire entry for the year 1628 was devoted to the Smotryc̆kyj affair:

> Dealing with us perfidiously in this year, Meletij Smotryc̆kyj revealed himself to be similar to his predecessor [i.e., Leontij Karpovyc̆] (who spoke one thing with his mouth, but had another thing in his heart). For in the Church of the Holy Miracle-Working Monastery of the Caves, during the feast of the Dormition of the Most Holy Virgin, suffering no compulsion, he himself voluntarily wrote a revocation, and in accordance with it, in the church during the Divine Liturgy (in the presence of a very large gathering of other clergy and of worthy and excellent men, both from the Crown and from Lithuania), immediately after the reading of the Gospel, he tore and burned his *Apology*; and still, having returned peacefully to Derman' Monastery, the wretch nonetheless returned *in vomitus suos* [to his own vomit], and that in order to gain a miserable few thousand *złotys*.
>
> He also harmed our Brotherhood by taking improperly, and keeping illegally, ecclesiastical apparatus of gold, silver, pearls, and precious

stones, also a great many books from our Brotherhood library—both Eastern and Western theologians, as well as various historians— which had been sent to him from our monastery at his urgent request; about all of which there have already been some court cases, and we will not hesitate to bring suit against him in its proper time and against whomever the law declares liable.[18]

I will return later to the specific allegations concerning Smotryc'kyj's behavior at the Kiev Council of 1628. What is important here is that the Orthodox explained the defection of their former archimandrite and archbishop by characterizing him as a man motivated above all by material interests. The Orthodox did indeed bring legal charges against Smotryc'kyj, and similar allegations would appear in other works of the period.[19]

The Uniate Smotryc'kyj himself responded to these charges by acknowledging that he did not lack for the things of this world in either Church, and thus he certainly would not have given up the known for the unknown if he had been interested only in improving his material lot:

And do not even you know, you hypocrite, that your Vilnius schismatic monastery was a greater trap of gold for me, which dressed me from head to foot in gold, than Derman' Monastery. My greed ought to have been greater there than here, for there the parishioners of the archbishopric of Polack from all of Belarus remembered me.[20]

And in a letter to the cupbearer of Volhynia, Lavrentij Drevyns'kyj, a political leader among the Orthodox laity, Smotryc'kyj made reference to his desire to reimburse the Brotherhood for some books and church apparatus, this perhaps a reference to the matter of the "stolen" books and materials.[21]

Finally, in a Greek encomiastic poem on Smotryc'kyj entitled ΜΑΙΣΤΟΡΟΣ, which was appended to Smotryc'kyj's *Paraenesis* of 1629, Mikołaj Żórawski, professor of Greek at the Jagiellonian University, devoted one line of verse to the archbishop's lack of interest in things of this world: "Nor is he wont to desire earnestly the things of the earth."[22]

Thus when Kortycki and Suša portrayed Smotryc'kyj's monastic life, they were not simply using somewhat conventional terms to reflect some real or desired qualities of their subject; they also were conscious that if they were to have a saint of Smotryc'kyj, they would have to answer an opposite, equally conventional depiction—and one which their side had had a hand in establishing. On this question and many others, Suša presented the most "optimistic" picture. In his *vita* there was no hint that even the Saul of Disunion was ever motivated by anything but the most spiritual—if misguided—of motives. Here we read that the young Smotryc'kyj's life as an Orthodox monk was exemplary,[23] and (as we have read above) that the older Smotryc'kyj improved the monastery's collection of ecclesiastical apparatus and books partially out of his own pocket (Suša 1666, 127). It is quite possible that both of these pieces of information were answers to specific charges to the contrary: the old Uniate allegation that the young Smotryc'kyj was motivated by a lust for power, and the new Orthodox allegation that the older Smotryc'kyj had stolen books and equipment from the Orthodox Brotherhood of Vilnius.

So who was Meletij Smotryc'kyj? Was he the vain and arrogant, plebeian upstart of the early Uniate depiction, the modest scholar-monk of his own Orthodox depiction, the greedy hypocrite of the later Orthodox depiction, or the saintly ascetic of the later Uniate depiction? We do not receive any enlightenment on these questions from the series of allegations and counter-allegations contained in the primary sources. In fact, it is largely because of the allegations that the question has been raised. Only one of the charges cited above—the theft of books and equipment—is subject in any way to verification. A recent catalogue of Smotryc'kyj's books found in the monastery at Derman' is able to tell us only that these particular objects seem not to have been stolen from Vilnius (Losievskij 1986, 88–89). We therefore still do not know whether Smotryc'kyj was a thief.

There are no "objective" sources of information on this question. In his grammar of Church Slavonic of 1618–1619, as an example of the use of the accusative case for the direct object of a transitive verb, Smotryc'kyj wrote: "I drank wine, and I slept soundly."[24] But this is hardly evidence that Smotryc'kyj had been a wine-bibber as an Orthodox layman. Court records of 1621 described the pomp and opulence of Smotryc'kyj's entry into Vilnius as the newly consecrated archbishop of Polack in November 1620 (see below, p. 78). But these testimonies were elicited from Orthodox burghers who were prisoners, at the moment, of the Catholic authorities in Vilnius, and the fact that they offered the version their interrogators wished to hear lessens their value as "disinterested" testimony.

One important point in all this is that the allegation of mercenary motives was a standard ploy in the polemics of this period. Anyone who converted to your religion did so only out of the most spiritual of motives; he had no interest in the richer benefice or promise of personal safety that your king or your archbishop had promised him. He had simply come to recognize the truth. But anyone who converted from your religion could only have been interested in temporal wealth. No other acceptable explanation could be found. As the Uniate Smotryc'kyj himself quite reasonably pointed out, the archimandrites of the (wealthy and influential) St. Michael's Monastery in Kiev and others were not (in Orthodox eyes) motivated by greed and lust for power; why should only the monastery at Derman' arouse these emotions?[25]

Consider the case of Smotryc'kyj's one-time opponent, the Uniate archbishop of Polack and martyr, Josafat Kuncevyč. The grand chancellor of Lithuania, Lew Sapieha, had written to him on 12 March 1622 in a letter that became widely known at the time: "Your Grace's actions [are] governed more by ambition and *privato odio* [by private hatred], than *fraterna charitate* [by brotherly love]."[26] But in a sermon delivered on 12 November 1646 (and printed in 1647 on the eve of the Xmel'nyc'kyj Uprising), Father Kazimierz Woysznarowicz, secretary to King Władysław IV, praised the martyr through a rhetorical denial of these same allegations, "And what raised our Josafat on high? Shall I say it was high titles? No. Then perhaps lordly incomes and preeminence? No. Then, finally, presumption concerning himself? No. Love of one's neighbor, this raised him up."[27]

Some images, formulations, modes of argumentation became commonplaces in the polemical literature of the time. Consider, for example, the image of the Orthodox children, who, without a proper Church hierarchy, were dying without baptism. The Orthodox cupbearer of Volhynia, Lavrentij Drevyns'kyj, employed this pathetic commonplace in his speech before the Polish Sejm in 1620 (see Bantyš-Kamenskij 1805, 66). Smotryc'kyj liked it and used it the next year in his *Verification of Innocence*.[28] Even the Catholic Lew Sapieha liked it and cited it in rebuffing Josafat Kuncevyč in a letter dated 22 April 1622.[29] In similar fashion, some putative qualities of Meletij Smotryc'kyj became commonplaces in the public and private discussions.

Which version, then, was the "real" Meletij Smotryc'kyj? It is possible, of course, that Smotryc'kyj was all these things at various times, or even at the same time: pious, arrogant, generous, mercenary, somewhat brave, somewhat cowardly, etc. But perhaps the more important question here is why we have continued to accept the "either-or" formulations which we have inherited from the contemporary sources. Why are we satisfied with cartoon depictions of serious people who lived in times of great change and were subject to a variety of motivations in making the difficult decisions required of them? My own impression is that modesty did not come easily to Smotryc'kyj, who had no doubts about his own abilities, at least when he compared them with those around him. Smotryc'kyj chose to represent himself to Patriarch Cyril Lukaris at one point by drawing on the well-known saying: "In the land of the blind, the one-eyed man is king."[30] This is typical of the mixture of arrogance and humility that shaped Smotryc'kyj's view of himself and his world. And as to the charge of materialism, it is not unthinkable that he sought to be as comfortable as possible once he converted to the Uniate Church, and that, at the same time, he wore a hair shirt and employed a fearful scourge to ease his conscience. We still do not know that his conversion, or his life in general, were characterized by one of these traits to the exclusion of another, or really that any one of them was foremost in Smotryc'kyj's character. And the thing I wish to stress here is that we certainly do not know these things from the sorts of allegations I have cited above.

We can continue the scholarly debate over Smotryc'kyj's life in the terms that have prevailed in the past, by asking what character trait caused his conversion. If we do so, however, we should be aware that we will be repeating, or denying, the allegations that were in the air during his life. We will either condemn him for inconstancy in betraying his faith (or his nation, or his culture, depending upon how we define those terms), or we will congratulate him for finally recognizing the truth. While we may certainly continue to argue whether Smotryc'kyj's actions were ultimately beneficial to the Ruthenian Church, the Ruthenian nation, or Ruthenian culture, we should be aware that by doing so we may not understand the man himself any better, or the problems he faced.

Called upon to judge primary sources that "distort" the record through a variety of sins of omission and commission, we might be tempted to sympathize with the sixteenth-century English magistrate who, exasperated with the regular recourse of Catholic offenders to mental reservation, exclaimed: "Yf this Doctrine should be allowed, it would supplant all Justice, for we are men, and no Gods, and can iudge but according to [men's] outward actiones and speeches, and not accordinge to their secrette and inward intentions."[31] But even in their silence, opacity, distortion, and mendaciousness, the sources do speak to us of Smotryc'kyj and his world. In the case cited above, the sources do not necessarily tell us whether Smotryc'kyj was wordly or spiritual, arrogant or humble. But they do tell us, at a minimum, that these allegations were made at the time, that he was subject to such allegations, and that they were useful in particular contexts to particular representatives of particular parties in attempting to control his public persona. The way Smotryc'kyj responded to these allegations shows, I believe, that he was not entirely ignorant of the allure of earthly things and that he was not—or, at least, did not wish to seem—governed by these considerations when he made important decisions.

How, then, to proceed in the face of these suspicions about the nature of the testimonies? I have decided to write in the first part of my book not so much a biography of Smotryc'kyj (although I hope the outlines of his life will appear here in more convincing form than in previous treatments), as an examination of the functioning of the rumor mill in the Smotryc'kyj affair, a history of the contemporary debate about the man and his allegiances. This sort of study will necessarily imply a certain repetition. Two possible schemes come to mind. I could either offer a series of contemporary treatments—more or less complete, as they happen to be—of Smotryc'kyj's life, or I could cover the main events of his life's course once in order, summoning all the witnesses as they speak to each stage in his life, thus jumping frequently from testimony to testimony and presenting them as a sort of dialogue within each chapter. The first scenario tells the story of competing representations of a controversial man; the second tells the story of a controversial man about whom there were competing representations. The differences are perhaps slight, but I have chosen the second method, above all other considerations because it maintains the object of representation, rather than the various representations themselves, at the center of attention.

But are there no other means to counter the tendency—given this mode of portrayal and the nature of the witnesses—of the object of investigation to dissolve into the conflicting representations that served the purposes of particular groups or individuals at particular moments?

Where is the "real" Smotryc'kyj to be found in the stingy documentation, in the distortions produced by the sources, in his conformity to the expectations of opponents and supporters? One answer is that these fragmented, unclear, and contradictory pictures also contain partial glimpses of the "real" Smotryc'kyj: his "outward actiones and speeches" as well as his "secrette and inward intentions" were often ambiguous, unclear, internally and mutually contradictory; and the "real" Smotryc'kyj did often conform to the authorities to which he had publicly given his allegiance. But another answer is that the tensions between program and practice, between outward behavior and internal intent (wherever we can infer this), between attempts to conform and failure to do so—in short, the contradictions themselves, can sometimes lead us by way of a kind of spiritual triangulation to some fruitful areas in which to search for further traces of the the "real" Smotryc'kyj.

My point of departure in the second half of this book (and one I will seek to make persuasive in chapter 10) is that Smotryc'kyj was well aware of the "rules of the game" involved in public pronouncements concerning himself and his beliefs about Ruthenian culture, faith, and nation; and above all, that he knew the levels of risks involved in any deviation from the various authorities to which he had publicly offered his allegiance. If we can catch Smotryc'kyj deviating from these authorities, if we can catch him taking certain risks (when he could have dissimulated or remained silent), then perhaps we will find a clue to something closer to the heart of his existence.

Thus, in the second half of my book I have sought to bring to light the ways in which Smotryc'kyj—in a variety of specific contexts from the realms of language and culture, faith and Church, nation and state—distanced himself and his views of himself and his nation from the authorities to which he had (or ought to have) given his allegiance. In other terms, in the second part of this book I will investigate the obscurities in Smotryc'kyj's allegiances (many of which will come to light in the first part) for clues to a more comprehensive understanding of his actions.

The excursuses that comprise the second half of my book grew out of minor details, observed peculiarities, deviations from what I had come to consider normal paths for Smotryc'kyj. The notion I have followed in each case is that each detail reflected something more far-reaching, a pattern of behavior that put Smotryc'kyj in a position of conflict, caught between authorities to which he needed to appear to conform (and to which he did conform, for the most part) and his own views, which were not always and in every detail identical with either of the increasingly rigid orthodoxies to which he declared his allegiance at various times.

I offer in this part of my study four excursions into areas of tension between conformity, dissent, and dissimulation in Meletij Smotryc'kyj's life and work. This approach, I have discovered, suits the materials and the state of our studies well. In the general absence of reliable authorities of our own—historical grammars and dictionaries, biographies and chronologies, histories of doctrine and political thought—we can exploit one of the properties of the culture we are studying: this was an age of well-established authorities for many walks of life, and the people of this time defined themselves as individuals and groups, defined their cultures, confessions, and nations, by their adherence to a particular set of recognizable authorities. Moreover, the authorities were accorded a hierarchy: this is to say, deviation from an authority at the higher end of the scale brought with it (or could possibly bring with it) a greater risk and a harsher penalty than deviation from an authority at the lower end of the scale (for example, heresy versus orthographic deviation, to choose an extreme example, in a culture that had ceased to make a direct connection between the two types of deviation).

What I will be investigating here is thus a type of aberrant behavior. My assumption is that in taking risks of these sorts, Smotryc'kyj may have revealed something of himself that was hidden in acts of conformity. Further, since these individual acts of deviation can be set against a hierarchy of authorities, we may be able to assign at least approximate values to acts of nonconformity.

This said, I need to make a number of qualifications. Smotryc'kyj did not reveal "himself" only in acts of nonconformity. The "real" Smotryc'kyj can also be found in acts of conformity to expectations, and I attempt to touch on this problem in these essays as well. Second, many authorities within the realm of Ruthenian Orthodoxy existed in theory but not in practice. For example, Ruthenian polemicists and cultural activists made reference in their debates with Catholics and Protestants, as well as in their internecine arguments, to a series of Orthodox authorities ranging from grammars of Church Slavonic to expositions of the Ruthenian faith. But in so doing, they were often aware that there was little practical agreement as to the nature of these authorities. A Ruthenian apologist began, then, with two things: a loyalty to, and pride in, Ruthenian Orthodox culture and a nagging sense of insufficiency prompted by an awareness that his culture was not as well defined as those of the opponents. Thus an Orthodox apologist faced a dilemma— he first had to defend the authority of his culture and, since he was frequently aware that there was no explicit agreement within his own side on some of the questions posed, he had at the same time to seek to define his authorities, often pretending that the definition he was offering was not his own ad hoc solution but the consensus of the ages. In this climate, the Orthodox apologist was nearly always on the defensive, since he had agreed to play the game according to the rules imposed by his opponents.[32]

In the chapters that comprise the second half of my book I have examined the way Smotryc'kyj played the game in three realms— languages and culture (chapter 11), Church and faith (chapter 12), and nation and state (chapter 13). In each case I have been interested in two things: the ways in which Smotryc'kyj established a set of Ruthenian Orthodox authorities, and the areas where he deviated from authority— either those he had himself established at the programmatic level or those espoused by the particular group to which he had declared his official allegiance at a given moment. In chapter 10 I examine evidence for Smotryc'kyj's understanding of the "rules of the game," his beliefs about the nature of authority, and his practice in the realm of conformity, dissent, and dissimulation.

The general purpose of this book is to discover what Smotryc'kyj and his contemporaries told us, directly or indirectly, about the ways in which the archbishop of Polack sought to represent and to shape himself and his culture in response to various pressures. My focus, then, will be not on the universal but on the specific: how was a given aspect of a persona, an article of faith, a grammatical precept, or a lexical item, and so forth, manipulated in a particular context? What was the contextual value assigned to it by those who made use of it? To what end was it exploited in the public and private debates?

The studies to which I have reacted are characterized by their proprietary nature toward Smotryc'kyj and his culture. This is something that they have inherited from the seventeenth-century sources. After all, it requires a sense of possession in order to feel a sense of loss. I begin by denying them ownership. Let us not assume that Smotryc'kyj or his culture was wholly defined by any of the sets of absolute oppositions that his apologists and detractors—including, on occasion, the man himself—have used in their efforts to describe, and thus to control, him.

But in denying possession to others I am, of course, staking a claim to my own version of Smotryc'kyj. In the first half of the book my vision is primarily a negative one. I seek to undermine our confidence in what the sources tell us about Smotryc'kyj and his allegiances. I construct a picture based not so much on what the sources directly reveal as on what they hide, not on certainties but on questions, ambiguities, contradictions. In the second half, my vision is a more positive one. I seek to determine what truths might be revealed by those areas of unclarity in Smotryc'kyj's cultural, confessional, and political allegiances.

In my search for the truth about who Meletij Smotryc'kyj was, I have sought to read the sources available to me the way a moderately suspicious person reads the newspaper or tries to make sense of the actions of his neighbors: with a willingness to see patterns in seemingly unconnected events, and with a readiness to concede that the patterns might, after all, be the result of the observer's need to interpret. Some will, no doubt, find the picture of Smotryc'kyj I offer the result of a "conspiracy mentality," others will be impatient with the caution I exercise in expressing my suspicions about his actions and motivations. Of course, I hope that my version of Smotryc'kyj and his world will be convincing. In an effort, however, to make my discussion useful to those who may wish to propose other visions of this enigmatic figure, I have attempted to maintain in the foreground a discussion of the nature of the evidence and of the ways I have arrived at my choice of testimonies and their interpretation. The truth about Smotryc'kyj that I will offer here will be a partial truth at best, and certainly one colored by my subjectivity. But still, I offer it as a truth about this complex individual, a reconstruction of some part of the past, subject to supplementation, confirmation, or rejection based on a more persuasive interpretation of the available testimonies in the Smotryc'kyj affair.

Part I

A Life in Controversy

Eastern Europe, 1619

CHAPTER 1

Birth

That he was born is one of the few aspects of Smotryc'kyj's life not shrouded in mystery or controversy. But even here the circumstances have been open to question. Naturally, not all aspects of his birth were subject to manipulation in the polemic of the time. Questions such as the date and place of his birth are of interest only to the scholarship of the last century or so. But the quality of his birth—was he of noble or plebeian stock?—a question considered solved for modern scholarship, was a hotly debated issue in the polemics of the 1620s. A reexamination of that controversy shows that here, as in many other cases, the matter was not as simple as we have come to believe.

First, then, when was he born? There are three pieces of information that may reflect contemporary views concerning the year of Smotryc'kyj's birth. And as so often in these documents, they provide conflicting evidence. Perhaps the most important is a letter Smotryc'kyj himself wrote to Pope Urban VIII on 6 July 1627 asking to be received into communion with the Roman Church. Smotryc'kyj introduced himself in the following terms:

> Behold, situated in the most remote appendage of the sinful world, born in the schism out of necessity, [I] wallowed in it for fifty years out of ignorance.[1]

This would place his birth in 1577. But the same letter was cited with a somewhat different reading by Smotryc'kyj's earliest biographer, Jakiv Suša, who claimed he had drawn on Vatican documents: ". . . born in the schism out of necessity, I wallowed in it for fifty years *of my own volition*" (emphasis added).[2] A modern Ukrainian Catholic scholar, Father Solovij (1977, 135–36), has drawn on this second reading to argue for an earlier date of birth. In his view we should set it at 1575 since the opposition of "out of necessity" ("ex necessitate") to "of my own volition" ("ex voluntate") implied that Smotryc'kyj had made a conscious choice to remain in the schism, and reason, according to Solovij, comes at the age of two. Moreover, Solovij continues, Smotryc'kyj converted not in 1627 but in 1625. But then, if I follow all this correctly (and it is not at all certain that Smotryc'kyj "converted" in 1625), we should subtract another two years and put Smotryc'kyj's birth at 1573. Ignoring the problem of the reading found in Suša's version of the letter (which may be a product of Suša's own alliterative emendation: "ex voluntate volutatus"), it is not clear from the context of the letter that Smotryc'kyj intended for Barberini to make all these complicated suppositions and calculations. He simply said to the pope that he had spent the last half century in the schism. The Uniate Metropolitan of Kiev, Josyf Ruc'kyj, wrote in his report to Rome, which apparently accompanied Smotryc'kyj's letter of 6 July, that the archbishop had begun to "grow cold in the schism" sometime after his return from Constantinople (i.e., early 1626 to the middle of 1627), at a point that marked fifty years of his life and of his life in the schism.[3] In any case, fifty is a nice round number. Probably too nice. Perhaps we had better allow for the possibility that it was an approximation and say that this piece of evidence indicates that Smotryc'kyj was born ca. 1577.

A second witness is found in a short biography of Smotryc'kyj written 21 September 1630—perhaps by Metropolitan Ruc'kyj[4]—for inclusion in the files of the Sacred Congregation for the Propagation of the Faith (*Propaganda Fide*). It placed his birth ca. 1580.[5]

A third piece of evidence poses more problems. A manuscript *Book of Derman' Monastery* contained information on the archimandrites of that establishment. The entry for Smotryc'kyj reported that he "passed on in the year 1630, fifty-eight years from his birth."[6] But all indications are that Smotryc'kyj died on 27 December 1633;[7] even the *Book of Derman' Monastery* indicated that the next archimandrite was appointed in 1634 (Korotkij 1987, 24). And yet, the number fifty-eight has the allure of specificity. Could this entry be incorrect on the year of death, but correct on the age at death? If so, then Smotryc'kyj was born in 1575. Unfortunately, since I have been unable to consult it directly, I can offer nothing about the age and reliability of the *Book of Derman' Monastery*.

In sum, all the evidence points to the conclusion that Smotryc'kyj was born between 1575 and 1580. The date ca. 1577 has the authority of stemming from Smotryc'kyj himself. The later in the decade we place his birth, as soon will become clear, the closer the chronology of his schooling fits the normal pattern for his age (see below, pp. 34–35). If he was born in 1577, then his two "conversions"—taking the habit in 1617 and his covert conversion to the Uniate Church in 1627—occurred in his fortieth and fiftieth years. Smotryc'kyj portrayed his becoming a monk as occurring when it was time for him "to order his life" (see below, p. 64). Was he perhaps conscious of an important birthday in this year?

Where was he born? Smotryc'kyj himself told us nothing other than the fact that Podolia and Volhynia were well acquainted with his father Herasym.[8] In the brief biography cited above we learn that he was born "in Russia," that is to say, in Rus', which is not very specific (Velykyj 1972, 218). Suša claimed in 1666 that Smotryc'kyj had been born in Podolia.[9] This may be true, but Suša altered so much for programmatic reasons that one wonders whether to trust him even in this sort of information. His surname may derive from the village of Smotryč in Podolia, and some later scholars have suggested that this was his birthplace; but surely the name alone is no guarantee that his mother— herself nowhere mentioned in the sources[10]—happened to be there when the time came for Meletij to be born. In fact, Herasym seems to have been connected with Ostroh at about this time (the Ostroh Bible appeared in 1580–1581). Perhaps Meletij was born there.

We have little information on Smotryc'kyj's family life, which is frustrating, since he may have belonged to one of the first professional literary families in Ukraine. His grandfather's name was Danyjil, probably the same "deacon Danyjil" who copied an anti-Hussite polemical work at Smotryč in the second half of the sixteenth century (see Myc'ko 1990, 13). Meletij's father Herasym Danyjilovyč, served the Ukrainian magnate and palatine (voievoda) of Kiev, Konstantyn Vasyl' Ostroz'kyj, primarily, it would seem, as a writer. Herasym was one of the editors of the Ostroh Bible, which represented the first printing of Church Slavonic Scripture; he may have been among the first to write verse in Rus'; he was the author of polemical works; he served Ostroz'kyj in some administrative capacity (Meletij said as castle scribe [1621c 110/454], Suša said as vice-starosta [1666, 14], and Myc'ko says as vice-treasurer [1990, 23]), perhaps in exchange for which he received from Ostroz'kyj the villages Borysivka and Baklajivka (see Suša 1666, 15–16). Tradition (see Myc'ko 1990, 39) and Suša (1666, 15–16) have seen in him an early, perhaps the first, rector of the school founded in Ostroh.[11]

Meletij had a brother Stefan (apparently an older brother, according to Suša [1666, 16]), who also was connected with the school at Ostroh (according to Myc'ko [1990, 42], from the end of the sixteenth century until 1636). Among other things, he copied the sermons of St. John Chrysostom and perhaps the *Kormčaja* (Myc'ko 1990, 40).[12] We do not know whether Meletij had other siblings.[13] Both Suša (1666, 16) and Petruševič (1874, 35) wrote that Herasym had two sons; but a document from the beatification process of Josafat Kuncevyč spoke of "*one* of [Meletij's] carnal brothers," thus implying that there might have been more than two sons, all told.[14] The sources also mention a somewhat younger Mytrofan Smotryc'kyj, perhaps a relative, who copied a *Xronograf* (see Myc'ko 1990, 18; Dobrjanskij 1882, 288). On 5 February 1635 Ruc'kyj wrote of a "fraternal nephew" ("nepos ex fratre") who had taken the habit in the Uniate Derman' Monastery (where Smotryc'kyj was archimandrite in his last years), and who wished to study in some seminary abroad. (Ruc'kyj suggested the Greek college in Rome.)[15] Was this Stefan's son? Ruc'kyj described the young man's father as "schismatic in name only." Stefan seems to have become a Uniate by the end of his life (see Myc'ko 1990, 112–13). A document of 1655 mentioned a Father Jeremija Smotryc'kyj, who resided at the Supraśl Monastery.[16] Finally, Andrzej Węgierski mentioned in his *Libri Quattuor Slavoniae Reformatae* (Amsterdam, 1679, 473) a certain "Georgius Smotrisius," apparently a contemporary of Meletij.

Meletij himself, however, had next to nothing to say about his family life or childhood experiences. In response to allegations that he and Metropolitan Jov Borec'kyj secretly preferred Turkish rule to that of the Polish king, Smotryc'kyj wrote in 1621 that both he and the metropolitan had "parents, brothers, sisters, and other relatives and in-laws in those lands nearer to the Foe, in Volhynia, Ukraine, Podolia, and in Pidhirrja."[17] Other than this passage, which was directly motivated by the polemic, the only other information we have from Smotryc'kyj directly concerning his family is his defense of his father in *The Defense of the Verification* (Smotryc'kyj 1621c, 109–110/453–54).

What was Meletij's given name? All later sources have told us that it was Maksym, Meletij being the name he adopted when he became a monk. Smotryc'kyj's own testimony, however, complicates the issue. The name Maksym appears in several early sources. The Uniates used this name in 1621 when they brought legal proceedings against

Smotryc'kyj for accepting "illegal" consecration from Theophanes, the "pseudo-patriarch" of Jerusalem (see Žukovič 1906, 547–48, 549, 866, 876); the point here was that, by using his given name instead of the name he had adopted some three years earlier when he took the habit, the Uniate authorities were refusing to recognize even Smotryc'kyj's tonsure, much less the fact that he was now a member of the Church hierarchy. On another occasion the Roman Catholic and Uniate side derided Smotryc'kyj by (mis)translating a Latin proverb into Polish using not the name Meletij but Maksym: "*stultorum plena sunt omnia* [fools are everywhere], the world is full of Maksyms."[18] Further, on 1 January 1628 the papal nuncio in Warsaw wrote a report to the Sacred Congregation for the Propagation of the Faith on the recent convert "Meletij, who was previously called Maksym."[19] And Suša wrote in 1666 of the arrival in this world of "Maximus," who, on account of the schism into which he was born, ought to have been called "Minimus."[20] But Smotryc'kyj himself said in 1616—that is, before he was tonsured— that his name was Maksentij: he wrote his name this way in one version of the preface to his Ruthenian translation of the *Homiliary Gospel* (Smotryc'kyj 1616, v^r/13). An Orthodox pamphlet against Smotryc'kyj, written most likely sometime between his conversion in 1628 and his death in 1633, told of "Meksentij or Maksym (for thus did he call himself)."[21]

Smotryc'kyj spelled his names in a variety of manners. In Cyrillic letters he signed his name Мелетий Смотриский, in Polish Meletiusz Smotriski, Smotrzyski, or Smotrziski, and in Latin Meletius Smotrickij, Smotriscky, or Smotrysky.

But was Maksym (or Maksentij) Herasymovyč Smotryc'kyj a nobleman? This is where the public manipulation of personal data came into play. Here as in many other aspects of Smotryc'kyj's life—at least as far as the contemporary sources were concerned—the answer has depended entirely on one's point of view: regardless of what the truth may have been, in public pronouncements he was what the given side required him to be for its own purposes at a given moment in the exchange of polemical tracts.

The Roman Catholic and Uniate side insisted in the period after his conversion that he was a nobleman. And on this particular detail all investigators of both sides have agreed, drawing their information, directly or indirectly—whether they are aware of it or not—from Suša's account.[22] But the matter is not absolutely clear: it is quite possible that here as elsewhere Suša and others stated that Smotryc'kyj was a nobleman because claims had been made—earlier by the Roman Catholics and Uniates themselves, and more recently by the Orthodox—that he was a plebeian interloper.

So let us back up. The year was 1621. Smotryc'kyj had recently been named archbishop of Polack and archimandrite of the Brotherhood Monastery in Vilnius; Jov Borec'kyj had been made Orthodox metropolitan of Kiev. The Uniate and Roman Catholic side challenged the legitimacy of the consecrations, arguing that the man who claimed to be Patriarch Theophanes of Jerusalem was in fact a spy sent by the Turks on a journey via Moscow to Rus' in order to gather information and to sow discontent among the Orthodox during a time of unrest between the Commonwealth and the Ottoman Empire; and, more important for us, that Smotryc'kyj and Borec'kyj, the two singled out as the leaders of the Orthodox side, had committed treason against the state by meeting with Theophanes and by allowing themselves to be consecrated by him.

These allegations had been made in legal charges brought by the Catholic authorities and by the Uniate hierarchy in the spring of 1621. They were in the air when Smotryc'kyj wrote his anonymous *Verification of Innocence* (Vilnius, 1621), in which he claimed that the honor (this was the crucial word in the discussion) of the entire Ruthenian nation had been besmirched in these allegations against the two Orthodox leaders.[23] Moreover, he dedicated the preface of a second edition of the work to four leading Ruthenian Uniate noblemen.

These four men responded by signing their names to a letter published in 1621 in which they showed that they were well aware who had written the *Verification of Innocence*. Furthermore, they answered Smotryc'kyj's main argument by defining the nation as the sum of its nobility and by charging that both Smotryc'kyj and Borec'kyj were from the plebs. Therefore, according to their reasoning, no harm had been done to the honor of the Ruthenian nation in the personal allegations brought against the two improperly consecrated churchmen.

> This (as throughout) is your side's—or yours, who published this *Verification*—evil and improper deed. . . . For where is there any mention of the Ruthenian nation? Only of Smotryc'kyj and Borec'kyj and of their own treason do they write and do the letters and universals of His Majesty the King speak. . . . Why should the noble Ruthenian nation be at fault on account of the evil actions of your volunteers for

ecclesiastical office? . . . And what are Smotryc'kyj and Borec'kyj in the Ruthenian nation—*fex populi et abiectio plebis* [the dregs of the populace and the refuse of the plebs]. How can there be a reflection upon the Ruthenian nation from these people?[24]

The Uniate Metropolitan of Kiev, Josyf Ruc'kyj likewise indirectly attacked Smotryc'kyj's genealogy by calling him the son of "Herasym the priest."[25] And the Uniates were still complaining at the Warsaw Sejm of 1623 that Smotryc'kyj and Borec'kyj were men "of the plebeian condition" (*plebeiae conditionis;* Golubev 1883a, 84). One could not really "dishonor" Smotryc'kyj or Borec'kyj, because they had been born without honor.

Smotryc'kyj responded directly to Ruc'kyj's accusations, stating that he would consider his birth just as noble if he actually had been born into a clerical family.[26] But since the other side had decided to make an issue of it, Smotryc'kyj provided the following defense of his lineage:

> Herasym Danyjilovyč Smotryc'kyj was known to Podolia, which bore and raised him, and had him as castle scribe of Kam'janec' under three Kam'janec' starostas. He was known to Volhynia, where he lived in the Konstantyn tract, provided with no small estate on his little field of land in Podolia by the Illustrious Grace, Prince of Ostroh, Palatine, of blessed memory, of Kiev. That man [i.e., Herasym], great in his time in the Ruthenian nation, seeing our Ruthenian nation inclining unto ruin on account of the simplicity and crudeness of those who ought to have been wise and learned, left his *munimentum* [bulwark] worthy of eternal memory . . . [27]

And Smotryc'kyj further referred to his father's "honorable birth" (Smotryc'kyj 1621c, 109/453: "vczciwe vrodzenie") and to his "noble dignity" (Smotryc'kyj 1621c, 109/453: "szlachecka poważność"). Later, in *Elenchus,* he took a different tack in responding to the *Letter:* here he argued that the servants (i.e., Borec'kyj and Smotryc'kyj) should not wish to be "better" than their Lord, about whom David had prophesied when he said (Ps. 22, 6) "I am a worm and no man; a reproach of men, and despised of the people (literally, "refuse of the plebs," again, *abiectio plebis*)."[28] But finally, also in *Elenchus,* Smotryc'kyj wrote of his "honorable, noble birth."[29] The reluctance, and the awkwardness, with which Smotryc'kyj finally spoke of his "noble birth" make me wonder whether he had some hesitations about pushing the issue. Smotryc'kyj's defenses of himself could place him among the *szlachta;* but they could also simply say that he was not of dishonorable parentage. His description of his father placed emphasis on his literary service to the Ruthenian magnate Prince Konstantyn Ostroz'kyj and to the Ruthenian Church. In fact, Herasym seems to have earned his material well-being through that service.[30]

We do not know the opinion of Smotryc'kyj's Orthodox coreligionists when the issue of nobility was first raised. All such Orthodox opinions that have survived about the pre-conversion Smotryc'kyj come from Smotryc'kyj himself. But here, as in so many other issues, the same allegations of plebeian status would surface again after his conversion, from the other side. Now it was the Orthodox who made Smotryc'kyj a member of the plebs. Unfortunately, the work in question here—an Orthodox *Reprotestation* written in answer to Smotryc'kyj's own *Protestation* (L'viv, 1628)—is not extant. But the Catholic response to that work—a tract entitled *Answer to the Reprotestation* (1629), which Golubev (1883, 351) ascribes with some reason to the Bernardine friar Felicjan Korzeniowski—gives a clear picture of the nature of the charges; and the parting shot gives an equally clear picture of the general level of the polemic:

> You make allegations about Father Smotryc'kyj's birth, not concerning his soul and virtue, but concerning the conception of his body. . . . But if he was not born in noble fashion [*po ślachecku*] or senatorial, he was born in regal fashion as nobly as Solomon. . . . And what about your own birth?[31]

Thus in the period after Smotryc'kyj's conversion it was now the Orthodox who dredged up the old allegations: your star convert has mud on his shoes. At least one figure on the other side—probably a Polish Catholic—was willing to grant the charge, but he denied the conclusion drawn: Smotryc'kyj's was an aristocracy of the spirit. So what if he was not born into the upper reaches of the aristocracy? This defense accorded well with Smotryc'kyj's earlier description of his father. If Herasym was a member of the *szlachta,* then he was not a wealthy one. The son of Deacon Danyjil—in Smotryc'kyj's account, as well as in Suša's—seems to have derived his income from service to Ostroz'kyj. And most accounts of Smotryc'kyj's education seem to have made him impecunious and talented, dependent upon the kindness of the Ostroz'kyj and the Solomerec'kyj families for his stipend.

The point is that we have come to know that Smotryc'kyj was a member of the nobility because Suša said so and others have repeated it, and—who knows?—maybe it was even in some sense true. (If true, however, he must have belonged to the recently ennobled: was Deacon Danyjil a шляхтичъ?) But the crucial and consistently overlooked fact is that we know this only because it became an issue in the polemic, because someone, at some point, decided that Smotryc̆kyj was vulnerable on this issue. This seems to have been a useful way to attack one's ecclesiastical opponent. Smotryc̆kyj's Uniate opponent as archbishop of Polack, Josafat Kuncevyč, was the target of a similar campaign mounted by the Orthodox nobleman Lavrentij Drevyns̆kyj, who claimed in a speech before the Sejm in 1620 that the future martyr was a *homo plebeius* (see Bantyš-Kamenskij 1805, 67). Suša and the Uniate author of the short report to the Vatican may well have been seeking to undo a specific aspect of the old Uniate and Roman Catholic campaign against Smotryc̆kyj. In fact, the Uniate and Roman Catholic side was still making this allegation as late as 1624.[32] It had already reversed its position by 1630. And as usual, Suša (1666, 14) went the extra mile in his effort, tranforming Herasym, whom Smotryc̆kyj had described as "castle scribe" (1621c, 110/454 : *grodzki pisarz*), into a "vice-starosta" (*vicecapitaneus*).

CHAPTER 2

Education

Schooling has been the point of departure for many attempts to define Smotryckyj and to explain his actions. This method of examination began during his lifetime and has continued into the present. Smotryckyj was the man he was—so his admirers and detractors, including Smotryckyj himself, tell us—because of the education he received at home and abroad. That he was one of the most learned men of his time and place is one of the few things that scholars of both confessional sympathies have been able to agree upon. But, as we will soon see, publicly his contemporaries could not agree even on this one point: in an age when an entire lexicon of philological invective stood at the ready for controversialists of all sorts, Smotryckyj's opponents were always eager to portray him as possessing the dullest of wits and the slowest of pens. Privately, however, these same opponents were often willing to grant Smotryckyj considerable learning and a persuasive prose style.

The real issue became the quality of Smotryckyj's education experience. Each side, especially in the later scholarly discussion, has tended to attribute the "good" in Smotryckyj to the time spent in their schools, and the "bad" to the pernicious influence of the opponents' teaching. There was, further, some general discomfort about his studies with the German Protestants. Following one of the lines of thought among the Orthodox of the early seventeenth century, the nineteenth-century Orthodox scholar Golubev looked with greater sympathy upon the Protestants than upon the Catholics and depicted Smotryckyj's studies in Germany as a sort of temporary antidote to the Jesuits:

> It was difficult to pass through the crucible of the Jesuit schools completely free from the direction that reigned in them. Without a doubt, neither did M. Smotryckyj avoid the influence of Jesuit pedagogy. But at first that influence was significantly weakened by Smotryckyj's travels through Germany. . . . Listening to lectures within

the walls of Protestant universities . . . exposed to Meletij the weak sides of the Latin West and temporarily distanced him from the Jesuits (Golubev 1883, 94).

The important point is that all later scholarship has seen Orthodox, Catholic, and Protestant schooling as fundamentally different and has blamed the character flaws it imputed to Smotryc′kyj—either the tardiness with which he came to acknowledge the truth, or his lack of steadfastness—in large part upon his varied educational experience.[1]

What do we know about the young Smotryc′kyj's course of studies? Here, too, Suša provided the most information, and it has been this version of events that has been repeated in most subsequent biographies. In Suša's *vita* we read that Herasym Smotryc′kyj was made rector of the new Orthodox school founded on the holdings of Prince Konstantyn Ostroz′kyj in Ostroh,[2] and that he had two sons, whose education he supervised. According to Suša, Maksym, together with his older brother Stefan, received his first training in Greek and Latin from Cyril Lukaris, future Patriarch of Constantinople.[3] The scholarly literature has followed the implications of Suša's account and has assumed that this occurred in Ostroh.

In 1601, according to Suša (and here his chronology is probably faulty), Prince Ostroz′kyj sent Maksym, along with the young Orthodox nobleman Jurij Puzyna, to the Jesuit Vilnius Academy. Smotryc′kyj spent several years there studying "rational philosophy and the higher sciences." But the "harsh germ of the schism" kept him from finishing his schooling with the Jesuits; he then accompanied a member of the Solomerec′kyj family (from other sources we know it was Bohdan[4]) to "Silesia, Wrocław, and thence to Leipzig, Nuremberg, and other cities and academies of non-Catholic Germany."[5] According to Suša he then returned to Lithuania in 1610, the year he published his *Thrēnos.*[6]

A brief Uniate biography of 1630 told much the same story as Suša, although it made Smotryc′kyj's parents, and not Prince Ostroz′kyj, the sponsor of his studies. Smotryc′kyj was sent, by his parents, and on account of his great promise, to study with the Jesuits in Vilnius where he completed the program of "lesser studies of letters, up to physics."[7] Thereupon, on account of his parents' concern over the type of instruction he was receiving, he was sent "to Germany, to the heretical schools," where he was infected with the heterodox poison. Upon his return he wrote many books against the Catholic faith, the most pernicious of which was his *Thrēnos* of 1610.[8]

Yet another document, a report of the papal nuncio in Warsaw on the recent convert, which was sent to Rome on 1 January 1628 (while Smotryc'kyj was still a covert Uniate), claimed that the future archbishop had studied at Vilnius Academy and had been expelled from there "on account of the schism." He then went to Germany, where, "practicing amongst the heretics, he composed a book full of heresies [i.e., *Thrēnos*], with which he seduced a great many persons."[9]

These sources—all of them Uniate or Roman Catholic and written after Smotryc'kyj had converted—told much the same story: Smotryc'kyj left Vilnius Academy for the heretical schools of Germany, whence he returned to Lithuania to publish his most dangerous anti-Catholic work, the *Thrēnos* of 1610. And yet, they did not tell quite the same story. Who sent him to Vilnius: his parents or Prince Ostroz'kyj? What happened at Vilnius Academy? One source (Suša) told us he studied "natural philosophy and the higher sciences" there, but the "harsh germ of the schism" sent him off to Germany. Another (the author of the short life, Ruc'kyj perhaps) said it was the parents who removed their son from the influence of the Jesuits and sent him to Germany. A third (the nuncio) claimed he was expelled from the academy (and that he composed *Thrēnos* in Germany). All this leads me to wonder whether the Uniate and Roman Catholic side was entirely comfortable with the Vilnius record of their most famous convert. As usual, Suša gave everything the most positive interpretation. Instead of "lesser studies of letters, up to physics," he wrote "natural philosophy [i.e., physics] and the higher sciences," perhaps seeking to give the impression that Smotryc'kyj had spent more time in Vilnius than he actually did.[10] And his explanation for Smotryc'kyj's departure was the haziest of the three; perhaps Suša, too, believed that, as the nuncio had reported, Smotryc'kyj had been expelled "on account of the schism." Vilnius Academy, as a Jesuit institution, existed, among other reasons, in order to educate the sons of Rus' in the ultimate hope of converting them. Smotryc'kyj must have been unusually forceful in his defense of Orthodoxy to have been expelled. It is entirely possible that Smotryc'kyj's studies in Vilnius coincided with the declaration of the Union of Brest in 1596. Did that event or Smotryc'kyj's reaction to it have anything to do with his expulsion from the academy (if he indeed was expelled)?

An Orthodox biography of Smotryćkyj, probably written sometime between 1628 and 1633, gave a more or less neutral account on this issue. Smotryćkyj studied "Latin philosophy"—a qualitative rather than quantitative term that does not indicate how much of the course he completed—at Vilnius Academy;[11] thereupon he went to German lands "for the sake of greater and deeper academic study."[12]

Smotryćkyj himself wrote about his education only after his conversion to the Uniate Church. There he acknowledged that he had been, as a young man, a student ("dyscypuł") of Lukaris.[13] He later lamented the fact that he had spent his young years "at the grave of Luther," studying at the academies of Leipzig and Wittenberg.[14] (Notice that subsequent biographers have repeated Suša's assertion that Smotryćkyj studied at the academies of Wrocław, Leipzig, Nuremberg, and other German cities, whereas Smotryćkyj said specifically Leipzig and Wittenberg.) But Smotryćkyj said not one word about his time in Vilnius. Is it being overly suspicious to consider this a curious omission? Would it not have been proper for the older Smotryćkyj, in reviewing his spiritual biography, to say a word of thanks to the Jesuit fathers for planting the seed of his future conversion? What was Smotryćkyj's relationship with the Jesuits and their academy in Vilnius? The Polish Jesuit Wojciech Kortycki, Smotryćkyj's confessor in his last days, assured the audience of his funeral oration that Smotryćkyj was a great friend of the order,[15] and at least one Orthodox investigator has portrayed him as a sort of double agent for the Jesuits all his life, enlisted into the service of the other side during his school days (see Demjanovič 1871, 207 ff). But Smotryćkyj, who singled out the Jesuits for special censure and derision in his *Thrēnos,*[16] had only little to say in their favor even after his conversion. In a pre-conversion Uniate representation, it was the work of the Uniate archbishop Moroxovśkyj, not that of the Jesuit Piotr Skarga, that convinced Smotryćkyj to renounce *Thrēnos.*[17]

Each side wished to have in Smotryćkyj a man whose allegiance was never in doubt, and Smotryćkyj himself often sought to portray himself in this manner. Therefore, the fact that his studies took him from the Orthodox center of Ostroh, to the Catholic center of Vilnius, and onward to various centers of Protestant Germany was a possible sore point: it required explanation by his supporters of the moment, and it was open to exploitation by his detractors who would seek reasons for his lack of steadfastness.

This type of argument was a part of the early competition for control of Smotryc'kyj's public persona. It would become one of the main aspects of later scholarship on the Smotryc'kyj affair, and one of the favorite explanations—by scholars on both sides of the issue—for Smotryc'kyj's hesitations in his choice of confessional allegiance. Very rarely could the Orthodox afford to acknowledge that they had had anything to do with the "heretics," and the charge of Protestant influence was often leveled against the Orthodox by Roman Catholic and Uniate polemicists.[18] The Orthodox Smotryc'kyj did not escape this sort of criticism.[19] But it was after Smotryc'kyj's conversion that the Roman Catholic and Uniate side made his schooling an integral part of its campaign, as if to say, were it not for his schismatic birth and early training, as well as his deviation to the academies of Germany, he would have been ours all along. The brief biography of 1630 (Velykyj 1972, 218) and Suša's *vita* of 1666 (p. 16) used the image of poison: thanks to the poison Smotryc'kyj imbibed during his years in Germany, it took him longer than it might have to obtain spiritual health.

Interestingly, the Orthodox sources of the time do not seem to have been particularly troubled by the fact that Smotryc'kyj studied in Vilnius *per se*. After all, in the absence of a higher institution of Orthodox learning, this was where many young Orthodox were sent to study. He was guilty, it is true, of the use of syllogisms,[20] and where could he have learned to use them if not among the Jesuits? But it was only in later Orthodox treatments that Vilnius Academy became a matter of controversy.

The question of chronology remains. Suša provided the only date in all the material I have examined so far, stating that Smotryc'kyj went to Vilnius in 1601. But is it likely that Smotryc'kyj arrived in Vilnius when he was over twenty years old (recall that the latest date of birth found in the sources is "ca. 1580") to spend "several years" pursuing studies that led only to "rational philosophy," in other words, physics? An average student would have had this much schooling under his belt at a much younger age. This chronology begins to make Meletij look like the class dunce. Another contemporary source may offer some help. The entry for the year 1600 in the Barkalabava Chronicle included—together with a report on the weather—the information that Smotryc'kyj had been made tutor to the sons of the Solomerec'kyj family;[21] perhaps it was shortly thereafter that Smotryc'kyj left for Germany with his charge, Bohdan

Solomec̄kyj. It is possible that this trip lasted until at least 1606: the name "Solomerecki" appeared in the matriculation list of Leipzig University for that year (see Kot 1952, 243). It thus is likely that Smotryc̄kyj's stay in Vilnius fell sometime in the late 1590s.

Further, we know that Cyril Lukaris was in the Commonwealth on two occasions: his first stay overlapped with the Council of Brest in 1596, and his second trip ended in 1601.[22] According to Rozemond (Lukaris 1974, 6–7), Lukaris first arrived in the Commonwealth in July 1594 (at age 23) with letters of introduction for L'viv. On 27 March 1595, Myxajlo Rahoza (the metropolitan of Kiev) made him archimandrite of the Holy Trinity Monastery in Vilnius; and on 2 February 1596, the Vilnius Brotherhood made him rector of their school. As far as I have been able to ascertain, the earliest evidence linking Lukaris with Ostroh came in Andrzej Węgierski's *Systema historico-chronologicum ecclesiarum Slavonicarum* published in Utrecht in 1652 (Myc̄ko 1990, 39). Węgierski claimed that the future Calvinizing patriarch of Constantinople was rector of the school in Ostroh in the period 1594 to 1600 (if this was the case, then obviously this must have been with interruptions). This is a rather late source. Where did Węgierski get his information? If Lukaris was connected with Ostroh, it must have been very briefly: during his first trip he was occupied most of the time in other places, and his second trip was short. If Smotryc̄kyj was a student of Lukaris at Ostroh, it must have been during the period 1594 to 1596. But this chronology still poses some problems. If Smotryc̄kyj was born in 1577, would he not have been rather old to study at Ostroh in 1595 (especially if his subsequent studies with the Jesuits in Vilnius brought him only as far as "natural philosophy")?

Perhaps Smotryc̄kyj encountered Lukaris elsewhere? Could Meletij have studied at the Brotherhood school in Vilnius? Or in L'viv? As a Uniate, Smotryc̄kyj would later claim that he had been present with Lukaris on one occasion at the residence of the Catholic archbishop of L'viv, Jan Dymitr Solikowski.[23] There are huge gaps in our knowledge of Smotryc̄kyj's activities before ca. 1617 (that is, before the fortieth year of his life). We should not rule out the possibility that Smotryc̄kyj, who led a highly peripatetic life, spent some time in L'viv in the 1590s. Smotryc̄kyj claimed in 1628 that he had "lived" with Jov Borec̄kyj for four years (see Smotryc̄kyj 1628b, Biv^v/634). Could it be that he spent a longer time in the 1590s in L'viv, and his presence there overlapped with that of the future metropolitan? On the other hand, by describing himself as Lukaris' "dyscypuł," he did not say very much about his relationship with the older man. Did Smotryc'kyj necessarily mean by this that he was a student under Lukaris' tutelage in organized school instruction? Perhaps (especially given the argument he was making here) Smotryc'kyj meant only that as a young man he had been fascinated by the "unionizing" strains in Lukaris' thought, especially as expressed in the letter to Solikowski.

Let us further take stock of a few historiographic commonplaces about Smotryc'kyj's education:

Smotryc'kyj studied at Ostroh. With his father. And with Lukaris. (These could be three separate assertions, but they often have been linked.) The only direct evidence that Smotryc'kyj studied at Ostroh comes from Suša. It makes good sense, assuming Herasym was indeed rector of the school (an assertion that is itself only "traditional" [see Myc'ko 1990, 39]), but is it accurate? Smotryc'kyj would later claim that he owed his schooling to the generosity of God, the Ostroz'kyjs, and the Solomerec'kyjs (in that order).[24] But the Ostroz'kyjs seem to have financed his education in Vilnius, thus this statement does not necessarily tell us anything about the school at Ostroh. That Meletij was in some sense his father's "student" seems likely. Unfortunately, we know absolutely nothing about the details of this transferal of knowledge. How much time did Herasym spend with Meletij? (When did Herasym die?) Was he in any official sense Meletij's instructor (in Ostroh or elsewhere)? What subjects did he discuss with his son?

It is clear that the young Smotryc'kyj (at about age 20) had some direct contact with Cyril Lukaris. But this does not necessarily mean that Lukaris was Meletij's teacher *sensu stricto* or that the contact between the two came in Ostroh. Assuming Smotryc'kyj was born in 1577 and that he began to study at the Jesuit academy in Vilnius around 1596, there are many years about which we know absolutely nothing, and there is enough evidence pointing to a stay in L'viv that we should be open to the possibility that he also studied at the Brotherhood school in that city for some time (and may have entered Lukaris' tutelage there).

Finally, *Smotryc'kyj returned from Germany with a degree in medicine.* This is a less widely spread, but still persistent historiographic misunderstanding. This claim is no doubt based on a misreading of the title page to the *Apology* of 1628: *An Apology for My Peregrination to the Eastern Lands, by Me, Meletij Smotryc'kyj, M. D. Archbishop of Polack . . .* [25] The title is in Polish, and the letters *M. D.* are indeed Latin, but they do not signify *medicinae doctor*; they mean rather *misericordia Dei*, or "by God's mercy." Smotryc'kyj himself told us as much in Polish a few pages further: "Meletij Smotryc'kyj, *by God's mercy* Archbishop of Polack." [26] I raise this small misunderstanding only because it refuses to go away. [27] Smotryc'kyj was certainly a learned man. On this all sides have now agreed, but there is no reason to exaggerate. For that matter, he may not have completed any course of studies. The expellee from Vilnius Academy (assuming this information is accurate) and the preceptor to Bohdan Solomerec'kyj may have amassed his considerable learning through his demonstrably wide reading. But, did he ever take a degree? It was, after all, the name Solomerec'kyj and not Smotryc'kyj that figured in the matriculation records in Leipzig for 1606 (Kot 1952, 243). Meletij's official status in Germany seems to have been preceptor to the young prince, and not exchange student.

CHAPTER 3

Works

 A more general question encompasses Smotryc'kyj's entire career: which works should we attribute to him? Because many works of the period appeared either under a pseudonym or anonymously, this question can be complicated. And even here, oddly enough, for Smotryc'kyj's contemporaries the question of which works to attribute to him could depend on one's point of view, a question of the needs of the moment. That is, Smotryc'kyj's opponents might be aware that the work they were answering was actually written by Smotryc'kyj, but they might, for various reasons, contrive to ignore that fact. Conversely, they might refer to the unnamed author of a work by Smotryc'kyj and to Smotryc'kyj himself as different persons, even though both the author and the audience of the work were aware that they were the same person. Smotryc'kyj could refer to himself in the third person in a variety of manners: as an anonymous author he would refer to "Father Smotryc'kyj" by name (even after the opposing side had identified him as the spokesman for the Orthodox); or, again as an anonymous author, he could refer to another work he had written anonymously, as if it had been written by someone else; and, as a Uniate author of works published under his own name, he would refer to his former pseudonyms as if these were people who enjoyed lives of their own. Thus we need to be alert to three related sets of questions: what works did Smotryc'kyj write; what works did his contemporaries know that he wrote, and when did they come to know it; finally, what use did they (and Smotryc'kyj) make of this knowledge for polemical purposes?

Before his secret conversion in 1627, Smotryc'kyj signed his name to only three printed works: in one version of the preface to the *Homiliary Gospel* of 1616, while still a layman, he laid claim to the translation of that work, and he probably also wrote all the other prefaces;[1] in 1618–1619 he published his grammar of Church Slavonic, signing his name Meletij for the first time (Smotryc'kyj 1618,)(1^r); and in 1620 he published under his new titles of archbishop of Polack and archimandrite of the Vilnius Orthodox Brotherhood Monastery of the Church of the Descent of the Holy Spirit separate Polish (Smotryc'kyj 1621a, 1ʳ/236) and Ruthenian (Smotryc'kyj 1620, 120) versions of his funeral oration on the death of his predecessor at the Brotherhood monastery, Leontij Karpovyč. Once Smotryc'kyj converted, he seems to have signed his name to all his works; in fact, he now made anonymity into the badge of dishonor worn by Orthodox writers.[2] As a Uniate—covert or overt—Smotryc'kyj printed four polemical tracts: *Apology* (1628); *Protestation* (1628); *Paraenesis* (1629); and *Exaethesis* (1629). In two of them, he gave lists of his polemical works before his conversion, publicly acknowledging his authorship of them for the first time: *Thrēnos* (1610); *Verification of Innocence* (1621); *Defense of the Verification* (1621); *Elenchus* (1622); and *Justification of Innocence* (1623).[3] These works, plus a manuscript tract (published in Studyns'kyj 1906 on the basis of what was apparently an autograph that went up in smoke with the Krasiński collection in Warsaw in 1945; see Waczyński 1937) and some twenty-four letters (see appendix A), are all the extant works that I have been able to find and can definitely attribute to Smotryc'kyj.[4]

Scholarship of the nineteenth and twentieth centuries has rendered the question of Smotryc'kyj's corpus of works even more difficult by making attributions with little or no basis for doing so. Some of these attributions have become so firmly entrenched in the scholarly literature that few investigators remain aware of their problematic nature. All of these questionable attributions deal with the period before Smotryc'kyj became a monk.

Kyrylo Studyns'kyj put forth the hypothesis that Smotryc'kyj was the author of the Orthodox polemical works that appeared in 1598–1599 under the pseudonym "Clerk of Ostroh": *Answer to the Letter by the Reverend Father in God, Ipatij,* published along with the *History of the Robber Council of Ferrara or Florence* (reprinted in Gil'tebrandt 1903, 377–476), and *In Response to the Second Letter of the Reverend Father Ipatij* (reprinted in Studyns'kyj 1906, 201–229). According to my hypothetical chronology of his studies, Smotryc'kyj could have been in Vilnius in these years and just over twenty years old. But this chronology is highly speculative and would not in any way exclude the possibility that he was the "Clerk of Ostroh." Studyns'kyj's argument (1906, xxxvii–l), however, is based solely on coincidences between the Clerk and

Smotryc'kyj (primarily in *Thrēnos*) at the level of theme, style, and borrowed phrases. This, of course, is insufficient evidence by itself. Did Smotryc'kyj offer evidence in any way? The following passage is perhaps the most important, and it is typical of the problems we face in examining these sorts of issues:

> Last year here in this land there departed from this world a man of no small reputation in the Ruthenian nation [i.e., Dem'jan Nalyvajko], both for the piety of his life and for his knowledge of the dogmas of the faith. Still living, however, are those honorable men, priests of the Ostroh *capitula* [chapter], in whose presence, at the mention of my lamentatious writing [i.e., *Thrēnos*], he said that it is equal to the writings of St. John Chrysostom as far as the authority of the truth of God described in it is concerned, and that it is fitting for us to pour out our blood and to lay down our lives for it. How many similar opinions were there, before the appearance of that lamentatious writing, about the works of Zyzanij and Philalet! I heard from the lips of that same now deceased man that he did not praise the Clerk's work, and that it was he who dissuaded the man whose city it was that the Clerk took as his title, from signing the work in his own name (and that is where, through the offices of the author of that work, the matter stood), giving this reason: if some cleric makes injurious reproach to your great and worthy name, how will you defend your account? And so at his advice, that work appeared under the name of the anonymous Clerk of Ostroh, so that if one cleric said something that did not suit another cleric, the harm would not be great.[5]

What do we learn for certain from this passage? That in 1628 Smotryc'kyj was willing to accept responsibility for writing *Thrēnos* and that, if he wrote the works published under the pseudonym "Clerk of Ostroh," he was still unwilling to take credit for them. In fact, the passage cited above could be enlisted in arguments in both directions. Everyone who participated in the polemics of the 1620s seems to have known who Theophil Ortholog was, and nobody equated him with the Clerk of Ostroh; this could be because they were different people, but it could also be because Nalyvajko's advice had paid off, and no one's reputation had been tarnished with the publicly attributed authorship of these works. (Actually, Nalyvajko's words seem to have been directed most immediately to Konstantyn Ostroz'kyj—"the man whose city it was that the clerk took as his title"—as the sponsor of the works.) The fact that Smotryc'kyj referred to the Clerk in the third person and as someone separate from Ortholog is of no help to us: he likewise often referred to Ortholog (a pseudonym to which he later confessed) in the third person and as someone separate from the author of other works he wrote while yet Orthodox. The point remains that we lack convincing evidence for Studynskyj's hypothesis, and the circumstantial evidence seems to be against it.

Studynskyj's argument in favor of the attribution is weak. How can we determine authorship of a polemical work of that age on the basis of something so general as shared thematics, shared sources, shared strategies of argumentation, etc.? These things were supposed to be the same from work to work. Why should we not assume that Smotryckyj also followed the literary code of the time by borrowing and imitating what he found worthy? Studynskyj seems to have made this attribution out of desire for definiteness, and because Smotryckyj—who had both motive and opportunity—could be made to fit the charges. But can we convict him? Our picture of the early seventeenth century is not so clear that we can rule out the existence of possible "clerks" who are otherwise absolutely unknown to us.

Few scholars have pursued Studynskyj's observations, so it is not the specter of the Clerk that haunts Smotryckyj studies. Far more frustrating is the persistent inclusion of an Orthodox polemical pamphlet called *Antigraphē* (Vilnius, 1609) in the Smotryckyj corpus. Those who have come to think that Smotryckyj wrote it base their knowledge, directly or indirectly, on the following passage from the *Apology:*

> Those are well aware of this who knew of my lucubrations against a work entitled *Union,* against *A Conversation between an Adherent of Brest and a Member of the Brotherhood,* against the *Resurrected Nalyvajko,* against the *Politics, Ignorance, and Rite of the New Churchmen of Vilnius,* written and prepared for release to publication in print already after the publication of the *Lament.*[6]

The title page of *Antigraphē* tells us that it was written by one of the monks of the Vilnius monastery and that it was directed against, among other things, a work entitled *Heresies, Ignorance, and Politics of the Priests and Citizens of the Vilnius Brotherhood.*[7] This might be the work that Smotryckyj mentioned above, and it is on the identity of the work responded to that the attribution of *Antigraphē* to Smotryckyj has been made.

But there are counterarguments. Smotryckyj was usually more careful in citing titles. Are these two necessarily the same works? And why did he not simply give the title of his own work, when it would have been easier, as he did elsewhere, to write the word *Antigraphē* in referring to this particular work? Notice also that these works were prepared for print (Smotryc'kyj did not say that they were actually printed), and—as we will see later (pp. 70–72)—that they seem to have been from a period when he had a hard time convincing himself to publish anything on dogma; and, more important, that they were prepared for print after the appearance of *Thrēnos* (in 1610).

Other counterevidence is even stronger. Consider the following passage from Smotryc'kyj's *Paraenesis* (Cracow, 1629):

> After Philalet, a certain anonymous Clerk of Ostroh does the same thing, who is fuller of blasphemies against the eternal preexistence of the Son of God, and of falsehoods about the Council of Florence, than he is of doctrine and truth. Thereafter the author of a work entitled *Antigraphē* does the same thing, who (*alias homo pientissimus* [otherwise, a most pious man]) in addition to other inconsistencies considers it *haeresis* [heresy] to confess that the Holy Spirit proceeds also from the Son. He praises and accepts the works of the Clerk and Philalet and acknowledges them as the writers for his side. Thereupon I do the same thing in my lamentatious work, which *totus fere Calvinizat* [almost totally Calvinizes].[8]

Here we find the entire Smotryc'kyj family (at least as Studyns'kyj would have it): it is, of course, not unthinkable that Smotryc'kyj referred to himself two or three times, once in the first person and otherwise in the third person. But the point is that Smotryc'kyj did not identify himself here with the author of *Antigraphē*. In fact, just the opposite: is it likely that in 1628, when he was spending much of his time beating his chest in public for his crimes as an Orthodox churchman, Smotryc'kyj would have bothered to inform his readers that the author of *Antigraphē* was "otherwise a most pious man," if he was indeed the author?

The objections to the traditional attribution of *Antigraphē* to Smotryc'kyj as outlined above follow the general lines of reasoning found in an undeservedly overlooked piece of literary detective work by Bogusław Waczyński (1949), and I think that his arguments are ultimately convincing. It is remarkable that not one of the authors of the several book-length treatments of Smotryc'kyj's life that have appeared since has read Waczyński's work (which is on prominent display in *Nowy Korbut*) or has reconsidered the evidence on his own. All of them have included *Antigraphē* in their discussions of Smotryc'kyj's works.

I have found two more witnesses in this matter, both unusually clear in their attribution of *Antigraphē*. Unfortunately, they are also mutually contradictory.

In answer to Smotryc'kyj's *Thrēnos* of 1610, the Polish Jesuit Piotr Skarga wrote an *Admonition* (Cracow, 1610), in which he identified the author of *Thrēnos* with the author of *Antigraphē:*

> Ortholog himself gives himself away—that the Nalyvajko Church of Vilnius sent him—when, in another of his books called *Antigraphē*, he signs himself a brother of the Vilnius church. . . . But certainly we can soon find out who he is and what his name is.[9]

But in Jakiv Suša's *vita* of 1666 we find a compendium in Latin of Smotryc'kyj's letter of 1627 to Patriarch of Constantinople Cyril Lukaris, in which the archbishop attributed *Antigraphē* to a certain "Azarias" (Azarij), which, according to some, was the pseudonym of Zaxarija Kopystens'kyj.[10] And a few pages later, Suša himself mentioned *Antigraphē* and attributed it to "Zacharias."[11]

Was it Smotryc'kyj or Kopystens'kyj? Or neither? Actually, neither testimony was unequivocal. Smotryc'kyj's letter to Lukaris existed in at least three versions: a Polish version (probably Smotryc'kyj's own Polish translation of his Latin original) included in *Paraenesis* of 1629 (Smotryc'kyj 1629a, 63–95/676–92); a Latin copy in the archives of *Propaganda Fide,* published recently by Father Velykyj (1972, 130–45); and the Latin compendium in Suša, which could stem either from a retranslation of the Polish found in *Paraenesis* or from another copy that Suša had found in Rome (Suša 1666, 70–81). Of these three, only the version published by Suša contained the attribution to "Azarias." And it is entirely possible that the attribution stemmed from Suša's reworking of his material, and not from Smotryc'kyj. But these facts do not necessarily diminish the value of this testimony. There may have been good reasons for Smotryc'kyj not to include the attribution in his *Paraenesis* which was intended for a Polish audience: it was sometimes part of the literary etiquette of the time to avoid attributing anonymous works to their authors in print. Moreover, Suša repeated (or accepted) this attribution by proceeding to attribute *Antigraphē* to "Zacharias."

But what about Skarga's attribution of the work to Smotryc'kyj? Let us proceed carefully here. This attribution belongs to the sort of libel that passed for confessional debate in the period. Skarga did not say that

Smotryc'kyj wrote it; he said that Ortholog wrote it. This is crucial.
Skarga did not know the identity of Ortholog at this time. The contextual
purpose of the paragraph from Skarga's work cited above was at least
twofold: to assert that *Thrēnos* was not a translation from Greek and
Slavonic—and thus not a work having pan-Orthodox authority—but the
original, Polish-language work of a local figure;[12] further, to smoke out
the author of *Thrēnos* by encouraging the Vilnius Brotherhood or the
author of *Antigraphē* to come forward and declare their ignorance of a
work the author of which faced criminal charges. Thus it remains highly
unlikely that it was Smotryc'kyj who authored *Antigraphē*. Perhaps it
was Kopystens'kyj.[13]

The opposite case is presented by the *Supplication* that was printed in
1623 in the name of the people of the Greek religion and directed to the
king and the Sejm gathered in Warsaw in that year.[14] This work followed
up on the polemical works written by the Orthodox in the years 1620–
1623 in defense of the Orthodox hierarchy consecrated by Patriarch
Theophanes in 1620—all of which were the works Smotryc'kyj later
acknowledged as his own. Smotryc'kyj and Borec'kyj were expected to
attend the Warsaw Sejm in 1623 in order to present their case. They seem
not to have appeared, however (see below, pp. 91–93), and they sent in
their stead a work entitled *Justification of Innocence,* written by
Smotryc'kyj in Borec'kyj's name. Petruševič (1874, 445) first suggested
that Smotryc'kyj might have been the author of the *Supplication,* but no
one has followed up this reasonable hunch. Since we have no hard
evidence that it is his, however, I will not include it in his corpus of works.

Recently, the editors of an anthology of Ukrainian poetry from the
late sixteenth and early seventeenth century have attributed to Smotryc'kyj
a number of verse works, mostly epigrams in his polemical pamphlets,
but also including an anonymous lament on the death of Leontij Karpovyč
(Kolosova and Krekoten' 1978, 166–79). They, too, make their attribution
on the basis of "the close ties that existed between Karpovyč and
Smotryc'kyj and the high level of literary ability and talent of the latter"
(Kolosova and Krekoten' 1978, 384). Once again, we have opportunity
and motive, but this certainly is not enough to convict. There is, however,
one other piece of evidence that might add to the case against Smotryc'kyj.
As we will soon discover, Smotryc'kyj often identified his otherwise
anonymous Orthodox polemical pamphlets by including a motto (the
same that appeared in the grammar and in the Uniate polemical

pamphlets—these also contained his name on the title page) that began with a capital M and ended with a capital S. The *Lament* does not contain this motto. It does, however, begin with an epigram attributed to the Attic poet and author of New Comedy Menander. And Smotryc'kyj referred to him as Μενάνδ. Στοβ., i.e., Menander, as cited in Johannes Stobaeus, the influential fifth-century anthologist of Greek literature. If Smotryc'kyj was the author, was he playing a humanistic game with his readers here by sneaking in his own init.als?

The Uniate Smotryc'kyj himself told us that in the 1610s, in a period of self-doubt after publishing *Thrēnos,* he had written several works, none of which, apparently, appeared in print.[15] They included a work (or individual works?) written in answer to the Uniate pamphlets entitled *A Conversation between an Adherent of Brest and a Member of the Brotherhood, The Resurrected Nalyvajko,* and *Politics, Ignorance, and Rite of the New Churchmen of Vilnius* (see Smotryc'kyj 1621b, 105/ 576); a series of theses in Polish representing Orthodox and Uniate/ Roman Catholic positions on the procession of the Holy Spirit (portions of which were published in Krevza's *Defense of Church Unity*);[16] and a "Palinode" or retraction of *Thrēnos* (see Smotryc'kyj 1628a, 105/576).

A minor mystery is Smotryc'kyj's catechism of the Orthodox faith, a work which formed a sort of leitmotiv in all his Uniate works. He claimed he had begun to work on it in 1621, and that he set off for the East, among other reasons, in order to have Lukaris and others act as censors for it (see Smotryc'kyj 1621b, 105–106/576). During the year that he was a covert Uniate (July 1627 to August 1628) he was showing the catechism to Ruc'kyj on the one side and to Borec'kyj and Mohyla on the other; and according to his letter to Ruc'kyj, the work was all but ready for print (see Kojalovič 1861, 366–67). He came to the Orthodox council in Kiev in August 1628 in order to have the Orthodox hierarchy pass judgment on it (see Smotryc'kyj 1628b, Aii[v]/628). Even after the setback that he met at the council, he continued to describe the catechism as ready for publication and a key to the reunification and the spiritual health of the Ruthenian nation (see Smotryc'kyj 1629b, 101[r]/803). What happened to it?[17]

The pages of Petruševič's chronicle offer a mixture of unlikely, possible, and probable attributions of otherwise unacknowledged works by Smotryc'kyj, all of them made with the same authority and all of them unidentified. Let me simply list them: *Institutiones linguae graecae,*

Cologne, 1615 (Petruševič 1874, 428; this belongs to the category of unlikely); a Cyrillic (apparently Ruthenian) version of *Thrēnos,* Vilnius, 1610 (Petruševič 1874, 417; possible, but I doubt it); *Лямептъ . . . на жалосное преставленіе . . . отца Леонтія Карповича*—that is, the work found in Krekoten' and Kolosova 1978 (Petruševič 1874, 477–78; possible, perhaps even likely, but how did he know?); *Fundamenta na których Łacinnicy jedność Rusi z Rzymem fundują* (Petruševič 1874, 477–78; not impossible, but what is it?).

A more interesting line of questioning, however, is: how soon were Smotryc'kyj's contemporaries aware that he had written the works we now attribute to him, and how did they (and Smotryc'kyj himself) exploit this information in the public debates?

Let us begin with the first work. Smotryc'kyj published *Thrēnos* in 1610 under the pseudonym Theophil Ortholog. It must have created quite a stir. A letter written by the papal nuncio, Francesco Simonetta, to Cardinal Scipio Borghese-Caffarelli on 18 August 1610 from Vilnius contained what was most likely a reference to *Thrēnos:* "I have not missed any opportunity to offer every fervent and efficacious service to help suppress this infamous Ruthenian book."[18] King Sigismund III Vasa soon forbade the buying or selling of the book on pain of a fine of 5,000 *złotys*, and he ordered the author and printers arrested (see *Akty* 1875, 93–95).

Smotryc'kyj apparently escaped punishment for writing the book, but how long did he escape notice as its author? Skarga seems in 1610 not to have known who wrote it since, as we saw above, he taunted the author by saying that the Uniate and Roman Catholic side would soon find out. Smotryc'kyj wrote in 1629 in his last Uniate work *Exaethesis,* that the secret was well kept, at least for a period: no one, except for a few in the Brotherhood, knew who Theophil Ortholog was.[19] And Moroxovs'kyj (1612, A2ᵛ) was still calling the author "anonymous" in 1612. The Uniate Smotryc'kyj was to claim that he had soon regretted having written the work and that he made several attempts to renounce it, including a performance at the Derman' Monastery.[20] The Orthodox side, at pains to discredit everything the new convert claimed, alleged he had never been in Derman' before 1621, and thus could not have made his public statement of regret.[21] The Uniates had already claimed in 1621 that Smotryc'kyj had expressed his regret to them a few years earlier. Again, they had their reasons for doing so: if true, the allegation might discredit Smotryc'kyj in Orthodox eyes. Out of all this disagreement the likelihood arises that it became known (at least by certain people on both sides) sometime in the mid 1610s, probably after 1612, that it was Smotryc'kyj who had written *Thrēnos*. The first public use of this knowledge, however, seems to have come in the polemic of 1621–1623. Smotryc'kyj's authorship of *Thrēnos* was by now an open secret that the Uniate and Roman Catholic side sought to exploit in its works.

Since, in the early stages of the polemic, the Roman Catholics and Uniates would often attribute authorship of an anonymous work to Smotryc'kyj on the basis of stylistic devices and mottoes, let us pause at this point to pose another question debated in the polemic of the time: was Smotryc'kyj a good prose stylist? This question may cause some surprise, since this is perhaps one of the few things upon which later scholarship on both sides of the issue has seemed to agree. But for Smotryc'kyj's contemporaries, as usual, it depended entirely on one's point of view. The Orthodox called Smotryc'kyj a second Chrysostom, in defense of whose works one might reasonably shed one's blood (see Smotryc'kyj 1629a, cited above, p. 40); the Uniate side called him a second Cicero and sent Latin translations of his works to Rome (see below, pp. 45, 153–54). But each side offered their respective high opinions of Smotryc'kyj's eloquence only while he was writing for their side. When he was writing for the other side, his style was subject to question, or rather, to ridicule.[22] This confessionally motivated evaluation of style has been continued in a few of the more recent scholarly investigations (see, e.g., Urban 1957, 197). To take a broader view of the issue, all this attention to Smotryc'kyj's style can be interpreted as a recognition of the persuasiveness of his prose and as an attempt to enhance or to neutralize its attraction.

The *Letter* written in 1621 in response to the second edition of the *Verification of Innocence* attributed that work to Smotryc'kyj by identifying his style:

> [The second edition of *Verification of Innocence* was dedicated to us] by your side, or rather by you alone, Smotryc'kyj, who . . . clearly gave yourself away in it by your affected style, by the childish-stupid phrasing, and by the confounded sense from the interwoven words (by which you pass yourself off as a wise one with the simpler people).[23]

The *Letter* returned over and over to ridicule Smotryc'kyj's "most wanton style and language,"[24] his love of neologisms or, as the *Letter* put it, his "invented morosophic words."[25] (The words "childish-stupid" and "morosophic" may themselves have been intended as a parody of Smotryc'kyj's style.) Moreover, according to the Uniates, his was a prose style that only the author could love:

> We looked even further in that book of yours, and we were amazed at the duplicity of the words and at their mass, at the incomprehensible confusion *sensus insensati* [of insensate sense], from which even the author himself would not be able to extract himself and comprehensible only when he sharply assaults and attacks someone.[26]

They also identified certain words that were characteristic of Smotryc'kyj's usage (e.g., *sequak,* pl. *sequakowie,* from the Latin *sequax,* i.e., attendant or follower); these would appear in other Roman Catholic and Uniate works as a way of identifying Smotryc'kyj.[27]

Moreover, it was on these same stylistic grounds that the *Letter* identified Smotryc'kyj as the author of a petition from the Cossack Hetman Petro Konaševyč-Sahajdačnyj to King Sigismund III:

> What sort of tumult, sedition, rousing of the people against the bishop in Polack [i.e., Josafat Kuncevyč], who had been established according to canon and according to the laws and authority of His Royal Majesty, and against the local palatine, were worked by means of the letters and patents and emissaries of the intruder upon that bishopric, the Reverend (as he titles himself) Miolentij? But that knightly people (that we return to it), brought by you to sedition, was convinced to undertake negotiations with Their Lord Graces, the Hetmans, concerning these bishops and the metropolitan, and to undertake a legation to His Royal Majesty. The recent embassy of *Pan* Sahajdačnyj to His Majesty the King gives you away. For he arrived with some monk of his (he names him in that legation) for the bishopric for which you are greedy, and the legation submitted in writing expresses all your emotion, and its entirety is about the Greek and about his deeds in Moscow and about you who were consecrated by him, as if that legation were written by you (which is certainly the case). For the entire content and the sense of your *Verification,* and even the style of the words, give you away. . . . This is all your handiwork.[28]

In order to identify Smotryc'kyj as the author of *Verification of Innocence* and the Cossack petitions, the authors of the *Letter* must have drawn on their knowledge of the style of some previous work. It was not necessarily *Thrēnos* that defined for them Smotryc'kyj's style. After all, he had already printed the *Homiliary Gospel,* the grammar of Church Slavonic, and the two versions of his funeral oration on the death of

Leontij Karpovyč, and all of them in his own name. I suspect, nonetheless, that the Uniates were referring here to *Thrēnos,* and that they did so in order to tie Smotryc'kyj, through his penchant for a highly rhetorical pathos, to activities that bordered on the seditious. This—and not idle literary curiosity—was after all the main reason for making Smotryc'kyj the author of Sahajdačnyj's petition.[29]

The authors of the *Letter* noted one similarity between *Thrēnos* and the *Verification of Innocence*: a list of Ruthenian nobility who had been "lost" to Rus'. The list found in *Thrēnos* (15^{r-v}/31) was a famous one, which readers in the 1620s would certainly readily recall. That found in the preface to *Verification of Innocence* (Smotryc'kyj 1621b,):(iii^v–iv^r) was much more modest and would not, in my opinion, necessarily evoke that earlier work. And yet the authors mentioned *Thrēnos* and made an obscure reference to its printer, "Lohvyn" (Leontij) Karpovyč[30]:

> Why should the noble Ruthenian nation be at fault for the evil deeds of your volunteers for Church authority. This does not concern us, who are descended from our ancient ancestors in the Ruthenian nation, nor the descendents of those whom you named in this preface, as once upon a time in the *Lament* published allegedly by Lohvyn.[31]

Here we have attribution by analogy, which, if *Thrēnos* was still as popular and as dangerous (for its author and printer) as it once was, may have sufficed to link the author of *Verification of Innocence* with the author of *Thrēnos*. There was a passage toward the end of the *Verification of Innocence* that could not have failed to evoke *Thrēnos:* this was a section entitled "Consolation of the Ruthenian Nation" ("Uciecha narodu ruskiego"), in which Smotryc'kyj adapted verses from Jeremiah 1–3 in an extended lament of the events that had recently occurred in Vilnius, after the Uniates had brought legal charges against those Church and city leaders who had been involved in the "illegal" consecration of the Orthodox hierarchy. The authors of the *Letter* did not mention *Thrēnos* in their treatment of this passage; but they did identify pathos as characteristic of one aspect of Smotryc'kyj's style, and they sought to neutralize it by accusing him of using rhetoric in an irresponsible manner:

> The "Consolation of the Innocence of the Ruthenian Nation," the "Admonition" to your side, the presentation of the Vilnius tragedy that occurred to the burghers, your *sequacks* [followers]—this your pathos

(in the "Consolation of the Innocence of the Ruthenian Nation"
through invented words taken from Holy Scripture), by which you
arouse the people, is not of any use except for tumults, rebellions,
seditions, which everyone will recognize who will wish to notice it.
And so, are you not the authors of sedition in the Commonwealth?[32]

Yet another response (apparently also last of the three, dated 10
August 1621 in the letter of dedication [A4^r]) to the *Verification of
Innocence,* Tymoteusz Symanowicz's *Examination of the False
Verification,* identified Smotryc'kyj directly (or almost directly) as the
author of *Thrēnos.*[33]

As the polemic of the early 1620s continued, the Roman Catholic-
Uniate side gradually escalated the war of words, placing special emphasis
on Smotryc'kyj's training and style. The *Twofold Guilt,* also written in
1621 in response to the *Verification of Innocence,* noted Smotryc'kyj's
predilection for unusual and invented words. Smotryc'kyj answered
with a *Defense of the Verification* (Vilnius, 1621), to which the other
side responded with an *Examination of the Defense* (Vilnius, 1621).
This second work sent the unnamed author of the *Defense* to read
Baronius' *Annales,* "if he will not be too lazy to finish it."[34] Why this
jibe? Because readers on all sides knew by now that Smotryc'kyj was
meant, and that the Orthodox side had made the fact of his learning a
weapon in their polemical arsenal. As the work continued, the references
to Smotryc'kyj became less veiled and sought more and more to neutralize
his erudition and eloquence. "Perhaps he did not know this," the
Examination resumed its ridicule, "but that is not surprising, since he did
not read this in his grammar."[35] From this point on in the polemic, for the
Roman Catholic and Uniate side the unnamed opponent would become
the grammarian: because, of course, Smotryc'kyj was the author of a
famous grammar of Church Slavonic; but, even more importantly,
because, by making Smotryc'kyj a grammarian, they would be able to
concede to him expertise in what they portrayed as a lowly science,
thereby denying him the right to take part in doctrinal debates. Smotryc'kyj
was for them the old grammarian and the new theologian;[36] he may have
known grammar, according to the Uniates—and even this was subject to
question—but he did not know dialectics.[37] In addition to this general
campaign to belittle Smotryc'kyj's literacy, the Uniates had a very
specific goal in mind: to goad Smotryc'kyj and the Orthodox side into
taking part in a public disputation (no doubt rigged by the authorities in

favor of the Uniate and Roman Catholic side). We will challenge your
learning and powers of persuasion, they seem to say, so that you will be
forced to demonstrate them to the world. What, according to the Uniates,
caused the Orthodox to refuse to debate?:

> . . . *crassa ignorantia et diffidentia causae* [crass ignorance and the
> diffidence of the cause]. You are ignoramuses (forgive us), having
> nothing firmly established in your heads; rather you only base
> yourselves on the words which, like parrots, you use stupidly in your
> sermons and in print.[38]

The name-calling reached lower and lower depths. The Uniates
translated the Latin proverb *stultorum plena sunt omnia* ("fools are
everywhere") into Polish with a reference to Smotryc'kyj's name before
he took the habit: "The world is full of Maksyms."[39] And amidst all this
personal invective, the Uniates continued to tie Smotryc'kyj to *Thrēnos:*

> Was it long ago when that [author of] *Appendix* [to *Elenchus*] published
> a book, allegedly translating from Slavonic into Polish, in which he
> rejected prayers to the Most Holy Virgin, Mother of God, and to all the
> saints. Had he himself not already been poisoned by the teaching of
> the heterodox? And did that poisonous spider not attempt to poison
> others with that teaching, until our pastors and their dogs sounded the
> alarm against that wolf?[40]

Here the indirect reference to the infamous book ("allegedly translated
from Slavonic into Polish") leads me to believe that in 1621 it was still a
dangerous book: dangerous to the faithful of the other side, but perhaps
also dangerous to the author, should he be identified by the authorities.

Smotryc'kyj himself added to the intrigue by including in all of his
works, beginning in 1621 with the second edition of the *Verification of
Innocence,* a motto—either at the beginning or at the end of the work (or
both)—which identified the work as his. The motto—in English: *My
life's only hope Christ JesuS*—appeared in Greek in his Orthodox works
and in Latin and Polish in his Uniate works. For example, in the *Defense*
it appeared in the following form, Μία ζωῆς ἡμῶν ἐλπὶς Ἰησοῦς ὁ
χριστὸΣ (Smotryc'kyj 1621c, 127/462), in the *Apology* as *Meae vitae
vnica Spes, IEsvs ChristvS* (Smotryc'kyj 1628a, *1ʳ/514), and in
Exaethesis as *Mego żywota iedyna nadzieia IEzvs ChristuS* (Smotryc'kyj
1629b,):(1ʳ/695). The first and last letters, which were always capitalized,
identified the author by his initials. And in case anyone had not figured
it out, Smotryc'kyj could have pointed to the fact that in 1618–1619 he

had closed his grammar of Church Slavonic, a work to which he signed his name on the title page, with precisely this motto in its Greek form. In fact, this was the first time this device had appeared in print. Thus, by using this motto in "anonymous" works, Smotryc'kyj was acknowledging these works as his without any doubt. By signing his polemical works in the name of all the fathers of the Orthodox monastery and by adding to that his personalized motto, Smotryc'kyj could exert some control over his anonymity: he could maintain the fiction that the works were written anonymously in the name of the entire Brotherhood, but he could also imply that no anonymous work without this motto was to be attributed to him with any certainty.

The Uniates got the message. But they also attempted to exploit the situation:

> But we do not make this our cause, nor will we: it is our gain and praise to suffer for Christ the Lord and for His truth. And time will tell, the Lord God granting, if the malice of man should arise, that we will be more eager for this [i.e., to suffer for the faith] than [the author of] the *Appendix* [to *Elenchus*], who, it is true, offered himself for this, but it soon became clear that his offer was not genuine. For someone reminded him about that *per tertias personas* [through third persons] with a staff for the dishonorable words, which both [the author of] *Elenchus* as well as [the author of] the *Appendix* [to *Elenchus*], in their wretched little writings against us, have placed upon us *plaustra integra* [by the cartload], to the point that he had to defend himself before everyone, renouncing, the poor wretch, even his work, for which he would be deserving of praise and gratitude; but instead, for his wolf-like humility, he ascribed this work to someone else, displaying some little schoolboy's Greek motto, the beginning of which is M and the end S, so that we might surmise the name and surname of that author. Dear [author of] *Appendix,* if that work is dear to God and praiseworthy among men, then why do you so urgently reject it? If it is evil, then why do you foist it upon your neighbor, yourself fleeing before it? I suppose the problem is the little wife, the dear children; *compatiar tibi* [may I pity you], poor thing; do not take upon yourself what you cannot manage; you have no reason to show yourself to the world: the dog can even safely bark in the corner under the bench, but on the street he may be punished with a staff, for which he himself will be at fault; or, that I speak more to the point, it is safer for the wolf to snatch sheep in the woods than in the field near the shepherd and the dogs, where he will be punished with a staff, and where it will not be easy for him to avoid the dogs.[41]

But what are we to make of this mysterious web of allegations? Was Smotryc'kyj being charged with writing the *Elenchus* and its *Appendix,* or wasn't he? Or were there supposed to be two different authors here?

The motto clearly identified him as the author, but in this passage Antonij Seljava (Sielawa) hinted that someone else had written it and had sought to place the blame on Smotryc'kyj. Even worse: this "someone else" had been subjected to some public humiliation—perhaps an event which the rumor mill had made known to much of the readership; and that someone had—or did not have—a wife and children. But Smotryc'kyj *was* the author of *Elenchus* (he acknowledged his authorship later as a Uniate), and Seljava must have known this: he had just told us as much by identifying the author of the *Appendix* with the author of a work allegedly translated some years ago from Church Slavonic into Polish and written under the influence of the heterodox (see *Antelenchus* 1621, 53/716–17). And the dig about schoolboy's Greek was reminiscent of the entire Roman Catholic and Uniate campaign against Smotryc'kyj.

So what was the point? It is entirely possible that this was one of those veiled references to the scandals of the day that will remain obscure for us. Was Smotryc'kyj secretly a family man?[42] Was he attacked with a club in public? Had Smotryc'kyj, when challenged directly, denied his authorship of the work? Had someone else—to whom these allegations applied—hidden himself behind Smotryc'kyj's initials? Were these two parts of *Elenchus* written by different authors? But is it not also possible that this tissue of—if I understand them correctly—partially contradictory allegations was simply another attempt to smoke out the author? It is possible that this was not so much a reflection of what the rumor mill was saying, as an attempt to direct that useful medium, so that Smotryc'kyj would be forced to step forward and take credit for all of his works, while denying that he or anyone connected with the *Elenchus* ever had a wife and children. However this may be, we can be certain of one thing: at this point Smotryc'kyj was still unwilling in public either to acknowledge that he had written *Thrēnos,* or to renounce it before the Orthodox as an authority on Church and faith.

Both sides would continue to play the game of names after Smotryc'kyj's conversion. Smotryc'kyj then acknowledged his authorship of the old works in infrequent acts of contrition, but for the most part he criticized the views of Ortholog as if he were a stranger to him.[43] The Orthodox side, for its part, defended "Ortholog," "Elench," etc., against the authors of *Apology* and *Exaethesis* as if the four had never met.[44]

This game of multiple identities also allowed both sides to revise their opinions of Smotryc'kyj's learning and eloquence. The old schoolboy, infatuated with words he did not understand would become for the Uniates a master of Polish prose, a Polish Cicero,[45] while the old heir to Chrysostom would become for the Orthodox an addict of macaronic style and empty syllogisms.[46] The secretary of *Propaganda Fide,* Francesco Ingoli, wrote on the back of the letter Ruc'kyj sent to Rome in 1627 with news of Smotryc'kyj's conversion that the archbishop was "the most learned man among them [i.e., the Orthodox] and a most experienced preacher in the Ruthenian language."[47] And the Greek motto, Smotryc'kyj's old badge of shame according to the Uniates, became in its Polish and Latin reincarnations—and for the same Uniate and Roman Catholic side—the mark of his honor.[48] Suša, as usual, even attempted to rehabilitate the young Smotryc'kyj: he was always eloquent, even too eloquent, since he used his pen for the wrong cause at first. The Orthodox, according to Suša, considered *Thrēnos* a work in defense of which one should be willing to die, treated it as an heirloom, and took it with them into their coffins.[49]

In Uniate historiography, two of Smotryc'kyj's works—*Elenchus* and *Exaethesis*—had careers far in excess of their intrinsic interest. In 1627, when Smotryc'kyj was about to convert, the Roman Catholic palatine of Braclav, Aleksander Zasławski, singled out *Elenchus,* next to *Thrēnos,* of course, for special disapprobation,[50] and Suša followed him in his evaluation.[51] And when the Uniate Smotryc'kyj gave lists of his Orthodox works that he considered relatively inoffensive, he often omitted *Elenchus* (and, of course, *Thrēnos*); or, conversely, when he criticized his past works he included *Elenchus* with *Thrēnos* among the unredeemable— and this on five different occasions.[52] Now, my point here is that there is little obvious difference in the works of 1621 and 1622, all of which were devoted to the defense of the recently consecrated Orthodox hierarchy, and none of which had much to say on specifically doctrinal matters. Perhaps Smotryc'kyj was seeking to conform to Zasławski's view of his work. And similarly, *Exaethesis,* a point-by-point refutation of Andrij Mužylovs'kyj's *Antapologia,* was later portrayed by the Uniates as a rhetorical masterwork (see Suša 1666, 121–22). The explanation is similar in both cases: as far as I can see, the Uniate and Roman Catholic side was seeking to place a more definitive break between Smotryc'kyj's Orthodox and Uniate careers (more definitive than Smotryc'kyj himself had made it, as we soon will see), and to portray Smotryc'kyj as now a full-fledged Uniate writer. Thus they chose to condemn his final Orthodox polemical work simply because it was final, and to praise his final Uniate work because it was the least ambiguously Uniate of his "Uniate" works.

Chapter 4

Lay Leader

We have relatively few records concerning Smotryc'kyj's activities before 1620, when (at age 43, more or less) he was consecrated archbishop of Polack. (The historical record improves somewhat after 1621, but not by much.) Still, there are indications that he must have been one of the leading laymen in Ruthenian culture in the period from his return from Germany to Rus' (probably sometime between 1606 and 1608) and until he took the habit in 1617–1618. Above all, we can infer this on the basis of three quite different works, each the Ruthenian masterwork of its genre: the *Thrēnos* of 1610,[1] a polemical tract that earned him both an unusually ardent following among the Orthodox and a threat of punishment from the Roman Catholic authorities; the *Homiliary Gospel* of 1616, the first Ruthenian version of a popular set of sermons, which, in this edition and in its revision of 1638, may have been read from Ruthenian pulpits and used in Ruthenian private devotion in many parishes for several decades in the mid-seventeenth century;[2] and finally, the grammar of Church Slavonic of 1618–1619, a frequently cited authority—well into the eighteenth century—on the liturgical language of the Orthodox Slavs in an area that included Rus', Muscovy, Serbia, and Bulgaria, as well as of the Glagolitic monks in Dalmatia and the Glagolitic printing house in Rome.[3] In terms of practical significance, these may have been the most important works of his life. It is worth noting here that the fragmented portrayals that have separated Smotryc'kyj's work as a grammarian from his other works have obscured the fact that the grammar was only one of his projects in the area of sacred philology in this period.

But what else do we know about the life of this leading lay figure during this crucial time in his life? With the exception of an incident (or series of incidents) which the Uniates would later use in an attempt to blackmail him, we know next to nothing. This period, when Smotryc'kyj was working on some of his more important projects, remains for us shrouded in mysteries: partially because of a lack of information, and partially because of the later controversies.

What is relatively certain about this period? Smotryckyj had returned from Germany to the Polish-Lithuanian Commonwealth at least by 1608–1609, since he published *Thrēnos* in 1610, and he later stated that the Vilnius Brotherhood had taken "more than a year" to censor it.[4] We do not know how long he had been back at that time. In the Orthodox *Pamflet* written sometime between 1628 and 1633 we read that Smotryckyj returned from Germany "after a few years"; if he did indeed go to Germany ca. 1601, then perhaps his return to Lithuania fell sometime around the middle of the decade. The name "Solomerecki" appeared in the matriculation records of Leipzig University for 1606 (Kot 1952, 243); if this was Bohdan, and if Smotryckyj was still acting as his preceptor, then he might have returned sometime between 1606 and 1608. (And perhaps, assuming Smotryckyj returned to Lithuania ca. 1607, we should take seriously the information found in the nuncio's report of 1628 [see Velykyj 1960, 298] that Smotryckyj had written, or had at least begun to compose, *Thrēnos* while still in Germany.)

Thrēnos, as is well known, met with the ire of the Catholic authorities. Writing on 1 April 1610 from his "camp near Smolensk," Sigismund III ordered the book confiscated, the printer and author imprisoned, and its reading banned. The printer was Leontij Karpovyč, who would become archimandrite of the Vilnius Brotherhood Monastery during the period when Smotryckyj became a monk there and published his *Homiliary Gospel* and his grammar of Church Slavonic at the press in Vievis.[5] Upon Karpovyč's death Smotryckyj would succeed him as archimandrite. Perhaps Smotryckyj was referring to Karpvoyč's role in the *Thrēnos* affair (though with what caution even ten years later!) when he wrote:

> He [had become] a confessor in essence and a martyr by will, when he had to die harshly every day for the Gospel truth throughout two entire years, tortured through harsh and cruel imprisonment in the dungeon. You, Orthodox Christians, are aware of the course of this matter; you are aware of the cause, aware also of the effect.[6]

From our present vantage point we know that *Thrēnos* was read and copied in Muscovy; it is worth noting, however, that Smotryckyj himself knew by 1620 that he was an author with an international reputation.[7] (In an effort to represent the printing of *Thrēnos* as a treasonous act, Skarga had placed the work in Muscovy at the time of the Polish campaign of 1610.[8])

Smotryc'kyj must have been tonsured sometime between 1616, when he signed his name as Maksentij to the *Homiliary Gospel,* and 1618, when the first copies of the grammar of Church Slavonic appeared with his monastic name Meletij on the title page. In 1621 the author of the *Examination of the Defense* claimed that four years had not passed since the period just before Smotryc'kyj took the habit. Thus it would seem likely that Smotryc'kyj received his monastic tonsure sometime late in 1617 or early in 1618. He later wrote that he had lived in the monastery for more than a year before becoming a monk;[9] thus he probably entered the monastery ca. 1616 (about the time he was publishing his *Homiliary Gospel* on the Brotherhood press in Vievis: all the prefaces but the one to which Smotryc'kyj appended his own name were signed in the name of the "monks of the Holy Spirit Monastery").

Where was he between 1610 and 1616? The sparse sources point toward a continued connection with the Solomerec'kyj family and toward activities in the Minsk palatinate. (Was he hiding out from the authorities there while Karpovyč served his time in prison?) According to Suša he gained the affections of the local people through the eloquence of his sermons (in Ruthenian, presumably, since the "simple and common people" were his audience).[10] (The Orthodox would later deny that he was ever much of a preacher: see below, p. 88.) In an Orthodox *Pamflet* we read the following concerning Smotryc'kyj's stay on the Solomerec'kyj holdings:

> After a few years, he returned again with the young prince [Solomerec'kyj] to Balkahrad, to his [the prince's] mother, Princess Jeva Korsakivna Solomerec'ka—a great adherent of Orthodoxy—who was by now already a widow. She held the aforementioned Maksym in great respect, and for the sake of Orthodoxy she gladly listened to him in many things. And he, doing much in defense of the Orthodox faith, was known and honored by the local church for his writings.[11]

Smotryc'kyj himself would later write that after his studies, and before he entered the monastery, he spent "a few years on courtly amusements as a sort of rest from the dust of the schools" (see Smotryc'kyj 1621c, 104–105/451). Was the "court" that of the Solomerec'kyjs?

What else was on Smotryc'kyj's desk in this period? Suša suggested that he took part as an editor in several other literary projects:

> Nor is it proper to pass over in silence here what was also worthy of praise in him. For indeed, bringing the Slavonic Psalter and New Testament into agreement with [copies in] the Greek idiom so laboriously, thus did he so beneficially reform the entire Ruthenian nation. By his care and industry there were edited in print, along with various divine offices and prayers, a breviary in that same language. He added to these lucubrations a lexicon and a grammar, likewise in Slavonic.[12]

We recognize the grammar, of course, but what about all these other works? These certainly are the sorts of things one might expect Smotryc'kyj to have been working on at the same time he was writing his grammar of Church Slavonic and translating the *Homiliary Gospel.* In fact, the question is not without interest for students of that grammar. In part, the grammar seems to have grown out of work on the correction of texts used in the Church Slavonic Bible[13]—this is especially clear in the section devoted to syntax. It would be useful to know which texts Smotryc'kyj examined, whether he also looked at liturgical texts in his work on the grammar, and whether any of the extant works of this sort stemmed from his workshop. Perhaps Smotryc'kyj was involved in the work on some of them. But then again, he may have been directly involved with none of them: we must never underestimate Suša's need to make a hero even out of the "Saul of the Disunion." Nonetheless, it is worth noting that in the early 1610s the Vilnius Brotherhood issued from its press in Vievis several works of the types Suša later attributed to Smotryc'kyj: for example, *Daily Prayers* in 1611 (including a catechism; see *Kniha* 1986, 84, No. 70); New Testament and Psalter in 1611 (*Kniha* 1986, 84–85, No. 71); *Horologion* (Canonical Book of Hours) in 1612 (*Kniha* 1986, 85–86, No. 73); *Anthology* in 1613 (i.e., an anthology of prayers; *Kniha* 1986, 86, No. 74); and, *Prayer Book* in 1617 (*Kniha* 1986, 88, No. 79). It would seem reasonable to suspect that Smotryc'kyj at least collaborated on some of these projects.

Smotryc'kyj's connection with the Solomerec'kyjs and with the Brotherhood printing house in Vievis and in Vilnius seems to indicate that he resided in Belarus and Lithuania in these years. But was he also rector of the school in Kiev during this period? It is often thought that Syl'vestr Kosov said that he was. Defending the legal right of the Orthodox to Latin schools in the Commonwealth and the need for Latin learning, Kosov wrote in 1635:

> And since those schools in which we now teach were always in our
> possession in the past, as they are now, and since Smotryc'kyj, Kasijan,
> and others, who taught in Latin without interruption until our times,
> were rectors over them—therefore, His Royal Majesty will deign to
> confirm this one [i.e., school] out of his gracious lordly mercy.[14]

But this evidence is inconclusive. In what year was Smotryc'kyj's
rectorship supposed to have fallen? Kasijan Sakovyč was rector of the
school in Kiev from 1620 to 1624. Did the order in which the names
were given imply that Smotryc'kyj preceded him? It is certainly unlikely
that Smotryc'kyj occupied this position once he had been made archbishop,
that is, after 1621. In 1617 Jov Borec'kyj held the position in question.
On another occasion Smotryc'kyj told us that he had "lived" with
Borec'kyj for four years (see below, p. 130). Could this mean that he was
in Kiev for four years at some time prior to 1616, when we find him in
the Vilnius Brotherhood? But when? Nimčuk (1979, 13–14) looked for
a period of four consecutive years and placed Smotryc'kyj's rectorship
of the Kiev school in the period 1614–1618. But Smotryc'kyj's *Homiliary
Gospel* appeared in Vievis in 1616, precisely in the middle of this
period, making it seem more likely that he was in Lithuania at this time.
We know that he lived in the monastery for a year before his tonsure in
1617–1618. Perhaps it was sometime between 1610 and 1616 that he
was in Kiev. The Brotherhood school was founded in 1615–1616, so
perhaps Smotryc'kyj was briefly its first rector. But the sources would
seem to imply that Smotryc'kyj was in Belarus after his return from
Germany and before he became connected with the Vilnius Brotherhood.
As we will soon see, Smotryc'kyj seems to have made a brief trip to Kiev
and Volhynia in about 1617, but this was probably only for a few weeks,
and the apparent purpose of his trip was not pedagogical but to talk with
leaders of the Orthodox side about the prospects for a reunification of
the nation. Perhaps the four years that Smotryc'kyj "lived" with Borec'kyj
were not consecutive. Thus we could look for a briefer period in the
1610s when Smotryc'kyj could have been present in Kiev, and for a
second, briefer period later on—perhaps 1623, before he went east, or
1626–1627, just after he had returned.

Let us, however, examine the question from another side: why is
everyone so certain that Kosov had the Kiev school in mind when he
mentioned Smotryc'kyj? After all, the passage cited above spoke of
schools in the plural, and Kosov mentioned four Orthodox schools in the

few lines preceding this passage: those in Vilnius, L'viv, Kiev, and Vinnycja.[15] It is true that the main thrust of the work was the latter two. But the passage did not say for certain that Smotryc'kyj was connected with the school in Kiev. What is more, there is no necessary reason to link Kosov's testimony to Smotryc'kyj's statement that he spent four years with Borec'kyj. Smotryc'kyj's accounts of his actions in this period omitted any direct reference to Kiev. Could Smotryc'kyj and Borec'kyj have resided for four years not in Kiev but in Vilnius? Or somewhere else? Is L'viv possible? (We know Borec'kyj was there before going to Kiev. There are plenty of gaps in our knowledge of Smotryc'kyj's activities before he went to Vilnius Academy ca. 1596 and again in the early 1610s.) Could they have resided for some non-consecutive period of four years, either in Kiev alone, or in Kiev and Vilnius (or somewhere else)? In any case, we should not be too certain Smotryc'kyj spent much time in Kiev in this period. Perhaps it was in Vilnius that he was rector, perhaps during the second half of the decade.

It seems likely that Smotryc'kyj was rector somewhere; wherever it was, we begin to form a picture of his activities in the period. His interests were homiletics, pedagogy, correction of the church books, and Church Slavonic grammar. All these activities fit together nicely in a complex, the center of which was a new Orthodox Ruthenian sacred philology.

The more interesting question, though, is whether Smotryc'kyj was firmly in the Orthodox camp in this period prior to becoming a monk in the Orthodox Church. This question first became an issue in the public debates of 1621–1622, after Smotryc'kyj and others had been consecrated to episcopal, archiepiscopal, and metropolitan sees by Patriarch Theophanes of Jerusalem. It was, of course, the Uniate and Roman Catholic side that initiated the debate—with an obvious purpose: to weaken Smotryc'kyj's position as the leader of the Orthodox side and the sole Orthodox participant in the pamphlet wars by encouraging doubts among the flock about the reliability of the shepherd.

The Uniates first sought to influence the rumor mill in this matter in 1621 in *Twofold Guilt,* a work often attributed to the Uniate Metropolitan of Kiev, Josyf Ruc'kyj. They began their allegations with a flourish guaranteed to appeal to the rumormongers:

> Concerning your Smotryc'kyj I can no longer keep silent about what, up until now, has not come out from our side in public as a public

declaration. And even now, not all will be told; a little something will remain secret. But it is absolutely necessary to mention what properly belongs to this matter.[16]

According to the Uniates, Smotryc'kyj negotiated for some time (this, as we will learn, was supposed to have occurred ca. 1617) "to see how he himself might come and might bring his group along with him, to union with us."[17] Smotryc'kyj had claimed he believed (at least in this Uniate account) all the same articles of faith as the Romans. "Proof" of this was the fact that some of the Orthodox had reported to the Uniates that Smotryc'kyj had asserted to his own side that "the Romans will be saved in their religion."[18] A further sign of his *bona fides* was the fact that he had allegedly encouraged the Uniates to attack the Orthodox, summoning them to a public disputation.[19] Moreover, Smotryc'kyj supposedly drew up "several tens" of theses on the procession of the Holy Spirit—presumably, in this Uniate account, in favor of the *Filioque*—and had urged the Uniates to publish them. The Uniates responded that there was too much material for inclusion in a Polish book but agreed to publish excerpts in Lev Krevza's *Defense of Unity.*[20] In spite of the fact that the Orthodox had refused to take part in a public disputation, Smotryc'kyj

> did not cease to negotiate with us, and he even attached to himself certain laymen, until he was found out. Thereupon everything was made public, and the poor fellow was in some trouble with those of little understanding. That man—if he is now of that same faith of which he was at that time—is our brother. If he is of a different faith, then he is a proper and true apostate, for he betrayed the faith that he had recognized and had already professed before people (and there were several of them there, both clergy and laity).[21]

The passage I have summarized and cited above is typical of much of the personal libel that informed the confessional polemics of the day. There is no real proof here. The strategy seems to have been one of piling layer upon layer of allegation so that the opponent would have to use great care in distinguishing for the readership between truth, half-truth, and lie, and thus appear more guilty in the process. Most important for us here is that, in this picture, in the period before the publication of the *Defense of Unity,* that is before 1617, in the year or so before he took the habit, Smotryc'kyj was represented as a kind of double agent: he was allegedly running back and forth between the Uniates and the Orthodox, seeking to bring the Orthodox to a public debate, and writing a set of theses on the procession of the Holy Spirit to aid the other side (portions of which were apparently published in the *Defense of Unity*), until he was caught by the Orthodox and, through fear of the ignorant Orthodox laity, forced to cease his direct dealings with the Uniates. But these allegations also contained a threat: if you do not do as we wish, so the Uniates seem to have been saying to Smotryc̆kyj, we will produce names of individuals involved and make even more damaging allegations. Here we have the picture of Smotryc̆kyj that would appear in the propaganda of both sides at various times: he was isolated, duplicitous, disloyal, cowardly, easily manipulated—a man who liked to have it both ways and was afraid to take a stand. But let us not forget that the Uniates drew this picture not so much to establish the truth about the past as to influence the future, to gain control over Smotryc̆kyj's actions. And at this point in 1621 the Uniate side wished, short of Smotryc̆kyj's conversion, or at least loss of credit with the Orthodox side, to blackmail him into taking part in a public debate. This must have been one of the reasons for withholding some piece of incriminating evidence with the not-so-veiled understanding that these things could and would be made public if Smotryc̆kyj did not do as they wished.

Smotryc̆kyj included in the *Defense of the Verification,* also published in 1621 in Vilnius, a third-person account of his actions in the period in question, which was offered as a defense against the charges I have outlined above:

> Father Smotryc̆kyj answers your allegations thus: if you had not mixed falsehood in among the truth, he would accept everything with which you filled your ninth chapter concerning him. But since some of this is said by you so deviously that, if it were not refuted by a proper answer, it could harm his reputation, . . . we record this account in his favor against your account.[22]

This preamble to a defense of his actions in 1617 is interesting to me, above all, for its recognition of the rules of the game: the Uniates had sought to tarnish Smotryc̆kyj's reputation with the Orthodox; his response was to take the same general set of facts—events he was apparently unable to deny—and place them in a different context, one that would portray him as firm in his allegiance to the Orthodox Church.

Father Smotryc̆kyj, we read, "spent his young years up to manhood on liberal arts, both here in the fatherland and in foreign countries." He then spent a few years "on courtly amusements as a sort of rest from the

dust of the schools"—this presumably a reference to the time spent in
the 1610s at the estate of the Solomerec'kyj's. When it then "came time
for him to order his life [precisely at age 40, if he was born in 1577] and
to employ, for his own benefit and that of his neighbors, the tool of the
studies that he had gathered for so many years—[he] had always planned
to enter the monastic order (for which he had an eager soul almost since
the days of his childhood) only when he had obtained certain knowledge
of the intended goal of both sides amongst the confounded brethren (for
that had bothered him for a long time)." And since, according to
Smotryc'kyj, he was aware of the "goal" of his own side but ignorant of
that of the other, he asked permission from his superior, Leontij Karpovyč,
to contact the Uniates in order to find out what they were about. At this
time Smotryc'kyj was living at the Vilnius Orthodox Brotherhood
Monastery of the Church of the Descent of the Holy Spirit without
putting on monastic vestments, "as the custom of the monastery has it,"
in a sort of novitiate. It was under these circumstances, and with the
blessing of Karpovyč, that Smotryc'kyj had meetings with Uniate youth,
and then, since the youth could not provide him with the information he
sought, with Ruc'kyj, Kuncevyč, and Krevza.[23]

What is of central importance here is that Smotryc'kyj's descriptions
of the meetings changed the power structure entirely with respect to the
Uniate representations:

> And through these three meetings with these individuals, he discussed
> with them not, as the *Redargutor* [i.e., the "Refuter" of *Verification of
> Innocence,* i.e., the author of *Twofold Guilt*] alleges, how he himself
> might come and bring his group with him to agreement with them, but
> what goal the Union had, and how, if it should come to a total [union]
> of our entire Ruthenian nation, the faith of our Eastern confession can
> remain whole in it, since without a patriarch, whichever direction that
> Union turns, we face an obstacle. And they can remember well for
> what reasons. He demonstrated to them the indignity [we suffer] from
> both their side and from ours; he demonstrated to them the destruction
> of those who confess their faith, by both them and by their Union: that
> by entire houses, the Uniates transfer from the Union to the Roman
> Church; that the [Orthodox/Uniate] churches on the estates of their
> Lords, the Romans, change into [Roman Catholic] churches; that it is
> permitted to come from the Ruthenian to the Roman religion, but that
> it is forbidden to go from the Roman to the Ruthenian; that they force
> you out of the Ruthenian towns, establishing their schools where your
> Uniate schools were supposed to have been, and such things. This is
> what the conversation of Father Smotryc'kyj was with them during his
> thrice held meetings with the superiors.[24]

Further, Smotryc'kyj claimed that, as far as the salvation of the "Romans" was concerned, he could reasonably say that "*Defectus fidei non excessus condemnat* [it is the defect in faith, not the excess, that condemns souls]"; and he went on to say that the other side was free to interpret these words as it saw fit.[25] These words, silently borrowed from the archbishop of Split and "arch-apostate," Marcantonio de Dominis—an important and unacknowledged fact to which I will return later—provided an unusually flexible polemical tool. Smotryc'kyj claimed he had said nothing more than that correct faith is defined by adherence to a minimum shared by many "particular Churches" and that believing less than that minimum (a "defect" of faith) caused heresy, whereas believing more (an "excess" of faith) was tolerable (see below, pp. 210–17). He claimed here that he had not said specifically to which group the Roman Catholics belonged, and thus they were free to interpret these words as they saw fit.

Smotryc'kyj would use de Dominis' definition of correct faith on several occasions. This pre-irenicist, pre-ecumenical view of Church and faith was a versatile polemical weapon for the Orthodox archbishop. On occasion he would direct it against the Roman Catholics, urging them to accept the Orthodox without the need for a new Union. But in this instance, his audience may actually have been the Orthodox. He could announce to the world that he had used this formula—remarkably unspecific in its terms—and that if the Latins had interpreted it to mean they could be saved in their Church, they were free to do so. For reasons I hope to make clear later (in chapter 12), I suspect this precise formula was not what Smotryc'kyj used in 1617, since it surely stemmed from de Dominis, and, as far as I have been able to ascertain, de Dominis first published this definition of correct faith in 1621. But Smotryc'kyj was already under de Dominis' spell in 1617,[26] and he may have rephrased his earlier argument in terms he had begun to use later. Smotryc'kyj had probably been arguing for some broad ecumenical view of Church and faith in 1617 and was now forced in 1621, once he had become a leader in one of the Churches, to use this fuzzy irenic formula not to argue for tolerance, but in an attempt to quell doubts on his own side about his *bona fides.*

Smotryc'kyj's response to the allegation that he had submitted theses arguing in favor of the *Filioque* took a similar tack. He admitted the "facts"—more or less—but denied their interpretation. Above all, his words offer an interesting insight into the workshop of the leading Orthodox controversialist of the day. Apparently Smotryc'kyj had drawn up several sets of theses presenting the positions of both (or various?) sides on several of the key dogmatic issues separating the confessional camps. And he looked to the tools of sacred philology to support the Orthodox position over the Uniate: the Latin argument was corrupt because it strayed from the words and sense of the Greek authorities.[27]

In their *Examination of the Defense,* the fifth work that appeared in the Vilnius pamphlet war of 1621, the Uniates raised the stakes in their campaign against Smotryc'kyj, as they had threatened to do:

> We mentioned the reason in *Twofold Guilt* why we did not write out everything there concerning Smotryc'kyj's negotiations with us, believing that this was sufficient at that time for an admonition to Smotryc'kyj. And now the [author of] *Defense* denies what we wrote there truly and without any exaggeration. We must say more—and the genuine pure truth—for the affirmation of this, even if it will not be to Smotryc'kyj's liking, obliging him in the fear of God to acknowledge, having consulted his memory (and he can remember, for it was not four years ago), whether it was not as we write here.[28]

Chief among the new pieces of incriminating evidence was the allegation that Smotryc'kyj had soon regretted writing *Thrēnos*— something he had supposedly repeated to the Uniates "about three times." This was no minor charge. Remember that the Orthodox had treated *Thrēnos* as a priceless jewel, an heirloom, a work equal to those of Chrysostom, a book worth taking to the grave; and yet, according to the Uniates, the new leader of the Orthodox had soon changed his mind. The Uniate account cited Smotryc'kyj's alleged words to them: "I have disgusted many . . . by means of that book; I wish to make it good to the Church of God through some significant service, by which as much would be corrected as was ruined." Further, the response by Illja Moroxovs'kyj, bishop of Volodymyr, had completely convinced him: "I had wished [he says in this Uniate allegation] to respond to it, but I could never bring myself to this in any way. There was an occasion, when I wished to respond, that a fear fell upon me; I cast my pen upon the table, and I myself broke into tears."[29]

The "significant service" that Smotryc'kyj had in mind, according to the Uniates, was the unification of Rus'. Many of Smotryc'kyj's actions in this period, in this Uniate portrayal, were directed toward this end. First, he converted one person in Volhynia to the Union who later went over to the Roman Catholic Church, for which a certain priest in Vilnius had chastised him. (The Uniates withheld the name but offered to make it known to the sceptical.)[30]

Worth noting here is the parenthetical Uniate disclaimer that "apparently there were not good Uniate priests in those parts." The Uniates were sensitive to the allegation that they were nothing more than a way station on the path from Orthodoxy to Roman Catholicism.[31] But to whom were they responding here, and why did they reveal to their readers that this convert had gone "all the way." Had Smotrycʹkyj perhaps made this complaint in his private talks with them, or were they engaging in preemptive damage control?

Second (in the Uniate representation), Smotrycʹkyj dwelled as a sort of crypto-Uniate spy with Archimandrite Leontij Karpovyč, for whose conversion he held high hopes, complaining only of the father's laziness. (This must be true, argued the Uniates, "for how would we know this secret, since we were not in communion with him there?")[32] Third, he submitted to the Uniates a plan for gaining all of Rusʹ for the Union: Smotrycʹkyj identified "the individuals upon whom he believed it depended," and he "promised that he would work with them and travel to those places where each lived."[33]

At this point the Uniates wrote, "here we will withhold yet another piece of information, so that we do not say everything; but we will also tell this, if he should remain so shameless and reject what we have cited above; at that time we must bring also the remainder to light, which properly remains secret; whence everyone will understand that it was difficult for us to know about their secret matters, except from one who was himself well aware of them."[34] Notice that the Uniate attempts to corroborate their story depended upon information withheld—a kind of blackmail, whereby they implied they possessed further incriminating evidence they would make public to Smotrycʹkyj's harm. The Uniate account may have been true, but we should note that (as far as I have been able to determine) the threat was not carried out—at least not in the next public stages of the polemic.

"He had contracted with us that he was to travel throughout all the Ruthenian lands so that he might arrange their hearts for mutual harmony and Church unity"—this is how the Uniates begin their account of Smotrycʹkyj's activities as a double agent. Smotrycʹkyj supposedly began his campaign in Vilnius, in an atmosphere of deceit and mistrust. He met secretly with the other side many times (not just the three times, as Smotryc'kyj had claimed), and eventually he was "caught" by an Orthodox shopkeeper at a meeting with the Uniates at the Bernardine friars, after which the Orthodox Brotherhood "vented its anger upon him," and he received a "solemn fraternal punishment" from the entire Brotherhood, including Leontij Karpovyč, with whose blessing (in Smotryc'kyj's version) he had begun to meet with the Uniates. Things finally came to a head when an Orthodox spy ("who, having cunningly inclined to us, found out about everything we had discussed among ourselves—and that is an important person among them") reported on Smotryc'kyj's continued dealings with the Uniates, and the Brotherhood demanded that he "either take the habit or depart from them."[35]

According to the Uniate account, the Uniates remained in contact with Smotryc'kyj, counseling him that "having put off lay clothing, he of his own accord put on the rasson that is the clerical dress in our rite." The next statement is characteristic of much of the Uniate allegations: "At our urging he traveled to Volhynia, to Kiev, still in lay attire, and we know that he returned the same person that departed from us."[36] This manages to make sinister (at least to the Orthodox side) an event that may or may not have had deeper significance. After all, it says nothing more than that Smotryc'kyj went to Volhynia in lay clothing, and that he returned the same as he left.

Thus, in this Uniate picture, Smotryc'kyj was on the verge of converting, and he would have done so, were it not for two things. The first brought with it the conventional charge of timorousness: the Orthodox Brotherhood began to attack him with its suspicions, insisting that he take the habit with them.[37] The second was unusually specific, and will deserve our attention at a later point:

> And at that time he was given the books from the conventicle of Marcantonio de Dominis, Archbishop of Split, the apostate. And having embraced them, he became what he is now. Such is the constancy of this man that one book of one apostate, who introduced a new, unknown sect, one that had not existed previously, and which sect the English Kingdom (to which he had gone) did not wish to receive, so altered him in every regard that *ab equis descendit ad asinos* [he descended from the horses to the asses]. And if, in all this, he should wish to be so shameless, we will convince him and we will name the individuals.[38]

Notice the theme of clothing in these charges and counter-charges. Whose uniform was Smotryc'kyj wearing when he went to Kiev, apparently just before he became a monk? It is curious that Smotryc'kyj had answered this seemingly minor charge before it was made. It is as if, when he told us in *Defense of the Verification* that it was normal for prospective members of the Orthodox Brotherhood Monastery to wear lay clothing during the quasi-novitiate, he knew that the Uniates would make a different interpretation of his behavior. However we interpret this detail, the picture we receive is of a sort of undercover lay brother. And the most important question still remained unanswered: whose side was he on?

The purpose of all these allegations was clearly to encourage doubts among the Orthodox about their leader by alleging that he had secretly regretted writing *Thrēnos,* that he had had conversations with the Uniates concerning the need for unification in the Ruthenian nation, and that he had begun to act under the Uniate banner. But, even assuming events similar to these did take place, Smotryc'kyj could have been speaking of union on his own terms. And indeed, he responded in his *Elenchus* by acknowledging the truthfulness of much that was alleged:

> We do not controvert what you said concerning the meeting of Father Smotryc'kyj with you: it is not customary to criticize in anyone the *pium intentum ad optimum finem* [pious intention toward the best end], through whatever *media* [means], so long as it be done honestly. Had he conferred with you in order to remain with you, he would have done that; but since he conferred with you in order to understand from you whether there would ever be any hope of your return whence you fell away, and since he did not see this in you, he left you alone, and he himself did what he was supposed to do. As far as the *Lament* is concerned (since you insist that he is the author), neither he nor we regret its publication; to the contrary, we delight in it, and we recommend it for the reading of all Orthodox and those who believe otherwise.[39]

But recall once again: Smotryc'kyj was writing for two audiences—the Uniates who had made the allegations and the Orthodox in whose eyes the Uniates had sought to discredit him. Let us pay special attention to what Smotryc'kyj felt he could admit and what he could not or would not admit. The fact that meetings occurred need not or (perhaps more accurately) could not be denied, at least in Smotryc'kyj's opinion, and especially since, according to him, the power structure was just the reverse of that in the Uniate allegations: it was Smotryc'kyj who sought to bring the Uniates into union with the Orthodox. Thus, we can be relatively certain, some sort of meetings did take place. Conversely,

Smotryc'kyj did not feel at liberty to acknowledge that he had doubts about his *Thrēnos;* he did not even fully acknowledge that he was the author of the work. Clearly, *Thrēnos* continued to be a problematic work. The Uniates felt they could compromise Smotryc'kyj first by linking his name with the work, and then by alleging that he had secretly renounced it. Smotryc'kyj could not, or would not, admit to the first (here his audience was the secular authorities of the Commonwealth) or to the second (here his audience was the Orthodox).

It is important to note that in this polemical exchange, as in the polemics devoted to many other questions, one of the most important bodies of opinion in this debate—the Orthodox side other than Smotryc'kyj—is practically mute to us in the extant sources. But we might suspect that some on the Orthodox side already held suspicions about their leader since the Uniates were attempting to exploit these doubts. Smotryc'kyj seems to have been mistrusted by all sides at some time or another, sometimes, apparently, by all sides at one and the same time.

We have, however, two more sets of documents on this period and these issues: Smotryc'kyj's own statements on his past after his conversion to the Uniate Church and statements from the Orthodox side written after the conversion but dealing with the earlier Smotryc'kyj. We must be aware here that the Uniate Smotryc'kyj could treat the Orthodox Smotryc'kyj as a semi-stranger: that is, the Orthodox Smotryc'kyj could be useful to the Uniate Smotryc'kyj in furthering his goals of the moment. Smotryc'kyj was just as adept as any of the other participants in the debate at putting his own public persona to use. Thus he could declare in 1628 that he had indeed done some of the things that the Uniates had alleged in 1621 concerning his behavior in 1617; but this did not necessarily mean that he did them, or that he did them in the manner claimed.

Writing in 1628, Smotryc'kyj was now seeking to explain why he "converted" when he did. His strategy was to portray the act of conversion as the result of a long period of soul-searching that had begun sometime soon after he published *Thrēnos* in 1610 and had continued throughout his years as a lay leader and as an Orthodox archbishop, culminating only in the late 1620s. According to Smotryc'kyj, witness to his period of self-examination were his "lucubrations written against the work entitled *Union,* against the *Conversation of the Adherent of Brest and a Member of the Brotherhood,* against *The Resurrected Nalyvajko,* against the *Politics, Ignorance, and Religion of the New Churchmen of the Vilnius Church,* which were prepared to be released for publication already after the publication of the *Lament.*"[40] These works were included in this autobiographical statement, however, not because they defended the Union (they were written *against* Uniate works, after all), but because they were less virulently anti-Uniate than *Thrēnos.* (Smotryc'kyj included his later works written in defense of the newly established Orthodox hierarchy in the same category: "I do not mention *Verification,* its *Defense, Elenchus, Justification,* and others similar, in which, one after the other, the further I proceeded the less I attacked genuine dogmas, the more I dealt with the affairs of the moment that had come up suddenly at those times."[41])

But what interests me most in this chapter are Smotryc'kyj's statements about his activities as a lay leader. He mentioned two works: a treatise on the procession of the Holy Spirit written in the Polish language "in the manner of the syllogisms that the Greeks are wont to use against the Romans, and the Romans against the Greeks, and which I had submitted for the reading of the archimandrite, my predecessor in that post" and a *palinōdia* (i.e., a revocation) written in response to *Thrēnos.* In proof of this assertion, Smotryc'kyj suggested that the treatise on the procession of the Holy Spirit might still be obtainable in the library of the monastery of the Orthodox Brotherhood in Vilnius; and he stated that he had presented the palinode to the Ostroh chapter and that it remained in the monastery at Derman'.[42] Why did he not publish them, we might reasonably ask? Smotryc'kyj answered: "My God, likely on account of the great affront caused Him by the *Lament,* did not allow me to come to the publication of the one or the other, having wished to keep me longer in this experience."[43]

We should not lose sight of the immediate context of these statements: Smotryc'kyj was seeking in 1628 to demonstrate to the world that he had been struggling with the same questions since the mid 1610s, and that his "conversion" had been a long process that had begun soon after he published *Thrēnos* and before he had become a monk in the Orthodox Church and then been made an archbishop. These are statements that would please neither side, as we will see later, but here the Orthodox were the main audience. Smotryc'kyj was no longer in a position where he had to prove to them his *bona fides,* and it was in the interests of his polemic to emphasize his "Uniate leanings" in that earlier period. And yet, the picture that Smotryc'kyj offered was not quite that which his Uniate opponents had put forth in 1621–1622. We find no mention here of Smotryc'kyj's dealings with the "other side," no suggestion that he was a sort of double agent. In fact, Smotryc'kyj said in 1628 of his theses on the procession of the Holy Spirit more or less what he had said in 1621: that they were an exercise presenting arguments for both sides, which he had offered to Leontij Karpovyč for general discussion. (The only difference was that in 1621 Smotryc'kyj had needed to claim— addressing himself here to the Orthodox—that the Uniate and Roman Catholic arguments were weaker.) The most important new piece of information on this occasion was that Smotryc'kyj now admitted he had soon regretted writing *Thrēnos.*

This picture rings truer than other portrayals of this period in Smotryc'kyj's life. By 1628 Smotryc'kyj was a "free man," at least with respect to the Orthodox side, and he no longer needed to please them in portrayals of his earlier self. We should not rule out the possibility that in some respects he was now offering a "cleaned-up" version of himself to please his new Uniate masters. But if that had been his main goal, he could have gone somewhat further in that direction. We tend to think of his *Apology* as a "Uniate" work; but this is not quite correct. Smotryc'kyj wrote it while he was "covertly" Uniate and "overtly" Orthodox. He still used all his old ecclesiastical titles here without the qualification "so-called" (*nuncupatus, rzeczony*), which he would be required to use in his overtly Uniate activities. Smotryc'kyj was somewhere in the middle here, not answering entirely to either side. For a number of reasons, which will become clearer below, I suspect Smotryc'kyj felt most comfortable during these in-between periods and revealed more of his "true self" at those times.

Among all the representations of Smotryc'kyj offered at one time or another, it is this that I find the most convincing: Smotryc'kyj was a man caught somewhere in the middle between two increasingly rigid orthodoxies which wished to claim his unqualified support. Probably the picture of a man internally torn, constantly occupied with soul-searching, edging first toward one and then the other side, is not too far from the truth.

With Smotryc'kyj's conversion to the Uniate Church we finally have the opportunity to sample Orthodox opinion of his behavior in the late

1610s. But we should again be aware that Orthodox opinions about the Smotryc̆kyj of the 1610s expressed in the late 1620s did not necessarily reflect Orthodox opinion in the period before Smotryc̆kyj's conversion.

According to Andrij Mužylovs̆kyj's *Antidotum* of 1628, the Orthodox were suspicious of Smotryc̆kyj from the start, and precisely in the period when, according to the Uniates, he was dealing with the other side:

> Everyone sees clearly that you are a hypocrite; which even your father in the Holy Spirit, Leontij Karpovyč, Archimandrite, of blessed memory, of the Vilnius Church of the Descent of the Holy Spirit, saw in you, wherefore he did not wish to receive you into the order, knowing that you would cause great turmoil in the Church of God. Only with the passage of time, at the demand of a few individuals who little knew the inner wolf, he had to receive you into the order whether he wished to or not; and having washed his hands, he is clean of this. Expecting your correction with time, everyone supported you.[44]

And elsewhere:

> And a sure sign of your future apostasy was the fact that, when you were admitted to the second baptism of holy repentance, the voice of the common people said that you would trouble the Church, lead astray the Orthodox people, add to trial and tribulation, submit the Orthodox doctrine of the Church to suspicion.[45]

Smotryc̆kyj responded to Mužylovs̆kyj by returning to a discussion of the period just before he became a monk. Here we read that Smotryc̆kyj arrived at the Holy Spirit Monastery (ca. 1616) already convinced of the fact that he had been in error in *Thrēnos,* especially on the issue of the *Filioque.* He brought with him his theses on the procession of the Holy Spirit, but he had to abandon his hope of an open discussion of them, since they (or his actions?—after all, he was also in contact with the Holy Trinity Monastery) had caused an uproar. Smotryc̆kyj finally acceded to monastic tonsure after many on the Orthodox side, including Leontij Karpovyč, had begged him to do so. (And here it was Smotryc̆kyj who named names: a certain Vasyl', who had taken the monastic name Varlam, would corroborate his story; all the Orthodox had to do was to ask him.)[46]

In yet another Orthodox document from the period we read that indeed Karpovyč, as well as Smotryc̆kyj, was a wolf in sheep's clothing (see *Synopsis* 1632, 17ᵛ/571). Perhaps this was the result of Smotryc̆kyj's claim that he had had Karpovyč's blessing in his dealings with the

Uniates. Both statements could reflect later attempts to reassert a kind of control over the situation by alleging that the Orthodox had never really trusted Smotryc'kyj anyway.

What did Smotryc'kyj himself tell us about the general question whether the common Orthodox people trusted him? Again, we obtain conflicting pictures depending upon the needs of the moment. In writing to the patriarch of Constantinople, Cyril Lukaris, asking him for guidance in what the Orthodox were supposed to believe, Smotryc'kyj claimed that he himself did not know the answer to this, and that this state was intolerable since *the nation looked to him for guidance.*[47] He had been "exalted unto heaven in glory, grace, and the love of his nation" because of the works he had written in defense of the Orthodox Church.[48] He was held "in such love by many of my nation that, in order to show their great gratitude toward me for those works and for my services, they were moved to display my image in their houses so that they would always have me before them."[49] But in seeking to explain why, on one occasion, Mohyla might have refused to receive him, he pointed to the fact that *the nation held him in suspicion.*[50] Which view was accurate? Probably both, to some degree; even in Smotryc'kyj's own usage, it depended which Smotryc'kyj was useful at the moment.

Chapter 5

Archbishop of Polack

Smotryc'kyj had been an Orthodox monk barely three years when, in October 1620, he rose to occupy the second most important position in the hierarchy of the Ruthenian Orthodox Church. When the archimandritehood of the influential Vilnius monastery was soon added to the episcopal see, he may well have rivaled Jov Borec'kyj, the metropolitan of Kiev, for importance in Ruthenian Church matters. He was, for all practical purposes, the sole spokesman for the Orthodox side in the controversy over the reestablishment of the Orthodox hierarchy in the years 1621 to 1623.

What were the circumstances of Smotryc'kyj's rise to power in the Ruthenian Orthodox Church? Let us begin with a general outline of the events. The Orthodox Church in Rus' had been without a full hierarchy since 1596 due primarily to the conversion of some of the clergy at the time of the Union of Brest and to the death of others. Thus in 1617 when Smotryc'kyj first took the habit in the Orthodox Church, most of the old bishoprics were vacant, at least from the point of view of the Orthodox. Only that of L'viv remained in Orthodox hands. All the other sees were occupied by Uniate clergy.

The Orthodox hierarchy was consecrated at a very delicate time in the political life of the Polish-Lithuanian Commonwealth—or, at least, this was how the Uniates and Roman Catholics would seek to portray the situation. The Commonwealth was engaged in frequent skirmishes in the east with its neighbors, Muscovy and the Ottoman Empire. Polish armies under Hetman Stanisław Żółkiewski were defeated by the Turks at the Battle of Ţuţora (Cecora) on 7 October 1620.[1] The Cossacks were a political and military force that the Polish authorities wished to control and exploit, but whose allegiance was never quite certain. These facts placed the Orthodox churchmen and burghers in a delicate situation: since they were co-confessional with the Cossacks and with the Muscovites, and since they were obedient to a patriarch who lived under

Ottoman rule, any sort of independent actions on their part could easily be represented to Polish-Lithuanian public opinion as acts of treason.

In 1620–1621, on his way from Muscovy (where he had installed the Muscovite Patriarch Filaret) back to Jerusalem, Patriarch Theophanes of Jerusalem spent some time in the eastern lands of the Polish-Lithuanian Commonwealth. His consecration of a new Ruthenian Orthodox Church hierarchy helped to set the stage for an escalation in the conflict between Uniates and Orthodox. Smotryc'kyj and others traveled to Kiev in the late summer or fall of 1621; there Smotryc'kyj was made archbishop of Polack, and bishop of Mscislaŭ and Vicebsk. On his return to Vilnius, where he discovered that Leontij Karpovyč had died, he was also made archimandrite of the Brotherhood Monastery. This must have occurred sometime before 8 November/18 November 1620, when Smotryc'kyj signed the preface to his funeral sermon for his predecessor using both his new titles.

The Uniate and Roman Catholic side sought to exploit the vulnerabilities in the Orthodox political position. Among the questions raised in the exchanges of polemical tracts were these: Who was the man who claimed to be Patriarch Theophanes of Jerusalem—was he an imposter? a Muscovite spy? a Turkish spy? What right, according to canon and secular law, did Smotryc'kyj and others have to accept consecration from him? What were the circumstances of the consecration? What were Smotryc'kyj's subsequent actions, motivations, and goals? What role were the Cossacks being given to play in all this?

As far as we can now determine, the struggle for control of public opinion on the matter of the new hierarchy began with Smotryc'kyj's return to Vilnius shortly following his consecration.[2] The earliest documents (a charter of King Sigismund III dated 1 February 1621 and a letter of the king to Bohdan Ohins'kyj dated 7 February) reflected a situation governed by the rumor mill: that Smotryc'kyj and Borec'kyj were Turkish spies, that Borec'kyj was hiding out with the Cossacks in Kiev, that Smotryc'kyj had his own armed forces in Lithuania (Žukovič 1906, 538–42). According to rumor, Theophanes was a Turkish spy, and Smotryc'kyj and Borec'kyj had come into an agreement with him "under the pretext of religion" in order to sow "harmful rebellions and uprisings among the people."[3] Furthermore, a certain "someone" (Ruc'kyj, according to Orthodox allegations), who was responsible for giving the king all this information, "was not ashamed" to allege to him that

Theophanes was "not a patriarch, or a bishop, but a simple monk."[4] Or as Tymoteusz Symanowicz phrased it in his *Examination of the False Verification:* this was the work of "a certain Theophanes, certainly a Greek by birth, and a Cretan in manners,"[5] in other words, one whose gifts one should beware, and certainly a liar (cf. Titus 1:12). Of course, there were reasons why Roman Catholic and Uniate apologists could make such charges and expect a receptive audience: Greek patriarchs did at times—for a variety of reasons—join forces with the Turks in a kind of anti-Polish alliance. Cyril Lukaris sent twelve agents to the Commonwealth in 1621 before the Battle of Xotyn (Chocim) (see Hering 1968, 58).

The Orthodox would later claim publicly that it was Metropolitan Ruc'kyj who had "informed," giving the king the "false" information—a charge that Ruc'kyj (or at any rate the author of *Twofold Guilt,* if he was not Ruc'kyj himself) would deny. A similar version of the King's original charter calling for the arrest of Borec'kyj and Smotryc'kyj was made known to a wider audience in the Grand Duchy on 6 February 1621. Probably the Uniate and Roman Catholic side saw to it that this document was spread in broadsheets and affixed to public places.[6]

Lithuanian chancellor Lew Sapieha was a voice for restraint among the authorities. The same man who would remind Josafat Kuncevyč that the Polish-Lithuanian tradition of toleration was incompatible with the future martyr's application of Lk. 14:23 (*compelle intrare:* "compel them to come in") against the Orthodox (see below, p. 227), now urged Ruc'kyj to exercise caution in publicizing the documents charging Smotryc'kyj and Borec'kyj with treason.[7] For the remainder of 1621 and 1622 the two sides jockeyed for position through court proceedings, rumors, and polemical pamphlets.

On 12 March 1621, at the complaints of Josafat Kuncevyč, who was Smotryc'kyj's Uniate counterpart as archbishop of Polack, and of Lev Krevza, his competitor as archimandrite in Vilnius, Metropolitan Ruc'kyj summoned Smotryc'kyj (under his secular name, Maksym Herasymovyč) to appear no later than 19 March before his ecclesiastical court.[8] When Smotryc'kyj did not appear, he was given until 27 March to show his repentance. (An open letter containing all this information was nailed to the doors of the Holy Spirit Monastery.) When Smotryc'kyj made no move toward meeting the Uniate demands, Ruc'kyj declared him excommunicated on 28 March and made this known through a solemn public ceremony and through publication of the decree of excommunication (Žukovič 1906, 547–51).

At this point a series of legal actions were begun on both sides. On 3 April 1621, four Orthodox city officials and twelve burghers were arrested, charged with *lèse majesté* and with treason, and, more specifically, with financially aiding Smotryc'kyj, a man who had entered into dealings with Turkish subjects (Žukovič 1906, 700–703). These were the events Smotryc'kyj had lamented *Thrēnos*-style in the "Consolation of the Innocence of the Ruthenian Nation," which he placed toward the end of *Verification of Innocence.* The records of the prisoners' interrogations are of interest here in that they reflect some of the same charges about Smotryc'kyj's behavior (but in much greater detail) that were to surface in the exchanges of printed polemical pamphlets.

The interrogation posed the following questions to the Orthodox prisoners: Were you present at his Liturgies? Who gave the money for his vestments and other accoutrements? What happens at the meetings of the Orthodox Brotherhood? What happens to the money they collect? Who sent Smotryc'kyj to Kiev? Who met him upon his return to Vievis, where he celebrated his first Liturgy? Who accompanied him to Vilnius? What women went about schismatic households collecting pearls and gold for Smotryc'kyj's vestments (Žukovič 1906, 704–706)?

Just under the surface of these questions we can see the outlines of the Uniate representation of Smotryc'kyj—he was a haughty, power-hungry, plebeian interloper, who had made himself archbishop solely for temporal gain.

As far as we can tell from the testimonies of the Orthodox (to the extent that they were reliable accounts, and not simply what the interrogators wished to hear), Smotryc'kyj did indeed make a grand entrance into Vilnius, led on both hands by Orthodox nobility, covered with robes, gold, and jewels, wearing a mitre that the Orthodox community of Vilnius had purchased in Toruń. Rumors had been flying at that time that Smotryc'kyj had been created not archbishop, but metropolitan of the Ruthenian Church. He is supposed to have assaulted verbally those who first met him on his return to Vilnius for not greeting him as befitted an archbishop (Žukovič 1906, 705–707).

The court cases dragged on with little concrete outcome. The Orthodox lay leaders were eventually released after a fire broke out in the town hall. (Some suspected arson [Žukovič 1906, 874].) The Great Circle found in favor of the Orthodox charges against Rucʹkyj and sent the case to the Sejm. The Lesser Circle found in favor of Rucʹkyj's charges against the Orthodox Brotherhood and sent the case to the Crown Court (Žukovič 1906, 711). Charges and countercharges continued, but with little practical result.

On 15 March 1621, Sigismund III had signed a universal for the arrest of Jezekijil Kurcevyč, Bishop of Brest and Volodymyr, and on 19 March for that of Smotrycʹkyj and Borecʹkyj (Žukovič 1906, 711), but on 6 May he wrote Sapieha asking his opinion whether it would be good to call Smotrycʹkyj before the Sejm Tribunal (Žukovič 1906, 864). As far as we know, Smotrycʹkyj was never arrested. And remember, this was the second time the king had attempted to have him apprehended. Which raises the question: were these arrest orders to be taken seriously? Surely the authorities knew by now who had written *Thrēnos*? Surely Smotrycʹkyj could have been arrested if they had wished to press the issue? I suspect, on the one hand, that the authorities were loath to arrest Smotrycʹkyj and others for fear of fanning the fires of Orthodox discontent in the towns and among the Cossacks. We could imagine Sapieha urging caution on this issue. On the other hand, I suspect that the orders were taken seriously enough for Smotrycʹkyj never to feel entirely secure. This is reflected on a number of occasions. He seems to have feared for his safety when he attended the 1622 Sejm in Warsaw; he did not attend that of 1623, even though he seems to have been expected to do so (see below, pp. 91–93). And he attributed the reluctance of Zaxarija Kopystensʹkyj and Peter Mohyla (on different occasions) to be seen with him to his standing with the Polish-Lithuanian secular authorities;[9] this same reluctance was expressed by the Roman Catholic palatine of Braclav, Aleksander Zasławski (see below, pp. 118–19). True, by that time (1627), Josafat Kuncevyč had been murdered and Smotrycʹkyj indirectly implicated in the actions of the citizenry of Vicebsk. Still, the picture we receive is of a man who, since 1610, had been most active in Ruthenian spiritual affairs, but who had always been in danger of apprehension by the secular authorities.

And yet, Smotrycʹkyj did remain active in representing himself and his nation to public opinion. He did this primarily through the printed polemical pamphlets and through letters to his flock in Polack and in Vicebsk. The first printed work, Smotrycʹkyj's *Verification of Innocence,* was an answer to allegations first made public in legal complaints entered into the castle books. The allegations had included two main points: First, that Theophanes was a Turkish spy, sent to the Commonwealth to encourage treason among the Orthodox during a time of conflict between Poland and the Ottoman Empire, and that by allowing themselves to receive consecration from this man, Smotryc'kyj and others were acting treasonously. And, second, that investiture belonged to the king, and that by accepting consecration without the king's prior investiture, the Orthodox were guilty of *lèse majesté*.

Rumors must have been circulating concerning Smotryc'kyj's life, character, parentage, and actions during this stage. These charges would become an important part of the polemic in the years 1621–1623. Central to the Uniate campaign was the portrayal of Smotryc'kyj as a man of the plebs, consumed with greed, pride, and lust for power, who had wrongfully arrogated to himself authority that could only be conferred by the king; and that only upon a man of the nobility.

Smotryc'kyj answered the legal charges brought against him and his fellow bishops in *Verification of Innocence,* but he chose here to ignore the personal attacks. He did, however, devote some attention in *Verification* to two questions that relate directly to my investigation of the methods and means that he and others used in representing his actions and motivations. First, the methodological question: Smotryc'kyj made *Verification of Innocence* into a critique of rumor and slander, and in so doing he devoted some attention to the workings of the rumor mill. His strategy—beginning with the title page citation from Justus Lipsius: "Nothing can be said so carefully or thoroughly that malice could not pick at it"[10]—was to portray slander as something so efficacious that its victims (in this case, Borec'kyj and himself, above all) had no certain defense. His "logic," to take his argument to the extreme, was this: we have been slandered, therefore we must be innocent.

Smotryc'kyj thus turned his opponent (Ruc'kyj, as he implied elsewhere[11]) into "someone . . . (we call him 'someone' because he hides himself),"[12] who sent out "false hourly reports"[13] from an "infernal forge."[14] The logic of the rumor mill, according to Smotryc'kyj, was that it allowed its users to shape the truth for their own purposes: "You must know, Kind and Gracious Reader, that if Borec'kyj were not metropolitan and Smotryc'kyj not archbishop, and if they had conversed even twice as much with that man [i.e., Theophanes], then that holy man would not be an imposter but the proper, genuine Patriarch of Jerusalem (as he is), and Borec′kyj and Smotryc′kyj would not be traitors."[15]

In *Verification of Innocence* Smotryc′kyj devoted his only lines (as far as I have been able to determine) to the theory and practice of the art of lying. I will discuss this aspect of Smotryc′kyj's perceptions of the "rules of the game" later (see chapter 10, below). Let me simply note that Smotryc′kyj's main point in this particular context was not that lying was evil because it was not the truth: lying was evil in this particular instance because it posed a threat to the security of the Commonwealth. This was Smotryc′kyj's response to Uniate charges that the actions of the Orthodox were a form of treason: how dare the Uniates lie "unto the confounding of internal peace in the Commonwealth during the military expedition against the enemy of the Christians and against the pagan Turkish emperor . . . "[16] Thus, in this Orthodox version of events, it was the actions of the Uniates, and not those of the Orthodox, that posed a threat to national security.

A second way of defusing Uniate allegations was to claim that there had been no particular plan for Smotryc′kyj to receive consecration. He had been sent by his superior Leontij Karpovyč, as the latter's representative.[17] No one, including Smotryc′kyj, knew that he was to receive consecration in Kiev.[18] Even the opponents could testify how little desire he had for the titles and benefices of Church office: the Uniates, according to Smotryc′kyj, had already offered him the same see of Polack, not to mention another see, which he—for polemical effect—declined to mention. (Was he hinting that they had offered him the metropolitanate?) Smotryc′kyj wrote that he had always been "alien to the harmful intrigue" of Church office, and had desired to avoid it his entire life (not even wishing to first take the habit), had it not been for "God's plan" and for "the voice of the people, which in such a matter is the voice of God."[19]

As an aside, we must ask when this offer occurred from the Uniate side. Josafat Kuncevyč had occupied the see of Polack since 1618. As we have seen, Smotryc′kyj had been engaged in some semi-covert discussions with the Uniates around 1617, just before he received tonsure. The Uniates would claim he was on the verge of conversion at that time. Perhaps they had "sweetened the deal" with a promise of high office among them? Was Josafat, then, their "second choice?" Or was this simply the impression Smotryc′kyj wished to leave with his readership?

It was crucial to Smotryc'kyj to portray his side (and himself) as innocent of any unpatriotic thoughts, and as victims, rather, of Uniate malice. Thus, Smotryc'kyj would argue, the Ruthenian hierarchy was consecrated well before the defeat of Hetman Żółkiewski's Polish-Lithuanian armies at the hands of the Turks at the Battle of Ţuţora in Moldavia on 6–7 October 1620.[20] (Actually, this seems to be false. According to Žukovič [1906, 580], Borec'kyj was consecrated on 19 October and Smotryc'kyj a bit later. The charges of treason may have led Smotryc'kyj to alter the facts here.) Smotryc'kyj, so he himself claimed, lived "openly, not surreptitiously" in Vilnius after his consecration, awaiting confirmation from the king.[21] If anything, it was the Orthodox who were under constant attack, not only in rumor campaigns, and court proceedings against Vilnius burghers, but even suffering all sorts of physical attacks against the Holy Spirit Monastery:

> They cause us the greatest pains they can, in word and in deed; they shoot stones from a slingshot at our monastery; they fling arrows from bows against the foundations and the buildings, and against the church they fling arrows lit with a sulphur wick; they cast lighted torches over the wall onto the square of that same monastery; into the cornerstones of the walls of the church they stick pieces of smouldering waxed cloth together with other incendiary preparations and wicks.[22]

The Uniate and Roman Catholic side continued to portray the reception of consecration from Theophanes as an act of treason. In 1633, in the climate of behind-the-scenes politicking before the election of Władysław IV as successor to his recently deceased father, Sigismund III Vasa, the Orthodox and the heterodox had made common cause. At this point, court preacher Fabian Birkowski accused all non-Catholics of un-Polish activities.[23] And he, too, returned to the events of 1620, portraying the consecrations as an act of treason directly connected with the defeat at Xotyn in 1621 (Birkowski 1633, 5), and as an attempt on the part of the Turks to drive a wedge between the Poles and the Cossacks (Birkowski 1633, 12).

The Uniates quickly identified Smotryc'kyj as the author of *Verification of Innocence,* and they found him the most vulnerable figure on the Orthodox side. Now they chose to make into a main theme what had earlier figured only on the margins: Smotryc'kyj's plebeian birth, his unseemly arrogance, his love of power and worldly goods. According to the *Letter* of 1621, Smotryc'kyj and Borec'kyj were self-created, self-adoring idols.[24] Smotryc'kyj was puffed-up by the spirit of ambition, an insignificant person who had arrogated to himself the decision of matters in the Commonwealth that belong to his betters.[25] He was the author of "tumults and seditions"[26] through the letters and emissaries he sent from Vilnius to his see of Polack.[27] And what was the instrument of Smotryc'kyj's arrogance? Here, as was often the case, the Uniate side played the Cossack card: Smotryc'kyj, according to them, urged the Cossacks ("that knightly people") to rebellion.[28] Both sides played this game. The Uniates and Roman Catholics could seek to portray the Orthodox hierarchy as inciting the Cossacks to rebellions and sedition, when, in the Uniate representations, the Cossacks were far from such activities. But, the Orthodox could also "defend" the Cossack's honor, with the implicit threat that they controlled Cossack actions, so that they should be treated well. Was this wishful thinking on both sides?

The picture painted of Smotryc'kyj as an ambitious, plebeian monk verged on parody:

> Did you stray far from monastic poverty, from humility, and monastic modesty when you became apostate? Seized by disgusting ambition, you force your way, against God and man, upon the thrones of the metropolitanate and bishoprics. And that of Polack appeals to you most of all: already Reverend Melentij usurps for himself the insignia and episcopal power of the archbishopric of Polack, against the power (pitiful thing) of His Majesty the King, since he did not submit or nominate him. He borrows the titles, submits them to print himself, revering himself (truly a ludicrous thing), celebrates not just in the episcopal garments but perhaps even in those of the metropolitan. He has episcopal seals cut for himself, he makes inscriptions on the chalices. He allows himself to be led by the hand of the aristocracy (*ne quid ambitioni et arrogantiae desit* [lest there be anything lacking in ambition and arrogance]), he himself being of the condition of which he is, and he glories in this. He appropriates the bishopric of Polack, and he does not see that in that same constitution of 1607 it was written that such dignities are to be given to noblemen.[29]

Josafat Kuncevyč wrote in a private letter to Lew Sapieha, "after the completed expedition against the Turks, the Cossacks had intended not to support the schism," but then "pseudo-bishops, especially Smotryc'kyj . . . aroused them (acting as their scribe) to send this petition to His Majesty the King, in order that their ambition might come all the more quickly to fruition."[30] (Sapieha responded that the fact that "a few of the rabble and of the Kievan gentry do not accept Borec'kyj and

Smotryc'kyj . . . is not yet a piece of evidence that will convince the schismatics."[31])

Twofold Guilt, also a Uniate work published in 1621, painted a similar picture of a man of mean birth who had taken for himself power which did not belong to him. "A certain Smotryc'kyj,"[32] so we read, made himself bishop, ordained priests (and not only to his own diocese), celebrated the Liturgy in pontifical manner, and sent letters and emissaries to Polack.[33] The common thread here was that Smotryc'kyj was a haughty intruder, who sat in Vilnius writing letters and sending spies to disturb the peace of his misappropriated diocese of Polack. The insistence that Smotryc'kyj celebrated the Liturgy "in pontifical manner," and that he had appropriated some of the rights of the metropolitan is particularly interesting here. The Uniates sought to discredit Smotryc'kyj in Orthodox eyes by painting him as power hungry even within the (in their view) illegitimate hierarchy. Smotryc'kyj, according to them, may well have harbored a desire to take for himself the powers that properly belonged to Borec'kyj:

> But Smotryc'kyj himself, having taken up residence in the Brotherhood Monastery in Vilnius, has behaved as haughtily as if there were not God in heaven, nor the king or any spiritual or temporal authority on earth. He made himself known publicly as bishop, and the other [Jov Borec'kyj] as metropolitan; he submitted it to print; he dressed not in episcopal, nor in archiepiscopal vestments, but in that which befits metropolitans—and not all metropolitans—according to the custom of the Eastern Church; he celebrated Liturgies in pontifical fashion; he ordained priests and deacons, not only for the diocese of Polack, but also—as a *universalis pastor* [universal pastor]—for the metropolitanate; either he himself, or his delegates, sent—when there were not enough monks—laymen in the monastic habit throughout various parts for rebellions, until they began to catch them and they admitted that they were laymen, having only the habit of monks.[34]

Again, we should be aware that part of the Uniate strategy may have been to create dissension within Orthodox ranks by portraying Smotryc'kyj as someone so power-hungry that not even his own side could really trust him. The Uniates may have sought here to exploit the confusion that reigned among the Orthodox upon Smotryc'kyj's first return to Vilnius as to whether he was now metropolitan and not just archbishop.

How did Smotryc'kyj respond to all these allegations? First, he sought through irony to counter the picture of an arrogant, power-hungry usurper:

> Smotryc'kyj sits not with an army in the Vilnius Brotherhood Monastery but only with a dozen or so fellow monks, not with some cannon but only with an episcopal staff.[35]

Notice, however, that he did "sit" in the Vilnius monastery. Was this an inadvertent usage, or does it give the picture that he did not stray far from the relatively secure confines of his monastery? Second, he denied that he could possibly have disturbed the peace in the diocese of Polack, since there was no peace to disturb. His Uniate counterpart, Josafat Kuncevyč—whom Smotryc'kyj portrayed as ambiguous or even duplicitous, and certainly unclear in his allegiance (these allegations should begin to sound familiar)—had already disturbed what peace there was. Kuncevyč "hid from them [his true allegiance] for all those times, and he did not openly renounce obedience to the patriarch until the moment came for that gold of yours [i.e., Josafat] to be rubbed against the *lydius lapis* [touchstone], then their Lordships, the citizens of Polack discovered he was brass." This happened (according to Smotryc'kyj) not through any letters he may have sent as archbishop, but somewhat before he was made archbishop, when Josafat refused to make the trip to Kiev to meet with Patriarch Theophanes of Jerusalem, the legate of the patriarch of Constantinople.[36]

And notice what this implies without directly saying it: Smotryc'kyj could not have set off for Kiev with the hope of being elevated to the see of Polack, since it did not become clear until Josafat did not go to meet Theophanes that he had completely withdrawn his obedience from the patriarch of Constantinople. It was in this context that Smotryc'kyj depicted a fluid, or at least poorly defined, confessional allegiance in the diocese of Polack. About life under one of his predecessors he wrote, "They had peace under Herman, since he was only slightly in the Union."[37] But even if we accept that the allegiances of Herman Zahors'kyj were not entirely clear, I wonder how much doubt there could have been concerning Josafat in 1620. Perhaps some doubt did exist. But perhaps it also suited Smotryc'kyj's needs at this point to portray his opponent as a recently discovered covert Uniate. This then would add evidence for Smotryc'kyj's portrayal of his trip to Kiev as one carried out as a representative of Leontij Karpovyč, and not to further his own ecclesiastical career.

The second part of Smotryc'kyj's defense dealt more specifically with the charge that he had directed a campaign against Kuncevyč's authority through his letters and emissaries:

> Father Smotryc'kyj did not send out any of his universals. He wrote to their Lordships, the citizens of Polack, but he wrote in answer, not to initiate the correspondance. That letter of Father Smotryc'kyj was

shown to His Grace, the Lord Palatine of Polack, it was carried further
to show others, in which deed there was nothing of the sort—by the
grace of God—which you, *Redargutor,* falsely allege. There were
letters from that place in which he is in charge even before these letters
to the nobility and to the burghers of all the counties who presented
themselves to them first with their letters and asked for some spiritual
counsel and teaching. But these letters were not termed universals, nor
was their teaching that of turmoil. Concerning the monks you mention
who were sent about: did you torture nearly unto death in his diocese
one monk until he confessed that he had been sent by Father
Smotryc'kyj? And the Lord God will require his blood at your hands
[Ez. 3:18, 20].[38]

Smotryc'kyj also denied the charges that he had usurped the powers of
metropolitan:

And what you allege concerning Father Smotryc'kyj, that he ordained
priests not only for the diocese of Polack but also for the metropolitanate:
with the exception of those who are on the foundations of the
Brotherhood, and the monks, you allege a falsehood.[39]

In the remainder of the debate over the newly consecrated Church
hierarchy, the circumstances of Smotryc'kyj's consecration ceased to
occupy center stage. Attention now focused on Smotryc'kyj's dealings
with the Uniates before he took the habit and on his learning, all of this
an attempt to provoke his entering into a public disputation. This is the
material I surveyed in the preceding chapter.

But with the death of Josafat Kuncevyč on 12 November 1623 at the
hands of citizens of Vicebsk, Smotryc'kyj's actions as the recently
consecrated archbishop of Polack again became a focal point in the
debate. I will deal with the particulars of this part of the polemic in
examining the controversy that surrounded Smotryc'kyj's conversion.
Let it suffice for now to note that in the course of the various processes
surrounding the beatification of Josafat in the late 1620s and 1630s, the
view became established that the citizens of Vicebsk had acted with
premeditation and that it was Smotryc'kyj's letters to his diocesans that
had led to Kuncevyč's martyrdom.

Oddly enough, the same questions were debated once again after
Smotryc'kyj's conversion. Now, in answer to Orthodox charges that he
had converted for personal gain, Smotryc'kyj could reiterate some aspects
of the Uniate picture of his earlier self living an opulent life in Vilnius,
being led by the Ruthenian nobility:

And do not even you know, you hypocrite, that your Vilnius schismatic
monastery was a greater trap of gold for me, which dressed me from

head to foot in gold, than the monastery of Derman'. My greed ought to have been greater there than here, for there the flock of the archbishopric of Polack from all of Belarus remembered me. There whatever I said—my word immediately became deed, without any trouble and care of mine, by those who did not even allow a speck of dust, as they say, to fall upon me. There in Vilnius pride and haughtiness ought to have overcome me, where during my celebration of the liturgy there was figured singing for four choirs, crowds of deacons and presbyters on both sides vested in blue and gold, where an innumerable throng of people surrounded me, where the high-born nobility led me by the hand. But as you saw nothing in me of these three things at that time, and, by the grace of God, I held my soul pure of all that, believe the same thing about me now as well.[40]

Here, in 1629, Smotryc'kyj *admitted* that he had enjoyed an opulent life in Vilnius, but this was not the same as granting the validity of the charges raised previously by the Uniates. The changes in the context altered the polemical strategy. In this instance, Smotryc'kyj was responding to Orthodox charges that his conversion had been motivated by a love of wordly things. He responded that he had had such things before, and that, as they had not been centrally important to him then, neither were they now.

According to the Orthodox polemicist Andrij Mužylovs'kyj, who wrote in 1629, there were three omens of Smotryc'kyj's future apostasy. I have already mentioned the first: that, at the time of his monastic tonsure, the common people raised the objection that he would disturb the Church. The other two omens referred to the period we are now examining: the second was that when Smotryc'kyj was to receive his consecration from Patriarch Theophanes, for lack of proper priestly vestments—lest it be said of him "Friend, how camest thou in hither not having a wedding garment? [Mt. 22:12]"—he had to put on Mužylovs'kyj's own robes;[41] and the third was that on the occasion of his last appearance in Vilnius, before his trip east, a column fell from the church.[42]

Smotryc'kyj's response to Mužylovs'kyj, his *Exaethesis* of 1629, lent support to several of the points that the archbishop had made about himself and his ambitions in 1621. He was sent to Kiev at the request of his superior, Leontij Karpovyč, who was already severely ill and, concerned with finding an appropriate successor to himself as archimandrite, seems to have chosen Meletij: he charged him with returning from Kiev a presbyter, and when Smotryc'kyj refused, he "fell upon my neck before the brethren, drenched with tears, and begged me to do this."[43] Smotryc'kyj's immediate goal here was to answer Mužylovs'kyj's claim that he had not enjoyed the trust of Leontij Karpovyč; thus his portrayal of himself as one not interested in ecclesiastical office—when this was no longer the main issue in the polemic—might seem to support his earlier representation of his ambitions. Further, according to Smotryc'kyj, he had had the necessary vestments—those of a deacon while he remained a deacon, and those of a presbyter when he became a presbyter. It had been rather Mužylovs'kyj who had first snatched the garments that had been prepared for Smotryc'kyj, so that when it came time for Smotryc'kyj's consecration, it was necessary to remove them from Mužylovs'kyj.[44]

In a similar vein, Diplic, who defended Smotryc'kyj the author of *Thrēnos* against Smotryc'kyj the author of *Apology,* argued paradoxically that the earlier Smotryc'kyj was an ineffectual "teacher," that is, preacher. The point, I suppose, was to show that it did not matter whether Smotryc'kyj as an Orthodox archbishop knew what he believed, since he rarely imparted his doctrinal knowledge to the people in the form of sermons. (Smotryc'kyj had claimed in *Apology* that he went to Constantinople because he was an archbishop in the Ruthenian Church and did not know what he believed.) All told, according to Diplic, Smotryc'kyj "taught" (i.e., "preached") in the church in Vilnius no more than five times—three times from the *cathedra,* including the funeral oration for Karpovyč, and twice from the pulpit; and he taught outside of Vilnius no more than five times. Even worse, according to Diplic, his performances were embarrassing: the funeral sermon was cribbed in large part from Latin; the second sermon was clearly unprepared; the third time was somewhat better, although it included nothing about doctrine.[45] Therefore—and this was Diplic's main point—Smotryc'kyj never taught heresies as an Orthodox archbishop![46]

Finally, one Orthodox polemicist—the same author of a *Reprotestation* who had taken up the earlier Uniate refrain alleging that Smotryc'kyj was a son of the plebs (see above, p. 28)—would, in the period after his conversion, make Smotryc'kyj responsible for the death of Josafat Kuncevyč.[47] Once again we have come full circle: Orthodox polemicists took up the previous Uniate charges once Smotryc'kyj had converted.

Chapter 6

Pilgrim

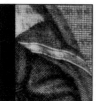 Smotryc'kyj spent his life in motion. The description he gave of himself on the title page of his grammar of Church Slavonic as one who was a pilgrim in temporary residence at the Orthodox Brotherhood Monastery of the Descent of the Holy Spirit in Vilnius[1] was not only an expression of the conventional view of the temporal life of the Christian as a pilgrimage on earth; it was also a fitting characterization of his existence. By 1618 Smotryc'kyj had traveled extensively in the eastern lands of the Commonwealth, including stays in Vilnius, L'viv, and Kiev (and no doubt Ostroh); his studies had also sent him to Leipzig and Wittenberg. He may have visited Cracow on his way to or from Germany. We know that he was in Warsaw at least once (in 1622) as a representative of the Orthodox hierarchy at the Sejm.

But his pilgrimages were far from over at that point. In 1623–1625 Smotryc'kyj traveled to Constantinople and to the Holy Land. In 1628 he published a work entitled *An Apology for My Peregrination to the Eastern Lands*. The title itself indicates controversy concerning his actions and motives. According to Smotryc'kyj's version, people on the Orthodox side were by that point (that is, early in 1628) questioning the reason for his trip. In fact, the trip may well have begun in an atmosphere of contention. Documents dating from just after his return show that there was a time when neither side accepted what would become his account of the events. Again, though, the views on each side could change in time, depending on the version of Smotryc'kyj that was required at the moment.

On 6 September 1626, the Ruthenian Uniate bishops who had gathered in Kobryn petitioned the king, among other things, to protect them from Smotryc'kyj, who had by then returned from his trip. According to them he had fled to Turkey after the death of Josafat Kuncevyč; the implication here was that Smotryc'kyj was directly responsible for the martyr's death and that he had left the Commonwealth to avoid the consequences of his actions (see Velykyj 1952, 64–65). Therefore, according to a Uniate document of 1626, Smotryc'kyj departed Ukraine under a cloud of suspicion, a fugitive from the secular arm of the Commonwealth. His statement in 1628 that the archimandrites of the Kievan Monastery of the Caves may have refused to receive him (Zaxarija Kopystens'kyj in 1626 and Peter Mohyla in 1628) in order to avoid displeasing the king, along with the evidence of Aleksander Zasławski's letter of 1627 that, as a senator, he could not risk associating with Smotryc'kyj the "dis-Uniate,"[2] lend credence to this view. Certainly, the author of *Thrēnos,* the "illegally" consecrated archbishop of Polack, and the author of "incendiary" letters to the citizens of Vicebsk shortly before the death of Josafat cannot have been in the king's good graces. And in fact, there is some evidence that he may have left Warsaw in 1622 (not 1623; see below, pp. 91–94), where he was present to attend the Sejm, precisely because he feared difficulties with the secular arm.[3]

But this was not the controversy Smotryc'kyj had in mind; his *Apology* had nothing to say about any of this. In fact, Smotryc'kyj remained absolutely silent about his relationship to the Josafat affair—this is an important point to which I will return. The *Apology* was composed, among other reasons, in answer to Orthodox objections to the pilgrimage that were apparently made public by 1628. The only written reference to early Orthodox objections came in Diplic's *Antapologia* of 1634, where he argued that some had urged Smotryc'kyj already in 1623 not to go east, saying that he could write a letter to Lukaris instead (as he did, in fact, after his return from Constantinople).[4] We should remember that this work was written in response to the *Apology* and thus may or may not have reflected earlier Orthodox opinions. In any case, it is not a very eloquent testimony. It offers no help on the important questions: Smotryc'kyj's stated goals at that time or Orthodox objections to them. Since we do not have written records of the Orthodox objections, we must use Smotryc'kyj's defense to reconstruct them. Orthodox responses to the *Apology* may, in turn, provide some corroboration.

What chronology can we establish for Smotryc'kyj's trip? On the title page of *Apology,* Smotryc'kyj stated that his trip occurred in the years 1623 and 1624. In *Paraenesis,* he stated that he was "a third year in that place whence our Ruthenian nation received the Orthodox Christian faith,"[5] and in *Apology* he wrote of having spent two years in the East.[6] All this information taken together would seem to suggest Smotryc'kyj spent two full years and some months in Constantinople and the Holy Land. But which two years and some months? The title page to the *Apology* said 1623 and 1624. But in the passage just cited from the beginning of *Apology* Smotryc'kyj wrote that "it is already the third year now" since he had returned from his "peregrination." And in another passage, he wrote that "it is already the third year now" that the "false brethren" had been criticizing his "pilgrimage."[7] Thus in the spring to summer of 1628 (the *Apology* was written during Lent and published in late August; see below, pp. 124–25), Smotryc'kyj had been back in Rus' for somewhat more than two years.

Our earliest record of Smotryc'kyj's return to Rus' is dated 26 February/ 6 March 1626: on the Sunday of Orthodoxy he and Jov Borec'kyj were together at a council in Kiev (Golubev 1883b, 280–83). We can assume that he had not yet returned by around 16 July/26 July 1625, the date of the preface to *Desiderosus* in which Kasijan Sakovyč wrote that Smotryc'kyj would answer allegations about his actions upon his return.[8] It therefore would seem that Smotryc'kyj returned to Rus' (Kiev, specifically, as we will see later) sometime late in 1625 or early in 1626, between 16 July/26 July 1625 (more or less) and 26 February/6 March 1626. This fits the chronology Smotryc'kyj offered in his *Apology*. For the sake of argument, let us assume that he returned around 1 January 1626. Thus, in the summer of 1628 he would have been back two and a half years.

When did he leave for the East? According to the traditionally accepted chronologies, Smotryc'kyj was in the Commonwealth most of 1623. He is supposed to have attended the Sejm, which met in Warsaw from 24 January to 11 March 1623 (these dates are taken from Žukovič 1907, 277), to have been somewhere in the Commonwealth on 12 November when Josafat Kuncevyč died in Vicebsk, and then to have stopped briefly in Kiev on his way to the East. (In the same preface to *Desiderosus,* Sakovyč wrote that Smotryc'kyj had resided in the Brotherhood Monastery in Kiev before leaving for Constantinople.)

There are several problems here. First, Smotryc'kyj and Borec'kyj seem not to have attended the Sejm in Warsaw in 1623. The *Justification of Innocence* was written in Borec'kyj's name and dated, probably with an old style date, 6 December (i.e., 16 December) 1622 in Kiev. In it Smotryc'kyj wrote that Jezekijil Kurcevyč had been sent by "us" in order to "give account of himself and of the two other calumnied persons."

(Kurcevyč was archbishop of Volodymyr and Brest. In 1621 Sigismund III had called for his arrest, along with that of Smotryc'kyj and Borec'kyj.) The king had received Kurcevyč well and had released him with these words: " . . . you have our favor; tell the others as well to do this and they, too, will receive our favor."[9] This makes it sound as if Smotryc'kyj and Borec'kyj were not present in Warsaw, had sent Kurcevyč in their stead, and were perhaps to appear the next year (1623). But then Smotryc'kyj wrote (again, in Borec'kyj's name) a few lines later that, having heard these words of the king (they must have been present— hiding out? —in Warsaw at the time), "we the accused willingly appeared *at the most recent Sejm*"—in other words, at that same Sejm of 1622; but they did not plead their case before the king at that time, because:

> [. . .] during such a great danger to the fatherland, it was proper for us to pay attention less to our own honor than to [the fatherland's] safety, both through our own counsel and through the counsel of those whom it befitted to give good advice—namely, that we not seem to anyone publicly to impede the cause of the Commonwealth in such an anxious and dangerous time with our own private matter (since unpeaceful heads were accustomed to present our most peaceful matters as disturbances)—we had to abandon for the time the matter we had undertaken, having commended it to a better time, if the Lord God should deign to lengthen our life and grant us health.[10]

Smotryc'kyj went on to write that "having first appeared (before the king) through our *Verification* and through our fellow bishop [i.e., Kurcevyč], who is as guilty in that calumny as we are), we now appear at this present Sejm [i.e., that of 1623] . . . through this *Justification* of ours . . . and we give this account of our innocence."[11] But Smotryc'kyj and Borec'kyj did not appear in person: the *Justification* was supposed to take the place of a personal appearance. At the end of the work Smotryc'kyj (in Borec'kyj's name) thanked the king for a letter of safe conduct to attend the "present" Sejm, and excused his lack of appearance at it due to "our insufficiency" and "my [i.e., Borec'kyj's] health."[12]

From this information, we can surmise that Smotryc'kyj and Borec'kyj were in Warsaw in 1622 and, for whatever reason, were reluctant to appear before the king at that time. This would seem to be the incident to which Zasławski referred, alleging that Smotryc'kyj had fled Warsaw fearing for his safety, when there was nothing to fear. (Notice that Smotryc'kyj exploited the anti-Orthodox rumors of 1621 in motivating his behavior: we could not speak of our private matters during such an unpeaceful time for the Commonwealth, since there are those who would interpret such actions as unpatriotic, if not treasonous.) Perhaps Smotryc'kyj and Borec'kyj returned together to Kiev in 1622. We know that Smotryc'kyj was there at least on one occasion during that year: he later claimed he had saved three Uniate monks from a martyr's death in Kiev sometime during 1622.[13] (And remember that we still need to account for four years—not necessarily consecutive—during which Smotryc'kyj "lived" with Borec'kyj.)

On 23 May/3 June 1623 Borec'kyj wrote a letter urging the faithful to discount the rumors the Uniates had been circulating, which claimed that he and Smotryc'kyj had relinquished their offices at the recent Sejm (that is, the Sejm that had ended on 11 March 1623; see Golubev 1883b, 265–68) in exchange for the king's forgiveness. Given the nature of communication in those days, it likely was not necessary for Smotryc'kyj and Borec'kyj to have attended that Sejm in person for the other side to consider them fair targets for these rumors. For that matter, this rumor could also have been an attempt to place an unwarrented interpretation upon the *Justification of Innocence,* the contents of which may not have been well known.

If we assume that Smotryc'kyj's trip lasted two and a half years, then perhaps he left for Constantinople around the middle of the summer in 1623. The chronology I am constructing differs here again from the traditional one in one crucial regard: it puts Smotryc'kyj out of the Commonwealth (perhaps already in Constantinople) on 12 November 1623, when Josafat Kuncevyč was martyred at Vicebsk. Golubev (1883a, 115), who was more thorough than most of the investigators of Smotryc'kyj's life, wrote that Smotryc'kyj arrived in Kiev late in 1623 on his way east. This claim is based on a number of assumptions that do not necessarily have to fit together: that Smotryc'kyj stopped by in Kiev on his way east (this information was from Sakovyč, and probably reliable), that Smotryc'kyj's trip had something to do with the year 1623 (judging by the information Smotryc'kyj himself gave on the title page to *Apology* and elsewhere), and that Smotryc'kyj was still in the Commonwealth on 12 November. This last assumption probably stems from the Uniate historiographic tradition that made Smotryc'kyj first responsible for Kuncevyč's death, and then ascribed his conversion to the martyr's intercession.[14]

Looking ahead, we should note that Smotryc'kyj himself never mentioned the martyr or his death in describing his own spiritual pilgrimage. The only contemporary piece of evidence (unknown to Golubev) that placed

Smotryc'kyj "at the scene of the crime" (or at least still within the Commonwealth) was the above-cited petition of Uniate bishops to the king (6 November 1626), which described Smotryc'kyj as having been the "primary cause" of Kuncevyč's death, and as having fled to Turkey in order to avoid the consequences. However, in light of the other evidence, which is more convincing, we can discount this document as testimony for chronology and add it to the body of Uniate literature that sought to link Smotryc'kyj with treason: since Smotryc'kyj was indirectly guilty in Kuncevyč's death, why not make his trip east a symptom of his guilt?

In an otherwise uncontroversial passage, Smotryc'kyj wrote that he heard a sermon delivered by a certain hieromonk Benedict, archimandrite of the Vatopedi Monastery, in the Great Church in Constantinople in 1623.[15] This passage and all of the different, independent chronologies found in various forms in various contexts in Smotryc'kyj's work seem to imply that he was in Constantinople for some large portion of 1623. Would it make sense, then, to describe his pilgrimage as having encompassed the year 1623 if he had set off for Kiev only on—let us say—13 November 1623, and then spent some time in Kiev before beginning his pilgrimage?

Gelazjusz Diplic wrote in his *Antapologia* of 1634 that Smotryc'kyj could not have heard Benedict preach in Constantinople because he was still in the Commonwealth in 1623 (Diplic 1634, 272). Nonetheless, we should not accept Diplic's argument for our chronology here. Diplic wrote a six-hundred-some page refutation of Smotryc'kyj's main Uniate works, *Exaethesis* and especially *Apology,* in which he sought to disprove every comma of his opponent's tracts; his attention was so focused upon the minutiae of Smotryc'kyj's arguments that he seems not to have noticed that his own findings were often mutually contradictory. In this particular passage, Diplic's goal was not to establish a chronology for Smotryc'kyj's actions, but to defend Benedict. He did this by "proving" that Smotryc'kyj could not have heard him preach in 1623, since he was in the Commonwealth then. I suspect that Diplic may have known that Smotryc'kyj was in the Commonwealth at some point in 1623 and may have used this fact to "prove" that, therefore, he could not have been in Constantinople in 1623.[16]

Let me now attempt a chronology of the years that included Smotryc'kyj's pilgrimage to the East. He attended the Sejm in Warsaw together with Jov Borec'kyj in 1622, where he received an invitation to an audience with Sigismund III, and whence he fled, apparently fearing for his safety. (Did he mistrust the king's intentions?) Perhaps he returned thereafter with Borec'kyj to Kiev, or perhaps he joined him sometime fairly soon. While in Kiev he resided in the Brotherhood Monastery. Perhaps he was already there on 6 December/16 December 1622, since the *Justification of Innocence* (written by Smotryc'kyj) was signed on that day from the Brotherhood Monastery church. Two things argue for placing Smotryc'kyj with Borec'kyj for some months in this period. First, Smotryc'kyj would later state he had "lived" with Borec'kyj for four years (see below, p. 130). Perhaps some portion of that time was in the period of late 1622 and early 1623. (We have seen that Smotryc'kyj was in Kiev on at least one occasion in 1622.) Second, Borec'kyj and Smotryc'kyj soon became linked in people's minds, and Borec'kyj would have to answer suspicions as to their actions. Perhaps these suspicions were fueled by the knowledge that Smotryc'kyj and Borec'kyj had been spending much time together in those crucial years.

And so, sometime in 1623, rather earlier than later, and apparently before Josafat was martyred on 12 November, Smotryc'kyj set off for the East, traveling first to Constantinople. The trip, according to Smotryc'kyj himself, normally took under six weeks.[17] Probably the itinerary took him over the "normal" route.[18] Smotryc'kyj wrote only of the "labors, dangers, and miseries, on land and on sea" that he experienced on his trip.[19] This does not tell us very much, and it may have been partially motivated by some Pauline self-stylization (cf. 2 Cor. 11:26) directed at Uniate readers.

In a letter from Borec'kyj to Smotryc'kyj's monastic deputy in Vilnius, Josyf Bobryc'kyj, dated 12 January/22 January 1625, we read that Smotryc'kyj was healthy, had completed everything necessary in Constantinople, and had left for Jerusalem on 17 August/27 August (i.e., 1624). He arrived at the Lord's Sepulcher twelve days later (i.e., 29 August/8 September), and was to remain there until Easter (i.e., spring of 1625), whence he would return to Rus' (Golubev 1883b, 234). The impression is that Borec'kyj was reporting on the basis of a letter from Smotryc'kyj himself.

Thus Smotryc'kyj was first in Constantinople from sometime in 1623 until 17 August/27 August 1624. What did he do during this time? We have only a few details from Smotryc'kyj himself. We know that during his stay in Constantinople, he "resided with [Lukaris]" for some ten weeks,[20] that he was taken sick during his stay in the city, that, due to

Lukaris' "great difficulties at that time," he was unable to discuss his
Ruthenian catechism with the patriarch as he had planned to do and that,
at Lukaris' suggestion, he set off for the Holy Land, even though he was
still not thoroughly recovered.[21] (Thus when he wrote to Borec'kyj that
he was healthy, he must have meant healthy *again,* recovered from his
illness.)

Smotryc'kyj painted a picture of "heretical terror" in Constantinople.
According to him, he was approached by a few "pious hieromonks,"
who "complained of [Benedict's sermon], but who could not undertake
anything."[22] He wrote further of two monks—from this same group?—
who were later forced to leave, and whom Smotryc'kyj met again on his
way back to Rus', during a stopover in Iași (Jassy). The first, a certain
Nicholas from Crete, "rebuked the patriarch, in the presence of many
metropolitans, that he taught, and allowed to be taught, such dogmas of
the faith that had never been heard of in the Eastern Church; for which
he was immediately ordered to leave the patriarchate." The second, one
Matthew from Athens, complained "also in the presence of many
metropolitans . . . of the evil customs of the unhappy Constantinopolitan
See and of its incumbents," who allowed men to be placed upon
episcopal and metropolitan sees that were neither trained in God's law
nor learned in other disciplines; those who had studied were "held here
in disregard and hatred: so long as he has a beard and a purse, make him
immediately a bishop and a metropolitan."[23]

For his trip to the Holy Land, Smotryc'kyj gave a somewhat more
detailed list of sights seen, a sort of pilgrim's guide to the main attractions
of the region.[24] He stated that he visited Zion, Jerusalem, Bethlehem, the
River Jordon, otherwise unspecified places where Christ taught and
preached, Golgotha, the Mount of Olives, and the grave of the Virgin
Mary in Gethsemane.[25] In Jerusalem he read a work against unleavened
bread by a certain Metropolitan Leontij of Rus' ("whether or not he was
ours, I do not know").[26] On at least one occasion he talked with Patriarch
Theophanes of Jerusalem, the man who had consecrated him archbishop
in 1620 (Smotryc'kyj 1629a, 83–84/686–87).

He then returned to Constantinople, sometime after Easter 1625,
where he seems not to have tarried long, since the plague was raging. He
saw Lukaris only a few times in passing on this occasion and was unable
to discuss with him the questions that had been troubling him.[27]
Smotryc'kyj stopped in Iași on his return trip (where he encountered the

above-mentioned Nicholas and Matthew), by now perhaps in the fall of 1625 (Smotryc'kyj 1629b, 9/709).

Did Smotryc'kyj perhaps return home by way of Rome? This is, on the face of it, a strange question, and it would certainly seem unlikely if Iași was on his return route. However, Kortycki made this claim in his funeral oration on Smotryc'kyj.[28] And a few scholars have repeated this information, so we need to consider it.[29] It is important to note that during Smotryc'kyj's lifetime, no one seems to have made such an allegation. This looks much more like the sort of symbolic spiritual biography that Smotryc'kyj's Roman Catholic and Uniate apologists sought to give him: Smotryc'kyj, the errant leader of Rus', wandering from Constantinople to Rome where he finally found the truth. Only one other somewhat contemporary source—Kasijan Sakovyč's *The Schismatic Council of Kiev,* published in 1641—made such a claim, offering Smotryc'kyj as a model for the emulation of the Ruthenian nation:

> Did not that Father Smotryc'kyj, of blessed memory, experience this in himself? . . . Wherefore, not having found the true faith in Turco-Greece, he had gone to [or perhaps simply "turned to," "had recourse to": *udał się do*] the Holy Apostolic See of Rome, and thence he received what his soul desired. I advise you, too, Ruthenian nation, to seek the true faith there and not in Turco-Greece among the Mussulmans.[30]

Again, this was a spiritual biography, and not necessarily a travelogue. It may well have drawn on Kortycki for its formulation.

Smotryc'kyj wrote that he had barely crossed the borders of the Commonwealth, when he was "all but crucified by envious ingrates,"[31] who began to spread calumny about his peregrination—as he phrased it on the title page to his *Apology*—"orally and in writing."[32] (To such an extent that, as Smotryc'kyj wrote to Lukaris in an open letter upon his return, he had thought of abandoning his "wretchedly fallen" and "dearly beloved nation" and returning to Constantinople, or even more, to Palestine and Jerusalem, to live out his days in those holy places.[33])

But the real controversy, as Smotryc'kyj well knew, was over the reason for the trip. The Uniates had claimed in 1626—that is, before Smotryc'kyj's conversion—that the reason was so that he might avoid taking responsibility for his actions. In this view, Smotryc'kyj was a criminal and a coward who went east to hide out among the infidels.

After his conversion, the Uniate side would accept—at least tacitly—the version of events contained in Smotryc'kyj's *Apology*. (But we must always keep in mind that the Uniate side would continue to stress the role of Josafat's martyrdom in Smotryc'kyj's spiritual biography, an element notably absent in Smotryc'kyj's own representations of himself.) Smotryc'kyj's public justification for his pilgrimage was fundamentally doctrinal, and here his audience was the Orthodox (the "envious ingrates") and not the Uniates. He went to the fount of the Eastern faith because he had discovered at some point that he, an archbishop and an archimandrite in the Ruthenian Church, to whom the faithful looked for leadership, did not know what he believed.[34] Thus, he went to the East in order to discover whether Rus' still believed according to the faith of its forefathers;[35] in order to present to Patriarch Cyril Lukaris for his censorship a Ruthenian-language catechism that he, Smotryc'kyj, had written;[36] and thereby, in order to obtain unity for the Ruthenian nation. Note also what, according to Smotryc'kyj was not among his reasons for going to the East. He did not set out at his advanced age on such a long and perilous journey merely for a change of air or scenery.[37] (Had anyone made this allegation? Or was he—more likely—seeking to emphasize the seriousness of his undertaking?) And, more to the point, he did not make this trip on his own initiative: the metropolitan and the archimandrite of the Kievan Monastery of the Caves were aware of his trip and, in effect, blessed it by sending along letters to the patriarch.[38] What is more, Vilnius, Kiev, and Ostroh were all aware that for eight years Smotryc'kyj had struggled with himself concerning the true faith; and since he had not been able to find the answers at home, he set off for the East.[39]

We have little precise information concerning Smotryc'kyj's experiences during his stay in Constantinople. He wrote that he had sought on several occasions to discuss his catechism with the patriarch, but that Lukaris was occupied with his own difficulties at the time.[40] It is worth observing here that the Orthodox side would accuse Smotryc'kyj of bad faith in airing dirty laundry in public by writing an open letter to Lukaris after his return to Rus', asking the patriarch's opinion on doctrinal matters, when he certainly could have discussed these issues in person. But we should not be too quick to accuse Smotryc'kyj of dishonest (or of only dishonest) behavior here. After all, when he wrote of Lukaris' "difficulty" (*trudność*), he could hardly have been acccused of exaggeration: on 2 October 1623 (about the time of Smotryc'kyj's arrival?) Lukaris had just been returned to his see after the first of five depositions in his stormy eighteen-year career.[41] Further, Lukaris gave Smotryc'kyj his own catechism to read, which Smotryc'kyj later declared heretical. Smotryc'kyj heard a sermon in Greek by the above-mentioned Benedict that adhered to Calvinist doctrine; and in conversation with Benedict, he discovered that he had studied in Wittenberg along with Zacharias Gerganos, the author of Calvinist Greek catechism. The general point of all these details was to show that Constantinople, the supposed center of Orthodoxy for Ruthenians, had lost its right to demand allegiance, since its leaders had not only ceased to be Orthodox but had become crypto-Calvinists.

Not surprisingly, in the period after Smotryc'kyj's conversion became generally known, it was the Orthodox side that challenged the reasons he had given for making a trip to the Eastern lands. Their first strategy was to deny Smotryc'kyj's premise: it was not true that Smotryc'kyj did not know what he believed; it was not true that the doctrine of the Eastern Church was contained in the works of its "new theologians," Philalet, Zyzanij, the Clerk, and Ortholog; it was not true that Smotryc'kyj went to the Eastern lands with the blessing of the Ruthenian nation (Diplic 1634, 14). Smotryc'kyj, according to them, was well prepared to discuss matters of the faith with Lukaris; why did he not do it on the spot instead of waiting to return and then send him the letter he published in Polish at the end of his *Paraenesis*?[42]

Thus, according to the Orthodox, Smotryc'kyj's pilgrimage was not made in good faith. What, then, was the reason for his trip in the eyes of the Orthodox? As often before, here too we encounter the charge of self-aggrandizement: Smotryc'kyj supposedly traveled to Constantinople and Jerusalem in order to betray the patriarchs,[43] as well as the Ruthenian nation, by convincing Lukaris to give him a letter granting him more power in the Ruthenian Church. According to Mužylovs'kyj, this was a letter that raised Smotryc'kyj's stature, that made him an "idol in Rus'."[44] The *Indicium* of 1638 contained more specific information: this letter made Smotryc'kyj patriarchal exarch in Rus'; thus all appeals were to be made through him and not directly to the patriarch:

> Look at the apostate Smotryc'kyj, who in the name of all Rus'—clergy and laity—having invented letters for himself from all Rus', went to Jerusalem and the patriarchs, and there, having easily deceived all the

patriarchs, having invented letters from them to Rus', obtained signatures for those letters so that thenceforth no appeals would be brought from our Rus' to the patriarch of Constantinople, but that they be referred by him as the exarch and representative of the patriarch. Whereby he intended to lead Rus' away from its obedience to the patriarch of Constantinople, and secretly to introduce the dishonorable Union, and that for fallible glory, so that subsequent ages would ascribe this to him and to no one else, as was the case with him who burned the temple of Diana in Ephesus [cf. the legend of Herostratos]. And when Rus'—unlearned as it is—barely caught him at this and gave him spiritual punishment for the fact that he had dared to act unto the deception of all Rus' without its knowledge, not wishing in his haughtiness and presumption to be meek, he went to Derman' and, trained in this error of the Union, he wickedly attacked the Holy Church, his Mother, with his works.[45]

What was really at stake here? Obviously the entire Ruthenian nation did not have the right to appeal directly to the patriarch without first appealing to the local authorities. But the brotherhoods that had received the so-called stauropegia did have such a right. And by returning with a letter from Lukaris removing the stauropegial rights, Smotryc'kyj was weakening the power of these lay organizations and strengthening the ordained Church hierarchy.

The nature of the letter that Smotryc'kyj had brought back from Lukaris must have played an important role in the rumors that were circulating at the time. Smotryc'kyj himself responded specifically to Mužylovs'kyj, but probably also indirectly to charges raised by others on this topic, with the following lines from the *Exaethesis* of 1629:

As far as . . . the letter brought by me from Father Patriarch is concerned: it was beneficial for our Ruthenian nation; it did not raise me, either personally or in my dignity, in the least. Your exarchs, of whom there were two in Kiev, a third in Stepan', a fourth in L'viv (you ought, anarchist, to have criticized that four-headed monster for their anarchy and ambition)—that that letter removed them, and ordered that an exarch be chosen by the entire Ruthenian Church, touched a wound, especially in Kiev. Those exarchs sent out messengers throughout the entire land of Rus', asserting to the people as certain, things of which not one iota was found in this letter. And through their greediness they submitted this letter to suspicion and disregard; and me you do not cease even until today to calumny on account of it.[46]

One of Smotryc'kyj's main charges against the Orthodox Church in the period after his conversion was that the power structure had been upended: the laity ruled over the clergy. The letter from the patriarch could be seen as part of a program to consolidate power in the Ruthenian

Church within the ordained Church hierarchy. In claiming that he went eastward with the knowledge and blessing of people like Jov Borec′kyj, Smotryc′kyj seems to have been implying that at least some of the hierarchy supported his attempts to limit the influence of the laity and the lesser clergy.

When Sakovyč wrote in 1625 that Smotryc′kyj had gone east, "whence power and permission for the pacification of *such* matters usually comes," he may well have been speaking of these same two issues: the question of ecclesiastical authority and organization (especially the issue of the ordained hierarchy versus lay confraternities) and the establishment of correct Orthodox doctrine.

But the central disagreement over the reasons for Smotryc′kyj's trip stemmed from the divergent interpretations of his conversion. And the events surrounding his conversion would make it impossible for the rest of the hierarchy—even those like Mohyla and Borec′kyj, who may have sympathized with some aspects of his program—to allow themselves to be seen as in any way connected with this "traitor" to Orthodoxy.

CHAPTER 7

Convert

 In a life filled with controversy, it was the change of allegiance from the Orthodox to the Uniate Church that was the paramount source of public scandal during his lifetime and was to remain the focal point of interest in the Smotryc'kyj affair. Two larger traditions of interpretation—one Uniate and Roman Catholic, the other Orthodox—grew up almost contemporaneously with the events. The Uniate and Roman Catholic historiography would soon characterize Smotryc'kyj's conversion by drawing on the formula of the "Saul of Disunion" converted to the "Paul of the Union" by the blood of Josafat Kuncevyč, the Ruthenian St. Stephen. Whereas early Orthodox representations did on occasion refer to Smotryc'kyj as a Judas, later Orthodox historiography has not made systematic use of this succinct formulation. It has been consistent, however, in its attempts to portray Smotryc'kyj as a traitor, who was inconstant in his allegiances and motivated above all by interest in personal gain. These are essentially the two schools of thought on Smotryc'kyj that have continued to prevail in scholarly literature, and it is important to realize that these formulations began very early—during Smotryc'kyj's lifetime—growing out of the polemical literature of the time which sought in particular contexts to portray Smotryc'kyj in particular manners for particular ends.

From the very beginning, the Uniate and Roman Catholic side insisted that Smotryc'kyj's conversion was nothing short of a miracle. In order to fully comprehend the significance of this particular polemical strategy, it is necessary to recall that Smotryc'kyj had been made at least indirectly responsible for Kuncevyč's martyrdom in the earliest documents relating to the affair. According to the Uniates and the Roman Catholics, it was Smotryc'kyj's letters and embassies sent from Vilnius to the citizens of Polack, in which he urged them to refuse obedience to the Uniate archbishop, that led to a general state of unrest in that diocese.[1] As late as 6 November 1626, exactly eight months before Smotryc'kyj's official conversion to the Uniate Church, the Uniate bishops who had gathered in Kobryn included in their petition to King Sigismund III Vasa the news that Smotryc'kyj, who had been the "primary cause" of the death of Kuncevyč, and who had fled to Turkey to avoid the consequences, had now returned to the fatherland and was continuing to stir up trouble. (The bishops invoked the specter of the Cossacks at this point.) The Uniates asked the protection of the king, lest another of them lose his life.[2]

A royal charter charged the citizens of Vicebsk with a premeditation in their murder of Josafat that allegedly dated back to 1621 (Žukovič 1907, 296, 302). Among the charges: the citizens of Vicebsk had ceased rendering obedience to Josafat in 1621; they had begun giving it to Maksym Herasymovyč, recently called "Melentij" Smotryc'kyj, who had been consecrated by "some Greek" Theophanes; Theophanes, in turn, was allegedly sent by the Turkish sultan to Moscow in order to convince the Muscovites to attack the Commonwealth in concert with the Ottomans (Žukovič 1907, 297–98). The accused testified that at first they had received Josafat, but then in 1621, "probably on account of our sins," a certain Meletij Smotryc'kyj sent a certain Syl'vestr in monk's clothing to Vicebsk with his charters, declaring himself the legally consecrated archbishop and Josafat an apostate (Žukovič 1907, 303–304). Smotryc'kyj's letters were "the first cause" of all the rebellions, as well as of the death of Josafat (Žukovič 1907, 301). (Against this characterization we can note that Smotryc'kyj wrote to Lev Horko, who presented the archbishop's charter at the city hall on 3 March 1621, urging him not to cause any unrest, to turn the other cheek [Žukovič 1907, 304].) The decision of the court was that the accused, aroused by the letters and envoys of Smotryc'kyj, had conceived the plan and carried it out (Žukovič 1907, 309). Nineteen were condemned to death (Žukovič 1907, 311).

The stage was thus set for the Uniate and Roman Catholic side to make of Smotryc'kyj the "Paul from Saul." A recent Ukrainian Catholic investigation (Solovij 1977, 264) has claimed that Smotryc'kyj himself often likened himself to St. Paul. Actually, this is not true. I have found only one or two passages in which Smotryc'kyj referred to his previous "persecution" of the Church and none where he attributed his conversion to the blood of the future St. Josafat.[3] I know of only one passage where the Uniate Smotryc'kyj mentioned the death of Josafat—this was in his

last work, the *Exaethesis* of 1629. But this occurred in the context of a
long list of acts of violence that had been committed in the strife over the
Union; and in this list Josafat immediately preceded those who were
condemned to death by the authorities for their part in the marytrdom of
the future saint.[4] The "Saulus-Paulus" formula was actually—and this
fact is crucial—the interpretation that the Uniate and Roman Catholic
side sought to give to the Smotryc'kyj affair; my impression is that
Smotryc'kyj did little to further this particular view of the events. As far
as I have been able to determine, this historiographic formula made its
first written appearance in a letter sent by Aleksander Zasławski to
Smotryc'kyj stating the conditions under which the Polish Roman Catholic
palatine of Braclav would give Smotryc'kyj control of the monastery at
Derman'. In a letter dated 19 February 1627, Zasławski wrote to
Smotryc'kyj:

> Who here does not remark Your Most Reverend Paternity's most
> forceful calling? I might truly dare to set it equal, that I not say to
> place it above, the calling of St. Paul, that most illustrious torch in the
> Church of God. For in the latter case, it confounded and bound the
> feet of the horse and cast down the rider himself; whereas in the other
> case, it bound Your Paternity's very sharp intellect, darkened your
> illustrious wit, restrained entirely your contrary will. And so, with
> external means did the Lord deal with the latter, and with Your
> Eminence he dealt with internal means.[5]

But while Zasławski's letter shows that the Roman Catholic and
Uniate side was eager to portray Smotryc'kyj as a Ruthenian St. Paul, it
was in a letter of Metropolitan Ruc'kyj written soon thereafter to Rome
(10 July 1627), informing the pope of the recent conversion, that we first
find written evidence that Josafat had been added to the scenario in the
role of St. Stephen:

> The Most Reverend Meletij Smotryc'kyj, nuncupate Archbishop of
> Polack, easily the prince of the schismatics in the North, renders
> obedience to Your Holiness through me and through his letters. And
> I ascribe his return only to glorious God and to the blood of the
> martyr Josafat. For what Paul was to Stephen, such was Smotryc'kyj
> to Kuncevyč; such that if we ascribe the conversion of Paul to the
> prayers of Stephen, thus shall we ascribe the conversion of Smotryc'kyj
> to Kuncevyč?[6]

And the same day Ruc'kyj wrote the following to the secretary of the
Sacred Congregation for the Propaganda of the Faith:

Meletij Smotryc'kyj, called [*nuncupatus*] amongst the schismatics Archbishop of Polack—the schism in these lands had no one more learned than him, nor more hostile to the Holy Union—has already rendered his obedience to me, and through me renders his obedience to Our Most Holy Lord. But how to procede with him Your Most Reverend Eminence will conclude from the included letters. I ascribe this conversion to nothing else but to the blood of the servant of God Josafat; for conversely, along with the *vox populi* [voice of the people], I attribute his death to the Most Reverend Meletij as to the original cause. Thus behold: from Saul, Paul; from a wolf, a lamb.[7]

Probably there were some rhetorical exaggerations here. The leader of the Uniate side, which six years earlier had publicly portrayed Smotryc'kyj as one of the duller Ruthenians, now introduced him in Rome as absolutely the most learned. And had there been no one in Rus' "more hostile" toward the Union? After all, the Uniate side had also sought six years earlier to reveal Smotryc'kyj as a closet Uniate. The point is that Meletij's conversion would make bigger headlines in Rome with the representation found in Ruc'kyj's letter, and not with that found in the Uniate polemical works of 1621–1622.

Ruc'kyj "accepted" what he portrayed as the popular belief that Smotryc'kyj had been responsible for the death of Josafat.[8] But this popular belief, the so-called *vox populi,* had not yet made the next step to attribute Smotryc'kyj's conversion to the martyr's death. After all, Smotryc'kyj was at this point a covert Uniate and would remain so for over a year. As late as 1629, after Smotryc'kyj had become an overt Uniate, Fabian Birkowski (though as court preacher under Sigismund III and Władysław IV, hardly the *vox* of the *populus*) published a sermon entitled *The Voice of the Blood of the Blessed Josafat Kuncevyč,* which still placed the Orthodox archbishop exclusively in the role of "wolf" to the martyr's "good shepherd."[9] The work continued the policy of denying Smotryc'kyj any official status in the Church (referring to Meletij as "Mr. Smotryc'kyj"), and of making Theophanes (the "pseudo-patriarch of Alexandria[!]") into a spy.[10] Here, too, we find Josafat in the role of St. Stephen.[11] But there was no hint of a positive role for Smotryc'kyj. Probably the sermon was delivered before Smotryc'kyj's conversion became public knowledge. The imprimatur of Sebastian Nuceryn (Birkowski 1629, A4ᵛ), who would approve Smotryc'kyj's own *Paraenesis* a half year later, was dated 3 January 1629—in other words, while Smotryc'kyj was still a covert Uniate. If this work indeed appeared in 1629, we can note that Birkowski did not revise his picture of Smotryc'kyj in any way to fit the new order of things.

Smotryc'kyj's conversion came at an opportune moment for Ruc'kyj and the Roman Catholic and Uniate side in the Ruthenian lands. A year later, in 1628, the first process of beatification for Josafat Kuncevyč was initiated; by claiming that the *vox populi* was attributing Josafat's death to the activities of Smotryc'kyj in 1621–1622, the stage was set for making the conversion of the latter into the most spectacular miracle of the former. And indeed, in the *bulla canonizationis* of 6 July 1867, Pope Pius IX drew on the formula first set down by Ruc'kyj two hundred and forty years earlier:

> just as through the prayers of the protomartyr Stephen, Saul, breathing murder and threats, was changed from a wolf into a lamb, thus, through the prayers of Josafat, Meletij Smotryc'kyj himself, the author, as we say, of conspiracy and the sharpest opponent of the Union, repenting of the deed, clung with ardent zeal to the See of Peter and the Roman Pontiff and, actively defending the Catholic faith, has seen the last day.[12]

As far as I have been able to ascertain, however, the Uniate and Roman Catholic *populus* was slow to draw on this formula. The closest thing we have to a record of what "the people" were thinking and saying at the time is the record of the various processes for Josafat's beatification. A first process was conducted in Polack in 1628, a second in Rome in 1629, and a third in Rome in 1632, that is, in the period from one to five years after Ruc'kyj's letter to *Propaganda Fide* and at a time when everyone knew of Smotryc'kyj's conversion and while Smotryc'kyj was still alive. In all of these first three processes, some twelve witnesses out of a total of well over a hundred mentioned Smotryc'kyj in their testimony. All twelve who had anything whatsoever to say about him testified that it was Smotryc'kyj who had sent the letters to Vicebsk urging the citizenry to withdraw their obedience from Josafat. Thus the purpose of mentioning Smotryc'kyj was to make him responsible, though perhaps only in an indirect way, for the death of Kuncevyč.[13] The connection between the two competing archbishops was quite distant in the minds of the witnesses. There was not one mention of Smotryc'kyj's conversion or of Kuncevyč's role in that affair in the testimonies that come directly from Rus', that is, in the documents from the Polack process of 1628. The single reference to Josafat's role in Smotryc'kyj's conversion during the latter's lifetime appeared in a testimony taken in Rome in 1629 and was likely influenced by knowledge of Ruc'kyj's original letters to Rome; it was thus not reflective of the Ruthenian *vox populi.*[14] In the second Roman process of 1632, the connection between Josafat and Smotryc'kyj did not appear at all. Thus, in sum, the Orthodox archbishop of Polack was a rather insignificant figure in Josafat's beatification processes of 1628–1632.

By the time of the second process in Polack in 1637 the situation was markedly different. The *populus* had the story down pat, and Smotryc'kyj's name appeared with some regularity. The following testimony was typical:

> I know this: that Smotryc'kyj, one-time pseudo-archbishop of Polack, was the chief cause of all the evils. . . . And nothing else converted Smotryc'kyj to the holy faith but the blood of the martyr; and, as I see, this saint made him a saint from such a thief and a wolf. *And all these things are public information and knowledge.*[15]

Here we find Smotryc'kyj not only in the role of the saint-maker, but also in that of a possible saint in his own right.

What had happened in the meantime? Two things, in my opinion, had a direct bearing here: Smotryc'kyj had died (27 December 1633), and his confessor in his last days, the Jesuit head of the now-Roman Catholic Ostroh chapter, Wojciech Kortycki, had delivered—and published to the world in print—a funeral sermon bearing the Pauline title (cf. 2 Tim. 4:7) *A View of the Fight Well Fought, the Course Finished, the Faith Kept* (Vilnius, 1634).

That Smotryc'kyj had died made it easier, I suspect, for the Uniate and Roman Catholic side to mount a campaign to control his public persona. As long as Smotryc'kyj remained active, his allegiance was subject to question; and he himself never made use of the Saulus-Paulus formula, at least not in any manner approximating that in which it would be employed by Roman Catholic and Uniate propagandists.

After Smotryc'kyj's death, however, Kortycki was able to popularize the new view that Ruc'kyj had first employed in his letters to Rome:

> For if we examine the prior way of life of both St. Paul and that most reverend man, both can say of themselves *persequebar Ecclesia Dei, et expugnabam illam, et proficiebam in Iudaismo* (and the latter can say *in Schismatismo*) *supra multos Coaetaneos meos in genere meo, abundantius aemulator existens paternarum mearum traditionum.* I persecuted, he says, the Church of God, and I conquered it, and I

surpassed many of my equals in the schism, ardently and insistently
defending my paternal traditions. Both persecuted, with only this
difference: that Paul persecuted with his tongue and sword, and
Meletij with his pen and tongue. I do not know which was the more
harmful. And so, what one great doctor says of St. Paul—If Stephen
had not prayed, the Church would not have Paul today—this can very
appropriately be said of this man: If Josafat, who as a martyr made
rose colored with his blood the beauty of Orthodox Unity—if he had
not prayed, the Orthodox [Uniate] Church would not have Meletij
today.[16]

And one witness after another in Josafat's second beatification process
held in Polack in 1637 was able to say two things about Smotryc'kyj: that
he was first a persecutor of the Church, responsible, however indirectly,
for the martyrdom of Josafat, and that, thanks to the blood and prayers of
Josafat, he was converted to the true Church. Many used the Saulus-
Paulus formulation, and some of the witnesses cited Kortycki as the
source of their knowledge. I suspect, given the formulaic nature of the
testimonies, that many more owed their knowledge to that source.[17]

Thus, by the time Jakiv Suša wrote his *vita* of Smotryc'kyj in Rome in
1666, no one misunderstood the title he gave his work: *The Saul and
Paul of the Ruthenian Union, Transformed by the Blood of the Blessed
Josafat, Or Meletij Smotryc'kyj*. Suša opened his biography with a
reference to Smotryc'kyj's posthumous miracle and called for an official
investigation—signs that the promotion of a beatification process might
have been one purpose of Suša's work.[18] Suša had subtly altered the old
view of Smotryc'kyj in order to make his allegiance to the Uniate Church
seem stronger, or at least of longer duration. For Suša, Smotryc'kyj was
in a sense a lifelong Uniate whose wanderings as a young man were due
to the influence of an Orthodox home and studies in Protestant Germany.
In this vein, Suša emphasized Smotryc'kyj's friendship with Ruc'kyj in
the late 1610s.[19] He further stated that Church and state investigations of
the Josafat affair had cleared Smotryc'kyj of direct complicity in the
murder; he was *only* guilty of indirect responsibility by virtue of the
letters he sent to Vicebsk.[20] For Suša, therefore, Smotryc'kyj was not so
much the convinced Orthodox, a persecutor of the true Church, who was
converted solely by divine intervention and the prayers of Josafat; rather
he was also the troubled seeker after truth, who, after eight years of
struggle with himself, finally came to a recognition of the true Church.

This may reflect the lingering feelings of uncertainty concerning the
firmness of Smotryc'kyj's confessional allegiance. Whether or not he

was aware of it, by emphasizing the constancy of Smotryc'kyj's piety in spite of his conversion, Suša was revising the earlier Uniate and Roman Catholic representation which had made inconstancy his hallmark. After all, this was the man who, according to earlier Uniate propaganda, was on the verge of announcing his allegiance to the Uniate Church, when one book, a work by Marcantonio de Dominis, changed his mind. There are some indications that these Uniate and Roman Catholic portrayals of Smotryc'kyj's conversion were directed at least as much toward putting forth a particular picture of Josafat Kuncevyč as of Meletij. Kortycki's sermon came in the midst of the various processes that would lead to Josafat's beatification on 16 May 1643.[21] The future saint may also have been Suša's primary concern. Suša had published a life of Kuncevyč the year before, in 1665. That account, too, had contained both central elements of the plot: Smotryc'kyj was the main cause of the martyr's death through his letters and emissaries (Suša 1665, 57–58); and Smotryc'kyj's conversion was one of Josafat's posthumous miracles (no. 27 of 100, to be precise; Suša 1665, 111–12). There Suša had promised his readers detailed information on Smotryc'kyj's own death and posthumous miracle in a work devoted to him alone—that is, the *vita* he was to publish the following year. Once again it seems that the Uniate and Roman Catholic side was operating with a certain set of priorities in mind. Suša was in Rome to solicit help for his flock in the period after the Xmel'nyc'kyj Uprising (1648). Smotryc'kyj, dead now for over 15 years, had interceded to protect the monastery at Derman' from the ravages of the uprising.[22] Perhaps first on the agenda was to hasten the progress of Josafat toward canonization; second was to rekindle interest in Smotryc'kyj's beatification.

The Orthodox, of course, had a quite different view. While the Uniate and Roman Catholic side was beginning to mount its campaign for Smotryc'kyj's beatification (and we can easily argue that Ruc'kyj's first letters to Rome on the issue of Smotryc'kyj's conversion in 1627 were already seeking to place him in the ranks of the "beatifiable" in the minds of his Roman readers), the Orthodox side was busy portraying him as a man who loved the things of this world, a heretic, a chosen vessel of the Antichrist. I have already mentioned the Orthodox allegations that Smotryc'kyj had been lured to the Uniate Church by the promise of Derman', by the promise of money. These allegations appeared in a number of works from the period (and even after Smotryc'kyj's death), and Smotryc'kyj himself felt a need to answer the charge that he had converted for Derman' in his *Paraenesis* of 1629.

The most complete, immediate response to the Uniate and Roman Catholic campaign was reflected in the anonymous, manuscript *Pamflet* against Smotryc'kyj, discovered by Golubev and published in 1875. Since it treated Smotryc'kyj as a traitor to the faith but made no mention of his death (and, in fact, held out some hope for his reversion to Orthodoxy[23]), the work was written most likely sometime between August 1628 and December 1633. *Pamflet,* too, emphasized the mercenary in Smotryc'kyj: he was moved by the love of money;[24] his sympathy was not with Lazarus, but with the rich man (cf. Lk. 16);[25] he was to the patriarch in Constantinople as Judas was to Christ.[26] Interesting here is the accusation of inconstancy. The Roman Catholic and Uniate side, in order to encourage doubts on the Orthodox side about the reliability of their leader, had made inconstancy one of the central points of their attacks in the early 1620s. In the late 1620s the Orthodox would now seek to return the favor. The pamphlet against Smotryc'kyj contained an "Admonition to the Holy Father, the Pope of Rome," concerning the sincerity of the recent convert. Here Meletij was put into the same category with Luther and Calvin.[27] Elsewhere *Pamflet* put it quite succinctly: "[He is] neither yours nor ours."[28]

But this later controversy over Smotryc'kyj's nature and the reasons for his conversion obscure a more interesting competition for control of his loyalty that was conducted partially behind the scenes and partially in public view while what we have come to call his "conversion" was still an ongoing process. A consideration of that competition brings to the fore several unexamined issues: What were the circumstances of Smotryc'kyj's conversion? How did the convert himself view—and represent—his conversion? Can we find any evidence that Smotryc'kyj's goals and representations evolved as the process of his "conversion" progressed?

Smotryc'kyj referred in his public works very sparingly to his conversion. In the only printed reference to the very act of conversion that I have found, Smotryc'kyj used the general term "change": "I suffered a change . . . "[29] True, in all the Uniate works (even in the *Apology,* where it was not yet official public knowledge that he had converted) he contrasted the old Smotryc'kyj—or rather the old Smotryc'kyjs, since he referred to the authors of his own Orthodox works separately—with the new Smotryc'kyj. But what was the difference? The older versions did not know what they believed, the new one did. The point when Smotryc'kyj came to this realization would then be an important stage in the process of his conversion as he viewed and presented it. But the archbishop offered conflicting evidence on this issue. At one point, he claimed he left for the East (in 1623) already what he was in 1629. But what was the thrust of this statement? To emphasize the early nature of his conversion? Or the relative stability of his present position? On the other hand, he said that he went to Constantinople with the knowledge that he did not know what he believed; but he also implied that the full realization of this fact came in his encounter with Lukaris. As the Orthodox would later point out, if he went to Constantinople with this knowledge, why did he wait until his return to pose his questions in epistolary form to Lukaris in 1628? So when did he convert according to this particular scheme? In 1623? 1625? 1627? 1628?

Let us attempt a chronology of Smotryc'kyj's "conversion" in its broadest sense. On some occasions Smotryc'kyj implied that the change he had undergone had taken place about the same time he was made Orthodox archbishop of Polack in 1620, or even somewhat earlier. Writing in 1628 for public consumption, Smotryc'kyj placed his "change" somewhat before 1621, and he implied a gradual process of "changing" that had prepared the way:

> I do not mention *Verification,* its *Defense, Elenchus, Justification,* and others similar, in which, one after another, the further I went the less often I attacked true dogmas, the more broadly I wrote about the everyday matters that had suddenly come up at those times. . . . After all this, in the year 1621, having decided to abandon the lamentatious errors and heresies, I undertook, not without the will of God, Whose special grace I experienced in this matter above my worthiness and readiness, the serious manner of investigating this truth, which we received in our ancestors from the Holy Eastern Church: that is, I began to write a catechism of the dogmas of the faith in the manner of a dialogue, having summoned the Lord my God for help.[30]

This picture of a gradual process of change, beginning as early as the 1610s appeared in several places in Smotryc'kyj's Uniate works. While he was still a layman, and while he was a simple monk in the Brotherhood Monastery in Vilnius, Smotryc'kyj talked with Leontij Karpovyč and others, arguing that the Brotherhood had done a great wrong lending its authority to the printings of the Ruthenian "new theologians," Zyzanij, Philalet, Ortholog, and others.[31] But he began to speak out publicly about this evil only once he had become a bishop,[32] and he became even more vocal after his return from the Holy Land.[33] On one occasion, Smotryc'kyj gave a precise date for the beginning of the process:

> For almost eight whole years I struggled at home with myself and with the blasphemies of those authors; and Vilnius is well aware of this, well aware is Kiev, well aware the Ostroh chapter, and many of those who seemed to be of some importance in our nation, with whom I conferred about this, purposefully convening with them for this very reason. And since I did not find what I sought at home, I set off to the East to seek this among my own.[34]

This would imply—if Smotryc'kyj set off for the East in mid 1623—that he had begun his search for the truth by late 1615.

The precise place in this continuum from ca. 1615 to 1627–1628 where the real "change" was supposed to have occurred seems to have varied as necessary in Smotryc'kyj's own representations. An earlier date seems to have suited his polemical strategies when he had an Orthodox audience in mind. Against the notion that he had converted to receive the archimandritehood of Derman' Monastery, Smotryc'kyj wrote that he had set out for the East already an adherent of the Union, and that the monastery already had an archimandrite (Jezekijil Kurcevyč) at the time.[35] However, as we will soon see, this strategy caused him problems with his new Roman Catholic and Uniate masters, and it may have been with them in mind that he twice offered hints of a "conversion-like experience" sometime during his trip to the East. First, Smotryc'kyj wrote that in Golgotha, at the scene of Christ's Crucifixion

> there was not within me any internal or external sense that did not take comfort, rejoice, be glad, that did not feel itself present at the place of the Crucifixion of its Savior. In my thoughts I was entirely—with all my soul—joy and comfort. Holy Golgotha was then for me paradise. . . . And immediately there, having subjected myself with all my soul and with my pure heart unto that ONE requested by Him from His Father [cf. John 17:11, 21, 22], I offered, pledged, and committed myself unto Him, as my Lord and God, for that service in His Holy Church, that I might declare His salvatory ONE unto my nation.[36]

Second, Smotryc'kyj again saw Patriarch Theophanes, now in Jerusalem, where he related a story he had heard while in Moldavia on his way back from Rus' (apparently in 1621, a few months after he had consecrated

Smotryc'kyj and the rest of the Ruthenian hierarchy) concerning the "conversion" of Metropolitan Matthew of Myra. Matthew had been the author of writings "vexatious *usque ad nauseam* [to the point of nausea] toward the Western Church and the Roman religion regarding the differences between the Eastern and the Western Churches."[37] But then, St. Peter appeared to him three times at noon "whether in a dream or through *extasis,* he himself could not discover." The first two times, St. Peter said to him: "Matthew, how did my see so offend you that you inveigh against it so shamelessly? I admonish you, desist from this." And the third time he added: "If you do not desist from this, I will summon you to the terrible divine judgment; there you will give account for this before the impartial Judge." Whereupon the metropolitan "came to his senses," "cursed his work," and "burned it in the presence of his people."[38]

Smotryc'kyj relayed the recounting of this story, but did this imply that he had already "come to his senses" by this point? He may have wished to give this impression to his Roman readers, but to Lukaris, to whom these lines were addressed, he described the experience of hearing this story only as having given birth to a "gnawing worm in his conscience" that began to "drill my heart penetratingly" since Smotryc'kyj, too, had written such works.[39] Again, there were several ambiguities in this presentation. Which works did Smotryc'kyj have in mind? Certainly *Thrēnos,* but did he mean here the others as well, or did they belong to the process of spiritual change? And was Smotryc'kyj still in some doubt? Had the doubts only then begun to take effect? Or was this only part of the fiction of his letter to Lukaris?

On the other hand, on a few occasions Smotryc'kyj used language reminiscent of the beginning of the lives of SS. Constantine-Cyril and Methodius—the ninth-century apostles of the Slavs—to describe his conversion, that of Lukaris (was this wishful thinking on his part?), and that of the entire Ruthenian nation. Thus, in *Paraenesis* Smotryc'kyj wrote of the conversion—and forced conversion at that—of the Ruthenian nation:

> Deign to cause it to happen, O Lord Jesus Christ, that the honorable, holy, and soul-saving opinion of that doctor, who was great in the Church of God [i.e., St. Augustine], occur for our Ruthenian nation from that power, unto whose government, industry, care, and defense the Lord God entrusted unto us, so that it might be praised through its advancement; and so that through the act of giving of this cause, you,

too, having acquired the wisdom granted unto you, might be wise and
might *come to the recognition of the truth.*[40]

Furthermore, in the open letter to Lukaris that he appended to *Paraenesis,*
Smotryc'kyj sought to influence the patriarch and to explain his own
actions using the same general terms:

> Wherefore, if I should be neglected by Your Holiness in my request
> and thrust away empty-handed, taking God as my witness, the Creator,
> Who examines the hearts and minds of man, then, *salvo tuo Paterno
> Honore* [saving your paternal honor], I would have to do what I
> perceived as bringing salvation to my soul, through the grace and help
> of my *God Who does not desire the death of the sinner* and Who grants
> conversion to man.[41]

These choices of biblical passages (cf. 1 Tim. 2:4; Ez. 33:11) were not by
chance in these contexts (the first at the culmination of the *Paraenesis*
proper, the second at a sort of false culmination near the end of the open
letter to Lukaris appended to the *Paraenesis*). In both instances Smotryc'kyj
paraphrased one of the key programmatic commonplaces of documents
connected with the Cyrillo-Methodian movement. Compare for example
the beginning of the *Life of Constantine:* "God is merciful and generous,
awaiting man's repentance, that all might be saved and might come unto
the understanding of the truth; for He does not wish death for the sinner,
but repentance and life."[42] In the only passage where Smotryc'kyj
explicitly made St. Paul the model for his "change," he drew on the same
Cyrillo-Methodian topos:

> There was a time when I persecuted the Church of God beyond
> measure, and wasted it, and profited in Rus' above many of my equals
> in my own nation, being more exceedingly zealous not of God's law,
> nor of the decrees of my fathers, which were pure, and are holy and
> immaculate, but rather of those errors and heresies, which were sown
> by our Zyzanijs in our Ruthenian Church while people slept. And my
> own works themselves, which I had intended for their defense, brought
> me, by the merciful grace of a merciful God, to notice and recognize
> them, such that I could no longer go against the truth of the Church
> with my writings, unless I had entirely prepared myself for receiving
> those errors and heresies and did not know myself to be, or call myself,
> any longer a son of the Eastern Church. My conscience, not without
> God's special compassion, nonetheless did not allow me to do this,
> even though I attempted many times as if to struggle with God's
> calling. For which let eternal thanks be to the living Lord, *Who does
> not wish the death of the sinner,* from me His miserable creature.[43]

But again, when was "that time": shortly after 1610, when Smotryc'kyj
wrote *Thrēnos,* or did it last until his covert conversion in 1627? The

immediate context would seem to imply the latter, were it not for the fact that it was only one page later that Smotryc'kyj himself placed the break in 1621 (see Smotryc'kyj 1628a, 105–106/576).

In a letter to Cardinal Bandini, written the same day he wrote to Urban VIII asking to be received into the Catholic Church, Smotryc'kyj again used the Pauline formulation: "Blessed be our God, the God of mercy, Who wishes mercy and not a sacrifice."[44] And in his last work, the *Exaethesis* of 1629, Smotryc'kyj used this same biblical passage to describe the reunion of Rus': "that many people repent and, despising your schism, betake themselves to Holy Church Unity—let God Almighty be praised, *Who does not wish the death of man.*"[45]

Smotryc'kyj knew the lives of SS. Cyril and Methodius (he cited them in his Uniate works), so these were probably not fortuitous usages. As an indication of a wider pattern of use, consider the ironic example found in the Orthodox account of the "anti-miracle" performed by Ipatij Potij after the Council of Brest:

> But God, Who wishes that all men be saved and come unto an understanding of the truth, showed their sacrifice to be entirely unclean and unacceptable, for immediately—O terrible miracle!—the chalice fell into pieces and the wine poured out.[46]

True, this passage represented a more literal citation of the beginning of the life of St. Cyril than those found in Smotryc'kyj's works; still I suspect Smotryc'kyj purposefully chose this biblical passage with such resonances for Orthodox readers and writers when he described the conversion of himself and his nation to Rome. By means of this allusion, Smotryc'kyj sought to place this new affirmation of spiritual allegiance in the same tradition as the original conversion of the Slavs to Christianity.

Again, however, these references belonged to the more subtle sort, and Smotryc'kyj seems to have avoided describing a clear break in so many words in his spiritual biography. In 1627 he presented to Aleksander Zasławski, the Roman Catholic palatine of Braclav, a spiritual biography that implied a gradual process of change beginning in the 1610s. Zasławski, who probably viewed these issues more in terms of "either-or," naturally desired to know why, if Smotryc'kyj had reached such an important turn in his life some ten years earlier, he had not converted at that time but had gone on to write even more works against the Roman Catholic Church?

> But you should remember your own words, that you recognized you
> were in error not six but more than ten years ago, that it was not the
> Spirit of God that was working in you, when you wrote the pestilent
> *Lament,* but it was through the spirit (if I may say so) of ambition, the
> spirit of heresy, which you contracted in heretical schools. But therefore,
> why did Your Most Reverend Paternity produce other books, in which
> you confirmed, praised, and persuaded everyone to ponder those
> things that are contained in the *Lament?*[47]

In what camp, then, should we place Smotryc'kyj on his return to the
Commonwealth (which came no later than the winter of 1625–1626)?
What did he do in the period between his return from the East and his
covert conversion to the Uniate Church in June 1627? He spoke of the
actions of the Vilnius Brotherhood in 1626 as something distant from
him and certainly not under his supervision.[48] Where was the archbishop
and archimandrite residing in 1626 and 1627? While the Uniate side
portrayed him to the king in their petition of 1626 as well-ensconced in
Kiev, exploiting the support of the Cossacks, other indications point to
growing suspicions toward him on the part of the Orthodox. Smotryc'kyj's
first three Uniate works, *Apology, Protestation,* and *Paraenesis,* were
all written with the purpose of answering the Orthodox rumor mill,
which had been making various allegations concerning his trip to the
Eastern lands and his behavior since his return. Both sides, it appears,
were mounting campaigns to exert more direct control over his behavior.

Smotryc'kyj seems to have spent at least part of the time between 1
January 1626 (the approximate date of his return to Rus') and 6 July 1627
(the date of his official petition to Rome, which could also have marked
the beginning of his tenancy at Derman') in Kiev with Borec'kyj. They
were together at the Sunday of Orthodoxy in Kiev that year (26 February/
8 March 1626). Borec'kyj seems to have come under the same suspicions
as Smotryc'kyj, perhaps for continuing to work in concert with him, when
others—Kopystens'kyj and Kopyns'kyj, for example—had become his
opponents.[49] Smotryc'kyj offered two different reasons why Kopystens'kyj
had refused him residence in any Kiev monastery on his return from the
East: according to the first account, either because he wished to avoid the
suspicion of the people who held Smotryc'kyj in suspicion or because he
wished to avoid the displeasure of the king for harboring an enemy of the
state, and according to the second account, because of the letter Smotryc'kyj
had brought back from Lukaris removing the stauropegial status of the
brotherhoods. The latter is more likely the key reason: Kopystens'kyj

challenged the patriarchal letter in Borec̕kyj's court on 26 June/6 July 1626 (Golubev 1883a, 135; 1883b, 289–90). Rumors once again must have been flying. On 9 May/19 May 1626 Borec̕kyj found it necessary to defend himself and Smotryc̕kyj from charges that the two of them had betrayed Orthodoxy: "neither have we had any agreement with the apostates . . . nor have we ever perfidiously made any agreements against the Ruthenian Church or against our nation, nor did we think to do it, nor can we think to do it, without the will of God and without the will of the entire Church of the Orthodox."[50] Smotryc̕kyj seems to have been by now unwilling, or unable, to return to Vilnius. He wrote 29 August/8 September 1626 from Mižhirrja to a Vilnius abbess and nuns, saying that he had waited until then to write in the hope (a vain hope, as we know with hindsight!) that the "contrary noise concerning him would quiet, and the troubled hearts of the pious be consoled."[51] His *Paraenesis* was an open letter to the Vilnius Brotherhood, an attempt to answer rumors that the members of the brotherhood cited to him, alleging that he was either a Uniate or a proponent of some third sect. On 8 November/18 November 1626, Bohdan Solomerec̕kyj gave Smotryc̕kyj control of the Barkalabava Monastery (*Arxeografičeskij* 1867, 31–380). Was this at the time of the funeral of Solomerc̕kyj's mother, when Smotryc̕kyj, who was present in Belarus, was (as the Orthodox *Pamflet* assures us) partially "unmasked" as a traitor to Orthodoxy (see below, p. 122)?

He was apparently once more somewhere in the middle. It seems likely that Smotryc̕kyj himself was in this period again actively discussing opportunities for a reunification of Rus' with leaders of both Churches: Ruc̕kyj and Zasławski, on the one hand, Mohyla and Borec̕kyj, on the other. True, in later documents he would portray his actions—here, I believe, addressing the audience of his new Uniate and Roman Catholic masters—solely as an attempt to bring the leaders of the Orthodox side into union with Rome. But this scenario should sound familiar by now. By 1628, Smotryc̕kyj had been unmasked by the Orthodox side and had been brought to the point of no return in his public confession of his new faith. He was, perhaps, putting a slightly new interpretation on those recent, somewhat ambiguous events in light of the new, clearer situation.

It is worth proceeding slowly here. In his first letter to Urban VIII, Smotryc̕kyj would use the image of the bright sun in describing the Barberini papacy. Certainly he wished to portray his new beliefs as something that could withstand examination under that light. But we should not focus solely on the clarity of the situation to which Smotryc'kyj later arrived (or wished to claim publicly that he had attained); also important are the shadows of the period when Smotryc'kyj's conversion was still a process. These shadows—these questions and ambiguities— are much more interesting and reveal some important and neglected aspects of the events of the period and of Smotryc'kyj's mind. If we define Smotryc'kyj's conversion as his public profession of faith—and this was the act that the Uniate and Roman Catholic side was to emphasize—then his conversion was indeed preceded by a series of partial steps that could be subjected to a variety of interpretations. Although Smotryc'kyj would later describe them all as leading inexorably to his official conversion, we should also allow for the possibility that they may have been somewhat more ambiguous in their original context.

On the eve of Smotryc'kyj's petition to Urban VIII on 6 July 1627 each side had its doubts about him. According to his own representations, he was discussing the question of Union—with what details, we cannot be certain—with Borec'kyj and Mohyla. But he had apparently been discussing the same things with the other side for several months. Was he firmly in either camp? We do not know this with certainty, but if we review the testimonies carefully, we see continued doubts on the Uniate and Roman Catholic side as well as among the Orthodox.

Smotryc'kyj asked for the use of the monastery at Derman', a holding of Prince Aleksander Zasławski. He had apparently been talking with Zasławski and, through him, with Ruc'kyj, about his views on the universality of the Church. Probably the Uniate side would have considered that it had heard all this from Smotryc'kyj before but had been unable to enlist his open support. This time, they may have felt, Smotryc'kyj was in a weaker position due to his part in the Josafat affair and due to the growing suspicions about him on the Orthodox side, stemming perhaps to a certain extent from rumors about the letters he had brought back from Lukaris. In any event, Ruc'kyj seems to have expressed some scepticism in the intial stages and urged Zasławski to demand Smotryc'kyj's conversion in exchange for Derman';[52] and Zasławski pointed out that it would be difficult for him, since he was a senator, to explain to the king why he was having any business with such an enemy of the public peace.[53] The cost of Derman', the cost of acceptance by Ruc'kyj and Zasławski, would be written evidence of Smotryc'kyj's conversion to the Uniate Church. The explicitness and insistance of this demand leads me to suspect that Smotryc̆kyj might have been seeking to avoid putting anything in writing. Zasławski, for his part, was quite straightforward in stating his reason for this demand:

> Therefore, since the will of man is changeable . . . until death, I would gladly have—for the sake of the peace of my heart (not that I would distrust Your Most Reverend Eminence, God forbid)—certainty in writing.[54]

Recall that Smotryc̆kyj had told Zasławski that he had already undergone a change in the 1610s, and that the palatine of Braclav had then desired to know why, if this was the case, Smotryc̆kyj had continued to write works against the Uniates. It was no doubt this difficulty in being certain of Smotryc̆kyj's allegiance that caused Zasławski to demand a written statement of allegiance. Zasławski's letter was dated 19 February 1627.

Thus, the next stage in the process of Smotryc̆kyj's conversion (at least from the point of view of the Roman Catholic and Uniate authorities) would be his compliance with Zasławski's demand for a written statement. This did not come until five months later, on 6 July 1627, when Smotryc̆kyj converted officially (but covertly) in Zasławski's house in the presence of Metropolitan Ruc̆kyj and wrote three letters to Rome, one to Pope Urban VIII, a second to Cardinal Ottavio Bandini, and the third to the Holy Office (see Velykyj 1972, 125–29).

First, Smotryc̆kyj's introduction of himself to the pope:

> That light of the sun, which illumines this entire mass of the earth with its rays, seems in these most lamentable times to be Your Holiness' fortunate pontificate of the Church of God, and all the more brilliant the more it is obscured by the clouds of so many heresies and schisms. Such that, as I ought to say of it, there is no one who can hide from its warmth. Behold, situated in the most remote appendage of the sinful world, born in the schism as out of necessity, having wallowed in it for fifty years out of ignorance, extracted from the pit of miseries by the rays of Your Holiness' benefices and compassion toward the Ruthenian Church, I am moved, my feet and hands bound, to throw myself in tears at the knees of Your Holiness and to kiss Your feet most humbly. And since, all ambiguity of words having been set aside and the schismatic heresy having been abjured, I render obedience to You, and I am able to say nothing besides: "Father, I have sinned against heaven, and before thee, and am no more worthy to be called Thy son [Lk. 15:18–19]." But You, indeed, Most Holy Father, forgive me everything I have sinned, with mind, mouth, and pen, against You and Your Holy See, as well as against the Holy Roman Catholic Faith; and I wish to retract all those things, without shame, God helping, so

that, by killing the sin in me that was mine, I might obtain grace in You, Most Holy Father, the life which is of God. May You deign to make me as one of your servants. I wish for this one thing, that, as I say from my heart with the holy sinner, "I have sinned against the Lord," thus, together with him, I might hear from You, Most Holy Father: "And the Lord has removed your sin from you."[55]

Unfortunately, we do not have a printed edition of Smotryc'kyj's letter to the Holy Office, if it is indeed still extant. But we do have a third-person report on the contents of that document. The important new piece of information here was that Smotryc'kyj requested permission to remain a covert Uniate for some time and to retain his old titles. It is not entirely clear whose idea it was for Smotryc'kyj to remain covert. The matter had appeared in Zasławski's letter to Smotryc'kyj before the latter included it in his petition to the Holy Office.[56] Zasławski's letter was, however, in large part the result of his personal discussions with the archbishop, and the suggestion may well have come from Smotryc'kyj himself. Smotryc'kyj made the idea his own in two ways: by demonstrating to the Holy Office his familiarity with the technique of dissimulation known as *reservatio mentalis* (he asked permission in his letter to continue commemorating aloud the name of the patriarch of Constantinople during the Divine Liturgy, with the understanding that he would silently be praying for his conversion); and, by staking claim to a territory on the mental map of the Holy Office and *Propaganda Fide,* where the same rules would apply as in Jesuit missions to India (see below, p. 173). Notice that with this maneuver Smotryc'kyj both drew nearer to Rome (by demonstrating his knowledge of the rules of the game) and distanced himself from it (by arguing that he was engaged in the sort of missionary activities in distant and strange lands where certain rules could be bent). For a period of more than a year (July 1627 to August 1628) both sides were supposed to think that Smotryc'kyj belonged to them. He was overtly Orthodox, while Rome had his assurances that he was inwardly Uniate. But what of the possibility that he was already dissimulating when he asked for permission to dissimulate? In the 1610s Smotryc'kyj had sought the sort of structures that would allow him freer access to both sides. Could he not have been doing something similar here?

If this was the case, then we would need to assume a certain level of dissimulation in Smotryc'kyj's letter to Urban VIII. There is no way to prove this. The conventionality of the language could be enlisted in arguments in either direction. The argument I hope to support is that

Smotryckyj did indeed dissimulate in so far as his vision, while no longer that of the rest of the Orthodox hierarchy, was not entirely that of Barberini's Catholic Reform either.

Was the image of the Barberini papacy as "the sun from which no one can hide" only a positive one for Smotryckyj? Why was it that he chose here and elsewhere to abjure the "ambiguity of words" and "the schismatic heresy" not personally and actively, but impersonally and passively, through an ablative absolute construction in his Latin? (And for that matter, was the mention of "ambiguity of words" itself some sort of slip of the pen?) These details by themselves are of little significance, but they may begin to carry more weight if they seem to be part of a more general pattern of behavior.

In this spirit note that, whether or not Smotryckyj was sincere in his declaration of allegiance, Rome did not fully trust him. Why not? Was this the natural distrust toward a former foe? Was it perhaps that Smotryckyj had shown himself too familiar with the art of *reservatio mentalis* in his first letter to the Holy Office? However this may be, Rome specifically left it up to Ruckyj to certify at some point that he considered Smotryckyj sincere in his conversion and thus a possible candidate for an official title within the Roman Church. And for a variety of reasons—about which presently—this certification did not come for well over a year. And even after his overt conversion, Rome continued to gather information about Smotryckyj's behavior.

What did Smotryckyj do during his year of covert Uniate activities? Almost all our information here stems from the conflicting versions of the proceedings of the Orthodox council held in Kiev in August 1628. By this point, some participants in what may have been ambiguous dealings in 1627–1628 seem to have felt that the lines between the two religious camps were again being drawn with great precision. This meant that they were now required to represent their actions as conceived absolutely in keeping with the goals of the authorities of that side to which they had finally pledged allegiance. This display of good faith was as much for their own side, as for the other. At the same time, both groups of participants—Smotryckyj on the one side, Mohyla and Boreckyj on the other—would seek to portray their former interlocutors as wavering and unreliable in their allegiances, perhaps as much to shake the standing of their new opponents with their respective sides as to establish the truth of the matter.

What happened at the Kiev Council of August 1628? Apparently Smotryc'kyj felt that the events of that meeting were potentially so damaging to his cause that it was necessary to impose his version of events immediately—before the rumor mill might be swayed in another direction—by publishing a *Protestation,* by writing to Lavrentij Drevyns'kyj, who was a leading Orthodox nobleman,[57] and by attempting to enter an official, legal protest into the castle books.[58] And indeed, at about the same time, if not a few days earlier than Smotryc'kyj's *Protestation,* the Orthodox side issued its own printed account of what had occurred, likewise seeking to influence public opinion in its favor.

An Orthodox pamphlet assured its readers that Smotryc'kyj had already been found out before the Kiev Council of 1628:

> he began to compose a book full of poison, calling it *Apology,* and the Fathers of the Kievan Caves Monastery charged him partially at a council, having unmasked him, although not entirely. After these events, when he was in Balkahrad at the funeral of the above-mentioned princess Solomerec'ka, who had departed in Christ, some of the Fathers unmasked him then as unorthodox, but they could not charge him openly, since he was held in great esteem by all, until they manifestly condemned him for the second time at the council in Kiev.[59]

Thus we learn from the post-conversion Orthodox version that the Orthodox monks in Kiev already had their suspicions, probably when Smotryc'kyj met with them around 8 September/18 September 1627 to discuss the next year's council; that he remained in generally good favor with the Orthodox people, at least in the area of Minsk, where they had known and respected him ten years earlier; and that he was finally "unmasked" at the Kiev Council of 1629. We might also wish to allow, however, for the possibility that the Orthodox now exaggerated their suspicions in order to assert a kind of retroactive control over Smotryc'kyj—as if to say, "we knew all along."

Nonetheless, it is entirely likely that suspicions would have arisen from the fact that Smotryc'kyj seems not to have been residing in Vilnius. How did the influential Vilnius Brotherhood view him in this period? There is some reflection of the suspicions in the opening lines to Smotryc'kyj's *Paraenesis* published in 1629 after the events of the Kiev Council. There Smotryc'kyj stated that, on the eve of the council in August of that year, his deputy in Vilnius, Father Josyf Bobryc'kyj, had handed him a letter from the Vilnius Brotherhood asking him to respond to rumors that had been circulating about him. Smotryc'kyj began his work by referring directly to doubts the Vilnius Brotherhood had harbored against him in the period before his "unmasking" at the council:

> Unable, through lack of place and time, to answer sufficiently Your Graces' letter of the thirteenth day of August of the present year 1628 when it was handed to me in Kiev by Father Josyf, my deputy (in which Your Graces ask me for a clear response: that I remove the suspicion which has arisen about me in Your Graces' hearts due to the repute carried in the mouths of men, some alleging that I am a Uniate, and others that I have invented something new and thus attempt to tear Rus' into a third part, whence there would finally arise a deception worse than the first); now, by the grace of God, having acquired a freer time and place, I answer at greater length than I had answered previously.[60]

Perhaps these suspicions had arisen (or had been encouraged) when Smotryc'kyj's dealings with the Uniates (particularly with Ruc'kyj) were discovered by the Orthodox side. On that occasion, as we will soon see, he wrote to the Vilnius Brotherhood portraying his activities in much the same light as when he was required in 1621 to answer similar charges about his actions and intentions in 1617: here again, ten years later, Smotryc'kyj claimed he was meeting with the Uniates in an attempt to bring them into union with the Orthodox under the Orthodox banner.

And still, one wonders, just how covert did he really intend to be? He had already circulated portions of his *Apology* to Borec'kyj and Mohyla; and Kasijan Sakovyč had printed some portions of it before the council convened. No one who so much as glanced at the chapter headings of the *Apology* could have retained any doubts about Smotryc'kyj's willingness to accept the licitness of Roman doctrine on key issues. For much of the Orthodox laity and lesser clergy at this time, this was tantamount to being a Uniate. Nonetheless, there was still the matter of Smotryc'kyj's titles: in the *Apology* he continued to use all his old Orthodox titles without the qualification nuncupate (*nuncupatus,* that is, "so-called," "in name only"), which would later be required of him by the Roman Church. From this point forward, that is, after the Kiev Council, Smotryc'kyj would always add the word nuncupate to his title; works published after his death, such as Kortycki's funeral oration and Suša's *vita,* would omit the nuncupate titles entirely—to which Smotryc'kyj always laid claim—and describe him simply as archbishop of Hierapolis and archimandrite of Derman′ Monastery, using only his post-conversion titles. This detail, small in itself, may add to our picture of Smotryc'kyj's frame of mind in this period. He may still have been somewhere in between, a sort of double agent who had not yet been forced into the open by one side or the other; he may still have felt he had opportunities for maneuvering in a variety of directions.

Smotryc'kyj's main goal in the opening pages of his *Protestation* was to show that the Orthodox leaders, Jov Borec'kyj and Peter Mohyla, had collaborated freely in discussions on Church union during the year preceeding the August council. Thus their later behavior could be portrayed as inconsistent, the result of improper pressures placed by the Orthodox lesser clergy and laity (with the Cossacks in the background) upon leaders who were weak and perhaps lacked real conviction. Smotryc'kyj's plan of action in this period was remarkably similar to that which in 1621 the Uniates had alleged concerning his actions in 1617: he had identified key targets, this time Borec'kyj and Mohyla, whom he hoped to win to his side through his personal intervention and persuasiveness. Once the pastors had been won, so the logic went, the flock would follow. At least this was the way Smotryc'kyj later portrayed his activities in the period. With this mode of action in mind, perhaps we should consider the possibility that programmatically Smotryc'kyj could have been more or less covertly Uniate, to differing degrees with different levels of Ruthenian society. He might thus have been more covert with the laity and lesser clergy, less covert with upper reaches of the hierarchy. Indeed, as we will see, Smotryc'kyj was later to express surprise at Mohyla's "change of heart" toward his ideas, since he had once expressed "even more" of his concerns directly to him than he now wrote in the *Apology* (see Smotryc'kyj 1628b, Ciii[r–v]/636–37).

In Smotryc'kyj's versions of the events, he met with the Orthodox hierarchy in Kiev in 1627 during the feast of the Nativity of the Most Holy Virgin Mary,[61] celebrated on September 8. (This was 18 September on the new calendar.) This means that Smotryc'kyj met with the Church hierarchy already a covert Uniate—a fact which, of course, he omitted from his account. Perhaps he timed his letters to Rome to coincide with the coming meetings of the hierarchy; in this way if things were to go sour with the Orthodox—as they eventually did—then he would have a sort of fallback position. It was presumably on this occasion that

Smotryc'kyj was partially discovered, at least according to the later opinion expressed in the Orthodox *Pamflet*.

At this meeting the leaders who were present, Borec'kyj and Mohyla (who was at that time still a layman), asked Smotryc'kyj to present to them for approval and publication the catechism that he had taken with him to Constantinople. Smotryc'kyj agreed to do so on the condition that he be allowed to publish first a series of considerations of the six major differences between the Eastern and Roman Churches. Smotryc'kyj received the consent of those present.[62] Half a year later, on the sixth Sunday of Lent in 1628, Smotryc'kyj was summoned to a gathering in Horodok (Gródek) that included Borec'kyj, Mohyla (who was by now archimandrite of the Monastery of the Caves), and Bishops Isakij Boryskovyč of Luc'k and Ostroh, and Pajisij Ippolytovyč of Chełm (Xolm) and Belz. Here, according to Smotryc'kyj, it was decided that a local council of the Ruthenian Church should be held; also, means for the reunification of Rus' would be considered. Borec'kyj was to send out private letters, and Smotryc'kyj was commissioned to write an appeal urging everyone to attend.[63] On that occasion the four churchmen present agreed that Smotryc'kyj might publish together with the call to the council his "Considerations" of the six differences between the two Churches.[64]

Meanwhile, Smotryc'kyj was secretly continuing his dealings with the Uniate side. On 2 March/12 March 1628 he wrote to Ruc'kyj from Derman' informing him of the progress of his talks with Borec'kyj and Mohyla. He thanked Ruc'kyj for the return of eight sexterns of his catechism (were these printed sexterns?) with Ruc'kyj's annotations and corrections, and he informed the metropolitan that he would ask Zasławski to make an edition of the works of St. Thomas Aquinas (to which the metropolitan had referred the archbishop) available to him, so that he might be able to continue with his work. According to Smotryc'kyj, twelve sexterns remained to be corrected.[65] This reveals that while Smotryc'kyj was preparing his catechism for approval by the Orthodox in Kiev in August of 1628, he was secretly having the same work censored by the head of the Uniate side.

Smotryc'kyj got down to work immediately after Easter; by Pentecost he had finished the work that had been commissioned by the Orthodox hierarchy, and he gave it the title *Apology*. He then had it recopied and sent around the Apostles' Fast to Borec'kyj and Mohyla in Kiev, together with letters which he later published in his *Protestation*.

Smotryc'kyj told Borec'kyj in the accompanying letter that he felt the
work could be printed in the course of about three weeks if two presses
were used. Borec'kyj and Mohyla responded through Smotryc'kyj's
messenger that they would read the work and give him their reactions.
Smotryc'kyj had heard nothing by the end of three weeks, and assuming
that silence indicated satisfaction and approval, he decided to go ahead
with the printing, which was to be done in Polish.[66] (The implication,
confirmed by the Orthodox *Apolleia,* was that the versions sent to
Borec'kyj and Mohyla were in Ruthenian.)

When the time came for Smotryc'kyj to travel to Kiev for the council,
he assumed that the leaders of the Orthodox Church, that is, Mohyla and
Borec'kyj, still held the same view of the purpose of the meeting as they
had all discussed in Horodok. Establishing this point was the main goal
of the introductory pages in the *Protestation.* Assuming this account is
accurate, in the first two years after his return to the Polish-Lithuanian
Commonwealth Smotryc'kyj must have had complete access to the
leaders of both sides. Rumors must have been flying concerning the
activities of the archbishop of Polack and archimandrite of Vilnius, now
residing at Derman'. The Roman Catholic and Uniate side seems to have
maintained some scepticism about the new convert's sincerity; but,
conversely, we should also realize that, by dealing with Smotryc'kyj at
all, Borec'kyj and Mohyla must have been demonstrating some openness
to ideas expressed by a man who stood under a cloud of suspicion, for at
one point during the year Smotryc'kyj was, apparently, almost found
out. On 2 March/12 March 1628 he wrote to Ruc'kyj that the news had
recently been "spread throughout all of Volhynia" that he had been
meeting with the Uniate metropolitan.[67] To the Orthodox Brotherhood
in Vilnius he wrote that on 20 October/30 October (apparently 1627) a
certain Ivan Dubovyč had come to Kiev, allegedly from Ruc'kyj, urging
Smotryc'kyj and Borec'kyj to meet with the Uniate side to discuss
"reunion" with them. According to Smotryc'kyj, the Orthodox leaders
responded that they were ready for union, but under the Orthodox
banner.[68] Smotryc'kyj (remember his account in 1621 of his actions in
1617) was certainly once again representing his actions to the Orthodox
in the most positive light, that is as most unambiguously "Orthodox."
Was he perhaps doing something similar in his letter to Ruc'kyj? Where—
if anywhere—did he place absolute allegiance at this point?

By the time of the council in August 1628, the Orthodox leaders would no longer show tolerance. The picture Smotryc'kyj painted of the atmosphere in Kiev is remarkable for its evocation of barely suppressed fear and tension. In Smotryc'kyj's representation, the proper power structure had been inverted, and the laity and the presbyters were giving commands to the bishops. The threat of violence on the part of the Cossacks was clearly presented, although Smotryc'kyj did not make it quite clear who, if anyone, controlled them. In this portrayal, all churchmen seem to have been unable to do anything without considering what the Cossacks might do, and for some of the churchmen this advanced their own goals.

The further course of events as Smotryc'kyj presented them is as follows. When he arrived in Kiev on 13 August/23 August 1628, all his former collaborators seemed to be avoiding him. First, Mohyla refused to receive him in the Monastery of the Caves, where he had gone directly upon his arrival in Kiev. Smotryc'kyj thought that this might have been because Mohyla wished to avoid being linked with someone the common people held in suspicion, a fact which Smotryc'kyj and Mohyla had often discussed; or, more likely in Smotryc'kyj's opinion, Mohyla refused to receive him, just as the archimandrite's predecessor had done, in order to avoid disfavor with the king. (This referred, presumably, either to Smotryc'kyj's part in the Josafat affair or to his long-standing habit of being in the king's bad graces.) And so, according to Smotryc'kyj, he went to the St. Michael's Monastery, where he was received with the respect befitting his station, little suspecting that Mohyla had had a change of heart.[69]

But then—and thus we learn how Smotryc'kyj became aware little by little that his position had dramatically changed—he received a visit from four presbyters of the Monastery of the Caves, who did not greet him in a manner befitting his station, in as much as they did not kiss his hand. From this exchange we learn that the council had already convened, either officially or unofficially, and had condemned the *Apology* as un-Orthodox. (Smotryc'kyj later reported that the actual condemnation of his work had occurred at 1 o'clock the next day, 14 August/24 August, on the eve of the Feast of the Dormition.[70]) Although Smotryc'kyj stated he stood by his work, he was willing to offer any sort of compromise, so long as he would be allowed to address the council directly. Even the fact of the book's existence could be neutralized: the printing could be halted, and the copies suppressed.[71] Smotryc'kyj seems to have placed all his hopes in being received by the council and to have been confident in his powers of persuasion (see Smotryc'kyj 1628b, Aiv^v–Bii^r/630–31).

As night fell on the 13th of August (23rd of August), Smotryc'kyj gradually became aware of the danger of his situation. His retinue began to receive threats; people pointed fingers at them, calling them Uniates, such that they became afraid to leave the monastery. On the next morning, Smotryc'kyj sent a letter to Jov Borec'kyj, in which he sought to discover the reason for the treatment he had been receiving. Was it because he had published to the world the errors of the Ruthenian writers? Or was it because he had showed a means for reconciling the brethren who had been set at odds? Smotryc'kyj could see no other possible cause for Borec'kyj's behavior. He asked Borec'kyj's help in what he felt should be the common undertaking of the Ruthenian nation in seeking medicine for its ailments (Smotryc'kyj 1628b, B1^v–Biii^r/631–32).

In the second letter that Smotryc'kyj wrote later that day, having received no answer from Borec'kyj in the meantime, he increased his deference to the metropolitan. What had happened in the meantime? Among other things, in Smotryc'kyj's account, the sense of personal danger had increased. Returning from delivering the first letter, Smotryc'kyj's retinue reported hearing the threat that they and their master would be condemned as Uniates the next day, and that "more than one of them would drink of the Dnieper."[72] Later, "at the dinner hour," Borec'kyj's brother Andrij joined some of Smotryc'kyj's retinue, the archpriest of Dubno, and Deacon Isaja, in addition to other clerics. He then said to them: "For God's sake, let His Grace, Father Archbishop, take care of himself; for coming now from the monastery village, I came upon quite a group of Cossacks, who in their deliberations, not noticing me as a person well known to them, swore they would not allow him to live, should the Council charge him with anything concerning the Union."[73] When Smotryc'kyj heard of this, he said:

> I see I have come upon a situation of anarchy, for my fathers and brothers will easily, through these people, have the better of me in debate. What am I to do in this matter? I would avoid them, since they are people who are not wise or useful in this matter. But I do not know how or where I am to go. I would go to the castle, but the vice-palatine is not there. I would return, but I fear an attack, for they are already announcing it. I could go to the city, to the monastery, but I would stir it up even more, for they declared that I was there even before my

arrival. And one must fear that they would not admit me, for there are already licentious, drunken people everywhere, as at a fair.[74]

In this frame of mind, sometime in the afternoon, Smotryc'kyj sent his second letter of the day to Borec'kyj.

"I wrote this letter—asking them to permit me to their common council—drenched with tears," Smotryc'kyj wrote, "since this was precisely the reason why I labored over my work, and it was for this very reason that I went there: to discuss with them the things described in it."[75] He stated that he hoped and expected to die in the Church that bore him, and he held out the possibility of suppressing the work if necessary: "What has already come into being through print cannot be undone; we can, however, still avoid having it spread throughout this entire state, through our mutual consideration and counsel."[76] Anything is possible, so Smotryc'kyj seems to have been saying, so long as the other side would agree to receive him at the council. He was apparently convinced that if they would receive him, he would be able to persuade them that his work described Orthodox doctrine. According to Smotryc'kyj, his opponents' goal was to condemn the *Apology* before he had a chance to defend it. Borec'kyj, so Smotryc'kyj came to hear, said when they discussed whether Smotryc'kyj should be allowed to speak with them: "Let the Devil speak with him."[77]

After sending this second letter, a Kievan Cossack by the name of Solenyk arrived. After greeting Smotryc'kyj, Solenyk read him "in Cossack fashion" a long lecture, which finished with the following statement: "We gained this Church by our blood; and we will seal it with our blood, or also with that of those who might dishonor it for us in any way, or abandon it."[78] Solenyk and another Cossack tarried with Smotryc'kyj for an hour. Shortly after their departure, Smotryc'kyj heard that Borec'kyj and three bishops had arrived and gone to the church. Smotryc'kyj went there, where he and Borec'kyj greeted each other "not fraternally, but as if we did not know each other very well."[79] When all who were in the church were asked to leave it, the two Cossacks who had visited Smotryc'kyj remained. Only after a long altercation with Borec'kyj did they agree to leave. On his way out Solenyk said to Smotryc'kyj in his Cossack dialect: "The devil take your mother. Just try to cheat us, just try. Both Peter and Paul will get what's coming to them here."[80]

At this point Borec'kyj leveled the charges of the Orthodox against Smotryc'kyj. The Orthodox were most disturbed by Smotryc'kyj's statement (in the *Apology*) that during the entire time when he was an archbishop in the Church, he did not know what he believed. And they accused him of introducing papistic heresies into the Church: the Manichaean, Sabellian, Apollinarian, and others (Smotryc'kyj 1628b, Ci^v/634). Here Smotryc'kyj expressed his amazement at what he portrayed as unexpected words from the metropolitan: after all, he had lived with him for four years and had heard no harsh words from him concerning the Roman Church or the Union. In fact, in Smotryc'kyj's version, Borec'kyj had seen only the new calendar as a hindrance, since the common people found this aspect of their culture the most inviolate.[81]

Then Mužylovs'kyj enumerated the errors found in the *Apology* and gave Smotryc'kyj a list of three demands: that he foreswear disturbing the Church; that he publicly recant, reading a prepared denial of the *Apology* from the pulpit; and that he not return to Derman', but remain in Kiev.[82] Here Smotryc'kyj received prepared "sermons" from three laymen, including the Cossack scribe. The clergy took part in this series of lectures only *pro forma*. Smotryc'kyj again asked to be allowed to present his *Apology* to the council for discussion point by point. But after an hour, toward dusk, he was sent a prepared statement of recantation. For many reasons he did not wish to spend the night in St. Michael's Monastery. He hinted that these reasons were important, but did not express them here (or anywhere else later on, as far as I have been able to determine). In an effort to please his Orthodox coreligionists, Smotryc'kyj attempted a compromise: he removed some passages from the proposed recantation, recopied it, and sent it back to them, but unsigned.[83] He then went directly to the Church of the Kievan Caves' Monastery, in the sanctuary of which he encountered his opponents, who demanded that he sign the recantation and not return to Derman':[84]

> I asked them to cease playing these games with me, that I could not in good conscience agree to the signature and to their conditions. Thereupon immediately, right there in the sanctuary, Father Archimandrite of the Monastery of the Caves [i.e., Mohyla] harshly attacked me with dishonorable words (who not long before had believed and spoken well and piously about the matter that I described in my *Apology;* and had praised the letter that I had written to His Holiness the Patriarch of Constantinople last year, in which is expressed *summatim* [briefly] all that is described in the *Apology,* and then some; for when I read it before him at Derman' and at our conference in Horodok, when we discussed the six differences between us and the Romans, he mentioned it and praised it before the spiritual authorities

who were there); that man, I say, of such good belief about this matter, attacked me venomously with words that are wont to be used against honorable people anywhere else but not in the sanctuary, and that by your average person. Whereupon there arose such a noise that both those within the sanctuary and those who were rather close to it, moved as if at some violent act.[85]

By this point in his *Protestation* Smotryc'kyj had set the stage for a description of the event, the public opinion of which he wished to control by writing this work: his public recantation of *Apology*. What had he achieved in this preparation? Above all, he had shown himself a man of good faith, who arrived in Kiev to find that his partners in what was supposed to have been a common effort for the good of the nation had come under the control of lesser clergy (Zyzanij and Mužylovs'kyj), laymen, and Cossacks. He himself, along with his retinue had been threatened with physical violence. And he had managed to portray the men who had been crucial to the success of his program—Borec'kyj and Mohyla—as weak and inconstant: they would now have been praising the Union publicly, as they had often done privately in the past, had they not allowed themselves, through fear and lack of real convictions, to come under the control of their inferiors. This argument begins to sound familiar. It was, after all, largely the same one that the Uniate side had employed against Smotryc'kyj in 1621, when it wished to distance the Orthodox leader from his followers.

In this account it was at this point that Smotryc'kyj signed the recantation and promised not to return to Derman'. He implied here that this was not because he feared for his life, but because he feared to cause an uproar in such a holy place.[86] All then went to vespers, including Smotryc'kyj, who little suspected what was to follow:

But after the reading of the Gospel, contrary to my expectation, my Vilnius deputy [i.e., Josyf Bobrykovyč] was sent to the pulpit. And the priests went out from the sanctuary to the pulpit. Father Archimandrite of the Monastery of the Caves gave each of the bishops sheets of paper and candles. Thereupon, he who was in the pulpit read the sheet and then tore up the page given him from my *Apology* and cast it down. And then Father Borec'kyj, with whom the one who is called of Luc'k [i.e., Isakij Boryskovyč] stood in the pulpit and, cast anathema against the law and, without a judgment, against that same *Apology* and at the same time also against Father Kasijan, Archimandrite of Dubno, a man unsuspect in the Orthodox faith and never convicted of, or caught in, any heresy with even one canon; and he tore up the sheet and put out the candles. And following him, all the bishops did the same.[87]

Smotryc'kyj concluded his work with the claim that, for his sins, God had denied him the martyr's crown for the time being.[88] Notice that this final element, that Smotryc'kyj should perhaps have refused to sign the revocation and accepted—if such was forthcoming—a martyr's death, appeared at the end of the discourse, almost out of the blue. After all, Smotryc'kyj had gone to great lengths to portray his behavior as resulting not from cowardice, but from a desire to salvage some part of his program, to preserve peace in a holy place, etc. And yet, Smotryc'kyj seems to have had a bad conscience; or at the least, he seems to have felt a need to aim his *Protestation* simultaneously at two audiences: at the local Ruthenian Orthodox audience, of course, but perhaps also at the Uniate and Roman Catholic authorities. For them, as we will soon see, the most important message would be that to which Smotryc'kyj only hinted in the last line of his work, but which he placed in a strange (strange, in that it was somewhat discordant with the work itself) prominence through his choice of the biblical citations that were featured on the title page: Rom. 14:4 ("Who art thou that judgest another man's servant? to his own master he standeth or falleth. Yea, he shall be holden up: for God is able to make him stand.") and Matt. 26:75 ("And Peter remembered the word of Jesus, which said unto him, Before the cock crow, thou shalt deny me thrice. And he went out, and wept bitterly."). This was the message that Smotryc'kyj intended for his Roman Catholic and Uniate audience, and, through Ruc'kyj's letters, this was the message they got. As we will soon see, though, they seem not to have been reassured by it as to Smotryc'kyj's reliability.

The main Orthodox account of the same events was offered in a work entitled *Apolleia of the Apology* which was signed in Kiev on 30 August/ 9 September 1628, about a week ahead of the *Protestation.* The works were practically contemporary, but neither was a direct response to the other. The Orthodox offered the following version of the council. First, apparently aware that Smotryc'kyj would present himself as having been led into a trap, and also certainly to distance the hierarchy from any hint of "unionizing," the Orthodox pamphlet claimed a completely different purpose for calling the council. The Orthodox began their work with an extract from the constitution of the recent Sejm, which implied that a more immediate, secular matter was the main purpose for gathering:

> And as to the Ruthenian clergy and non-Uniates, they are to confer
> amongst themselves before the coming Sejm, so that, following the

example of our clergy and of the Uniates, they, too, according to their
obligation, might contribute to the present salvation of the
Commonwealth.[89]

This reason for the council—the need to rally all sectors of the
Commonwealth to its defense against the Turks—was repeated in a
paragraph that was entered into the castle books of Kiev (*Apolleia*
A1[r–v]/305–306). There was no mention of this reason for the council—
either in its planning stages, or once it had begun—in Smotryc'kyj's
Protestation, and he would later express his surprise that this was the
reason the Orthodox gave.[90]

This strategy did several things to further the Orthodox cause. It
portrayed the Orthodox as good citizens of the Commonwealth, which
was always a *desideratum* for Orthodox polemical strategy. It removed
any notion that Mohyla and Borec'kyj could have been collaborating
with Smotryc'kyj in the preparation of the council. Finally, it made
Smotryc'kyj seem ludicrously out of step with the business of the
Orthodox hierarchy.

Smotryc'kyj, according to the Orthodox, arrived two days ahead of the
Feast of the Dormition, and he stopped at St. Michael's Monastery as
planned.[91] This insistence may be of some interest. Smotryc'kyj, recall,
had written that he had expected to be received by Mohyla at the Caves
Monastery, and that he had gone to St. Michael's Monastery when turned
away there. The Orthodox could not have read the *Protestation* before
writing their work. Why the discrepancy in this small detail? Is it
possible that this event belonged to some larger pattern? For sake of
argument, let us consider the following scenario: Mohyla and Borec'kyj
had been having conversations with Smotryc'kyj in 1627 and 1628 in the
genuine hope of finding some means of reunification under a banner that
would be acceptable to them and to their constituencies. At some point,
however, they were given an ultimatum by the rest of the hierarchy and
by influential portions of the laity that made it impossible for them to
continue any contacts or even to admit that there had been any in the first
place. This might help explain the attempts to keep Smotryc'kyj away
from Borec'kyj and Mohyla, as well as the virulence of the attacks of the
metropolitan and archimandrite upon their former colleague (at least this
was what we read in Smotryc'kyj's representation of the events). It also
raises the question of who was ultimately responsible for the *Apolleia*:
Borec'kyj and Mohyla, or their "opponents" (at least in this hypothetical

picture) on the Orthodox side? Smotryc'kyj ascribed the work to the lower clergy or even to the laity.[92]

According to the *Apolleia,* Smotryc'kyj's book, which he had sent ahead, had already been condemned. Several persons, sent as representatives from the council, discussed matters amicably with Smotryc'kyj.[93] On the following day, Smotryc'kyj wrote to Borec'kyj. The letter given here in a Ruthenian version corresponded to the second letter Smotryc'kyj included in his Polish-language version of the events (*Apolleia* 1628, A2[r]–3[r]/307).

That afternoon, on the eve of the feast day, a meeting took place in Mohyla's residence. After the discussion, all went their own way with the agreement that a revocation be written and read on the next day from the pulpit. Actually, the revocation had already been written, but Smotryc'kyj did not accept that one; rather, according to the Orthodox, he recopied it and agreed to read the following:[94]

I, Meletij Smotryc'kyj, by the grace of God Archbishop of Polack, having been charged by our Ruthenian Church with the suspicion of apostasy from the Orthodox Greek faith of the Catholic Eastern Church, and having been submitted all the more so to the suspicion of the same apostasy through the appearance in print under my name of the book published under the title *Apology,* through this my announcement to my entire Ruthenian Church, through Your Graces present here at this time in the Holy Monastery of the Caves in this Holy Church dedicated to the Dormition of the Most Pure Virgin, Mother of God, report the following: that I myself am subject partially to such a straying from Orthodox dogmas, but that I acknowledge that, to a greater extent, such a straying occurred through the wanton plan of that person to whom that *Apology* was entrusted for publication in print in the Polish language, and namely, through the evil plan of Kasijan Sakovyč, who is the superior in the Dubno Monastery of the Lord's Transfiguration. And having recognized and acknowledged that this incautious behavior, both as far as my own sin is concerned, and as far as the harmful entrusting is concerned, is against the Orthodox dogmas of the Eastern Church, I voluntarily beg the Lord God to be merciful toward my sin, and I voluntarily promise my entire Ruthenian Church of that same merciful God that henceforth I will avoid this with all my heart, giving in this Holy Church knowledge of my desire through this sign, that before the eyes of all Your Graces I dishonor, tear, and cast under my feet my work entitled *Apology,* under the oath that I made unto the Lord God at the time when, in the presence of my Most Reverend Lord [i.e., the metropolitan] and the other hierarchs [i.e., bishops] of our Ruthenian Church, I was elected and consecrated to the episcopate in the obedience of the Most Holy Patriarch of Jerusalem, Father Theophanes. On this 14th day of August of the year 1628.[95]

To this statement, according to the Orthodox, Smotryc̆kyj affixed his episcopal seal and his signature.[96] (Remember that Smotryc̆kyj claimed he returned it unsigned.)

After signing this document, Smotryc̆kyj was allowed to take part in the council, the main purpose of which—the Orthodox repeated—was to express support for and to seek ways to further the defense of the fatherland. At this point, the Orthodox printed a letter written by Borec̆kyj and signed by the assembled churchmen describing Orthodox support for the general undertaking in defense of the Commonwealth (*Apolleia* 1629, A4ᵛ–5ᵛ/310–13). The letter was dated 16 August/26 August, the day after the Feast of the Dormition. (Smotryc̆kyj's name was missing from the signatures. Had he returned to Derman' by this time? Or was he no longer included in any of the deliberations?)

Immediately following the conclusion of the council and Smotryc̆kyj's departure, rumors began to reach Kiev (certainly encouraged in their spread by Smotryc̆kyj himself) which alleged that only presbyters had taken part in the ceremony at which the *Apology* was condemned and pages from it burned. To counter these accounts, Borec̆kyj wrote a letter dated 24 August/3 September which stated:

> I make it known unto every Orthodox person and unto all who wish to know: that no one else, having read together with the other clergy, but we, the metropolitan and the bishops, in the presence of our lord and concelebrant himself, Lord Father Meletij Smotryc̆kyj, Archbishop of Polack, Bishop of Vicebsk and Mscislau̇, Archimandrite of Vilnius and Derman', who, in full episcopal vestments, concelebrated with us the Divine Liturgy, after the procession with the crosses, in the Church of the Dormition of the Most Pure Mother of God, which is in the Holy Great Kiev Monastery of the Caves, in the pulpit after the Gospel and the lesson from the cathedra publicly tore, stomped, and consigned to fire by the power given to us by the council (anathematizing both the book and Kasijan) sheets published now in print and written in his own hand by His Grace; and Lord Father Archbishop himself tore, and burned, and consigned to anathema both the book and Kasijan before the entire Church.[97]

The letter was signed by Borec̆kyj and other, lesser, members of the clergy, but lacked Mohyla's signature. It ended with a warning not to read any copies of *Apology* or to have anything to do with Kasijan Sakovyč.[98]

What were the points of disagreement between the two works, which represented not statement and answer, but two independent accounts of the same events? The major descrepancy, of course, had to do with the purpose of the council and of Smotryc'kyj's trip to Kiev. In Smotryc'kyj's account, it was to discuss his catechism and his *Apology*. According to the Orthodox, it was to discuss matters of public defense. Smotryc'kyj felt he had been slighted by Mohyla and went to St. Michael's Monastery because—for reasons he claimed were unclear to him at the time— Mohyla refused to receive him. According to the Orthodox, Smotryc'kyj stayed in St. Michael's Monastery as planned. According to Smotryc'kyj, his work was condemned not so much by the authorities of the Church, that is, the metropolitan and archbishops, as by the lower clergy and laymen; the presence of the Cossacks had exerted improper lay influences on Church matters. According to the Orthodox, the entire hierarchy took part in all the events. Crucial was the matter of coercion. According to Smotryc'kyj, he accepted the recantation out of fear for the public order; he took part—passively, according to this version, since it was his Vilnius deputy who appeared in the pulpit—in the ceremony at which the *Apology* and Sakovyč were condemned, not realizing what was to come. According to the Orthodox, Smotryc'kyj willingly signed a document of recantation and willingly took active part in the ceremony in which he anathematized his collaborator Sakovyč, blaming the problems with the *Apology* in large measure on him. Smotryc'kyj portrayed the Orthodox as attempting to keep him a sort of hostage in Kiev. The Orthodox were silent about this.

A couple of points are worth noting. The revocation was a shameful document. Did anyone require of Smotryc'kyj that he place the greater blame for the *Apology* on Kasijan Sakovyč, who, as far as we know was only engaged in printing the work? Smotryc'kyj left us with the not-quite-clearly expressed implication that some problems had crept in when Sakovyč took the Ruthenian manuscript and made from it a Polish book. And he made some reference in his *Protestation* to the fact that Kasijan had been badly treated by the council; but I do not find that he prepared his readers for the possibility that he himself was the one who, through his "public abjuration" had put the blame on his collaborator. He told us, for example, that the condemnation "was executed upon a different person, as I said, and upon my *Apology*."[99] Did this muddy, impersonal formulation hide (or almost hide) guilty feelings?

Smotryc'kyj may have made a few other maneuvers to render the experience somewhat less dangerous to himself. Toward the end of the *Protestation* he wrote:

> I maintained whole during that very time my faith given to my God
> and promised to Him *per obedientiam* [by obedience], and my heart
> never gave its consent to their anathema cast upon my work in an un-
> Orthodox heart, nor could it give its consent piously. Whence it was
> that they condemned my Orthodox Catholic work, which I had written
> for them with great consideration, and thoroughly and authoritatively
> supported, explained, and strengthened each thing in it with Holy
> Scripture and the doctrine of the doctors of the Church, both Eastern
> and Western. And I cursed the blasphemies, errors, and heresies of
> their sowers of chaff, the Zyzanijs, who were refuted by me in my
> work; them did I tear; upon them did I put the candles out; and them
> did I cast under my feet.[100]

In other words, Smotryc'kyj told his readers that he had practiced
dissimulation, again a kind of *reservatio mentalis* or amphibology, in his
condemnation of the *Apology,* and thus he had kept his heart and mind
free from heresy (from the Uniate and Roman Catholic point of view).

But was he also seeking at the same time to render himself less
culpable with the Orthodox? Recall that Smotryc'kyj had made some
small corrections to the revocation before returning it to Mohyla. Without
the possibility of comparing the two versions, we can have no certainty
what they were. Nonetheless, there is one interesting locution that might
possibly have resulted from Smotryc'kyj's efforts to moderate the charges.
This is the phrase "suspicion of apostasy" (*подозрѣніе отстунства*),
which he used twice in describing the crime with which he had been
charged. This, I suspect, was a technical term. I only suspect this, since
we are never quite sure what was the authority—if there was one—for
Ruthenians (whether they wrote in Ruthenian or in Polish). "Suspicion
of heresy" and "suspicion of apostasy" were technical terms wherever
the Roman Inquisition had reached, however, and their significance was
described in inquisitorial handbooks. Smotryc'kyj used the term
"suspicion of heresy" (*podzór haerezyey*) on one occasion in another
context.[101] This was, in the larger scheme of things, a lesser charge:
Smotryc'kyj had not admitted to having been charged with apostasy, but
only with suspicion of apostasy. The handbooks treated of people
"suspected of heresy or apostasy" in three degrees: "slightly"
(*leggiermente*), "vehemently" (*vehemente*), and "violently" (*violente*).
Smotryc'kyj had not specified that his was of the slight variety, but
neither was it specifically vehement or violent.[102] I suppose this
formulation could have stemmed from Mohyla or Borec'kyj. But it is
certainly hard to imagine that, if Zyzanij or Mužylovs'kyj knew of its

significance, they would have chosen this formulation rather than a more serious charge: vehement suspicion or apostasy, pure and simple. Had the Ruthenian Orthodox Church adopted the lexicon of the Roman Inquisition? Whichever side the term originated on, we are justified in asking ourselves whether it implied a familiarity with the lexicon of the Inquisition and whether it indicated a certain attempt to salvage bilateral contacts. Was blame shifted to Sakovyč in order to make it possible to avoid an absolute break?

Notice also that neither the *Protestation* nor the *Apolleia* gave a satisfactory account of the end of the council. Smotryc'kyj wrote his *Protestation* from Derman', so obviously we can conclude that he was not long kept under house arrest in Kiev as Mužylovs'kyj had demanded. Not only did the *Apolleia* not mention this aspect of the events, but it sought to give the impression that "all was well," relatively speaking. Apparently, so long as the Orthodox did not read the *Apology* and had nothing to do with Sakovyč, everything could return to the state of affairs before the council. Smotryc'kyj, at any rate, was still accorded all his Orthodox titles in this work.

How far had Smotryc'kyj's "conversion" progressed at this point? By late August to early September 1628 the situation was becoming increasingly clear. Smotryc'kyj (for whatever reason) had cast his lot with the Uniate Church and with the Roman Catholic authorities, and once he had been "found out" by the Orthodox, he would have to remain there. Borec'kyj, and especially Mohyla, who was about to make his dramatic rise in the Ruthenian Orthodox Church, had to find their ways through the minefield of interests and power structures represented by the lesser clergy, the gentry and burgher class, and the Cossacks. It seems likely that during 1627–1628 Smotryc'kyj, Borec'kyj, and Mohyla had a series of discussions on the reunification of Rus' (although the terms may not have been quite as Smotryc'kyj later described them). I suspect that the reasons these contacts dwindled almost to nothing lay not only—perhaps not even primarily—in the wills of the participants, but in the demands of the powers to whom each was beholden. I see the activities of all three leaders in the period after the Kiev Council (after August 1628) as motivated now to a lesser degree by an attempt to keep some doors open to the other side, and to a greater degree by the desire of each to prove his *bona fides* to his own side. All of them, after all, had "sins" on their consciences: Smotryc'kyj the re-apostasy (from the Uniate and Roman Catholic point of view) at the Kiev Council, and Borec'kyj and Mohyla the secret meetings with an apostate in order to discuss the betrayal of the Church (from the Orthodox point of view).[103]

In fact, the events of 1628 may have revealed some preliminary skirmishing for control of the Ruthenian Church after the passing of Borec'kyj. Mohyla had become connected with Smotryc'kyj in the minds of many Kievans (despite his actions in August of that year), and Mužylovs'kyj's candidacy as metropolitan was supported by the Cossacks.[104] According to a "manuscript of (the Uniate) Metropolitan Lev Kyška" (1714–1729), which Petruševič used in his "chronicle," the Orthodox council that convened in Kiev on 9 July 1629 in preparation for the coming L'viv Council was dispersed the next day by the Cossacks, who forbade the Orthodox hierarchy under threat of death to have anything to do with the Uniates; "the archimandrite of the Caves Monastery (i.e., Mohyla) wept, and Borec'kyj spent the night with him" (apparently in fear for his life).[105]

This may have been Uniate disinformation. Still, Smotryc'kyj behaved for a while as if he had not lost access to the Orthodox side. On 28 September/8 October 1628, soon after he had experienced what he had portrayed in his *Protestation* as a harrowing ordeal in Kiev, where the Orthodox, according to him, were on the verge of placing him under a sort of house arrest (if not worse), he mentioned in an offhand fashion in a letter to the Orthodox nobleman and cupbearer of Volhynia, Lavrentij Drevyns'kyj, that a minor and mundane matter the two had discussed might be taken care of sometime soon in Kiev, as Smotryc'kyj planned to meet his Vilnius representative Josyf there at Epiphany (6 January 1629 O.S., i.e., 16 January).[106] This is, of course, a small issue in itself, but it certainly shows that we should be slow to draw the definitive barrier between the two camps: the most notorious defector from the Orthodox faith seems to have planned to return to Kiev on a sort of business trip soon after he had publicly confessed to "suspicion of apostasy" from the pulpit of the cathedral church of Ruthenian Orthodoxy, and perhaps even after he had made his public confession of allegiance to the Uniate Church. (If Smotryc'kyj had not yet made his public confession, did this letter show that he still held out hope for working directly with the Orthodox?) In this vein it is perhaps worth noting that the events marking the definitive break—Smotryc'kyj's public profession of the

Uniate faith and his removal from his see by the Orthodox side—are reflected in the sources only in the most indirect fashion.[107]

Now, however, propagandists for both sides, including on occasion the main actors in the events, devoted much of their attention to dispelling any remaining public ambiguities. For the Orthodox side, the *Apology* and Smotryc'kyj's actions during and immediately following the Kiev Council were the first official confirmation of the suspicions that their former leader had gone over to the other side. And borrowing a page from the earlier Uniate historiography, the Orthodox would now emphasize Smotryc'kyj's lifelong inconstancy. According to Mužylovs'kyj, writing a year later in 1629, Derman' was taken away from Smotryc'kyj after word of his "apostasy" (from the Uniate point of view) in Kiev became known; thereupon, in order to regain his position, Smotryc'kyj was forced to make a public declaration that he stood by his *Apology*.[108] Mužylovs'kyj cited a Polish version of the revocation Smotryc'kyj had made in Kiev and explained the archbishop's later abjuration of that revocation by invoking the notion of private, temporal gain:

> Having done such a holy thing pleasing to God and all people [i.e., having renounced his *Apology*], when they asked you whether you stand by the *Apology* or by the revocation, then, for the sake of a miserable income, you preferred to abandon the latter, which you made out loud and of your own free will in episcopal vestments. Is this your piety, is this your constancy in your old age? But then, who of us does not know himself to be a mortal man and inclined to sin?[109]

From this Orthodox account of what must have been Smotryc'kyj's public profession of the Uniate faith, we learn little more than what was repeated over and over in the sources of the period: one man's convert was another man's apostate. All agreed that Smotryc'kyj acted out of coercion, fearfulness, and an interest in personal gain. After all, according to Smotryc'kyj's would-be "controllers" (to borrow a term from the realm of spy thrillers), this was only human nature. But the question is— when was it that he acted in this fashion? Here we find no agreement. Notice the increasing frequency with which both sides sought to obtain from Smotryc'kyj written or public affirmation of his allegiance to their own party: Zasławski did it in July 1627, then the Orthodox in 1628, and soon thereafter the Uniates would require *public* confirmation of Smotryc'kyj's allegiance. Mužylovs'kyj's account may have reflected some of the distrust the Uniate and Roman Catholic side seems to have felt after the archbishop's performance in Kiev. (Unless, of course, it was simply slander aimed at encouraging such feelings of distrust.)

The Orthodox manuscript *Pamflet* from this same period also emphasized Smotryc'kyj's duplicity and love of temporal things in its account of his public profession of the Uniate faith:

> And he even requested forgiveness, but not in truth renouncing his work, that is *Apology,* which in church upon the pulpit he tore, burned, spat upon, and anathematized. And the council received his request. But before this council, wishing to elevate his status and standing, not satisfied with the brethren, the friends, the benefices, and the entire Church, and especially his eparchy, for help—that is, for bread and vestments—rather, through the help and intercession of the Uniates, with whom he had agreed to deceive the faithful, this so-called Meletij attained the Orthodox monastery of Derman'. And having returned there from here [i.e., from Kiev], when he was at the Council, he openly renounced the Orthodox patriarchs. And having received the Uniate heresy, he was removed from the episcopal office.[110]

(But was he "removed from the episcopal office?" I have found no other document, official or unofficial, confirming this allegation.)

Other Orthodox works of the period explained Smotryc'kyj's apostasy by focusing more exclusively on the theme of personal gain. For example, the *Synopsis* of 1632 repeated the account that Smotryc'kyj had voluntarily retracted his *Apology* in Kiev, but that he went to Derman' in order to gain temporal goods:

> Dealing with us perfidiously in this year, Meletij Smotryc'kyj revealed himself to be similar to his predecessor (who spoke one thing with his mouth, but had another thing in his heart). For in the church of the Holy Miracle-Working Monastery of the Caves, during the Feast of the Dormition of the Most Holy Virgin, suffering no compulsion, he himself voluntarily wrote a revocation, and in accordance with it, in church during the Divine Liturgy (in the presence of a very large gathering of other clergy and of worthy and excellent men, both from the Crown and from Lithuania), immediately after the reading of the Gospel, he tore and burned his *Apology;* and still, having peacefully returned to Derman' Monastery, nonetheless the wretch returned *in vomitus suos* [to his own vomit], and that in order to gain a miserable few thousand *złotys.*[111]

(Notice that now Smotryc'kyj was not only supposed to have signed the revocation but to have written it; he claimed he had only recopied it and had first returned it unsigned.)

Smotryc'kyj himself responded to the allegations against him in a variety of manners. First, he argued that they made no sense: if he was interested in personal gain, why would he have given up his not inconsiderable position and influence in the Orthodox Church for an uncertain position in the Uniate Church? He expected "hatred, abuse, shame" for his conversion; but he bore them gladly since he did not care about such things.[112] And he brought forth a new counter-allegation: while he was at the council in Kiev, the Orthodox had sought to bribe him to stay on their side:

> You allege of me that I conceived a love for the world, that I fell in love with it, and that I allowed myself to be imprisoned by it. But all three, by the grace of God, are as far from me as evil is from good. I knew that I would be last with my present side, I who was almost the first amongst you. Do you call this loving the world? This could more properly have been ascribed to me, had I remained with you. I, who knew no economic burden or care, and boasting and delighting in the fact that I was an archbishop, the first after the metropolitan in the Church, a hierarch of your side, thus would I have fallen in love with this world and with myself. And at that council of yours in Kiev you offered me three thousand *złotys* in hard cash on an annual basis, from certain places and from certain even honorable persons from amongst you, along with the appropriate maintenance of eight persons—clerical and lay—to attend to me, and with a dwelling place in the Monastery of the Caves. And having this from your side as if in my hands, if I were chasing after this world, and if I had come to love this present age, I would have settled on that, and I would vainly have unfurled my banners wider there than here. Especially since I already had the good earnest of glory that was caused by my writings, both with my own people and amongst foreigners, as a material for falling in love with myself.[113]

Notice that Smotryc'kyj's allegation "outdid" that of his opponents in its specificity. He could state the terms offered him by the Orthodox in great detail (3,000 *złotys* *per annum,* a staff of eight, and a dwelling place in the Monastery of the Caves), whereas the Orthodox were able to refer in general terms only to an offer from the Uniate side of "a miserable few thousand *złotys.*"

But while the Orthodox were publishing accounts of Smotryc'kyj's erratic behavior, the Roman Catholic side was also carefully watching its new convert, and many documents went back and forth between Rus' and Rome with questions and answers on the matter. There seems to have been genuine concern that Smotryc'kyj was not a sincere convert, or that he might be coerced or enticed back to the other side. If Smotryc'kyj was aware that he had missed a chance to acquire the martyr's crown, so were his new superiors. On 9 January 1629, Ruc'kyj wrote to *Propaganda*

Fide informing them (but with quite a delay) of Smotryc'kyj's recent lapse:

> Your Most Illustrious and Reverend Eminences direct me in your letter of 8 April of the preceding year that, after Meletij Smotryc'kyj should have shown himself through words and deeds to be such that there remained no doubt concerning his sincere conversion, then it would be necessary to see about his episcopal title, and you bid me notify him of this. This could not be done so soon on account of his absence, for he was rather far from us, that is, in Kiev, at a conventicle of the schismatics, where he was inflicted with great dishonor, contempt and ignominy, and suffered well nigh unto death for the Catholic faith, which he openly confessed in a book that was published and which I examined; and even if he did not obtain the martyr's crown there for his public confession of the faith and for this reason should incur amongst us the reproach of instability, nonetheless aided by divine help, he raised himself up and displayed, and even now displays, many apparent testimonies of his true conversion to his God.[114]

Ruc'kyj probably was attempting to "package" the information concerning Smotryc'kyj's recent re-apostasy by emphasizing that he now had the missing "proof" of the convert's sincerity, his public confession of faith. On 8 April 1628 (well before the Kiev Council), Cardinal Ludovisi had written to Aleksander Zasławski urging, among other things, that Smotryc'kyj make a *public* profession of faith (see Šeptyc'kyj 1971, 657). In late September 1628 *Propaganda Fide* once again urged Smotryc'kyj to "come in from the cold." On 25 September the Congregation entered into the *acta* an expression of its desire that Smotryc'kyj become an overt Uniate,[115] and on 30 September it sent a letter to the nuncio in Warsaw, Giovambattista Lancellotti, containing instructions to that effect.[116] Certainly *Propaganda Fide* was still unaware of the recent events in Kiev at this point. By delaying his report for four months, and by presenting the material in the manner and order he employed, Ruc'kyj was able to offer Rome a "good news-bad news" story (leading off with the "good news").

But this did not remove the distrust on the part of the Roman authorities. On 13 March 1629 the papal nuncio in Warsaw Antonio Santacroce wrote concerning the same events to Cardinal Bandini in Rome, and in his name to the Congregation for the Propagation of the Faith:

> I have had information from the agent of the Uniates mentioned by me in other letters, which I had already requested from Monsignor the

Metropolitan at that time. Some indistinct rumor of the following deed
came to this court, that is . . . that Meletij Smotryc'kyj, in this past year
leaving the schism, came to the Union, in order to signal more greatly
this action as much for the benefit . . . of his own soul, as for the
gaining of others; for the value that they placed in his opinion while he
was among the schismatics, he wished to go and profess the Union
publicly, and to renounce everything he had previously taught and
written against it at a council that the schismatics had gathered in
Kiev, where, being threatened by those schismatics, astonished, not
only did he not carry out his good intention, but he also said that
he . . . renounced [?] the Union, and that the true religion was theirs,
and he prom[ised] . . . to adhere to this one in the future. When the
council was finished, he returned to the above-mentioned metropolitan,
and with great sadness and copious tears, bitterly wept, chiefly regretting
that through his excess he had lost such a good opportunity to acquire
the palm of martyrdom. Then in the main church, unto the hands of
this metropolitan, he made his public profession of the faith, and he
confessed that he had done this because he had feared for his life, not
because he had thought that the religion to which the Uniates adhere
was not the true religion. And he did all this with the greatest feeling,
and for the greater authentication he printed in the Polish language a
protest in which he amply made the above-narrated declarations.[117]

We are dealing here with rumors of rumors of events. Even Ruc'kyj,
writing from nearby Dubno in Volhynia, had represented the things that
happened in Kiev in his report to Rome as something far away from
him.[118] (Possibly the metropolitan counted on the fuzzy notions of
Ukrainian geography held by his Roman correspondents in order to
"explain" the tardiness of his report on Smotryc'kyj's Kievan apostasy.)
Elsewhere we read that the nuncio considered Warsaw distant enough
from Ukraine to make the gathering of exact information a difficulty.[119]
And yet, Smotryc'kyj's possible "re-apostasy" was a significant enough
event to require a report from the nuncio to *Propaganda Fide.* But notice
that the Congregation did not receive an absolutely clear picture of the
events. Was it Smotryc'kyj's intention to "profess the Union publicly" in
Kiev in August 1628 exactly the way the nuncio in Warsaw may have
conceived this action, or was he still thinking in terms that, while not
anti-Union, did not make him party-line Roman, either? (For example,
did he still have hopes for the Ruthenian patriarchate, which figured
largely in the *Apology* and in *Paraenesis,* but was to disappear in
Exaethesis?) Smotryc'kyj's *Protestation,* written in Polish, and thus
generally unintelligible in Rome, did not exactly make the "above-
narrated declarations." Someone at some stage—was it Smotryc'kyj?,
Ruc'kyj?—seems to have decided that the message Rome should receive

should deal only with what was conveyed in the biblical citations on the title page and in the last few lines: Smotryc'kyj's feelings of regret for having missed an opportunity to acquire the martyr's crown and his re-establishment of his *bona fides* with the Uniate Church. It was perhaps implied on the margins of Smotryc'kyj's work; but more importantly, it was the message Rome wished to receive, and it seems to have been the main message Rome did receive.

Propaganda Fide was very much interested in Smotryc'kyj's "progress" in the faith. The Congregation first discussed his lapse on 8 May 1629. Apparently they had before them the two letters cited above. The Congregation acknowledged the facts of the matter and expressed the hope that these events would make of Smotryc'kyj an even stronger defender of the faith:

> As to the lapse of Meletij, nuncupate archbishop of Polack, who, having gone to the council of the schismatics in order to confess the Catholic faith publicly, seized by fear of death, again affirmed the schism; and who thereafter, having returned to the metropolitan of Rus', and repentant for the deed, and lamenting the opportunity for martyrdom shamefully lost, with bitter tears again publicly abjured the schism and published a book for the renunciation of his lapse and the confirmation of the Catholic faith: the Sacred Congregation, which has compassion for human weakness, and turns its mind to the example of St. Peter the Apostle and of St. Marcellinus, Pope and Martyr, has conceived great a hope that Meletij will be hereafter the best Catholic and will work strenuously for the propagation of the Holy Union.[120]

The expressions of sympathy for Smotryc'kyj and of awareness that man is, by nature, weak sound strangely familiar: they were expressed at about the same time by Mužylovs'kyj, an Orthodox participant in the council, in his refutation of *Apology*. (Mužylovs'kyj, of course, asked understanding not for Smotryc'kyj's abjuration of the *Apology*, but for his revocation of his abjuration, and his comments must have been at least partially ironic. But was *Propaganda* wholly sympathetic, or did it wish to convey a message of moderate disapproval?) Again on 13 July 1629, Cardinal Bandini related the news of Smotryc'kyj's reaffirmation of the Union and reabjuration of the schism, apparently drawing his information from Ruc'kyj's letter.[121]

This public profession of faith, which perhaps was what Mužylovs'kyj had portrayed as the statement extorted from Smotryc'kyj as the price of Derman', brought to a close the process of conversion. The actual deed must have occurred sometime between Smotryc'kyj's return to Derman' in late August 1628 and Ruc'kyj's letter of 9 January 1629. By this time Smotryc'kyj was no longer in any sense a covert Uniate, and Ruc'kyj attested on this basis that the final criterion had been met, and that Smotryc'kyj was sincere. From the point of view of the Uniate and Roman Catholic authorities, this public profession of faith was the definitive act of conversion. It is worth noting that Smotryc'kyj himself never referred to this event in his public works or in the letters which have survived. Only at this point have we reached the stage of relative clarity in Smotryc'kyj's allegiances. And yet, even here, in spite of Ruc'kyj's attestation, many of the communications between Rome and Rus' in the last years of Smotryc'kyj's life betrayed abiding doubts about the steadfastness of their prize convert.

CHAPTER 8

Archbishop of Hierapolis

 On 5 June 1631, Pope Urban VIII made Smotryc'kyj archbishop of the "Church of Hierapolis, which is *in partibus infidelium* under the patriarchate of Antioch."[1] This is a certainty, but ambiguities abound. How are we to view this appointment? What degree of respect did it bestow upon the recipient? What was the purpose of the consecration? How did Rome view this action? And the Ruthenian hierarchy? Smotryc'kyj himself? Here, again, we enter a world of highly obscure statements and actions.

The fact that when Smotryc'kyj converted to the Uniate Church, his title as Orthodox archbishop of Polack could not simply be transferred created a practical problem. This problem could then be exploited in adopting public postures. In its public propaganda, the Roman Catholic and Uniate side had never acknowledged the legitimacy of the appointments made by Patriarch Theophanes of Jerusalem. In Catholic documents, he figured only as the "pseudo-patriarch," a lay interloper and a tool of Turkey and Muscovy. More importantly, a Uniate archbishop of Polack already existed. After all, it was, in a sense, the conflict between the two archbishops of Polack that had led to the martyrdom of Josafat Kuncevyč and eventually, in the Uniate and Roman Catholic representations, to Smotryc'kyj's conversion. Thus, at least in colloquial usage, before his conversion Smotryc'kyj was for them the "pseudo-archbishop of Polack." After his conversion he was the "nuncupate archbishop of Polack." But the more crucial, behind-the-scenes problem was that whatever confidence Rome had originally had in Smotryc'kyj was shaken by his behavior in Kiev in August 1628. After word of those events reached Rome, Meletij entered what Šmurlo has called a "three-year quarantine" (1932, 517).

Rome was not sure "what to do with Meletij."[2] Despite his statements that he would rather be a layman in the true Church than an archbishop in the schism,[3] there are indications that Smotryc'kyj was concerned from the very beginning about his standing in the Uniate Church and may even have requested permission to retain his titles. When he petitioned the Holy Office on 6 July 1627 to be received into the Catholic Church, one of his requests was that he be allowed to remain for some time a covert Uniate; related to this was his petition to be allowed "to use the archiepiscopal title that he had unjustly usurped for himself, consecrated for the position of another who was legitimately elected and who is still living,"[4] as the third-person summary found in the archives has it. Did Smotryc'kyj himself use the expression "I unjustly usurped" ("iniuste usurpavi") in the original first-person version of his letter? For a variety of reasons—to which I will return later—I doubt it; and even if he did use this expression for this particular audience, I doubt that he was sincere.

In any event, the problem of Smotryc'kyj's title was also on Ruc'kyj's mind when he wrote to Urban VIII on 10 July 1627, four days after the first communication on this matter:

> Furthermore, since I know for certain that he had been consecrated a bishop in the schism, I humbly beg your counsel whether we should secure for him some cathedra from the Most Serene, or whether he should be made suffragan of someone else's cathedra, or whether he should be given to some title *in partibus infidelium*.[5]

Notice that Ruc'kyj acknowledged here, in a private letter to Rome, the legitimacy of Theophanes' consecrations, thus giving the lie to one aspect of the official Uniate and Roman Catholic campaign against Theophanes and his consecration of the Orthodox hierarchy. Note also that the suggestion of a title *in partibus infidelium* came last. This seems to have reflected the status of such a title relative to a regular appointment in the local Uniate hierarchy, and perhaps even relative to the second possibility (making Smotryc'kyj "suffragan of someone else's cathedra"). In that letter Ruc'kyj used the formula to which Smotryc'kyj would adhere as an overt Uniate: he referred to him as "Meletius Smotricius nuncupatus Archiepiscopus Polocensis" ("Meletij Smotryc'kyj, nuncupate Archbishop of Polack"). After his public abjuration of the schism, Smotryc'kyj would call himself either *nuncupatus* or *dictus* in Latin, *nuncupowany* or *rzeczony* in Polish, that is to say "so-called."

What was lacking for Smotryc'kyj to be given a new title in the Catholic Church? Apparently the first step—one dictated by *Propaganda Fide* in a letter to Ruc'kyj dated 8 April 1628 (i.e., before Smotryc'kyj's "re-apostasy" in Kiev)—was for Ruc'kyj to state to Rome that the convert had shown "in words and deeds" that he was indeed sincere.[6] In his letter of 9 January 1629 describing the events following the Kievan Council in August of 1628 (in other words, one year after Smotryc'kyj had first written to Rome), Ruc'kyj declared that Smotryc'kyj had now shown his true faith—by suffering disgrace at the council, by returning to Derman' and rejecting the schism, and, most importantly, by making a public profession of faith—and that it was now time seriously to consider which title would suit him:

> Your Most Illustrious and Reverend Eminences direct me in your letter of 8 April of the preceding year that, after Meletij Smotryc'kyj should have shown himself through words and deeds to be such that there remained no doubt concerning his sincere conversion, then it would be necessary to see about his episcopal title, and you bid me notify him of this.[7]

But which title? At this point, Ruc'kyj suggested the archbishopric of Halyč, but his coadjutor, Rafajil Korsak (who was archbishop of Pinsk; and note that the see of Halyč had been joined to the see of Pinsk on the Uniate side), preferred some title *in partibus infidelium*. Ruc'kyj wrote:

> I have thus resolved—and I beg most earnestly that it be confirmed by His Holiness through Your Most Illustrious and Reverend Eminences— that the title of Halyč, which my coadjutor Rafajil [Korsak] now uses, be given to him [Smotryc'kyj], and since that see was archiepiscopal from of old, before the title of the archbishop of Halyč was joined with the archbishopric of Kiev (whereas Halyč itself retained the name of bishop and now has a schismatic bishop), let Meletij have the title of archbishop of Halyč. My coadjutor, however, foresees some title *in partibus infidelium*, or, if this should not be acceptable, then let Meletij be given some vacant archiepiscopal title, lest someone in the schism rejoice that an archiepiscopal title of worse condition was obtained on account of his conversion to the Catholic faith. That, therefore, I obtain one of all these things, I desire Your Most Illustrious and Reverend Lords to be intercessors with His Holiness, and I beg most earnestly that this might be.[8]

Again, we are left with more questions than answers. This document seems to reflect some discord between Korsak and Ruc'kyj, or perhaps between Korsak and Smotryc'kyj. Again, did the qualifier "some" ("aliquis") reflect the lower standing of a title *in partibus infidelium?*

After first hearing of Smotryc'kyj's reaffirmation of the Catholic faith and reabjuration of the schism, *Propaganda Fide* ordered on 7 August

1629 that the documents for a title for Smotryc'kyj *in partibus infidelium* be sent to the Congregation of the Consistory.[9] Here it might seem that things were under way. And yet, after receiving Ruc'kyj's second letter, and noting Smotryc'kyj's "true" conversion, his public abjuration of the schism, and his progress in the Catholic faith, on 1 February 1630 *Propaganda Fide* decided first to write to the Warsaw nuncio, Cardinal Santacroce, for information and for his opinion.[10] On 9 July 1630 the Congregation heard from Santacroce concerning Smotryc'kyj's continued exemplary behavior, and they ordered at this point that precedents be sought for Smotryc'kyj's case.[11]

This sequence of communications seems to have reflected some behind-the-scenes foot-dragging in Rome. The tone of Ruc'kyj's next letter on this matter makes me think that he, too, may have viewed the proceedings in this light. In a letter of 1 December 1630 to *Propaganda Fide*, Ruc'kyj again raised the issue of Smotryc'kyj's title, noting that it was perhaps unnecessary to make any decision, since by now (two years had passed since Smotryc'kyj had become an overt Uniate) all had become accustomed to using his old titles with the qualification nuncupate:

> As far as the title of the Most Reverend Meletij is concerned, I would consider it to be left to the pleasure of the Sacred Congregation: whether another title should be given to him, or whether he should be left with the same, which perhaps seems more appropriate, for since he is already called by this name by everyone in general (that is, nuncupate archbishop of Polack), and since this title with such an addition could not be offensive to the regular [archbishop] himself, and finally since he could, in brief, be promoted to one of our vacant bishoprics, that I omit the difficulty of this new title, which has been examined in the Roman Curia for so long and not brought to completion. Let Your Most Reverend Eminence do what seems best to you in the Lord.[12]

By this point, Smotryc'kyj had made the claim (certainly for propagandistic reasons, but perhaps not only) that he had converted knowing that he would occupy the lowest of episcopal positions in his new Church.[13]

Finally, on 19 December 1630 the Consistory announced its finding, and on 3 February 1631 *Propaganda Fide* acknowledged that report, in which it was decided that Smotryc'kyj could be given "some episcopal title in the patriarchate of Antioch, in the parts subject to the realm of the Persians."[14] This choice of see was apparently made by Francesco

Ingoli, the secretary of *Propaganda Fide,* who had first suggested another bishopric *in partibus infidelium:* that of Christopolis, in the vicinity of Mt. Athos, so that Smotryc'kyj could go there and work toward the conversion of the Orthodox monks.[15]

How are we to interpret this appointment? The urgency felt in Ruc'kyj's first letters seems missing in the last. He had first argued that an appointment would make Smotryc'kyj all the more ardent in his defense of the faith. Clearly *Propaganda Fide* had some doubts about the sincerity of Smotryc'kyj's conversion and was hesitating at the beginning. Did Rome still retain some doubts concerning the legitimacy of Smotryc'kyj's consecration by Theophanes? Or was this only a canon-law pretext for foot-dragging? Certainly Smotryc'kyj's lapse in Kiev made them wary of giving him too much legitimacy. In any event, there is no indication that Rome ever considered anything other than an appointment *in partibus infidelium.*

Was there a significant difference between a see in Rus' and a titular see? The former would certainly have given Smotryc'kyj a role of greater direct importance in local Church matters. In Korsak's argument against giving Smotryc'kyj the title of archbishop of Halyč, and in Rome's final decision to give him the title *in partibus infidelium,* there may well have been an attempt to honor Smotryc'kyj without giving him any real power in the local Church. The qualifier "aliquis" used in referring to "some" title *in partibus infidelium* may have been an expression of a sort of condescension on the part of the granters. Even Ruc'kyj, by the end, seems to have seen the convenience of allowing Smotryc'kyj to be known as the nuncupate archbishop of Polack. Was this perhaps a way of bringing Meletij under a certain control, of receiving him on the Uniate side, without giving him any real power at the local level?

By choosing this solution, Rome created such an effect. The documents do not tell us in so many words that this was a consciously desired effect. They do tell us, however, that some in Rome and in Rus' had their doubts about Smotryc'kyj's trustworthiness. As we will see, the Uniate and Roman Catholic side continued to maintain surveillance over Meletij. It may have been Smotryc'kyj himself who was behind Ruc'kyj's initial insistence on a regular title. He asked to be allowed to keep his former titles in his first correspondence with the Holy Office. While it is true that this could be explained solely by the needs of his status as a covert

Uniate, it is also true that he continued in all his works and correspondence as a Uniate to use all of his old titles, with the addition of "nuncupate" before the title of archbishop of Polack. (His first Roman Catholic and Uniate biographers, on the other hand, Kortycki and Suša, dropped all the old titles and used only the title archbishop of Hierapolis.) Smotryc'kyj himself had written to Rome on 12 June 1631 (one week after he had been made archbishop of Hierapolis, but certainly before he was aware of the fact), saying that he desired a real cathedra, and one in Rus', rather than *in partibus infidelium.*[16]

Perhaps the curious wording of a letter from *Propaganda Fide* that may have accompanied the papal breve provides a clue to attitudes on both sides. *Propaganda Fide* wrote to Smotryc'kyj on 7 June 1631, two days after he had been made archbishop of Hierapolis:

> As soon as you receive the above-mentioned breve, you should thank His Beatitude for this honor and title, inasmuch as this sort of singular kindness on the part of His Holiness demands this as a duty, and His good will and benevolence toward Your Grace requires this recognition.[17]

Did this letter imply that *Propaganda Fide* had some doubts as to whether Smotryc'kyj would think to express gratitude on his own toward Urban VIII? Did it imply that Smotryc'kyj might not see this as a great honor?

I have found no evidence that Smotryc'kyj ever did write to Pope Urban VIII thanking him for the honor, if such it was. In fact, I have found no document written after he would have received the papal breve, and thus no document in which Smotryc'kyj himself used his new title. There is, however, some evidence that Smotryc'kyj continued to think of himself as a legitimately appointed archbishop of Polack (see chapter 9).

Meletij's new title was not the only subject of discussion between Rus' and Rome during his "three-year quarantine." On the one hand, we should note that *Propaganda Fide* seems to have come to view him as an important new expert for their side on the "Eastern Question." He was consulted on a number of matters including the feasibility of a plan to reunite all of Orthodox Slavdom with the Roman Church by beginning at the monastic center, Mt. Athos. Smotryc'kyj wrote in 1628 that this plan would not work for three reasons: First, the Turks would block it, since they would consider a union of East and West the beginning of an all-Christian campaign against them. Second, the present patriarch, an outright heretic, would not allow it. And, third, the entire Greek people, clerics and lay, and especially the monks in Mt. Athos, considered the Latins heretics.[18] He urged elsewhere, in a letter to Urban VIII, that Rome concentrate its efforts on Rus', which, as the vanguard of a revival of Slavic Orthodox spirituality, would be able to lead the rest of Orthodox Slavdom to Rome.[19]

From these documents it seems that Rome viewed Meletij as a kind of special informant on Orthodox Slavic matters. In fact, Rome sought to aid him in what it saw as an effort to discredit Lukaris. For some time part of the program of *Propaganda Fide* had been to portray Lukaris to the world as a crypto-Calvinist.[20] *Propaganda* wrote to Smotryc'kyj on 7 October 1628, asking him for the original or a copy of the famous letter that Lukaris had written to the Roman Catholic archbishop of L'viv, Jan Dymitr Solikowski, in which he had stressed the affinities of the Eastern and Western Churches and the distance of both from the Protestants.[21] Smotryc'kyj's letter to the patriarch, published in Polish at the end of his *Paraenesis* fit their plans nicely: Lukaris would appear to the world a Calvinist whether or not he answered it. But it is also possible that Smotryc'kyj genuinely sought to bring Lukaris and his patriarchate to Rus' in a move that would have given a united and Uniate Ruthenian Church more autonomy.

Word of Smotryc'kyj's conversion, according to Suša, caused great rejoicing in the Vatican.[22] The request that Smotryc'kyj submit his works and Latin translations of them for deposit in Castel Sant'Angelo has often been posited as further evidence for the high esteem accorded to Smotryc'kyj within the Catholic Church.[23] Kortycki included this episode in his funeral sermon, asking his listeners whether there was any other "Doctor of the Northern lands" whose writings Rome itself had requested.[24] But this request was an ambiguous honor at best. Castel Sant'Angelo was the headquarters of the Holy Office, the congregation that directed the Inquisition. Marcantonio de Dominis, whose books Uniate apologists had credited in 1621 with keeping Smotryc'kyj from converting a few years earlier, had died in 1624 in the prison that formed part of this building, while he was under investigation by the Holy Office. The requests for Latin translations have been represented as expressing a recognition of Smotryc'kyj's literary talents. But one of the primary motivations behind the request was certainly that, with Latin translations in hand, the Roman authorities interested in Smotryc'kyj's missionary activities in Rus' would have a better chance to keep tabs on the orthodoxy of the new convert. Smotryc'kyj wrote back to express his gratitude for the honor, and he politely refused the request, claiming that his Latin was not up to the task. He referred to his "scanty knowledge and rare use" ("exiguam cognitionem rarumque usum") of Latin (Velykyj 1972, 223). Was this likely? Was this the real reason for his reticence? Was his Latin really weak? Perhaps he, too, felt Rome's watchful eye and enjoyed the distance— geographic and linguistic—from the center of power. Ruc'kyj certainly realized that it was dogmatic orthodoxy that was at issue here, and not Smotryc'kyj's status as a semi-Polish Cicero: he responded that the works had been read and censored by Ruc'kyj himself, by Sebastian Nuceryn, Catholic censor in Cracow, and by the Uniate bishop of Volodymyr, Illja Moroxovs'kyj, who was, as Ruc'kyj assured *Propaganda Fide,* a good theologian.[25] This may not have allayed Rome's doubts. Rafajil Korsak, the main opponent to conferring upon Smotryc'kyj the archbishopric of Halyč, made some sort of compendium of Smotryc'kyj's works and sent them to the Holy Office.[26] Was his Latin better than Smotryc'kyj's?

Smotryc'kyj seems to have been aware of his shaky standing in Rome, and he made several attempts to establish his *bona fides.* He took part on the Uniate side in the failed Uniate-Orthodox council held in L'viv on 26 October 1629.[27] Our only piece of information on Smotryc'kyj's participation in that synod is not particularly eloquent. Still, it is somehow haunting to have this picture of a man who appears here as an "unmasked" double agent, now working openly, and only, for the other side. Smotryc'kyj is supposed to have addressed a mixed crowd of Orthodox and Uniates, including Lavrentij Drevyns'kyj, that had gathered at the house of the protopresbyter after the closing of the failed synod: "it would be good, Fathers, if you were us and we were you, and if you walked along the path we have laid out."[28] Gone in this utterance is the old shifting back and forth between inclusive and exclusive definitions of the national and personal identity.

Smotryc'kyj seems to have authored a letter "forged" in the name of Orthodox Rus' to Cyril Lukaris on 30 October 1629, just two days after the L'viv synod. The work contains no direct internal indication of authorship. It was signed in the name of Lukaris' "most obedient sons in the Spirit" (Hofmann 1929, 87). It has been published three times. Hofmann (1929, 75) described it as a letter from the "Ruthenians to Lukaris." Šeptyc'kyj (1965, 98) and Velykyj (1972, 186) both identified it as a letter by Smotryc'kyj "in the name of the disunited [i.e., non-Uniate] Ruthenians." Although this is certainly true, it deserves comment. The work is full of the phraseology of the Uniate Smotryc'kyj, but the author pretended to write in the name of "schismatic" Rus', which had refused only two days earlier to participate in the synod at L'viv. Ruc'kyj sent the letter to Rome on 18 February 1630. He explained that this attempt by Orthodox Ruthenians to discover whether their patriarch was a Calvinist had been composed by "us" (that is, by Smotryc'kyj) and had been signed by them.[29] Rome wrote back on 24 September 1630 and asked for an attested copy of the letter signed by the Orthodox, stating that they would then have the letter translated into Greek and Arabic, printed, and disseminated throughout Eastern Christendom.[30] Apparently no such "authenticated" version of the letter was to be had. In a subsequent letter (dated by Hofmann to ca. 1633), Lukaris wrote to Rus', urging the Ruthenians to remain firm in the faith and to beware of Smotryc'kyj, who had "pretended to be Orthodox," and had, like Judas, given the patriarch the "false kiss of peace," but who, upon his return to the Commonwealth, had made clear his intent to compete with Lukaris for the allegiance of the Orthodox.[31]

When Uniate Ruthenian churchmen wrote to Rome in this period, they often included reports of Smotryc'kyj's activities, assuring Rome that the convert continued to be zealous in his defense of the true faith. These statements had a funny ring to them, coming, as they did, in the context of reports on a variety of other matters.[32] Was Smotryc'kyj under some kind of surveillance within his own Church? Notice that the "quarantine" did not end with Smotryc'kyj's consecration to the see of Hierapolis but continued until his death. What, specifically, might have been troubling to the authorities in Rus' and Rome, other than the perhaps lingering general sense that this man's allegiance could never be taken for granted?

From the Roman point of view several possible areas of concern existed. First, there were indications that Smotryc'kyj continued to have some contacts with the Orthodox side. He wrote in his *Exaethesis* of 1629 (offering yet more "proof" that he had not converted for Derman') that he still received letters from the Brotherhood in Vilnius, offering him domicile there.[33] And he received letters from other Orthodox monks.[34] Had he really cut himself off from his "Orthodox past?"

Second, there was the matter of the Ruthenian patriarchate. True, Smotryc'kyj had not invented this idea, and many on the Uniate side had spoken in its defense. But Smotryc'kyj's forceful advocacy of this notion as the linchpin of a Ruthenian national union in *Apology* and *Paraenesis* might have struck Rome as placing matters of local interest before allegiance to the Church of Rome. This topic was notably absent in Smotryc'kyj's last work, the *Exaethesis*. Had he been told by his new masters to cease advocating this idea in public?[35]

Third, there was the matter of de Dominis. The Uniates had argued that Smotryc'kyj was under his spell in 1621. Smotryc'kyj never mentioned him while he was on the Orthodox side. But in 1629 Smotryc'kyj responded to his Orthodox opponent Mužylovs'kyj's use of de Dominis not by denying authority to the archbishop of Split, but by arguing that Mužylovs'kyj had not studied him carefully enough (see Smotryc'kyj 1629b, 89–90/791–92). I find this qualified defense of de Dominis remarkable. Recall that de Dominis had died only four years earlier in the prison of the Holy Office. Worse, he had been tried posthumously for heresy—*praesente cadavere*—and he had been condemned retroactively, his remains ceremoniously consigned to the stake, and his ashes cast into the Tiber. Smotryc'kyj could not have been unaware of this, and yet he went out of his way to cite de Dominis in his final work against his Orthodox opponent Mužylovs'kyj, using language reminiscent of passages in the Orthodox works of 1621–1623. No wonder he did not wish to send it to Rome. Was he counting here on the fact that the authorities in Rome, for the most part, did not read Polish? It would be useful to know whether Korsak included this passage in his Latin compendium. In any event, we should consider whether Smotryc'kyj remained under the spell of a vision that emphasized the unity of all Christian confessions and minimized the significance of doctrinal and ritual differences between them.[36]

Fourth, the extremity of his request that the pope together with the secular arm impose a union upon the Ruthenians may well have caused the authorities to wonder about the reliability of the new convert. He may have gone a bit too far, even for the Catholic secular and religious authorities, in his pleas with them to compel the Orthodox to unity: King Sigismund III rejected the plan (perhaps more on grounds of practicality than licitness).[37]

Finally there is the related question of whether Smotryckyj in his own mind had truly cut himself off from all his past. Did he still, in some fashion, regard himself as a legitimately consecrated archbishop of the Eastern Church? After all, in his own post-conversion spiritual autobiography, the line of demarcation in his life came not between the works of 1623 and 1628, when he made his covert and overt conversions, but in the period after *Thrēnos* and up to his consecration as archbishop in the Orthodox Church.

CHAPTER 9

Death and Posthumous Miracles

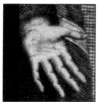Even in death Meletij Smotryc'kyj remained controversial. In 1638, five years after his demise, the Orthodox side wrote in its *Indicium:* "And so, living in a doubtful manner, he ended his life, having taken into his hands the letters from the Patriarch and from the Pope."[1] This peculiar statement was immediately transparent for anyone attuned to the rumors of the Smotryc'kyj affair.[2] It represented a critical response to a Uniate and Roman Catholic campaign, which sought to attribute to Smotryc'kyj a posthumous miracle, thereby confirming once and for all his exclusive allegiance to the Church of Rome. Also, perhaps more important for the immediate purposes of Uniate and Roman Catholic propaganda, it made Josafat's capabilities as intercessor all the more impressive.

Wojciech Kortycki, a Polish Jesuit, was Smotryc'kyj's confessor in his last days. He provided the first printed account of the miracle in his funeral sermon delivered on 29 Jaunuary 1634 (see Kortycki 1634, A1ʳ). This became the basis for public knowledge of Smotryc'kyj's death and posthumous miracle or miracles. According to Kortycki, when Smotryc'kyj saw that he was about to die, he asked his monks to "vest his body in the habit of the Order" and to

> place in his hand, as soon as he had died, the letter from the Most Holy Father URBAN VIII, the pope of Rome, who not only counted him among the faithful through that letter of his, but gave into his power and control the metropolis of Hierapolis as pastor and archbishop, that—I say—they place in his hand this letter or papal privilege, and bury him with it.[3]

Smotryc'kyj died, and his monks washed his face and hands ("as is the custom of the Order") and dressed him in the "vestments he had commanded them to make ready while he was still alive."[4] So far, so good. But, they all completely forgot about the letter from the pope, whether because of the heart's grief (as can happen), or through some sort of dispensation of the Lord's. Only nearly five hours later, when all the limbs had already stiffened, did they remember and attempt to place the desired letter in his already wooden hand. All the fingers were extended and straight, so that they barely managed to squeeze the letter in between the thumb and the forefinger. Here something happened similar to a divine miracle: right there, in the presence of the brethren, the cadaverous hand so grasped the letter with all its fingers that the parchment was wrinkled. Those present were astounded at this incredible thing, and, having grown bold, when they wished to pull that letter away from him so that he might hold it smoothly and properly in his hand, they could move it in no fashion, such that whenever anyone pulled upwards on the letter, the hand, not letting go of the letter, would rise with the pull. Whoever wished could discover this during several weeks: the very enemies of holy unity discovered this, checking to see whether the letter was not sewn or glued on to the hand of the deceased, and seeing this manifestly divine miracle, they went away in amazement. It is the opinion of worthy, noble men, that the body itself would have been pulled from the coffin by that letter, which he allowed no one to tear away from him, as if, no longer with the mouth, but with that hand, he cried out: *Fidem servavi*, I have kept the faith of the Universal Church and of its highest ruler.[5]

This, in Kortycki's account, was the main stage of the miracle. A second stage directly involved Metropolitan Ruc'kyj, who had arrived by this time[6] at Derman':

But one miracle was not enough to demonstrate the great virtue of such a holy father. Look, I ask you, what happened then. Informed about the death of the deceased, the Most Reverend Father Metropolitan arrived in Derman', whom the deceased himself, already in that illness, as he told me, invited with a humble epistle to come see him. Here, gazing with sorrow upon the dead brother and with amazement upon that truly miraculous thing, he ordered that the letter be removed from his hand. Wondrous thing! The hand stiffened, as if it understood the order and will of the elder, and it immediately allowed the letter to be taken from it.[7]

Kortycki introduced information concerning another aspect of the miracle somewhat later in his account:

I omit what was also worth noting in this matter: that when, soon after his death, a letter from the patriarch of Jerusalem was placed in his other hand, he did not receive it with [even] one finger. But this I leave to your consideration, gracious listeners.[8]

Next Kortycki told his listeners and readers that the first miracle was repeated several times:

This, too, is a miraculous thing, as if affirmed by a repeated miracle: that when, at the order of His Grace, Father Metropolitan, that same letter was again placed in the same hand, he again grasped it so that it was impossible to move it by any pulling, by any lifting.[9]

And, finally, Kortycki added the only piece of information to which he could attest as an eyewitness:

It is also worth marvelling at the fact that, a few days before the burial, the cadaverous hand became so fresh and free, that each finger allowed itself to be turned individually, and to be straightened out, and to be bent, just as if it were the hand of someone sleeping, which I myself, along with several priests, saw yesterday evening.[10]

It was this first account—along with the ever-active rumor mill—that formed the basis for public knowledge of Smotryc'kyj's posthumous miracle. Several main points should be kept in mind when reading other reports on the events. First, Smotryc'kyj himself asked that as soon as he was dead he be dressed in the habit of his order, that is the Order of St. Basil the Great, and that he be given the breve from the pope, who had received him into the Catholic Church and had made him archbishop *in partibus infidelium*. (But which letter? We have two separate letters, one of 7 October 1628, which received Smotryc'kyj into communion with Rome [Velykyj 1953, 467], and a second of 5 June 1631, which made him archbishop [Velykyj 1953, 482]. Did Kortycki conflate the two for dramatic effect?) Second, in the confusion after Smotryc'kyj's death the monks at Derman' had forgotten to follow his request. Only five hours later did they attempt to place the breve in Smotryc'kyj's hand—which hand was not specified—when rigor mortis had already set in. Third, the stiffened hand moved to grasp the papal breve with all its fingers and would not let go, even when the curious and the sceptical—including the Orthodox—sought to pull it out of his hand. Fourth, Smotryc'kyj released the breve only when Ruc'kyj, the pope's representative in Rus', asked him for it. Fifth, Smotryc'kyj refused, in those same first hours just after his death, to receive in similar fashion a letter from the patriarch of Jerusalem in "the other hand." Sixth, at Ruc'kyj's request Smotryc'kyj again received and released the papal breve. And seventh, the hand regained its suppleness just a few days before burial.

Perhaps to offer an answer in advance to sceptics who would be troubled by the familiar conventionality of Smotryc'kyj's miracle, Kortycki—apparently drawing on Ruc'kyj's words at the time[11]—made of Smotryc̆kyj a Ruthenian St. Alexis, who showed his allegiance by releasing the proper document to the proper authority:

> But it seems to me that, in this hand, Almighty God deigned to renew the miracle by which he brought the city of Rome to amazement at the death of His servant Alexis. For when the dead Alexis, holding in his hand the page on which his life was written, did not wish to release it to anyone, not even to his parents, he released it only to Pope Innocent in the presence of Emperor Honorius—in the same manner Meletij released the privilege of his dignity and the testimony of his unity and faith to no one else but to the highest and universal bishop of His Vicar.[12]

This account was given a measure of authority by the "attestation" of Metropolitan Ruc̆kyj that preceded Kortycki's sermon. The metropolitan, who played a major role in the second stage of the miracle, signed his name to the following statement:

> Whatever is said in this sermon about the fact that, after his death, the Most Reverend Father Meletij Smotryc̆kyj received and held the papal letter, and that he released the same in my presence and again grasped it, and finally about the fact that this hand, previously stiff and ossified, became marvelously ruddy: I attest that all this is the absolute truth, as the one, who, both by the duty of my pastoral care and my obligation, as well as by my own experience obtained infallible knowledge about this. And since no doubt remains about it, in my opinion such a miraculous thing, to the praise of God, ought not remain in silence.[13]

Notice that the account provided by Kortycki contained much information not specifically vouchsafed in Ruc̆kyj's attestation. Kortycki himself was able to attest by firsthand knowledge only to the seventh point, the suppleness of Smotryc̆kyj's hand just before burial. Ruc̆kyj was present for, and attested to, points four (the release of the breve), six (the repetition of the miracle with the papal breve), and seven (the returned suppleness of the hand), which occurred some weeks after all the other points. The only point to which he attested without direct knowledge was the initial reception of the breve.

Missing in Ruc̆kyj's attestation was the letter from the patriarch. According to the Orthodox *Indicium* of 1638, Smotryc̆kyj died holding it along with the papal breve. There was something odd about the way Kortycki had dealt with this matter. He told his audience of Smotryc̆kyj's refusal to accept the letter from the patriarch of Jerusalem out of chronological order and with a certain amount of awkwardness or reticence ("I omit what was also worth noting in this matter . . . "; "But this I leave to your consideration . . . "). Ruc'kyj said nothing at all about a letter from the patriarch; thus neither did he attest to this information nor did he deny it, although a cursory reading of his attestation might have given the impression that he had vouched for the veracity of the entire account of the miracle.

Ruc'kyj offered another, almost contemporary, semi-public account of the events in an open letter dated 16 January/26 January 1634 (first printed by Golubev in 1877).[14] He made no mention here of the wishes Smotryc'kyj expressed shortly before his death concerning the papal breve. He related simply that the monks—and let us take note of this formulation, since it will come up again—"forgot to do one thing: to place in his hands the papal letter."[15] Thereupon, they "placed [in his hands] the letter from the patriarch. . . . He did not take it with even one finger."[16] Thus, we should note, on 16 January/26 January Ruc'kyj told the story of both letters, but when it came time to attest to Kortycki's account, he mentioned only the papal breve.

Ruc'kyj, however, added information here that would not appear in Kortycki's sermon. Most important was the allegation that Smotryc'kyj had been poisoned by the Orthodox. According to Ruc'kyj, "a certain noble senator, well known to all" (who was he?), when passing through Mežyrič (Międzyrzecz), reported to the local Franciscans that he had heard that the schismatics were boasting that Smotryc'kyj would be poisoned, and he urged the monks to warn the archbishop.[17] If Smotryc'kyj received the warnings, he ignored them. In any event, Ruc'kyj stated that Smotryc'kyj had employed a deacon from Kiev, "who had good handwriting," as a scribe.[18] Soon thereafter (1 August/11 August 1633), Smotryc'kyj began to experience pains in his spleen. He went to a doctor in nearby Ostroh and submitted to a cure for two weeks. When he returned, much weakened from his *febris hectica,* the "deacon had vanished, and no one knows where he is."[19] On 8 November/18 November, Smotryc'kyj ordered a coffin made.

The other major public account of Smotryc'kyj's death and posthumous miracles came in Suša's *vita* of 1666. Suša drew on Ruc'kyj's open letter and Kortycki's sermon, thus including the allegations of poisoning for the first time in a public account of Smotryc'kyj's last months. Suša mentioned the rumors repeated by the unnamed senator to the Franciscans of Mežyrič and the ominous, disappearing deacon from Kiev. On 11

August 1633 (Suša gave new-style dates) Smotryckyj began to have pains in his spleen, for which he saw a doctor in Ostroh. After he returned to Derman', he soon (actually, three months later) died.[20] Suša did not mention the allegations of poison again in the body of his text, but the implications were clear: if Smotryckyj had been poisoned by the Orthodox, then he would receive the martyr's crown that had eluded him at the Kievan Council of 1628. And he did go so far as to place in the marginal commentary the information: "Meletij sick, probably by poison."[21]

From this point on, Suša's version of the miracle followed, by and large, that found in Kortycki. Smotryckyj asked his monks to dress him in the habit of the order and to place the papal breve in his hand after his death.[22] Through the confusion of the moment, or, in Suša's opinion, more likely through divine dispensation, the monks neglected to do this. Five hours later, they attempted to slip the document between the thumb and the index finger of the right hand (this detail was first made public in Suša's version), whereupon the hand became animate and grasped the parchment so firmly that it wrinkled the document.[23] Here—in correct chronological order—Suša included as an integral part of his narration something that Kortycki had mentioned out of order, only in passing, and with some hesitation, and that Ruckyj had not officially confirmed. This was the fact that by chance or, more likely, through divine dispensation, the monks thought of attempting to place a second letter— now it was from the patriarch of Constantinople, Cyril Lukaris (this, apparently, was Suša's embellishment on the tale)—in the left hand, but with no success.[24] In Suša's version when the doubters and scoffers arrived, they attempted not only to remove the breve from Urban VIII from the right hand, but to insert the letter from Lukaris into the left.[25] The remainder of the account ran much as in Kortycki's version.

Kortycki told his readers quite clearly that the letter—if indeed there was one—was from the patriarch of Jerusalem. Suša's emendation was not, however, without its dramatic motivation: a fitting counterbalance to the reception of a breve from Urban VIII by the right hand was the rejection of a letter from Cyril Lukaris by the left hand. But what letter could be placed on the level of the breve from Urban VIII? (Recall, we do not really know from either of these public accounts which letter from Urban VIII was intended here.) Lukaris, as far as we know, did not answer the letter Smotryckyj wrote him upon his return to Rus' and

published in Polish at the end of *Paraenesis.*[26] Was it perhaps supposed
to have been the controversial letter he brought back with him from
Constantinople, in which Lukaris removed the stauropegial status of the
brotherhoods?[27] Where was the letter supposed to have come from?
How did the monks, who were too busy to remember the papal breve,
locate—in the confusion of the moment—a letter from Lukaris? And
what is the significance of Kortycki's embarrassment and Ruc'kyj's
silence on this matter?

Another source of information on Smotryc'kyj's alleged posthumous
miracle was the behind-the-scenes investigation conducted by the Church
authorities soon after the death of the archbishop. Rome, especially the
Congregation for the Propagation of the Faith, was immediately interested
in obtaining reliable information on the events. On 5 June 1634, according
to the *acta* of *Propaganda Fide,* one of the topics of discussion was the
need for instituting a process concerning Smotryc'kyj's death and
posthumous miracles. On 2 August 1634, Ruc'kyj addressed to the
Congregation an official report on the affair:

> The three who had been assigned to take care of the body forgot to do
> one thing that the deceased ordered: that is, they did not place in his
> hands the apostolic breve concerning the archbishopric of Hierapolis,
> conferred upon him by the contemporary supreme pontiff, which the
> deceased himself charged them to do. Therefore, one of them took the
> aforementioned breve and, since the hand which was stretched out
> over the chest had already grown stiff, they placed the breve between
> the thumb and the palm. Thereupon they placed the letter of ordination
> from Theophanes, patriarch of Jerusalem, in the other, that is, in the
> left hand; and behold, the fingers of the right hand, which had been
> stretched out, grasped the breve so forcefully that the parchment of the
> breve was wrinkled, such that, when they noticed it, they wished to
> reposition the breve better so that it might be without wrinkle.
> Meanwhile, they see that the hand which had been stretched out has
> contracted; they ask each other who had contracted it; they answer
> negatively; they seek to pull the fingers back, but they are no longer
> able to do so; they seek to extract the breve from the thumb and from
> the finger, but they are unable to do so; they pull the grasped parchment
> upward, and behold the entire hand is lifted on high; they became
> stupefied; but the other hand, in which the parchment of the patriarch
> had been placed, had been drawn down proportionately and fell down
> at the left side, and that letter which the left hand had not touched
> remained on the chest.[28]

This was Ruc'kyj's second, and certainly the more official, attestation.
On this occasion, he put his name to things he could not have known

firsthand. What did he tell us this time? That the monks—and there were
three of them—forgot to do one thing that Smotryćkyj had asked of
them: to place the papal breve in his hand. This passage may take on
added significance in light of other documents I am about to examine.
For example, why this peculiar wording (which he repeated from the
Ruthenian letter of 16 January/26 January 1634): did Smotryćkyj ask
them to do other things as well? (And did they also forget to do any of
them?) Moreover, the strange syntax completely obfuscated the question
of whether they were to place the document in his hand before or after
his death. This time (as opposed to his letter of recommendation that
accompanied the printed version of Kortycki's sermon) Rućkyj attested
to the story of the patriarchal letter and told us that the papal breve went
on the right, the patriarchal letter on the left. These are the details we
found in Suša, and perhaps Suša got them here, if they were not his own
independent embellishment. Here, too, we find the first specific
identification of the patriarchal letter: it was the document given to
Smotryćkyj by Patriarch Theophanes of Jerusalem in 1620 in Kiev
when he made him archbishop of Polack. Moreover, the papal breve was
the one which made him archbishop of Hierapolis, and not that which
received him into the Catholic Church. This fact highlights a different
aspect of the papal breve. When, in Suša's version, a letter from Cyril
Lukaris, patriarch of Constantinople, was opposed to a breve from Pope
Urban VIII, it was the positions of these two men as heads of the Eastern
and Western Churches, respectively, that were emphasized; the common
"link" was to be sought in the antithetical relationship between the
senders. In Rućkyj's version, when the letter from Patriarch Theophanes
of Jerusalem was opposed to the same papal breve, it was Smotryćkyj as
the recipient who formed a real link between them: the first letter made
him Orthodox archbishop of Polack, the second made him Catholic
archbishop of Hierapolis.

On 16 December 1634, a meeting of *Propaganda Fide* was devoted
to Smotryćkyj's posthumous miracles,[29] and a call was made for the
nuncio in Warsaw, Onorato Visconti, to become involved in the matter
(see Šeptyćkyj 1974, 112). (Rome, from the initial stages of its
investigation, believed—probably on Rućkyj's word—that Smotryćkyj
had been poisoned by the Orthodox ["veneno a Schismaticis propinato
vita functo"] and thus fully deserving of the martyr's crown. Why was
so little polemical hay made of this point in Uniate and Roman Catholic

public propaganda?) On 30 July 1635, the case was remitted to *Propaganda Fide* (Velykyj 1953, 148), and on 3 October 1635 it sent out a call for copies of the letters describing the miracles.[30]

Visconti's reports contained three references to the affair. On 31 August 1634 the nuncio wrote that he had "heard tell of several unusual things," but that he had hesitated to write to Rome until he was able to obtain more reliable information.[31] On 12 September 1634, he mentioned once again the fact that rumors were circulating concerning the affair. And on 28 March 1635, thanks to the Sejm, which had brought to Warsaw two witnesses to the event, he was finally able to offer Rome some more reliable information. One of the witnesses was again Ruc'kyj, who offered essentially the same story to which he had attested earlier (see Velykyj 1961, 189–90). But the other was Isaja Rodovyč, who, unlike Ruc'kyj, was also present for the first half of the events. The nuncio's letter read like a police report:

> Father Vicar, Isaja Rodovyč, through the interpreter Father Ivan Dubovyč [apparently the same emissary from Ruc'kyj who had almost blown Smotryc'kyj's cover in the spring of 1628: see above, p. 126], makes his claim in the following form: "Archbishop Meletij, just a little before his death throes, ordered me, in the presence of Father Mytrofan Ferenčovyč (?) and Stefan Neubescki (?) and Stefan Glossosotti (?), to place—I do not remember well whether after he had died or during his death throes—in his right hand the letter of the pontiff by which he was created archbishop by His Beatitude and in his left hand the patriarchal letter from the patriarch of Jerusalem."[32]

From this point on, the account ran more or less along the lines to which we are now accustomed. But this preamble contained an interesting, new piece of information: the only extant report from an eyewitness to the intial stages of the story (and the man to whom the archbishop had directed his deathbed request) stated clearly that Smotryc'kyj himself had asked specifically both for the papal breve that had made him a Uniate archbishop and for the patriarchal letter that had made him an Orthodox archbishop.

This document may help to clarify some issues. Ruc'kyj had interviewed Rodovyč and certainly knew his story. Kortycki may well have known it, too. Perhaps even Suša, who wrote his *vita* in Rome and had access to Vatican documents, knew of this detail. And perhaps the rumor mill had made it still more generally known. (The Orthodox were making this allegation in their *Indicium* as late as five years afterward, in

1638.) In any case, this detail might help to explain Ruc'kyj's initial silence on the patriarchal letter, Kortycki's apparent discomfort with the event, and Suša's disregard for the facts. The problem was not the fact of the letter *per se,* or even of the patriarch—whether Theophanes or Cyril Lukaris; after all, in the public accounts given, the deceased's left hand had finally rejected the document. It would have made little difference to Uniate and Roman Catholic apologists whether Smotryc'kyj rejected obedience to Lukaris or rejected his consecration by Theophanes. The crucial point was the rejection. What might have made Uniate and Roman Catholic apologists uncomfortable was the suggestion that Smotryc'kyj himself had asked for both documents, and that this was the last recorded act of the new convert. It was, after all, the patriarchal letter that had placed Smotryc'kyj in conflict with Josafat Kuncevyč and had led, in the Uniate and Roman Catholic view of events, to Kuncevyč's martyrdom. It is possible that this document was among the things that hindered the campaign to make a saint of Smotryc'kyj. And perhaps it was the rumor of this event that motivated the use of the past active participle in the Orthodox allegation found in the *Indicium:* Smotryc'kyj died, after he had taken into his hands (i.e., of his own volition) both the papal and the patriarchal documents. (From the wording of Rodovyč's testimony it might seem that Visconti—on whose direction it is not clear—had specifically asked him whether he was to have placed the documents in Smotryc'kyj's hands before he died or after his death.)

Propaganda Fide's final report (ca. 1636) incorporated Rodovyč's testimony: Smotryc'kyj asked for both documents and, once dead (*Propaganda* omitted the story of the delay of five hours in carrying out the deceased's wishes), he grasped the breve and dropped the patriarchal letter.[33]

As we have seen, most of the sources for a biography of Meletij Smotryc'kyj reflect a competition for control of his public persona, and the events immediately following his death were part of this same struggle. Ruc'kyj wrote on 16 January/26 January 1634 that he had already received word of the miracle while staying with Albrycht Stanisław Radziwiłł, grand chancellor of the Grand Duchy of Lithuania, on his way to Derman'.[34] When he reached the town, he had difficulty gaining access to Smotryc'kyj because Aleksander Zasławski had secured the monastery and its holdings and was not allowing anyone, lay or clergy, into the area.[35] This directly contradicts Kortycki's statement that all, even the schismatics, were allowed to come see the miracle for themselves. Here we have struggle for control of public knowledge that depended even upon physical force! What was different in this chapter in his life was that Smotryc'kyj himself had ceased to play an active role in that competition. He had moved from the category of subject to that of object, or at least this is how he appears to us in the sources. This is, of course, not surprising for the period after his death. But Smotryc'kyj had practically ceased to be an active participant in the controversies after the L'viv Council of October 1629. Thus for four more years we find reports to Rome from Smotryc'kyj's new coreligionists on the "neophyte's" progress in the Catholic faith and assurances that he was busy writing many works in defense of the Union (which were never published). With the exception of a long letter to Urban VIII, in which a frustrated and perhaps desperate Smotryc'kyj urged the application of force to solve the confessional problems in Rus',[36] this man, who had stood at the center of attention and controversy for twenty years, became silent during the last four years of his life in the affairs of his nation and Church.

For us, who read the documents some three hundred and fifty years later, there are certain inadvertently grotesque, sinister, or humorous aspects in the descriptions of the events surrounding Smotryc'kyj's death: the long lines of doubting Thomases, who check to see whether the breve was "sewn or glued" onto Smotryc'kyj's hand, and their attempts to yank the document away without pulling the entire corpse from the coffin; Smotryc'kyj, "probably poisoned by the Orthodox," who sees a doctor in Ostroh about pains in his spleen; Kortycki, who, in an atmosphere of possible poisonings, informs his audience—the corpse no doubt lying at his feet—that, even in his weakened state, Meletij had reluctantly agreed, "but only for a very short time," to add to his drinking water the wine that his Jesuit "friend" was urging upon him.[37] Even the traditional iconography of Smotryc'kyj has a grotesque aspect to it: these images of an apparently live and healthy archbishop actually tell the story of his posthumous miracle.[38]

What renders these details grotesque, or sinister, or humorous is the fact that, in the final chapter in his biography, Smotryc'kyj had become— at least so it appears in the documents that have come down to us—what both sides had been seeking: a passive (actually, almost passive) object to be exploited in their public propaganda. Almost passive, because the last recorded statement of Smotryc'kyj's wishes and intentions once again added the question mark to public pronouncements concerning the exclusivity of his confessional loyalty. Thus, Smotryc'kyj died as he had lived: unclear in his allegiances—at least from his contemporaries' point of view—and the object of campaigns from both sides to represent him in unambiguous terms and to exploit his public persona for goals that may not quite have been his own.

Vera Effigies Serui Dei Meletij Smotriscij Archiepi Hierapolitani O.D.B.ä
Archimandritæ Dermanen immanis Parricidij D IOSAPHAT
Authoris sub URBANO viii. Pont. Max. conuersi & defun=
cti gloriose MDCXXXIII Decembris XXVII.
Romæ 1665   A.C.f.

Quæ fit Meletio facies ? commonstrat imago :
Ingenium quod fit ? posthuma scripta probant :
Quæ pietas illum decoret ? gerit iste libellus :
Quæue fides ornet ? Mortua dextra docet .

Portrait of Meletij Smotryc′kyj from Jakiv Suša's 1666 biography.

SAVLVS
ET PAVLVS

RVTHENAE VNIONIS

Sanguine Beati

IOSAPHAT

Transformatus

fiue

MELETIVS SMOTRISCIVS

Archiepifcopus Hierapolitanus Archimandrita Dermanenfis Ord. S. Bafilij Mag.

PER

IACOBVM SVSZA

Epifcopum Chelmenfem & Belzenfem cum S. R. E.
Vnitum eiufdem Ordinis, ex tenebris
in lucem prolatus.

*Blafphemus fui , & perfecutor & contumeliofus , fed
mifericordiam Dei confecutus fum , quia ignorans
feci in incredulitate .* 1. Timoth. 1. 13.

ROMÆ, Ex Typographia Varefij. MDCLXVI.

SVPERIORVM PERMISSV.

Title page from Jakiv Suša's 1666 biography, *Saulus et Paulus Ruthenae unionis sanguine B. Josaphat transformatus. Sive Meletius Smotriscius.*

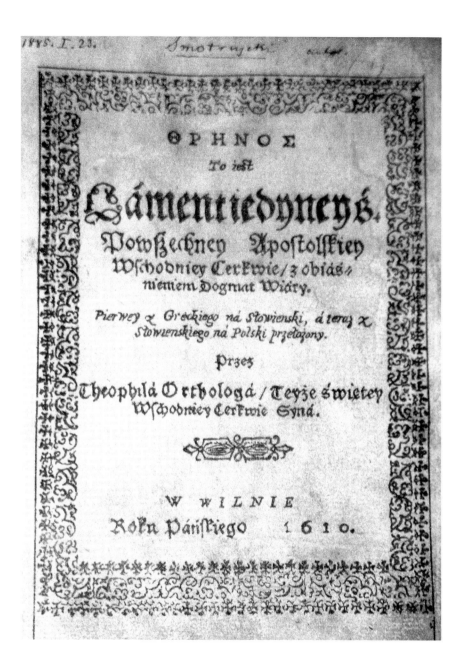

Title page from Smotryćkyj's 1610 ΘΡΗΝΟΣ. *To iest Lament iedyney ś. Powszechney Apostolskiey Wschodniey Cerkwie.*

Map of Jerusalem from Christiaan van Adrichem's 1613 *Theatrum Terrae Sanctae et Biblicarum Historiarum.*

(By permission of the Houghton Library, Harvard University)

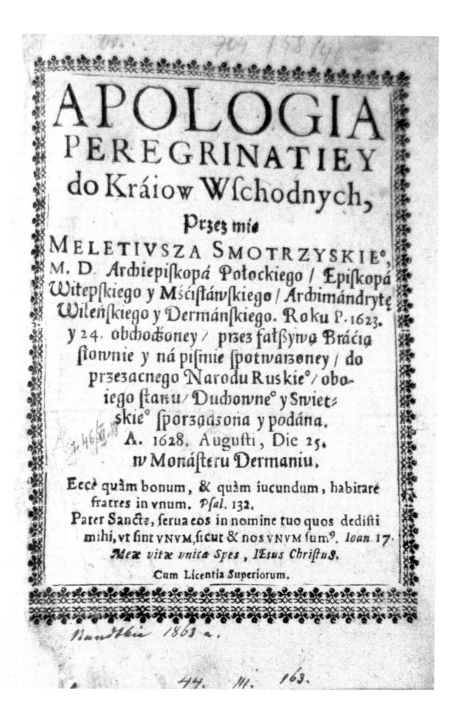

APOLOGIA

PEREGRINATIEY

do Kráiow Wſchodnych,

Przez mię

MELETIVSZA SMOTRZYSKIE°,
M. D. Arɖiepiſkopá Połockiego / Epiſkopá
Witepſkiego y Mśćiſtáwſkiego / Arɖimándrytę
Wileńſkiego y Dermánſkiego. Roku P. 1623.
y 24. obɖoɕoney / przez fałſzywą Bráćią
ſtownie y ná piſmie ſpotwarzoney / do
przezacnego Narodu Ruskie°/ oboiego ſtatu / Duɕowne° y Swiet-
skie° ſporządzona y podáná.
A. 1628. Augusti, Die 25.
w Monáſteru Dermaniu.

Ecce quàm bonum, & quàm iucundum, habitaré
fratres in vnum. Pſal. 132.
Pater Sanɕtę, ſerua eos in nomine tuo quos dediſti
mihi, vt ſint VNVM, ſicut & nos VNVM ſum⁹. Ioan 17.
Meæ vitæ vnica Spes, IEsus Chriſtuʒ.

Cum Licentia Superiorum.

Title page from Smotryćkyj's 1628 *Apologia peregrinatiey do Kraiow Wschodnych.*

PARÆNESIS,

ABO

NAPOMNIENIE,

OD

W BOGV WIELEBNEGO

MELETIVSZA

SMOTRZYSKIEGO,

Rzeczonego Archiepiſkopá Połockiego, Epiſkopá Witepſkiego y Mśćiſłáwſkiego, Ar-
chimándrytę Wileńſkiego y Der-
máńſkiego :

D O

Przeżatnego Bráctwá Wileńskiego, Cerkwie S. Duchá ;

𝔄 w oſobie iego / do wſſyſtkiego tey ſtrony
Narodu Ruſkiego vczynione ;

Anno 1628. Decembr: 12.

Cum licentia Superiorum.

W KRAKOWIE,

W Druk: Andrz: Piotrk:Typogr: J.K.M. Roku 1629.

Title page from Smotryckyj's 1629 *Paraenesis abo Napomnienie.*

Portrait of Josafat Kuncevyč from Jakiv Suša's 1665 *Cursus vitae et certamen martyrii, B. Iosaphat Kuncevicii, Archiepiscopi Polocensis Episcopi Vitepscensis et Miscislauiensis.*

Part II

Conformities and Deviations

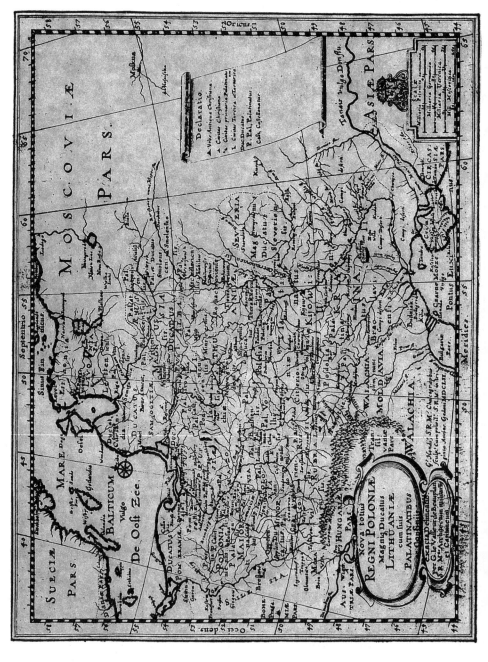

Guillaume le Vasseur, Sieur de Beauplan. *Nova Totius Regni Poloniae . . . exacta Delineatio*, 1652.

(Reproduced with the kind permission of Dr. Tomasz Niewodniczański)

CHAPTER 10

The Rules of the Game

On 6 July 1627, Smotryckyj addressed three letters to Rome. The first was to Pope Urban VIII, asking forgiveness for his sins and reception into the Catholic Church (Velykyj 1972, 125–26). The second went to Cardinal Ottavio Bandini, who was an influential member of both *Propaganda Fide* and the Holy Office. It declared Smotryckyj's desire "not to depart by a hair's breadth from the will of Our Most Holy Lord [that is, as we can see from the larger context, Pope Urban VIII] and of Your Eminence."[1] A third was sent to the Holy Office, in which, among other things, he specifically requested permission to remain for some time a covert Uniate, and to practice a number of types of dissimulation in the interim, in the hope of remaining in close contact with his former coreligionists and finally leading them into union with Rome (Velykyj 1972, 128–29).

All three letters, either directly or indirectly, raise questions of conformity and dissimulation. Specific aspects of Smotryckyj's requests to the Holy Office in particular betrayed a familiarity with codified techniques of lying. Especially interesting in this regard is his petition that he be allowed to continue commemorating aloud the patriarch of Constantinople when he celebrated the Divine Liturgy, but with the understanding that at the same time he would silently pray to God for Lukaris' conversion.[2] This was nothing more than a request for permission to employ a type of dissimulation known as *reservatio mentalis*. Further in his petition, Smotryckyj argued that by keeping his real allegiance hidden he would be behaving as did the Jesuits in India, where a certain amount of latitude had been permitted to Catholics in the pursuit of their mission.[3]

Mental reservation was only one of the more frequently practised types of licit lying that were described in the many handbooks on the *ars dissimulandi* (art of dissimulation) produced throughout Europe in the age of confessional debate. In the *Tractatus quintus de juramento et adjuratione* of his commentary on St. Thomas, the Spanish Jesuit Francisco Suárez (1548–1617) gave examples of the practice of mental reservation. Among other things, one could swear "I did not do it," followed by an inaudible "today"; or one could say "I swear," then say inaudibly "that I am swearing," and complete the oath with an audible "I did not do it" (see Zagorin 1990, 183).

We have an interesting Polish-Lithuanian example of the proposed use of mental reservation in this period and at the highest level. In 1634, when Władysław IV was about to take the oath to uphold the freedoms and liberties he had recently promised to the "dissidents" (the Protestants and the Orthodox) at the Election Sejm, the Grand Chancellor of Lithuania, Albrycht Stanisław Radziwiłł, whispered into the king's ear, urging him to employ the technique of mental reservation so that, without actually lying, he would nonetheless not be obliged to keep his promise: "Let Your Royal Majesty not have that intention," he said. The king, however, refused to dissimulate: "To whomever I swear with my lips, I also swear with my intention."[4]

In his letter of 19 February 1627, Aleksander Zasławski had urged Smotryc'kyj to remain for some time a covert Uniate, and he mentioned several of the traditionally cited precedents in defense of this practice, above all that of Nicodemus.[5] But, as we will see shortly, Smotryc'kyj had been reading in the rules of licit lying long before his conversion. Elements of Zasławski's letter bear the imprint of his conversations with the archbishop, and the idea of remaining a covert Uniate and of practicing dissimulation may well have originated with Smotryc'kyj.

Smotryc'kyj's letter to the Holy Office was not the only occasion upon which he had recourse to the art of dissimulation. In his attempt to convince his new Uniate (and Roman) masters that he had not renounced the faith when he participated in the solemn ceremony at Vespers in the Kievan Monastery of the Caves on 14 August/24 August 1628, during which pages of his *Apology* were cast under foot, and the work and its printer anathematized, Smotryc'kyj wrote:

> For during that very time I maintained whole my faith given to my God and promised to Him *per obedientiam* [by obedience], and my heart never gave its consent to their anathema cast upon my work in an un-Orthodox heart, nor could it give its consent piously. Whence it was that they condemned my Orthodox Catholic work, which I had written for them with great consideration, and thoroughly and

authoritatively supported, explained, and strengthened each thing in it with Holy Scripture and the doctrine of the doctors of the Church, Eastern and Western; and I cursed the blasphemies, errors, and heresies of their sowers of chaff, the Zyzanijs, who were refuted by me in my work: them did I tear; upon them did I put the candles out; and them did I cast under my feet.[6]

Here, too, we are in the realm of mental reservation. While Meletij was overtly tearing, stomping, and burning pages from his *Apology*, he was covertly doing the same to the errors and heresies of the Ruthenian "new theologians." These lines were, of course, directed in large part to the Uniate and Roman Catholic authorities. Smotryc'kyj drew on the art of dissimulation to "prove" that he had kept the faith: his outward actions were impious, therefore (so the "logic" went) he must have been dissimulating, since his heart "could not piously give its consent" to these proceedings.

Finally, to cite just one more piece of evidence that he often "reserved" his true beliefs: Smotryc'kyj expressed his amazement in 1628, after the events of the Kiev Council, at what he sought to represent as Mohyla's sudden, unexpected antagonism to the Uniate ideas found in the *Apology*. After all, the archimandrite of the Monastery of the Caves had approved the open letter Smotryc'kyj had written to Lukaris, in which, according to the archbishop, he had expressed "even more" of his (true) beliefs (Smotryc'kyj 1628b, Ciii[r–v]/636–37).

The Roman authorities acknowledged the possibility that Meletij had been dissimulating in their direction as well, when they charged Ruc'kyj with attesting that the archbishop had shown himself a sincere convert "in words *and deeds*" (see above, p. 149).

All these examples of "lying by the book" came from Smotryc'kyj's Uniate or, more correctly, covert-Uniate period. I have found evidence, however, that he had been studying the rulebook earlier in his career. In the *Verification of Innocence* of 1621, Smotryc'kyj devoted—as far as I have been able to determine—his only lines to the theory and practice of the art of lying. Here he argued that his opponents had been lying, and he rejected their lies in these terms:

But they say that there are three sorts of falsehoods (for that is how the apostate theologians, who were rebuked for this malice, defend themselves): *officiosum, jocosum, perniciosum* [helpful, humorous, malicious]. Does any one of these three allow one to lie against the honor and the blood of your neighbor? Are humorous and helpful lies of the sort that cause harm?[7]

He then went on the cite Ex. 23:1, Lev. 19:11, Mt. 12:36, Rom. 3:8, 1
Th. 5:22, Ps. 5:5–6—all of them directed against lying. And he concluded:
". . . their theology allows them these things. We and the Church of
God do not have that custom."[8]

Let us pause over this passage for a moment. At first glance, it might
seem that Smotryc'kyj was answering some specific Uniate work when
he cited the defense allegedly offered by the "apostate theologians." But
this is hardly likely. The *Verification of Innocence* was written not in
response to any particular Uniate polemical work, but in answer to
rumors, the king's universals, and the arrest of the Orthodox burghers of
Vilnius. Further, the Uniate side cannot have justified itself by recourse
to the rules for the art of lying: in its portrayal of events it was not telling
licit lies, which would have been self-defeating, but the simple truth.
This passage is instead an example of the polemical sleight of hand that
Smotryc'kyj often used in setting up straw men to knock down: "Perhaps
my opponents will argue that their recourse to lying belongs to the licit
sort . . . ?" ("And perhaps no one will notice immediately the premise:
that my opponent, by continuing the debate on my terms, has just
admitted the charge of lying and is now pleading to the lesser charge of
'licit lying,' but I will not allow him even this.")

Smotryc'kyj had engaged here in confessional stereotyping: "Your
apostate theologians (read: pupils of the Jesuits) justify lying; the
Church (read: our side) rejects it." But in so doing he also showed
himself well-versed in the theory of this sort of casuistry. After all, the
standard tripartite taxonomy of lies that he attributed to the "apostate
theologians" ("officiosum, jocosum, perniciosum") must actually have
stemmed from his own reading of the handbooks: St. Thomas Aquinas
had first provided this categorization of the various types of lies in his
Summa theologiae, and his words on the topic were often cited by
sixteenth-century authors of the *artes dissimulandi* (see Zagorin 1990,
30). Smotryc'kyj could have had it, for example, from Suárez'
commentary on Aquinas.[9] (Suárez was Smotryc'kyj's older contemporary,
and his works may well have been known to the Orthodox churchman:
Marcantonio de Dominis had written a work against Suárez in defense
of the Church of England in 1620, and Smotryc'kyj, as we will see in
chapter 12, seems to have known this work well.) But probably this
reference to Aquinas occurred in other sixteenth-century handbooks as
well. Smotryc'kyj, need not have taken it precisely from Suárez. The

point is that as an Orthodox churchman Smotryc'kyj had been reading works justifying lying, which he attributed to the theologians of the other side. Once he had gone over to that other side, he would show himself an adept practitioner of the theory that, as an Orthodox, he had attributed to the Roman Catholics and the Uniates. Was this a sort of confessional stereotyping at the level of his self-representation?

Thus, in reading of Smotryc'kyj's desire not to depart a "hair's breadth" from the will of Bandini and Urban VIII, we are permitted to question whether he was not actually expressing his sincerely held desire not to appear to have departed from the party line. Similarly, we also are entitled to wonder whether the statements of subjection to the pontiff were in any way conventional pieties, which he hoped he believed, or hoped he seemed to believe, but which actually expressed much more ambivalent feeings toward the holder of an office he had earlier described as that of a secular tyrant, equivalent in his rule of the Catholic Church to "the Turk" in the secular polity.[10]

Smotryc'kyj lived in a world in which "truths" from the realms of culture, faith, and politics were—like those he sometimes offered concerning his own persona—regularly used in campaigns to manipulate public opinion. Most important for my argument, Smotryc'kyj was aware of the contingency of these truths. He expressed this awareness, however, only in the context of a critique of the other side's behavior. Here he attempted to undermine his opponents' positions by revealing the ad hoc nature of the "truths" to which they subscribed. Let us revisit some of those places where the Uniate Smotryc'kyj unmasked the Orthodox subterfuge. The Orthodox, according to the Uniate Smotryc'kyj (and he ought to have known, since he was writing in part about his "former self"), did not examine their authorities for the truth of their claims concerning the faith. It sufficed for Orthodox readers to know that Theophil Ortholog (i.e., Smotryc'kyj himself) criticized the pope; they would then accept the other "truths" he offered without asking questions.[11] The Orthodox, according to the Uniate Smotryc'kyj, were engaged in an "unequal fight" with the Romans; therefore, they (for Smotryc'kyj, "we") had gone to their ("our") enemy's enemies for help in the struggle, making these enemies' heresies into their ("our") faith.[12] The Orthodox, again according to the Uniate Smotryc'kyj, considered themselves Orthodox to the degree they set themselves apart from the Romans.[13] "It is the custom of all Christian sects," the Uniate Smotryc'kyj wrote in 1629, "to call apostates or renegades those who, having abandoned their sect, join another one; and Jews, too, call apostates those who leave their midst and through baptism enter into communion with Christians."[14] (Somehow, I would have expected Smotryc'kyj to write of those Christians who had left their original sect and joined not some other "sect" but the "true Church." Was the "truth" contingent for him to this degree?) Finally, the Orthodox—again according to the Uniate Smotryc'kyj—traditionally had recourse to an "excuse," according to which, but for their superior secular authority, it would be the Romans, and not the Orthodox, who were the schismatics; in other words, the Orthodox were schismatics—in this Orthodox view of the world (here cited and rejected by the Uniate Smotryc'kyj)—"on account of their [the Romans'] power, and not on account of our property."[15]

This view of the contextual nature of the "truth" informed public disputation and appeal to authority in polemical arguments. Authorities were chosen not necessarily because they were thought reliable, but because the opponents were obliged to consider them reliable. The Orthodox Smotryc'kyj appealed to Latin authorities, and the Uniate Smotryc'kyj appealed to Church Slavonic authorities. A document was first deemed authoritative (because of the argument that could be made from it, not because of what it was), and then the lexicon of sacred philology was mustered in its defense. Smotryc'kyj could find philological arguments to establish or undermine the authority of any given document, depending upon its usefulness in the argument of the moment. Take, for example, the famous and disputed letter from the Ruthenian hierarchy and Metropolitan Mysajil supposedly written in 1476 to Pope Sixtus IV.[16] The Uniate Metropolitan of Kiev, Ipatij Potij, presented himself on 15 June 1605 with a copy of the letter, which he had found in the church in Kreva (Krewo), and demanded that it be entered into the castle books (see Scepuro 1898, 357). This was no matter of interpretation. Since the letter—if authentic—was unambiguous testimony for the earlier existence of a Uniate Ruthenian Church, the Orthodox Smotryc'kyj drew upon his supply of philological arguments to undermine its authority. Like the *Donatio Constantini* (to which Ortholog had devoted the immediately preceding pages) the letter from Mysajil was a pious forgery, revealed as such by a consideration of its style and content: even its proponents had to admit that none of the writings of the new or old doctors of the Roman Church contained such an exaggerated praise of the pope.[17] The Uniate

Smotryc'kyj was obliged, of course, to defend the authority of the same work: one copy was "found in the church in the village of Vilbijna near Ostroh," written "in old script," "already half moth-eaten";[18] a second was "found in the church in Kreva, in the house of God, among the church books" and "published to the world illustriously in print."[19]

Or consider the question of historiographic authorities. The Orthodox Smotryc'kyj argued his point not from "some anonymous writers of annals [*latopiscy*]," but from "certain, illustrious, trustworthy chroniclers [*kronikarze*] of worthy name and good repute."[20] To the first category belonged "authors" of Slavic Orthodox manuscript chronicles (whenever they did not prove his point); and to the second category belonged the Polish sixteenth-century classics of printed historiography: Marcin Kromer and, above all, Maciej Stryjkowski. The Uniate Smotryc'kyj would base his argument on testimonies from his "ancestors in Rus', from the Greeks, and the Romans, and from the foreigners," thus placing Rus' historiographers at the head of a list that also included other equally ancient and venerable witnesses—the Greeks and the Romans.[21] Did a witness seem to speak against Smotryc'kyj's argument of the moment?—then it must have been the result of falsification (probably programmatic falsification by Zyzanij).[22]

In fact, this free manipulation of a philological lexicon could be employed to bolster or undermine the authority of any given text. If a document was useful, then it could be described as old, moth-eaten, stylistically correct, accepted in the East, accepted in the West, printed or manuscript (both terms could be construed to lend authority); if a document spoke against your cause, then it was "snatched from under the bench," stylistically incorrect, manuscript rather than printed (when these two terms were opposed, printed texts usually enjoyed greater prestige), the result of conscious falsification.

Where are we to find the truth in this hall of mirrors? (I ask this as a student of Meletij Smotryc'kyj, in particular, but these comments may apply by extension to many aspects of Ruthenian culture of the late sixteenth and early seventeenth centuries.) How are we to reconstruct a past reflected in such distorting testimonies? One method might be to focus precisely upon this aspect of the documents. In the following three chapters I will seek to examine Smotryc'kyj's public programs and private views on issues of language and letters, faith and Church, nation and state as they were delineated within a field of tensions partially defined by authority, on the one hand, and by conformity, dissimulation, or dissent, on the other. Smotryc'kyj was well aware of the role authorities of various sorts played in his life and of the risks involved in deviating from them. Our first task in attempting to answer the question who Smotryc'kyj was is to determine what were the rules, what were the authorities to which he publicly adhered in these three areas of his life. The second task is to attempt to follow him as he played the game, to observe his public adherence to the rules, his exploitation of any loopholes in the rules, any areas of diminished authority, and to catch him when he "cheated," when he expressed his allegiance to the required authorities publicly but did another thing privately—in other words, when he dissimulated. (And as we have seen, even dissimulation occupied a certain position within the rules of the game.) Some parts of the truth about Smotryc'kyj can be found in the tensions between his will to conform—or at least to seem to conform—to the various authorities he established for himself at various times throughout his career and the ways in which he nonetheless often deviated, with greater or lesser risks, from these norms.

CHAPTER 11

Polonica Orthodoxe

"O nieporządnego, o przewrotnego, o niezbożnego rąk wkładania obyczaiu" (Smotryc'kyj 1610, 14ʳ/30: "Oh, the disorderly, oh, the perfidious, oh, the impious custom of laying on of hands!"). In this way Smotryc'kyj—using the pseudonym Theophil Ortholog—caused the Holy Mother, the Eastern Church, to lament the ordinations being made among her sons in the *Thrēnos* of 1610. And the important thing here is that he used the genitive case to do it. This was abnormal usage in Polish, even for a Ruthenian; but even more important is the fact that it was willfully abnormal, the result of a pattern of behavior on Smotryc'kyj's part that had analogues in other, "more risky" areas of his life, namely those of the Church and the state. When Smotryc'kyj ventured from secular rhetoric into sacred philology, his deviations from the various possible norms could carry great risks. And this may offer additional clues as to who the man was.

How can we describe Smotryc'kyj's Polish usage? What criteria can we use to determine normality and abnormality? Once we have determined where the deviations lie, how are we to evaluate them? There is little secondary literature here to help us. Smotryc'kyj's Polish—or that of any of the Ruthenians of the late sixteenth and early seventeenth centuries—has largely escaped scholarly attention. Because of the division of cultural patrimonies according to contemporary notions of nations and peoples, the Polish usage of Ruthenians has fallen through the cracks, often treated on the one side solely as an oddity or an example of a regionalism, and on the other side as something for which to apologize, a symbol of shame, at best as the use of the language of the politically stronger party as a sort of expediency.[1] I propose a somewhat different approach for Smotryc'kyj—to examine the linguistic behavior of this "marginal" user of the "dominant" language (both culturally and politically dominant) for evidence that he purposefully reshaped it to suit his own needs and interests.

The one study of Smotryc'kyj's Polish of which I am aware is a recent treatment by Stanisław Urbańczyk, who, in addition to according Smotryc'kyj a generally correct Polish usage (1983, 372), gives many examples of types of peculiarities in his usage: Church Slavonicisms connected with the Eastern rite, and thus motivated by the topics of Smotryc'kyj's works; compound nouns either borrowed from Church Slavonic or modeled on that usage, along with many other borrowings from or imitations of Church Slavonic (1983, 374–75); and a series of words that "were then rather uncommon; probably they were already going out of use. Their evaluation is difficult, for they are either unknown to the dictionaries, or only in a few examples."

Urbańczyk's criteria for identifying the "abnormalities" of Smotryc'kyj's Polish stem from the realm of historical linguistics. Thus, he finds most of his material in the best developed areas in this field (that is, in phonology, morphology, and lexicon), and the fewest in the least developed area, syntax. It seems to me that one of the key issues in the evaluation of "unusual usage" in Smotryc'kyj's works is touched upon in Urbańczyk's concluding remark. He states that Smotryc'kyj, his contemporaries and successors, "entered into the sphere of influence of the Polish language . . . and began to exert an influence upon the Polish language, to collaborate in creating Polish literature . . . " Smotryc'kyj's "abnormalities" therefore are observable, for the most part, on the basis of their Ukrainian or Church Slavonic reflexes, and are evaluated (or rather, would be evaluated—Urbańczyk does not carry his study this far) on the basis of their role in the formation of the Polish literary language.

A different way for describing and evaluating Smotryc'kyj's Polish usage is possible. What interests me, above all, is the behavioral component: what did Smotryc'kyj think he was doing when he deviated from accepted norms? I believe that—seen in these behavioral terms— Smotryc'kyj's use of Polish was not simply a manifestation of the Polish influence in Rus', nor an example of the importance of the borderlands in the formation of the Polish literary language (although it may also have been both of these things): viewed from within, Smotryc'kyj's Polish usage was an attempt, within the limits imposed by the rules of the game he was playing, to create something new and something of one's own. This was an appropriation of the Polish language for Orthodox purposes, an establishment of an Orthodox Polish rhetoric and sacred philology to compete with the Protestant, and especially, Catholic variants. I, too, use the tools of historical linguistics to identify possibly interesting forms, words, contructions, but I do not limit myself to them: a seemingly "normal" Polish word or phrase may also turn out to fit this pattern of behavior. I am not particularly interested whether Smotryc'kyj's usages gained acceptance in the Polish literary language at large or even whether they became the norm or were always noticed by other Orthodox Ruthenians. I am interested, for now (for now, since a wider study of this phenomenon will be, I think, an important desideratum for the entire corpus of Ruthenian Polish), in the usage of one important individual and in what this usage can tell us about how he lived in the world.

Let us begin by returning to the "genitive of remorse or surprise" cited at the outset. This was not "normal" Polish usage at the time. One assumes that if a writer of this period wished to exclaim about the downfall or the pitiful state of something, he would use the vocative case in Polish as an equivalent of the accusative of exclamation in Latin. In any event, he would not use the genitive case.

When Lev Krevza, archimandrite of the Holy Trinity Uniate Monastery in Vilnius, exclaimed in 1617 "o bezrozumne wierzanie!" (Krevza 1617, 51/29: "oh, senseless belief!"), or when Josyf Ruc'kyj, Uniate metropolitan of Kiev and one of Smotryc'kyj's opponents in the pamphlet wars of 1621–1623 over the "illegal" restoration of the Orthodox hierarchy, cried out "o bezrozumne głowy!" (*Sowita* 1621, 28/463: "oh, senseless heads!"), they probably were thinking in terms of the vocative case. In his response to Smotryc'kyj's *Thrēnos,* the Uniate polemicist Moroxovs'kyj wrote in his *Parēgoria* "o licentiam furoris" ("oh, boldness of rage") using the accusative case in the Latin, which he then "translated" into Polish with the vocative: "O niesłychana śmiałości!" (Moroxovs'kyj 1612, 11: "oh, unheard-of audacity!").

The Orthodox Smotryc'kyj himself rendered the Latin saying "o tempora, o mores!" (which was, no doubt, the accusative) with what probably was the vocative in Polish: "o czasy, o obyczaie!" (Smotryc'kyj 1621b, 23/341). And the Uniate Smotryc'kyj wrote in Latin in deriding his Orthodox opponent the archpriest of Sluck, Andrij Mužylovs'kyj, "o te Iudicem iniquissimum! o Forum importunissimum!" (Smotryc'kyj

1629b, 19ᵛ/720: "Oh, thou most unjust judge! Oh, most unsuitable forum!"). Again, this was the accusative case, as Latin grammars required.

The genitive of remorse or surprise that Smotryc'kyj used in similar situations in his Polish was thus in some sense a deviation, though perhaps one that brought with it little risk. The "aberration" here was in looking to Greek and Church Slavonic models for a new Polish rhetoric, rather than to the more customary model provided by Latin. The genitive of remorse, used to lament the state of something (often there was an implied comparison with a former "golden age"), was a standard feature of Greek and Church Slavonic, and Smotryc'kyj knew it as such. Eight years after he had first introduced it in his Polish usage in *Thrēnos* he would include it in his discussion of Slavonic syntax:

> On the syntax of the interjection. Rule 1. *"Ole"* and *"o"* of remorse and *"o"* of surprise require the genitive, as, for example, *"O,* I am a wretched man" and *"O,* Your most wise judgments, O Christ," etc.[2]

Although Smotryc'kyj wrote his *Thrēnos* in Polish, he attempted to give the work a more Orthodox pedigree by claiming on the title page that it had been written in Greek, and then translated from Greek into Church Slavonic and from Slavonic into Polish. The use of genitives of exclamation thus should be seen as an effort on Smotryc'kyj's part to include "Orthodoxisms" in his Polish oratory.[3] In *Thrēnos* we might be tempted to ascribe this unusual formulation to the fiction that the work had been translated from Greek to Church Slavonic to Polish; the genitives of remorse could then be seen as a conscious imitation of "translator's Polish," remnants of the "original" in the new version. Similarly, in the Polish version of his funeral sermon for Leontij Karpovyč, we could argue that the Ruthenian "original" (if this is the correct term) had influenced the Polish version (although this would beg the question of the Ruthenian "norm" for such constructions).[4] But Smotryc'kyj used this construction in other, original Polish works as well, and throughout his career, both Orthodox (Smotryc'kyj 1621b, 65ʳ/ 390: "O nieznosznego praeiudicium") and Uniate (Smotryc'kyj 1629a, 48/669: "O skarania Bożego! o ślepoty tych ludzi!"). This is clearly "non-Polish." Evidence for its "intentionality" is found in the fact that it is used in highly rhetorical passages, that in similar rhetorical situations, other Ruthenian polemicists would use the accusative or the vocative, and that Smotryc'kyj himself would also use the accusative or the vocative on occasion.[5] This deviation betrays a particular programmatic motivation, because it established an opposition between a Polish rhetoric based on Latin models (that is, the "norm"—and note that Polish writers themselves were well aware of the "artificiality" of this "norm"[6]) and a Polish rhetoric based on Greek and Church Slavonic models.

How did Smotryckyj view Polish? To what degree did he consider it open to the kind of purposeful shaping for which I argue? What was its relationship to the other linguistic media he used? Above all, we should bear in mind the peculiarities of the boundary between Polish and the "Ruthenian vulgar tongue." Although users of the languages spoke of them as two different media between which one could translate in both directions, the boundary actually was quite porous. Textual material in one language could easily be exploited in the other through a process of transposition that was almost automatic at the graphemic and morphemic level, and included few lexical and syntactic substitutions.[7] A Ruthenian preacher could stand at the pulpit with a Polish book and preach from it in Ruthenian.[8] Smotryckyj, too, drew directly upon Polish literary material in composing his Ruthenian works.[9]

But the boundary was porous in both directions. We often assume, given the higher cultural status of Polish, the greater availability of "standard" works in Polish, and the more "closed" nature of Polish in comparison with Ruthenian, that the transferal was all in one direction: Polish to Ruthenian. Yet, there are indications that this was not always or necessarily the case. In his *Protestation* of 1628 Smotryckyj wrote that he had finished his *Apology,* had had two fair copies made and sent to Boreckyj and Mohyla, and then had sent a copy to Kasijan Sakovyč, so that he might see to having the work printed in Polish.[10] This implied that the versions Smotryckyj sent to Boreckyj and Mohyla (in a sense, the "original" versions) were written in Ruthenian. And the contemporary Orthodox pamphlet called *Apolleia* confirmed this impression.[11]

The boundary between Polish and Ruthenian was potentially so porous for those who regularly used both languages that we may be led astray if we always think in terms of searching for an "original." Smotryckyj published his funeral sermon on the death of Leontij Karpovyč, his predecessor as archimandrite of the Vilnius Brotherhood Monastery, in two versions. The Ruthenian version probably appeared first (preface dated 8 November/18 November 1620), the Polish shortly thereafter (preface dated 17 February/27 February 1621). As this was a sermon first delivered before an Orthodox audience, it would also seem likely that the Ruthenian version was the "original," and the Polish the "translation." But do these terms really apply here?

Consider the case of Smotryc'kyj's usage of the word *бесѣда/biesiada* (in both versions) to describe his funeral sermon on the death of his predecessor as archimandrite of the Vilnius Brotherhood Monastery, Leontij Karpovyč.[12] Did this usage constitute an "-ism"—for example, Ruthenianism, Slavonicism, Orthodoxism, general stylism—of any sort in either language? In the Polish case, we might be inclined to say yes, since the "normal" meaning of "biesiada" is "convivium" or "banquet, feast." Smotryc'kyj had given the word the meaning found in its Church Slavonic cognate *бесѣда,* i.e., "sermo" or "sermon." Since the word looked the same in Ruthenian as in Church Slavonic, we might be inclined *not* to treat it as an "-ism" in the Ruthenian version.

Neither of these evaluations reflects the peculiarities of Polish and Ruthenian usage for contemporary users such as Meletij Smotryc'kyj. First, the Polish usage: in describing his sermon as a "biesiada," Smotryc'kyj was again actively seeking to create an Orthodox Polish rhetoric. This was not a case of "translator's Polish" or an inadvertent slip on the part of a not-quite native speaker. Smotryc'kyj knew well the "normal" Polish usage of the word "biesiada," as he wrote in *Thrēnos* (to chose a work of unimpeachably Orthodox credentials) of "revellings and drunkenness" (Smotryc'kyj 1610, 65ʳ/81: "biesiady y piiaństwa") or of "luxurious revellings and banquets" (Smotryc'kyj 1610, 170ʳ/186: "roskoszne biesiady y bankiety"). Or in the *Sermon* itself, where he cited Gal. 5:21 according to the Wujek Bible: " . . . murders, drunkenness, revellings, and such like" (Smotryc'kyj 1621a, B4ᵛ/244: " . . . Mężoboystwa, Piiaństwa, Biesiady, y tym podobne . . . ") Here, the Ruthenian version (Smotryc'kyj 1620, B3ᵛ/133) cited Scripture in Church Slavonic, thus creating another stylistic level altogether: " . . . оубійства, піянства, бесчинни кличи, и подобная симъ . . . "

Conversely, how do we know that "бесѣда" was not an "-ism" in Smotryc'kyj's Ruthenian? Without any clear notion of a "normative Ruthenian" in this period, and given evidence indicating that Smotryc'kyj was engaging in stylistic artifice in his use of "biesiada" in the meaning of a sermon in Polish, should we not entertain the possibility that even in his Ruthenian usage "бесѣда" was a sort of "stylism," a semantic Orthodoxism. He entitled his work, after all, *Казанье/Kazanie* and not

Бесѣда/Biesiada. If our goal is a contextual evaluation of usage, our notions, drawn from the realm of historical grammar, of "standard" usage for Polish versus Ruthenian/Ukrainian or Church Slavonic, or West versus East Slavic, can only be approximate guides, and then only to help isolate those cases worth further investigation.

Another example occurs in a translation from St. John Chrysostom, which the Orthodox Smotryc′kyj included in his *Verification of Innocence* of 1621 (30ᵛ/355):

> Co ieśli kto z Prawosławnych za rzecz lekką poważy, y mimo siebie puści, on vyrzy: Ia lekce nie ważę, ale *czuć o tym y dbać chcę.*

> [And if anyone of the Orthodox should consider this an insignificant matter and take no heed of it, let him see: I do not count it lightly; rather *I will watch for and take care* of this.]

This probably was a Church Slavonicism. The word *chcę* here does not have the "normal" Polish meaning here of "I wish" but serves, after the model of Church Slavonic (perhaps Smotryc′kyj was translating from a Church Slavonic source rather than Latin or Greek), to form the compound future tense together with the infinitive. I suspect, again, that Smotryc′kyj had intentionally employed an "Orthodoxism" in translating the Greek Father into Polish. He certainly knew the "normal" ways to form the future in Polish ("proof" of this assertion can be found on every page of his prose), but he chose several times to make this Church Slavonic construction a part of his Polish rhetoric. Here, as in the case of the genitive of remorse, it is the rhetorical quality of this usage that argues for its intentionality: in the examples I have found, Smotryc′kyj used the construction to round out an assertion that something always had been, was then, and would forever be: "You inclined, you incline, and you will incline" (Smotryc′kyj 1621b, 57ᵛ/372: "Skłaniałeś, skłaniasz, y skłaniać chcesz"); "it presented itself, presents, and will present itself" (Smotryc′kyj 1621b, 59ʳ/383: "stawił, stawi, y stawić chce"); "we were, we are, and, by God's help, we will be" (Smotryc′kyj 1623, 8ʳ/518: "byliśmy, iesteśmy, y być za pomocą Bożą chcemy"); "we were, . . . we are, and God willing, we will be" (Smotryc′kyj 1623, 8ʳ/518: "Byliśmy, . . . iesteśmy y być da Bog chcemy").

Or consider the following (again from Smotryc′kyj's Orthodox *Verification of Innocence* of 1621, 18ᵛ–19ʳ/337):

Nie to zaiste Czytelniku Miłościwy, co w słowach *praetenduie*, na
vmyśle ten *Calumniator* knuie: Iż z pomienionych od niego przyczyn
intentowane Maiestatu Krola Iego M: nieuszanowanie stanąć nie
mogło, przyszył do nich potwarz: aby iednego o drugie vderzeniem,
skry zamyszlonego przez się, w Oyczyźnie pożogu wykrzesił: Ludzi
niewinnych, łapaniem, więzieniem, y morderstwem podżarzył: y po
wszytkich Koronnych y Litewskich Państwach y Ruskich rospłomienił,
a potym krwią niewinną *tuszył y gasił.*

[In truth, dear reader, that *calumniator* {i.e., the "someone" who had
portrayed Smotryc'kyj and the newly consecrated Ruthenian hierarchy
as Turkish spies and traitors} schemes in his intent not what he
pretends in his words: since, from the reasons mentioned by him, an
intended disrespect for the majesty of His Majesty the King could not
be drawn, he tacked calumny onto them, so that, through the striking
of one against the other, he might strike in the fatherland the sparks of
the conflagration which he had himself invented; so that he might set
innocent people on fire through seizure, imprisonment, and murder; so
that he might spread the flames throughout all the domains of the
Crown, Lithuania, and Ruthenia; and then, so that he might *quell and
extinguish* the fire with innocent blood.]

For *tuszyć* the lexicographic authority M. Samuel Bogumił Linde cites
only the standard meanings in modern Polish: "expect, anticipate, hope"
(1859, 743). He notes the Russian cognate *тушить,* with the meaning
of "extinguish, put out," but he gives no examples of Polish usage in this
sense (1855, 29). Yet, it is clear from the context that Smotryc'kyj used
the word as a near synonym for *gasić,* as it occurs in the modern
Ukrainian *тушити.*

Or this example from Smotryc'kyj's Uniate *Paraenesis* of 1629 (60/
675):

Postępek ten święty po wszytkich Miastach ze wszytkim narodem
naszym vczyniony, nie będzie, y słusznie nie może, za mus y gwałt
bydź sądzony, ani od Bogu miłych, ani od samego Pana Boga. Nie
gwałt czyni lekarz gdy pacyentowi swemu wywinioną z stawu rękę
abo nogę, z niemałym iego bolem naciąga: toż się będzie dziać y z
nami. Bo ieśli wy y nie przyznawacie sobie z Cerkwie Pana
Chrystusowey wywinienia się, to iest, z schizmy, *vwierzyć was y
vpewnić* iście w tym maią puchliny y strupy, staw ten wywiniony
osiadłe, to iest, błędy y Herezye: ktorych wy też sobie przez lat
dwadzieścia y ośm, iak się poczęły wysadzać, nie przyznawali.

[Once that holy deed has been done {i.e., the forced reunification of
Rus'} unto our entire nation throughout all the towns, it will not and
cannot properly be judged as force and violence, either by those who
are dear to God or by the Lord God Himself. A doctor does not inflict
violence when, with no small pain to the patient, he pulls on an arm or

a leg that has become dislocated from the socket. The same thing will happen to us. For if you do not acknowledge that you have become dislocated from the Church of Christ the Lord (that is, on account of the schism), the swellings and scabs (that is, the errors and heresies) that have settled on the socket must certainly *cause you to believe and assure you* of this, although you have not acknowledged them to yourselves for these twenty-eight years that have passed since they began to swell.]

Linde gives only "to believe" as the meaning of *wierzyć* (*uwierzyć* is the perfective form of this verb in Polish [1860, 310–11]), but he notes the Russian usage *увѣрять/увѣрить*, which he glosses under *upewnić*, i.e., "to assure" (1860, 149). Here again, context tells us that it is the "Orthodox" meaning of the word that we are looking for, as found in the work of Smotryc'kyj's contemporary, the Ruthenian lexicographer Pamvo Berynda (1961, 136): "оувѣряю: оупевнаю."[13]

The two examples cited immediately above have one thing in common: in each case we are dealing with "synonymical" pairs of words, which are in fact synonymical only if we give one member of the pair not its "normal" Polish meaning (both words exist in "normal" Polish), but its East Slavic, "Orthodox" meaning. In each case the ambiguous word comes first, so that its actual meaning becomes completely clear only when we reach the second member of the pair. In other words, we are dealing with a sort of bilingual pun.

Two comments are in order here. First, in both instances the synonymical pairs were clearly used to mark the progress of a rhetorical period. In the first case, the doublet indicated the end of the larger syntactic unit, and in the second case it introduced the final "then"- clause. Again, it is this rhetorical quality that leads me to suspect that the usage was intentional.

Second, Smotryc'kyj did make jokes. It is important to establish this fact in order to place these synonymical pairs in a context of linguistic behavior. One of Smotryc'kyj's jokes in particular drew its humor from precisely this sort of punning juxtapostion of the local Ruthenian, non-Polish form with that belonging to "normal" Polish.

Smotryc'kyj's Uniate opponent in 1621, Metropolitan Josyf Ruc'kyj, had taken a position similar to that found in the eleventh-century authority on canon law Ivo of Chartres (1040–1117). Smotryc'kyj responded by citing a passage directed against Ivo from the *Annales ecclesiastici* of Cardinal Cesare Baronio (Caesar Baronius) (1538–

1607) and by then imagining what the cardinal (a nearly contemporary authority in the Roman Catholic Church) might have said to his Uniate colleague Ruc'kyj:

> Ieśli tak Baroniusz do *Iwona,* Męża w Kościele Rzymskim iako sam mowi, wielkiego, y Stolicy Apostolskiey zasłużonego, w tey własney o *Inuestiturach* przełożonym świetskim Krolom, Xiążętom, y Wielmożam zabronionych sprawie mowi: co by nie rzekł do tego marnego *Iwana,* nierzkąc Stolicy Apostolskiey nie zasłużonego, ale w Kościele Rzymskim albo mało albo owszeki nie znaiomego (Smotryc'kyj 1621c, 16/407)?

> [If Baronius speaks thus to *Ivo,* a man who was, as he {i.e., Baronio} himself said, great in the Church and of service to the Holy See in precisely this matter concerning the investitures that are forbidden to kings, princes, and magnates, what would he not say to this wretched *Ivan,* who has not only not been of service to the Holy See but is little known or entirely unknown in the Roman Church?]

Note that the name Ivan was clearly marked for Smotryc'kyj and his audience as an "Orthodoxism."

There are many other examples of the jocular use of "Ruthenianisms" in Smotryc'kyj's Polish. Consider the following example:

> Nakazałli kiedy Patryarcha Synod pomiestny, stawić sie na nim był powinien Metropolit: a nakazałliby go Cesarz, Metropolit by Ruski *na to ani hunął.* Bo skarać go, władzy nie miał, y w cudzym Państwie mieć nie mogł. Ktorego władza poty, poki granicy Państwa iego. A zwierzchności Duchowney władza, poki granicy Cerkwie powszechney: to iest, po wszytkim świecie (Smotryc'kyj 1628a, 58/552).

> [If the patriarch {of Constantinople} ever convened a local council, the metropolitan was obliged to appear for it; but if the emperor convened it, the metropolitan of Rus' *never even gave it a second thought.* For he did not have the power to punish him, nor could he have had in another's domain, since his power reaches only as far as the borders of his domain. But the power of the spiritual authority reaches as far as the borders of the Universal Church, that is, throughout the entire world.]

The word *hunął* is the issue here. Linde cited it, referring only to this passage from the *Apology,* and called it a Ruthenianism (from *гунути*), with the implication that it was the inadvertent result of interference (1855, 191). I would ask whether this is not another conscious "Orthodoxism" on Smotryc'kyj's part? Most important is the way he used the word. He certainly could have chosen a more "normal" Polish expression here, but instead he switched codes to emphasize the lack of authority that the Byzantine secular power had over the Church in Rus'. Smotryc'kyj had the metropolitan of Rus' switch from "standard" Polish to a Ruthenian regionalism in order to express his disdain for the outsider's pretentions.[14]

Urbańczyk raises the question of the nature of Smotryc'kyj's spoken Polish and concludes that—although it was not reflected in his orthography—it was probably the well-known "borderland dialect" ("dialekt kresowy") with its peculiar forms and intonations (1983, 373). In the background of Urbańczyk's study and Linde's entries lurks the problematic assumption that Smotryc'kyj's "mother tongue" was Ruthenian and that Polish was for him a "foreign language." But are these descriptions really applicable here? Although we cannot hope to answer questions like this in any convincing way, I think it would not hurt for a moment to try to imagine listening to Smotryc'kyj—say, in Warsaw, at the preparations for the Sejm of 1622—where he might have had to address a variety of groups representing different constituencies and in different languages: Polish, Ruthenian, perhaps Latin. In Smotryc'kyj's case, the boundary between spoken Polish and Ruthenian must have been exceptionally tenuous, perhaps a question of gradations rather than of an absolute border. I imagine him switching between the two languages and between stylistic levels of the two languages, depending upon his audiences, using the sorts of puns and jokes I have cited here as road signs along the way. How Smotryc'kyj spoke and wrote (and especially his displays of verbal wit) may have been part of the way in which he defined his public identity.

Thus, I would argue, we should be slow to ascribe other Ruthenianisms and Church Slavonicisms in Smotryc'kyj's Polish to an inadvertent foreign influence and be rather inclined to suspect that they, too, were part of a program to create an Orthodox variant of Polish. This observation applies especially to the compound nouns noted by Urbańczyk. If we view Smotryc'kyj's use of words such as *serdcowiedzca* ("knower of hearts"), *hymnopisec* ("writer of hymns"), etc. (Urbańczyk 1983, 374) against the background of a broader linguistic behavior that aimed at the "orthodoxification" of the Polish language, then we might be inclined to see them as consciously aberrant, and not the result of inadvertent interference. From the point of view of those who saw (or now see) the language as tending toward toward the closed, well-defined end of the scale, Smotryc'kyj was guilty of "linguistic deviation." This sort of deviation carried with it little risk: at the worst, he might be dismissed as a provincial.

Another type of active shaping of Polish, however, carried with it a somewhat greater risk in that it was subject to judgment according to authorities that were not only philological but also ecclesiastical. The problem was this: Smotryc'kyj cited Scripture in Polish frequently in his Polish polemical works. Which version did he use? This was a question that went far beyond (or, perhaps more accurately, had little to do with) issues of taste and style. Smotryc'kyj was active at the end of the great flourishing of Polish sacred philology. He had a wide range of translations from which to choose. By accepting a particular version (or by opting to make his own translation) he would make a practical statement that had far-reaching implications for an Orthodox program of Polish sacred philology. By writing Scripture in Polish in one manner and not another, he would take a stand on issues of authority and doctrine, and thus would enter into an area of possible risk.

In order to evaluate this risk, we need to take a look at the authorities to which Smotryc'kyj could have adhered, and those to which, as an Orthodox or a Uniate, he should have adhered. Ruthenian ideas about language and languages in the late sixteenth and early seventeenth centuries were shaped in large measure by a need to respond to the Protestant and Catholic programs for sacred philology that had been elaborated in the sixteenth century. What was the general outline of this challenge? Here we must begin with the question of authorities. The Western Church had long adhered to a trinity of sacred languages that comprised Hebrew, Greek, and Latin. For scriptural justification it drew on John 19:19–22, which stated that these were the languages in which the inscription "Jesus of Nazareth, King of the Jews" had been placed above Christ's cross. They were also the languages of the most authoritative texts of Scripture in the Western Church: the Hebrew Old Testament, the Greek New Testament, and the Latin Vulgate translation of the Bible. Greek and Latin were the languages of the most authoritative interpreters of Scripture. But while the Western Church in the Middle Ages was aware at some level that Hebrew and Greek were the "original" languages of its cultural tradition, it had no difficulty according a nearly absolute practical authority to the Latin Vulgate. In the absence of any broader knowledge of Hebrew and Greek it was convenient, after all, to have one set of programmatic authorities and another orientation on the practical level.

It was only with the Renaissance, when the "homo trium linguarum" became the goal of one type of education, that the traditional authority of the Vulgate came under sustained attack. The basic outlines of that development from Valla's *Adnotationes* through Erasmus's *Novum Instrumentum* to the biblical philology of the Reformers are well known.[15] Of crucial importance was the fact that this attack on the authority of the Vulgate was couched in terms of the newly revived textual criticism that lay at the heart of Renaissance Humanism. The Reformers inherited this in large measure from Valla and Erasmus. The Protestant program was simple and—at first glance—convincing. It drew a strict line of demarcation between "original languages" or "original texts," on the one hand, and translations, on the other hand, arguing that the descrepancies between the Vulgate Latin translation as compared with the "originals" found in the Hebrew Old Testament and the Greek New Testament proved the former corrupt. On issues of authority, it did not distinguish between "languages" and "texts" in those languages. Absolute authority was therefore to be accorded to the "original languages."

The Roman Church now faced several new problems. The decree of the fourth session of the Council of Trent in April 1546 offered what was essentially an internal compromise among Catholics by declaring the Vulgate—out of all the Latin versions then in circulation—authoritative "for faith and morals."[16] It did not specify whether the Hebrew and Greek texts were also authoritative and if they were, whether they were more, or less, authoritative than the Latin. This somewhat unclear situation made for a variety of responses on the Catholic side to the Protestant challenge and even to some occasional sparring within the Catholic side.

There were two general types of Catholic responses to the Protestant argument, which—to borrow the terminology of Werner Schwarz (1955)—might be described, respectively, as "philological" and "inspirational."

The philological camp pointed out the weaknesses in the Protestant argument on its own terms. The Protestants were guilty of a fundamental textual-philological error when they equated original languages with original texts. Why must the extant manuscripts in the original languages reflect the faithful transmission of original texts? What if the Hebrew texts of the Old Testament had been subject to neglect and to the malicious intervention of the Jews, who had sought to weaken the Christian argument that Jesus was the Messiah foretold by the prophets? What if the Greek texts of the New Testament had been subject to neglect and to the malicious intervention of the Greeks, who were notorious heretics and had sought to have scriptural authority for their heresies? And what if the Latin Vulgate had been translated carefully, and early on, from as yet uncorrupted Hebrew and Greek sources, by a highly trained philologist, and had been transmitted faithfully by the Roman Church, which had been entrusted with its keeping? Could we not then argue that indeed philology itself controverted the Protestant position? An argument such as the one I have outlined above could be—and was—used to deny all authority to the extant Hebrew and Greek texts of Scripture. But it could also be used to argue that all three versions possessed some authority and that, while the Vulgate remained the main practical authority, Catholic theologians and controversialists might in certain instances draw on the Hebrew and Greek testimonies, since the Vulgate remained, after all, a translation, however faithful.

The inspirational argument, which could be employed by itself or in addition to the philological argument, held that the Vulgate translation—much like the Septuagint—was the result not only of skilled philology (in this case that of St. Jerome), but also of the intervention of the Holy Spirit, Who had guided the translator's pen. Thus the Vulgate was at the outset just as authoritative as the Hebrew and Greek originals.[17] And at this point the argument could switch from the "inspirational" to the "philological" by pointing out that the Latin text—unlike the Hebrew and Greek—had been transmitted faithfully.

Closely linked to the question of scriptural authorities was that of the authority of Scripture: how much of Church doctrine was defined by Scripture, and who had the right to interpret it? Luther and, following him, many of the Protestant polemicists said all of it and potentially everyone. Of course this was a programmatic statement. In practice, it gave Luther the right to reject any interpretation that did not agree with his own: "If I were the only one in the entire world to adhere to the Word, I alone would be the Church."[18] But the principle of *sola Scriptura* could also be made into the central argument for the translation of Scripture into the vulgar tongues. If Scripture was the sole foundation for faith and morals—and even if the Hebrew and Greek texts should remain the ultimate authority—all Christians should have direct access to the Bible in some form, whether read or heard.[19]

The Roman Church responded by reasserting the importance of the "unwritten traditions." As the decree from the fourth session of the Council of Trent had put it, the Church received both Scripture and unwritten traditions as authoritative for faith and morals.[20] On the question of translation no agreement was reached, and the council fathers decided to allow for the different customs and needs of different countries.[21] Translations had to be approved by Rome and often included an interpretative apparatus that gave the reader the "unwritten traditions," that is, the interpretations handed down by the Church. While the practical difference between Protestant and Catholic versions might be minimal, the programmatic difference was fundamental. For the Catholics, only the Church had the right to interpret Scripture. Or, as St. Augustine had put it in what was to become a favorite text of Catholic controversialists: "For my part, I should not believe the Gospels except as moved by the authority of the Catholic Church."[22]

By the time Smotryc′kyj published his first work, there existed two well-defined Polish programs for sacred philology: one non-Catholic and the other Catholic.[23] The non-Catholics all began from the position that Scripture was to be accorded absolute authority and should therefore be translated into the vulgar tongues. For the most part, they still employed the philological argument that the Hebrew and Greek texts as the "originals" should be the supreme authority for interpretation and translation. Nonetheless, Marcin Czechowic's response to Szymon Budny's criticisms of the reliability of the Greek New Testament showed that, for some non-Catholics, the Greek text had become a sort of Protestant Vulgate, the textual authority of which was founded upon the authority of that Church or group of local Churches.[24]

The Polish Catholic response was complete by 1599 when the entire Bible was published in a revision of the translation by the Polish Jesuit Jakub Wujek. The *Apparatus sacer* that preceded this edition contained an extensive review of Protestant positions—general European and local Polish—along with the authoritative Polish Catholic statement on matters of sacred philology. Several points here will be of interest to us. First, the original Wujek translation had aroused controversy within the Jesuit ranks. Wujek's New Testament of 1593 and Psalter of 1594 were, in the opinion of some, too reliant on the original languages, strayed too far from the Vulgate, and paid too much attention to Polish style. The Wujek Bible of 1599 appeared after the translator's death and was the result of a thorough revision that brought it more in line with the Vulgate. Second, by containing a ban on reading all previous non-Catholic editions, the 1599 edition established a kind of relative authority for this particular version among all Polish translations.[25]

What did Polish Protestant and Catholic debates over sacred philology have to do with the Rus'? First, both of the Western camps had, since the late sixteenth century, been competing in the eastern lands of the Polish-Lithuanian Commonwealth for the souls of the Orthodox. The first printed works in the Ruthenian vulgar tongue were catechisms and confessional tracts published by Protestants and Catholics. The Ruthenians soon became a part of the Polish-language reading public.[26] Thus, Polish works by Protestants and Catholics could also be shaped with an eye for a Ruthenian readership. This definitely was the case with Bible translations: beginning with Szymon Budny's Bible of 1572, all Polish versions of Scripture contained the Orthodox pericope headings or зачала, since, as Czechowic put it, "the brethren of the Ruthenian lands demanded this of us especially."[27] Thus when the Orthodox Ruthenians began to play an active role in the confessional battles, they knew well the Protestant and Catholic programs in their Polish versions, and they had several practical models on which to draw in formulating their response.

The problem for Smotryc'kyj was this: the Orthodox Ruthenians were, for a variety of reasons, writing more and more in Polish by this time, but they possessed no Orthodox program for Polish sacred philology and no Orthodox standard of Scripture in Polish. There were several competing Catholic and non-Catholic norms, many of which seem to have been familiar to Smotryc'kyj: the Leopolita Bible of 1575 (a revision of the original 1561 edition), the Budny Bible of 1572 and New Testament of 1574, the Czechowic New Testament of 1577, the Wujek New Testament of 1593 and Bible of 1599, to mention only those versions I am certain Smotryc'kyj consulted. Smotryc'kyj thus had several possibilities. He could have provided his own translation in Polish. He could have chosen a version of Polish Scripture, Protestant or Catholic, that suited him best and adhered to it. Or he could have compromised by choosing an existing version as a model and adapting it to his own needs.

Almost all of Smotryc'kyj's Polish biblical citations came in polemical works; even the 1620 *Sermon* on the death of Leontij Karpovyč is not without its connections to the polemic over the resurrection of the Orthodox hierarchy. This may explain why we find no heterodox scriptural models here, even though, based on Greek as they were, the heterodox versions of Polish Scripture might seem closer to the heart of an Orthodox Slav: not because he would not use them on other occasions, but, I suspect, because he could not allow his Uniate and Catholic opponents to catch him using heterodox texts. Whatever the reason, there were three scriptural models in Smotryc'kyj's Polish citations, all of them Catholic: the Leopolita Bible of 1575, the Wujek New Testament of 1593, and the Wujek Bible of 1599. With the exception of the *Sermon* of 1620, all Smotryc'kyj's Polish works from *Thrēnos* (1610) through *Defense of the Verification* (1621) drew on the Leopolita Bible in its revised version of 1575 or 1577 (the text being the same). In the *Sermon,* and in all Polish works beginning with the *Elenchus* (1621), some version of the Wujek translation was the model: in most instances, this seems to have been the posthumous edition of 1599; in his final work, the *Exaethesis* (1629), Smotryc'kyj seems to have drawn on the New Testament of 1593 for New Testament citations and on the Bible of 1599 for those from the Old Testament. (I offer material in support of my findings in appendix B1.) These were all versions—the Leopolita of 1577 and the Wujek versions of 1593 and 1599—that were announced as, and had been in fact, translated from the Latin Vulgate. Only the Wujek New Testament of 1593 defended occasional recourse to the Greek text. This is behavior that might have required some explanation in the Orthodox Smotryc'kyj, but certainly would have raised no eyebrows among his later Uniate and Roman Catholic masters.

What kind of authority did Smotryc'kyj allot Greek texts in his consideration of languages and letters? At the programmatic level, at least for the Orthodox Smotryc'kyj, Greek was the supreme authority. This, of course, comes as no surprise. The Orthodox Smotryc'kyj defined himself and his nation in part by their allegiance to the "Greek faith" and to the "Greek nation." On the one occasion that he made explicit reference to his recourse to Greek sources, he couched his discussion in philological terms: his argument against the fire of Purgatory was better than that of his opponent because it drew on Greek interpreters who had recourse to the original languages; his opponents' arguments could not be as good because they were based on interpretations of the Latin translation, at best one step removed from the genuine sources:

> You cite the testimony of the Blessed Augustine or someone else among the Roman doctors of that age who understood those Pauline words differently and used that passage to prove the fire of Purgatory. And we answer them thus: If it is proper for Greeks to interpret Greek writings—since you cannot deny that Greeks know their common language better by birth than people of another nation by learning, and since the Apostle wrote in Greek—then certainly none of the Latins could understand that passage more appropriately and interpret it more aptly than St. John Chrysostom. Therefore one ought rather call upon the opinion of those who are greater, than the opinion of the Latin doctors, who made such an interpretation, either through the insufficiency of the Latin language in the expression of the property of Greek words, or else, in opposing a greater evil they gave way to a lesser evil.[28]

Moreover, Smotryc'kyj wrote elsewhere in the same work, the Latin Church was guilty of willfully corrupting texts—both Greek and Latin—in order to bring them more in line with (false) Latin doctrine.[29]

But if we put these two arguments together, we see that Smotryc'kyj was not exactly defending the printed Greek texts of the Latin West, since, in his representation, many of them (along with Latin texts) had been corrupted by the Roman Church. Thus what he was defending here—and recall that in *Thrēnos* Smotryc'kyj was writing in the first person as a personification of the Greek Church—were those Greek texts (presumably manuscript) of Holy Scripture and the Greek Fathers that were the sole "possession" of the Eastern Church. This reasoning was similar to one aspect of an argument found later in the seventeenth century in Muscovy: the Old Believers, who opposed Nikon's correction of the church books according to new, printed Greek texts, claimed that the correction was really a corruption, since it was based on Western printings of Greek texts, and the Latins had taken the Greek texts from Constantinople, printed their own corrupt versions, and destroyed the originals.[30] In both cases, the "source" for this history of Greek texts in the early modern period could have been Maksim Grek.[31]

This argument was likely motivated by the fiction of the rhetorical strategy Smotryc'kyj chose to employ in *Thrēnos*. I do not know how many Greek manuscripts he had at hand, but he likely had few. All indications are that his philological workshop was that of a Western-trained sacred philologist, and his texts of Greek Scripture and Greek Fathers were primarily those available in Western humanistic editions.[32]

In responding to Smotryc′kyj the Polish Jesuit Piotr Skarga seems to have recognized (or chosen to focus upon) the common points between the Orthodox and the Protestants on the question of the authority of Greek Scripture; thus he was able to draw on the repertoire of Catholic anti-Protestant arguments in his response:

> Not against the Roman or the Latin Church, but against the Greek [Church] is the old taunt *Graeca fides* ("Greek faith"), and the old accusation that they falsify the books not only of the Doctors, but even the words of Holy Scripture, and in their place they interpolate heretical ones, and they cast out the Catholic ones. Which is not said of good people. The Bible that was first translated into their language, which we call the LXX, has been wondrously falsified by the Greeks through deletion, addition, and corruption, as St. Jerome asserts. Origen, Lucian, Esychius, and Jerome (who consulted the Hebrew text) corrected this Bible. But it has again become so confused and corrupted by the Greeks that it is nearly destroyed and one can barely find its remnants. And the Roman Church had to have recourse to the Hebrew text, abandoning the Greek, whence arose our Vulgate, with the exception of the Psalter which had already become so well established in all the Churches. And the Latin Church maintained this Vulgate with wondrous diligence, and truth-loving Greeks have to have recourse to our Latin Bible. The same thing happened with the New Testament, which was also falsified by the Greeks, especially by the heretics, for whom that language was always an unhappy mother. The Greeks threw out of the Gospel the story about the adulteress and the final chapter of St. Mark. And they added to the Lord's Prayer "Thine is the Kingdom and the power and the glory for ever," which is not found in any Evangelist. As you can see in Tertullian, Cyprian, Ambrose, Jerome, who interpreted the Lord's prayer without that addition. That is a greater addition than that of "and from the Son."[33]

Notice that Smotryc′kyj had focused on the Fathers, but Skarga aimed his weapons at Greek Scripture, the place where the Orthodox and Protestant arguments had common ground. We have, in a sense, come full circle. Arguments first directed by the Latins against the Greeks, and then by the Catholics against the Protestants, were now again employed by Polish Catholics against the Orthodox Slavs. The specific examples Skarga gave (the *pericope de adultera,* the final chapter of Mark, the Greek "addition" to the Lord's Prayer) had become by then part of the standard Catholic argument against Protestant adherence to Greek authorities.[34]

Other than these two passage from *Thrēnos,* we find in Smotryc′kyj's work only the implications of a program informed by submission to Greek (both texts and language) as the highest authority. Smotryc′kyj offered on several occasions a trinity of sacred languages: Greek,

Slavonic, and Latin. It is probably not by chance that Greek always appeared first. For example, *Thrēnos* was allegedly translated from Greek into Slavonic and from Slavonic into Polish.[35] The *Homiliary Gospel* of 1616 was translated from Greek to Slavonic to Ruthenian.[36] Schools in Rus' were to train their students in Greek, Latin, Slavonic, Polish, and Ruthenian.[37] Smotryc'kyj's grammar of Church Slavonic began with the assertion that Slavonic possessed grammaticality, like Greek and Latin:

> It will depend upon your dutiful zeal, diligent teachers, that the benefit of grammar, which, in the Greek and Latin languages, has been shown through experience itself to be clearly significant, be felt in the Slavonic language as well, and, in time, through a similar experience, be proved significant. For you who have studied the art of Greek or Latin grammar know what it brings to an understanding of the purity of the language, as well as of the correct and fine spelling, writing, and understanding of written works according to the properties of the languages. Every benefit that the grammars of the above-mentioned languages commonly bring, the Slavonic grammar is surely capable of bringing in its Slavonic language.[38]

But to what extent did this reverence for Greek make itself felt beyond the programmatic level? I have already pointed to the fictive motivation of Smotryc'kyj's defense of Greek in *Thrēnos*. A quick examination of Smotryc'kyj's schooling or of his library is enough to convince anyone that Latin stood supreme in his learning at the practical level.

Still, there are indications of the practical importance of Greek authorities in Smotryc'kyj's critical use of Scripture. I stated above that Smotryc'kyj's use of Polish Catholic versions throughout his career might have required some explanation on the Orthodox side (were it not for the fact that there was no Polish Orthodox version available), but would have raised no eyebrows among his later Uniate and Catholic masters. That is, it would have caused no surprise, were it not for the fact that he did not cite his sources verbatim: he "corrected" his Polish sources according to some version of the Greek New Testament that belonged to the tradition of what is now known as the *textus receptus*.[39] (Support for these claims is given in appendix B2.) What is more, Smotryc'kyj's "critical use" extended beyond the New Testament to encompass all of Holy Writ. While Smotryc'kyj may have borrowed at some points from the heterodox in articulating his adherence to Greek authorities, he differed from the heterodox in that he made Greek Scripture—here the Septuagint—the basis not only for his correction of citations from the New Testament, where it was the "original language," but also in the Old Testament, where it was a translation. (See appendix B3.) This may offer further insight into Smotryc'kyj's Orthodox program for Polish sacred philology. Smotryc'kyj nowhere articulated his reasons for drawing on the Greek translation in the Old Testament. He once—as a Uniate—derided his opponent, Andrij Mužylovs'kyj, for his pretensions in citing Hebrew readings (probably drawn from Wujek's critical apparatus, even though Smotryc'kyj pointed to Calepinus), but this could be explained as motivated by the needs of the moment. Mužylovs'kyj, of course, drew on the testimony of the Hebrew text because it was in an "original language." Smotryc'kyj's response was simply *ad hominem:* someone like Mužylovs'kyj had no business pretending he could read Hebrew.[40] Smotryc'kyj never explicitly criticized the reliability of the Hebrew Old Testament, nor did he explicitly defend the reliability of the Septuagint.

That he drew on the Septuagint was not surprising: Greek Scripture was the foundation of the Greek faith. He had defended recourse to Greek before with a philological argument: it was the "original language." But original of what? Here we may find a clue. It was not only the original language of the New Testament; it was also the traditional language of old Greek interpreters, the Greek Fathers. Smotryc'kyj likely viewed the Septuagint and the Greek New Testament as a kind of Vulgate for the Eastern Church. Even in this "traditional" Orthodox stance, Smotryc'kyj could have found certain kinds of support in the programs of the Catholics and the Protestants. The Catholic notion of a text authoritative partially by virtue of a tradition of exegetical use within the Church was employed by Protestants such as Marcin Czechowic, who sought to reestablish the authority of the Greek New Testament in the face of the philological challenge mounted from such different corners as the Catholic establishment and the radical Antitrinitarian Szymon Budny: for Czechowic the Greek New Testament was "the text . . . long received and approved by all," thus a kind of Protestant Vulgate.[41] In similar fashion, for the Orthodox—and here Smotryc'kyj was no exception—the entire Greek Bible was an Orthodox Vulgate, defendable, like the Latin Vulgate, in "inspirational" or "philological" terms according to need.

But now, perhaps the more crucial question: were there any differences between Orthodox and Uniate programs and practices for Polish sacred philology? At the local, programmatic level, the Uniates were especially vulnerable to the charge that they had abandoned Greek (and Slavonic) for Latin. In this spirit, the Orthodox side claimed that the soon-to-be Uniate Smotryc'kyj had celebrated the Divine Liturgy in Slavonic when he was in the Holy Land not, as he had alleged, out of love for his nation, but because he wished to keep his intentions secret from his (non-Slavic speaking) companions, and because his Greek was weak, and he was afraid he might make a mistake.[42]

In fact, at least at the programmatic level, the Uniates may have been in something of a quandary here, caught between Rome, which was becoming, in response to the Protestants, more and more insistent on the sole authority of the Vulgate, and the Orthodox, who were quick to allege Uniate deviations from Greek traditions. In response to charges of Latinophilia, the Uniates would exaggerate their adherence to Slavonic;[43] on Greek they were less forthcoming.

Only the Orthodox Smotryc'kyj explicitly defended adherence to Greek authorities. According to the Uniate Smotryc'kyj, the decrees of the Council of Trent contained the authoritative explications of doctrine for the Ruthenian Church. While there was some room for disagreement on the Roman side, even the most "Grecophiliac" among Catholic sacred philologists (for example, Robert Bellarmine and Jakub Wujek) saw a very limited role for Greek Scripture in biblical exegesis and translation.

Bellarmine (and Wujek following him) delineated four areas where it was permissable for a Catholic exegete to consult the Hebrew and Greek texts. But even for them (and they represented the most "liberal" portion of Catholic opinion on this issue) there could be no question of the correction of the text of Holy Scripture according to the "original languages."[44] As a Uniate, then, should Smotryc'kyj have transferred allegiance from Greek to Latin texts? Should he have drawn only on the Wujek Bible of 1599 as his authority for Scripture in Polish? Probably this was one of those gray areas that had been left undefined by the articles of the Union. Smotryc'kyj himself, however, had publicly declared the decrees of the Council of Trent—and specifically those from the fourth session devoted to the authority and canon of Scripture—binding for all Orthodox.[45]

Thus, it was in at least partial contradiction of his own stated Uniate program that Smotryc'kyj's practice of correcting Polish versions according to Greek texts did not alter when he converted to the Uniate Church. Skarga had sought to compromise the Orthodox Smotryc'kyj by finding a borrowing from Czechowic; in similar fashion, Orthodox controversialists would now seek in the post-conversion period to find a predilection for the Vulgate in Smotryc'kyj's work.[46] But this was generally unfair. True, Smotryc'kyj would now draw on the authoritative Polish Jesuit versions, but he had started to do so well before his conversion; and he would continue—even as a Uniate—to subject them to a revision according to the Greek texts. (See appendix B4).

An exception to this general policy of textual emendation will help demonstrate the pattern I am seeking to delineate in Smotryc'kyj's behavior. In the Uniate *Exaethesis* of 1629, where Wujek's New Testament of 1593 served as the source for New Testament citations, Smotryc'kyj made no emendations among the twenty-nine passages I have examined. On the other hand, he made two emendations in this same work among the Old Testament verses where the Bible of 1599 remained the source. In the Uniate *Apology* of 1628, where Smotryc'kyj used the Bible of 1599 for quotations from both Testaments, I have found that ten of forty-three New Testament passages had been corrected. Once again, two emended passages appeared among the Old Testament citations.

Smotryc'kyj's respect for the authority of the Greek text caused him to treat passages from the Bible of 1599 more critically, while giving a sort of approbation to the New Testament of 1593. What we know of the genesis of both versions fits this picture well. Wujek had been criticized by his censors for giving too much attention to the Greek text in his translation at the expense of the Vulgate.[47] As the title page of his work indicated, Latin and Greek had been placed at an almost equal level. Perhaps in an effort to quiet his critics, Wujek was careful to state that he did indeed accord highest authority to the Vulgate (the Louvain version, since the fate of the *Vulgata Sixtina* had not yet been decided):

> So that you have here, dear Reader, the entire New Testament in Polish, simultaneously translated from the Greek and from the Latin, such that at one glance you will see immediately where there is something different, or more, or less, in the Greek than in the Latin. This is the only difference, however: that the Latin, as the more

> reliable, we place in the text itself; but the Greek, wherever it differs somewhat from the Latin, we signify in the margin.[48]

In spite of these assurances of good faith, Wujek continued to draw criticism, especially from Father Stanisław Grodzicki, for straying too far from the Vulgate. Grodzicki became a member of the committee that edited Wujek's translation of the entire Bible, published in 1599 after the translator's death. As the title page of the new edition indicated, the editors had restored the Vulgate to a position of absolute authority. In their concluding remarks the editors specifically criticized Wujek for relying too heavily on the Greek text:

> For in the first edition, in a few matters, the Greek text was followed, for the sake of those who desired this. Since this has now all been rejected, you have here in its pure form the Latin text as it is.[49]

The result was an authoritative Polish Catholic translation based on the by now officially approved Clementine Vulgate.

Thus by favoring the Wujek New Testament of 1593 over the Bible of 1599, that is, by leaving the former uncorrected and by subjecting the latter to correction according to the Greek text, Smotryc'kyj was continuing—even as a Uniate—to demonstrate a practical allegiance to Greek authority. Recall that in *Thrēnos* Smotryc'kyj had explicitly defended the reliability of Greek texts over Latin in order to reject the fire of Purgatory. In practice, he continued to favor Greek texts, even after he had acknowledged the acceptability of Roman doctrine on this issue. And on one occasion as a Uniate he even pointed out the fact that his argument (this time, nota bene, in favor of Purgatory) was supported by the Greek reading rather than the Latin (see appendix B5). Adherence to Greek seems to have been more than just programmatic for Smotryc'kyj, since he so consistently corrected his Polish models (and not just—also his Church Slavonic texts; see appendix B6) according to that text, even after his conversion. But it was also connected with programmatic issues. The Uniate Smotryc'kyj was always in the more delicate position since he needed to prove his "Orthodoxy" to the Orthodox without raising suspicions about his "Catholicity" with the Catholics. This may help to explain why he continued to adhere to Greek models but did not stress the point explicitly, even after he was attacked by the Orthodox.

By correcting the Vulgate readings in the authoritative Polish Catholic version of Scripture (Old Testament as well as New) according to Greek authorities, and by continuing to do so as a Uniate, Smotryc̆kyj made his strongest statement at the level of language and letters and took his greatest risk in deviating from the norm: here he had left the realm of secular rhetoric and had entered that of sacred philology in order to create an Orthodox Polish program and version of Scripture that were in partial opposition to those of Polish Protestants and Catholics.

What emerges from all this heterogeneous material is a pattern of "willfully deviant behavior." Smotryc̆k·j's linguistic practice, I argue, was part of a larger pattern of behavior that sought, within the "rules of the game" imposed by the competition with the better established "opponents" (i.e., Latin-Polish culture, the Roman Catholic religion, and the Polish-Lithuanian state), to find those areas of acceptable differentiation in which a kind of Orthodox Ruthenian "otherness" could enjoy a certain autonomous existence. In other words, some of the peculiarities in Smotryc̆kyj's usage were a reflection of, and—more importantly—part of the arsenal for, the confessional, cultural, and political competion with Polish Protestants and Catholics. In Smotryc̆kyj's Polish I find not only (if at all) the regionalisms of a non-native speaker, or only a symbol of subjugation, but also the ultimately unsuccessful attempt to "co-opt" the language of a dominant culture for the goals of the subordinate. And not entirely unsuccessful, at that. Smotryc̆kyj won a kind of unacknowledged, posthumous victory by gaining M. Samuel Bogumił Linde as one of his more influential readers. How many times does Linde cite Smotryc̆kyj as the sole witness for an unusual word or usage! In this manner some of Smotryc̆kyj's conscious Orthodoxisms made their way into the standard nineteenth-century lexicographic authority for the Polish language.

CHAPTER 12

Fides Meletiana

 In an open letter to Patriarch Cyril Lukaris published as an appendix to his *Paraenesis* of 1629, Smotryc'kyj asked: "in all the above-named articles [of faith], are we in agreement with the Romans or the Protestants, or do we adhere to and confess some third, middle thing."[1] The question was, of course, not entirely in good faith; by offering Lukaris these three choices on these particular articles of faith (that is, those that had been defined by the various Protestant confessions and by the Council of Trent[2]), Smotryc'kyj was giving the patriarch a chance to describe himself to all the world either as a Catholic, a "heretic" (i.e., a Protestant), or a "schismatic" (i.e., an Orthodox). Or at least this was how Smotryc'kyj's new Roman masters would represent the issue: *Propaganda Fide* had been seeking to portray Lukaris to the Christian world as a crypto-Calvinist for some time, and Smotryc'kyj's letter was received in Rome with great gratitude, as a contribution to the general campaign.[3]

But I also suspect strongly that Smotryc'kyj's question was not entirely in bad faith either. A "totalizing" biography, one that seeks one main question in all of Smotryc'kyj's life, could focus on his various attempts to discover "what do we, Rus', believe?" *Thrēnos* (Smotryc'kyj's only positive statement about the "Ruthenian" faith) was in its entirety an answer to those who "err in ignorance" about what Rus' believed.[4] At the end of *Thrēnos,* Smotryc'kyj published a sort of catechism of the "Ruthenian" faith. And he began in 1621, "having decided to reject the lamentatious errors and heresies," to write a new *Catechism of the Holy Eastern Church,* with which he set off for the East in 1623 in order to have the work censored by Lukaris (Smotryc'kyj 1628a, 105–107/576–77). This search for doctrinal authority was in the background of all his activities as a Uniate.

What did Rus' believe? If we examine the discussion of this question as it was conducted in the public domain, we will see that both sides (and thus, both Smotryc'kyjs) tended to phrase their answer in these terms: "Rus′ believes what it (that is, "we") have always believed." Here the definition of faith was almost always expressed in exclusionary terms for the present and in inclusive terms for the past: "We believe as Rus′ has always believed. (Your side no longer holds these articles of faith, or offers this obedience, but it used to do so.)"

The individual article of faith was not the only, or perhaps even the most important thing: first came a decision to declare one's allegiance to a particular vision of the national Church, then the various arguments— cultural, political, and dogmatic—were manipulated in an effort to convince others to rally around a particular national banner. This is not to say that specific aspects of spiritual life—the calendar, the primacy of the pope, and the Eucharist, among the most important—could not arouse extremely emotional responses. And still, dogmatic arguments were often mustered to prove not the dogmatic point itself, but to defend something much more general: a multi-faceted vision of national identity. This type of "national consciousness" was defined to a great extent in negative terms, by defining oneself in terms of not being another: "We are not you; we do not believe as you believe." The early Smotryc'kyj said, in effect, "the Orthodox are not Roman Catholics";[5] the later Smotryc'kyj said "the Orthodox are not Protestant."[6] But who were they?

If we begin with Smotryc'kyj's exposition of doctrine in *Thrēnos,* we note that here he seems to have been primarily concerned with defining and defending Orthodoxy in opposition to Roman Catholicism. Often what he presented as Orthodox faith followed "mainstream" Protestant thought—Lutheran and Calvinist—steering a passage between Roman Catholic positions on the one side and Anabaptist and Antitrinitarian positions on the other. Most of the time Smotryc'kyj acknowledged only the positions he was rejecting, and not those he silently emulated. The closest he came to announcing a sort of Protestant-Orthodox solidarity was in praising the Protestants for rejecting the primacy of the pope, but in lamenting the fact that they had not yet recognized the One Holy Eastern Church.[7]

The fundamental difference between the Eastern and the Western Churches in Smotryc'kyj's first representation of the matter boiled down to the Protestant-Catholic argument over the authority of Scripture. Again, I must repeat this point, Smotryc'kyj presented this not as a borrowing from those debates (he did not even mention them), but simply as a description of the main disagreement between the Greek and the Latin Churches. The Greek Church made Scripture its authority for faith;[8] it permitted the reading of Holy Writ by all; and it allotted interpretation to the "local Church." The Latin Church denied all this, reserving authority for its own interpretations and for the so-called "traditions."[9] And on many occasions in *Thrēnos,* Smotryc'kyj implicitly appropriated the principle of *sola Scriptura,* claiming that his argument was based on the "pure Word of God"[10] and not on the papal traditions,[11] the Roman "fables."[12]

In similar fashion, a rhetorical invocation of the old Orthodox Fathers couched in the "ubi sunt" topos ("Where now are those Fathers as of old, who would . . . ") sought new Orthodox teachers who would help the Eastern Church sail past the Scylla of those who say there was a time when Christ was not (the most immediate referent being local Antitrinitarians) and the Charybdis of those who placed traditions over Scripture (and everyone knew whom Smotryc'kyj meant here; see Smotryc'kyj 1610, 5^r/21).

This approach allowed Smotryc'kyj to offer "Orthodox" answers to all the questions that had been raised in the confessional debates of the sixteenth century between Reformers and Catholics, even in the absence of an authoritative Orthodox statement on the issue. Smotryc'kyj thus was himself speaking as that Orthodox authority, and he offered a short summary, a kind of Orthodox catechism at the end of *Thrēnos.*

In a sense, this was the last time Smotryc'kyj published (so far as we know) a positive statement about what Rus' believed. As a Uniate, he was later to argue that in his Orthodox works of 1621–1622 "the further I proceeded the less I attacked genuine dogmas, the more I dealt with the affairs of the moment that had come up suddenly at those times."[13] This was essentially correct: it would be difficult to recreate a positive statement of faith on the basis of those works devoted primarily to the question of the legality of the new Orthodox hierarchy. But Smotryc'kyj's reticence continued into and throughout the Uniate period as well.

A kind of doctrinal exposition is to be found in the Uniate works, but this exposition was likewise more negative than positive. It said, in short, Theophil Ortholog (Smotryc'kyj's pseudonym as author/ "translator" of *Thrēnos*) and all the other Ruthenian "new theologians"— Christopher Philalet, the Clerk of Ostroh, Zyzanij, etc.—were wrong in their doctrinal and historical statements, and they were wrong in two ways: both in their positive statements about the dogmas of the faith and in their negative statements that portrayed the Roman faith as illicit. The most positive of Smotryc'kyj's declarations in this period were of the sort "the Roman Church is not incorrect in its faith. (Therefore, what would it hurt you to be in union with it?)" Smotryc'kyj did not exactly (and certainly not authoritatively) say in these works what the Eastern Church believed: he said what it did not hold as incorrect. In so doing, of course, he contradicted many of the positive doctrinal statements he had offered in *Thrēnos.* Thus, in the view of the Uniate Smotryc'kyj the Eastern Church did not consider it incorrect to accept the so-called traditions alongside Scripture as authorities for faith and morals (see Smotryc'kyj 1628a, 23/535, 118/582); to confess that the Holy Spirit proceeded "also from the Father" (see Smotryc'kyj 1628a, 133–46/589–96); to administer the Eucharist under one species, and so on (see Smotryc'kyj 1628a, 167–75/606–610).

This new approach of the Uniate Smotryc'kyj led to (or was in part prompted by?) a reappraisal of the relationship between the Greeks and the Protestants. Now it was the Germans who had infected Greece (and very recently, at that—thus "Greek" authority was preserved) with the heresies Smotryc'kyj found there during his trip and which the Ruthenian new theologians had helped to propagate: "that the interpreter of Holy Scripture is the same Scripture itself. . . . That the traditions are unnecessary,"[14] and so forth.

What gets lost in all this is Smotryc'kyj's desire for—and apparent inability to produce—a positive statement on Ruthenian belief. This quest motivated his polemical defense for his trip to Constantinople: to find out from the supposed source (Lukaris, above all) what the Eastern Church believed. And on the margins of all Smotryc'kyj's actions was the Ruthenian catechism he had long seen as one of the primary desiderata for the spiritual good of the Ruthenian nation. He supposedly had begun work on it (or at least on a new version of "it": remember that *Thrēnos* had also contained a "catechism") around 1621. He had traveled with it to Constantinople in order to have Lukaris pass judgment on it. He had promised to submit it to censorship at the Kiev Council of August 1628. And in the meantime he had been working further on it and secretly submitting it to Ruc'kyj in order to receive his blessing. From the exchange of letters between Smotryc'kyj and Ruc'kyj, one gets the impression it was all but ready for print. Yet neither side—nor Smotryc'kyj himself, if we consider him at certain times a somewhat independent player—published the work, even though both sides clearly desired something like this.

What happened to this statement of the Ruthenian faith? Why did it cause Smotryc'kyj so much difficulty? Why did it take him so long to complete it? I suspect part of the reason was a real uncertainty, once the Western rules of the game had been accepted, as to what the Eastern Church believed. Although the Uniate Smotryc'kyj would once claim that the Council of Trent described the faith of the Universal Church, he could not simply have presented Bellarmine's *Great Catechism* as Orthodox doctrine. My impression is that part of Smotryc'kyj's dilemma here was that he operated with conflicting goals in mind: he saw a need for a catechism, as he often said, but he tried to find a solution acceptable both to Ruc'kyj, on the one hand, and to Borec'kyj and Mohyla, on the other hand; in short, he felt that someone (and if not he, then who?) needed to produce a positive statement on Ruthenian doctrine, but, for a number of reasons, he had long been leery of such positive statements. One of the reasons for his leeriness lay in his own way of viewing faith and the Church.

What did Meletij Smotryc'kyj believe? I have found one interesting detail that may help us come closer to the core of the man, so often hidden behind layers of deceit, conformity, and convention, or obscured by gaps in the stingy documentation. In this particular case, an interesting "near silence" on Smotryc'kyj's part might lead us out of the realm of *argumentum ex silentio* and to some fruitful avenues of speculation and some partial answers on what he actually believed.

I refer here to a major and—most importantly for my argument— controversial contemporary of Smotryc'kyj, Marcantonio de Dominis, the archbishop of Split (Spalato). Smotryc'kyj referred to him only once, but it is clear that he drew more substantial spiritual nourishment from him than this meager menu would suggest. Smotryc'kyj's penchant for writers whose books had found their way to the Index may have been one of the reasons for the bilateral caution of his relations with Rome after his conversion. Moreover, the fact that—in the face of probable negative reactions from his readers on both sides—he was not quite silent about this controversial writer may provide some clues to his beliefs.

Actually Smotryc'kyj's lone reference to the Spalatene archbishop came in his last published work, the *Exaethesis* of 1629. But the story began at least a decade earlier. In the polemic of the years 1620–1623 over the "illegal" restoration of the Orthodox hierarchy, the Uniates sought to discredit Smotryc'kyj as a leader of his side by revealing more and more about his alleged dealings with them in the years just before he took the habit. According to their version of events, around the year 1617[15] Smotryc'kyj was meeting regularly with Uniate leaders, was himself a convinced "unionizer," and had agreed to attempt to bring his side with him into union with Rome. And he would have done it, too, according to the Uniate complaints, had it not been for his general timorousness, his fear of scandal, his lust for fortune and power, his lack of real convictions, and so forth. These charges are so familiar in the Smotryc'kyj affair—and indeed in contemporary accounts of the lives of anyone who converted (or almost converted)—that one is tempted to consider them all nothing more than commonplaces. But one reason given by the Uniates had the allure of specificity:

> And at that time he was given the books from the conventicle of Marcantonio de Dominis, Archbishop of Split, the apostate. And having embraced them, he became what he is now. Such is the constancy of this man, that one book of one apostate—who introduced a new, unknown sect, one that had not existed previously, and which sect the English Kingdom (to which he had gone) did not wish to receive—so altered him in every regard that *ab equis descendit ad asinos* [from horses he descended to asses].[16]

Smotryc'kyj answered almost all the charges brought against him by admitting the substance, but by altering the power structure: it was he, Smotryc'kyj, who had wished, with the blessing of his superior at the Vilnius Brotherhood Monastery, Archimandrite Leontij Karpovyč, to discover what the Uniates were about and to see if there were a way— acceptable to the Orthodox—to bring about a reunification of all Rus' (see Smotryc'kyj 1621c, 104–106/451–52; Smotryc'kyj 1622a, 48ᵛ–49ʳ/ 511). But on de Dominis not a word.

Who was Marcantonio de Dominis?[17] What was the new sect he had invented? Could Meletij have been a secret "member" of it? Let us consider, by way of introduction to the problem, the "circumstantial evidence," the probable affinities between the two archbishops. First, there was the minor but not uninteresting issue of the Slavic connection: de Dominis, after all, had defended his Dalmatian parishioners' access to the Slavonic liturgy against Counter-Reformation linguistic policy.[18] Could this have been of interest to the author of the *Syntagma?* Second, there was the Jesuit past. De Dominis was an ex-Jesuit and a product of their schools, Smotryc'kyj an unfinished product, if we believe the contemporary account of his expulsion from Vilnius Academy (see Velykyj 1960, 298). Third, there was the habit of talking with all sides about a general Church union. De Dominis' world can be evoked by the capitals and leaders that appeared on his spiritual map, and between which he shuttled, either in person or through letters: Rome, Split, Venice, Constantinople, London (and back to Rome); Paolo Sarpi, Patriarch Cyril Lukaris of Constantinople, King James I of England, Pope Urban VIII. Smotryc'kyj's spiritual and physical pilgrimages took him hardly less far afield, and Lukaris and Barberini played important roles in them. Fourth, there were de Dominis' conversions, his switches of allegiance: with Venice in the pamphlet wars against Rome; with England against the Spanish Jesuit, Francisco Suárez; with Rome against the "schismatics." Could the writings of other confessional wafflers have been of interest to Smotryc'kyj?

Two autobiographical quotations from de Dominis may help to convey some of the intangibles, some of the reasons why we might wish to take seriously the Uniate allegations about the importance of the archbishop of Split for the archbishop of Polack:

> From the earliest years of my priesthood I had an almost innate desire to see the union of all Christ's Churches: I could not regard the separation of West from East, South from North, with equanimity, and I anxiously desired to discover the cause of such great and frequent schisms, and to see if it were possible to find out some way to bring all Christ's Churches to their true and ancient unity.[19]

And further:

> I laugh at those who, risking enormous practical difficulty and danger, cross over from one side to the other. . . . The only people who do it wisely are those who want to talk and write freely about the abuses, superfluities, and errors of one of the sides, where they may do so without hindrance.[20]

Smotryc'kyj did not cite these passages, but I suspect that he might have nodded at them in recognition. And, as I hope to show in a moment, it is more than likely that he had, in fact, read both of them.

Actually, de Dominis converted twice, once to the Church of England and then back again to the Church of Rome. Each time the event was presented to the world as great confessional theater: de Dominis' public abjuration of schism and affirmation of faith to the applause of his side of the moment and charges of greed, lust for power, and lack of real conviction on the other side. And much as they treated Smotryckyj, his side of the moment praised him in public, but had private doubts. Sir Dudley Carleton, Viscount of Dorchester and English legate in Venice, said of de Dominis: "I cannot say he is so much a Protestant as his writings shew he is not a Papist" (see Malcolm 1984, 61); this statement is typical of the perplexities felt by those who found de Dominis' allegiance hard to gauge. Catholic doubts continued after de Dominis' final return to Rome in 1623, and they would lead to his imprisonment by the newly reinvigorated Inquisition in Castel Sant'Angelo on 18 April 1624, during the first year of the papacy of Urban VIII. One of the reasons given for his imprisonment was that he was once again propounding his peculiarly inclusive view of the Universal Church, denying the power of the Council of Trent to determine articles of faith (see Malcolm 1984, 78). In any event, he died there an unrepentant heretic—"of natural causes," as the Catholic sources insisted—on 9 September 1624; but even this did not save him from trial for heresy. In one of the great spectacles of the Catholic Reform, de Dominis was tried—*praesente cadavere*—in the Church of Santa Maria sopra Minerva before the Supreme Tribunal of the Inquisition, declared a heretic, his books and bodily remains burned on 21 December 1624 at Campo dei Fiori, and his ashes thrown into the Tiber.

One could easily understand why Smotryckyj—both Orthodox and Uniate—would avoid using this name too much in public. The Uniate charges thus become all the more intriguing: had Smotryckyj been under the spell of de Dominis' unusually inclusive vision of a Universal Church in 1617, and had he been shaping his talks with the Uniates (or—equally interesting—also with the Orthodox?) in terms borrowed from the Dalmatian archbishop?

So far I have offered an allegation and some circumstantial evidence. Was there any specific subject of suspicion that might lead us from the domain of slander into that of direct, provable influence of de Dominis upon Smotryckyj?

My suspicions first led me to the following passage from Smotryckyj's Orthodox *Defense of the Verification* of 1621, where he had offered an ecumenical view of the Church:

> Is not the Church of God the name of the Christian and Catholic Church? This you cannot deny. But His Majesty the King, Our

Gracious Lord, in a universal given to Patriarch Jeremiah (whom we
have mentioned here) calls our Ruthenian Churches in the obedience
of the patriarch, Churches of God. Why do you wonder then that in the
privilege which he gave us, he sees fit to call us people of the Christian
Catholic religion? For if so, you say, he would have been denying that
he himself is of the Catholic faith. You are mistaken Mr. *Redargutor*
[i.e., Metropolitan Ruc'kyj, author of *Twofold Guilt*, which was the
refutation of Smotryc'kyj's *Verification of Innocence*]. I would say
that His Majesty the King is better able to define what the One Holy
Catholic and Apostolic Church is than you are. But I do not dare to
compare your stupidity to such a high intellect. His Majesty the King
is pleased to know that both our sides, the Eastern particular Church
and the Western, are contained in the Holy Catholic Church, which is
one in its reins, in which the particular Churches were conceived and
to which both have the same right. And since they are united by the
unity of mutual love, both sides beg the Lord God that He paternally
remove and eliminate what separates them, that is, whatever has come
between them as a difference *non per defectum* [not by defect], but *per
excessum* [by excess]. And since, as they say, *defectus fide non utitur,
excessu[s] fide abutitur,* therefore His Majesty the King finds no
defect in our Holy Greek faith, nor in his own Roman faith. Whereby,
when he is pleased to call us people of the Greek Catholic Christian
religion, he does not deny himself the same Catholic Christian title.
Therefore the Refuter is much mistaken in arguing the opposite, not
wishing to know that *neque in excessu, neque in defectu* [neither in
excess or in defect] (if he can also say this of his own Church) has the
Holy Eastern Church left the Catholic Church.[21]

Two main, interrelated points are of importance in this passage. First,
this was an inclusive definition of faith that refused to exclude from the
Church anyone who believed the minimum (that is, who has no "defect"),
and that looked with tolerance upon the "excesses" in faith that might
differ somewhat among individuals or groups of individuals (e.g., views
on transubstantiation, the procession of the Holy Spirit, leavened or
unleavened bread, communion under one or two species, the primacy of
the bishop of Rome, the number of the sacraments, and other such
"indifferent" matters). Second, this was a view of a Universal Church
that included all the "particular" Churches that had no "defect," even if
they differed somewhat in their "excesses" of faith. This was the general
sense of Smotryc'kyj's somewhat obscure argument cited above. But
more importantly, as I hope to demonstrate in a moment, it was the core
definition of de Dominis' monumental chief work, *De Republica
Ecclesiastica* (London-Hanover, 1617–1622).

As far as I have been able to determine on the basis of the subject
indices and some not entirely random searching, de Dominis first

formulated his definition of orthodoxy and catholicity in his defense of the Church of England against the Spanish Jesuit Francisco Suárez which he published following Book VI of the *De Republica Ecclesiastica.* Part 2 of the *De Republica Ecclesiastica,* which included Books V and VI, along with the answer to Suárez, appeared in London and in Frankfurt in 1620, early enough—although not by much—for Smotryćkyj to have drawn on it in 1621. In the passage that interests me here, de Dominis referred ahead to Book VII, which appeared only in 1622. Book VII was devoted in part to the question of the schism between East and West, and as such would certainly have interested Meletij (and I know that he had read it by 1629); although it made broad use of this definition of correct faith that centered on "defects" and "excesses," it could not have been Smotryćkyj's source in 1621.[22]

What is most important to me here is the nature of the arguments both de Dominis and Smotryćkyj made. How did de Dominis defend the Church of England? A man who started with an *exclusive* definition of faith would have said "The Church of England is correct in what it believes," and he would likely have gone on to add "And the Church of Rome is wrong." De Dominis, whose definition was unusually *inclusive,* said simply "The Church of England is not wrong in what it believes, and for that matter," he would continue on many occasions, "neither is the Church of Rome, nor are the Lutherans, or the Calvinists, or the Greeks." In fact, among the Christian confessions de Dominis would exclude very few, primarily the Puritans and the "Arians," new and old.

A few passages from de Dominis may help to convey the flavor of his thought and argumentation:

> For faith is believing everything that one must believe, whereas infidelity is to believe none of those things. But heresy is to believe some of the things one must believe, but to deny others or not to believe them, or to disbelieve them, whether they be positive or negative. To believe all of them, however, and something in addition, but which, nonetheless is not set forth by God to be believed, even were it false, and were it believed as true and as a thing of faith, I do not consider to comprise in itself either infidelity or heresy, but rather an error, unless, as I said, this bring with it a rejection of the value of some truth revealed by God. And in consequence, to reject, and not to believe as divine faith, those additions that God has not revealed for us to believe, but which men have added, even if they be otherwise true, and not false, does no detriment to true faith, nor does it comprise heresy, nor is there a sin from this, so long as the thing, as it were, not be believed as an article of faith.[23]

> Let us adhere, nonetheless, to the distinction already given: that Catholic faith can suffer detriment either in defect or in excess. Through defect it is truly either destroyed or diminished; through excess, it is not destroyed, rather it is corrupted and disfigured.[24]

> Here I wish again to cut short superfluous disputations, and I offer another most common and familiar distinction: it is one thing to speak of the Universal Church, another of the particular Churches. . . . Moreover, I understand that Church to be Universal which embraces absolutely all the particular Churches, none excepted, nay rather all the faithful, no one excepted.[25]

And the examples could easily be multiplied.

Neither side in the Ruthenian debates can have been completely satisfied with this definition of orthodoxy and catholicity (regardless of the fact that Smotryc'kyj tried to pass it off as common knowledge, indeed proverbial ["iako mowią"], and as the personal belief of that "high intellect," the Vasa King). Probably it displeased his Orthodox coreligionists.[26] Certainly the Uniate response was negative; it would have been anyway, but one of the central reasons the author of *Examination of the Defense* (Vilnius, 1621) disagreed with Smotryc'kyj can be found in the conflict between inclusive and exclusive definitions of correct faith:

> And he [i.e., the author of *Defense of the Verification,* i.e., Smotryc'kyj] gave us his *axiomata* [axioms] as if *ex communi sensu Theologorum* [from the common understanding of theologians]: *Defectus fide non utitur, Excessus fide abutitur.* Both the *axiomata* and the *distinctio fidei* [definition of faith] are new and unheared of amongst theologians. And they were invented by a new theologian and an old grammarian.[27]

According to the author of the *Examination,* both the extremes of excess and defect should be avoided since "virtue is always contained in the mean."[28] Thus the Uniate response not only rejected the terms of Smotryc'kyj's argument, but it also rejected its status as "common knowledge," characterizing it as the unhappy invention of the author of the *Syntagma* (this was a way of "respecting" the fiction of anonymity while showing the other side that the ploy had not worked), who ought to have had the sense not to venture from the realm of grammar into that of theology. (It is worth noting that the Uniates seemed unaware of de Dominis' influence here; perhaps they had not yet read Part 2 of the *De Republica Ecclesiastica.*)

But Smotryc'kyj stuck by his definition the next year in *Elenchus* (42ᵛ–43ʳ/505), and he added new examples in its defense. Interesting in this regard is the fact that he attributed "defects," and thus heresies, to Nestorius, Sabellius, Arius, and Euthyches (see Smotryc'kyj 1622a, 44/ 506), two of whom were charged with precisely these transgressions by de Dominis in the context of that first passage I cited from his response to Suárez.[29]

In its *Antelenchus* of 1622, the Uniate side devoted, in turn, an entire chapter to the question: "Does an Excess in Faith Damn [Souls]?" Here again, the Uniates rejected the definition of correct faith given by Smotryc'kyj (and ultimately by de Dominis), stressing that correct faith meant to believe each and every thing revealed by God, neither more nor less. If God revealed one hundred things, then both he who believed ninety-nine of them, and he who believed all of them plus some new thing of his own invention, sinned against the faith.[30] Or to rephrase this objection in Spalatene-Meletian terms: "our 'excesses' are *de fide;* your 'excesses' are actually 'defects'."

As late as 1624, in a report to Rome dated after 6 May of that year, the Uniate authorities wrote that "the pseudo-bishop of Polack [i.e., Smotryc'kyj] constantly reads and recites well-nigh from memory" the works of de Dominis.[31]

I have little doubt that de Dominis provided Smotryc'kyj with the crucial definition of faith and Church and with one line of argumentation with which he sought to defend the newly consecrated Orthodox hierarchy throughout the pamphlet wars of 1621–1622. But the nagging question remains: did he believe it? Such a manner of reasoning was ideally suited to defending a politically weaker Church against a politically dominant Church, especially in the Polish-Lithuanian Commonwealth, where Smotryc'kyj could point out that this sort of mutual confessional toleration was supposed to be the foundation of the political federation.

Perhaps I will be closer to an answer to this question if I can show that de Dominis was in Smotryc'kyj's spiritual baggage when he made his way across the great confessional divide. The lone overt reference to de Dominis in Smotryc'kyj's work came in his last published pamphlet, the *Exaethesis* of 1629. In that tract Smotryc'kyj responded to Andrij Mužylovs'kyj's *Antidotum* of 1628 that had been written, in turn, against Smotryc'kyj's own *Apology* of 1628. At one point, in answering his opponent's arguments on the procession of the Holy Spirit, Smotryc'kyj exclaimed: "you sucked all that out of the Spalatene; swallow it together with him."[32] And he wrote in the margin: "In proving this absurdity, the schismatic Antidotist drew upon the schismatic Spalatene."[33] Hardly positive language about the Dalmatian heretic, it is true, but one could not really expect otherwise from the recent convert who was being watched so carefully by his new brethren; and, besides, there were interesting extenuating circumstances that we should note.

First, Mužylovs'kyj had made no mention of de Dominis. This is important. At the very least, we can say that Smotryc'kyj publicly betrayed a familiarity with the arch-heretic when, especially in the first few years after his public conversion, he might just as well have kept silent about the man to whom the Uniates had sought to link him some seven years earlier, and who had become much more dangerous to mention in the interim.

Second, this material on the *Filioque,* plus other arguments Smotryc'kyj made immediately thereafter, are from Book VII of the *De Republica Ecclesiastica,* which had appeared in print only in 1622. At the very least, this shows that Smotryc'kyj continued to read de Dominis. In fact, we begin to get the impression Smotryc'kyj read every installment of de Dominis "hot off the presses." In any case, his only overt reference to de Dominis shows that he was still reading him after the pamphlet wars of 1621–1622, perhaps even after the posthumous heresy trial of 1624 and after his own conversion to the Uniate Church.

But most important is the fact that, after a fairly weak jab at de Dominis, Smotryc'kyj went on to enlist his authority against Mužylovs'kyj. This, of course, was standard fare: you always sought to turn your opponent's authority against him. But Mužylovs'kyj had not put de Dominis forward as an authority; he had not even mentioned him. And Smotryc'kyj used here exactly the argument he (and de Dominis) had made in 1621: the Roman Church was not heretical, not necessarily because it was "correct," but because it was "not wrong"; because it had no "defects," only what, according to Smotryc'kyj, de Dominis called "excesses." This is the argument that Smotryc'kyj's Uniate opponents had rejected in 1621–1622.

But did Smotryc'kyj realize that he was drawing upon the work of a convicted heretic? I am nearly certain that he did. Smotryc'kyj seems to have been an eager reader of de Dominis over the ten years preceding 1629, and all of Europe was informed periodically (and in timely fashion), in Latin and in vernaculars, of the archbishop's sensational confessional journey. First, upon his arrival in England, there was his famous *Profectionis Consilium;*[34] then, with his return to Rome in 1623, there were two more apologies for his latest switch in allegiance.[35] The final chapter in his life was made into a public spectacle in Rome, and it was reported to the entire Latin-speaking world by a Pole. Father Abraham Bzowski (Bzovius) was the continuator of Cardinal Baronio's *Annales,* and he had included an account of de Dominis' posthumous adventure in vol. XVIII, which appeared in Cologne in 1627. Writing in 1629, Smotryc'kyj must have known he was citing Europe's most infamous heretic of recent memory.

Still, he called him "the Spalatene schismatic." This is not an insignificant detail. These were not general terms of disapproval and no one—least of all Meletij Smotryc'kyj—would confuse a schismatic with a heretic. In a fit of frustration you might ascend the ladder of terms of abuse until you got your opponent's attention: "thou schismatic, heretic, infidel, Jew, Turk, Anabaptist," etc. But did anyone ever descend the scale? We might quibble over the order of the terms at the top, but the bottom was fixed.[36] From the point of view of the Roman Church, de Dominis had died a heretic—no doubt about that.

Revealing this kind of familiarity with banned books and banned authors (especially one who had been burned by the Inquisition so recently—and with such ceremony) was no small matter. Smotryc'kyj must have known that the reading of banned books could bring him under "suspicion of heresy" from the Roman side. (And de Dominis was not the only author of banned books on Smotryc'kyj's syllabus.) For Havryjil Kolenda (Uniate archbishop of Polack from 1655 to 1674 and metropolitan of Kiev from 1665 to 1674) to receive permission to read "heretical" and other banned books—in order to refute them—the decision of a commission of five cardinals was required; and after his death, his books were burned (see Isaievych 1981, 128).

According to Ruc'kyj, Smotryc'kyj spent three whole days in the fall of 1633, shortly before his death, secluded in his cell with the caretaker (*сторожъ*), who carried no wood for fire to other rooms during that period, but instead aided the archbishop in burning the heretical and schismatic writings (including his own?) that were in his possession; Smotryc'kyj paid him ten *zloty*s for his efforts.[37] (Ruc'kyj mentioned here that Smotryc'kyj had written a testament, which, unfortunately, we do not seem to possess.) On 18 February 1630, Ruc'kyj wrote to *Propaganda*

Fide, stating that he was sending to Rome a copy of a letter of 1618 from Cyril Lukaris to de Dominis (published in Legrand 1896, 329–40), which Lukaris had himself copied and sent, together with de Dominis' books (presumably Part 1 of the *De Republica Christiana*) to the Vilnius Orthodox Brotherhood.[38] Was it Lukaris who first introduced Smotryc'kyj to de Dominis? Perhaps Smotryc'kyj had retained the letter and given it to Ruc'kyj as part of his attempt to discredit Lukaris: in the same package, Ruc'kyj sent the letter to Lukaris of 30 October 1629 that Smotryc'kyj had forged in the name of the Orthodox Ruthenians (see above, pp. 154–55). *Propaganda Fide* was eager to use the fact that Lukaris had written to a convicted heretic in its campaign to discredit him, but it sought attestations of the authority of the letter.[39]

And yet the Uniate Smotryc'kyj even cited de Dominis' own words (giving the reference to book, chapter, and page) in "proving" that the pope could not be the Antichrist. And he concluded his argument against Mužylovs'kyj, saying "by this advice of your adviser [i.e., de Dominis], O Antidotist, you ought to have betaken yourself to Holy Unity, and ought not to have led yourself and others astray into the deeper abyss of the most abominable schism."[40]

What was this all about? I suspect that Smotryc'kyj still adhered to some degree—and perhaps this belief was something he "mentally reserved" in large part—to his old Spalatene way of viewing correct faith and the Universal Church. Of course, he was required, in a public work, to place de Dominis in a negative light; but calling him a schismatic—and that only in a marginal note—was being unusually gentle about it. (I might add that Smotryc'kyj was not too delicate in other contexts to call a heretic—for example, Patriarch Cyril Lukaris— a heretic.) And still he found it possible—against all reason—to employ the Spalatene definition of faith in his response to Mužylovs'kyj. His argument was this: de Dominis had "falsely" treated certain things—the bloodless sacrifice, the mercy seat, transubstantiation, the adoration of the Eucharist, the number of the sacraments set at seven, fast-days established by the Church, the veneration of images, the invocation of the saints, the veneration of the relics of the saints, and so on—as excesses to be tolerated, and so they should be tolerated, especially since the Eastern Church believed them, too.[41] This reasoning is remarkably confused. Disapproval—mild at that—was expressed in the adverb "falsely, hypocritically" ("obłudnie"), but then Smotryc'kyj proceeded to make his point as if he had ignored his own qualifier. Were these things "excesses" or were they not? Were they or were they not *de fide?* The confusion, the inherent contradiction of this argument, may reflect Smotryc'kyj's dilemma, caught between the inclusive definition of faith he mentally "reserved" and his need to prove the exclusivity of his "orthodoxy" to his new Catholic masters.

Perhaps de Dominis himself can offer us a clue to an understanding of Smotryc'kyj's ability to convert and argue the other side so fervently. First, recall de Dominis' statement that the only reason for converting was to be able to criticize the abuses of the other side in relative peace. There are some indications that this was a way of thinking Smotryc'kyj found congenial. Second, a crucial motivation for de Dominis' return to Rome was his horror of schism, together with his realization that the English secular and religious leaders did not share his ecumenical views: "The Protestants really cannot claim that they left the Roman Church justifiably because it was schismatical. It did not make a schism, it *suffered* a schism."[42] Smotryc'kyj would argue more or less along these same lines as a Uniate: if the Roman Church is not heretical (if it only insisted a bit too fervently on a few *excessus fidei,* he may have mentally reserved), then the Eastern Church could not separate itself from the Western, barring some heresy on the part of the Romans, without becoming schismatic:

> In the sundering of one Church from the Church, that particular Church suffers the sin and shame of schism, which, not having any proper reason, does not wish to unite with the other Church, even though it is summoned to do so. And there can be no other proper reason for this but heresy itself.[43]

Even here, in using the term "particular Church," Smotryc'kyj may have been thinking in Spalatene terms.

Consider the following passages, the one from de Dominis, the other from Smotryc'kyj, each explaining why he had reverted/converted to the Roman Church:

> I would to God, that they to whome folishly I fled, would acknowledg their most miserable spirituall estat, not only for heresies, but also for their schisme to be most desperate: from which schisme now I have shewed that they cannot be excused, because they haue vnlawfully separated themselues from the true Church of Christ, which is our Catholikè Roman Church. And this poynt affrighted me, because schismatiks are excluded from being the Children of God: for *Deum*

non habent patrem (saith S. Cyprian) *qui Ecclesiam (veram) non habent matrem* (cited according to de Dominis 1978, 74–75).

. . . since I know well that it is a more useful thing to be a lay person in the Catholic Church than an archbishop in the schismatic Church, I do not care about that in the least. For lay people in the Church of God are its *legitimi* [legitimate] sons and the natural heirs to the Kingdom of Heaven; but bishops in the schism are not *legitimi*, nor do they have the right of inheritance of the Kingdom of Heaven. *Non potest Deum habere Patrem qui Ecclesiam non habet Matrem* [He who does not have the Church as his Mother cannot have God as his Father] says St. Cyprian. . . . Therefore, knowing about this, I do not care in the least for what you offer me, satisfied as I am with the exaltation I receive from the fact that I am in the Church of God, and therefore I have the Church of Christ the Lord as Mother and God as Father, which I could not have had in the schism, even as an archbishop.[44]

The similarities here could, of course, be nothing more than shared conventions: the use of the citation from St. Cyprian may have been simply common fare under the structural conditions of this particular sort of polemic. And yet, there is every chance that Smotryc'kyj, the avid reader of the *De Republica Ecclesiastica,* had also read de Dominis' re(re)cantation. However this may be, the point here is that when Smotryc'kyj converted to the Uniate Church, he was still using a type of reasoning that he had in common with de Dominis. When each man found himself in Rome (the one physically, the other confessionally), they each motivated their discussion in the following terms: Church unity is the highest good; the Roman Church is not wrong, therefore it is not right to be separate from it.

Once again, this was an argument that could please neither side; it remained far too "inclusive." De Dominis—whether a direct borrowing from him or simply an affinity with him—helps explain why no one was ever quite certain what Smotryc'kyj believed or whether he could be trusted. As an Orthodox (except in *Thrēnos*) he argued, in essence, "we do not have a defect of faith, and any excesses we have are not heretical, so leave us—your fellow particular Church of the Universal Church—in peace" (see Smotryc'kyj 1621c, 77–78/437–38). The other side of this coin was that when his Uniate opponents of the pre-conversion period tried to discredit him by claiming "But you said we could be saved in our Roman Church," he could respond with something along the lines of "Of course I did, and so you can: leave us alone" (see Smotryc'kyj 1621c, 106/452). Conversely, as a Uniate he now said to his Orthodox opponents, in effect, "The Roman Church is not incorrect in its faith, so what would it hurt you to live in unity with it" (see Smotryc'kyj 1629a, 49–52/669–71)? As a Uniate, Smotryc'kyj's argument was always "Ortholog was wrong (as also Philalet, Zyzanij, etc.); the Romans are 'not wrong'."[45]

But if Smotryc'kyj was unequivocal in his later rejection of Ortholog, he was less clear in his attitude toward his career as Orthodox archbishop of Polack. His own conflicting statements about his conversion testify to this. At times he spoke of his heretical writings (in the plural) and of the fact that he, an archbishop of his Church, did not know in 1623 what he believed, and that this was what compelled him to go to Constantinople for answers to his questions.[46] This would make the divide correspond more or less to his official switch in allegiance. But on a few occasions— and with more risk, in my opinion, since this was guaranteed to raise suspicions with his new masters—Smotryc'kyj placed the break sometime after the writing of *Thrēnos* in the 1610s (see above, pp. 111–19). This biography could satisfy no one on either side. It said in effect "I was never entirely yours" (this directed to the Orthodox), "and I am now not entirely yours" (this directed to the Uniates). And the switch that occurred in this period—note well, Smotryc'kyj may have been struggling with these ideas a year or two before he first read de Dominis in 1617— was likely a switch from the exclusive definition of faith he had produced (and insisted upon) in *Thrēnos* to the inclusive definition of faith that was a part of his way of thinking for the rest of his life. On matters of Church and faith there were many fundamental points of agreement between Smotryc'kyj's writings of 1621–1622 and those of 1628–1629, and on occasion the archbishop himself said so.

Smotryc'kyj seems to have presented just this spritual biography to Aleksander Zasławski in 1627 when he was considering joining the side of the Uniates. Zasławski, whose definition of faith was probably exclusive, naturally desired to know why, if Smotryc'kyj had reached this turn in his life in the 1610s, he had not converted at that time but had gone on to write even more works against the Catholic Church?[47] This seems to have been one of the things that caused Zasławski to demand written proof of faith and allegiance from Smotryc'kyj. And yet, Smotryc'kyj repeated this statement of his *curriculum vitae* in public on a few occasions after Zasławski had voiced his concerns in private. Again, we must ask whether these statements, along with his use of de Dominis, contributed to Smotryc'kyj's reluctance to send Latin translations of his works to Rome? Did he strive to keep a certain distance from his new masters?

In characterizing the importance of de Dominis for Smotryc'kyj, it is important to bear in mind that *De Republica Ecclesiastica* was a grab bag of ideas for polemicists of various stripes, above all for those who were antipapal. Among the Orthodox alone, we know of its importance for Zaxarija Kopystens'kyj's *Palinodija* (see Petrov 1879, 350) and, if we believe Smotryc'kyj, for Andrij Mužylovs'kyj's *Antidotum*. And probably it was more widely known than this. But the crucial difference between Smotryc'kyj and the others—and this, I believe, lay at the heart of the archbishop of Polack—was that he drew not primarily (if at all) upon the antipapal arguments, but upon the inclusive definition of faith and Church that, in turn, lay at the heart of de Dominis.

In view of the fact that the post-conversion Smotryc'kyj exhibited a certain desire to conform, we will probably never be entirely certain what other ideas he may have borrowed from de Dominis. I suspect, nonetheless, that the Uniate Smotryc'kyj continued to think in Spalatene terms when he wrote of faith and Church. For example, let us ask ourselves what the Uniate Smotryc'kyj meant when he wrote of the "Universal Church" (*Cerkiew Powszechna* or *Kościół Powszechny*)? At one level, by Universal Church he meant simply Catholic Church. And here he could follow the usage of the Polish Jesuits who had, about a generation earlier, introduced the term *powszechny* as a literal translation of the word "Catholic" in order to reassert claims of universality or catholicity for the Roman Catholic Church (see Górski 1962, 258–60). Smotryc'kyj thus could use this term and expect (or hope?) that Polish Catholic authorities would assume he meant thereby exactly what they did: that the Universal Church and the Church of Rome as defined by the Council of Trent were coterminous. But the term was ambiguous, and this may not have been quite what Smotryc'kyj meant, had he felt free to state his views more directly. As a Uniate, Smotryc'kyj would continue to use the general conceptual framework of a Universal Church comprising several particular Churches that he first attributed to that "high intellect," King Sigismund III Vasa, but which he really had from de Dominis.[48] And there are some indications that certain aspects of Smotryc'kyj's thoughts about, and hopes for, a reform of the Universal Church were in line with those of de Dominis. Both men eventually would acknowledge the primacy of the pope, but both gave much attention to a structure of Church order that would, in practice, limit the pontiff's role. Smotryc'kyj, like de Dominis, seems to have thought in terms of a Universal Church composed of many local or particular Churches, where a national patriarch and councils of bishops would rule, and where the differences, the "excesses" of each national Church would be tolerated.[49] Thus the Uniate Smotryc'kyj's constant call for episcopal synods and for the foundation of a Ruthenian national Church under the jurisdiction of a local patriarch may also have been encouraged in part by the writings of the Spalatene heretic. Consequently, to come full circle, when Smotryc'kyj wrote of the "Universal Church," he may have had the Jesuits' *Kościół Powszechny* in mind, but he may also have been thinking of de Dominis' *Ecclesia Universalis*.

But Smotryc'kyj was not de Dominis. While neither man's inclusive vision extended beyond the Christian confessions, de Dominis excluded only the radical reformed groups; Smotryc'kyj—at least in his public pronouncements—excluded all of the reformed. Further, de Dominis had been intolerant in his insistence upon mutual toleration, and he had paid the price. Smotryc'kyj survived, surrounded by the suspicion and mistrust of his new colleagues, writing ever stronger defenses of Rome to his Orthodox compatriots and ever more obsequious letters to Rome and to Urban VIII. Smotryc'kyj's tolerance extended to his demands for toleration. In now asking his former coreligionists to tolerate the "excesses" of the Roman Church, he was, of course, well aware that this meant tolerating the Roman insistence that some of them—the primacy of the pope above all—were *de fide*.

De Dominis' thought has been characterized as "utopian" (see Cantimori 1960). This is probably a reasonable assessment. His program for Church union relied upon a considerable amount of flexibility and good will on all sides: the will to be united along with the will to tolerate, the will of the flock to follow the chief shepherd along with the pontiff's will to relinquish power to the local councils of bishops. There was quite a lot of hopeful thinking here. My impression is that Smotryc'kyj hoped for some of these same things, and sought on occasion to bring some of them about, but that he had also made himself more dependent upon the "real" world than had de Dominis, and that his career tells the story of continually frustrated hopes.

Smotryc'kyj's covert inclusivity when it came to matters of dogma may help to explain why he had so much difficulty producing a catechism and why his statements on doctrine after *Thrēnos* were all of the negative sort. Perhaps this was the change Smotryc'kyj hinted at in his later biographical statements and placed somewhere in the years 1615 to 1621: a "conversion" from an exclusive to an inclusive definition of faith, which brought with it a retreat from offering positive definitions of correct dogma to a reliance upon a new sort of *via negativa.*

CHAPTER 13

Tolerance and Toleration

On 16 February 1630, in one of his last surviving writings, Smotryc̆kyj once again addressed a letter—this time a rather lengthy one—to Pope Urban VIII. In this epistle he put forth a "new" plan for bringing Rus' into union with Rome: *"compelle intrare:* compel them to come in." This was the proof text (from Luke 14:23) for the licitness— even the necessity—of using force in the conversion of heretics and schismatics. Actually, Smotryc̆kyj had already mentioned this notion publicly in his open letter to the Vilnius Brotherhood, where he had pleaded with the remaining nobility of the Ruthenian nation to convert now voluntarily, while the nation could still retain some of its rights and privileges, before—as a nation of peasants—it be "justly" compelled to do so.[1] A crucial component in the plan Smotryc̆kyj presented to the pope was the union of ecclesiastical and secular power: Church authorities were to exert their influence upon Catholic magnates to impose the Union upon the Orthodox monasteries and churches on their lands.[2] In other words, the pope and the king were to do on a large scale what Ruc̆kyj and Zasławski had done to Smotryc̆kyj alone: demand conversion to the Uniate Church in exchange for the retention of their monasteries.

What had happened to the doctrinal indifferentism that characterized Smotryc̆kyj's views on correct faith? In the context of the polemics on the "illegal" restoration of the Orthodox hierarchy, Lew Sapieha had already rebuked Josafat Kuncevyc̆ in an open letter of 12 March 1622, saying that "in our Commonwealth" the Gospel saying "compel them to come in" had no validity as a proof text for the licitness of confessional compulsion.[3] Smotryc̆kyj himself seems not to have been entirely at home with this method of "persuasion." He had argued against it, of course, when he was on the politically weaker Orthodox side.[4] And in the same passage of his 1628 letter to the Vilnius Brotherhood, he cited St. Augustine first as authority for the notion that opponents should be converted by verbal persuasion and not by force.[5] But, according to

Smotryc'kyj, St. Augustine later changed his mind on this issue, having realized in his struggle with the Donatists that force was sometimes licit, according to the Scripture: "give opportunity to a wise man, and wisdom will be granted to him" (see Prov. 9:9).[6] Smotryc'kyj thus was thinking and writing on the subject of tolerance and the means of persuasion at the same time that he was threatening and urging the use of force. The tone of Smotryc'kyj's last major extant writing, the letter to the pontiff, may have troubled some of his contemporary coreligionists. Sigismund III—probably motivated more by a sense of what was practically feasible, and less by a sense of what was theologically licit—responded negatively to Smotryc'kyj's plan.[7] What had happened in Smotryc'kyj's life to cause him to acknowledge the licitness—even to espouse the use—of force in the conversion of opponents?

Perhaps a contributing factor can be found in the realm of conformity and dissent. Smotryc'kyj's letters to Rome were all motivated by the desire not to depart "a hair's breadth" from the wishes of Urban VIII (see above, p. 173). Perhaps in putting forward this plan Smotryc'kyj wished, in part, to prove his *bona fides* to his Roman superiors. And yet, this program for the forced conversion of Rus' was present not just in his letters to Rome, but also in his last Polish-language works, where he seems to have felt a lesser need to conform. When Smotryc'kyj wrote in his *Paraenesis* of 1629—somewhat mysteriously (or ominously?) in this immediate context—that the "pope would say 'let it be,' and his word would become deed," he must have had in mind the plan for forced reunification he would present to the pope a year and a half later.[8] This was, after all, exactly what he would say to the pope: "you, the head, say to your arms, which you have in this most illustrious Kingdom of Poland, some secular, some spiritual: 'Let there be Union in the Kingdom of Poland'— and sooner than said, the completed Union will be seen."[9] And if there was a sense of the carrot and the stick in Smotryc'kyj's address to the nation ("convert voluntarily, before it is too late"), in his letter to the pope it was all stick ("compel them to come in; you have the power to do so").[10]

Smotryc'kyj seems also to have been in earnest, at some level, about his call to "compel them to come in." Assuming that this element both belonged to the "real" Smotryc'kyj and was paradoxical in the context of other aspects of his "real" self that tended toward tolerance, ecumenicism, irenicism—I think both assumptions are justified—then how are we to "explain" this paradox? Whence this strain of intolerance in a man of tolerance (or indifference, depending upon your point of view) toward many doctrinal differences?

I suspect that Smotryc'kyj's intolerance grew, in part, out of a sense that, whereas he might allow himself privately a certain indifferentism, nonetheless, publicly—before the nation—he needed to give a positive, exclusive statement on dogma. Thus, it is conceivable that Smotryc'kyj's public intolerance increased together with his private doubts concerning correct doctrine. I also suspect, though, that there was a political element that contributed to his conversion and his recourse to compulsion. Smotryc'kyj's public intolerance grew as well out of a series of frustrated attempts to effect a reformation of the Ruthenian national Church, and thereby of the Ruthenian nation. His letter to the pope reflects, in my view, a last-ditch attempt at national salvation that had as many implications for the political realm as it did for that of doctrine. Therefore, I posit a certain amount of good faith in Smotryc'kyj's argument which made allegiance to the Uniate Church into the means, with the preservation of the political nation being the goal.

To understand this we should begin with the embattled concept of a "Ruthenian nation." One major disagreement has been over whether we can speak of national consciousness among the Ruthenians of this period, and if so, to what degree. Polish scholars—often citing Stanisław Orzechowski's well-known description of himself as *gente Ruthenus, natione Polonus*—have sought to focus on the creation of the "political Pole" and have minimalized the importance of expressions of Ruthenian allegiance that were in any way distinct from expressions of allegiance to the Polish-Lithuanian state.[11] Other approaches, including an important body of work by Frank E. Sysyn, have begun with the notion—correct, in my view—that the witnesses reflect something more than a sort of nostalgic search for Ruthenian roots on the part of new Polish citizens, and have sought to examine the ways in which a growing sense of Ruthenian identity was expressed in a variety of cultural artifacts.[12] I find this completely persuasive: Sysyn's studies do not seek to posit an anachronistic, full-blown nationalism, nor do they ignore the ways in which a sense of community was beginning to find expression.

I disagree with Sysyn, however, when he argues: "because the Orthodox took upon themselves the role of defenders of the national tradition, theirs is the dominant, if not the only, concept of nation" (1986, 398). We can argue about which side held the "better" concept of Ruthenian "nationhood"; still, it seems to me, there were certain internal and external constraints to the game being played by both the Uniate and Orthodox that required each side to offer a version of Ruthenian nationhood, but allowed neither to overemphasize Ruthenian separateness—or at least not without radically changing the rules of the game.

Two things are important here. First, the "internal constraints." If any given party—Uniate or Orthodox—was going to wage a successful campaign for Ruthenian hearts and minds, it was required to offer a vision of "national" allegiance that included linguistic, religious, and historical-political aspects; this fact reveals in itself the presence of some sort of "national consciousness." The "external constraints" worked in the opposite direction. The Union of Brest had brought with it the necessary conditions for the creation of the public image of a "good Ruthenian" and a "bad Ruthenian." Much of the polemical literature of the time sounds oddly like an argument between siblings, both of whom knew a parent was listening in, but both of whom—for polemical effect—had decided to pretend they were unware of this third, more powerful party to the dispute. Both sides tried to do everything possible to portray the other side as the bad boys who had disturbed their parent's repose: the one side (according to the other) by spending too much time with the Cossacks, the other (according to the first) by bringing court cases and by running to "father" to tell lies about "brother." In sum, this meant that, while neither side could afford not to offer a vision of Ruthenianness, neither side could afford to be too insistent on questions of local rights and limited autonomy—again, as long as they wished to play the game by the old rules, which included "concern for the good of the Commonwealth" as one of the ground rules.

Here, too, the sources programmatically lied. They do not necessarily tell us whether Smotryc'kyj or any one of his contemporaries wished to see the "Ruthenian nation" (*naród ruski*) attain the status of a full-fledged nation-state; but they do allow us to follow the process of the manipulation of aspects of a national vision in given contexts for specific purposes. And they tell us that, at least in their public pronouncements, both sides continued to play the game by the old rules during Smotryc'kyj's participation in the debate (1610–1633).

Leaving aside for the moment the question of the ways in which definitions of Ruthenian nationhood were manipulated for programmatic and polemical effects (and the related question of whether Smotryc'kyj's version of Ruthenian nationhood changed or evolved in any way), let us first examine the generally uncontroversial aspects of Smotryc'kyj's definition of it. At the cultural and confessional level, the Ruthenian nation was a subset of the "Slavonic nation." Smotryc'kyj expressed by the term "the Slavonic nation/nations" (*naród słowieński/narody słowieńskie*) the confessional and linguistic community that is implied in Riccardo Picchio's term *Slavia Orthodoxa*.[13] In referring to the "Slavonic nation," Smotryc'kyj emphasized the supranational community of Orthodox Christians who used the "the Slavonic language" (*język słowieński*) in the liturgy.[14] But Smotryc'kyj's definition also reflected the fact that the supranational community was beginning to break up into smaller communities: by employing the term "Slavonic nations," he could shift emphasis to the smaller, "national" units that made up the "Slavonic nation," all of which used the (Church) Slavonic language for liturgical purposes.[15] Smotryc'kyj wrote that when he was at Golgotha, he celebrated the Divine Liturgy in the "Slavonic language" so that he might beseech God for the "Ruthenian nation" and for "all those nations that praise, glorify, and worship their Creator in the Slavonic language" (whom he again identified as the "Slavonic nations").[16]

Within the supranational confessional and cultural structure of the "Slavonic nation," Smotryc'kyj distinguished several individual nations. Most importantly for the local discussions, Smotryc'kyj and his contemporaries drew a line between the terms "Ruthenian nation" and "Muscovite nation" (*naród moskiewski*). In fact, in Smotryc'kyj's usage the terms *ruski, руский, rosieyski, россійскій, Rus', Русь, Rossystwo*,[17] *Rossia, rossiacus,* and *ruthenus* all pertained only to the Ruthenian nation. They were to be considered distinct from the terms *moskiewski, Moskwa, Moschovia,* and so forth, all of which pertained to the "Muscovite nation." "There used to be riches in our Ruthenian nation," Smotryc'kyj wrote; "there are even now in the Muscovite nation. The Lord God, however, did not allow schools to be raised either here among us, or there in Muscovy."[18]

But Rus' was also a "member nation" of a supranational political community. First, we know from Smotryc'kyj's Latin letters that he thought of the Ruthenian nation as a *gens,* since he consistently used *naród ruski* and *gens Rossiaca* as corresponding terms.[19] I have not found any instances where Smotryc'kyj used the word *natio* to refer to the Ruthenians. Furthermore, he viewed the Ruthenian nation as a consituent part of the Polish-Lithuanian Commonwealth. Smotryc'kyj used the term *oyczyzna* (*patria*, "fatherland") in reference to the Commonwealth as a whole and not to the Ruthenian nation in particular.

Consider, for example, in the following passage from *Verification of Innocence*, where Smotryc'kyj drew a clear line between the notions of nation (*naród*) and fatherland (*oyczyzna*):

> Whom from our Ruthenian nation, by the living God, would that not hurt? Whom even of its fellow citizens will that not move to commiseration? In this regard, even all of the non-Christian sectarians who do not have any access to the enjoyment of the liberties of these domains are freer than are we, a free nation, as we said, an independent nation, a nation born in one fatherland with the two others, and which bears equally with them all its burdens, a nation genuinely faithful to God's anointed, the Kings, Their Gracious Lords, and which eagerly pours out its blood at their every command.[20]

Here and elsewhere the Ruthenian nation was treated as one of the three nations (Polish, Lithuanian, and Ruthenian) that together formed the Commonwealth.

How, then, was the Ruthenian nation distinguished from the other two? As Sysyn has noted (1981, 457), "to be a part of the Rus' people, one had to profess the Rus' faith." (But we should always remember that one could exploit this definition in different manners, depending upon the needs of the moment and the definition given to the term "Rus' faith.") Smotryc'kyj, too, followed the common code of the age of the Reformation and the Counter-Reformation, which emphasized religious identification as a major "national" characteristic. It was quite normal for Smotryc'kyj to refer to the "Catholic nation" (*naród katholicki*) or "Polish (i.e., Catholic) faith" (*wiara lacka*), to the "Ruthenian (i.e., Orthodox) religion" (*religia ruska*), or even to the "nobility of the Ruthenian religion" (*Russkiey Religiey Szlachta*). "In our Ruthenian Church, that is to say our Ruthenian nation . . . "[21]—this qualification is typical of many passages in which Smotryc'kyj made confessional allegiance the major component of national consciousness.

The range of meaning of the word *naród* and the close identification of the Ruthenian nation with the members of the "Ruthenian Church" can best be seen in Smotryc'kyj's various discussions of the place of the Ruthenian nation within the Polish-Lithuanian Commonwealth. Consider, first, the following passage from *Justification of Innocence:*

> For those above-mentioned honorable deeds and audacious acts of
> courage that the noble Ruthenian nation rendered to the Grand Dukes,
> their Lords, [and] Their Majesties the Kings of Poland, it has been
> given the freedom by them to sit in senatorial dignity equally with the
> two, Polish and Lithuanian, nations, to give counsel concerning the
> good of their states and of their own fatherland, and to enjoy all the
> dignities, prerogatives, the call to offices, freedoms, rights, and liberties
> of the Kingdom of Poland.[22]

In such cases the term "Polish nation" generally referred to the Roman
Catholic citizens of the Polish Crown, while "Lithuanian nation" referred
to the Roman Catholic citizens of the Grand Duchy. "Ruthenian nation"
then referred to the Orthodox citizens of the Commonwealth as a whole.

In other passages, Smotryc'kyj shifted emphasis from the political-
administrative autonomy of the "the Polish and Lithuanian nations"
(*narody polski y litewski*) in their functions as the Polish Crown and the
Grand Duchy of Lithuania to their confessional unity as a part of the
single "Catholic nation, both Polish and Lithuanian" (*naród Katholicki,
Polski y Litewski*). In this case the Commonwealth contained only two
nations—the Catholic nation formed by Poland and Lithuania, and the
Orthodox nation, which was Rus':

> What did the Ruthenian Church lose that it had these metropolitans
> consecrated not only not by the patriarch, but even against the will of
> the patriarchs, and that it obeyed one who was consecrated by the
> pope? What harm did it do to the Ruthenian nation, its Orthodox faith,
> and its rights and freedoms (to which you now pretend)? None at all.
> What harm can it do now when, for many highly proper and important
> reasons, it withdraws from that obedience and, following the model of
> the nations I have mentioned, creates for itself a separate archbishop
> or even a patriarch? Not only will this not harm it in the least, but it will
> bring with it great and salvatory benefits, to wit: it will unite it in faith
> and love with the Catholic nation, Polish and Lithuanian, and thereby
> cleanse it of the errors and heresies of your Zyzanijs.[23]

In another passage Smotryc'kyj demonstrated that he was well aware of
the possible range of meanings in the term *naród* by writing of "the
harmony and love of these two or three nations, i.e., of the Eastern and
Western Churches within the domains of our Fatherland."[24]

It is clear, moreover, that in many instances, especially in discussing
the "rights, freedoms, and liberties" that pertained to the Ruthenian
nation, Smotryc'kyj was referring only to that portion of the nation upon
which those rights could be bestowed, that is, the nobility.[25] Indeed,
many of the laudatory epithets that Smotryc'kyj used in referring to the

Ruthenian nation (for example, *cny, zacny, przezacny,* or *szlachetny*) called attention to its noble qualities. One of Smotryc'kyj's major concerns, as shown by his polemical works, was that the Ruthenian nation not lose its integrity or its honor.[26] According to Smotryc'kyj, one of the most deleterious effects of the discord within the Ruthenian nation was the loss of noble families to the Latin Church or to the various heterodox groups.[27]

Terms which, since the nineteenth century, have become identified with national units, such as *Litwa* ("Lithuania"), *Biała Ruś* ("Belarus"), and *Ukraina* ("Ukraine"), were used by Smotryc'kyj in a jurisdictional or geographic sense. Thus he was able to speak of members of the Ruthenian nation who resided in each of these areas. Consider, for example, his concern that the controversy over the restoration of the Orthodox hierarchy in 1620 not harm the reputation of the Ruthenian nation in "Lithuania" and "White Russia."[28]

Finally, all the nations I have mentioned so far—Poland, Lithuania, Rus', as well as the other "Slavonic" nations—could appear in lists of the nations of Europe.

These, then, were the general components of a definition of "Ruthenianness" to which both Smotryc'kyjs and, indeed, both sides— Uniate and Orthodox—adhered in their public debates. But there were several ways in which these definitions could be rendered controversial, in which they could be exploited in the public debate. First, by opposing a vision of a "Commonwealth of Three Nations" (a "Reczpospolita Trojga Narodów," as it were) to the dominant notion of a polity of two nations (the accepted Rzeczpospolita Obojga Narodów), both Uniate and Orthodox apologists had entered into an area of potential conflict with the Roman Catholic authorities. By insisting that Rus' had "voluntarily" united with Poland and Lithuania, Ruthenian controversialists were coming close to subverting the concept of the polity held by the other, more powerful "nations" with whom they had "freely" united. Second, definitions of Ruthenianness could also be employed as polemical tools within the internecine quarrels. Each side had identified a portion of this general definition to which it considered the other open to criticism, and that other side would then need to respond by emphasizing their own "strengths" on this issue. (Sometimes they also revealed a sense of guilt or vulnerability by focussing on the question at issue without a specific provocation). The Orthodox

Smotryc'kyj devoted much attention to representing his own side as that which adhered to the Pauline precept that "every soul be subject unto the higher powers" (Rom. 13:1), thus emphasizing the good standing of Rus' in the Polish-Lithuanian Commonwealth.[29] The Uniate side drew attention to its adherence to Slavic Orthodoxy, to its use of Slavonic authorities, thus emphasizing its membership in the "Slavonic nation."[30] Even the Catholic authorities had to play the game whenever they needed to "pacify Rus'" or guarantee the military services of the Cossacks.

The uncontroversial definitions of Ruthenian nationhood could be made controversial according to the needs of the moment. The definitions could be couched in inclusive terms, if the polemical strategy required at that particular point a vision of Rus' that included the other side ("Our common home: let us preserve it"—this sort of thing), or in exclusive terms, if that was more useful in making a particular argument ("We are the true Rus', and you are not: therefore, the rights, freedoms, and liberties guaranteed to Rus' belong to us alone"). Smotryc'kyj was a master at subtle switches—even within an argument of one paragraph—between inclusive and exclusive definitions of Church and nation. Problems in interpreting a *locus classicus* in Smotryc'kyj's work devoted to a definition of Ruthenianness can be solved in part if we bear in mind that the author has switched subtly for polemical effect in this passage (and in many others) between inclusive and exclusive definitions of Rus':

> If they are truly Rus', as they ought to be and must be (for whoever changes his faith does not immediately also degenerate from his blood; whoever from the Ruthenian nation becomes of the Roman faith does not become immediately a Spaniard or an Italian by birth; rather he remains a noble Ruthenian as before. For it is not the faith that makes a Ruthenian a Ruthenian, a Pole a Pole, or a Lithuanian a Lithuanian, but Ruthenian, Polish, and Lithuanian blood and birth); if, then, they are truly Rus', as they are (of which nation and blood there is, by the grace of Almighty God, no smaller number than from the other two member nations honored with the senatorial dignity at the side of God's anointed, the King our Gracious Lord. Most noble Ruthenian blood excels in these times in the spiritual and secular Lithuanian Senate; most noble Ruthenian blood has in these days entrusted to it the priceless jewels of the Lithuanian Commonwealth: the seal and the staff); if, then, they are truly Rus', that we say it for yet a third time, as they are, then, by God, with what heart can they bear such a hideous stain upon their nation which has always been faithful, pure, and never in any way suspect to Their Majesties the Kings of Poland and the Grand Dukes of Lithuania, Their Gracious Lords?

With what ears can they bear to hear this horrible shame that infects
unto ruin the health as well as the honor of its worthy nation?[31]

Here Smotryc'kyj used the concept of "blood" to refer to an "ethnic"
community (but only to the nobility—only to those to whom the concept
of "noble blood" applied) that was also a confessional community. Rus'
and Ruthenians were characterized, at least originally, by their Orthodoxy;
Spaniards and Italians, or Poles and Lithuanians, by their Catholicism.
Smotryc'kyj's appeal to ties of "blood" derived in this passage from the
fact that his addressees were noble converts from Ruthenian Orthodoxy
to the Roman Catholic or Uniate Churches. These converts he elsewhere
termed "apostates"—apostates obviously from the Orthodox Church
but also apostates from the Ruthenian nation.[32] Smotryc'kyj was appealing
to and trying to claim (or reclaim) for the Ruthenian nation such
illustrious "expatriots" as the Sapieha, Chodkiewicz, Tyszkiewicz,
Czartoryski, and Wiśniowiecki families. If we were to ask Smotryc'kyj
whether the noble families he included in his list in the first chapter of
Thrēnos were or were not a part of the nation, his answer would be that
it depended upon the needs that had been created by the public polemic
of the moment.

Given the external and internal constraints placed upon definitions of
Ruthenian nationality, and given the fact that most of our sources reflect
the manipulations of these "truths" for specific polemical goals, how are
we to corroborate or falsify claims often made in the scholarly literature
that Smotryc'kyj's conversion brought with it a fundamental switch in
his vision of national identity? One traditional view (held on both sides
of the divide) has it that the Orthodox Smotryc'kyj defended Helleno-
Slavonic-Ruthenian cultural values, Eastern Orthodoxy, and Ruthenian
national interests. The Uniate Smotryc'kyj, on the other hand, defended
Latin-Polish cultural values, Roman Catholicism, and the Polish-
Lithuanian status quo. If we were to ask Smotryc'kyj himself, we would
find that the Orthodox Smotryc'kyj adhered to Latin authorities,[33] was a
"Catholic" and a "Uniate," and was one of the more ardent Polish
patriots; and conversely, that the Uniate Smotryc'kyj adhered to Helleno-
Slavonic authorities,[34] was "Orthodox," and had a vision for Ruthenian
"autonomy." In each of these cases, Smotryc'kyj answers were motivated
in great measure by polemical strategy and can be seen as direct answers
to specific claims, allegations, objections to the contrary, which the
opposing side had made, would make, or might conceivably make.

Where, then, are Smotryc'kyj's "real" beliefs to be found? One indication lies behind the public arguments, in the common denominator between the two polemical postures: both Smotryc'kyjs adhered to a sense of Ruthenian otherness that informed their reasoning and provided each with a point of departure and a goal. The Orthodox Smotryc'kyj made a definition of Rus' distinctiveness into the point of departure for an argument that the nation had been accorded certain rights, freedoms, and liberties. Conversely, the Uniate Sn.otryc'kyj made preservation of that distinctiveness, and thereby of those rights, freedoms, and liberties, into a central reason for embracing the Union.

The Orthodox Smotryc'kyj emphasized the equality of the Polish, Lithuanian, and Ruthenian nations. In his representation of things, Rus' had "freely" united with Poland and Lithuania in much the same way Lithuania had freely united with Poland. Through its union with Poland and Lithuania—sometimes Smotryc'kyj implied "as a condition for uniting," other times he implied "as a result of uniting"—Rus' maintained or received (depending on your point of view) "rights, freedoms, and liberties" that set it equal with the other two "brother" nations: it bore an equal responsibility in the defense of the Commonwealth, and because of its past services in the defense of Ruthenian princes, Lithuanian grand dukes, and Polish kings, it now had the right to hold office in the Commonwealth and to deliberate concerning its good.[35] Part of this, of course, served the polemical purpose of the moment for the Orthodox Smotryc'kyj. But it seems to have been more than that. If Smotryc'kyj's only goal had been to represent Rus' to the authorities as an obedient citizenry, he could have found other ways to do so that placed less emphasis on Ruthenian autonomy.

The Uniate Smotryc'kyj's appeals to the "nation" were addressed to two major groups, the Church hierarchy and the nobility, and they were couched in terms of national preservation. For the Uniate Smotryc'kyj, this preservation would come from the concentration of power: spiritual power in the hands of the hierarchy, secular power in the hands of the nobility. The threat to the nation came then on two fronts: from the laity and lesser clergy that had upset the ecclesiastical order, and from the "rustification" of the nation, from the loss of nobility. With the loss of the noble class came, in Smotryc'kyj's view, the loss of the "rights, freedoms, and liberties" of the Ruthenian nation (which had been won by, and pertained to that class in particular).[36] This was, of course, a question of authority: who had the right or power to write on questions of dogma, and who had the right or power to determine the cultural and confessional authorities for the nation?

This concern for Ruthenian "otherness" appeared at all levels of Smotryc'kyj's work and throughout his career: in his "Orthodoxification" of the Polish language, in his concern that Rus' have its own collections of homilies, lives of saints, "spiritual exercises" (rather than continue to use Polish Catholic "classics," as both Orthodox and Uniates had done), in his search for a Ruthenian catechism (rather than accept Hosius or Bellarmine outright),[37] in his concern for a Rus' polity through maintenance of its gentry class.

One way in which Smotryc'kyj sought to preserve Ruthenian "otherness" within the Commonwealth was through a plan for an independent Ruthenian patriarchate. In some regards he seems almost to have identified the idea of Union with the idea of the new patriarchate. In the text of *Paraenesis,* Smotryc'kyj discussed what the establishment of an independent patriarchate would bring to Rus';[38] but in the margin at this point he wrote of the benefits that the *Union* would bring to Rus'.[39] Smotryc'kyj offered several models or precedences for his plan: the various autocephalous Orthodox Churches, beginning with that of Muscovy.[40] But his plan, in some of its formulations, went even beyond this: to transfer the see of Constantinople to Rus'. If it is true, Smotryc'kyj argued, that "Rome is where the pope is," then it would also become accepted that Constantinople is where the ecumenical patriarch is.[41] With or without Lukaris, Smotryc'kyj envisioned a leading role for the Ruthenian Church in a renovation of Eastern Christendom. Rus'—in words Smotryc'kyj attributed to Zasławski—was the only nation among the Eastern Churches in a position to take on this role, since it alone was both free (so long as it maintained its nobility) and learned. Muscovy was free, but ignorant. The rest were both in servitude and ignorant.[42]

There is a prevalent opinion that the idea of the independent Ruthenian patriarchate could only serve the goals of the Uniate and Roman Catholic side (see Ploxij 1989, 45–47). I am not certain that this was the case in the views held by the participants in the debates in the late sixteenth and early seventeenth century. I would suggest that the idea of the independent patriarchate was often attractive to those whose visions of the Commonwealth were, for whatever reason, "sixteenth-century," that is to say (by this time) somewhat outmoded. The patriarchate was sometimes seen as a means to preserving peace at "home" (and that meant in the Polish-Lithuanian Commonwealth) together with the "rights, freedoms, and liberties" of Rus′ in particular. But the plan depended on a certain amount of tolerance on the part of the authorities in the Commonwealth toward confessional differences, and (in the Uniate variant) tolerance on the part of the Orthodox toward communion with Rome.

Smotryc′kyj's argument as an Orthodox archbishop (that is, after he had rejected his "lamentatious errors and heresies") had been, in essence, that Rus′ tolerated Rome; all that was required for peace at home was that Rome tolerate Rus′. There was considerable wishful thinking here in both directions, and I suspect that the Orthodox Smotryc′kyj was required to moderate his toleration of Rome in order to please his constituency in Rus′. His Uniate career can be seen as a series of efforts to bring about a variant of the same vision. There is no reason to assume that Smotryc′kyj's goals were exactly party-line Uniate throughout this period, or that they did not change throughout this period (i.e., 1627–1633) in order to accommodate each succeeding defeat and to attempt to salvage some portion of his vision. When Smotryc′kyj wrote to Lukaris in 1627, begging him at the end to come to Rus′ to be the *restaurator* of the Ruthenian Church and the *restitutor* of the freedoms of the Ruthenian nation,[43] he made the usual argument: if you (we) do not do something quickly, the nation (i.e., its nobility) will disappear, swallowed up by the Uniates and the Roman Catholics.[44] (And actually, it was here in his letter to Lukaris, dated 21 August 1627, that Smotryc′kyj first used the phrase "compel them to come in": if Lukaris did not act quickly, it would be only to the common people—"and almost properly so"—that these words would be said.[45]) How are we to interpret this statement on the part of the covert Uniate that he feared the loss of his Church and nation to the Uniates and the Roman Catholics? If it had appeared only in the actual letter addressed to Lukaris, we might ascribe it to dissimulation alone: Smotryc′kyj was still playing Orthodox to the patriarch. But how Orthodox would any "real" Orthodox be likely to consider him, having read the contents of the rest of the letter? And besides, this was not just the version sent to Lukaris (which most likely was in Latin); this was the Polish adaptation published to the nation as an appendix to his open letter to the Vilnius Brotherhood, and published after his *Apology* had been anathematized by the hierarchy in Kiev. How are we to interpret this slip of the pen? Or was it no mistake?[46]

I take the statement at least partially at face value. In this period from 1627 (and probably earlier) to 1629, Smotryc'kyj's "real vision" of Uniate Orthodoxy and Orthodox Unity was *potentially* acceptable, but *practically* unacceptable—as more details became known—on both sides. He seems to have seen the Ruthenian patriarchate not only as a way to capture the good will of the Orthodox, but also as a way to co-opt the Uniate Church in Rus', to render it more "Orthodox." This would require a willingness on the part of the Orthodox to tolerate Rome, to acknowledge the primacy of the pope and the non-heretical status—"the orthodoxy"— of the beliefs of the Church of Rome, along with a willingness on the part of Rome to tolerate a certain degree of autonomy for the Church of Rus', to tolerate a view of Church order that foresaw a Universal Church comprising several "particular Churches" with a greater degree of authority concentrated in the local episcopal councils. But the will to tolerate such a vision, as Smotryc'kyj was to discover, was lacking on both sides. In my view, then, Smotryc'kyj's reasons for urging the creation of an independent patriarchate were not the same as those of the Uniates who seem (at least in their representations to Rome—but were they, too, dissimulating here?) to have been motivated by calculation: the patriarchate was for them an expediency to gain the Orthodox common people (see Krajcar 1964, 74).

The shape of Smotryc'kyj's program for national revival (survival?), some of the motivations for his move from tolerance to intolerance, and the cause of his ultimate failure can be sought in his attitude toward authority: it sufficed, in his view, to win the elite (secular and ecclesiastical) for any particular vision of the nation, the "people" would (as they should) follow. This seems to have been his *modus operandi* throughout his career. In 1617 and again in 1627, Smotryc'kyj was engaged in a highwire juggling act, attempting to bring the leaders of the two sides together through his powers of persuasion. And some of the leaders seem to have been willing to consider the plan; it was at least partially due to the pressures exerted by the flock that the shepherds of the Orthodox side had to retreat.

But the question remains: why was Smotryc'kyj doing this in 1627 with at least one foot planted in the Uniate camp? I suspect that Smotryc'kyj's considerations in this period on the nature of power may have held a clue. Smotryc'kyj's vision of a strong national Church within the Polish-Lithuanian Commonwealth, independent from Constantinople, with perhaps some degree of autonomy with regard to Rome, required a tolerance that was lacking on both sides. The only side with the power to compel "toleration" was the Polish Catholic side. When Smotryckyj cited (note well, in order to refute it) the "usual" Orthodox objection that it would be the Romans who were the schismatics, if it were not for their superior secular power, I suspect he had set up a straw man that—in his own view—had more flesh and blood than usual.[47] As long as we are schismatics to the Poles and Lithuanians, we will also be rebels and traitors;[48] and as the weaker party, it was Rus' who would ultimately lose the battle. (Or as Smotryckyj had pointed out at the doctrinal level: Rus' was engaged in an "unequal battle" with the Romans.[49]) All these arguments seem to have been formulated by a man who had been turning his thoughts not to dogma but to power, not to what was the truth but to who had the power to impose their vision of the truth. Therefore, Rus' must "freely" unite with Rome on the confessional level, as it had "freely" united with the Poles and Lithuanians as a polity: only in this manner could Rus' maintain its "otherness." Smotryckyj employed here the image of the political federation of the Polish-Lithuanian Commonwealth as a model for Church union for Rus':

> Let us take an example from the secular union of the Polish Crown and the Lithuanian Grand Duchy, and we will see what sort of creature a union is. The foundation of the union of these two domains is for both these domains to know one lord, to collaborate in counsel and in industry about them, and for each of them to enjoy its own proper rights, freedoms, and liberties. And the foundation of a spiritual union is to know one superior pastor of the Church of Christ the Lord, to collaborate with him in faith and love, and for each local Church to enjoy its customs, rights, ceremonies, and rites, as far as the Church order is concerned.[50]

This was, of course, part polemical ploy, but again—not only so. Smotryckyj's hierarchical view of his Church was in accord with his view of the nation: the one could not exist without the other. (And the premise of his argument was that even his Orthodox opponents of the moment would share his vision of the secular union.)[51]

Smotryckyj's first three Uniate works were those of a man of a certain optimism, but they were also suffused with a sense of urgency. He seems to have viewed this period as a "last chance" for his nation, and to have been confident of his power to persuade. In the *Apology,* at the Council of Kiev in August 1628, even in the *Protestation* and in the

Paraenesis, Smotryc'kyj was speaking to the nation from the middle ground of a covert Uniate, urging them to follow his program for national survival before—through the loss of the nobility—there was no nation left. The Council of Kiev was the first broader test (he had been "testing" throughout 1627 and 1628 in his meetings with Borec'kyj and Mohyla) and was the first major defeat to his program. It was immediately thereafter, in his *Paraenesis,* that Smotryc'kyj sketched for the nation the outlines of his "Plan B"—"compel them to come in."

After the autumn of 1628, Smotryc'kyj appeared to the nation as an overt Uniate: the Orthodox side had had time to declare him as such, and he had apparently made his public profession of faith to the satisfaction of the Uniate authorities. He was no longer in a position to go between the two sides. In the one—not particularly eloquent—testimony to Smotryc'kyj's participation in the abortive national Synod in L'viv (28 October 1629) we can perhaps see a man who had little hope of salvaging his former vision. He had now to acknowledge the divide between "we" and "you" and to place himself publicly on one side of that divide.[52] When the Orthodox side did not appear in L'viv, Smotryc'kyj saw his last chance to win through persuasion disappear.

It was at this point (16 February 1630), after all these defeats, that Smotryc'kyj acted on his earlier threat, writing to Urban VIII and urging him, in concert with King Sigismund III, to impose unity upon Rus'. In my view, this was an act of desperation. Smotryc'kyj saw this as the last chance to "save" his nation. It would have been better if his compatriots had freely chosen salvation (again, I emphasize: a salvation that was as much political as religious); but since they had not, it was necessary to impose salvation upon them while there was yet someone to save. Smotryc'kyj tended toward medicinal metaphors in these contexts (which must have made his readers wince):

> A doctor does not inflict violence when, with no small pain to the patient, he pulls on an arm or a leg that has become dislocated from the socket; the same thing will occur with us as well.[53]

> A harmful ulcer is sometimes cut out, sometimes burned out, and the patient must suffer this. And if anyone does not wish to suffer this, but rather prefers to die from this ulcer, he is bound by those who care for him, and against his will he is briefly afflicted so that through a short suffering, having become cured for the rest of his life, he might not suffer that pain any more.[54]

Smotryc'kyj might have summarized his spiritual journey on this topic since 1620 in this manner: Rus' does not tolerate Rome, and thus we are not tolerated; in order to ensure that Rus' be tolerated, it is necessary that the power impose tolerance upon us; in this manner we can preserve a Ruthenian political nation and, through the Ruthenian patriarchate, a certain distance from Rome. This is, of course, a simplification, and it pertained to only one aspect of Smotryc'kyj's thought, but it is a crucial aspect, in my view, for understanding his motivations.

This reasoning was paradoxical. But it is, in my opinion, a paradox that evokes something of Smotryc'kyj's nature. At this point, it may be worth noting that a leading European theoretician of the parodox of tolerance and power, Justus Lipsius, was also on Smotryc'kyj's reading list. This, of course, was nothing particularly unusual in itself. Lipsius had a far-reaching sphere of influence. There were many Polish Lipsians, why not a Ruthenian Lipsian?[55] What interests me here, however, is the Flemish scholar's attitude toward tolerance and power; perhaps as a type of response to issues that Smotryc'kyj also faced, it could help us to understand the archbishop's behavior. At the least, we will see that the type of paradoxical reasoning for which I have argued here was a possible response in this period.

In short, Lipsius converted even more frequently than de Dominis, seemingly with each change of academic appointment. In each institution—Lutheran Jena, Catholic Cologne, Calvinist Leiden, Catholic Louvain—Lipsius managed to convince his colleagues that, at a minimum, he was not against them. Most of his friends seem to have believed he was on their side, and Lipsius allowed them to maintain their beliefs as long as possible.[56] After a life of constant change and a final return to Louvain and Catholicism, Lipsius came to the paradoxical conclusion that the only means to protect peace and religious tolerance was to impose it: one religion in one state.

This idea—a version of the old *eius religio, cuius regio*—was, of course, nothing new. But it was perhaps unusual in the mouth of a man of Lipsius' religious "indifferentism." Lipsius' behavior shows us, at the least, that it was possible for a man of considerable confessional indifferentism to tolerate intolerance in the name of the political good of the commonwealth.

But Lipsius may have been more than just a type in Smotryc'kyj's life. Smotryc'kyj referred to Lipsius only once (another of his near silences), but his references to Tacitus and Seneca (not necessarily the spiritual property of Lipsius, but—for a man of Smotryc'kyj's generation and formation—practically so), along with the general neo-stoicism of his letters of dedication to *Thrēnos* and the *Homiliary Gospel,* help to increase the impression of the importance of this political thinker for the archbishop of Polack. And the solitary reference to Lipsius may again have been one of Smotryc'kyj's calculated risks.

This reference came on the title page to *Verification of Innocence:* the name Lipsius, followed by the text in Latin and in Polish "Nothing can be said so carefully and thoroughly that malice could not pick at it."[57] Smotryc'kyj did not identify his source other than by giving the last name of the author. This is perhaps suspicious in itself, since Smotryc'kyj usually identified his sources with some precision, with more precision—in any event, than many of his contemporaries. As it turns out, this passage came not from Lispius' *De calumnia* (where I first looked, since calumny was the main theme of *Verification of Innocence*), but immediately following that passage from the *Politicorum, sive civilis doctrinae libri sex* (Leiden, 1589) where Lipsius had put forth his program for the enforced preservation of religious "toleration":

> Therefore it is firmly our opinion that one religion is to be maintained in one kingdom. Nevertheless, two things can be asked: whether those who dissent are always to be punished, and whether all of them. But if I discuss this matter, it is not curiosity that moves me, but public benefits and the current state of Europe, which I am not able to contemplate without tears. O greater part of the world: what torches of discord has religion set on fire for you! The heads of the Christian Republic contend among themselves, and several thousands of men have perished and are perishing by the pretext of piety. Who will remain silent here? Not I. . . . *Nothing can be said so carefully and thoroughly that malice could not pick at it.*[58]

The *Politica* was the main reason Lipsius' works were put on the Index in 1593, and in spite of his efforts to revise the treatise in a way acceptable to the Catholic authorities, it was to remain there (see Saunders 1955, 43). Did the Orthodox Smotryc'kyj neglect to identify the source of his citation fully because of its controversial context?

In a sense, tolerance and toleration were not the central issues here, at least not in the usual meaning of these words. Smotryc'kyj was tolerant of the doctrinal differences between the Eastern and Western Churches. But as long as he remained in the Orthodox camp, he could count on no support from either side for this attitude of confessional indifferentism. By switching allegiances, he could hope for support (and, perhaps, political enforcement) for his view of the Universal Church from the Roman Catholic secular authorities and from the Uniate and Roman Catholic Church authorities. But here, too (as in other aspects of his cultural work), it may be that Smotryc̆kyj had sought to co-opt his former opponents' position by joining them, by making their position his and by subtly changing their position in the process.

The later Smotryc̆kyj offered a view of his nation and Church that was highly hierarchical. Secular and ecclesiastical polities for Smotryc̆kyj resembled tree structures, each with one head (king and pope), but with several levels of branches beneath (Crown, Grand Duchy, and Rus', each comprising groups of Polish, Lithuanian, and Ruthenian gentry, burghers, and peasants; or national, "particular" Churches, each headed by a patriarch and comprising councils of bishops: the "common people" and the "laity" stood at the bottom of each branch and "communicated" with the "power" along the lines of the tree structure). This view of hierarchy and power displayed both conformity and dissent on Smotryc̆kyj's part. On the one hand, he would use it to wrest power from the Ruthenian laity[59] and to vest it in the regular Church hierarchy of the Ruthenian nation (which was to owe its ultimate allegiances to Rome and to Warsaw). But on the other hand, through "regularizing" this sort of relationship with the secular and religious power, Smotryc̆kyj seems to have hoped to guarantee Ruthenian otherness by reserving for it a separate branch in the tree and by interposing at least one node of power between the Polish king and the citizens of Rus', and between the bishop of Rome and the Ruthenian faithful. Rome certainly viewed the establishment of an independent patriarchate as a threat to Church order. The notion of "immediate subordination to the Patriarch of Constantinople [or, eventually, of Kiev] and mediate subordination to the Supreme Pontiff," as the Uniate report of 1624 had phrased it,[60] was unacceptable in Rome. According to Krajcar (1964, 78): "The current interpretation of the *plenitudo potestatis* did not leave space to intermediate hierarchs between the bishops and the centre of ecclesiastical unity."

Conclusions

"Who was Meletij Smotryc'kyj?" I return again to the question that I have posed in different fashions throughout this work. Smotryc'kyj's first posthumous biographer, the Jesuit author of his funeral sermon, Wojciech Kortycki, tells us that "With himself alone, with himself alone did Meletij wage a fierce battle every day, every hour, every moment."[1] I agree with this evaluation to a certain extent—perhaps I would take exception to the word "alone." I also agree, for example, with the frequently expressed Orthodox assessment that he was characterized by a certain confessional indifferentism.[2] But I do not agree with these statements in the *contexts* of their arguments. I do not mean by them what their authors meant. For Kortycki, the inner struggle was one that led finally to a recognition of the truth, to an end of the conflict; for me, the conflict ended only with Smotryc'kyj's death (and, in a sense, not even there). For Golubev, Smotryc'kyj's confessional indifference was a sign of weakness of character, something that made him subject to the allure of wealth and power; for me, it was what put him in a position to attempt various programs to resolve the "Ruthenian Question" and what caused him—in a world that insisted more and more at the public level on an exclusive choice of allegiance—ultimately to fail in his attempts.

I marvel at the confidence with which many of these students of Smotryc'kyj have been or are able to offer a "total" picture of a man, when I find mostly fragments—especially since I still find myself drawn to the gaps in our documentation. There are a great many individual scenes that we can suppose to have taken place, but about which we can know little or nothing. What kinds of things did Meletij and his father, Herasym, discuss over the dinner table (assuming that they shared this kind of conviviality)? What was the bearing of the young Orthodox student at the Jesuit Vilnius Academy? What sort of impression did the trip through Poland to Germany make upon him? What sort of impression

did he make upon his academic colleagues in Germany? Did he take part
in any sort of Protestant-Orthodox discussions about points of mutual
agreement? Did he learn to speak German? (With a Saxon accent?) To
what extent did he lead his life in Lithuania after 1610 like a fugitive—
in the king's ill graces first for writing *Thrēnos,* second for accepting
consecration from Patriarch Theophanes, and third for his part in the
martyrdom of Josafat? What did he do (for about forty years!) before he
took the habit? (And what were those "courtly amusements" to which he
devoted himself in the 1610s.) What finally caused him to become a
monk? How did his bearing change when he returned to Vilnius as the
second most important person in the Ruthenian Orthodox hierarchy?
When and why did he decide to travel to Constantinople and the Holy
Land? What were the circumstances of his trip? Did he meet with the
Jesuits there? In what language(s) did he converse with Lukaris? With
other Greek ecclesiastics? With the churchmen in Wallachia? When he
spoke with his fellow Ruthenians, how did his speech resemble what he
wrote down as Ruthenian? How did he perform in situations—for
example, at the Sejm in Warsaw and its smaller attendant groups—
where he might have had to address in short succession all the confessional
and political groups that defined his life in the Polish-Lithuanian
Commonwealth: was he able to move with some fluency from group to
group? How closely was he being observed in his last years by his
Uniate and Roman Catholic colleagues?

These questions (and many more) suggest themselves from a reading
of the sources and their context, but I have either incomplete information
on them, hopelessly contradictory information, or simply no way to
know. To assemble a "picture" of Smotryc'kyj from the many fragments
I have brought together requires a considerable amount of imagination
from the historian (and good will on the part of the reader). Thus, I
remain sceptical of the portraits of Smotryc'kyj—whether Orthodox or
Uniate (or their secular variants)—that have been produced over the
years, and my impression grows that they were written in answer to the
need to "explain" his conversion, in order to make of him a hero or a
traitor. Thus, I begin to seek in these treatments not traces of Smotryc'kyj
but motivations that stem from the personal beliefs of the individual
scholars and their allegiances (to Orthodoxy, to the Uniate Church, to
the Roman Catholic Church, to "Western" culture, to "Eastern" culture,
to Poland, to Rus', to the elite, to the lower classes).

Yet, I too ask the fragmentary testimonies what they can tell me about the man who left them. Within the figure of Smotryc'kyj (or within what they have created of him in their investigations), most of my predecessors have been drawn to, and emphasized, that which has "lasted": his contributions to resolving the Ruthenian question, the connections between Smotryc'kyj and those who continue to deal with the "same" questions. Again, I stress that these are important and interesting issues. By defining themselves as heirs to Smotryc'kyj—either in negative or positive terms—these scholars have established a direct connection, and this is the nature of tradition and self-representation. One aspect of scholarship must always be to follow up the links. But this type of scholarship may not necessarily tell us everything we can know about Smotryc'kyj himself. In fact, it may sometimes tell us more about the would-be heirs than about the putative ancestor.

I have been drawn in my investigation—in addition to these things— to the idiosyncratic, to the "one-time" occurrences, to that in Smotryc'kyj's life which, for whatever reason, failed and perished (and to the fact that it failed and perished), to the moments of hesitation and deviation on the overarching path that took him from Orthodoxy to the Uniate Church. The contradictions—the disjunctions when Smotryc'kyj was supposedly firmly planted one one side of the fence—have interested me, as have the continuities that linked his views and actions on both sides of the fence. I have been intrigued by that which distanced Smotryc'kyj's life and work from those who (students of the present among them) have chosen to see in him an ancestor. This, too, is "who Meletij Smotryc'kyj was," and it is an aspect of his life that has not received much attention so far. This does not mean that new heirs to Smotryc'kyj will not become apparent. But it does (if I have come to understand correctly the rules by which Smotryc'kyj played the game) call into question the several sets of binary oppositions that his would-be descendants and estranged progeny have used in assessing the life of their supposed ancestor.

The rules of the game to which Smotryc'kyj adhered removed any exclusive opposition between Greek-Slavonic and Latin-Polish culture, between Eastern and Western Churches, between Ruthenian nation and Polish-Lithuanian Commonwealth. They required Smotryc'kyj (and all Uniate and Orthodox players) to express their allegiance to Greek-Slavonic culture. But there is no doubt that at the practical level, Smotryc'kyj's education in Vilnius and in Germany (and probably also in Ostroh) served to make of him an Orthodox man of Western Latin learning. As the Uniate Smotryc'kyj would point out, the Greek part of studies in his days had come through an Italian intermediary, anyway.[3]

The rules of the game required at the programmatic level a choice of Church: in Smotryc'kyj's world, this meant either Uniate or Orthodox (although conversion to Roman Catholicism or the various heterodoxies were among the ways to "exit" the game). But for most of his life (after the mid 1610s) this choice did not necessarily imply an exclusive choice between East and West. Smotryc'kyj offered a series of configurations on the question of confessional allegiance throughout his life: first, the Orthodox Church is correct, and the Roman Catholic (and Uniate) Church is wrong (see *Thrēnos*); second, the Orthodox Church is correct, and the Roman Catholic (and perhaps the Uniate) Church is (perhaps) not incorrect (see the works of 1621–1623); or, third, the Roman Catholic (and thus the Uniate) Church is not incorrect, therefore, "we" (that is, "you") must be incorrect (see the works of 1628–29). The game required here an exclusive choice at the programmatic level, but this public stance could be used to further other more-or-less inclusive views of a Universal Church.

No opposition was permitted (again at the programmatic level) that espoused the interests of a Ruthenian nation to the detriment of (or separate from) those of the Polish-Lithuanian Commonwealth. Here Smotryc'kyj could argue as an Orthodox archbishop that what was good for the Ruthenian nation was good for the Commonwealth, and as a Uniate that what was good for the Commonwealth was good for the Ruthenian nation. But in public pronouncements there could be no exclusive opposition between the two communities (except, of course, to the detriment of the Ruthenian nation).

These were the rules to which Smotryc'kyj adhered. Within this general framework, what has interested me the most have been those glimpses of the ways in which Smotryc'kyj played the game in some "creative" fashion. My impression (and this is in disagreement with Orthodox historiography—but not, therefore, necessarily in agreement with the Uniate) is that his goal throughout his life was to create—within the constraints of these rules—a Ruthenian culture, Church, and political community that maintained what set it apart from the Poles and Lithuanians. Hence, my fascination with those grey areas, and the ways in which Smotryc'kyj exploited them to loosen the grip of the rules from time to time in realizing his vision.

In examining Smotryc'kyj's life and works in this manner, it has become clear to me that identifying the influences (and here I mean Western influences) in the program is only the first step. It is an important first step, and we certainly need many more studies before we have a clear picture of the spiritual forces at work in Ukraine in the early seventeenth century. But this is a relatively easy task. In many cases, and certainly in that of Smotryc'kyj, we can *suspect* at any given juncture that whatever books, ideas, and people were important to Western European intellectuals were also important to their Ukrainian counterparts. And since much of Western culture was in this period characterized by the high level of its explicit codification, we may often be able to prove the presence of the Western influence in Ukraine. From the life of Smotryc'kyj we see that, when evaluated according to several standards—use of humanistic grammars, use of the entire range of Protestant and Catholic authorities in attempts to answer the questions raised in the Protestant-Catholic debates of the sixteenth century, knowledge of the vocabulary of the Inquisition, recourse to the art of dissimulation (and the list continues)—the eastern boundary of the Western European sphere of spiritual influence extended into Ukraine by the beginning of the seventeenth century.

The difficulty comes in evaluating the "Eastern" portion of Ukrainian culture. It certainly was present at the overt, programmatic level. What was its significance at the practical level? Here we are hampered by three things: the fact that Eastern culture was less well codified (sometimes programmatically so), the fact that the state of our knowledge about Orthodox Slavic culture up to the early seventeenth century can in no way rival that of our knowledge about the West, and the fact that we are only beginning to understand what people like Smotryc'kyj knew about the culture of Orthodox Slavdom.

We are not alone, however, in facing this dilemma. People like Smotryc'kyj were also aware that a spiritual and cultural border ran somewhere through Ukraine and that they occupied a spiritual territory where the rules that defined the world to which they increasingly looked began to lose their hold. In many cases, Smotryc'kyj and his contemporaries simply did not know the "Eastern," or "Greek" and "Slavonic" answer to the question posed by the West; they did know, however, that they had agreed to play the game by the Western rules (i.e., to try to answer all the questions posed by the Catholic and Protestant West), and that there thus *had* to be an Orthodox answer to the question. In some cases, there may have been no "correct" Orthodox answer to the question, because the question itself was new, was one which had been posed in these precise terms, or with this sense of urgency, only in the recent Protestant-Catholic debates.

Thus, instead of studying only the "influences" (and again: this part of the task is not over for Ukrainian culture as a whole, or, no doubt, for Smotryc'kyj in particular), we should also attempt to play the game along with them: we should try to follow the creative aspects of their "cultural plagiarism," the ways they sought to master the rules and to exploit the areas of "laxity" in producing a modern, Orthodox Slavic national culture.

Many investigators have been troubled by the "mixed" quality of the various languages used by Smotryc'kyj and other Ruthenian writers of the late sixteenth and early seventeenth century. This, I believe, is a misplaced purism, if our goal is to understand Smotryc'kyj's usage, the behavioral, intentional aspects of his linguistic performances. My comments on his use of Polish apply in general terms to his other languages. Smotryc'kyj's goal was a late-humanistic, Ruthenian Orthodox Slavic literacy. The word "goal" is important. Smotryc'kyj's grammar of Church Slavonic is not completely described if we apply to it the term "prescriptive," in opposition to "descriptive." It was both of these things: descriptive of good, corrected texts of Church Slavonic (whether or not they existed in 1618) and prescriptive of the ways those texts should be corrected in the future. But it was more than this. It was a "desiderative" grammar, an expression of a wish that Orthodox Slavic society might some day speak and write Slavonic the way Western Europe then spoke and wrote Latin. Thus, the question of "influences" (again, if we are interested in the way Smotryc'kyj *used* his languages), as well as the opposition of Polish to Ruthenian, Latin to Greek and Slavonic, was excluded in a sense by the rules of the game. All of these languages had roles to play (some more at the programmatic level, others more at the practical level), and aspects of one could be incorporated in the other in order to render Polish more "Orthodox," Church Slavonic and Ruthenian more "late-humanistic." The way Smotryc'kyj played this aspect of the game underwent no changes with his switch in allegiance.

The rulebook required a choice of confession. But even here, Smotryc'kyj seems to have sought out those areas where the rules could be temporarily eluded. Most crucial are those periods in the middle 1610s and the middle 1620s when Smotryc'kyj had purposefully created situations for himself that were unclear, when he was least subject to any one particular authority, and when he could afford for himself the greatest access to leaders of both sides. These are the periods from which we have no immediate records: Smotryc'kyj published no confessional works in these periods; his later pronouncements about them were quite definitely colored by his need at the moment to portray himself as absolutely unmoveable in his beliefs and allegiances. Several things encourage me to look to the periods of unclarity for hints about the real Smotryc'kyj. In the material I have presented in the second half of this book, we can see the outlines of a man who was well aware of the authorities between which he needed to choose, of his own need ultimately to conform to one or the other, but also of his need to find ways to loosen the authorities to which he conformed in order to make room for his view of himself and his nation; and he was further aware of the levels of dissimulation required (or permitted) in order to live with these authorities.

Several times Smotryc'kyj raised the issue of whether his world was divided into two, or more than two, camps. His point of departure in *Paraenesis* was to answer rumors and allegations that he was now seeking to introduce some third sect into his nation, which was already divided in two.[4] In his letter to Patriarch Cyril Lukaris of Constantinople he asked (probably not *entirely* in good faith): "are we in agreement with the Romans or with the Protestants, or do we adhere to and confess some third, middle thing?"[5] And in *Exaethesis* he wrote that he had been uncertain "which faith was that pure and immaculate faith: that, which I and our other writers before me had described, or that one to which the Uniate responses pointed us, or finally some other, third one."[6] The precise definition of the three differed—Protestants, Catholics, and the "other"; or Uniates, Orthodox, and the "other." But the general structure of the situation remained the same. In each case, Smotryc'kyj left the question at least partially unanswered, allowing his readers to draw their own conclusions. Since he rejected the Orthodox "new theologians," most would assume that he sided with the Uniates and Roman Catholics, implicitly rejecting the unspecified third possibility. Probably he did believe that he was supposed to think this way. I suspect, however, that a key to understanding Smotryc'kyj's dilemma was that he was a man who—like de Dominis—felt more at home with some "third" way, but that he was at some level a conformist who—like Lipsius—had a need to submit to authority. In dedicating his *Apology* of 1628 to Aleksander Zasławski, Smotryc'kyj praised him for being a man who knew how to steer a middle course between the demands of the Catholic authorities and the things acceptable to their Orthodox subjects.[7] This *modus operandi* likely described the archbishop of Polack at least as well as it did the Catholic senator.

In matters more easily hidden from view, Smotryc'kyj sought all his life to define at some practical level—in language, faith, and nation—that "third, middle thing," partially by borrowing from the other two confessions and cultures, which were better defined. In that same letter to Lukaris, Smotryc'kyj asked: "Am I to follow the decree of the Council of Trent concerning these divine matters, or of that side, against which that Council worked in these articles of the faith."[8] Again, the question was probably not entirely in good faith, but it is nonetheless revealing of Smotryc'kyj's dilemma. Was there no third way in matters of faith? What did the Orthodox believe, if they did not believe what their "new theologians" had taught them?

Those mysterious, poorly delineated periods in Smotryc'kyj's life—ca. 1613–1617 and 1623–1627—were, in my opinion, the times when Smotryc'kyj sought to realize most actively a third way: the first time, perhaps, to convince everyone that the Union of Florence (correctly interpreted) was all the union the Commonwealth really needed, and that it was worth respecting (on both sides); and the second time, that the Ruthenians should establish their own independent patriarchate.

There were some structural similarities in the two periods. After each hiatus Smotryc'kyj wrote a series of polemical works in quick succession. In the first works in both instances (*Verification of Innocence* and *Apology*), he devoted some of his attention to those things that included both sides, and in the later works to those things that divided the two. One reason could be increasing frustration with the other side. Another reason could be growing suspicion concerning his *bona fides* on his own side. Thus there were two periods of negotiations with both sides—perhaps informed, in part, by considerations of these two topics—the first ca. 1617, the second ca. 1627, both followed the next year by Smotryc'kyj's attempts to prove his unwavering allegiance, the first time to the Orthodox side, the second time to the Uniate side. And both times there are indications that, Smotryc'kyj's public protestations to the contrary notwithstanding, neither he nor his masters of the moment were entirely comfortable with the results. Note Smotryc'kyj's reluctance—in the face of considerable outside pressure—to declare absolute allegiances, to take the habit, to accept consecration, to convert overtly. Smotryc'kyj seems to have sought to delay these actions and to have regretted their finality. If Smotryc'kyj was born in 1577, then we should note the collateral importance of key anniversaries in motivating his "conversions": he became a monk at age 40 and converted (covertly) to the Catholic Church at age 50.

But was not the choice of confessional camp at least partially a result of strategical considerations at the cultural and political level? In Smotryc'kyj's rulebook, there was no escape from the political framework of the Polish-Lithuanian Commonwealth. And he may even have believed that this was—*realistically speaking*—the best thing for his nation. In his grammar of Church Slavonic, in a passage with no polemical coloring whatsoever, Smotryc'kyj gave as an example of prolepsis the kind of quick symbolic survey of the Federation that one might expect from Adam Mickiewicz: "My brothers have died, Jakov in Vilnius, Stefan in Cracow, Nikolaj in Kiev."[9] Thus, the question, perhaps even at some not-quite-conscious level may have been this: under which confessional banner will the Ruthenian nation have the best prospects for salvation—at all levels: cultural, ecclesiastical, political—within this general political constellation?

In the first period of indecision on Smotryc'kyj's part, ca. 1613–1617, his argument seems to have been based on an outdated vision of the Polish-Lithuanian Commonwealth, where each member nation could expect that its freedoms of conscience would be respected. The second period—and perhaps this was the real motivation for the change of allegiance—was based in part on a more pragmatic view of the possibilities for toleration in the Commonwealth of the late 1620s. Thus, the idea of the Ruthenian patriarchate and the local councils of bishops may well have been for Smotryc'kyj a means to that third end, a compromise, a way of winning peace from the stronger party while maintaining some degree of distance from Rome.

Referring to the work of Frances Yates, Hugh Trevor-Roper (1978, 218) has suggested that we think in terms of a sort of early international ecumenical "movement" that began to grow in the period of relative peace in the early seventeenth century, and which might include such disparate figures as Richard Hooker, Justus Lipsius, Jacques-Auguste de Thou, Isaac Casaubon, Hugo Grotius, Lancelot Andrewes, Paolo Sarpi, William Laud, and Cyril Lukaris. 1618 is the symbolic date for the end of the irenic hopes of the these early ecumenicists; after the beginning of the Thirty Years' War, each of these figures had to find their way in the new, harsher reality. Of course, Marcantonio de Dominis also belongs in this group. In the picture that is beginning to emerge from less partisan treatments, the archbishop of Split is no longer presented as the faithless opportunist, but as, in a sense, the first martyr of the "pre-ecumenical" movement of the early seventeenth century.[10] We could perhaps also add Georg Cassander to the list, among those early ecumenicists who played some role in Smotryc'kyj's spiritual formation.[11] I would like to suggest that a more useful way of viewing Meletij Smotryc'kyj and the dilemma of his life is to place him as a member of this ecumenical international and to examine his life's work, including his conversion, as yet another way a "pre-irenicist," "pre-ecumenicist" (these are terms suggested by Cantimori [1960]) made his way in the Europe of the 1620s.

The dilemma of Meletij Smotryc'kyj was this: although he may have believed in a world, felt most at home in a world, that comprised more than two camps, of which more than one was—in Spalatene terms—"not wrong," he nonetheless realized later in life that he was actually living in a world that was neatly divided into two camps, of which—by virtue of the power structure that was coming increasingly to the fore in the Polish-Lithuanian Commonwealth—one was "right," and the other was an undifferentiated amalgam of all those who were "not right." Thus, Smotryc'kyj may have reasoned, "in order to defend my nation, its Church and culture, and in order to see them survive and take their places among the nations and Churches of the Commonwealth and of Europe in the early seventeenth century, it is necessary that they be aligned with the 'right.'"

The irony of Smotryc'kyj's solutions was that all his attempts were wrong. There was no acceptable way at that moment—acceptable to Orthodox society and to the Catholic powers—to be an "inclusivist," "unionizing" leader of the Ruthenian Orthodox Church. There were not two Smotryc'kyjs, as contemporary propaganda and later scholarship would have it. There was one Smotryc'kyj, at least after the rejection of

Thrēnos in the 1610s—with many public faces. His career, from the mid-1610s to the end of his life, with all its contradictions and about-faces, was a series of frustrated attempts to define and defend a Ruthenian Church, nation, and culture that was "inclusive" and still "included," tolerant but yet tolerated. He was thwarted by the society he wished to defend, which could not always recognize itself in his definition of it, and by the powers to which he wished to defend it, who would not accept the level of autonomy he accorded his local Church, nation, and culture.

Is it, then, not likely that the conversion *per se*, the switch of allegiance from the patriarch of Constantinople to the bishop of Rome applied more to external things than to faith? That Smotryc'kyj simply exchanged one set of *excessus fidei* (as de Dominis would have put it) for another? And that he was motivated not so much by considerations of correct doctrine, or of fame or temporal wealth, as by considerations of political power, and by a realization that the Orthodox lacked the will to be united and that the Catholics lacked the will to tolerate an independent Ruthenian Orthodox Church? In the end, Smotryc'kyj may have felt a need to be aligned with the side which, for whatever reasons, had the will to be united and had the political power to try to compel the other side to be united with it.

Smotryc'kyj's real "conversion" was an almost lifelong process and included many stages that are discernible to us at this distance, and doubtless many others about which we will never know. There was some sort of break with old ways sometime in the 1610s, after he had begun to have doubts about having published *Thrēnos*. This break probably included in it some aspects of the issues I have raised here: above all, a switch from an "exclusivist" to an "inclusivist" view of Church and faith, and a desire that the bishops exercise more of their power over the local Church.

But Smotryc'kyj "lost" the game he was playing. Why? Perhaps, in part, because, in spite of his musings about and occasional use of the art of dissimulation, he did not dissimulate enough, or at the right times. He seems to have had too great a regard for the "truth." He seems really to have believed that through his powers of persuasion, either in person or through his polemical works, he would be able to make the elite—secular as well as religious—see the "truth," and once the elite were all heading in the right direction, the rest would follow. That is to say, he lacked political sense. And he also had the disadvantage of having a public career that coincided almost exactly with the last twenty years of the reign of Sigismund III Vasa.

Smotryc'kyj's efforts did not "perish entirely," however, to the extent that Peter Mohyla succeeded. Mohyla possessed some of the things Smotryc'kyj had been lacking: a more refined political sense, an apparently greater capacity to dissimulate, and a knowledge of when he needed to do so. Moreover, his task was perhaps somewhat easier, since his career coincided rather with the reign of Władysław IV. Smotryc'kyj's program was not in conflict with that of Mohyla (and Smotryc'kyj said so in 1628, at least partially in order to discredit Mohyla in the eyes of the Orthodox). In many areas, Mohyla carried forward the program for a Ruthenian national culture that Smotryc'kyj had only started or projected. At the level of language and letters there would have been no important oppositions between the two. (Mohyla even issued in 1638 a "corrected" version of Smotryc'kyj's *Homiliary Gospel* of 1616—without any mention of the first translator.) How different from Mohyla's catechism could Smotryc'kyj's have been?—both recognized the need to remove the Ruthenian "new theologians" from the center of attention, and both sought to limit Lukaris' influence on matters of the faith.[12] Smotryc'kyj's political program—one which Mohyla brought into being—heralded the switch from a power base dependent on the Cossacks and the Brotherhoods to one that favored the Ruthenian nobility and the regular Church hierarchy. And Mohyla, too, gave some thought to the feasibility of a Uniate Ruthenian Church, under an independent patriarchate (which office he himself would occupy). The differences between the two men did not necessarily go the heart of the program: on the one hand, under Władysław IV the authorities were willing to tolerate more autonomy on the part of the Ruthenian Orthodox nation than they were in Smotryc'kyj's day under Sigismund III and, on the other hand, Mohyla had a better sense of how far his "constituency" would follow him in moves toward agreement with Rome.

I cannot, however, *prove* many aspects of the picture of Smotryc'kyj I have offered here. The interpretation of a historical record this fragmentary and this mendacious—and this is in itself an assertion I cannot really prove, but one I hope I have made convincing—requires a kind of schooled impressionism to determine which statements are lies and which half-truths; which statements are pretexts governed by the needs of the polemic and which reflect (to whatever degree) real beliefs; which silences or near-silences are key pieces in the puzzle and which are simply fortuitous gaps in the documentation. It requires the development of an ear for subtle changes in tonality. But it also requires an awareness of just how tenuous such an interpretation must be.

I find the paradoxical, fragmentary, unclear picture of Smotryc′kyj I have offered more convincing than the reigning "clear" pictures on either side of the confessional or national divide. I do not find convincing evidence that Smotryc′kyj's conversion brought with it any fundamental change in his attempts to shape a Ruthenian Orthodox response to the cultural, doctrinal, and political challenge of the local Reformation and Counter-Reformation. Nor do I find that he was ever quite Orthodox or quite Uniate in the way many of his contemporaries and most of his students have expected him to be. But, again, I cannot prove it. I cannot find absolutely unequivocal evidence that what I have chosen to place in the center of attention was not the polemical subterfuge on Smotryc′kyj's part, and that what I have attributed to the requirements of conformity were not Smotryc′kyj's real beliefs. Did Smotryc′kyj argue for the establishment of an independent Ruthenian patriarchate in order to put some distance between the pope and Rus′? Or did he do it in order to make the idea of union palatable to the Orthodox? Or was he (as I suspect) motivated by a program for "national survival," and did he thus have both considerations in mind? I have, however, found collateral corroboration for my picture of Smotryc′kyj in the attitude of his contemporaries: no one ever completely trusted him. There must have been good reason for this.

I have not "pinned Smotryc′kyj down" (to use the lepidopterist's metaphor, with which Trevor-Roper [1978, 214] evaluated the best recent study of Cyril Lukaris): Meletij, like the Calvinizing patriarch, "flutters still." But I have, I hope, placed these "flutterings" at the center of the archbishop's life and sought its meaning in them. As students of the seventeenth century in Eastern Europe, we would do well to be less scandalized by the fact of such sorts of switches in allegiance and more sensitive to what these hesitations can tell us about the spiritual fault lines that resulted from the entry of Rus′ and the other Orthodox Slavic nations into the world of early modern Europe.

I end with a fragment, one of the many images that have contributed to the composite we call Meletij Smotryc′kyj, and the image he himself *sought* to leave when he gave instructions for composing his deathbed scene. Let us picture—in conscious opposition to the two reigning iconographies—a man who, holding his letter of consecration from the patriarch of Jerusalem in his left hand and that from the bishop of Rome in his right, had attempted with mixed success to find a way for an Orthodox Slav to maintain his identity in the early modern West.

Notes

INTRODUCTION

1. On Smotryc̀kyj's grammar of Church Slavonic, see Aničenko 1973; Baumann 1958; Baumann 1956–1957; Čexovyč 1934; Dietze 1974; Dylevskij 1958; Frick 1986; Horbatsch 1974; Horbatsch 1964; Kociuba 1975; Makaruška 1908; Mathiesen 1981; Nimčuk 1979; Nimčuk 1982; Pugh 1987; Pugh 1985; Sjöberg 1966; Weingart 1923; Zasadkevič 1883.

2. Among the Orthodox interpretations of Smotryc̀kyj's life, see Anuškin 1962; Askočenskij 1856; Bantyš-Kamenskij 1805; Demjanovič 1871; Elenevskij 1861; Evgenij 1827; Golubev 1883; Jaremenko 1984; Jaremenko 1986; Kojalovič 1859 and 1861; Korotkyj [Korotkij] 1984; Korotkyj [Korotkij] 1987; Korowicki 1935; Osinskij 1911; Prokošina 1966. For Ukrainian Catholic and Roman Catholic interpretations, see Čubatyj 1934; Fedyšyn 1934; Grabowski 1916; Pobihuščyj 1934; Sabol 1951; Siarczyński 1828; Solovij 1977–1978; Urban 1957. Most treatments, both Orthodox and Catholic, have relied heavily on the 1666 Uniate *vita* by the Bishop of Chełm Jakiv Suša.

3. Sysyn is also the author of a fascinating picture of another important cultural, confessional, and political fence-sitter from this period—Adam Kysil, a leader of the Orthodox, who would become a senator on the eve of the Xmel'nyc̀kyj Uprising. See Sysyn 1985.

4. Smotryc̀kyj 1621c, 114–15/456: "Mieli pokoy za Hermana, bo był tylko cieniem w Vniey: Popow ni do czego nie przymuszał . . . "

5. This is to say, the sum of the sources that I have been able to assemble from seventeenth-century printings and from later printed versions of manuscript materials. The new scholarly ferment in Ukraine, Belarus, and Lithuania will probably add a few new pieces to the puzzle.

6. See the recent study by Zagorin (1990) for several chapters in the history of the theory and practice of "lying" in early modern Europe. See also Ginzburg 1970.

7. Kortycki 1634, D2^r: "a tu proszę słuchaczow moich, niech teras nie tylko wszy chętliwie, ale y oczy ku mnie skłonią. Znaliście, cni słuchacze, Iego Mości Oyca Meletiusa Smotryskiego Archimandrytę Dermańskiego? znaliście męża świątobliwością, mądrością y dostoynością Arcybiskupią Prześwietnego? Znaliście człowieka, ktory pracą vstawiczną stargany, y kłopotami codziennymi prawie wysuszony zaledwie duszę w sobie trzymał? Znaliście one postami wysuszone członki, one kości chorobami, y frasunkami niemal wyschłe, ciało

ono prawie wywiędłe? Znaliście. Poyrzyciesz, proszę, iakiego oręża na ciała swego karność vżywał."

8. Kortycki 1634, D2ʳ: "*Tu Disciplinę iego niewidaney srogości, z drotowatych stryczkow we dwa troki skręconą, y węzłami twardemi trefnie nawiązaną z ambony ludowi pokazano.*"

9. Suša 1666, 130–31: "Flagrum, quo saepe saepius abscondite suum castigans corpus, vt Paulus alter, inseruitutem redigebat, horrorem menti memoria incutit sua: quod oculos quondam omnium perculit spectatorum; cum pro rostris ab Alberto Cortiscio in funebri Meletij encomio productum fuisset."

10. Suša 1666, 144–45: "Vnum Iosepho Archiepiscopo cessit, Flagrum eius horribile, thesauro monasterij illatum, in exemplum successoribus, in memoriam Meletianam."

11. Kortycki 1634, D1ᵛ: "Naprzod Oręże iego było, Praca vstawiczna a iakoby bez wytchnienia, tak że y pokarmu zażywaiąc, nawet, y w chorobie ciężkiey, vstawicznie, co do nauki zbawienney służyło, abo rozmawiał, abo rozmyślał, abo y pisał. . . . y zda mi się iakoby do tego był przyszedł, że mu ciężey było nie robiąc odpoczywać, aniżeli pracować."

12. Kortycki 1634, D1ᵛ: "Drugie oręże było iego surowe, a ledwie wytrwane posty, abo raczey rzekę post, gdyż y samo branie pokarmu iego tak szczupłe było, że się vstawicznym, y iakby iednym postem nazwać bespiecznie życie iego zakonne może. Od czasu, ktorego się w Zakonie Ś. Panu Bogu zaślubił, iarzynek tylko prostych, abo rybek trochę, y to drobiazgu zażywał. Wina rzadko barzo y ledwie co skusił. W tey samey chorobie gdym tak osłabionego widział, że zaledwie tchnął, wmowiłem to weń, żeby dla zawzięcia iakiego posiłku kieliszeczek wina wpołudnie y wieczor brał, posłuchałci mię wprawdzie ale na czas barzo krotki."

13. Kortycki 1634, D1ᵛ–D2ʳ: "Trzecie oręże iego Ostra włosienica, ktorey zawsze miasto płotna vżywał. . . . A iako żołnierz stoiąc w sprawie zbroie nie składa, tak y on szat, ktorych vżywał, nigdy nie składał, tylko gdy abo dnia siodmego włosienicę odmienić było potrzeba, abo się biczować."

14. Suša 1666, 129–30: "A regressu ad S. Ecclesiam, ad extremam vitae aegritudinem, vino vix vnquam vsus. . . . Caeterum toto septimano annorum poenitentium Dermani studio, nullo alio patriae vsus potu, nisi ceruisiae: et quidem singulis diebus, tertia tantum parte ollae, quae puerum non reficeret."

15. Suša 1666, 127: "Lignea istic Religiosorum fuere habitacula, quibus deiectis, e cocto latere vniuersa, tam priuata quam communia aedificia, fieri curauit. . . . Librariam Sacris codicibus, et interpretibus, Synodorum concilijs Sanctorum Patrum, Latinorum Graecorumque lucubrationibus, Ecclesiasticae Historiae voluminibus, praecipue cumulauit. In quae non solum e peculio monasterij, sed etiam proprio, multum aeris appendit. Ecclesiae imagines, altaribus vasa sacra, sacerdotibus ornamenta, splendidiora quam debuit, cum dispendio indigentiae suae contulit."

16. *List* 1621, 26–27/752: "Drzecie się Bogu y ludziom, omierzłą ambitią obięci, na przestoły metropolii y władyctw. A Połockie naybarziey smakuie: iuż insignia y władzę władyczą wielebny Mielenci połockiego archiepiskopstwa sobie przywłaszcza, mimo władzą (żałosna rzecz) K. Jego M., że go nie podawał, ani nominował. Tytułow zażywa, w druk ie podaie sam, siebie (śmieszna rzecz zaprawdę) wielbiąc, w ubiorach nie władyczych tylko, ale snać metropolich celebruie. Pieczęci sobie władyckie ryie, na kielichach napisy czyni. Pod rękę się szlachcie (*ne quid ambitioni et arrogantiae desit*), sam będąc iakiey iest condicii, wodzić dopuszcza y tym się pyszni."

17. Smotryc'kyj 1621c, 104–105/451: "Ociec Smotrzyski, ktory młode lata swe aż do lat męża, y tu w Oyczyźnie, y w Cudzoziemskich kraiach, na naukach wyzwolonych vcziwie przewiodł, gdy mu po kilkorocznych dwornych zabawach, miasto nieiakiego odetchu po prochu szkolnym przeżyłych, żywot postanowić, y przez tak wiele lat zbieranego *studiorum* sprzętu w pożytek swoy y bliźnich zażyć przychodziło. Miał to w vstawicznym przedsięwzięciu, aby nie pierwey do Zakonu Mniskiego (do ktorego od lat niemal dziecinnych ochotną duszę miał,) wstąpił, ażby o namierzonym w rozrożnioney braci (bo go to wielce po wszytkie czasy trapiło) obudwu stron celu wziął wiadomość pewną."

18. *Synopsis* 1632, 17ᵛ–18ʳ/571–72: "W tym roku podstępnie z nami idąc Meletius Smotrycki, podobnym się być antecessorowi swemu (ktory inszego co usty mowił, a inszego co na sercu miał) obiawił. Lubo to publice w cerkwi ś. cudotworney Pieczarskiey na fest Zaśnienia Przenaświętszey Panny, żadnego na się gwałtu nie maiąc, ale sam dobrowolnie napisawszy revocatią, według niey, wpośrzod cerkwie na liturgiey ś. (przy bardzo wielkim zgromadzeniu duchowieństwa inszego y przybytności, tak z Korony, iako y z Litwy wielu godnych y znamienitych ludzi) zaraz po przeczytaniu Ewangelii *Apologią* swą szarpał, palił, a iednak zwrociwszy się spokoynie do monastera Dermańskiego, wrocił się znowu nieborak in vomitus suos, a to dla intraty biednych kilku tysięcy złotych.

"Bractwu też naszemu w zabraniu nienależnym y zatrzymaniu nieprawnym od złota, srebra, pereł y drogich kamieni, apparatow cerkiewnych, y tym podobnych ozdob: niemniey y bardzo wiele xiąg z biblioteki naszey Brackiey, Theologow tak Wschodnich iako z Zachodnich, tudziesz y rożnych historykow, przy inszych wszytkich rzeczach, z monastera naszego za usiłowną iego proźbą onemu przesłanych, na kilkanaście tysięcy złotych zaszkodził. O co wszytko zaszły iuż y processa niektore prawne, y czasu swego z nim samym y z kim prawo drogę ukaże prawem czynić pewnie nie omieszkamy."

19. The charges that the Vilnius Brotherhood brought against Smotryc'kyj on 9 August/19 August 1629 are reprinted in the addenda to Golubev 1883a (384–86). An anonymous pamphlet against Smotryc'kyj, which must have appeared sometime after Smotryc'kyj's conversion became apparent in August 1628, and most likely before his death in December 1633, also emphasized greed and arrogance as the explanations for his conversion. See *Pamflet* 1875, 562.

Diplic (1634, 57) repeated the allegation that Smotryc̆kyj had stolen some books from the Brotherhood: "Zwłaszcza że ia też Doktorow Cerkiewnych pism nie mam, oprocz niektorych pism iednego y drugiego Doktora Cerkiewnego, y to na Sławieński ięzyk przetłumaczonych. A snać, choć na czas ten, kiedy to piszę, mogłbym mieć od Ich MM. PP. Braci Wileńskich, Doktorow świętych pisma, gdyby nie tenże Apologiuiący Autor, korzystaiąc w ich dobrym, v siebie tych ksiąg ich, mimo słuszność nie zatrzymywał, iako y inszych rzeczy onychże."

20. Smotryc̆kyj 1629b, 67ʳ/767: "Zaż sam ty tego obłudniku nie wiesz, że Wileński wasz Schysmatycki Monaster, więtsza złota moia sieć była, ktory mię vbrał od głowy do nog we złoto, niż Monaster Dermański. Więtsze moie tam by miało być łakomstwo, niż tu: Bo tam ze wszytkiey Białey Rusi Archyepiskopiey Połockiey Parochyanie, pamiętali na mię."

21. Golubev 1883b, 322: "Зъ стороны книгъ и аппаратовъ постерегаю того, абы на нихъ тые чіи суть не шъкодовали, до споряженя реестру, за отъездомъ отца Антоніевымъ пріити не моглемъ: еднакъ спорядити его хочу и дай Богъ самъ въ Кіеве господину Отцу Іосифу намѣсникови моему Виленскому отдать его, если намъ ведлугъ намовы на празникъ Богоявленіе ставитися тамъ прійдетъ."

22. Smotryc̆kyj 1629a, N3ʳ/693: "Μηδὲ λιλαιόμενος γήϊνα δὴ πέλεται."

23. Suša 1666, 19: "Non eo tamen inficias, eum hoc in claustro, multis insudasse corporis afflictionibus: molestis nimirum cilicijs, insomnibus vigilijs, durae quieti, pallidae ieiunitati, nudae pauperiei, morum componendorum exercitationi, et si quae in statu a vera fide alieno, comperiri potest, pietati."

24. Smotryc̆kyj 1618, Ч3ʳ: "Пихъ вино и спахъ сонъ сладок[ъ]"

25. Smotryc̆kyj 1629b, 68ʳ/768: "Nie czynią iako baczę v ciebie temu co siedzi w Monasteru Michałowskim Kijowskim: ni owemu, co siedzi w Monasteru Stepańskim: ni temu, co w Milcach, ni onemu co sobie poza Dnieprskich Monasterach dinduie, Monasterze ich ni bielm, ni kłamstwa, ni ognia piekielnego, pychy y hardości: ni w świecie Dymasowego rozkochania sie: Tylo ieden Monaster Dermański to wszytko z sobą nosi."

26. Żychiewicz 1986, 161: "Wści postępki barziey ambicyą *et privato odio*, niż *fraterna charitate* rządzące się . . . "

27. Woysznarowicz 1647, Divʳ: "A coż wyniosło wzgorę naszego Iozaphata, rzekę że tytuły wysokie? nie. toć podobno intraty Pańskie y preeminencye? nie. toż na ostatek presumpcya o sobie, nie. Miłość bliźniego ta go wyniosła."

28. Smotryc̆kyj 1621b, 52ʳ⁻ᵛ/376–77: "Stąd Cerkwi pieczętowanie, nabożeństwa zabrona: Dziatek bez Chrztu, doszłych bez zbawienney Ciała y Krwie Syna Bożego Świątości z tego świata ześcia."

29. Żychiewicz 1986, 177–78: "By ciż Święci na tak wielką krzywdę Bożą za żywotów swych tu na świecie patrzali, na iaką ia tu teraz patrzam w Połocku, że

chłopstwo grube, tak wiele dziatek bez krztu, tak wiele dorosłych bez Spowiedzi i używania Sakramentu Ś. do piekła posyła y posyłaią."

30. Smotryc'kyj 1629a, 81/685: "*Inter coecos, et monoculus Rex.*"

31. Cited according to Zagorin 1990, 191.

32. Of course, on some of the older questions (such as the procession of the Holy Spirit) the Orthodox position was long established, and an Orthodox polemicist could draw on an authoritative tradition in formulating his own stance. But what was the Orthodox position on the authority of Scripture, transubstantiation, and other questions that had become focal points in the confessional debates of the sixteenth century in the West? For that matter, even in rejecting the *Filioque*, Orthodox polemicists often felt a need to acquaint themselves with the arguments of the Antitrinitarians (especially Polish Antitrinitarians) on the Godhead, although they rarely admitted that they had done so.

CHAPTER 1

1. Velykyj 1972:125: "Ecce ego in ultima peccantis terrae appendice situs, in schismate velut ex necessitate natus, in eodem per annos quinquaginta ex ignorantia volutatus . . . "

2. Suša 1666, 65: " . . . in schismate velut ex necessitate natus, in eodem per annos 50. *ex voluntate volutatus . . .* " (emphasis added).

3. See Kojalovič 1861, 363: "Occiso autem Josaphat 'timens sibi' in Graeciam accessit atque inibi trienno exacto, rediit: 'et visis miseriis non tantum corporalibus, sed etiam spiritualibus,' ut patet ex ipsius postulatis tepescere in schismata coepit Anno suae aetatis suique schismatis quinquagesimo."

4. This is the opinion of the recent editor of Vatican documents on Ruthenian matters, Father Velykyj (1972, 218).

5. Velykyj 1972, 218: "Meletius Smotrziski natus in Russia ex nobilibus parentibus, sed schysmaticis, circa annum Domini 1580mum."

6. See Korotkyj 1987, 23–24: " . . . преставился року 1630 от рождества своего в 58 лет." Korotkyj gives his information in what, I assume, must be his own Russian translation.

7. Suša 1666, 138: "Decembris vigesima septima, vt colligere mihi licuit . . . " The year 1633 is given elsewhere in Suša's chronology (see Suša 1666, Biiʳ).

8. Smotryc'kyj 1621c, 110/454: "Znało Herasima Daniłowica Smotrzyskiego Podole ktore y rodziło go, y wychowało. . . . Znała Wołyń."

9. Suša 1666, 14: "Vitalem Spiritum Meletius hausit, in Podolia e nobili prosapia."

10. Unless we consider the example of agreement of compound subjects Smotryc̆kyj gave in his grammar of Church Slavonic (Smotryc̆kyj 1618, ѿ1ʳ) as evidence for his attitude toward his own mother: "Отецъ и мати честна ми еста: и, Братъ/ сестра/ и чадо любезни ми суть."

11. A study of Herasym's life work remains an important desideratum. On Herasym, see Kolosova 1985.

12. Petruševič (1874, 35) cited as an entry for the year 1608 in his chronicle page 612 of a manuscript that had been in the possession of the eighteenth-century Uniate Metropolitan of Kiev, Lev Kyška: "Basilius Konstantynowicz Ostroski anno aetatis 83 moritur, ejus mandato Stephanus Smotrzyski parochus Ostrogensis tituli Natae Mariae, filius Gerasimi Smotryski de Kamieniec scripsit Prawiła."

13. Smotryc̆kyj himself gave the following example of prolepsis in his grammar of Church Slavonic (Smotryc̆kyj 1618, Ъ1ʳ): "Братїе мои измроша, Іаков[ъ] в[ъ] Вилни, Стефан[ъ] в Краковѣ, Нїколай в Кіевѣ." Did he also have brothers Jakov and Nikolaj, in addition to Stefan? (But Stefan Smotryc̆kyj seems to have outlived his more famous brother, so perhaps this grammatical example contained an exaggerated account of Stefan's demise and offers no reliable information concerning the Smotryc̆kyj brothers.)

14. Velykyj 1955, 70: "Io non ho conosciuto Miletio Smotricio, ma ho ben inteso dire da un suo fratello carnale che egli fosse ordinato per Arcivescovo Polocense dal sudetto Herrone, asserto patriarca Hierosolimitano."

15. Šeptyc̆kyj 1974, 117–18: "Nepos ex fratre piae memoriae archiepiscopi Meletii, qui accepit habitum religiosum et iam fecit professionem in eodem monasterio Dermanensi, petit ut possit studere in exteris regionibus in aliquo seminario si potest esse Romae ultra alios quatuor in collegio Graeco, quaeso, procuret in memoriam tanti viri, R.da D.tio Vestra. Parens ipsius iam videtur nomine tantum esse schismaticus et non re, vult ipsi dare viaticum et si quae alia erunt necessaria."

16. *Arxeografičeskij* 1870, 214. Jakiv Suša mentioned in 1686 a Ieremias Smotrzycki, who was a member of the Order of St. Basil the Great (see *Akty* 1900, 375).

17. Smotryc̆kyj 1621b, 42ʳ/366: "Iak y na te nowopoświęcone dobrego sumnienia duchowne Osoby, Oyczyznę swoię miłą, iak Duszę swoię miłuiące, Rodzice, Bracią, Siostry, y insze krewne y powinowate w tamtych temu Nieprzyiacielowi bliższych krainiach, na Wołyniu, na Ukrainie, na Podolu, y na Podgorzu maiące, mimo wszelką prawdę, niebacznie się mieczesz?"

18. *Examen* 1621, 19/574: "*stultorum plena sunt omnia*, pełen świat Maximow." Actually, the Uniate were answering Meletij here, who, in his "anonymous" *Defense of the Verification* had written (Smotryc̆kyj 1621c, 18/408): "*stultorum enim plena sunt omnia*: pełen świat głupich."

19. Velykyj 1960, 298: "... Meletio, chiamato prima Massimo ... "

20. Suša 1666, 14: "Maximus in Baptismatis lumine dictus est; cum potius quod e Schismaticis prodijsset tenebris, minimus esset dicendus. Nihilominus praesagio quodam, eo vocatus est nomine, quod diuina Metamorphosi, in virum post euaserit maximum."

21. *Pamflet* 1875, 564: "сей [Herasym Smotryckyj] імяше сына именемъ Мексентія или Максима (сице бо самъ нарицашеся)."

22. Suša 1666, 14: "Vitalem Spiritum Meletius hausit, in Podolia e nobili prosapia. ... Progenitor eius Erasmus Smotryski, Vicecapitaneus Castri Camenecensis, plurimo egit tempore." In this case, Suša was not the first Uniate to give this information: the brief biography of 1630, probably from the pen of Ruckyj for the information of *Propaganda Fide*, tells us that "Meletij Smotryckyj was born in Rus′ of noble parents, though schismatic." (Velykyj 1972, 218: "Meletius Smotrziski natus in Russia ex nobilibus parentibus, sed schysmaticis.")

23. Smotryckyj 1621b, iᵛ/315: "... ten Przezacny y święty Mąż, Patriarcha Ierozolimsky, a przy nim insze vczciwe Osoby: z ktorych *reflexiue* wszytek Zacny Narod nasz Ruski taką zmazę, ktora oraz y zdrowie y vczciwe iego razi, tłumi, y zgubi ... bezwinnie ponosi, y cierpi."

24. *List* 1621, 5–6/736–37: "To (iako we wszytkim) zły y nieprzystoyny wasz, albo twoy, ktoryś tę Verificatią wydawał, postępek. ... Bo gdzie iest tam o narodzie Ruskim? Tylko (o) Smotrzyskim a Boreckim, a perduellii ich samych piszą y brzmią listy zawarte Jego Kr. M. y uniwersały. ... Narod zacny Ruski, coż ma być przywinien za złe sprawy tych ochotnikow waszych do przełożeństwa cerkiewnego? ... A coż Smotrzyski y Borecki w narodzie Ruskim fex populi et abiectio plebis: iakoż od tych ludzi reflexia na Ruski narod?"

25. *Sowita* 1621, 69/492: "Wszytkiego tego dowiedziemy, gdy kto po nas tego będzie potrzebował; Nie wspominam dawnieyszych, ktorzy przede dwudziestą lat pisali y pisma swoie podali w Druk, Theologow waszych, iako Zyzaniego, Suraskiego, Harasima Popa ktorego synem iest wasz Smotrycki, y Philaleta ktory był Nowokrzczeńcem, Cleryka Ostroskiego, y inszych tym podobnych."

Ruckyj referred here to a certain deacon Herasym, who was active in the Vilnius Brotherhood in the 1590s. (See Scepuro 1898, 86, 89, 92.) Could Ruckyj really not have known who Meletij's father was? Was this rather an intentional slight? Or does our fragile sense of who was important in those days distort our views of what must have been common knowledge?

26. Smotryckyj 1621c, 109/453: "... rozumiesz żeś to miał zawstydzić y obelżyć Smotrzyskiego, synem go Popowskim być powiedziawszy gdy przez to raczey małżeństwu Presbyterskiemu, przymawiasz. Za iedno dobro, miedzy inszemi vczciwego vrodzenia swego dobry ważył by to sobie Ociec Smotrzyski, by się był z Męża na służbę Bożą wydzielonego vrodził."

27. Smotryc̈kyj 1621c, 110/454: "Znało Herasima Daniłowicza Smotrzyskiego Podole ktore y rodziło go, y wychowało: y Grodskim Pisarzem Kamienieckim za trzech Starostow Kamienieckich miało. Znała Wołyń, gdzie od Ś. pamięci Iaśnie Oświeconego Xiążęcia Ostrozkiego, Woiewody Kiiowskiego, przy swym ziemiańskim na Podolu szpłachciku, nie pogardzoną maiętnością w Konstantynowskim Trakcie opatrzony mieszkał. Ten wielki swego czasu w Ruskim narodzie mąż, widząc nachyloną do vpadku Cerkiew naszę Ruską, prze prostotę y hrubiaństwo tych, ktorym mądrym być należało y vczonym, zostawił *Muniment* swoy wieczny pamięci godny."

28. Smotryc̈kyj 1622a, 7ʳ/469: "A że Oyca Boreckiego y Oyca Smotrzyskiego Męże vczciwe w narodzie Ruskiem, *fecem populi et abiectionem plebis* nazywacie, nie dziwuiemy się. Coż bowiem sługa ma mieć nad Pana? Chrystus Pan ich, od wam podobnych tak miał być nazywany: iako o nim w osobie swey Prorok Boży mowi, *Ego autem sum vermis non homo, opprobrium hominum et abiectio plebis.* Ia iestem robak a nie człowiek, pośmiewisko ludzkie y odrzucenie pospolstwa."

29. Smotryc̈kyj 1622a, 30ʳ/492: "Oycu Smotrzyskiemu wziąć tego nikt y z Władyctwem słusznie nie może, co mu vczciwe iego Szlacheckie vrodzenie bez Władyctwa słusznie dało."

30. Suša (1666, 16), too, described Herasym's service to Ostroz'kyj, including our only evidence that Herasym was rector of the Ostroh school, stating that he was given two villages for his labors: "Cui etiam dignos labore census designauit, villasque insuper Baklaiouka, et Borisouka e Ducatu Ostrogiensi adiecit." If this was the case, the younger Smotryc̈kyj seems to have been unable to draw on the income from these villages to fund his schooling.

31. Golubev 1883b, 350: "Zadaiesz o urodzenie O. Smotryckiemu nie na duszę y cnotę ale na początek ciała. . . . ale ieśli się nie vrodził po ślachecku, albo senatorsku, urodził się po krulewsku tak zacnie iako Sołomon. . . . A twoie urodzenie iakie?"

32. Velykyj 1952, 267: " . . . Maximus Harasimovius, homo plebeiae conditionis, qui se cognominaverat Meletium Smotricki . . . "

CHAPTER 2

1. For Orthodox views, see Golubev 1883, 94; Osinskij 1911, no. 7–8, 441; Prokošiną 1966, 38–40; Elenevskij 1861, 116. For Roman Catholic and Ukrainian Catholic views, see Solovij 1977, 140–41; Urban 1957, 140–41, 168.

2. Suša 1666, 15–16: "Inde Ostrogiae liberali effuso aere, non Slauonicae duntaxat linguae, sed Graecarum iuxta, atque Latinarum artium, erexit palaestram. In qua Ruthenam multam, qua nobilem, qua plebeiam aluit iuuentutem. Caeterum videns dictum Erasmum Smotryski, Vicecapitaneum

Camenecensem, eruditionis Ruthenos inter haud spernendae, authoritate sua tantum apud eum perfecit, vt relicto publico honore, eius gymnasij Rectorem subierit."

3.   Suša 1666, 16: "Erasmus duos habens filios, cum eos pro sua tenuitate, seuera morum disciplina excoluisset, magistro e Graecia, per Ducem dictum euocato Cyrillo, ad Constantinopolitanam post euecto sedem, in Graecis Latinisque litteris erudito, imbuendos tradidit. Sub quo Maximus, aetate licet minor eruditione maior, in vtroque idiomate apparuit."

4.   See Smotryc'kyj's dedication of the *Homiliary Gospel* of 1616 to Bohdan Solomerec'kyj (Smotryc'kyj 1616, "iʳ/7).

5.   Suša 1666, 16: "Iuniorem cum Georgio Puzyna, e primaeuo nobilitatis Volhiniensis flore iuuene, sanguineque sibi iuncto, sub annum 1601. Vilnam pro tractandis liberalibus disciplinis, ad Patrum Soc. Iesv, direxit Academiam. Isthic aliquot moratus annis, rationalique exacta Phylosophia, cum altioribus scientijs, vti durum Schismatis germen prohiberetur, curando tyrocinio magnae notae iuuenis, atque e Principibus oriundi, sed Schismatici Solomerecij, admotus est. Quo cum in Silesiam, Vratislauiam, inde Lypsiam, ac Norimbergam, aliasque in Ciuitates, et Academias acatholicae Germaniae demigrauit."

6.   Suša 1666, 17: "Quandoquidem Laicus adhuc, quasi magnae authoritatis in fide Magister, Vertente iam anno 1610. Volumen virulentum concepit: eidemque nomen, Theophili Orthologi Lamentum, indidit."

7.   Velykyj 1972, 218: "Puer, ob eximiam indolem, a parentibus Patribus Societatis Jesu in disciplinam traditus, absolutis minoribus litterarum studijs ad Physicam usque, inter illos profecit."

8.   Velykyj 1972, 218: "Sed anxijs parentibus, ne ex consuetudine Patrum Societatis, deserto avito Schismate in Catholica Religione perseveret, mittitur in Germaniam ad Scholas Haereticorum, ubi haeretico veneno infectus rediens in Russiam, adhuc saecularis existens, multos edidit libros contra fidem catholicam ac Unionem Ruthenorum cum S. R. E., sed inter caeteros unum pestilentissimum, inscriptum *Lamentatio Ecclesiae Orientalis.*"

9.   Velykyj 1960, 298: "Meletio, chiamato prima Massimo, havendo studiato nell'Academia di Vilna in Lithuania, fu poi per causa dello Scisma escluso da quella, onde andatosene in Germania e pratticando fra Eretici compose un libro pieno d'heresie, col quale ha sedotto moltissime persone."

10.   The Ukrainian Catholic scholar Solovij (1977, 141) made Suša's "natural philosophy" into "philosophy" pure and simple. Thus, in his view, Smotryc'kyj would have spent four years in Vilnius. Since Smotryc'kyj seems not to have studied philosophy in Vilnius, perhaps he did not spend as many as four years at the academy.

11.   *Pamflet* 1875, 564: "и града Вилна достигъ въ тамошной Академіи Езуитской латинскую философію навершалъ."

12. *Pamflet* 1875, 565: "вящшего ради и глубочайшаго ученія Академичнаго."

13. Smotryc̆kyj 1629a, 68/679: "zwłaszcza iżem ia też (iako z młodych lat Dyscypuł Wieleb: twey) Wielebności twey skryptow nie mnieyszym powodem, w tę taką myśli rostargninę, y opiniy gmatwaniny przyszedł."

14. Smotryc̆kyj 1628a, 95–96/571: "Kto był Theophil Ortolog? Lutrow Zwolennik Ktory w Akademiey Lipskiey y Witemberskiey, przy grobie Lutrowym wiek swoy młody na naukach trawiwszy, skwarow Luterańskich dymem okopciały do Lytwy przybył, y Ruś Lamentuiąc tymże czadem zaraził."

15. Kortycki 1634, A3ᵛ: "Na koniec znaiąc osobliwy a wielce miłosny w Christusie affekt, y vfność przeciwko mnie, y wszytkiemu zakonowi naszemu Prześwietnego tego, y Przeświętego Męża, ktorego czcigodne ciało przed sobą widzicie."

16. Smotryc̆kyj punned, referring to Rome as the head ("caput") that seizes ("capit") everything, and to the Jesuits not as *Jezuici* but as *"Wyzuwici,"* from the verb *wyzuwać/wyzuć*, meaning "to despoil, deprive." See Smotryc̆kyj 1610, 77ʳ/93: "Abowiem Rzym *caput quod omnia capit*, a Iezuita wyzuita, co z dobr ludzi wyzuwa."

17. *Examen* 1621, 44/591: "[Smotryc̆kyj] Powiedział, że Xiążka Iego M. Ojca Władyki Włodzimierskiego, Respons na ich Lament nazwana, Parigoria we wszytkim mu dosyć vczyniła."

18. Cf. *Antelenchus* 1622, 49/717: "Waszeć to naymilsze y teraz obcowanie iest z Inowiercami, naymilsze rozmowy y zasiadania, consultacie z nimi, czytanie ksiąg ich, posyłanie dzieci do szkoł ich, chowanie ich v siebie. Czy nie wyż to właśnie, istotnie y rzeczywiście Inowiercow nauką truć się ludziom swoim, iako mowi *Appendix*, dopusczacie? y przed tym iescze dawno za przodkow waszych wam podobnych, Ruś była dobrze potruta, przed Vnią był Skoryna heresią Hussyta, ktory wam księgi po Rusku drukował w Pradze. Przyimowali ich wdzięcznie, dosyć na tym że się zwał Rusinem z Połocka, iako się podpisał. Smakowali sobie iego druki, człowiek godny, mowili; a Rusin brat nasz to drukował. Symon Budny, y Laurenty Krzyżkowski iad swoy Ariański po Rusku drukowawszy, rozsiali miedzy Popy, przyięli to za lekarstwo, tak iż y teraz mamy iescze trudność z Popami odeymuiąc im te księżczyska z rąk."

19. *Antelenchus* 1621, 49/716: "Ieśliż ten sam [i.e., Smotryc̆kyj] nie był iuż struty nauką Inowiercow?"

20. *Pamflet* 1875, 567: "но вся елико унѣяти мудрствуют хваляше и паче онѣх силогизмами Оригенскими услаждаше, православних злословяше."

21. *Polnoe* 1975, 185: "Того року была зима люта и снежная. Благовещение было на святой недели в [пя]ток. Почали орати по святе на четвертой недели. Того ж року, месеца апреля у понеделок на святого Мартина папы римского, взявши з науки от Лаврентия зараз дано до

науки латинския до пана Максима Герасимовича Смотрицкого."

22. Skarga 1610, 108: "Był ten Cyrillus na Brzeskim Synodzie, na ktorym się vnia sstała, y iam go tam poznał, roku Pańskiego 1596. . . . drugi raz roku Pańskiego 1601. wysłany tu był."

23. Smotryc'kyj 1629a, 69/679: " . . . nim do wiadomości mey doszedł List Wieleb: twey, przy X. Demetryuszu Solikowskim, godney pamięci Arcybiskupie Lwowskim, (v ktorego y mnie z Wieleb: twoią czasu iednego bydź zdarzyło się) Roku 1601. *Ianuarij* 24. *die*, we Lwowie zostawiony . . . " Smotryc'kyj was referring here to the famous letter Lukaris had left with Solikowski on his second departure from the Commonwealth, in which he had emphasized the areas of unity between the Orthodox and the Catholics, and the areas of disagreement between those two groups and the Protestants. This letter was first published in its original Latin version and with a Polish translation in Skarga 1610, 108–113.

24. Smotryc'kyj 1616, v^r/13: "То бовѣмъ все щоколвек в розумъ могу, если що могу, по ласце Б[о]жой, и по ласце Ясне Освецоных Кнж. Острозскихъ, ласце и добродѣйствам В. Кнж. М. домовства, приписовати повинен найдую ся: которого при боку и тубытных и чужоземских Академій вызволеных наукъ вдячности, ведлуг мѣлкого довтѣпу моего, звѣдати здарил ми Г[оспо]дъ Богъ."

25. Smotryc'kyj 1628a, *1^r/517: "*Apologia Peregrinatiey do Kraiow Wschodnych, Przez mię Meletivsza Smotrzyskiego, M. D. Archiepiskopa Połockiego . . . sporządzona y podana.*"

26. Smotryc'kyj 1628a, 1/523: "Meletivs Smotrziski *Z miłosierdzia Bożego* Archyepiskop Połocki . . . " [emphasis added].

27. Consider, for example, the two most recent book-length studies. Jaremenko (1986, 9) falls into the old trap, whereas Korotkyj (1987, 27–28) realizes that this is unlikely, but comes up with the wrong solution, interpreting M.D. as "Magni Ducatus," or "of the Grand Duchy," and he interprets this as an expression of Lithuanian patriotism.

CHAPTER 3

1. I assume that Smotryc'kyj authored all the prefaces since they are all elaborate reworkings of the same themes and verbal material; moreover, the other prefaces were signed in the name of the Orthodox Brotherhood, in exactly the same fashion as the polemical works he wrote in the period 1621–1623. See Smotryc'kyj 1987b, xx–xxii.

2. See Smotryc'kyj 1628a, 24/535: "Ieśli nie co inszego, tedy to samo tych Ciemnych Authorow naukę y pisma w podeyrzenie nieprawdy podać nam było

miało, że żaden z nich imienia swego do tych swych bałamutni nie podpisał, ale tylko zmyślone. Ktory kiedy rodzic poczciwego swego spłodku wstydził sie, iak sie ci swoich zrodkow wstydali, że sie do nich znać nie zezwolili: przez co za pewne to o sobie, y o nich wiedzieć dali, że niepoczciwego łoża spłodki na świat puścili." But Smotryc'kyj had made this argument before in his Orthodox incarnation. (It was a common polemical ploy on both sides of the fence.) The (anonymous!) author of the "Preface to the Reader," and presumably the "translator" of the *Thrēnos* attributed by him to "Theophil Ortholog" (i.e., Smotryc'kyj himself in each instance), addressed the following words (Smotryc'kyj 1610, () () ()ivᵛ/13) to the Uniate author(s) of *Nieiakiś Nalewayko* and *Relatia albo vważenie spraw ktore się Roku 1609 Działy w Wilnie:* "Ieśli ieszcze iaka w tobie boiaźni Bożey, Cnoty y wstydu przyrodzonego iskierka została, wynidź na iawią, zrzuć tę maszkarę z twarzy, obiaw imię swoie, wyźrzysz ieśli tego ze wstydem y wieczną hańbą nie zażyiesz?"

The pseudo-Orthodox polemicist Diplic (1634, 614–15) answered Smotryc'kyj's lines cited above from the *Apology* by arguing that Philalet, Ortholog and others did not sign their real names in order to avoid persecution from the Catholic secular authorities ("the stronger side"): "Po wtore to mowię, że drudzy, iako Philalet y Ortholog, imion swych własnych do pism swych nie podpisali, nie ta iest przyczyna, aby się oni mieli byli prac swoich wstydać, gdy ie na świat wypuszczali: ale że chcieli wyść niebeśpieczeństw, ktore zwykły potykać, te, co przeciwko stronie potężnieyszey ważą się co pisać, y na nie nacierać."

3.   See Smotryc'kyj 1628a, 105/576: "nie wspominam verificatiey, obrony iey, Elenchu, Iustificatiey, y tym podobnych. w ktorych iedney po drukiey, im daley, tym rzadszy byłem w następowaniu na dogmata prawdziwe, szerszy w rzeczach potocznych, pod te czasy nagle przypadłych"; Smotryc'kyj 1629a, 22/656: "ponieważ dosyciem się iemu iuż był przez Lament, werifikacyą, obronę iey, Elench, iustyfikacyą, y insze prace moie znaczne, bydź nieco okazał . . . "

Notice that the lists are slightly different, that both are incomplete, and that in both instances Smotryc'kyj laid claim to "other" unspecified works.

4.   According to Myc'ko (1990, 112), Smotryc'kyj translated (into Ruthenian?) Marcantonio de Dominis' *Profectionis consilium* from the Polish version of P. Blastus-Kmita. Myc'ko writes of a unique copy of the Polish translation—apparently unknown to Polish bibliographers—in L'viv. Smotryc'kyj's translation (if it was his), *Причини отъеханья зе Влох*, was printed anonymously by the Vilnius Brotherhood printing house between 1618 and 1623. (See *Kniha* 1986, 94–95; see also Myc'ko 1984). I have not seen this work.

5.   Smotryc'kyj 1629a, 7/648: "Przeszłego Roku zszedł z tego świata tu w tym kraiu, mąż w narodzie Ruskim, tak w pobożności żywota, iako w wiadomości Dogmat wiary, nie lada exystimacyey: są iednak żywi ci poważni mężowie, z Ostrogskiey Kapituły Świeszczennicy, przy ktorych obecności, w głos o

Lamentowym skrypcie to mowił, że iest w poważności opisaney w nim prawdy Bożey, pismom ś. Złotoustego rowny: za ktory krew swoię nam wylewać, y duszę zań pokładać godzi się. Nuż co tych tym podobnych głosow było, przed wyszciem tego Lamentowego skryptu, o Skrypcie Zyzaniego y Philaletowym? O skrypcie Klerykowym, z vst tegoż zeszłego męża słyszałem, że go nie chwalił: y iż on był, ktorym odwiodł od tego, że się imienno do tego Skryptu nie podpisał ten, czyie było to miasto, ktorym się ten Kleryk otytułował; (na czym iuż przez Authora Skryptu tego, rzecz była stanęła) daiąc tę przyczynę: że gdy wielkiemu y zacnemu imieniowi twemu, lada Klecha karczemne słowo zada, czym tę swoię powieść wesprzesz? Y tak ten skrypt za iego radą, na bezimiennym Kleryku Ostrogskim stanął: że by dobrze Klecha Klesze co nie w smak przymowił, nie wielki miał bydź vraz."

6. Smotryćkyj 1628a, 105/576: "Świadomi są tego dobrze ci, ktorym wiadome były moie lucubracie naprzeciw scriptu Vnią otytułowanego. naprzeciw rozmowie Brześcianina z Bratczykiem. naprzeciw zmartwychwstałego Nalewayka. naprzeciw Politice Ignorantiam y nabożeństwu nowo Cerkwian Wileńskich napisane y do publikowania przez druk iuż po wydaniu Lamentu, puszczone bydź, nagotowane."

7. See Gil'tebrandt 1903, 1149: ΑΝΤΙΓΡΑΦΗ *albo ODPOWIEDŹ na script vszczypliwy . . . ktoremu tituł: "Heresiae, ignoranciae y Politika popow y mieszczan bractwa Wileńskiego" . . .*

8. Smotryćkyj 1629a, 89–90/689–90: "Po tym Philalecie, toż czyni nieiakiś bezimienny Kleryk Ostrogski, ktory pełnieyszy iest bluźnierstw naprzeciwko przedwieczności Syna Bożego, y fałszu o Synodzie Florentskim, niż nauki y prawdy. Toż czyni potym Autor Skryptu mianowanego, *Antigraphe*, ktory (*alias homo pientissimus*) przy inszych inkonweniencyach, Ducha ś. y od Syna pochodzić, wyznawać, *Haeresim* bydź mieni. Kleryka owego, y onego Philaleta skrypta chwali, prziymuie, y za swey strony Skrybenty przyznawa. Potym czynią toż y ia w swym skrypcie Lamentowym, ktory *totus fere Caluinizat.*"

9. Skarga 1610, 2: "Sam się wydaie Ortholog, iż go Wileńska Nalewaykowska Cerkiew wysłała, gdy się w inych książkach swoich, Antygrafem nazwanych, bratem Cerkwie Wileńskiey pisze. . . . A my rychło się pewnie dowiedzieć możem, kto iest, y iako go zowią."

10. Suša 1666, 80: "Existimare se insuper, pari plectendos decreto, iam dudum fuisse, Philaletum Caluinum, cum suis blasphemijs, Clericum Ostrogiensem, cum suis mendacijs, ignominem Azariam, cum sua antigraphe . . . "

11. Suša 1666, 87: "Denique vt mittam Basilium Surazki, Zachariam Antigraphes authorem . . . "

12. Skarga declared the notion that *Thrēnos* was a translation to be a fiction: the author was a local product, well-versed in obscure heretical Latin tracts (unknown, in part, even to Skarga), and certainly trained by the heretics. (See

Skarga 1610, 3: "Ostatnie y grube kłamstwo ten tytuł ma: gdy daie znać, iż te książki w Grecyey po Grecku pisano, a on ie z Słowieńskiego na Polskie przetłumaczył. Kto temu vwierzy gdy czyta v niego w tym piśmie Łacińskie pisarze ciemne, z podławia gdzieś od heretykow podrzucone, o ktorych nie tylo Grekowie, ale y my nie słychaliśmy. Gdy też poiedynkowie Ruskie dzieie y domy Książąt y szlachty wylicza: y gdy X. Skargę y inne wspomina, o ktorych Grekowie nie wiedzą. . . . Zdrada tedy iest w tych książkach, wszytko iego są wymysły, ktory się tu wychował, y Łacińskiego ięzyka nawykł, y iadu się aż do gardła heretyckiego nabrał y wszytkie w nim heretyki przewyższa.") Moroxovs'kyj also wrote that Ortholog was a pseudonym, and that *Thrēnos* was not written in Greek or Slavonic. (See Moroxovs'kyj 1612, A2ᵛ: " . . . przez iakiegoś Anonima, pierwey iakoby z Greckiego na Słowieński, a teraz z Słowieńskiego na Polski przełożone. . . . Bowiem tego nigdy po Grecku [chyba dialecto Cretensi, ktorego on zażywa] ani po Słowieńsku nie było.")

13. Bohdan Struminsky has argued that "Azarij" was not Kopystens'kyj. See Krevza 1987, xxxiii–xxxxiv. Here Struminsky and others have been concerned primarily with the authorship of the *Книга о Вѣрѣ*, which was written by "Azarij." Perhaps this other, neglected reference to Azarij in Smotryc'kyj's letter will add to the debate. Did Kopystens'kyj ever reside in the Vilnius Brotherhood Monastery? If not, then it would seem unlikely that Azarij was Kopystens'kyj. Perhaps we should look for some other Zaxarija as author of *Antigraphē*. Smotryc'kyj himself gave a rehearsal of Orthodox authors and works in *Apology* (150/598: "Zyzani, Wasili Surazki, Antygraphe, Azarias") that listed *Antigraphē* and Azarias separately. But this does not necessarily mean he thought they were two different authors. Smotryc'kyj was listing works here and adhering to the convention of respecting pseudonyms and anonymities. Petruševič (1874, 414), whose chronicle is a gold mine of potentially interesting, but nearly always unattributed information, made Kopystens'kyj the author of *Antigraphē*. How did he know?

14. This work has been reprinted in Kojalovič 1865, 230–31.

15. Smotryc'kyj 1628a, 105/576: "Bog moy, podobno za vczynioną iemu przez Lament wielką obrazę, w tym doświadczeniu dłużey mię mieć chcąc, przyść mi ni do owego, ni do tego publicatiey nie dopuścił."

16. Smotryc'kyj 1628a, 105/576: "Niemal y teraz nayduie sie w Bibliotece Monastera Bractwa Cerkiewnego Wileńskiego Traktat o pochodzeniu Ducha Ś. sposobem syllogismow od Graekow Rzymianom, y wzaiem Graekom od Rzymian zadawać sie zwykłych, polskim ięzykiem napisany."

17. Petruševič claimed (1874, 446) he possessed a manuscript copy of a portion of Smotryc'kyj's catechism. The Orthodox side claimed in 1644 that it possessed an autograph of the catechism. See *Lithos* 1644, 188/180.

18. Velykyj 1959, 53: "Non ho mancato di far sempre ogni caldo et efficace officio per aiutar la suppressione di quel nefando libro ruteno." This, of course,

does not tell us that *Thrēnos* was written in the Ruthenian language.

19. Smotryc'kyj 1629b, 70ʳ/770: "Ponieważ bowiem coby zacz był Ortholog, ktory to pisał, nikt na on czas, procz niektorych z Bratstwa Wileńskiego przednieyszych ossob: nie wiedział."

20. Smotryc'kyj 1628a, 105/576: "Przyszło było czasu swego y do tego, żem był y Palinodią na Lament napisał, ktorą do rąk Kapitule Ostrozskiey w tym Monasteru, w ktorym teraz residuię y to piszę, podana ode mnie bywszy zaległa."

21. Diplic 1634, 52: "Względem wtorego świadectwa, ztąd się o tym vpewniam iż on, iako mię doszło wiedzieć, dostąpiwszy vrzędu Episkopskiego y Archiepiskopskiego, przed tym, y w 1621 Roku, w Dermaniu nie był: zaczym ani tam Palinodiey swoiey podawać mogł."

22. A part of this polemical strategy is the type of criticism that might be called philological invective, whereby a writer would claim that his opponent lacked the basic, philological tools of the trade. According to Moroxovs'kyj, the Uniate respondent to Smotryc'kyj's *Thrēnos*, the future grammarian of Church Slavonic distorted the evidence, partially out of bad faith, and "partially out of a lack of knowledge of the Slavonic language." (Moroxovs'kyj 1612, 88: " . . . częścią z nieumiętnością ięzyka Słowieńskiego fałszywie przekłada.")

The Protestant polemicist Gelazjusz Diplic (who masqueraded as an Orthodox) sent Smotryc'kyj to read Cnapius' (Grzegorz Knapski) entry for "mixed speech" so that he might learn that unnecessary macaronisms were in bad style. According to Diplic, Kasijan Sakovyč had taken lessons in macaronism and solecism from Smotryc'kyj (Diplic 1634, 32–33, 42).

23. *List* 1621, 1/733: "Od was, albo raczey od ciebie Smotrzyski, ktoryś w niey affectatione styli, dziecinogłupią phrasi, y z przeplatanych słow, zawikłanym sensem (czym u prostszych ludzi za mędrka się udaiesz), znacznie wydał . . . "

24. *List* 1621, 36/760: " . . . petulantissimo styli et lingua . . . "

25. *List* 1621, 8/738: " . . . wynaydzione głupiomądre słowa."

26. *List* 1621, 28/753: "Wglądaliśmy y daley w tę xiążkę waszę y dziwiliśmy się obłudności słow y ich zgromadzeniu, niepoiętey mieszaninie sensus insensati, a takiego, z ktorego by się sam autor nie wyplotł y tylko tym zrozumiany, gdy kogo uszczypliwie tknie y urazi."

27. The Uniates claimed this was a peculiarity of Smotryc'kyj's style. See *List* 1621, 16/744: " . . . sequakowie (iż *verbo vestro utemur*)"; *Sowita* 1621, 55/ 482: "y mieli sequakow swoich (że Polszczyzny Bractwa waszego na ten czas zażyię) liczbą 14700." Smotryc'kyj used it throughout his career: "Apostasii swey Sequakow nie naydzie" (Smotryc'kyj 1621a, 239); "bez ordy sequakow moich" (Smotryc'kyj 1629, 13ʳ/713).

28. *List* 1621, 13–15/742–43: "W Połocku iaki tumult seditią, concitatią populi, przeciwko władyce, canonice y według praw y zwierzchności Jego Kr. M. postanowionego, przeciwko woiewodzie tamesznemu, przeciwko commisarzom Jego Kro. M., przez listy y patenty swe et submissas personas, natręt na to władyctwo wielebny (iako się sam tytułuie) Miolentij uczynił. Ale lud ten rycerski (iż się do niego wrocimy), przywiedziony od was w seditią, do contractow z ich mościami Pany hetmany o te władyki y metropolitę y do legacii Jego Kr. Mści namowili się. Świeże p. Sahaydacznego poselstwo do Jego Kr. M. wydaie was. Bo z swym iakimś czerńcem (mianuie go w tey legatii) na władyctwo ktoreś łakomym przyiachał y legacia na piśmie dana wszytek affekt wasz wyraża y wszytka iey summa o Graeczynie y sprawach iego w Moskwie y o was poświęconych od niego: tak iakoby od was (y tak iest pewnie) pisana to legacia. Bo wszytka rzecz y sens tey waszey Verificatii, nawet stylus z słowa wydaie. . . . Fabricia to wasza wszytko."

29. Skarga had already (in 1610) represented the writing of *Thrēnos* as an act of treason to the Commonwealth. *Thrēnos* had been published "quietly and without official knowledge, right at the time of the departure and campaign of His Majesty the King against Moscow." (Skarga 1610, A2^r: "cicho y nad vrzędową wiadomość, prawie pod wyiazd y wyprawę Krola I.M. do Moskwy.") The book itself made its way to Moscow, and just at the time of the Commonwealth's campaign against Muscovy. (See Skarga 1610, A2^v: "ale iż . . . daleko się rozsiewaią, y do samey Moskwy książki iego: zganić ie y potłumić było potrzeba. A zwłaszcza iż teraz Krol I.M. bogoboyny y miłościwy Pan nasz z Moskwą sprawę y woynę ma.")

30. See the letter of Sigismund III dated 6 May published in *Akty* 1875, 95: "Ażeby y na potem takowych pasquillusów y calumniy drukować nie mogli, aby drukarnią y typam tego bractwa zabrać, a drukarzów y autorów tych pasquillusów y correctora ich Łotwin [*sic*, but his name was Lohvyn] Karpowicza, zwłaszcza ieśli nie iest szlachcicem, o czem w.w. łacno się między sobą dowiedzieć możecie, na ratuszu, albo w więzieniu iakiem do nauki naszey zatrzymać kazali."

31. *List* 1621, 6/736–37: "Naród zacny Ruski, coż ma być przywinien za złe sprawy tych ochotnikow waszych do przełożeństwa cerkiewnego? Nas, ktorzy z przodkow starożytnych naszych iesteśmy narodu Ruskiego, to nie obchodzi, y tych potomstwa, ktorycheście w tey przemowie, iako niegdy w onym Lamencie wydanym wrzkomo od Lochwina, mianowali."

Cf. also Symanowicz 1621, F4^r: "Wszak w onym Nagrobnym Lohwinkowym Sarra się wasza do woli rzegocze? y drugich, żeby iey tego dopomagali, wzywa: y nie omyliła się pewnie."

32. *List* 1621, 17/745: "Uciecha niewinności narodu Ruskiego—napominanie do swoich, przekładanie przed oczy tragediey Wileńskiey z mieszczany, waszemi sequakami. To wasze pathos (w uciesze niewinności narodu Ruskiego, słowy wymyślnymi, z Pisma Ś. wyiętemi), ktore commovetis w ludziach, ku żadney

potrzebie inszey się nie ściąga, tylko ku tumultom, buntom, seditii, uzna kożdy, kto uważyć będzie chciał. A nie ieseście autores seditionis w Rzeczy Posp?"

33. Symanowicz 1621, B2ʳ: "Przepiekły się niegdy, Lamenty vszczypliwe Harasimowiczowe, w ktorych Bogu, y dobrym ludziom brzydką, ciężką, niezbożną, Bissurmańską niewolą śmiał zalecać; bluźnierskie Heretyckie nauki, przeciwko wierze powszechney Chrześciańskiey pod Tytułem świątobliwym Cerkwie wschodniey, do narodu naszego Ruskiego wwodzić: y wiele innych rzeczy tym podobnych pisać, drukować, y po wszytkiey Rusi, y W.X. Litewskim rozsiewać."

34. *Examen* 1621, 8/566: "Sprawi się lepiey, czytaiąc wszytkę tę Historyą, ktorey iest na arkuszow kilkanaście, ieśli się nie poleni."

35. *Examen* 1621, 12/569: "Snadź tego nie wiedział, acz nie dziw: bo w Grammatice swey tego się nie doczytał."

36. *Examen* 1621, 26/579: "*Defectus fide non vtitur, excessus fide abutitur:* A snadź, żeby to w *disquisitią* nie przychodziło, powiedział, że rozum nasz (mowiąc do nas) tego poiąć nie może. Nowe v Theologow i niesłychane tak *axiomatha*, jako i *distinctio fidei*. Od nowego też Theologa, a od dawnego Grammatyka wymyślone."

37. *Antelenchus* 1621, 33/703: "bo się na Dialectice tak znacie iak świnia na pieprzu." See also *Antelenchus, 38/708:* "Mowi daley że ta figura iest *Zeugma;* my że się znamy na Grammatykach (iako nam przyznawa tamże tenże *Elenchus*), tego Grammatyka odsyłamy do szkoły gdzie, go nauczą, że *Zeugma* nie ściąga się *ad tempora*: raczey może bydź *Solecismus*, ale o taką figurę chrostem daią *in forma posteriorum Analiticorum* w Grammatyce."

38. *Examen* 1621, 43/590: "... *Crassa ignorantia, et diffidentia causae:* Nieukowieście (odpuśćcie nam), nie maiący nic we łbie gruntownie włożonego, a tylko się na słowach sadzicie, ktorych, iako Papugi, na kazaniach i w druku głupie zażywacie."

39. *Examen* 1621, 19/574: "*stultorum plena sunt omnia*, pełen świat Maximow."

40. *Antelenchus* 1621, 49/716–17: "Dawnosz temu, iako sam ten *Appendix* wydał książkę wrzkomo przekładaiąc z Słowieńskiego na Polskie, w ktorey wyrzucił Modlitwy do Panny Naświętszey Bogarodzicy, y wszytkich Świętych. Ieśliż ten sam nie był iuż struty nauką Inowiercow? y tąż nauką potruć drugich iadowity paiąk nie vsiłował? aż okrzyknęli tego wilka Pasterze naszy y pieskowie ich."

41. *Antelenchus* 1621, 54–55/721–22: "ale oto nie czynimy, y czynić nie chcemy: nasz to iest zysk y chwała vcierpieć za Chrystusa Pana, y prawdę iego, y czas to da Pan Bog vkaże, ieśli złość ludzka nastąpi, że ochotnieyszemi na to będziemy, niż *Appendix*, ktory ofiarował ci się na to, ale się prętko vkazało, że to ofiarowanie iego nie prawdziwe było, bo ktoś mu y to *per tertias personas* o

kiiu przypomniał za słowa bezecne, ktorych iako Elenchus, tak *Appendix*, w marnych scripcyskach swych przeciwko nam *plaustra integra* nakładli, aż się on przed każdym sprawować, odrzekaiąc się chudak y prace swoiey, za ktorą godzien by był pochwały y podziękowania, y owszem z pokory swoiey Wołczey tę pracę drugiemu przypisał, vkazawszy sentencykę iakąś żakowską Grecką, ktorey początek *M.* a koniec *S.* żebyśmy się domyślili imienia y przezwiska tego authora. Miły *Appendix*, ieśli to praca Bogu miła, y v ludzi chwalebna, czemu iey tak pilno zapierasz? ieśli zła, czemuż na bliżniego wkładasz y w niebespeczeństwo go wdaiesz, sam vchodząc przed nim? Idzie podobno o żonkę, o miłe dziatki, *compatiar tibi* nieboże, nie podeymuyże się szaszku legawego pola, kiedy serca nie masz, po co się na świat pokazuiesz, pod ławą w kącie pieskowi beśpieczne y szczekać, ale na vlicy może się mu dostać kiiem, w czym sam sobie będzie winien, abo że podobniey rzekę, beśpieczniey Wołkowi szamotać owce w lesie, niż w polu przy Pasterzu y psach, gdzie mu się y kiiem dostanie y od psow niełacno vyść będzie mogł."

42. The only information we have on this topic is a marginal annotation written in a seventeenth-century hand in a copy of *Thrēnos* discovered by Studynśkyj in Cracow in 1898 (see Jaremenko 1986, 54). This note claimed that Smotryćkyj entered a monastery after his bride was stolen away: "Meletius Smotriski. Rapta sponsa Al. H. monasterium ingreditur." Studynśkyj argued that the initials Al. H. stood for Alisija Hulevyčivna, daughter of a Volhynian nobleman, and he wrote a historical drama on this subject (*Dvi zori*, L′viv, 1937).

43. Smotryćkyj wrote of "your Ortholog" (Smotryćkyj 1629a, 36–37/663: "Gdzież tu [in the Roman confession] z tego takiego prawdziwego Katholickiego ich wyznania, lub Manicheyskie dwa początki, lub Sabelliańskie dwu osob zlicie? Zaiste, nie Rzymskiey to wiary Herezya, ale twego Ortholoza, abo y przed nim czyie insze wymysły y kalumnie."). And on one occasion he charged Ortholog with falsely citing the words of St. Basil the Great so that they would support his own views on the Trinity (Smotryćkyj 1628a, 73–74/560: "takowy na koniec porządek, iaki nam Ortolog, iakoby z Basiliusza ś. omylnie przełożył, Oyca do Syna y do Ś. Ducha: a Synowi y świętemu Duchowi do Oyca, ŚŚ. Doctorow Cerkiewnym nie iest znaiomy, ale iest nowo zmyślony."). Smotryćkyj ought to have known, one would think. But what had happened here? Was Smotryćkyj now admitting that he had twisted testomonies as a young Ortholog? Did he only realize his "error" later on? Or was he now twisting the "facts?"

44. See, for example, Diplic 1634, 453: "przystępuię do vważenia błędow y hereziy Theophilowi Orthologowi od tegoż Apologiuiącego zarzuconych: tey nadzieie będąc, że Autor ten ni w czym y z niego triumphu nie odniesie . . . "

45. Suša 1666, 121–22: "Exethesis ea partus est praenobilis Smotriscij, qui dum dictas tuetur Considerationes, fortissimis eas fulcit argumentis; rerum autem veritatem et vim rationem, splendida exornat eloquentia. Vt recte a grauissimis viris ob eam Exethesim, Cicero Polonus dici meruerit."

46. See Diplic 1634, 33: "A dla ozdoby też kłaść Makaronizmy, iako ie

nazywaią, abo mowy mieszaney vżywać w takich pismach, co Pielgrzym ten w skryptach swoich, Łacińskie słowa wtrącaiąc zwykł czynić często, co mi za rozsądek? Niechay czyta Knapiusza pod słowy, ieśli się nie mylę, *mieszana mowa*, o Makaronizmach; azali się nauczyć będzie mogł, że mieszać mowę z mową bez potrzeby, iest rzecz nieprzystoyna, y naśmiewania godna."

47. Šmurlo 1932, 566: "... il più dotto tra di loro, et in lingua Ruthena praedicator emeritissimo."

48. See Kortycki 1634, D4ᵛ: "Pisma swoie, zwłaszcza w iedności Ś. będąc nie inaczey, iedno od Christusa zaczynał, ten herb, abo charakter Księgom swoim daiąc, *Meae vitae spes vnica IESVS CHRISTVS* Mego żywota iedyna nadzieia Iezus Chrystus, Do tego kresu wszytkim dusze swoiey pędem bieżał, a iako słusznie spodziewać się mamy, iuż dobieżał."

But Kortycki had twisted the facts a little: Smotryc̆kyj used this motto in *all* his works, Orthodox and Uniate, beginning with the second edition of *Verification of Innocence*, and not only "especially" those written in support of the Union.

49. See Suša (1666, 18–19) on the reception among the Orthodox and heterodox of *Thrēnos*: "Quot ibi verba, tot crudelia vulnera: quot sensus, tot lethalia toxica. Et quia insigni Polonicae linguae cultu, quasi dulci pharmaco condita, eo magis noxia. Adeoque non Schismatici modo istud lamentum, sed etiam haeretici, laetis terebant manibus, pleno fouebant sinu, demum corde suo penitus defigebant. Fuere qui illud quasi precio diues, arte praesigne Cimelium, suprema voluntate in suos deriuandum posteros, testatum reliquerint. E clero autem Schismatico non postremi, authoritate descriptae quasi in eo veritatis diuinae, monumentis Chrysostomi aequiparandum, sanguinemque pro eo fundendum censuere. Nec inglorium aestimatum, cuidam personae haereticae, cum eodem in aeuiternum lamentabili modo sepeliri."

50. See Suša 1666, 46: "In Elencho partu suo anni 1622. non solum illorum, quae in lamento anno 1610. quae in defensione verificationis 1621. scripsit, non solum inquam illorum, Vestram Reuerendissimam Paternitatem non piguit, poenituitue, verum etiam postposita sua palinodia, Spiritus S. instillante exarata maledicentiae suae Colophonem, vt aiunt imposuisse visa est."

51. Suša 1666, 21: "adiecit Elenchum, Librum vt infra videbitur perditissimum."

52. See Smotryc̆kyj 1628a, 90/568: "Bo poki twoy tobie iest Zyzani, Philalet, Ortolog, Klerik, Azary, Elenchus, Antygraph, Suraski, y tym podobni, poty ty w występku fałszu, kłamstwa, potwarzy, bluźnierstw, błędow, y Haereziy."; Smotryc̆kyj 1628a, 90–91/568–69: "Ia pod tymże samym Boga y zbawienia mego miłości obowiązkiem, z części mey każdego z was przestrzegam, vwiadomiam, y vpewniam, Że ktokolwiek z narodu naszego Ruskiego, dla tey wiary, ktorą naszę bydź Zyzani, Philalet, Ortholog, Klerik, Azary, Elenchus, y tym podobni opisali, traci co, abo vmiera: na swoię szkodę traci: y nadaremnie vmiera: zatraca duszę swoię, a nie zbawia."; Smotryc̆kyj 1628b, Ciʳ⁻ᵛ/634–35: "A co powiedziałem, żem nie wiedział, co po te lata moie wierzyłem: prawdę

powiedziałem. Świadkiem tego są scripta moie Lament, Elenchus, y insze: w ktorych to pisałem, com wierzył: a pisałem w nich Hęretycko, Hęretycko przeto y wierzyłem."; Smotryc'kyj 1629b, B1ᵛ/700: "Co każdy całego rozumu człowiek łacno obaczyć może, skoro scripta nieVnitskie z Vnitskimi zniesie, *Apocrysin z Antiresim*: Lament z Parigorią, abo z przestrogą: Kleryka z obroną Synodu Florenskiego: Elench z Antelenchem: y to teraźnieysze Antidotum z Apologią."; Smotryc'kyj 1629b, 4ᵛ/705: "Oto tymi swymi Antidotami, Elenchami, Apocrisisami, Lamentami, Antigraphami, Azariaszami; y tym podobnymi na krew Bratnią podżogami."

CHAPTER 4

1.   On *Thrēnos* and its rhetorical models, see Frick 1987.

2.   On the *Homiliary Gospel*, see Frick 1988.

3.   It is true that the grammar was printed soon after Smotryc'kyj had taken the habit. But it was still the result of his labors as a layman.

4.   Smotryc'kyj 1629b, 70ʳ/770: "ten Lamentowy sc[r]ipt więcey niż rok na Censurze był Bratstwa Wileńskiego, y miał nie lada Censora."

5.   Following the printing of *Thrēnos*, the press in Vilnius was closed, equipment and books confiscated, and some portion of the run was burned. Karpovyč was arrested and incarcerated; Smotryc'kyj apparently escaped punishment. See Anuškin 1970, 184–85; *Akty* 1875, 193–94: "Mamy wiadomość, iż w drukarni ś. Ducha ruskiey pasquilluse iakieś przeciwko zwierzchność y xięgy potaiemne drukuią, stąd w podeyrzenie do nas przychodzą. . . . chcemy mieć y rozkazuiemy, abyście dowiedziawszy się o tem, wielebnemu w Bodze biskupowi y iaśnie wielmożnemu woiewodzie Wileńskim donieśli, do których w tey mierze piszemy y za dołożeniem się ich takowe pasquilluse y xięgi podeyrzane popalili, durkarza y tych, którzy tych pasquillusów y xiąg podeyrzanych są autorami, do więzienia osadzili y do dalszey nauki naszey zatrzymali."

     The Vilnius Brotherhood entered a complaint into the tribunal books on 28 July 1610 (printed in Golubev 1883b, 183–85).

6.   Smotryc'kyj 1621a, D3ʳ⁻ᵛ/250–51: "Wyznawcą samą istotą, a Męczennikiem zezwoleniem zostawszy: gdy mu przez całe dwie lecie, srogim y okrutnym ciemnicznym więzieniem trapionemu, na każdy dzień dla Ewangelskiey prawdy ciężko vmierać przychodziło: Wiadomy wam Praw: Chrześcianie sprawy tey postępek, wiadoma przyczyna: wiadom y skutek."

7.   Smotryc'kyj 1621a, D4ᵛ/252: "Wszytko to iednak chutliwą, iakom rzekł, duszą święty ten Mąż przez całe dwie lecie znosił, byle tylko Ewangelskiey prawdzie poważne świadectwo był wydał: iakoż za łaską dobrotliwego Boga

wydał takie, ktore nie zmieściwszy się w granice Państw naszych, w Cudzoziemskie się krainy, y w pograniczne nam Krolestwa rozlało, a w nich Katholickiey Prawosławney Wiary naszey pobożność, niepokalaną być oświadczyło."

8. Skarga 1610, A2^v: "Nie dbalibyśmy o tego w pokrytym y zmyślonym imieniu Orthologa, tako od rozumu odpadłego: ale iż się od Graekow y Patryarchow wschodnych vdaie, y oszukać wiele prostych Ruskich ludzi kłamstwy swemi może, y daleko się rozsiewaią, y do samey Moskwy książki iego: zganić ie y potłumić było potrzeba. A zwłaszcza iż teraz Krol I.M. bogoboyny y miłościwy Pan nasz z Moskwą sprawę y woynę ma: ktora się barzo Rzymską y Katholicką wiarą brzydzi, y dla niey łaską Krola I.M. gardzić, y z tego czytania zapalić się do większego vporu, boiąc się o naruszenie nabożeństwa swego Graeckiego, może."

9. Smotryc'kyj 1629b, 15^{r-v}/715–16: "A potym mieszkaiąc w Monasterzu tym dłużey niż rok po świecku, byłem częstokroć sollicitowany y proszony tak od wszystkiego Bractwa, iak osobliwie od Nieboszczyka Przodka mego na tym Archimandrytstwie, o przyięcie habitu Zakonnego."

10. Suša 1666, 17: "Solomerecio Minscum sat celebrem et vetustam Ruthenisque obsitam Ciuitatem, quia proximam, saepius commeans, populum simplicem et rudem, intime sibi conciliauit. Quocirca ad illum veluti ad oraculum confluere, ab illius ore in dogmatibus fidei, vniuersi pendere, de illo vti de fonte quodam, doctrinam haurire; sed quia infecto, minime salutarem."

11. *Pamflet* 1875, 565: "по нѣвеликих лѣтех возвратися со князем юным паки въ Болкоградъ къ матери его, вдовѣ уже сущей Княгинѣ Соломирецкой Евѣ Корсаковнѣ, велицей благочестия ревнительницѣ, у нея же предреченный Максимъ во велицей чести бысть, и во мнозѣ ради благочестия послушаше его во сладост. Онъ же много поборая по благочестивой вѣрѣ писаніями всею здѣшнею церковию знаем и чтимъ бѣ."

12. Suša 1666, 19: "Nec tamen sileri hic congruum, quod insuper etiam tum, laude in illo dignum fuit. Etenim Psalterium, et nouum testamentum Slauonicum, ad Graecum idioma concinans, vt laboriose, sic toti genti Ruthenae proficue reformauit. Ipsius cura et industria typis editum, cum varijs officijs diuinis, et precationibus eiusdem linguae breuiarium. Adiunxit hisce lucubrationibus, Lexicon, et Grammaticam itidem Slauonica."

13. I offer a few examples of Smotryc'kyj's correction of Church Slavonic Scripture according to the Greek in appendix B6. See also p. 204.

14. Kosov 1635, 445: "A że te szkoły, w ktorych teraz uczymy, przed tym zawsze były y są u nas in possessione, gdyż był nad nimi przed tym rektorem Smotryski, Kassyan y inszy, ktorzy po łacinie uczyli sine interruptione aż do nas; ergo, tę ztwierdzać raczy i. k. mść z miłościwey łaski swey pańskiey."

15. Kosov 1635, 445: "Na ostatek ten Codrus przed ludźmi wielkimi taką wyćwierkuie o nas notą: nigdy Rusi naiaśnieyszy krolowie polscy szkoł nie pozwolali; ergo, y teraz pozwolone być nie maią. My neguiemy antecedens, a tobie, iako praw ruskich idyocie, tak płacimy: są prawa od świętey pamięci krolow polskich, mianowicie, od naiaśnieyszego Zygmunta Trzeciego nadane naszym na szkoły łacińskie w Wilnie, we Lwowie. Ergo tu hallucinaris y musisz przyznać, że nie nowina krolom polskim na szkoły łacińskie przywileia Rusi dawać; y na te szkoły, w ktorych my teraz w Kijowie y w Winicy uczymy, dyplomate pomazańca Bożego, krola niezwyciężonego, monarchy Władysława Czwartego y wszys[t]kiey Rzeczypospolitey konsensem są stwierdzono."

16. *Sowita* 1621, 69/492: "O waszym Smotryckim iuż zamilczeć nie mogę, co dotąd *in publicum* od nas *ex professo* nie wychodziło, y teraz iescze nie wszytko się powie, zostanie cokolwiek w taiemnicy, ale co do tey rzeczy właśnie należy, wspomnieć koniecznie potrzeba."

17. *Sowita* 1621, 69/492: "Ten długi czas znosił się z przełożonemi naszymi, przy czym bywali y niektorzy Świetcy, iakoby sam przyiść y gromadę swoię mogł przywieść do zgody z nami."

On the planned meeting of Orthodox and Uniates in 1617, see also Krevza 1617, A2ʳ/3.

18. *Sowita* 1621, 69–70/492: "Zawarł to z naszymi, że on wierzy wszytko, co wierzy kościoł Rzymski, to iest o pochodzeniu Ducha ś. O zwierzchności Papieskiey, y o wszytkich inszych Artykułach Wiary, a nie słowy tylko to mowił, ale rzeczą samą dosyć iaśnie, że szczyrze z nami postępował, wyświadczał: mowiąc z niektoremi swoich, od ktorycheśmy potym słyszeli, że Rzymianie w Wierze swoiey będą zbawieni."

19. *Sowita* 1621, 70/492–93: "Y to znakiem było szczyrości iego, że nas pobudzał, żebyśmy nastąpili na nie wzywaiąc ich na rozmowę y sposoby, iakoby do tego przyiść podawał, y przez pewną Osobę nam, y sobie dobrze znaiomą, przestrogi nam w słowach y na piśmie posyłał, y iuż był swoich przywiodł z nami do rozmowy, aż zły iakiś wiatr powionął, y czarnemi chmurami światło słoneczne, żeby na nie nie patrzyli zakrył: A gdy się iuż tak z nami stawić na rozmowę, trzema tylko dniami przed nią odmowili, a przez dwie całe Niedziele nas y przednich Senatorow prożną cieszyli nadzieią, onże radził przełożonym naszym, żeby przecie ich wezwali, choć przyidą, choć nie przyidą, Ksiąg samych Słowieńskich to coby było potrzebno do Obrony iedności vkazali, y stało się tak: Duchowni ich nie przybyli, ale Świeccy ludzie zacni, oboiey płci będąc z osobna wezwani od nas, przybyli y ochotnie słuchali. A iż nas, oniż sami prosili, żeby to w Druk wydano było; wydaliśmy."

20. *Sowita* 1621, 70–71/493: "Przy tym do kilku dziesiąt Theses ręką swą własną spisawszy, o Taiemnice Troyce Przenaświętszey, a mianowicie o pochodzeniu Ducha ś. Smotrycki posłał do nas, persuaduiąc żebyśmy y to przy tamtey Książce wydali: Myśmy, acz trudność czynili, że się nie zdało przy Polskiey książce, w ktorey y inaksza materia była Drukować tego, tak wielką

liczbę. wybrawszy iednak cośmy rozumieli potrzebnieyszego, Drukowaliśmy y nazawaliśmy tę Książkę Obrona Iedności."

21. *Sowita* 1621, 71/493: "Nie przestał się on znaszać z nami, y owszem przysposabiał do siebie niektorych świeckich, aż go spotrzeżono. Wyiawiło się zatym wszytko y był chudzina v małorozumnych w zatrudnieniu: Ten człowiek, ieśli teyże wiary iest teraz ktorey w ten czas był, to brat nasz: Ieśli inakszey to on własnym y istotnym Apostatą iest, bo odstąpił od poznaney y iuż przed ludźmi (a kilka ich tam było Duchownych y świeckich) wyznaney Wiary."

22. Smotryc'kyj 1621c, 104/451: "Na to tobie Ociec Smotrzyski tak odpowiada: gdybyś był między prawdę fałszu nie namieszał, wszytko by to ohułem, czymeś o nim ten dziewiąty twoy Rozdział natkał, przyznał. Ale że iest ni co od ciebie tak zdrożnie powiedziane, że gdyby przystoyną odpowiedzią nie było zniesione, *Reputaciey* iego dobrey . . . szkodzić by mogło . . . taką na tę twoię powieść, my za niego donosimy."

23. Smotryc'kyj 1621c, 104–106/451–52: "Ociec Smotrzyski, ktory młode lata swe aż do lat męża, y tu w Oyczyznie, y w Cudzoziemskich kraiach, na naukach wyzwolonych vczciwie przewiodł, gdy mu po kilorocznych dwornych zabawach, miasto nieiakiego odetchu po prochu szkolnym przeżytych, żywot postanowić, y przez tak wiele lat zbieranego *studiorum* sprzętu w pożytek swoy y bliźnich zażyć przychodziło. Miał to w vstawicznym przedsięwzięciu, aby nie pierwey do Zakonu Mniskiego (do ktorego od lat niemal dziecinnych ochotną duszę miał,) wstąpił, ażby o namierzonym w rozrożnioney braci (bo go to wielce po wszytkie czasy trapiło) obudwu stron celu wziął wiadomość pewną: swey strony takowego celu niewiadom nie był: Drugiey strony, był niewiadom: y gdy mu iuż to święte przedsięwzięcie stanu Zakonniczego skutkiem wypełnić do zamysłu przychodziło: do Wilna przyiachał, y do Monasteru naszego Wileńskiego wstąpił, aby się w nim y swey do Zakonu tego sposobności, y naszemu pożyciu przytomny przez iaki czas (iako to zwyczay Monasterski niesie) bez przyodzienia przypatrzył. Gdzie od wszelkich tegoświetnich zabaw vwolniony mieszkaiąc, do wzięcia wiadomości od przeciwney strony namierzonego w ich przedsięwzięciu celu, vmysł skłonił, zaczym takowych sposobow szukał, aby y im do niego, y iemu do nich chodzenie y z sobą rozmowa od starszego (ktorego woli y władzy iako posłusznik podlegał) była pozwolona. Co łacno otrzymawszy, iak wiele razow był nawiedzany od strony przeciwney z młodszych, wiedząc to sami dobrze: gdzie y z nim y z Błog: pamięci Przodkiem iego Archimandritem naszym bywała im rozmowa Duchowna częsta. A że mu nie do młodzieży w tym przedsięwzięciu był *intent*, ktora go w tym, w czym on potrzebował, pewnym vwiadomieniem sprawić nie mogła. Widział się z Xiędzem Ruckim dwa razy, z trzeciego *condictaminu*, że się X. Rucki nie stawił, widział się z X. Iosaphatem, y Kreuzą."

24. Smotryc'kyj 1621c, 106/452: "Po ktore trzykrotne z tymi Osobami widanie się, znosił się z niemi, nie iakoby sam, iako vdaie *Redargutor*, przyść, y gromadę swoję mogł przywieść do zgody z niemi: ale coby za cel był Vniey, y

iak się w niey Wiara wyznania naszego Wschodniego, ieśliby do zupełney wszytkiemu Narodowi naszemu Ruskiemu przyszło, cało ostać może: Ponieważ bez Patriarchi, ktorędy się kolwiek ta Vnia obroci, wszelako hakiem się ku nam stawi. A z iakich przyczyn, pomnieć mogą. Okazywał im zniewagę y od swych y od naszych: okazywał niszczenie przez nie, y przez ich Vnię wyznawcow ich, że się całemi domami z Vniey do Rzymskiego Kościoła Vnitowie przenoszą: że Cerkwie po maiętnościach PP. Rzymian na Kościoły się przemieniaią: że z Ruskiey Relligiey do Rzymskiey przystępować wolno: a z Rzymskiey do Ruskiey zakazano: że was z Ruskich miast wyciskaią, tam szkoły swoie zakładaiąc, gdzieby wasze Vnickie być miały: y tym podobne. O tym było Oycu Smotrzyskiemu z niemi za po trzykrotnym tym z starszymi widaniem się rozmowa."

25. Smotryc̆kyj 1621c, 106/452: "A co się Zbawienia dotycze wyznawcow wiary Rzymskiey, mogł to bespiecznie rzec, że *defectus fidei non excessus condemnat*: a zatym, kto to od niego słyszał, to co się iemu podobało, według swego pożądania *inferować* mogł."

26. According to Myc̆ko (1990, 112), Smotryc̆kyj translated de Dominis' *Profectionis consilium* into Ruthenian some time between 1618 and 1623.

27. Smotryc̆kyj 1621c, 108/453: "Co się dotycze *Theses* o Pochodzeniu Ducha Ś. były, y są *exercitium* Oyca Smotrzyskiego *Scholasticum*: nie na Disputacię, ale na vważenie ich zebrane y napisane: ma on tego z vstawicznych swych *lucubracij* wiele. z ktorych że y przeciwna strona vżyła co, wolno to iey było. Widział ie abowiem Ociec Smotrzyski być potężne, a przeciwney strony własne: widział ie też zaraz y barzo *corrupte* zażyte: mimo wole y sens Doktorow Świętych: indzie w słowiech, indzie w punktach, indzie w przekładzie z Graeckiego na Łaciński: aby stąd iaśniey prawda okazałą stanęła: gdyby y te *Theses* w swey *corrupteli* były poznane y zniesione."

28. *Examen* 1621, 43/590–91: "O znaszaniu się Smotrzyskiego waszego z nami, żeśmy w Sowitey Winie nie wszytko wypisali, tamżeśmy przyczynę pomnienili, rozumieiąc, że tego na on czas na vpomnienie Smotrzyskiego dosyć było. Teraz zaś i Obrońca neguie, cośmy tam prawdziwie y bez żadney przesady napisali, na potwierdzenie tego musimy, lubo to nie w smak będzie Smotrzyskiemu, więcey powiedzieć, a szczyrą istotną prawdę, zawięzuiąc go boiaźnią Bożą, żeby, zebrawszy się z pamięcią (a może pomnieć, bo czterech lat temu nie masz), przyznał, ieśli nie tak było iako tu piszemy."

29. *Examen* 1621, 43–44/591: "Żałował tego a powtorzył to razow ze trzy, że Xiążkę, Lament nazwaną pisał, wielum powiada tą Xiążką zgorszył, żal mi tego, chcę to nagrodzić Cerkwi Bożey posługą iaką znaczną, ktorą by się tak wiele naprawiło, iak się wiele zepsowało, a taką sprawę powiadał być ziednoczenie się nasze: O ktore on się chciał starać, porozumiawszy się z nami. Powiedział że Xiążka Iego M. Ojca Władyki Włodzimirskiego, Respons na ich Lament nazwana, Parigoria we wszytkim mu dosyć vczyniła. Chciałem prawi

był odpisać na nie, alem nigdy nie mógł się zebrać na to: był ten raz gdym chciał począć odpisować, trwoga iakaś padła na mię, vderzyłem piorkiem o stoł, a samem zapłakał, iakoż y po dziś dzień nie odpisano."

30. *Examen* 1621, 44/591: "Powiedział y to, że nawrocił na Wołyniu do Vnij iednego, ktory potym (znać że w tamtym kącie Kapłanow dobrych Vnitow nie było) przeszedł do nabożeństwa Rzymskiego, o co mię pry strofował Pop ieden w Wilnie, nie mianuię go na ten czas, ale kto nas spyta, powiemy imię iego. Za vpomnieniem iego pisałem powiada do tamtego człowieka, mowiąc: żem żartował (ale tamten, zaszedłszy żartem do Pana Boga, *serio* został przy Nim)."

31. The Uniate Smotryc̆kyj would insist upon adherence to the decree *De non transitu*, which banned Uniates from converting to the Latin rite. The decree was controversial and not always taken seriously in Rome and by the Polish Roman Catholics.

32. *Examen* 1621, 44/591: "Przy Leontym, ktorego oni tam mieli za starszego w zgromadzeniu swoim, mieszkać chciał do czasu, dla pozyskania iego, o ktorego skłonności dobrey czynił nadzieie, na lenistwo się tylko iego, że nie był pracowity, vskarzał, skąd żebyśmy tę taiemnicę wiedzieli, my tam z nimi nie obcowali to znać, że nieprawda."

Smotryc̆kyj had said of Karpovyc̆'s diligence in his funeral oration that "there was not a moment for that holy man in which he was not doing something so that either God conversed with him or he with God (Smotryc̆kyj 1621a, E4ʳ/256: "nie było minuty v tego świętego Męża, w ktorą by cokolwiek czynił, żeby albo Bog z nim, albo on z Bogiem nie rozmawiał."). So perhaps he was only apparently lazy? The information about Karpovyc̆'s laziness was corroborated, however, by an anecdote concerning Smotryc̆kyj and the archimandrite found in Peter Mohyla's notes (see *Arxiv* 1887, 58). Even if we come to the conclusion that he was indeed lazy, this still does not prove that Smotryc̆kyj had precisely these conversations with the Uniate side.

33. *Examen* 1621, 44/591: "Podawał sposob przeyścia do zgody, mianował osoby, na ktorych rozumiał że należało. Obiecał sam z nimi pracować w tym, y iachać do tych mieysc, gdzie ktory z nich był."

34. *Examen* 1621, 44–45/591: "(tu się ieszcze kęs zadzierzemy, żebyśmy nie wszytko powiedzieli, wszakże y to powiemy, kiedy on będzie tak niewstydliwy, a będzie się zapierał tego cośmy wyższej położyli, w ten czas musiemy y ostatek wynurzyć, co właśnie iest taiemnego, skąd każdy zrozumie, że trudno nam było o rzeczach ich taiemnych wiedzieć, tylko od takiego ktory ich y sam był dobrze wiadomy)."

35. *Examen* 1621, 45/591–92: "Zawarł był z nami, że miał iachać po wszytkich Ruskich kraiach, żeby disponował serce ludzkie do zgody zobopolney, y iedności Cerkiewney, a wprzod to miał począć w Wilnie, iakoż iuż był y począł, wiadomiśmy tego dobrze. Iuż się y tamte osoby Mieszczanie Wileńscy z ich strony schadzać z nami byli poczęli. Raz go przechyra iakiś Kramnik przestrzegł

v Ojcow Bernardynow gdy był z nami, za co zaburzyło się było ich wielebne
Bractwo nań, y miał o to Correctionem Fraternam solenniter, nie tylko od
Bractwa y od spowiednika swego, ale y od tego Leontego, o ktorym obrońca
powiada, że się za iego wiadomością znaszał z nami.

Powiedział nam to na
inszey schadzce (bo nie trzy tylko schadzki miał z nami, iako prawi), za czym
przyszło się nam namawiać o inszym mieyscu dla schadzek y o czasie żeby nas
nie postrzeżono, w czym słuchaliśmy zdania iego y swoieśmy też powiedzieli.
Nakoniec, kiedy ostrze następować nań w Bractwie poczęto, za oskarzeniem
iednego szalbierza ich sekty (ktory chytrze skłoniwszy się do nas, wszytkiego
się dowiedział, cośmy traktowali z sobą, a ten iest osobą znaczną miedzy nimi),
żeby abo habit brał, abo precz od nich vstępował."

36. *Examen* 1621, 45–46/592: "radziliśmy mu, żeby, świeckie odzienie
złożywszy, sam przez się Rasę włożył, ktore jest odzienie w nabożeństwie
naszym Clerickie. Z teyże namowy naszey ieździł na Wołyń, do Kijowa, w
habicie ieszcze świeckim, y wiemy, że tymże się zwrocił nazad, czym wyiachał
od nas."

37. *Examen* 1621, 46/592: "iedno iako go w podeyźrzeniu w Bractwie mieć
poczęto, tak się tego podeyźrzenia przymnażało, y nań vsilnie następowano, że
też habit Zakonny prziął."

38. *Examen* 1621, 46/592: "A w tym czasie poddano mu Xięgi ze Zboru Marka
Antoniego, Arcybiskupa Spalateńskiego Apostaty, za ktorą się chwyciwszy,
został tym czym teraz iest. Taki statek tego człowieka, że iedna Xiążka iednego
Apostaty, ktory nową sektę w Chrześciaństwie dotąd niebywałą, wprowadzał,
i ktorey sekty Krolestwo Angielskie (do ktorego się był vdał) prziąć nie
chciało, tak go we wszytkim odmieniła, że *ab equis descendit ad asinos*. A ieśli
w tym wszytkim będzie chciał być tak niewstydliwym, przeświadczamy go, y
mianować osoby będziemy."

39. Smotryc'kyj 1622a, 48ᵛ–49ʳ/511: "O znoszeniu się z wami Oyca
Smotrzyskiego nie *controuertuiemy: pium intentum ad optimum finem*, przez
iakieżkolwiek *media*, tylkoby *honesta* szło, ganione być ni w kim nie zwykło.
By był w ten koniec z wami *conferował*, aby z wami zostawał, vczynił by to
był: ale że *conferował*, aby z was wyrozumiał, ieżeliby kiedy nadzieia waszego
nazad wrocenia się była, zaś tam, skądeście odpadli. Ktorey po was nie
obaczywszy, zaniechał was: a sam to vczynił, co mu należało. Co się *Lamentu*
dotycze, (ponieważ iego *Authorem* mieć go chcecie,) y on y my wszyscy
wydania iego nie żałuiemy: y owszem cieszymy się z niego, y czytać go
wszytkim Prawosławnym y inowiercom zalecamy."

40. Smotryc'kyj 1628a, 104–105/575–76: "Rzecze mi snać kto: miałeś z tym
poczekać do Soboru, przy iuż powiedzianey przyczynie, zapytam go, ieżeli mię
on mogł vpewnić w tym, żem przed tym, mnie y wszytkim nam niewiadomym
Soborem vmrzeć nie miał? Rzecze powtore: czemużeś nie uczynił tego dawniey?
odpowiem mu y na to. Vczyniłem to tegdy, kiedy Pan Bog zezwolił, y zdarzył.
A vczyniłem po wielkim moim wybadywaniu, y doświadczaniu. Świadomi są

tego dobrze ci, ktorym wiadome były moie lucubracie naprzeciw scriptu Vnią otytułowanego. naprzeciw rozmowie Brześcianina z Bratczykiem. naprzeciw zmartwychwstałego Nalewayka. naprzeciw Politice *Ignorantiam* y nabożeństwu nowo Cerkwian Wileńskich napisane y do publikowania przez druk iuż po wydaniu Lamentu, puszczone bydź, nagotowane."

41. Smotryc̄kyj 1628a, 105/576: "nie wspominam verificatiey, obrony iey, Elenchu, Iustificatiey, y tym podobnych. w ktorych iedney po drukiey, im daley, tym rzadszy byłem w następowaniu na dogmata prawdziwe, szerszy w rzeczach potocznych, pod te czasy nagle przypadłych."

42. Smotryc̄kyj 1628a, 105/576: "Niemal y teraz nayduie sie w Bibliotece Monastera Bractwa Cerkiewnego Wileńskiego Traktat o pochodzeniu Ducha Ś. sposobem syllogismow od Graekow Rzymianom, y wzaiem Graekom od Rzymian zadawać sie zwykłych, polskim ięzykiem napisany, y Przodkowi memu na mieyscu tym Archimandritowi do czytania podany. Za ktorym na ten czas mieysce to tak sie było poruszyło, że aż, na większy gomon, niż na zbawienny pożytek zaniosłey sie sprawie, milczeniem złożyć musiałem. Przyszło było czasu swego y do tego, żem był y Palinodią na Lament napisał, ktorą do rąk Kapitule Ostrozskiey w tym Monasteru, w ktorym teraz residuię y to piszę, podana ode mnie bywszy zaległa."

43. Smotryc̄kyj 1628a, 105/576: "Bog moy, podobno za vczynioną iemu przez Lament wielką obrazę, w tym doświadczeniu dłużey mię mieć chcąc, przyść mi ni do owego, ni do tego publicatiey nie dopuścił."

44. Mužylovs̄kyj 1628, 6ᵛ: "każdy to na oko widzi, żeś hypokrita, co y Ociec twoy w Duchu Ś. pamięci, Błogosławiony Leontiusz Karpowicz Archimandrita, Cerkwie zesłania Ducha ś. Wileńskiey, w tobie widział, dla czego y do Zakonu cię prziymować nie chciał, zniaiąc żeś ty miał wielkie turbatie Cerkwi BOżey czynić, tylko czasowi schodząc, na żądanie niektorych osob, ktorzy wnętrznego Wilka mało znali, rad nierad prziiąć musiał do Zakonu, y ręce vmywszy czyst iest od tego, spodziewaiąc się iednak wszyscy za czasem poprawy po tobie, wkładali sie za tobą."

45. Mužylovs̄kyj 1628, 11ᵛ: "A tego przyszłego odstępstwa twego był znak pewny, gdyś do wtorego krztu Pokuty ś. był przypuszczany, głos ludu pospolitego, że Cerkwią zaturbuie, zawiedzie lud prawowierny, nabawi frasunku y kłopotu, poda w podeyźrenie prawowierną naukę Cerkiewną."

46. Smotryc̄kyj 1629b, 16ʳ⁻ᵛ/715–16: "Znam to, że gdy przybywszy do Wilna do Monastera Bratskiego Świętego Ducha, z przedsięwzięciem do stanu Zakonniczego, napisałem był y podałem miedzy Zakonniki Traktat o pochodzeniu Ducha Świętego chcąc o tym y z Starszym y z Młodszymi, ktorzy by tey rzeczy *Capaces* byli, Conferować: bo mię iuż Lamentowe w Traktacie o pochodzeniu Ducha Świętego na Mayestat BOży, rzucone bluźnierstwa za duszę były wzięły. Z czego gdym postrzegł, że więtszy gomon, niż szukany przez mię pożytek wynidź miał, poniechałem. A z tego mego Traktatu Propositow

napisawszy, do teraźnieyszego Iaśnie Oświeconego y w BOgu przewielebnego Oyca mego w Duchu y Pana, do Ś. Troycy Monastyra Wileńskiego odesłałem: ktore *perpolitę* przy obronie Iedności Ś. z druku są wydane. A potym mięszkaiąc w Monasterzu tym dłużej niż rok po świetcku, byłem częstokroć sollicitowany y proszony tak od wszystkiego Bractwa, iak osobliwie od Nieboszczyka Przodka mego na tym Archimandrytstwie, o przyięcie habitu Zakonnego: Czego Dobrze świadom Warlaam, bywszy Wasili pop Bratski: y wiem że inaczey nie rzecze: za ktorego prośbą y perswasyą, iako na ten czas Duchownika mego, obietnicę vczyniłem, y dzień wstąpienia do Zakonu naznaczyłem. Z iaką zaś radością, z iakim weselem y vciechą wszystkiego Bractwa Duchownych y świetckich, byłem do Cerkwie pod ten Akt y z Cerkwie prowadzony, Salutowany, honorifikowany, y Festem vczczony, świadomeś tego *Iniquissime obtrector* y ty dobrze."

47. See Smotryćkyj 1629a, 81/685: "Nie skłamam zaiste, ieśli y tak rzekę, że się ogląda na mię po niemałey części y wszytka Cerkiew Ruska. Mowię to nie w chlubę, ani w hardości (nie day tego Boże) ale mowię według dawney przypowieści: *Inter coecos, et monoculus Rex.*"

48. Smotryćkyj 1629a, 22/656: "y ieślibym tego przez chwałę Vniey szukał, abym się nieco w narodzie moim bydź okazał, czyniłbym to *praepostere,* y nadaremnie: ponieważ dosyciem się iemu iuż był przez Lament, weryfikacyą, obronę iey, Elench, iustyfikacyą, y insze prace moie znaczne, bydź nieco okazał; y przyczyny tey sławą, łaską, y miłością narodu mego aż pod niebo, iako mowią, wynoszony byłem."

49. Smotryćkyj 1629a, 23–24/656–57: "Rzekłem do nich [the Orthodox side at the Kievan Council of 1628], na insze ich do mnie słowa; że nie iestem omartwiały, abym nie czuł od strony swey honoru, poszanowania, sławy, y dobrego imienia: y żebym nie vważał, żem iuż w tey stronie lata moie do szedziwego włosu przepędził: że ku obronie iey wiele pisałem: wiele y na inszych Cerkiewnych Duchownych pożytkach pracowałem; przez co v wielu z narodu mego w tak okazałą miłość porwany byłem, że na oświadczenie wielkiey swey za te prace y vsługi moie ku mnie wdzięczności, konterfekty osoby mey, aby mię przed sobą zawżdy mieli, w domach swych wystawiać poruszyli się."

50. Smotryćkyj 1628b, Biʳ/630: "Ia będąc tego rozumienia, że to Iego Mość Ociec Archymandrita vchyla się mey przytomności, dla podeyźrzenia v ludzi, (bo sie to w rozmowach naszych trafiało często:) . . . "

CHAPTER 5

1. On Hetman Żółkiewski and the Battle of Ṭuṭora (Cecora), see Prochaska 1927, 234–69.

2. I draw much of the information that immediately follows (i.e., that part which is *not* from the printed polemical pamphlets of the time) from the survey of the legal documents published by Žukovič in 1906.

3. Smotryc'kyj 1621b, 3ʳ⁻ᵛ/321–22: "Mimo dobre sumnienie, z samey lekkości vmysłu, na zamieszanie wnętrznego Rzeczyp. pokoiu, pod czas woienney Expediciey z nieprzyiacielem Chrześciańskim, Poganinem Cesarzem Tureckim, do Krola Iego M. Pana naszego M. . . . około dnia siodmego Lutego, w Roku teraźnieyszym 1621 . . . donieść y vdać nie wstydał się, ani się obawiał: iakoby Przewielebny Ociec Patryarcha Ierozolimski, ktory w Państwach K. Iego M. przez cały niemal przeszły 1620. Rok był, y za wiadomością Iego Kr. M. w nich mieszkał y wyiachał, miał być *Impostorem* na szpiegi do Państw Iego K. M. od Cesarza Tureckiego wysłanym: a Borecky y Smotrzisky, przez tegoż *Impostora*-Patryarchę Ierozolimskiego z Cesarzem Tureckim zrozumiawszy się, pod *praetextem* Relligiey y Nabożeństwa, bunty y rostyrki miedzy ludźmi szkodliwe czynili y rozszerszali."

4. Smotryc'kyj 1621b, 28ᵛ/353: "a złośliwy ktoryś ięzyk nie wstyda się do tegoż Krola iego M. P. naszego M. vdawać go, nierzkąc za niePatryarchę, nie za Władykę, ale za prostego Czerńca: a ku temu za Szpiega y Zdraycę."

For another summary of the allegations (where this time, according to Smotryc'kyj, Theophanes had been portrayed as a layman), see Smotryc'kyj 1622b, 10ʳ⁻ᵛ/520–21: "Nie pośpiał za granice, . . . ali go, tak wielkiego . . . pasterza, niepohamowny ktoryś ięzyk do Maiestatu Waszey Krolewsk. M., Pana naszego M., podał za szpiega Tureckiego, za człowieka prostego, layka, państwam Waszey Krolewskiey M. nieprzyiaciela głownego; a podniesioney od niego Hierarchiey osoby, Metropolitę y Episkopy, za zdraycy oyczyzny, ktorzy by na zmowie przez tego szpiega z Turczynom, to przedsię wzięli, aby Państwa waszey K. M., Pana naszego miłościwego, a swoię miłą oyczyzną do rąk pogańskich wydali."

5. Symanowicz 1621, B3ᵛ: "Nieiakiś Theophan Graeczyn pewnie rodem, y obyczaiow Kreteńczyk . . . "

6. See Smotryc'kyj 1622b, 11ʳ/521: "nie tylko uniwersały te z kancellariey Waszey K. M. wydane w kożdym mieście po wszytkiey niemal Litwie y Białey Rusi, na insze osoby przy trzech specialiter wyrażonych przeformowane, przybiiać roskazowali; ale wszytkę zgoła tę Ruś, ktorzy pod zwykłym nam posłuszeństwem Patriarchy Konstantinopolskiego zostaiemy, pod te, o zdradę z roskazania Waszey Krol. M. wydane uniwersały zaciągnąć ważywszy się,— całe miasta, całe woiewodstwa, całe bratstwa, za teyże zdrady complices, pod swym y pod cudzym imieniem, do xiąg Bracławskich grodskich, ieśli y nie gdzie indzie, w Wiel. Xięstwie Litew. podali."

7. See Žukovič 1906, 540. Sapieha's letter of 9 February 1621 is published in *Arxeografičeskij* 1867, 30–31.

8. This document was printed in Sapunov 1883, 214–15. See also *Arxeografičeskij* 1869, 357–58.

9. Smotryćkyj 1628b, B1ʳ/630: "... a większą cześcią rozumiałem, że sie tego ochraniał [Mohyla] vczynić: aby sie nie podał w niełaskę Kro: Iego M. obcuiąc z nami: bo to czynił przed nim przodek iego Archymandrita Pieczerski [i.e., Kopystenśkyj]."

10. Smotryćkyj 1621b,):(1ʳ/313: "Nihil quidquam tam probe aut prouide dici potest, quod non vellicare malignitas possit."

11. See Smotryćkyj 1622a, 8ᵛ/471: "On to iest [i.e., "your metropolitan"], ktory starsze nasze za zdraycy vdał Tureckie, ktorzy by smakowali sobie panowanie Moskiewskie, lepiey iednak Tureckie: y ktorych zamysły pewne, na zgubę Oyczyzny. on Oyca Boreckiego wiazd do Wilna na Bohoiawlenie: a Oyca Smotrzyskiego do Połocka na *Epiphanię* rozgłosił: ktorym tak się wiele śniło o tym, iak y o zdradzie."

12. Smotryćkyj 1621b, 3ʳ/321: "Zapomniawszy ktoś boiaźni Bożey, (Ktosiem go zowiemy, bo się tai) . . . "
    But then Smotryćkyj sought to spread a rumor for the Orthodox side—that Rućkyj was no longer living. Smotryćkyj 1622a, 8ᵛ/471: "Metropolit wasz, ktorego żywym być powiadacie, (ieśli żywy iest,) . . . " Perhaps Rućkyj had not shown himself in public for some time.

13. Smotryćkyj 1621b, 50ᵛ/375: "Rozdarlić na nas vsta swoie Odstępcy naszi, strachem y sidłem, y cogodzinnemi fałszywemi nowinkami."

14. Smotryćkyj 1621b, 42ᵛ/367: "Gdyby kto twoim codziennym piekielney kuźnie nowinam wiarę dawać chciał, żywo duszę puścić by się musiał."

15. Smotryćkyj 1621b, 25ᵛ/344: "Wiedzieć masz Miłościwy y łaskawy Czytelniku, że gdyby Borecki nie Metropolit, a Smotrzyski nie Archiepiskop: by dobrze sowito tak wiele, z tym Mężem byli *conuersowali:* y ten święty Mąż byłby nie *Impostor*, ale własny prawdziwy, iaki iest, Patryarcha Ierozolimski: y Borecki y Smotrzyski byliby nie zdraycy."

16. Smotryćkyj 1621b, 3ʳ/321: "Mimo dobre sumnienie, z samey lekkości vmysłu, na zamieszanie wnętrznego Rzeczyp. pokoiu, pod czas woienney Expediciey z nieprzyiacielem Chrześciańskim, Poganinem Cesarzem Tureckim . . . "
    Cf. also Smotryćkyj 1622b, 9ᵛ/519–20: "A w iaki czas? Pod iakie Państw Waszey Krolewskiey M. postanowienie? Kiedy nieprzyiaciel krzyża ś. ogniem y mieczem na chrześciany dyszał. Kiedy Bisurmianin osobą swoią z niezliczonemi woyski do państw Waszey K.M., oyczyzny naszey miły, ciągnął,—w ten czas ten nieszczęsny człowiek nas y wierny narod nasz Rusky religiey Graeckiey starożytney wszytek za zdraycy oyczyzny z poganinem porozumiałe, do prześwietnych uszu Waszey Krolew. M. podał. Z iakiey słuszności? Z iakiego occasiey cienia?"

17. Smotryćkyj 1621b, 13ʳ/331: " . . . od Starszego mego, iako Posłusznik w nawiedzenie iego zesłany byłem."

18. Smotryc̆kyj 1621b, 25ᵛ/344: "Pogotowiu o te tak okrutne więzienie vczciwym mieszczanom Wileńskim nie przyszłoby było: ktorzy o Oycu Smotrzyskim, że tym czym teraz iest, miał był przyiachać, lub aby po to miał iachać, tak wiele wiedzieli, iak wiele o tym oboim y sam on wiedział."

19. Smotryc̆kyj 1621b, 25ᵛ–26ʳ/344: "Wiedzą to sami Przeciwnicy naszi, iak do tego wysoce znamienitego w Cerkwi Bożey Dostoieństwa dusza iego skłonna była: że y pierwszych stopniey *sacri Ordinis* na się wziąć, wielu *instanciam* Cerkiewnym odmawiał. Iak mu też Dostoieństwa tego *Beneficia* (ktore się teraz od niekogoś *ambitią* dobr, titułow, y *Honoru* iemu przypisuią,) smakowały, sami ciż Odtępcy naszi y tego dobrze są świadomi: ktorych barzo łacno mogł był dostąpić tegdy, gdy mu od samych tych, na ktorych miedzy niemi należało, *vltro* offiarowana była ta sama Archiepiskopiey Połockiey Stolica: Drugiey potym offiarowaney nie wspominamy. Ale on od tak wysokich w Cerkwi Bożey, zwłaszcza sumnieniem zawiedzionych, dostoieństw vbiegał, y aż do końca żywota swego, iako od szkodliwey *intriki* tey wszelako *alienus,* vbiegać w przedsięwzięciu miał. Y by nie rada Boża, ktorey ludzka z potrzeby vstępuie: y nie głos ludzki, ktory w takim dziele głosem iest Bożym: nigdy by z woli iego samego do tego było nie przyszło."

20. Smotryc̆kyj 1621b, Givᵛ/347: "Mowią na koniec y to, ieśli tey zmazy vyść byli chcieli, czemu pod tak ciężki na Oyczyznę czas, kiedy ią krwawą ręką nieprzyiaciel z porazki Wołoskiey zasmęcił, tego dostępować ważyli się? a co więtsza, od Szpiega Tureckiego? Y na to odpowiedamy: że pierwey byli poświęceni, niż to się zstało."

21. Smotryc̆kyj 1621b, 14ᵛ/333: "Czekać chcąc cierpliwie na łaskę Boga wszechmogącego, y na Miłościwą łaskę y obietnicę Kr. Iego M. na Seymie Roku 1607. vczynioną, y na tym przeszłym Reassumowaną w pokoiu, bez żadnych buntow y Sedicij, na iawi nie pokątnie w Państwach Iego Kr. M. żyiąc."

22. Smotryc̆kyj 1621b, 41ᵛ/366: "Przykrości iakie nawiętsze mogą słowem y dziełem wyrządzaią: na Monaster nasz kamieńmi z proc rzucaią: strzały z łukow na grunty y domy, a na Cerkiew z knotem siarczystym zapalonym napuszczaią: Na placy tegoż Monastera zapalone głownie przez mur wyrzucaią: Miedzy węgły ścian Cerkiewnych, ogniem zatleione sukna vwoszczone, z inszemi ogień żarzącemi przyprawami y knotami wtykaią."

23. Birkowski 1633, 2: "*Nie masz bałwanow, ani wroźbitow, ani wieszczkow w Izraelu.* Czy możecie to mowić Panowie Nieunici o swoiey Religiey Ruskiey, ktorey pospołu z Dyssydentami na zgubę Oyczyzny naszey wieczną dopinacie." Birkowski 1633, 5: "Kozacy odeydą od Lachow: Niemcy z dawna nie miłuią Polakow; Ci Heretycy, a tamci Schizmatycy; ktorzy wolą lada Kozaka mieć za Archimandrytę, niż nauczońszego Vnita."

24. *List* 1621, 9/739: "Sami się utworzywszy, iako idola iakie, w swych dostoieństwach niedostoynie adoruiecie, wielbicie y przewielbiacie: Wielebny Mielenci, Przewielebny Iow."

25. *List* 1621, 11/740: "Ale oto y daley, spiritu ambitionis nadęty, urągasz, wydawco tey Verificatiey, że gdzie u unitow stołki senatorskie? . . . A ieteście wy tanti, aby wam, ludziom lekkim, sądzić należało, kto w R. P. urastać ma?"

26. *List* 1621, 11/740: "tumulty y seditie."

27. *List* 1621, 13–14/742: "W Połocku iaki tumult seditią, concitatią populi, przeciwko władyce, canonice y według praw y zwierzchności Jego Kr. M. postanowionego, przeciwko woiewodzie tamesznemu, przeciwko commisarzom Jego Kro. M., przez listy y patenty swe et submissas personas, natręt na to władyctwo, wielebny (iako się sam tytułuie) Miolentij uczynił."

28. *List* 1621, 13/742: "A żebyście przy tym ostawali, przez większe nefas usiłuiecie, w ziednoczeniu z inowiercami ufność kładziecie, potęgę kozakow, ludzi rycerskich, na ochronę swego takiego zuchwalstwa zaciągacie."

29. *List* 1621, 26–27/752: "Dalekoście tedy odstąpili od czernieckiego ubostwa, od pokory y smirenności czernieckiey, iakoście apostatowali? Drzecie się Bogu y ludziom, omierzłą ambitią obięci, na przestoły metropolii y władyctw. A Połockie naybarziey smakuie: iuż insignia y władzę władyczą wielebny Mielenci połockiego archiepiskopstwa sobie przywłaszcza, mimo władzą (żałosna rzecz) K. Jego M., że go nie podawał, ani nominował. Tytułow zażycza, w druk ie podaie sam, siebie (śmieszna rzecz zaprawdę) wielbiąc, w ubiorach nie władyczych tylko, ale snać metropolich celebruie. Pieczęci sobie władyckie ryie, na kielichach napisy czyni. Pod rękę się szlachcie (ne quid ambitioni et arrogantiae desit), sam będąc iakiey iest condicii, wodzić dopuszcza y tym się pyszni. Władyctwa się Połockiego dopina, a tego nie widzi, że w teyże constitucii 1607 napisano, iż ludziom szlacheckim takie dostoieństwa dawane być maią."

30. See Kojalovič 1861, 337: "Wiem od person wiary godnych, że kozacy po skączoney expedycey z Turkami, nie myślili popierać schizmy. Lecz pseudoWładykowie ich, zwłaszcza Smotrycki, widząc znaczny respekt na niektórych ich Mości P.P. senatorów, pobudza ich (będąc pisarzem u nich) aby tą petitią względem schizmy J.K.M. przydawali, jakoby tym prędzey ambitia ich do skutku przyszła."

31. Żychiewicz 1986, 160: "Boreckiego y Smotrzyckiego, że kilku Czerńców y Kijowskiey szlachty nie przyimuie, ieszcze to nie *conclusio contra Manichaeos*, ieszcze nie dokument na przekonanie Syzmatyków."

32. This is the language of the legal charges brought against Smotryc'kyj in the spring and summer of 1621: "a certain Smotryc'kyj," "Maksym Herasymovyč, or as he calls himself, Melentij Smotryc'kyj," etc. The strategy, of course, was to deny Smotryc'kyj's standing by refusing to recognize his name. It is hardly likely that the author of *Thrēnos* and of the grammar of Church Slavonic was unknown to the reading public in Lithuania and in Rus'.

33. *Sowita* 1621, 63/487: "oznaymili Kr. I. M. to co na on czas w Wilnie naleźli, że nieiakiś Smotrycki vczynił się Władyką Połockim, święcił Popy, nie tylko do Władyctwa Połockiego, ale y do Metropoliey y wszytkie insze sprawy

Episcopom należące odprawował, celebruiąc *publice Pontificaliter* w Wilnie, Vniwersały y posłańce swoie rozsyłał po rożnych stronach w Wielkiem X. Lit. Oznaymuiąc, że Metropolita y Władykowie teraźnieyszy są wyklętemi, a oni są na mieyscach ich postanowionemi."

34. *Sowita* 1621, 76/496–97: "a sam Smotrycki osiadszy w Wilnie w Monastyrzu Brackim, tak hardzie sobie poczynał iakoby Boga w Niebie, Krola y żadney zwierzchności Duchowney y świeckiey na ziemi nie było; publikował siebie Władyką, drugiego Metropolitą, w Druk to podał, w vbiory nie Episkopskie, ani Archiepiskopskie, ale Metropolitom samym y to nie wszytkim według zwyczaiu Cerkwie Orientalney służące vbierał się, Liturgie *pontificaliter* celebrował, Popy, Diakony nie tylko do Władictwa Połockiego, ale y do Metropoliey iako *Vniversalis Pastor* święcił, Czerńcow gdy nie stało, ludzi świeckich w habicie Zakonnym, czyli on sam czyli delegatowie iego, po rożnych stronach na bunty rozsyłali, aż też ich łapać poczęto, y przyznali się, że świeckiemi byli, habit tylko maiąc zakonny."

35. Smotryc'kyj 1621c, 104/451: "Smotrzyski nie z woyskiem siedzi w Monasterzu Wileńskim Bratskim, ale z kilkunastą tylko braci Zakonnikow, nie z armatą iaką, tylko z posochem."

36. Smotryc'kyj 1621c, 114–16/456–57: "Ile do pokoiu, a potym niepokoiu Połockiego, z ktorych on y przypisuiesz pasterzowi tameyszemu, a niepokoy Smotrzyskiemu. O tym nie z nami rozmowa. PP. Połoczanie maią lata, sami za siebie odpowiedzą. . . . Co zaś za pokoy mieli, ktory ty tak bardzo wynosisz za tego twego świętobliwego, iako gi mianuiesz, Pasterza: daią znać słowa, ktoremi go PP. Połoczanie witali, gdy do niego miedzy inszemi, to w głos mowili. Ieśli do nas nie z Vnią, iak Anioła Bożego ciebie przyimuiemy; ieśli z Vnią, iak Przepastnika czuramy się. Taki pokoiu tego był początek, ktory trwał po wszytkie te trzy lata nie inakszy, w vstawicznych od Mieszczan przymowkach, y niesnaskach, z ktorą się on po wszytkie te czasy przed niemi taił: y posłuszeństwa Patriarszego iawnie nie zrzekał się: aż gdy przyszło temu twemu złotu *ad lydium lapidem* otrzeć się, tegdy go miedzią być PP. Połoczanie doznali: nie z vdania Vniwersałów iakichsi niebyłych od Smotrzyskiego rozesłanych, iako *Redargutor* fałszywie vdaie, ale z owey przyczyny: Po częstych rozmowach y wybadaniach z Władyką swoim PP. Mieszczanom Połockim, gdy go zapewne wyrozumieć nie mogli: coby zacz był, Vnit, lub Prawosławny. Occasię do doświadczenia iego, przybycie Oyca Patriarchy Ierozolimskiego podało im: o ktorym oni posłyszawszy, co przednieyszi nie tylko PP. Połoczanie, ale y PP. Mohilewcy, do Władyki śli, oznaymili mu o przybyciu Patriarszim, prosili go, ieśli iest Prawosławnym ich Episkopem, za iakiego się vdaie, aby z niemi na ich koszcie Oyca Patriarchę nawiedził: pozwolił, przyrzekł, rękę im na tym dał: Vcieszył ich przez tę swoię obietnicę wszytkich: rozniosł się wyiazd Władyczy do Oyca Patriarchi, po wszytkim mieście: lud pospolity wszytek w radości: że się nie oszukał na Pasterzu prawosławnym. Ci ktorzy mieli z nim iachać, o strugach, (bo Dnieprem ku Kiiowu puścić się, z namowy stanęło było: y o podróżnych potrzebach myślili:

O hoy: gdy przyszło do skutku ręki daniem stwierdzonego słowa: aż moy Władyka przerzeczone dumy w miech: zaleciały go skądyś inąd muchy: że mu głowę rozbrzukały, y przedsięwzięcie rozdmuchały. Nie Smotrzyski tedy przez swoie iakie Vniwersały (iako ty niebylicę iakąś powiadasz) do ohydy: y do iawnego okazania się tym czym iest, Pasterza (iako gi ty mienisz) Połockiego PP. Połoczanom y wszytkiey iego *Diaecesiey* podał: ale oto ten iego podstępny postępek."

37. Smotryc'kyj 1621c, 114–15/456: "Mieli pokoy za Hermana, bo był tylko cieniem w Vniey." And of Hedeon Brolnyc'kyj Smotryc'kyj alleged that he had "publicly declared that the Union disgusted him" (Smotryc'kyj 1621c, 115/456: "*publice* głosił, że mu mierziała Vnia").

38. Smotryc'kyj 1621c, 116–17/457: "Vniwersałow swych Ociec Smotrzyski żadnych nie rozsyłał. Pisał do PP. Połoczan: ale *resalutował,* nie *salutował.* Był ten Oyca Smotrzyskiego list pokazowany Iego M. Panu Woiewodzie Połockiemu, był wożony dla pokazania, y daley: w ktorym nic z tego za łaską Bożą, Co ty, *Redargutorze,* omylnie vdaiesz. Pisywano z mieysca tego, na ktorym on Przełożonym iest, y przed tymi listy do Szlachty y do Mieszczan we wszytkie powiaty, ktorzy się im z listami swoiemi pierwey *praesentowali,* a o radę y naukę, iaką Duchowną prosili: Niechrzczono iednak listow ich Vniwersałami, ani rady y nauki ich turbacyą. O Czerńce, co przypominasz rozesłane: męczyliście wszak, aż niemal do śmierci, w tegoż *Dioecesiey* iednego Czerńca, zaż się przyznał od Oyca Smotrzyskiego być zesłanym? ktorey krwie z rąk waszych Pan Bog poiskiwać będzie."

39. Smotryc'kyj 1621c, 117/457: "A co vdaiesz o Oycu Smotrzyskim, iakoby Popy nie tylko do Władyctwa Połockiego, ale y do Metropoliey poświęcał: wyiąwszy tych, ktorzy na gruntach Brackich są, y Zakonnikow, fałsz vdaiesz."

40. Smotryc'kyj 1629b, 67^r/767: "Zaż sam ty tego obłudniku nie wiesz, że Wileński wasz Schysmatycki Monaster, większa złota moia sieć była, ktory mię vbrał od głowy do nog we złoto, niż Monaster Dermański. Większe moie tam by miało być łakomstwo, niż tu: Bo tam ze wszytkiey Białey Rusi Archyepiskopiey Połockiey Parochyanie, pamiętali na mię. Tam co rzekłem, to słowo moie natychmiast dziełem sie stało, bez żadnego mego kłopotu y pieczołowania, od tych ktorzy na mię y prochu iako mowią, paść nie dopuścili. Tam w Wilnie pycha y hardość opanować by mię miały były. Gdzie y do Cerkwie y z Cerkwie Setnicami wprzod y o zad idących prowadzony byłem. Gdzie przy obchodzie nabożeństwa mego śpiewanie Figuralne było na Chory cztyry: Dyakonow y Presbiterow bławatno y złoto odzianych obostronnie gromadami: Gdzie ludzi *frequentia* niezliczona otaczała mię: Gdzie mię Rodowita Szlachta pod ręki wodzili. Ale iakoś na on czas ze wszytkiego tego troyga nic we mnie nie widział, y czystą z łaski Bożey miałem duszę moię od tego wszytkiego: toż rozumiey o mnie y dziś."

41. Mużylovs'kyj 1629, 11^v–12^r: "Znakiem było y to, gdy cię na Iereystwo, stan wielki powoływano, y iuż święcono, Iereyskieyć szaty nie dostawało, na

ktory czas ieszcze mogł być był Chrystus rzec, po coż tu bracie przyszedł nie
maiąc szaty weselney, A toć zcierpiał twoiey pokuty y vpamiętania czekaiąc,
azali sie nawrocisz, y azali sie vpamiętasz: Co sie iednak słusznie o Apologiaru
może rzec dnia dzisieyszego tobie: Po co sie bracie wdzierasz do Cerkwi
Wschodniey: po co tu bracie przychodzisz nie maiąc szaty takiey, iakiey
Cerkiew matka potrzebuie, ktorey gdy nie będziesz miał za matki, nigdy Boga
nie będziesz miał za Oyca: ktorego też czasu (aczem sie zdziwił) iednak
słabością człowieczą będąc ziętym, rozumiałem coś to być *fortuitum*, sam tylko
w stycharu kończąc Służbę Bożą, przy Wielebnym w Panu Bogu Oycu Patryarsze
Ierozolimskim Theophanie, Ryzy swoie na ciebiem włożyć musiał."

42. Mužylovs'kyj 1629, 12[r]: "Nie przestaiąc na tym, daley znacznieysze znaki
twego przyszłego vpadku P. Bog wyiawiał, gdyś z Wilna żałosną Bracią
żegnał, a naybarziey tych ktorzy z twego zaturbowania dla Cerkwi ś. podziemne,
y Ratuszne niewinnie więzienie spaniałym animuszem znosili, dla niey vmierali,
dla niey maiętności tracili, vrągania, przymowiska, gorzey niż poganie, (o Boże
wszechmogący) skromnie przyimowali: A drudzy z Magistratu rugowani
zostaiąc, supersedować y po dziś dzień ieszcze muszą, a teraz niestatkiem
swoim z niestatecznego Oyca będąc zrodzony, wielu pogorszyłeś: Biada tedy
człowiekowi przez ktorego pogorszenie bywa. Stąd P. Bog żadney nadzieie nie
zostawuiąc w tobie, gdyś *vltimum vale* w Cerkwi ś. *publice* czynił, y na mieyscu
ś. hipokritsko sie Panu Bogu kłaniał, Filar (za zrządzeniem tegoż Boga) będący
przy Obrazie Zbawicielowym wypadł, (na co patrząc y sameś sie zdumiał)
znacząc: iż kogo lub Prowowierny teraz sobie rozumie za Filara Cerkiewnego,
dla pychi y swey hardości vpadnie, y z Cerkwi wyłączony wielom będzie
pogorszeniem."

43. Smotryc'kyj 1629b, 9[v]–10[r]/710: "Przodka mego Archimandrity Wileńskiego:
iaka była ku mnie dusza, po wszytkie czasy mieszkania mego z nim, słowa iego
gdy mię pod bytność Patriarchi Jerozolimskiego do Kijowa wysłał, mowione
świadczą: Ktory przekładaiąc mi chorobę swoię ciężką, (bo w tey chorobie
świat ten pożegnał,) y Sukcessora potrzebę vkazuiąc exhortował mię y prosił,
abym do Wilna nie wracał sie, ieno iuż Presbyterem. Czego gdym mu odmowił:
napadszy przed Bracią, na szyię moię łzami oblany, prosił mię o to."

44. Smotryc'kyj 1629b, 15[v]–16[r]/716: "Pamiętam y to, że ty . . . pod czas
poświącania mego na Iereystwo, to odzienie Iereyskie ktore dla mnie nagotowane
było, porwałeś, y siebie nim przyodziałeś. Lecz gdy tego przy chirotoniey
potrzeba vkazała, abym na wierzch stychara Dyakońskiego Iereyską Ryzą był
przyodziany, to co mnie a nie tobie należało, z grzbieta twego było zewleczono,
a na mię włożono. . . . Ia pokim był Dyakonem, miałem szatę weselną
Dyakońską; a gdy zostawał Presbyterem, przyodziany byłem szatą weselną
Presbyterską, tak, że y iednego punktu bez należney mnie weselney szaty nie
naydowałem sie. A ty pod same Krolewskie przyszcie zostałeś iak oszarpany
knecht. Z cudzego z licem y w Ołtarzu cię rozebrano."

45. Diplic 1634, 54–55: "W Wilnie kazanie miał trzy razy z Kathedry, a dwa z
Ambonu. Z kathedry pierwsze kazanie miał nad ciałem ś. pamięci Oyca y

przodka swego: podał ie y do druku: a iakom słyszał przepisawszy po niemałey części z Łacińskiego, ktore wypuścił na świat ieden z Oycow Dominikanow. Drugie gdy powiedał w Roku P. 1621 . . . mało było czego słuchać: bo na co się był nagotował, to mu z pamięci było snać wypadło . . . "

46. Diplic 1634, 55: "Ale iednak we wszytkich tych trzech kazaniach swoich o wiary dogmatach nie vczył, ktore teraz heretyckiemi być mieni."

47. The Catholic author of the *Answer to the Reprotestation* wrote (Golubev 1883b, 349): "Mowisz, że on (i.e., Smotryc'kyj) był przyczyną śmierci ś. pamięci Josaphata . . . "

CHAPTER 6

1. Smotryc'kyj 1618,)(1ᵣ: " . . . при храмѣ сошествіа Прес[вя]таго и животворящаго Д[у]ха, назданномъ странствующаго."

2. Suša 1666, 54: "Ponderet ergo quo animo, etiam meam, Regia Maiestas, vti Senatoris cum Vestra Reuerendissima Dominatione, continuam accepturus esset consuetudinem?"

3. See the same letter of Zasławski as cited by Suša (1666, 54): "Leges nostrae, de extinctione candelae nos edocent. Hinc facile colligere ipsi licuerit, quomodo Maiestas Regia, eidem sit addicta? de cuius affectu, iam tum, ante effrenem Vitepscentium licentiam subdubitauit, quando Borecius, cum Vestra Reuerendissima Dominatione Varsauia, licet nihil metuendum erat, quasi declinato euaserit corpore."

4. Diplic 1634, 14: "A ieżeli się mu o co Oyca y starszych zopytać podobało było: mogł to tak sprawić, iako potym vczynił, y iako mu ci radzili ktorzy mu tey peregrinacyey odradzali."

5. Smotryc'kyj 1628b, 21/655: "Byłem to trzeci Rok tam, skąd narod nasz Ruski Chrześciańską Prawosławną Wiarę otrzymał."

6. Smotryc'kyj 1628a, 1/523: "Iuż to rok idzie trzeci Przezacny narodzie Ruski, iakom się z przedsięwziętey do wschodnich kraiow, y vciesznie nie bez dusznego y cielesnego pożytku mego za łaską Bożą przez dwa roki obchodzoney peregrinatiey, do Oyczyzny zaś wrocił."

7. Smotryc'kyj 1628a, *6ʳ/522: "Apologią ten moy Script ztąd mianowawszy, iż go puszczam częścią na zatkanie vst Łżebraci, ktorzy moie na Wschodne strony pielgrzymowanie, iuż to trzeci rok zazdrościwym Theonowym zębem gryzą."

8. See Golubev 1883a, 123, and Sakovyč's preface to Wilkowski 1626,)()(1ʳ⁻ᵛ: "O'ktorey ksiąszki zaleceniu bym dobrze nic nie powiedział, to samo

wielką iey v każdego z nas powagę ziednać może, iż ią tak wiele narodow w Europie naszey swoiemi ięzykami przetłumaczoną chcieli mieć, aż też z Polskiego ięzyka na nasz Ruski wiele ich sobie przekładaią y przepisuią, nawet w Monasterzech przy Trapezach do stołu braciey Nowicyuszom ią czytywaią, iakośmy w Kiiowskim Bratskim Monasterzu, za rezydenciey Oyca Smotrzyckiego człeka wielmi godnego czynili, (ktorego niech Bog w pobożnych zamysłach iego szczęści, ktore *amore veritatis in causa pacandae nostrae religionis* w serce swe zawziąwszy, *lubens libensq[ue] suscepit*, odieżdżaiąc tam, skąd moc y dozwolenie na vspokoienie takich spraw zwykło wychodzić, ktory z spokoynym swoim do nas się zwroceniem, może znieść opaczne o sobie rozumienie)."

9. Smotryckyj 1622b, 15ᵛ/525–26: "Stawił się z pośrzodku nas przed Maiestatem Waszey Kr. M., Pana naszego M., pod blisko przeszły sejm dla dania o sobie y dwu inszych spotwarzonych sprawy, od nas posłany oyciec Ioseph Kurcewicz, na Episkopstwo Włodzimierskie y Brzeskie poświęcony Episkop; ktorego . . . z takimi słowy od Maiestatu swego Krolewskiego Wasza Kr. M., Pan nasz M., odpuścić raczył: *masz łaskę naszę: powiedz y drugim, aby to uczynili, też łaskę naszę odniosą.*"

10. Smotryckyj 1622b, 15ᵛ–16ʳ/526: "To takie W. Kr. M., Panu naszego M., słowa, my obwinieni słyszawszy, na seym blisko przeszły ochotnie stawiliśmy się, przytomni dać W. Kr. M., Panu naszemu M., sprawę z słow tych, iakoby z ustnego roskazania W. Kr. M., przedsięwziąwszy. Lecz że nam pod tak wielkie oyczyzny niebezpieczeństwo nie więcey na honor swoy niż na całość iey baczenie mieć należało, za radą tych y swoią, ktorym o tym zdrowo radzić godziło się, abyśmy się nie zdali komu sprawą tą naszą priwatną publicznie Rzeczypospolitej sprawy pod tak ciasny y ten niebespieczny czas zatrudniać, (ponieważ niespokoyne głowy y naspokoynieysze nasze sprawy za turbacie podawać zwykły): przedsięwziętey sprawy tey swey na ten czas zaniechać musieliśmy, szczęśliwszemu ią czasowi, ieśli by nam Pan Bog żywota przedłużyć y zdrowia użyczyć raczył, poruczywszy."

11. Smotryckyj 1622b, 16ʳ/526: "Za ktorą za pomocą Bożą na tym teraźnieyszym seymie przed W.K.M., P. naszym M., (stawiwszy się pierwszy przez *Verificacię* y przez społEpiskopa naszego tak wiele w tey calumniey, iako y my winnego,) przez tę oto *Justificacię* naszę stawimy się, y w uniżoney powolności y w cały uprzeymości, iako wierni poddani Waszey Kr. M., Panu naszemu M., o niewinności swey taką sprawotę czynimy."

12. Smotryckyj 1622b, 21ᵛ/532: "Należało mi zaprawdy przytomnemu społecznie z oycem Meletiuszem Smotrzyskim, archiepiskopem, do Maiestatu Waszey Kr. M., Pana naszego M., stawić się, a za miłościwą łaską Pańską W. Kr. M., Panu naszemu M., uniżenie podziękować, za gleyt nam od Waszey Kr. M. przysłany. Lecz y niedostatek nasz y wielka zdrowia mego niesposobność stać się temu nie dopuściły."

13. Smotryc'kyj 1629b, 4^r/704: "Onych trzech Zakonnikow od Ś. Troycy w Roku 1622. z Wilna do Kijowa przybyłych, bym ia był do Męczeńskiey korony nie przeszkodził, twoi Kaimowie za inszą ich Bracią zażby byli nie posłali?"

14. The Ukrainian Catholic scholar Kurylas (1962, 62) ascribed Smotryc'kyj's decision to make his trip east to the shock of the Josafat affair. The Soviet scholar Prokošina (1966, 136) argued Smotryc'kyj went to the East because of his "fear of the people, of their strength and hatred." (She treated the martyrdom of Josafat as a class uprising.) The Roman Catholic scholar Żychiewicz (1986, 109) wrote "when Kuncevyč was killed in Vicebsk, Smotryc'kyj was shaken and could not regain his equilibrium. . . . The blood of him who was killed cried out to him from the earth." I do not think it happened that way: Smotryc'kyj was already gone on the day in question.

15. Smotryc'kyj 1628a, 120–21/583–84: "A ia w Konstantynopolu w Roku P. 1623. będąc, *publice* z Kathedry, przez nieiakiegoś Hieromonacha Benedicta, Konstantynopolskiey Cerkwie Wiel: Didiscala, ktory przy tym był tytułowany y Archimandritem Monastera Watopedskiego W św. Gorze. Przez tegoż tedy wielkiego wielkiey Cerkwie Konst. Didaskała *publice* z Kathedry przepowiadane słyszałem, owo, że modlitwy za vmarłe, iak pożytku zeszłym z tego świata Duszam żadnego nie czynią, tak też y w Cerkwi nie są potrzebne."

16. Diplic dedicated his work to Mohyla, but the new metropolitan, worried that the Orthodox side might be further compromised by the "heresies" that were again passed off as Orthodox doctrine, placed anathema on the book and its author, then ordered the book burned. See the Uniate report of 1635 to Rome in Šmurlo 1928, 113–14: " . . . Gelazius Diplica tipis mandatus, praefato metropolitae Kioviensi Mohila dedicatus, satis blasphemus, et erroribus repletus. Hunc librum postquam ad notitiam pervenerit, publice congregatis Mohila episcopis igni tradidit Luceoriae tanquam haereticum publicavit, et ne legatur vel habeatur is autor sub anatemate prohibuit, tam spiritualibus quam saecularibus, et excommunicationem tipis mandavit."

17. This is the amount of time he was willing to allow in his calculations of when Patriarch Cyril Lukaris ought to have answered the letter he had written to Lukaris on 23 August 1627. See Smotryc'kyj 1628b, 62/676: "Ktory [i.e., the letter] rąk iego od daty za Niedziel sześć pcwnie doszedł."

18. The "normal route" seems to have led through Moldavia into the Black Sea at the mouth of the Danube, thence through the Bosporus to Constantinople. Rozemond posits this itinerary for Cyril Lukaris on the basis of Georgius Dousa, *De itinere suo Constantinopolitano* (Leiden, 1599, pp. 18–21). See Lukaris 1974, 11.

19. Smotryc'kyj 1629a, 64/677: " . . . tak wiele podrożnych na szedziwy moy wiek, y na strudzone zdrowie, z vymą iego niemałą, prac, niebespieczeństw y bied, na ziemi y na morzu podiąwszy . . . "

20. Smotryc'kyj 1629b,)(3^r/697: "Byłem przed piącią lat w Kostantinopolu,

widziałem teraźnieyszego Patriarchę Cyrilla: mieszkałem przy nim Niedziel kilkanaście."

21. Smotryćkyj 1629a, 76/683: "Aż mię potym za dopuszczeniem Bożym za grzechy moie, choroba tamże zięła, przez ktorą, y przez wielkie Wieleb: twey na ten czas trudności, do poważney o tym rozmowy z Wieleb: twoią przyść nie mogłem; ale za radą Wieleb: twey, y nie wyzdrowiały dobrze, do Palestyny puściłem się, rzeczy te moie do rozmowy z Wieleb: twoią oznaczone, na zwrocenie da Bog moie z Palestyny, odłożywszy."

22. Smotryćkyj 1629b,)(3ʳ/697: "Przychodzili do rozmow ze mną niektorzy Hieromonachowie pobożni, ktorzy na to stękali, ale począć nic nie mogli."

23. Smotryćkyj 1629b, 8ᵛ–9ʳ/709: "Byli temi dniami kiedym ia był w Konstantinopolu, w Patriarchiey dwa Didaskałowie, Mathfiey Hieromonach Atheńczyk: y Mikołay Presbyter bezżenny, Kreteńczyk. pierwszy y Gręk był y Łacinnik: drugi po Łacinie nie vmiał ci z Konstantinopola z takich przyczyn vstąpić musieli. Mikołay przymowił Patriarsze przy bytności wielu Metropolitow, że takich wiary Dogmat vczj, y vczjć pozwala, iakie w Cerkwi Wschodney słychane nie były nigdy. Za co mu zaraz z Patriarchiey vstąpić kazano. Matfiey, ten miedzy wielą też Metropolitow, vskarżaiąc sie na złe zwyczaie nieszczęsney stolice Konstantinopolskiey, y na iey przełożone: że w tym wybioru y baczenia nie maią, aby na stolcach Episkopskich y Metropolitańskich sadzeni byli męże w Zakonie Bożym ćwiczeni, y w naukach vmiętni: ktorzy tu są w zniewadze y w nienawiści: ale byle ieno kto miał brodę a kaletę, wnet Episkop, y Metropolita. Zaczym tak nań Metropolitowie o swe kalety y brody nastąpili: że musiał y ten za pierwszym z Patriarchiey wędrować. z ktorymi obiema nazad iadąc widziałem sie w Iasiech."

24. Smotryćkyj would seek to convince the Orthodox of the licitness of the Latin positions by pointing out (Smotryćkyj 1629b, 10ʳ/710) that these shrines, so important to Orthodoxy and indeed to all Christianity, were now in the care of Western custodians—no doubt a fact of little consolation to his collocutors.

25. Smotryćkyj 1628a, 4–5/525: "Byłem w Syonie Ś. zkąd wyszedł zakon Boży: y w mieście Ieruzalem zkąd wyszło słowo Pańskie. . . . Tam byłem, gdzie sie iednorodzony Syn Boży, Bog Słowo z Przeczystey Panny narodził, gdzie sie Krzcił, gdzie zbawienną swoię Ewanyelią przepowiadał, gdzie nauczał y cuda sprawował, gdzie vcierpiał y vmarł, y trzeciego dnia zmartwychwstał, y zkąd wzniosł sie na niebo, y na prawicy Boga Oyca swego vsiadł. . . . Całowałem y grob Przeczystey świętey Paniey naszey Bogarodzice zawżdy Panny Mariey w Gethsemani."

26. Smotryćkyj 1628a, 43/545: "Lub mu sie też trafiło było na takiż script napaść, iaki y mnie przed trzema laty w Ieruzalem będącemu czytać przydało sie po Gręcku, pod imieniem nieiakiegoś Leontego Metropolity Ruskiego, (ieżeli on był nasz, tego nie wiem) wydany . . ."
    On the identity of "Metropolitan Leontij," see Podskalsky 1982, 171.

27. Smotryc'kyj 1629a, 76/683: "Ale ponieważ według pospolitego przysłowia: *Homo proponit, Deus disponit;* Bog wszechmogący to moie com był postanowił, inaczey, nie iakom ia chciał y rozumiał, odmienił, a przyiazd moy z Palestyny do Konstantynopola pod ciężkie a straszliwe powietrze bydź rządził, dla ktorego ia do tych przedsięwziętych, y we mnie postanowionych z Wieleb: twoią rozmow, przyść żadnym sposobem nie mogłem, y z niczym, kilka kroć z Wieleb: twoią iakoby mimochodem widziawszy się, odiachać musiałem."

28. Kortycki 1634, B3[r–v]: "Zabiega do Thracyey, zabiega do Palestyny, zabiega do Włoskiey ziemie, wszędzie wyrozrzewnieniu dusze pytaiąc Pana, Panie, co wżdy czynić? dopiero w mieście Rzymskim zrozumiał czego Pan chciał, iakoby to iemu było rzeczono: *Vade in ciuitatem,* Bież do miasta, a tam ci powiedzą, coć potrzeba czynić."

Kortycki 1634, E3[v]: "Iako gołębica z korabia Noego wypuszczona, za pierwszym razem nie znalazła gdzie by noga iey odpoczęła, wypuszczona drugi raz odpoczęła na oliwnym zielonym drzewie, gdzie y gałąskę zieloną vszczknąwszy, do korabia na znak pokoia, y dni lepszych przyniosła: tak y ten Przewielebny Ociec zwiedziwszy Thracyą, przebiegszy Palestynę, tak wielką część Europy, y Azyey morzem, y lądem, nie mogł znaleść gdzie by bespiecznie stanąć mogł, aż za powodem Boskim, trafił na obfite drzewo oliwne, trafił na VRBANA Naywyższego, y Powszechnego Chrystusowego Namiestnika."

29. See Stebeľsʹkyj 1782, 221. According to the Orthodox historian Askočenskij (1856, 96), Smotryc'kyj had *planned* all along to go to Rome; his trip to Constantinople was nothing more than a pretext.

30. Sakovyč 1641, 45–47: "Aza nie sprobował tego na sobie on świętey pamięci ociec Smotrzyski. . . . Zaczym, nie nalazszy w Turkogrecyey prawdziwey wiary, do stolice świętey apostolskiey Rzymskiey vdał się y ztamtąd otrzymał to, czego pożądała dusza iego. Tam y tobie radzę, narodzie Ruski, szukać prawdziwey wiary, a nie po Turkogrecyach z Bissurmany."

31. Smotryc'kyj 1629a, 64/677: "Tamem nic nie sprawił, a tu gdym się do Oyczyzny zwrocił, od zazdrościwych niewdzięcznikow tylko co vkrzyżowany nie byłem."

32. Smotryc'kyj 1628a, *1[r]/514: "Apologia Peregrinatiey do Kraiow Wschodnych, . . . przez fałszywą Bracią słownie y na piśmie spotwarzoney . . . "

33. Smotryc'kyj 1629a, 65/677: "zamysł był biednie vpadłego, a mnie serdecznie miłego narodu mego odbieżeć, y do Wieleb: twey, lubo na śś. mieysca Palestyńskie, ktore mnie prze pożycie na nich Zbawiciela naszego, iak dusza moia miłe są; zaś odwrot vczynić, y tam grzechow się mych cięszkich, przykładem pobożnych mężow śś. Oycow naszych, poki by ducha mego w ciele moim Bog moy, ktory mię stworzył, mieć mi pozwalał, płakać."

34. Smotryc'kyj 1628a, 11/528: "To mię dolegało, odpowiem temu, że ia Episzkop, ba y Archiepiszkop w Cerkwi narodu mego Ruskiego nie wiedziałem

com wierzył. . . . Nie miałoż mię to Episcopa dolegać? y nie byłoż mnie słuszney do tey moiey tak pracowitey peregrinatiey przyczyny?"

35. Smotryćkyj 1628a, 2/524: "Po to mowię do Oyca naszego y do starszych naszych Cerkwie Wschodney chodziłem, abym się od nich dowiedział y nauczył, o dogmatach pobożności, o wierze nadzieie naszey, w ktorey y doczesną szczęśliwość y wieczne błogosławieństwo nasze założone y vfundowane bydź rozumiemy y wierzymy. to iest o to pytać chodziłem, ieżeli taż iest nasza teraz, ktora za przodkow naszych wiara była, ktora cd nich z woley Bożey do nas była zawitała, ktora nie odszedszy od nich, nas była w przodkach naszych doszła."

36. Smotryćkyj 1628a, 105–106/576: "Po wszytkim tym, w Roku 1621. Lamentowe błędy y Harezye porzucić vsądziwszy, wziąłem przed siebie, nie bez woli Bożey, ktorego w pracy tey osobliwey łaski, nad godność y gotowość moię doznawałem, poważny sposob dochodzenia tey prawdy, ktorą my w Przodkach naszych z Cerkwie ś. Wschodniey przyięli: to iest, sposobem Dialogu Katechism wiary dogmat pisać, Pana Boga mego na pomoc wziąwszy, począłem. Ktory we wszytkich wiary dogmatach swoim methodem sporządzony, za tegoż dobrotliwego Boga pomocą, w Roku 1623. skończyłem; A zaraz o correctiey y o censurze iego pomyśliwszy, gdym iuż był dobrze wziął wiad[om]ość o cztrech księgach przez godney pamięci Meletiusza Patryarchę Alexandryiskiego o wiary dogmatach napisanych, chcąc ie mieć swemu Katechismowi za Censora, Directora, y Correctora: A w głowach samego na ten czas Ś. Konstantinopolski Patriarchalny Thron prawiącego, puściłem sie z nim na Wschod."

37. Smotryćkyj 1628a, 1/523: "miawszy to w vmyśle moiem dobrą pamięcią obięte, abym w tak dalekie, niebespieczne, a na moie podeszłe lata y płoche zdrowie trudne kraie zapuściwszy sie nie powietrze tylo odmienić szukał, y odległość mieysca sobą zmierzył, ale oto w nich, abym sie postarał, tak dla siebie, iak więcey dla ciebie, coby mnie v Boga łaskę v ciebie miłość, a tobie przed Bogiem, y przed wszystkim światem Chrześciańskim, zbawienia y nieśmiertelną sławę ziednało."

38. Smotryćkyj 1629b, 7^v–8^r/708: "Zaczym pewność wiadomości Wiary, iuż mi sie tu pomieszać musiała: Gdyżem *Cognitione speciali* nie wiedział, ktora by Wiara, tą czystą y niepokalaną wiarą była. Ta, ktorą ia, y Ci naszy przede mną scriptorowie opisaliśmy: lub ta, na ktorą nam vkazowały rescripta Vnitskie: Abo też ktora insza, trzecia. Takiey wiadomości Wiary nie miałem. Ktorą moię wiary mey wiadomość y niewiadomość tak y ty *fraudulente Sophista* rozdzieliwszy, *linguam tuam dolosam* powściągni: y Ważney przyczyny Peregrynatiey Moiey *Cauillis perstringere* poniechay: *Alieno malo sapere edoctus.* Ktorą ia obchodziłem nie swowolnie, iako ty mię swowolnie pomawiasz: ale za wiadomością zezwoleniem y błogosławieństwem tego, na On czas starszego mego, ktoremu o tym wiedzieć należało: y za wiadomością tego czasu Archimandrity Pieczerskiego, y iego Kapituły. Od Ktorych dwu osob y listy miałem podrożne. a od pierwszy y do Oyca Patriarchi."

39. Smotryc'kyj 1628a, 89/568: "Bo przez lat niemal ośm całe z samym sobą y z tymi oto Authorow tych bluźnierstwy doma biedziełem sie: Czego świadomo dobrze Wilno, świadomy Kijow, świadoma Kapituła Ostrogska, y wiele z tych, ktorzy się zdali bydź czym w Narodzie naszym: z ktorymi ia o tym conferował, z vmysłu do nich dla tego samego zieżdżaiąc. A żem doma tego, czego szukałem, nie naszedł. szukać tego v swoichże na Wschod puściłem sie." But eight years before which date? Before 1628, the year he wrote the *Apology*? Perhaps before 1624, the year he set out for the East? A case could be made for the latter, since 1616 coincides more or less with the period when, in the representations of the Uniates in 1621 and of Smotryc'kyj himself in 1628, he had been involved in great soul-searching.

40. Smotryc'kyj 1629a, 76/683: "Aż mię potym za dopuszczeniem Bożym za grzechy moie, choroba tamże zięła, przez ktorą, y przez wielkie Wieleb: twey na ten czas trudności, do poważney o tym rozmowy z Wieleb: twoią przyść nie mogłem."

41. For the date and details, see Hering 1968, 58.

42. Diplic 1634, 5: "A że on był gotowy na to dobrze, aby zburzyć y znieść nie powstydził się przez gruntowne dowody, co mimo nadzieie swoie w Katechizmie Patryarszynym wyczytał, ztąd wiem. Naprzod, że Palinodią niekiedyś był na Lament swoy napisał. Powtore, że w Roku P. 1621. Lamentowe błędy y herezye, iako on rozumie, porzucić vsądził."

43. *Pamflet* 1875, 566: "дойде Константинополя и Іерусалима и бысть у Патриарховъ, и сбыстся съ нимъ якоже со Іюдою предателемъ."

44. Mužylovs'kyj 1629, 6ʳ: "boś tam nic tego nie czynił, po coś peregrinował, według wyszey rzeczonego od ciebie: to znać żeś nie po to chodził, tylko abyś tu nas, y tam oszukał, nie conferowałeś z nim o Wierze, ktorey ieszcze nie miałeś, ale raczey wyprawiłeś oszukawszy niezbożnie Oyca y Pasterza swego affectem życzliwym, prosząc v niego, aby cię listem iakim nadarzywszy Boszkiem v Rusi vczynił, y wyprawiwszy to bez żadnych rozmow o Wierze Ś."

45. *Indicium* 1638, 16ʳ⁻ᵛ/794–95: "Obacz apostata Smotrzyskiego, ktory imieniem wszystkiey Rusi, duchownych y świeckich, zmyśliwszy sobie listy od wszytkiey Rusi, do Ieruzalem y patriarchow poszedł, a tam wszystkich patryarchow łatwo oszukawszy, listy od nich do Rusi zmyśliwszy, podpisy do tych listow otrzymał w ten koniec, aby od tego czasu żadne appellatie do patriarchi Konstantynopolskiego nie byli donoszone z Rusi naszey, a od n[i]ego, iako exarchi y namieśnika patriarszego, byli referowane. Przez co intendował Ruś od posłuszeństwa patriarchi Konstantynopolskiego odwieść, a unią bezecną potaiemnie wprowadzić, a to dla sławy omylney, aby to iemu, a nie komu inszemu czasy potemne przypisali, iak owemu, co kościoł Dyanny w Ephezie spalił. A gdy się w tym Ruś—nieuka—zaledwo postrzegła y onego duchownie strofowała, że się tego krom wiadomości na oszukanie wszystkiey Rusi ważył, nie chcąc się w hordości y praesumptiey upokorzyć, udał się do Dermania y w

tym błędzie uniey wyuczony cerkiew ś., matkę swoię, skryptami niezbożnie szarpał."

46. Smotryćkyj 1629b, 8ʳ⁻ᵛ/708–709: "Co się . . . listu przez mię od Oyca Patriarchi przyniesionego dotycze. Ten był Narodowi naszemu Ruskiemu pożyteczny: mnie ani z Osoby mey ani z dostoieństwa mego namniey nie wywyższał. Exarchowie waszy, ktorych było w Kijowie Dwa: w Stepaniu trzeci: we Lwowie czwarty: (to czworogłowne *Monstrum* miałeś nierządniku z tego ich nierządu y ambitiey strofować) iż ten list znosił, A od wszytkiey Cerkwie Ruskiey obranemu bydź Exarchowi nakazował: ruszył ie w sadno, zwłaszcza Kijowskich: Ci rozesłali po wszytkiey Ziemi Ruskiey przepowiedniki, to do ludzi za rzeczy pewne vdaiąc, co w tym liście y iedną literą nie naydowało sie. Przez ktore łakomstwa swe, y list ten do podeyrzenia y zniewagi podali: y mnie oń potwarzać y po dziś nie przestaiecie."

CHAPTER 7

1. See Velykyj 1952, 13, for a document from 1623–1624: ". . . in quas Sacerdotes Schismaticos, ab illo Pseudo Episcopo Smotricio quasi ordinatos, introducit, qui populum contra legitimum Pastorem turbaverint, et Unionem labefactantes in Schismate continerent." See also Velykyj 1952, 53, for a document from 12 September 1624: "Smotricius assidius velitationibus ad perniciem verae religionis imbutus, Polocensem antistitem impudenter agens, alienam ditionem invadit, sincerae fidei lumen in omnium animis extinguere conetur, et subdolis verbis cunctos ad defectionem sollicitat."

2. Velykyj 1952, 64–65: "Pseudo Metropolita[!] Smotricki, qui, dum peniebantur alii ob interfectionem Archiepiscopi Polocensis, cuius ille primarius author fuit, fugerat in Turciam, et nunc iterum rediit, turbatque iurisdictionem Metropolitae et aliorum Episcoporum Unitorum cum interitu animarum. Chioviae, adiutus a Cosakis, per vim occupavit ecclesiam Unitorum. Brevi timendum quod iterum aliquem Episcopum Unitum vita privabit, vel aliquam seditionem magnam in Regno faciet in Caput Unitorum, iterumque fugiet. Bonum igitur esset, si Nuntius Apostolicus serio de hac re cum Serenissimo Rege tractaret nomine Suae Sanctitatis."
    On the Uniate Council of Kobryn, see Fedoriv 1974.

3. The following is the only passage I have found where Smotryćkyj made the direct comparison between his experience and that of St. Paul (Smotryćkyj 1628a, 103/575): "Był ten czas iżem nad miarę prześladował Cerkiew Bożą, y burzyłem ią, y postępowałem w Rossystwie nad wiele rowiennikow moich w narodzie moim będąc większym miłośnikiem nie zakonu Bożego, ani vstaw moich oyczystych, ktore były czyste, y są, święte y niepokalane: ale oto tych błędow y Hęreziy, przez owe nasze Zyzaniae w Cerkiew naszę Ruską, gdy ludzie spali, nasianych."

The entire passage was an adaptation of Gal. 1:3–4; Smotryćkyj placed direct reference to St. Paul in the margin: "Tak y Paweł Ś. czynił." Smotryćkyj himself never put Josafat in the role of St. Stephen.

4. Smotryćkyj 1629b, 3ᵛ:704: "Zaż nie woła na twoie Kaimy niewinna krew Brata naszego Abla: Błogosławioney pamięci Iosaphata Archiepiskopa Połockiego? Ba y tych, ktorych za to *parricidium* pakarano?"

5. Printed in Suša 1666, 42–43: "Quis hic genuinam Vestrae Reuerendissimae Paternitatis, et nimis potentem, non aduertat vocationem? Sane aequiparare eam ausim, ne dixerim anteferre, D. Pauli vocationi, praelustris in Ecclesia Dei facis. Illic enim turbauit ligauitque equi pedes, ipsum deiecit sessorem; hic vero Vestrae Paternitatis peracrem ligauit intellectum, illustre offuscauit ingenium, refragantem toties repressit voluntatem. Denique externis cum illos medijs, cum V. Dominatione agit Dominus internis."

6. Velykyj 1956a, 195: "Reddit B.V. per me ac suas literas obedientiam R.mus Meletius Smotricius nuncupatus Archiepiscopus Polocensis, Schismaticorum in Septentrione facile princeps; Cuius ego reditum soli Deo Glorioso et sanguini Martyris illius Iosaphat adscribo. Enimvero quod Paulus fuit Stephano, id Smotricius Chuncevitio; quid si ergo sicut conversionem Pauli adscribimus orationibus Stephani, ita conversionem Smotricii Chuncevitio tribuamus?"

7. Velykyj 1956a, 196: "Meletius ille Smotricius nuncupatus apud Schismaticos Archiepiscopus Polocensis, quo neminem doctiorem aeque ac Unioni S. infestiorem Schisma in his partibus habuit, mihi iam reddidit et per me S.D.N. reddit obedientiam. Sed quomodo cum illo processum ex inclusis literis colliget D.V.R.ma. Ego nulli alteri quam sanguini Servi Dei Josaphat hanc conversionem adscribo; sicut e converso mortem eiusdem tanquam causae originali R.mo Meletio cum voce populi attribuo. Ecce ergo ex Saulo Paulus, ex lupo agnus."

8. See Rućkyj's letter to Urban VIII written in 1627 (the exact date is unclear), cited in Kojalovič 1861, 353 ("R-sum Meletium Schismaticos parricidas tum scriptis tum dictis contra pastorem suum excitasse . . . ") and also p. 357.

9. Birkowski 1629, 10: "Ale y z drugiey miary widzę ia wielką miłość w Iozaphacie błogosławionym, gdy wszystek na tym był, iakoby do świętey iedności kościoła Katholickiego wszystkę bracią swoię przywiodł, zwłaszcza owce dyecezeyy swoiey. Rosproszone były niedawno od wilka Smotryckiego, ktory się vdawał za pasterza nowego owieczek iego, y pod czas Seymu, na ktorym był pasterz, y wpadł iako wściekły przez listy y zwodniki niektore, szarpaiąc y drapiąc owieczkie Chrystusowe; o iako prędko przybieżał Ociec nasz święty, aby ginących ratował."

10. Birkowski 1629, 12: "Wyrwie się lada kto, lada szpieg, bez listow, bez świadectwa do was . . . a wy zaraz do niego."

11. Birkowski 1629, 11: "A nasz ś. Iozaphat do iakich? mało lepszy byli oni, ktorych fałszywy Patryarcha Alexandryiski pozwodził, y świętokradzkim obyczaiem na Władyki poświęcił: mało lepszy byli y oni Czerńcowie, ktorzy iako psi wściekli od Pana Smotryckiego nasłani, Połocką dyecezyą, włość Chrystusowę, szarpali; kupy to były apostatow, wybieglcow, konfederatow dusznych. Do takich z Warszawy przypadł, takich nawracał od odszczepieństwa przeklętego, iako niegdy Szczepan ś. Żydom mowił: *Twardey chrzczyce y nieobrzezanego serca, czemu to Duchowi ś. ieste*ś*cie przeciwni* [Acts 7:51]?"

12. Velykyj 1967, 435: "sicuti ad preces Stephani protomartyris Saulus caedis et minarum spirans e lupo in agnum commutatus est, ita Iosaphat precibus, ipse Meletius Smotricius, conspirationis uti diximus auctor, atque acerrimus Unionis oppugnator, facti poenitens, Petri cathedrae Romanoque Pontifici ardenti studio adhaesit, catholicamque fidem strenue asserens diem vidit supremum."

13. See, for example, Velykyj 1952, 83: "Dum haec ille ageret homo quidam, Patriarcham Hierosolymitanum se vocans, ex Moschovia in fines Regni Poloniae venit, Pseudo Metropolitanum pro Metropoli Kiioviensi, et alios Pseudo Episcopos pro omnibus Episcopatibus Ruthenis legitime unitis, et inter caeteros pro Polocensi Meletium Smotricium creat, qui confestim per totam Polocensem dioecesim ad Unionem conversis literas scribit, ne Josaphat uti illegitimo Pastori, papistae, haeretico, sed sibi vere orthodoxo, et a legitimo Pastore ordinato obedientiam praestent. Mittit cum his monachos quosdam et sacerdotes saeculares, qui omnes ab obedientia S. Antistitis, tum Warsaviae in Comitiis Ecclesiae, et Unionis firmandae gratia commoranti, reduxerunt, et persuaserunt, ut dictum Meletium ad se vocarent, Josaphat vero pellere constituerunt."

For other testimonies from the Polack process of 1628, see also, Velykyj 1952, 93, 125, 127, 155, 198, 202, 205, 206, 209, 210.

14. Velykyj 1955, 21; "Novi quoque Meletium Pseudo Archiepiscopum, primarium authorem seditionis contra Servum Dei, qui nuper fuit conversus ad fidelem catholicam, et SS.mo Domino per litteras reddidit obedientiam, cuius conversionis non aliam opinor fuisse causam, quam orationes Servi Dei."

15. Velykyj 1955, 282, 285: "Hoc scio quod Smotricki, quondam Pseudo Archiepiscopus Polocensis, caput fuit omnium malorum. . . . Smotricium autem nullus alius ad S. Fidem convertit, praeter sanguinem Martyris, et ut video hic Sanctus Sanctum eum ex tanto latrone et lupo efficit. *Et haec omnia notoria sunt et publica.*" (Emphasis added.)

16. Kortycki 1634, A4^{r-v}: "Bo weyrzymyli na pierwszą konwersacią tak Pawła Ś. iako y tego Przewielebnego męża: obadwa rzec o sobie mogą *Persequebar Ecclesiam Dei, et expugnabam illam, et proficiebam in iudaismo* (a ten rzec może *in Schismatismo*) *supra multos cooetaneos meos in genere meo, abundantius aemulator existens paternarum mearum traditionum.* Prześladowałem prawi, kościoł Boży, y burzyłem go y przechodziłem w Schizmie siła rowiennikow moich, gorąco y natarczywie zastawiaiąc się za Oyczyste podania moie. Obadwa prześladowali, ta tylo rożnica, że Paweł

ięzykiem, y mieczem, a Meletius piorem, y ięzykiem, nie wiem ktory szkodliwiey: Więc co o Pawle Ś. wielki ieden Doktor mowi By się był Szczepan nie modlił, kościoł by dziś Pawła nie miał: toż barzo przystoynie rzec się o tym mężu może, By się był Iosafat, ktory śliczność iedności prawosławney krwią swoią iako Męczennik zarożył, by się był nie modlił, cerkiew prawowierna Meletiusa by dziś nie miała."

17. See Velykyj 1955, 228, 241–42, 255, 271–72, 282–85, 299, 310, 329.

18. Suša 1666, B1ᵛ: "Ne memorem tot etiamnum viuentium, recentem vitae eius, et horum memoriam prodigiorum, ex quibus infallibilis eorum et Diuina, percipi facile poterit probatio et certitudo, dummodo de ijs sancta inquirere lubuerit Ecclesia."

19. Suša 1666, 17: "Inierat tum Smotriscius singularem cum Archiepiscopo Russiae Iosepho Rutscio notitiam, et intima eius vsus est consuetudine. Rutscius etiam tam commoda laetus occasione, de vnione cum eo Catholica perfrequens egit, qui eius emolliret pectus, deuinciret animum, et dotibus naturae egregijs insigniti viri lucraretur salutem."

20. Suša 1666, 24: "Enimuero in neutro testium examine, de mandato S.R. Ecclesiae Polociae transacto, imo neque in regali Vitepscensi, sanguinis Iosaphat vindice iudicio, patuit Smotriscium, eo nequitiae processisse, vt sanguinem tanti sitiret Archipraesulis. Verum quia praeferuido calamo, imperitae saeuaeque multitudini, Iosaphat reijciendum, se amplectendum, vt uerum persuasit Pastorem; tum illa ad tumultus ciendos praeceps, ad hauriendum sanguinem praecox, neque imperata ab eo, neque cogitata, crudelius, quam pretimesceret, peregit."

21. The *breve beatificationis* has been published in Velykyj 1967, 119–21.

22. Suša 1666, 144: "Non sine singulari loci protectione in omnibus Tartarorum, Schismaticorum, et Cosacorum incursionibus, cum a linea Cosatica, Horin videlicet fluuio, istud monasterium, vix duabus distet leucis, et inuiolatam in ea vsque tempora, Catholicae Vnionis fidem conseruet."

23. *Pamflet* 1875, 567: "Его же част (*аще не покается*) со Іюдою предателем и злочестивым Аріем и протчими еретики, благочестію сопротивляючимися."

24. *Pamflet* 1875, 562: "Сѣдинами честными украшаемъ, а сребролюбіем помрачаемъ . . ." Cf. 1 Tim. 6:10.

25. *Pamflet* 1875, 562: "со богачем а не со Лазарем жити изволил еси."

26. *Pamflet* 1875, 566: "дойде Константинополя и Іерусалима и бысть у Патріарховъ, и сбыстся съ нимъ якоже со Іюдою предателем."

27. *Pamflet* 1875, 563: "Престрога до отца с. Папежа Римского. О великій Пастыру великаго престола римскаго, рци ти кого непщуеши

имѣти себѣ достовернаго Мегментия Смердицкаго, яко нѣкгды Лютера богохульнаго, или Януша Калвина, упившагося безбожия вином не от истиннаго плода лознаго, но от своего разума суемернаго, невѣрь невѣрь, таковаго отступника стяжечи себѣ хулника."

28. *Pamflet* 1875, 562: *"нѣ Вамъ нѣ намъ."*

29. Smotryc̄kyj 1629a, 24/657: "Żem tedy pod zeszły moy wiek, pod lata moie stare, gdy iuż iedną nogą stoię w grobie, y gdy z tym światem co godzina rozstać mi się przychodzi, *poniosłem odmianę* . . . " (Emphasis added.)

30. Smotryc̄kyj 1628a, 105–106/576: "nie wspominam verificatiey, obrony iey, Elenchu, Iustificatiey, y tym podobnych. w ktorych iedney po drukiey, im daley, tym rzadszy byłem w następowaniu na dogmata prawdziwe, szerszy w rzeczach potocznych, pod te czasy nagle przypadłych. . . . Po wszytkim tym, w Roku 1621. Lamentowe błędy y Haerezye porzucić vsądziwszy, wziąłem przed siebie, nie bez woli Bożey, ktorego w pracy tey osobliwey łaski, nad godność y gotowość moię doznawałem, poważny sposob dochodzenia tey prawdy, ktorą my w Przodkach naszych z Cerkwie ś. Wszchodniey przyięli: to iest, sposobem Dialogu Kathechism wiary dogmat pisać, Pana Boga mego na pomoc wziąwszy, począłem."

31. Smotryc̄kyj 1629a, 5–6/647–48: "O czymem ia w Monasterze MM. Waszych Wileńskim, y świetcko y zakonniczo mieszkaiąc, często z tym, z kim należało, mawiał, y z wielą inszymi, po inszych Ziemie Ruskiey krainach, poważnymi mężami konferowałem: vkazuiąc to rzeczywiście, że Bractwa naszego Wileńskiego, przez druk wydani Skrybentowie, wielką szkodę Cerkwi Ruskiey czynią; Wiary prawosławney prawe dogmata, na Luterskie y Kalwińskie błędy, y Herezye, zmieniaią, y nimi lud tego złego niewiadomy, y postrzedz nieumieiący, na duszy zabiiaią."

32. Smotryc̄kyj 1629a, 6/648: "O tym wszystkim acz często po tamte czasy, iednak nie głośno mawiałem: a to z tey przyczyny; żem był Laik, Zakonnik prosty. . . . Lecz zostawszy z woley Bożey w Cerkwi Ruskiey Episkopem, znaiąc powinność swoię, y w niey się za pomocą Bożą poczuwaiąc, a temu pomienionemu, na wszystek Ruski świat przez cię nasianemu złemu, aby więcey duszom ludzkim na zbawieniu ich nic szkodziło, zabiegaiąc, (bom się też y sam do tego złego, przez lamentowy moy skrypt, znacznie był przyłożył: co mię nabarziey bolało) głośno o tym mowić począłem."

33. Smotryc̄kyj 1629a, 7/648: "Żem tedy ia te tych takich Skrybentow pisma, głośno iuż, za każdą o tym okazyą, mienił bydź Heretyckiemi, bluźnierstw przeciwko wierze prawowierney, a za tym y na Pana Boga, y na Maiestat iego ś. pełnymi, (a nabarziey to czyniłem, gdym się iuż z Peregrynatiey moiey do Ziemie ś. obchodzoney zwrocił . . .)."

34. Smotryc̄kyj 1628a, 89/568: "Bo przez lat niemal ośm całe z samym sobą y z tymi oto Authorow tych bluźnierstwy doma biedziełem sie: Czego świadomo

dobrze Wilno, świadomy Kijow, świadoma Kapituła Ostrogska, y wiele z tych, ktorzy sie zdali bydź czym w Narodzie naszym: z ktorymi ia o tym conferował, z vmysłu do nich dla tego samego zieżdżaiąc. A żem doma tego, czego szukałem, nie naszedł. szukać tego v swoichże na Wschod puściłem sie."

35. Smotryćkyj 1629a, 22/656: "Ktory [i.e., Derman'] na ten czas, kiedym się ia do wschodnych kraiow iuż z vmiłowaną z łaski Bożey Vnią puszczał, miał swego Residenta pewnego, żywego, y zdrowego; pod ktorym żywym, abym go miał kiedy dostąpić, iak rzeczy v mnie niepodobney, y na myśli nie miałem." Kurcevyč was Archbishop of Brest and Volodymyr and was the other Church figure for whose arrest, along with that of Smotryćkyj and Borećkyj, the Catholic authorities had called in 1621. Kurcevyč became the most infamous "defector" to the east of his generation: while Smotryćkyj was in the Holy Land, Kurcevyč found asylum in Muscovy, where he was to spend the rest of his days. See Xarlampovič 1914, 32–39.

36. Smotryćkyj 1628a, 6–7/526: "Nie był we mnie żaden wnętrzny y zewnętrzny zmysł, ktory by sie nie cieszył, nie radował, nie weselił: ktoryby nie iak przytomnego na mieyscu tym vkrzyżowanego Zbawiciela swego czuł. Wszystek duszą moią w myślach moich radość byłem y vciecha. Ray mi była tegdy Ś. Gołgota. . . . Gdzie zaraz siebie podawszy całą duszą y czystym sercem moiem w to proszone przez niego v Oyca swego IEDNO, iemu iak Panu memu v Bogu, na tę w Cerkwi iego Ś. posługę siebie ofiarowałem, poślubił, y oddał, abym zbawienne iego to IEDNO w narodzie moiem opowiadał."

37. Smotryćkyj 1629a, 83–84/686–87: "a potym toż słyszałem y z vst Oyca Patryarchy Ierozolimskiego *Kiiz* [*sic*] Theophana w Ieruzalem; ktoremu o tym w Multańskiey ziemi, gdy tam z naszey krainy Ruskiey był zawitał, sam vstnie ten Metropolit Mirski powiadał, z iakiey przyczyny swoie skrypta popalił, w ktorych zachodniemu Kościołowi y Religiey Rzymskiey, względem tych miedzy wschodną y zachodną Cerkwią rożnic, *vsque ad nauseam* był molestny."

38. Smotryćkyj 1629a, 84/687: "ktoremu o południu, przez senli, lub przez *extasim*, y sam wiedzieć nie mogł, okazował się ś. Apostoł Piotr po trzykroć, pierwszą razą y drugą mowiąc do niego: Mattheuszu, coć tak barzo przewiniła Stolica moia, że ią tak niewstydliwie łżysz? napominam cię, poprzestań tego. A to rzekszy, nie było go. A za trzecim razem do tych słow pierwszych przydał y owe: gdzie tego nie poprzestaniesz, na sąd cię on straszny Boży pozywam, tam mi się tego przed nielicemiernym Sędzią sprawować będziesz. Czym przestraszony bywszy Metropolita, a k sobie przyszedszy, y tey takowey swey prace, za ktorą groźny sąd Boży miał był ponieść, złorzeczywszy, popalił ią przed swymi."

39. Smotryćkyj 1629a, 84/687: "Co powiadane gdym i vsłyszał, vsłyszane w sobie vważał, vrodził mi się w sumnieniu moim gryźliwy mol, y raźliwie toczyć począł serce moie . . . ".

40. Smotryćkyj 1629a, 61/675: "Ktorego poważne, święte, y duszezbawienne tego w Cerkwi Bożey wielkiego Doktora zdanie, nad naszym narodem Ruskim

od tey władze, ktorey nas Pan Bog w sprawowanie, w przemysł, w opiekę, y w obronę podał, aby samym w dziele postępkiem chwalone było, zdarzyć racz Panie Iezu Chryste. Za ktorey przyczyny daniem, aby y wy przydaney wam mądrości nabywszy poczuliście, *a do poznania prawdy przyszli*." (Emphasis added.)

41. Smotryc̆kyj 1629a, 81–82/685–86: "Za czym, gdziebym od Wieleb: twey w tey prośbie moiey był przebaczon, y z niczym odepchnion, Bogiem stworzycielem, wnętrzności ludzkich wybadaczem, oświadczywszy się, to bym, *saluo tuo Paterno honore*, czynić musiał, co bym swey duszy zbawiennego bydź, za łaską y pomocą Boga mego, *śmierci grzesznikowey nie pożądaiącego, y nawrocenie człowiekowi daruiącego, vpatrzył.*" (Emphasis added.)

42. See Lavrov 1966, 1: "Богъ милостивый и щедръ, жадаа на покааніе чловѣче, да быша спасени въси были и въ разоумъ истинныи пришли, не хощетъ бо съмръти грѣшникомъ, но покааніа и животоу."

On the importance of this motif in the early Cyrillo-Methodian documents, see Picchio 1982.

43. Smotryc̆kyj 1628a, 103–104/575: "Był ten czas iżem nad miarę prześladował Cerkiew Bożą, y burzyłem ią, y postępowałem w Rossystwie nad wiele rowiennikow moich w narodzie moim będąc więtszym miłośnikiem nie zakonu Bożego, ani vstaw moich oyczystych, ktore były czyste, y są, święte y niepokolane: ale oto tych błędow y Hęreziy, przez owe nasze Zyzaniae w Cerkiew naszę Ruską, gdy ludzie spali, nasianych. w ktorych obaczenie y poznanie, same pracy, moie ktorem na obronę ich przed sie brał, za dobrotliwą miłosiernego Boga łaską, przywiodły mię, żem iuż więcey pismy moimi, wprzeciw Cerkiewney prawdzie iść nie mogł, tylo, aż ieślibym sie wszelako na przyięcie tych błędow y Haereziy, był rospasał: y więcey Synem Cerkwie Wschodniey ani sie znał, ani sie zwał. na co sumnienie moie, nie bez osobliwego miłosierdzia Bożego, wielą razow, iakoby w zapasy z powołaniem Bożym iść kusiwszy sie, owszeki pozwolić nie zezwoliło. Za co żywiącemu PAnu, *śmierci grzesznikowey niepożądaiącemu*, niech będzie ode mnie nędznego iego stworzenia, wieczne podziękowanie." (Emphasis added.)

44. Velykyj 1972, 127: "Benedictus sit Deus noster, Deus misericordiarum, qui misericordiam vult et non sacrificium."

45. Smotryc̆kyj 1629b, 16^r–v/716–17: "wiele ludzi obaczaią, y Schizmą waszą pogardzaiąc, do Iedności Ś. Cerkiewney vdaią się, niech ztąd będzie pochwalony *BOg wszechmogący, Ktory zginienia człowieczego nie pożąda.*" (Emphasis added.)

46. Golubev 1883a, 355: "но Богъ хотяй всѣмъ человѣкомъ спастись и въ разумъ истины пріити, отнюду же и жертву ихъ скверну и непріятну быти изъяви: абіе бо—оле страшнаго чудеси!—потиръ разсядесь и вино истече."

47. Zasławski's letter to Smotryc̆kyj (dated 16 February 1627) was included in

Suša's *vita* (1666, 45): "Verum meminisse suorum velit verborum, se non a sexennio, sed plusquam a decennio agnouisse errorem, non spiritum Dei in se operatum, cum pestilens scripsisset lamentum; Sed spiritu, pace eius dixerim, ambitionis, spiritu haereseos, quem in scholis attraxisset haereticis. Ecquid ergo Vestra Reuerendissima Paternitas, alios procudit libros? in quibus ea quae in lamento continebantur, confirmabat, collaudabat, et reuoluere cuique suadebat."

48. See the opening lines of *Paraenesis* (Smotryc'kyj 1629a, 3–4/646–47).

49. On 28 June 1628 Metropolitan Ruc'kyj wrote to *Propaganda Fide* informing the Congregation that Bishop Isaja Kopyns'kyj of Przemyśl had been sending out letters urging the Orthodox to have nothing to do with Borec'kyj or Smotryc'kyj. See Velykyj 1956a, 206: " . . . Isacius nuncupatus Praemislien. . . . misit literas encyclicas per totam Russiam, praecavendo ne cum Job Metropolita et Meletio Archiepiscopo habeant ullum commercium . . . "

50. Golubev 1883b, 280–81: "Кгдымъ мы ласкою всесилного Бога и его помоцю святою при церкви святое восточное православіи святѣйшихъ патріарховъ благословеніи и послушенствѣ, якосмы святыню приняли и неотмѣнне завше держали и при церкви восточной стояли такъ и теперь стоимо и моцно держимо и за помочю тогожъ творца держати и стояти до смерти сподѣваемся; ани зъ апостатами жадного поразуменья и здрады ихъ участництва немѣлисмо, ани противъ церкве руское и противъ народу своего нѣкгды намовъ жадныхъ подступно нечинилисмо, ани чинити безъ волѣ Божое и безъ волѣ всее церкви православныхъ не мыслилисмо, ани мыслитъ можемо."

51. Golubev 1883b, 285: "Многыми напастьми отъ лжебратій напаствованъ бывши, и за превосходячее терпливостъ мою оклеветаніе по сесъ часъ якъ въ забвеніи ходивши, до честности твоей писати не успѣлемъ, але якобы зъ умыслу занехалемъ, ажъ бы ся былъ той противный о мнѣ шумъ утишилъ и засмученыи благочестивыхъ серца зостали утѣшены."

52. Kojalovič 1861, 363: "'His et aliis id effecit Rud-smus Metropolita ut non priius Smotriscio Monasterium Dermonense conferre promiserit quam ea, quae unitum decerent, praestaret.'" But who was the author of this "report to the pope," which was apparently written shortly after Smotryc'kyj's conversion? Ruc'kyj? The nuncio in Warsaw? Perhaps it was the latter, since the passage cited above seems to have been a commentary on Ruc'kyj's actions and words.

53. Suša 1666, 54: "Ponderet ergo quo animo, etiam meam, Regia Maiestas, vti Senatoris cum Vestra Reuerendissima Dominatione, continuam accepturus esset consuetudinem?"

54. Suša 1666, 52: "Quoniam itaque ambulatoria est voluntas humana . . . vsque ad mortem; libens vellem, propter cordis mei pacem, (non quod diffidam Vestrae Reuerendissimae Dominationi, absit) habere certitudinem in scripto."

55. Velykyj 1972, 125–26: "Solare illud lumen, universam hanc mundi molem suis collustrans radiis, videtur his deploratissimis temporibus esse Ecclesiae Dei foelix Beatitudinis Vestrae pontificatus, eo splendidior, quo magis tot haeresum et schismatum nubibus obtegitur. Ita, ut de illo dicere debeam, non est qui se abscondat a calore eius. Ecce ego in ultima peccantis terrae appendice situs, in schismate velut ex necessitate natus, in eodem per annos quinquaginta ex ignorantia volutatus, eo beneficiorum et affectus Beatitudinis Vestrae erga Rutenam Ecclesiam radiis ex miseriarum lacu extractus attrahor, ut pedibus manibusque revinctis, ad genua Beatitudinis Vestrae cum lachrymis prosternar et eius pedes humillime deosculer. Et quoniam omni verborum ambage seposita et haeresi schismatica abiurata illi obedientiam reddo, nil amplius dicere possum, quam quod: Pater, peccavi in coelum et coram te! Non sum dignus vocari filius tuus. Tu vero, Beatissime Pater, dimissis mihi omnibus, quaecumque contra te, Sanctamque Petri Sedem ac sanctam fidem Romanam catholicam mente, ore et calamo peccavi, eaque omnia sine pudore, Deo iuvante, retractare volo, ut in me occidendo peccatum quod meum fuit, in te, Beatissime Pater, consequar gratiam, vitam quae Dei est: facere me digneris sicut unum de mercenariis tuis. Hoc unum opto, ut sicut ex corde cum sancto peccatore dico: Peccavi Domino; ita cum eodem a te, Beatissime Pater, audiam: Et Dominus transtulit a te peccatum tuum."

56. Suša 1666, 55: "Quia tamen respicio, ne scripta V. Reuerendissimae Dominationis, minus accepta sint schismaticis, ideo malim et desiderarim, vt cum se merum et sincerum probauerit vnitum, schismatis seipsum veste obuelare velit. Non enim obfuit Nicodemo occultus discipulatus Christi. Neque Apostolis, non statim post Ascensionem Domini praedicauisse; sed propter metum Iudaeorum sese occlusos tenuisse; vsque dum S. super eos descendisset Spiritus. Vestra porro Dominatio non metu id faceret, sed quia eiusmodi ratione, plures in viam salutis deducere possit."

57. This letter is published in Golubev 1883b, 317–22.

58. Smotryc'kyj wrote to Drevyns'kyj (Golubev 1883b, 319–20) that he had attempted to enter his protestation into the castle books at Luc'k. When his protestation was not accepted, he decided to write to Drevyns'kyj and to print his *Protestation*.

59. *Pamflet* 1875, 566: "начат составляти яда исполненную книжицу, Апологію сію нарицая, егоже ощутивше Кіево-печерскіи отцы, соборнѣ отчасти обличиша, но не до конца. По сих же сущу ему при погребеніи тѣла преставлшіяся о Христѣ вышереченныя Княгинѣ Соломирецкия въ Болкоградѣ, и тамо ощущаху его нѣцыи от отецъ яко неблагочестивъ, но не возмогоша явѣ его обличити, занеже у всѣх во велицей чести бѣ, дондеже вторицею на соборѣ въ Кіевѣ явственнѣ его обличиша."

60. Smotryc'kyj 1629a, 3/646: "Na List MM. Waszych, Dnia 13. *Augusti*, Roku tego teraźnieyszego 1628. mnie w Kiiowie przez Oyca Iozepha Namiestnika mego oddany; na on czas prze niesposobność mieysca y czasu,

dostatecznie odpisać nie mogszy (w ktorym mię MM. WW. o wyraźną Rezolucyą proszą, abym vprzątnął tę o sobie suspicyą, ktora się z sławy w vstach ludzkich noszącey się, w sercach MM. WW. o mnie vrodziła, że mię owi vdaią za Vnita; a drudzy, że coś nowego zamyślam: y tak na trzecią część Ruś rozerwać pokuszam się; skąd by bydź musiało oszukanie ostatnie gorsze, niż było pierwsze) teraz za łaską Bożą, czasu y mieysca wolnieyszego nabywszy, MM. WW. na to odpisuię obszerniey, niżem iuż odpisał."

61. Smotryćkyj 1628b, Aii^v/628: "Roku przeszłego 1627. nakazany był nam Episkopom Sobor, o Święcie Narodzenia Panny Naświętszey w Kijowie."

62. Smotryćkyj 1628b, Aii^v/628: "Gdzie gdym sie z powinności dostoieństwa mego stawił, byłem od tych na ktorych tam przodkownie należało, a osobliwie od Iego Mści Oyca Iowa Boreckiego (inszi Episkopowie na ten Synod nie przybyli) y od teraźnieyszego Iego Mści Oyca Archimandrity Pieczerskiego, na on czas ieszcze człowieka świetskiego, proszony y sollicitowany, abym ten moy Katechism, z ktorymem do Wschodnych kraiow dla censury y Correctury iego ieździł, (ponieważ on tego tam nie dostąpił,) podał pod Censurę Cerkiewnikom narodu naszego Ruskiego, aby za tym niemieszkało do vżywania Cerkwie Ruskiey, przez druk mogł bydź podany. Na co ia Ich Mościom odpowiedziałem, żem to gotow vczynić, tylko o to iedno proszę, aby pierwey, niż go pod vważenie y Censurę podam, wolno mi było wydać *Consideratiae* tych sześciu roźnic, ktore sie miedzy Cerkiew Wschodną, y Zachodną przywnoszą, aby tym łacniey y szczęśliwiey ta Censura obeyść sie mogła. Na co od Ich Mściow: y od inszych na ten czas przytomnych pozwolenie łacno otrzymałem."

63. Smotryćkyj 1628b, Aii^v–iii^r/628: "Z tym pozwoleniem czekałem na pogodę. Ali iakoby w puł roka potym, szostey Niedziele w Post wielki, obie te wyż mianowane osoby, Ociec Borecki, y Ociec Archimandrita, iuż w stanie Duchownym, maiąc z sobą dwu Episkopow Oyca Isakiego y Oyca Paisia, przybyli tu na Wołyń do Grodka maiętności Pieczerskiey: do ktorych za nakazem ich, przybyłem y ia. Gdzie o Cerkiewnych duchownych sprawach namowę miawszy, vpatryliśmy wielką potrzebę Synodu pomiestnego wszytkiey Cerkwie Ruskiey tak z stanu duchownego, iak y z świetskiego, zawołania Szlacheckiego y Mieyskiego. Na ktorego zwołanie Ociec Borecki listy miał rozesłać prywatne, a mnie zlecili to napisać, przez co by sie kożdy łacno dał pociągnąć, na ten wielce gwałtowny potrzeby ziazd, stanowić sie. A w ten naprzednieyszy koniec, abyśmy miedzy sobą na tym Synodzie w miłości y w pokoiu, vważyć y obaczyć mogli, ieżeliby sie mogł iaki sposob, bez naruszenia wiary naszey Praw y Przywileiow, wynaleść ziednoczenia Rusi z Rusią: to iest nievnitow z Vnitami."

64. Smotryćkyj 1628b, Aiii^r/628: "Z ktorey przyczyny tamże zaraz od wszytkich tych pomienionych czterech osob, pozwolono mi było, przy ogłaszaniu przyczyny Synodu, napisać y te wyż pomięnione sześciu miedzy Wschodną y Zachodną Cerkiew zachodzących roźnic *Consideratiae*, ktoreśmy z sobą tam vważali, y za niewielkie roźnice bydź sądzili: y pospołu oboie wydać."

65. Kojalovič 1861, 152, 366–73: "Dnia 29 Februarij listy Wiel. Twey od X-cia Jego M-ci przesłane pospołu z ośmią sextermionow katechismowych, doszły mię; przy nich y annotationes censoriae: w ktorych odsyła mię Wiel. twoja do pism R. Thomae Aqu. a ja ich nie mam: piszę do X. J. M-ci, aby mi ich do tey potrzeby użyczyć roskazał jeśli się w Bibliotece Dubienskiey [znajdują?]. Dialogum de processione Spiritus S. secundum mentem annotationum Wielebn. Twey poprawiłem. Tegoż katechismu posyłam teraz do Wieln. Twey sexternionow siedmi przy mnie zostało ieszcze nieskorygowannych dwanaście: y te za okazią pewną przeszlę."

66. Smotryc'kyj 1628b, Aiv^v/630: "Na te Listy Ich Mość: Przez mego Posłańca do mnie odpisali, że skoro po przeczytaniu tey prace mey, mieli swe o niey zdanie naroczyto, y dostatecznie, (ich słowa są) mnie oznaymić. Iż czekawszy na to Ich Mościow zdanie Niedziel trzy, a mieć go nie mogszy, tego rozumienia będąc, że się to Ich Mościom podobało, iako ze mną częstokroć o tym rozmawiaiąc, dobrze wyrozumieć mi się byli dali, posłałem ią dla wydrukowania ięzykiem Polskim."

67. Kojalovič 1861, 367: "teraz niedawno w wielkich gomonach od braci zakonnikow Monastera mego Dermońskiego byłem, którzy wziąwszy wiadomość o tym, że[m?] się z Wieleb. Twoją w Dubnie widział (chłopięta Wiel. Twey memu Heliaszowi Jlkowskiemu powiedzieli, a on inszey braci), oraz niemal wszyscy odbiegli mię byli, y po wszytskim Wołyniu rossławili."

68. *Arxiv* 1883, 605–606: "Дня двадцатаго октобра прибылъ сесъде до Киева Іванъ Дубовичъ, инокъ уницькій, поведаючи быти себе посланымъ отъ ксендза Руцъкого. . . . бо если есть щирость, бегати намъ того не потреба, кгдыж есмо по нихъ болше ничого не потребовали, толко абы се тамъ вернули, отколь выпадли."

69. Smotryc'kyj 1628b, Bi^r/630: "Ali 13 dnia *Augusta* podpołudnie, gdym sie był prosto ku Monasterowi Pieczerskiemu zapuścił, y do Iego Mości Oyca Archymandrity, ktory mię *solenniter* przez list swoy z Bracią swoią na ten Zaśnienia Panny naświętszey *fest* prosił, czeladnika swego posłał: iachać mi tam nie pozwolono: vkazano mi do Monastera Michałowskiego: Ia będąc tego rozumienia, że to Iego Mość Ociec Archymandrita vchyla sie mey przytomności, dla podeyrzenia v ludzi, (bo sie to w rozmowach naszych trafiało często:) a większą częścią rozumiałem, że sie tego ochraniał vczynić: aby sie nie podał w niełaskę Kro: Iego M. obcuiąc z nami: bo to czynił przed nim przodek iego Archymandrita Pieczerski: na odmianę vmysłu iego w sprawie tey namowioney anim pomyślił. y iachałem do Monasteru Michałowskiego. Gdzie od namiestnika y Braci przyięty byłem w Cerkwi iak Archijerey."

70. Smotryc'kyj 1628b, Civ^r/637: "A potym w Wigilię Święta Zaśnienia przenaświętszey Panny, o iedney godzinie tę sprawę we stu y pięciu punktach Episkopom trzem, ktorzy o tym dniu tam do Pieczerskiego Monasterza byli wezwani, przełożyli: y ieden z nich po swym zdaniu zdanie wszytkich Episkopow concludował: A drugi zdanie wszytkich Presbyterow . . . "

71. Smotryćkyj 1628b, B1ᵛ/631: "Odpowie [Mużylovśkyj]: Ale o to iuż w druku. Rzekłem, coż z tego? temu sie łacno zabiec może."

72. Smotryćkyj 1628b, Biiᵛ/632: "Ten taki list napisawszy, do Oyca Boreckiego przez wyż pomięnionego Diakona posłałem, 14. *Augusti*, rano, Po ktorego przesłaniu, czeladź moia rozmaite nowiny donosiła mi, ktore miedzy nie rozsiewano: miedzy inszemi y to, że o iutrzeyszym dniu y Pan wasz, y wy z nim iak Vnitowie będziecie przeklęci: nie ieden sie z was y Sławuty napije."

73. Smotryćkyj 1628b, Biiᵛ/632: "Dla Boga niech o sobie Iego Mość Ociec Archyepiskop radzi: gdyż iadąc teraz ze wsi Monasterskiey, nadiachałem kupę niemałą Kozakow, ktorzy w radzie swey, mnie iako sobie dobrze znaiomego nie wystrzegaiąc sie, sprzysięgli sie nie żywić go, ieśli co o Vnią nań od Soboru przewiedziono bedzie."

74. Smotryćkyj 1628b, Biiᵛ–iiiʳ/632: "trafiłem, iako baczę na nierząd: boć mię tak ci Oycowie moi y Bracia przez te ludzie łacno przedisputuią. Coż by w tym czynić? Vchyliłbym sie im, iako ludziom w tey mierze niebacznym y nieużytym. Ale nie wiem iak, y dokąd. Zszedłbym do Zamku, Pana Podwoiewodzego nie masz. iachałbym nazad, obawiam sie zasacki, bo iuż o niey głoszą. Do Miasta do Klasztoru, ale ie barziey zaiątrzę: bo iuż mię ieszcze przed przyiazdem tam bydź głosili, bać sie też potrzeba ieżeli mię y dopuszczą: bo iuż ludzi swowolnych, pijanych iako na kiermaszu, pełno wszędzie."

75. Smotryćkyj 1628b, Biiiᵛ/633: "Ten list aby mię do rady swey spolney dopuścili, łzami oblany prosząc pisałem. Gdyż dla tego nad tym moim scriptem y pracowałem: po to tam y iachałem, abym o opisanych w nim rzeczach z nimi namawiał."

76. Smotryćkyj 1628b, Biiiʳ⁻ᵛ/632–33: "To co sie iuż stało przez druk, rozstać sie nie może: wszakże aby sie to po wszytkim tym Państwie nie rozleciało, zabiec sie temu ieszcze może, za zobopolną w tym namową y radą naszą."

77. Smotryćkyj 1628b, Bivʳ/633: "Ociec Borecki (iako mię wiedzieć doszło) na to sie odezwał, Niechay z nim Dytko mowit. Otoż masz Oyca: y krotko, y nie k rzeczy."

78. Smotryćkyj 1628b, Bivʳ/633: "Ktory po przywitaniu sie ze mną, vczynił do mnie po kozacku, iak sie mu podobało, długą lekcyę: a zakończył ią tym, że my tey Świątynie nabyli krwią naszą: krwią też naszą pieczętować ią chcemy: abo y tych, ktorzy by ią nam iakokolwiek znieważali, y od niey odstępowali."

79. Smotryćkyj 1628b, Bivʳ/633: "przywitaliśmy sie nie po bratersku, ale iakoby mało sobie znaiomi."

80. Smotryćkyj 1628b, Bivʳ⁻ᵛ/633–34: "nu bies u waszey matery, machluyte machluyte: dostanet sia tut y Pawłu y Gawłu."

81. Smotryćkyj 1628b, Bivᵛ–Ciʳ/634: "Ia słyszawszy to, prawie otrętwiałem, z nowości słow tego człowieka nievważnych, ktory przez lat mieszkania mego

z nim cztery (powiadam to o nim pod świadectwem Bożym) mało w czym Rzymskiemu Kościołowi, o ktorymeśmy częste z sobą mowy miewali, przymawiał, y w wierze iego żadney Hęretyckiey przygany nie naydował: y o zgodzie z nim Rusi zawsze dobrze słowił: y sposob do Iedności ś. barzo łacny bydź vkazował, by sie tylo mogło w samym Kalendarzu pomiarkować: ktory do pociągnienia prostych ludzi narodu naszego, iest nieprzystępny."

82. Smotryc'kyj 1628b, Ciii^r/636: "Gdym iuż był w Cerkwi y w ołtarzu, przysłali do mnie, abym ten kartelusz podpisał, i żebym zaraz pod sumnieniem przyrzekł, iuż z Kijowa do Dermania nie iachać."

83. Smotryc'kyj 1628b, Ciii^r/636: "A w tym iakoby w godzinę po tym, iuż o zmierzku, napisany zrzeczenia sie sposob, ieżelibym na nim zezwolił przestać, y do nich przybydź, przysłali do mnie. Ia też tey nocy w Monasterzu Michałowskim, z wielu ważnych przyczyn, ktorych na ten czas nie wyrażam, zostawać nie chcąc, a przytomnością moią miedzy niemi, zaiątrzone ich ku mnie serca chcąc vmitygować, ten przysłany do mnie kartelusz, z wielu twardszych nieprzystoyności ociosany, zły iednak, y przepisany, a niepodpisany, Posłańcowi ich dałem."

84. Smotryc'kyj 1628b, Ciii^r/636: "Gdym iuż był w Cerkwi y w ołtarzu, przysłali do mnie, abym ten kartelusz podpisał, i żebym zaraz pod sumnieniu przyrzekł, iuż z Kijowa do Dermania nie iachać."

85. Smotryc'kyj 1628b, Ciii^{r-v}/636–37: "Prosiłem ich aby tych lekkości ze mną stroić poniechali: i że ia na ten podpis, y na te ich conditie dobrym sumnieniem pozwolić nie mogę. W tym zaraz, tamże w ołtarzu, słowami niepoczciwemi surowie rzucił sie na mię Ociec Archymandrita Pieczerski (ktory niedawno przed tym dobrze y pobożnie o tey sprawie, ktorą ia w tey moiey Apologiey opisał, y rozumiał y mowił; y list ten, ktory im do Iego Mści Oyca Patriarchy Konstantynopolskiego w przeszłym roku pisał, w ktorym summatim wszystko to, y ieszcze więcey iest wyrażono, co iest w tey Apologiey opisano, chwalił: bom go v mnie w Dermaniu przed nim czytał: y na tym zieździe naszym Grodkowym, gdyśmy o tych sześciu miedzy nami y Rzymiany Rożnicach rozmawiali, zmiankę przed tymi przełożonymi Duchownymi, ktorzy tam byli, czynił, y dobre słowo iemu dawał.) Ten mowię, tak dobrego o tey sprawie rozumienia człowiek indzie gdzie, a nie w ołtarzu, y to od lada kogo, na ludzie poczciwe mowić sie zwykłymi słowy, iadowito rzucił sie na mię. Zaczym stał sie taki hałas, że sie y ci co w ołtarzu, y ci co ołtarzowi bliższemi byli, iakoby na gwałt iaki poruszyli."

86. Smotryc'kyj 1628b, Ciii^v/637: "Ia też widząc, że sie do niepohamowanego złego rzecz ta niesie, y aby do wielkiego rozruchu, y krwie rozlania winney y niewinney (iako sie w takich razach, a ile w nocy, dziać zwykło) w Cerkwi tey Przezacney Pieczerskiey nie przyszło, kartelusz ten według woli ich, mimo wolą moię podpisałem: y do Dermania nie iachać, przyrzekłem. y tak sie ten huk y szmer vśmierzył."

See also Smotryc'kyj 1628b, Div^r/641: "Nie dla tych, mowię strachow y zniewag w to pogorszenie, miłosierdziu Bożemu poruczywszy sie puściłem sie; ale częścią dla tego, aby to mieysce ś. krwią, iakom rzekł, niewinną y winną nie było oblane. A większą częścią, że sprawoty mey słuchać nie chcieli: y mowić mi nic w obronę tego mego scriptu nie dopuścili."

87. Smotryc͞kyj 1628b, Ciii\ʳ–iv\ʳ/637: "Ali po przeczytaniu Ewangeliey, nad oczekywanie moie, zesłany był na Kazalnicę Wileński moy namieśnik. Duchowni też z Ołtarza ku Ambonie wystąpili. Rozdał każdemu z Władyk Ociec Archymandrita Pieczerski karty y świece. W tym ten co był na katedrze kartelusz ten czytał, a potym daną sobie z mey Apologiey kartę rozszarpnął, y rzucił. Zatym Ociec Borecki, z ktorym stał na Ambonie ten co sie nazywa Łuckim, na tęż Apologię, a przy niey zaraz, y na Oyca Kassiana Archymandritę Dubieńskiego, człowieka w wierze Prawosławney niepodeyrzanego, y ni iednym Prawem Duchownym w żadnym Hęretyctwie nigdy nie konanego, ani posoczonego, bez prawa y bez sądu Anathemę rzucił: kartę rozszarpnął, y świece zgasił. Toż za nim czynili wszyscy Władykowie."

88. Smotryc͞kyj 1628b, Div\ʳ⁻ᵛ/641–42: "Byłać mi za tym ich takim na mię następem Wyznawce, ieśli nie y Męczeństwa zaraz korona, do rąk moich podana, ale niestety, Bog moy, w ktorego ręku y śmierć moia y żywot, za tym takim moim respektowaniem sławie Mayestatu iego, iako baczę, niemiłym, wypaść mi iey z rąk moich pod ten czas dopuścił. Czego ia z dusze mey ciężko żałuię, y poki żywota we mnie, żałować y prosić o nie nie przestanę."

89. *Apolleia* 1628, A1ᵛ/303: "А Штося тычетъ Духовныхъ Роускихъ неОунитовъ, Тедыся маютъ передъ Сеймомъ пришлымъ знести зъ собою, якобы прикладомъ Духовенства нашого и Униатовъ ведлугъ здолности тежъ приложилися до ратунку теперешнего Речипосполитои."

90. Smotryc͞kyj 1629a, 8/649: "przyczynę ziazdu naszego do Kiiowa na Sobor, nie tę daie, ktora się miedzy nami w Grodku, maiętności Monastera Pieczerskiego, była namowiła, y postanowiła; y iakobym się ia dla tey od nich pomienioney przyczyny, do Kiiowa stawił: o ktorey ia anim wiedział, anim słyszał. W czym mię y same tego listy, ktory mnie, y insze narodu Ruskiego osoby, kilką Niedziel przed skończeniem, ba y przed zaczęciem Seymu, nierzkąc przed wydaniem y wyszciem Constitucyey, na ten Sobor wzywa, wyświadczą."

91. *Apolleia* 1628, A4ᵛ/306: "въ монастыри с[вя]т[о]го Михаила Золотоверхового мешканье назначоное одержалъ."

92. Smotryc͞kyj 1629a, 8/649: "ten Duchowny stan, w napisie tey swey *Pohibeli* [i.e., the *Apolleia*], abo Episkopy, y ich Przełożonego z stanu Duchownego niemądrze wyzuwa, abo ludziom świetckim Starszeństwo Cerkiewne nierozsądnie przypisuie . . ."

93. *Apolleia* 1628, Б1ʳ/306: "долго розмавляли, а то все въ любви зъ собою отправуючи, розышлися."

94. *Apolleia* 1628, Б2ʳ/308: "въ Навечеріе южъ Праздника зъ зезволеньемъ

на то, абыся ревокаціа написала, и Публице зъ Каθедры дня завтрешнего читаная была: въ правдѣ было то же зъконципованная была и написаная. Лечъ его милостъ отецъ архиепископъ на оную не зезволивши, своею власною рукою овую натерминовалъ, Переписалъ, и читати на Божественной Литургіи позволилъ."

95. *Apolleia* 1628, Б2ᵛ–3ʳ/308–309: "Я Мелетій Смотрискій Милостію Божіею Архіепископъ Полоцкій, бывшій взятый отъ всея Церкве нашеи Рускои въ подозрене отступства отъ Вѣры Православнои Греческои Соборнои Церкве Въсточнои: А выйстьемъ подъ именемъ моимъ зъ друку выданои Апологіею отитулованои Книжки, еще барзѣй въ тогожъ отступства подойзрене поданои презъ сее мое оголошене всей Церкви моей Рускои черезъ Милостъ вашу притомныхъ на сесъ часъ въ Святой Обители Печерской и въ Храмѣ семъ Святомъ Пречистои Дѣвы Богородицы Успенію посвяченномъ до вѣдомости доношу: ижъ зъ части нѣкоторои таковому отъ Православныхъ догматъ облуженію самъ подлегаю, зъ болшеи еднакъ части тое такое облужене сталоеся быти признаваю зъ своволного домыслу особы тои, которой тая Апологіа языкомъ Полскимъ зъ Друку быти выдана была отъ мене повѣрена: меновите зе злого умыслу Касіана Саковича въ Монастыру Дубенскомъ Преображенія Господня старшенствуючого. Которое неосторожное облуженеся, такъ иле до самого моего погрѣшеня, якъ и иле до шкодливого повѣреня противно Православнымъ Восточнои Церкве Догматомъ быти познавши, и признавши: милостива быти погрѣшенію моему Господа Бога умоляю, а всей Церкви моей Рускои тогожъ Добротливого Бога моего доброволне обецую же южъ на потомъ всею душею моею выстерегатися того хочу, даючи въ сей Святой Церкви вѣдомостъ того моего жалованя презъ знакъ овый, же передъ очима Милостій вашихъ всѣхъ той мой Апологіею названый скриптъ зневажаю, шарпаю и подъ ноги моѣ помѣтаю: подъ клятвою учиненною Господу Богу на онъ часъ кгдымъ былъ при Преосвященномъ Господинѣ моемъ и прочихъ Церкви нашей Россской Архіереахъ на Архіерейство отъ Святѣйшаго Патріархи Іерусалимского Господина Отца Θеофана подъ послушенство Святѣйшаго Патріархи Константинополскаго произвоженъ и Рукополаганъ. Року а҃х҃к҃и҃ [1628], Августа д҃і [14] дня."

A Polish version of this text was published in Mužylovs'kyj 1629/41ʳ⁻ᵛ. According to Golubev (1883a, 400), Smotryc'kyj's recantation was also published separately in print.

96. *Apolleia* 1628, Б3ʳ/309: "У того Листу Печать Архіепископская притиснена естъ одна. А подписъ руки тыми словы: Мелетій Смотрискій, Архіепископъ Полоцкій, Епископъ Витепскій и Мстиславскій, Архимандритъ Виленскій и Дерманскій Власною Рукою."

97. *Apolleia* 1628, В2ᵛ–3ʳ/314–15: "Кождому Православному и хотячому вѣдати то ознаймуемъ: ижъ не хто иншій впродъ прочитавши зъ иншимъ духовенствомъ але мы Митрополитъ и Епископове, при бытности

самогожъ господина и съслужителя нашего господина отца Мелетіа Смотриского Архіепископа Полоцкаго Епископа Витепскаго и Мстиславского, Архимандріта Виленского и Дерманского, который Литургію Божественную по обхожденіи съ Кресты въ Храмѣ Успеніа Пречистои Богородицы въ Святой Великой Лаврѣ Печерской Кіевской будучомъ въ всемъ Архіерейскомъ одѣню зъ нами сполне целебровалъ. Публице на Амвонѣ по Евангеліи и читаню зъ Каѳедры на писмѣ карты зъ Друку выданои теперъ, а рукою власною отъ Его Милости написанои шарпалисмо, допталисмо и огню властію собѣ отъ собора даною (проклинаючи и книжку и Касіана) предавалисмо, и самъ Господинъ Отецъ Архіепископъ шарпалъ, палилъ, и Анаѳемѣ якъ Книжку такъ и Касіана предъ лицемъ всеи Церкви отдавалъ."

98. *Apolleia* 1628, B3^{v}/316: "нехай читаня онои овшеки занехаетъ, яко тои которая от самогожъ *Autora* еи подоптаная, пошарпаная и Проклятству отданая ест. Зъ Кассіаномъ тежъ жадного сполькованя мѣти не потреба, яко зъ тымъ который въ Церкви Въсточной мѣстца южъ не маетъ."

99. Smotryc'kyj 1628b, Civ^{v}/638: "Lecz na inszey osobie, iakom powiedział, a na mey Apologiey iest exequowany."

100. Smotryc'kyj 1628b, Diii^{v}/641: "Bogu memu daną, y iemu *per obedientiam* szlubioną wiarę moię y pod ten samy czas cało zachował: y serce moie na tę ich, na ten moy script nieprawowiernym sercem rzuconą Anathemę nigdy nie zezwalało, y zbożnie zezwolić nie mogło. Zkąd było, że oni klęli moy prawosławny Katholicki script, ktory im ia z wielkim vważeniem pisał, y każdą rzecz moię w nim pismem Ś. y Doktorow Cerkiewnych Wschodnych y Zachodnych nauką dowodnie y poważnie sparł, obiaśnił y zmocnił. A iam klął ich kąkolosiewcow Zyzaniow, refutowane przez mię w tym moim scripcie, bluźnierstwa błędy y Hęrezye: te darłem, ne te świecę zgasiłem, te y pod nogi moie rzuciłem."

101. Smotryc'kyj 1628a, 130/588: "Bo ieśli kto nieprawo wyrozumiawszy wiary iey dogmata, nieprawo o nich mowi y pisze, a przez swoy błąd w *podzor sie Haerezyey podaie*, ten taki sam w wyrozumieniu swym nieprawym hańbę ponosi." (Emphasis added.)

102. For a contemporary discussion of the possible charges that could be brought forward by the Inquisition, see Masini 1665, 229–60. I had access to the second edition; the first edition was published in Genoa in 1621. Galileo, to cite the case of Smotryc'kyj's more famous contemporary, had been found "vehemently suspected of heresy." See Finocchiaro 1989, 14–15, 38. De Dominis, to cite another contemporary who was put on trial by the Inquisition, had been convicted of heresy outright. See Redondi 1987, 110–18.

103. Illja Kopyns'kyj, the same who had earlier spread allegations about Smotryc'kyj and Borec'kyj, would now charge that Mohyla lacked religious convictions (Golubev 1898a, 47–48).

104. This is the implication of the letter from King Sigismund III to the palatine of Kiev, Janusz Tyszkiewicz, of 23 June 1631 urging him to oppose the candidacy of Mužylovs'kyj, but carefully, lest the Cossacks take the opportunity to revolt. See Golubev 1883b, 431: "Masz tego iednak Uprz. W. przestrzegać, żeby się tym postępkiem przyczyna nie dała do rozruchu iakiego między kozakami."

105. Petruševič 1874, 291: "Sesio reiecta ad 10-am, qua die archimandrita Peczarensis concessit synodum, sed legati Leopolienses non permiserunt, justifikowali się podsądek i czesnik składaiąc winę na X. Bakowieckiego ale zaraz okrzykneli grożąc Kozacy y tak rozeszli się. Archimandryt Peczarski płakał u ktorego i Borecki nocował. Die quarta ab inchoata Synodo in monasterio Pustynensi congregati Borecki prosił Ostrozskiego o radę z płaczem co czynić, ponieważ szlachta protestowała się nec comparet, a kozacy śmiercią grożą postanowili nie zezwolić na synod, lubo duchowni chcieli synodować i podziękowali królowi za łaskę, i prosili aby ten synod seymem był naznaczony, aby się zniesli z Patryarchą, aby było mieysce sposobne y bez presidentow religionis latinae."

This document sounds like an early seventeenth-century testimony. Thus, when Petruševič wrote of a "ms. *of* Metropolitan Kyška," he may have meant nothing more than "in the metropolitan's possession." But here, too, we have no way of knowing what Petruševič has given us.

106. Golubev 1883b, 322: "Зъ стороны книгъ и аппаратовъ постерегаю того, абы на нихъ тые чіи суть не шъкодовали, до споряженя реестру, за отъездомъ отца Антоніевымъ пріити не моглемъ: еднакъ спорядити его хочу и дай Богъ самъ въ Кіеве господину Отцу Іосифу намѣсникови моему Виленскому отдать его, если намъ ведлугъ намовы на праздникъ Богоявленіе ставитися тамъ пріідетъ."

107. Sometime before 7 August 1629, *Propaganda Fide* took cognizance of Ruc'kyj's report on the event. See Šeptyc'kyj 1971, 726: "Quando quidem Meletius Ruthenus, qui nuper accessit ad Unionem, dedit signa verae conversionis, emittendo iterum fidei catholicae professionem coram populo . . . "

108. Mužylovs'kyj 1629, 39ᵛ: "na ktorym Soborze y twoia Apologia iako Cerkwi Prawosławney przeciwna szarpana y palona była od Przewielebnego w Bogu Oyca Metropolity, Archiepiskopow, y Episkopow, y od ciebie samego, ktory poznawszy swoy błąd y nie vmieiąc vst otworzyć, prosiłeś o przebaczenie. ale gdyć Dermań po zwroceniu sie twoim z Kiiowa odeymowana, znowuś sie wrocił do Apologiey: dla czego ia żałością ziętym będąc, nie tak dalece na Xiążkę twoię odpisuiąc, iako pokazuiąc twoy niestatek, w porywczą to światu podaię, ponieważ ona przez sie (iako od ciebie samego wyklęta) tego nie iest godna, a żeby temu wierzono, list twoy kładę y Reuocatią, ktora własną ręką twoią po dziś dzień pisana znayduie sie tam gdzie iey należy, z podpisem ręki twoiey y pieczęcią twoią własną."

109. Mužylovs'kyj 1629, 42ʳ: "Vczyniwszy taką rzecz świętobliwą Bogu y

wszytkim ludziom miłą, dla *intraty* mizerney, gdy cię pytano ieśli stoisz przy Apologiey albo przy Reuocatiy: tedyś wolał tego odstąpić coś dobrowolnie w vbierze Archiereyskim w głos vczynił, azaż to twoia pobożność, aza to twoia stateczność w leciech szedziwych: Lecz ktoż z nas nie zna siebie być człowiekiem y skłonnym do grzechu?"

110. *Pamflet* 1875, 566: "Онъ же еще и прощенія просихъ, но не истиннѣ отрицаяся писанія своего сирѣчь Апологіи, юже во церкви на амвонѣ терзаше, паляше и оплеваше и проклинаше, соборъ же прощенію его сподобляет; прежде же того собор сей рекомый Мелетій хотя сродство свое и родство возвысити, не довляяся братиею, други, благодѣтелми и всею церковию паче же и Епархиею своею еже на потребу сирѣчь хлѣба и риз, но помощию и ходатайством униатским, съ ними же он на соблазнь вѣрный согласися, достигаетъ благочестиваго монастыря Дерманя, и оттуду, егда бѣ на соборѣ паки тамо возвратився, явственно отречеся благочестивих Патриарх и пріем Ересь униатскую, сана святительскаго обнажися."

111. *Synopsis* 1632, 17ᵛ/571–72: "W tym roku [1628] podstępnie z nami idąc Meletius Smotrycki, podobnym się być antecessorowi swemu (ktory inszego co usty mowił, a inszego co na sercu miał) obiawił. Lubo to publice w cerkwi ś. cudotworney Pieczarskiey na fest Zaśnienia Przenaświętszey Panny, żadnego na się gwałtu nie maiąc, ale sam dobrowolnie napisawszy revocatią, według niey, wpośrzod cerkwie na liturgiey ś. (przy bardzo wielkim zgromadzeniu duchowieństwa inszego y przybytności, tak z Korony, iako y z Litwy wielu godnych y znamienitych ludzi) zaraz po przeczytaniu Ewangelii *Apologią* swą szarpał, palił, a iednak zwrociwszy się spokoynie do monastera Dermańskiego, wrocił się znowu nieborak in vomitus suos, a to dla intraty biednych kilku tysięcy złotych."

112. Smotryc′kyj 1629a, 22/656: "czego z pochwały Vniey, wiedząc, iak on iest iey affekt, od niego nie spodziewałem się, y owszem nienawiści, łaiania, y hańby więtszey, niż inszy Vnitowie czekałem: ktore iuż z vciechą dusze mey, bo o nie nie dbam, ponoszę."

113. Smotryc′kyj 1629b, 3ʳ⁻ᵛ/703–704: "Wkładasz na mię, żem vlubił świat, zakochałem sie w nim, y iemum sie w niewolą oddał. co wszytko troie, za łaską Bożą, tak iest dalekie ode mnie, iako iest daleka złość od dobroci. Wiedziałem ia, że v teraźnieyszey mey strony miałem bydź ostatni, ten ktory byłem v was niemal pierwszy: y tożem vlubił świat? Właśniey by mi to przypisano bydź mogło, bym był v was zostawał: Ktory żadnego gospodarskiego ciężaru y pieczołowania nie doznawaiąc, a tym, żem iest Archiepiskop, pierwszy po Metropolicie w Cerkwi, strony waszey Archierey, chlubiąc sie y ciesząc, w świecie tym y w sobie samym kochałbym sie. Ktoremu na każdy rok z pewnych mieysc, od pewnych y zacnych z miedzy was osob, po trzy tysiąca złotych gotowego grosza, na tym zborze swym w Kiiowie ofiarowaliście, y wychowanie na ośm przy mnie Duchownych y świetckich osob przystoyne, z pomieszkaniem w Monasteru Pieczerskim. Co Ia od Strony waszey iak w ręku

maiąc, bym sie za światem vganiał, y ten teraźnieyszy wiek vmiłował, na tym bym był vsiadł, y tam proporce moie w prożnocie szyrsze niż tu rospościerałbym. Zwłaszcza dobry iuż zadatek sławy y v swoich y v obcych ku materiey kochania sie w sobie y w świecie, przez scripta moie sprawiony maiąc."

114. Velykyj 1956a, 223–24: "Praecipiunt Ill.mae ac Rnd.mae Dominationes Vestrae in suis ad me octava Aprilis anno superiori datis literis, ut postquam Meletius Smotricius verbis ac factis talis apparuerit, ut nulli dubium de sincera ipsius conversione relinquatur, tunc agendum esse de titulo ipsius episcopali et iubent me hoc ipsi significare; hoc fieri tam cito non potuit propter absentiam ipsius; fuit enim remotior a nobis, scilicet Chioviae, in conciliabulo Schismaticorum, ubi magnis opprobriis, contemptu et ignominia affectus et ferme extrema passus est pro fide catholica, quam professus fuit libro in lucem edito et a me examinato et licet ibi non obtinuit coronam Martirii per apertam fidei confessionem et hoc nomine incurrerit apud nos in notam instabilitatis, tamen divino adiutus auxilio erexit se et multa evidentia testimonia verae suae ad Deum eiusque conversionis exhibuit et modo exhibet."

115. See Velykyj 1953a, 67: "Denique eidem Nuntio scribendum, ut Meletii conversionem ad Religionem Catholicam publicet, eique praecipiat, ut se palam Catholicum profiteretur, cum hac de re a Metropolita Russiae fuerit admonitus."

116. See Šmurlo 1932, 510: "Quando V.S. sará avvisata dal medesimo metropolita e da Meletio nuovamente convertito a publicar la di lui conversione, et ad ordinargli, che palesamente si professi cattolico, desidera la medesima Sac. Cong-ne ch'ella faccia quel tanto ch'in questo particolare eglino scriveranno a V.S."

117. Velykyj 1961, 8–9: "Dall'Agente degli Uniti mentovato da me nell'altre lettere ho havuto informazione, della quale havevo già richiesto Mons. Metropolita fin d'all'ho[ra] . . . à questa Corte giunse qualche indistinto rumore del seguente fatto, cioè, . . . che Meletio Smotricio, qual'l'anno passato lasciando lo Scisma, venne all'Unione, affine di segnalar maggiormente quest'azzione così per utile . . . [dell'] anima sua, come per acquisto dell'altri, che per il valor di lui facevano gran conto della sua opinione, mentre egli era frà scismatici, volle andar à professar publicamente l'Unione, e disdirsi di quanto contro essa aveva prima predicato, e scritto, in una Sinodo, che li Scismatici havevano congregato in Chiovia; dove essendo da detti Scismatici minacciato, attonito, non solo non essequì il suo buon proposito, ma disse d'[i non] . . . abbracciar l'Unione, et esser vera relligione la loro, e prom[ise] . . . seguitar quella in avvenire. Finita poi la Sinodo ritornò al detto Metropolita, e con gran dolore, e copiose lagrime pianse amaramente . . . rammaricandosi principalmente, che per sovverchia sua . . . s'havesse perduta si bella occasione d'acquistar la palma del martirio. Nella Chiesa poi principale in mano di esso Metropolita fece publicamente la professione della fede, e confessò d'haver fatto quello per timore della vita, non perchè dubitasse, che non sia la vera relligione quella, che

tengono gli Uniti. Et il tutto fece con grandissimo senso, et per authenticazione maggiore, ha stampato in lingua polacca una protesta, nella quale fà amplamente le sopranarrate dichiarazzioni."

118. See Velykyj 1956a, 224: "... fuit [i.e., Smotryćkyj] enim remotior a nobis ..."

119. See Velykyj 1960, 300: "... ma per la gran distanza de luoghi, e per il poco commercio, ch'è fra quei, e questi avviene che molto difficilmente si possono haver lettere loro et in tutto il tempo che sono quà, non ho ricevuto dal Metropolita di Russia altro che una lettera per negotio suo particolare, nè mai m'ha dato aviso della ricevuta di tant'altre mie scrittegli, nè di quelle che venivano mandate a me di cortà per esso lui."

120. Velykyj 1953a, 76–77: "Quoad lapsum Meletii Archiepiscopi Polocensis nuncupati, qui ad Synodum Schismaticorum profectus, ut fidem catholicam publice profiteretur, terrore mortis correptus, iterum Schisma asseruit, et deinde ad Russiae Metropolitam reversus, factique poenitens, ac dolens de martyrii occassione turpiter ammissa, amaris lachrymis Schisma publice iterum abiuravit, et in detestationem sui lapsus confirmationemque eiusdem fidei catholicae libellum evulgavit, Sac. Congregatio humanae fragilitati compatiens ad exemplumque S. Petri Apostoli, et S. Marcellini Papae, et Martyris animum convertens, spem magnam concepit, eundem Meletium optimum deinceps fore catholicum, et pro Sancta Unione propaganda strenue laboraturum."

121. Velykyj 1953a, 80: "Referente eodem Ill.mo D. Card. Bandino literas Metropolitae Russiae de iterata, ac solemni abiuratione Schismatis a Meletio, Archiepiscopo Plocensi, pontificalibus inducto facta, Sac. Congregatio iussit commendari factum Meletii, et animari ad prosequendam Schismaticorum Unionem."

CHAPTER 8

1. Velykyj 1953b, 482: "Ecclesia Hierapolitana, quae in partibus infidelium sub Patriarchatu Antiocheno consistit."

2. Thus Rućkyj was too optimistic in his first communication with Rome on the matter of Smotryćkyj's conversion (Velykyj 1956a, 196): "Sed quomodo cum illo processum ex inclusis literis colliget D.V.R.ma."

3. Smotryćkyj 1629a, 23/656: "... wiedząc ia to dobrze, że pożytecznieysza iest rzecz bydź w Cerkwi Katholickiey Laikiem, niż w Cerkwi Schizmatyckiey Archiepiskopem."

4. Velykyj 1972, 128: "ut utatur titulo archiepiscopali, quem sibi iniuste usurpavit, consecratus in locum alterius legitime electi et adhuc viventis."

5. Velykyj 1956a, 195: "Itemque cum certo sciam illum consecratum fuisse in schismate Episcopum, consilium humillime peto an illi apud Serenissimum aliqua Cathedra procuranda, an alicuius Cathedrae Suffraganeus constituendus; an titulo aliquo in partibus infidelium donandus."

6. Šeptyc'kyj 1971, 657: " . . . ut postquam Meletius verbis ac factis talis apparuerit, ut nulli dubium de syncera ipsius conversione relinquatur, vel ab Amplitudine Tua, si vacantem titulum ad suam provisionem spectantem habuerit, ad episcopalem promoveatur dignitatem, vel a Sanctissimo D.no Nostro in concistorio, prout solet, de aliquo titulo in partibus infidelium provideatur . . . "

7. Velykyj 1956a, 223–24: "Praecipiunt Ill.mae ac Rnd.mae Dominationes Vestrae in suis ad me octava Aprilis anno superiori datis literis, ut postquam Meletius Smotricius verbis ac factis talis apparauerit, ut nulli dubium de sincera ipsius conversione relinquatur, tum agendum esse de titulo ipsius episcopali et iubent me hoc ipsi significare."

8. Velykyj 1956a, 225: "Ego sic constitui, quod confirmari a Sua Sanctitate per Ill.mas ac Rnd.mas Dominationes Vestras etiam atque etiam rogo, ut titulus Haliciensis, quo nunc utitur Coadiutor meus Raphael, detur ipsi et quia illa Sedes fuit archiepiscopalis ab antiquo tempore antequam uniretur Archiepiscopatui Chioviensi titulus Haliciensis Archiepiscopi ipsa autem Halicia nomen Episcopi retinuit et nunc Episcopum habet Schismaticum, sit Meletii titulus Archiepiscopi Haliciensis; Coadiutori autem meo provideatur de aliquo titulo in partibus infidelium, vel si hoc non placuerit, detur ergo Meletio titulus aliquis archiepiscopalis vacans, ne qui in Schismate gaudebat titulo Archiepiscopi deterioris conditionis efficiatur propter conversionem ad fidem catholicam. Ut igitur alterutrum horum omnium obtineam vos Ill.mi ac Rnd.mi Domini apud suam Sanctitatem Intercessores esse cupio et ut hoc fiat, etiam atque etiam rogo."

9. Velykyj 1953a, 81: "Referente eodem Ill.mo D. Card. Sixti instantiam Metropolitae Russiae de titulo Archiepiscopali in partibus infidelium pro Meletio Archiepiscopo Polocensi nuncupato, Sac. Congregatio iussit adiri Congregationem Concistorialem."

10. Velykyj 1953a, 85: "Referente eodem Ill.mo D. Card. S. Sixti instantiam Metropolitae Russiae de titulo Archiepiscopali pro Meletio, attentis eius vera conversione, publica Schismatis abiuratione, et denique progressibus ipsius in propaganda Cath. Fide, Sac. Congregatio censuit prius scribendum esse Cardinali S. Crucis pro informatione, eidemque iniungendum, ut etiam sententiam suam significet."

11. Velykyj 1953a, 88: "Referente eodem Emin.mo D. Card. Ubaldino instantiam Metropolitae Russiae pro titulo archiepiscopali in partibus infidelium conferendo Meletio Archiepiscopo Polocensi nuncupato, Rutheno unito, et nuper a Schismate converso ad catholicam fidem, et simul testimonium D. Cardinalis Sanctacrucii de praefati Meletii . . . , moribus e continuatione in fide

catholica, S.mus iussit perquiri a R.mis DD. Datario, Cariophylo, et Maraldo, et a D. Petro Arcudio exempla, ex quibus constet Romanos Pontifices aliquoties Graecos fecisse Episcopos, vel Archiepiscopos titulares in partibus infidelium ordinatos, vel ordinandos ritu graeco."

12. Velykyj 1956a, 245–46: "Quod attinet ad titulum R.mi Meletii ad libitum S. Congregationi reliquendum putarem; utrum scilicet alter illi titulus dandus, vel cum eodem reliquendus; quod fortassis magis consonum videretur; tum quia iam passim ab omnibus hoc nomine (scilicet nuncupatus Archiepiscopus Polocensis) vocitetur, tum quia hic cum tali addito titulus nec ipsi odiosus esse possit Ordinario, tum demum quia posset ad aliquem ex nostris vacantem Episcopatum brevi promoveri. Ut omittam difficultatem huius novi tituli in Curia Rom. tanto tempore examinatam necdum absolutam. Faciat D. Vestra R.ma quod sibi in Domino videtur."

13. Smotryc'kyj 1629b, 3ʳ/703: "Wiedziałem ia, że v teraźnieyszey mey strony miałem bydź ostatni, ten ktory byłem v was niemal pierwszy."

Smotryc'kyj had earlier reported that this was one of the arguments the Orthodox had employed at the Kiev Council of 1628 in encouraging him to remain on their side: that the Uniates would make him a "bishop out of an archbishop, and that of some dusty title" (Smotryc'kyj 1629a, 23/656: "że ze mnie Archiepiskopa vczyni Episkopa, y to iakiegoś zatchłego tytułu.")

14. See Šeptyc'kyj 1965, 123 for the report of the Consistory and Velykyj 1953a, 97 for that of *Propaganda*: "Referente eodem Emin.mo Domino Card. S. Sixti Decretum Sac. Congregationis rerum Concistorialium, in quo fuit resolutum, dandum esse Meletio Smotricio, Rutheno unito, titulum aliquem episcopalem in Patriarchatu Antiocheno, in partibus Regni Persarum subiectis, et simul referente reperire sub dicto Patriarchatu Hieropolim, Urbem Cyrristicae regionis, titulo archiepiscopali insignitam, illoque posse honorari Meletium, Sac. Congregatio censuit, si S.mo placuerit, dictum Meletium titulo praedicto insigniri posse."

15. See Šmurlo 1932, 514, 516. Ingoli had noted on 7 August 1629 (Šeptyc'kyj 1971, 726): "Essendo stato arcivescovo, se li potrebbe dar un titolo arcivescovile in partibus infidelium, ove bisognando potesse andare a risedere, et a mio giuditio se li potrebbe dar la metropoli Christopolitana con titolo d'arcivescovo di Christopoli, essendo quella città in Macedonia, ov'è il Monte Santo, al qual si potrebbe andar a suo tempo Meletio, per ridurre all'unione li 3 gran monasteri de Rutheni, che sono in detto Monte, e colà starebbe nella sua provincia."

16. Velykyj 1972, 223–24: "Superest, me gratias immortales agere SS.mo D.no Nostro, quod Sanctitas Sua curam mei inutilis sui servi gerens, pro titulo archiepiscopali mihi conferendo fuerit paratissima, nisi ab aliquibus Patribus mota fuisset ea de re difficultas. Hanc ego, Em.me D.ne, difficultatem, ut planum mihi est, prorsus omnem aliam ea de re imposterum difficultatem sustulisse invenio. Minus enim honestum est extra terminos Ecclesiae Rossiacae titulum quaerere nudum, si sese is intra eam cum throno offerat. Cui, si Dei et

Superiorum meorum sententia impar iudicatus fuero, minus extraneo par esse per memetipsum iudicari potero. Quo ego summae Summi Dei providentiae relicto, me meaque humillima obsequia tuae Eminentiae commendata esse volo."

17. Šeptyc'kyj 1971, 871: " . . . de quo honore ac dignitate Beatitudini Suae gratias agere, cum primum praefatum breve receperis, debebis, nam et huiusmodi singulare Sanctitatis Suae beneficium id officii exigit, et illius affectus ac benevolentia in Amplitudinis Tuae recognitionem hanc expostulat."

Ruc'kyj had written to *Propaganda Fide* on 25 November 1628, asking whether the pope could write a breve congratulating Smotryc'kyj on a job well begun and urging him on, "ut quod sua eloquentia, ac doctrina in stabiliendo Schismate perdidit, eisdem in extinguendo Schismate reparet" (see Velykyj 1953a, 65–66). There seems to have been a lot of urging in both directions. Were there doubts about the commitment of the participants?

18. See Velykyj 1972, 173: "I. Quod unionem Graecorum cum Romana Ecclesia Turcae habent pro certissima coniuratione omnium christianorum contra Turcam. II. Quod patriarcha modernus sit infensissimus Pontificibus Romanis, imo haereticus. III. Quod tota plebs Graecorum, non solum spirituales, sed etiam saeculares, habent Latinos pro blasphemis haereticis, et maxime (quod ego probe novi) in collo Montis Sancti."

Ruc'kyj had written to *Propaganda Fide* on 28 June 1628 urging them to listen to Smotryc'kyj on the proposed mission to Mt. Athos "as one who is so expert in these parts and who has much experience" (Velykyj 1956a, 208: "tanquam rerum perito in illis partibus et habenti multam experientiam"). The nuncio in Warsaw, Antonio Santacroce, had also written in 1628, stating that Smotryc'kyj was the man to ask: "est enim vir iste tantae authoritatis in illis partibus" (see Velykyj 1960, 332).

Propaganda responded on 7 October 1628 that no grandiose plans concerning Mt. Athos would be undertaken without first consulting Smotryc'kyj. See Hofmann 1929, 73: "Consilium Amplitudinis Tuae circa missionem ruthenorum ad Montem Sanctum uti rationibus validissimis subnixum, unanimi Sanctitatis Suae et Ill. Patrum consensu comprobatum fuit; quinimo tanti illud ab eis factum est, ut facile nobis persuadeamus S. Congregationem nihil magni momenti esse in Graecia molituram, nisi prius audita Amplitudinis Tuae sententia."

19. Velykyj 1972, 211: "Hae duo, Pater Sanctissime, si tu vivida tua pastorali in omnes auctoritate reipsa effeceris, en optatam Unionem in Rossia nostra ad manus habes; qua potitus, suppone te per tuos Rossos brevi temporis successu in omnibus nationibus, Orientalis Ecclesiae nomine in schismate esse jactantibus, eam obtinuisse."

20. *Propaganda* had met on 13 November 1627 to discuss the Lukaris question. See Hering 1968, 110.

21. Hofmann 1929, 73: "Literarum Cyrilli exemplum aut originale ipsum,

quod Leopoli conservatur, et quo Amplitudo Tua eiusdem Cyrilli apertas in dogmatibus fidei contradictiones convicit, desideramus, si illud absque incommodo haberi poterit, ac Romam miserit [Amplitudo T.] rem gratissimam Sacrae Congregationi faciet."

22. Suša 1666, 83–84: "Dum haec in Russia agerentur, Romae circa initia mensis Octobris, anni eiusdem, conuersio Smotriscij Sanctae enotuit Ecclesiae. Et mirum quantum eam de filio conuerso Matrem vidisses laetantem. Etenim frequente Purpuratorum corona, cuius summum, Vrbanus VIII. decore, amplitudine, pietate, sapientia, gloriose illustrabat, lectae Smotriscij litterae."

23. The nuncio reported on 14 September 1629 that he had three of Smotryc'kyj's works (presumably the Polish originals of *Apology*, *Protestation*, and *Paraenesis*, although *Exaethesis* might be one of them), which he would send "con qualche occasione," since they were too large for the post (Velykyj 1961, 36, 40).

24. Kortycki 1634, Hiiiʳ: " . . . niektore pisma iego, ktore na łaciński ięzyk przetłumaczywszy do Rzymu był posłał, Ociec Naświętszy tak pochwalił, że ie ozdobniey przepisane pospołu z Originałem nieboszczykowskim *in Castro Angeli in selecta Bibliotheca Apostolica* z pilnością chować rozkazał, czego nie czynią tylko wielce wybornym pismom ludzi abo wielce świętych, abo nader vczonych. Czy ziawił się tych wiekow w kraiu połnocnym Doktor, abo Theolog iaki, ktorego by stolica Apostolska tak vczcił?"

25. Velykyj 1956a, 235: "Libros Rev.mi Meletii Smotricii, quos edidit contra Schismaticos, misi ego Ill.mae ac Rev.mae Dominationi Vestrae [nuncio in Warsaw]; ultimum etiam qui adhuc sub praelo est, mittam quando in lucem prodibit. Unum ego revidi, et R. D. Nucerinus, censor librorum per Episcopatum Cracoviensem, et mitto hoc exemplar. Ultimum porro, quod nondum prodiit, examinavit Rev.mus Episcopus noster Vladimiriensis, qui est bonus theologus, ita ut non videatur esse opus versione latina, quae multum temporis insumeret. Tres hucusque libellos edidit, ex quo ipse est nobiscum, quos omnes puto me misisse. De Apologia optime recordor misisse me, de aliis non item; propterea nunc mitto duos, ad vertendum enim in latinum cuperem, ut non obligarentur, quia est longi temporis negotium. Si tamen Sacra Congregatio his opus habet, et replicabit adhuc semel, obedientiae cedent omnia. In posterum vero si volet Sacra Congregatio, ut libri nostri, quos contra Schismaticos forte scribemus, maxime provocati ab ipsis, committat id Ill.mis Nuntiis Apostolicis, ut examinari faciant ab illis, qui norunt linguam polonicam."

Smotryc'kyj's *Exaethesis* of 1629 bore Moroxovs'kyj's imprimatur dated 10 June 1629 (Smotryc'kyj 1629b, 102ᵛ/805).

26. Velykyj 1956b, 10, 11: "[Korsak] Vitam Josephi conscripsit, quamvis non perfecerit. Scripta Meletii ad voluntatem Urbani VIII in Vaticanum transferenda latine reddidit. . . . Pontificis eiusdem iussu doctissima atque utilissima Meletii Smotrischii, Polocensis Antistitis, opera de rutheno in latinum sermonem vertit. Quorum etiam exemplar in Vaticana Bibliotheca fuit collocatum."

According to Šmurlo (1932, 518) rough drafts of the Latin versions of the *Apology,* together with the "Considerations" that form its second half, and *Paraenesis* are preserved in the Neapolitan National Library (IX.A.52). Were these the compendia made by Korsak?

27. The Orthodox side was almost unrepresented. Both sides had met earlier at separate, unilateral synods to prepare for the bilateral meeting. Here, again, it is not unlikely that Borec̆kyj and Mohyla wished to take part in the L'viv Council under certain conditions, but were convinced not to do so by the strongly negative opinions expressed at the Orthodox synod in Kiev by the lesser clergy and the Cossacks (see above, p. 139). On the synods of 1629, see Žukovič 1911, Xoma 1973, Krypjakevyč 1913.

28. *Akty* 1848, 158: "dobrze by, ojcowie, żebyście wy my, a my wy byli, i drogą nami utorowaną chodzili."

29. Hofmann 1928, 88: "Scripsi ante unum trimestre a nunnullis praecipuis schismaticis medium fuisse oblatum, ut scriberent ad suum patriarcham de suis miseriis tam spiritualibus quam corporalibus, ut sic responsum eis obtineretur et intelligeretur, sitne calvinista, prouti nos affirmabamus, litteras autem ipsorum scribendas esse a nobis et ab ipsis subscribendas, obsignandas et Constantinopolim transmittendas. Rev.mo Melitio nostro demandatum est hoc munus; scripsit, et harum litterarum exemplar mitto . . . "

30. Hofmann 1929, 89: " . . . ut Sanctitas Sua eas in linguam graecam et arabicam verti ac imprimi et disseminari per Graeciam et Syriam cogitaverit, idque faciemus, si Amplitudo Tua alteram praedictarum litterarum copiam authenticam, hoc est ab eisdem non unitis subscriptam sigillisque munitam ad nos mittere dignata fuerit, de qua re tota Sacra Congregatio enixe rogat Amplitudinem Tuam."

31. Hofmann 1929, 95: "Profectus ad nos semel Meletius Smotritius simulans se esse orthodoxum nos omnes fefellit, imo ut Iudas falsum osculum pacis dedit, sed intentio, quam celabat, erat totam ecclesiam vendere. . . . Quando hic erat, non se declarabat; regressus in Poloniam, appetitus ei venerat homini ocioso, mecum competere et se clariorem in sua apostasia pontificiis monstrare."

32. See Velykyj 1956b, 73 for a letter of Korsak to Ingoli (1 February 1630) reporting (jocularly?) on "R.mus Meletius noster Neophitus . . . " and Velykyj 1956b, 90 for a letter of Korsak to Ingoli (5 July 1632): "R.mus Meletius in Unione S. constantissimus, Monasterio suo Dermanensi sese inclusit suaeque vacans saluti, libris quibusdam pro S. Unione post typo vulgandis ordinandis insudat." The documents published in Velykyj 1953a, 125 ("7. Quod Meletius Archiepiscopus in monasterio Dermanensi scribit contra Schismaticos") and Velykyj 1953a, 131 ("Referente Emin.mo Domino Cardinali Barberino de libris Meletii, Archiepiscopi Polocensis nuncupati, contra Graecos schismaticos ex polonica lingua in latinam translatis, et de litteris eiusdem Meletii ad Patriarcham Cyrillum Constantinop. pro defensione Catholicae Fidei, Sac.

Congregatio nihil rescripsit") show that *Propaganda Fide* took cognizance of these reports on Smotryc'kyj's activities, also in a context of reports on a variety of subjects.

33. Smotryc'kyj 1629b, 67^v/768: "Wiesz, że mi wolno było y do tych czas w Wilnie tey takiey Duchowney Pompy, dostatkow wszelakich, y Codzienney ludzi oboiego stanu assystencyey zażywać. O co mię często samo Bratstwo Wileńskie y przez listy, y przez posłanniki swe sollicytowało. Owey też teraźnieyszey moiey strony Zwierzchność Duchowna, za prośbą Bratską mieszkania mi w Monasteru ich, z zawieszeniem na ten czas spraw Archyereyskich, nie broniła."

34. Smotryc'kyj 1629, 77^v/778: "Piszą do mnie niektorzy z pobożnych y nabożnych Zakonnikow waszych . . . "

35. On the history of discussions over the Ruthenian patriarchate, see Krajcar 1964. *Propaganda* wrote to Rus' in the later seventeenth century admonishing the Ruthenian clergy to cease talking about the independent patriarchate. But Rome seems to have been cool to the idea from the start. (See Krajcar 1964, 82.)

36. See chapter 12.

37. See chapter 13.

Chapter 9

1. *Indicium* 1638, 16^v/795: "A tak wątpliwie żyiąc żywot skończył, wziąwsy w ręce list patriarszy y papieżski."

2. Rumors of Smotryc'kyj's evil demise were still circulating in Muscovy in the second half of the seventeenth century. See Subbotin 1885, 81, 283.

3. Kortycki 1634, F3^v–4^r: "Przy częstym vżywaniu, ciała Pańskiego, y inszych nabożeństwach, widząc czy z osłabienia sił przyrodzonych, czy z iakiego natchniena przyrodzenie przechodzącego że godzina ostatnia blisko, nie zaniechał też pogrzebu. A przywszy Braciey, ktorzy mu osobliwie przytomni bywali, roskazał, aby mu wszystko coby do pogrzebu, a zwłaszcza do pokrycia ciała służyło, prętko zgotowano. Żałosne to Braciey rozkazanie było, bo go iako Oyca miłowali, przetoż nie życząc aby mu się to rychło zgodzić miało, co gotować kazał, nieco omieszkiwali, życząc aby się iak naywięcey żywot Oyca miłego przedłużył: aż gdy vstawicznym iego dokuczaniem wszystko iuż gotowo przed sobą widział, roskazał, aby gdy skona, ciało wedle zwyczaiu zakonnego vbrawszy, List Naświętszego Oyca VRBANA VIII Papieża Rzymskiego, ktory go nie tylko miedzy prawowierne poczytał swoim onym listem, ale y Metropolią mu Hierapolską, krwią, y Męczeństwem Filipa Apostoła Pańskiego wsławioną iako Pasterzowi, y Arcybyskupowi w moc, y władzą podał, ten mowię list, abo

przywiley Papieski w rękę sobie skoroby vmarł włożyć, y z nim się, pogrześć roskazał."

4. Kortycki 1634, F4^r: "skonał mile, y świętobliwie iako Zakonnik, kapłan, y Biskup święty z wielkim żalem synow swoich, ktorzy omywszy twarz, y ręce iego (iako zwyczay zakonny) vbrali ciało w one szaty ktore sobie ieszcze za żywota zgotować kazał."

5. Kortycki 1634, F4^{r-v}: "A o liście Papieskim, czy przez żal serdeczny, iako to bywa, czy z iakiego zrządzenia Pańskiego wszystkim z pamięci wyszło. Dopiero w pięć prawie godzin, gdy iuż członki wszytkie skościały, wspomniawszy, list on pożądany w prawą rękę iuż prawie zdrewniałą włożyć vsiłowali. Palce wszystkie wyciągnione były, y zproszczone, tak że zaledwie miedzy wielki, a wtory palec list wciśniono. Tu rzecz cudowi Bożemu podobna, tamże zaraz przy Braciey ręka strupiała list wszystkimi palcami tak ścisnęła, że się pargamen pomarszczył: Zdumieli się na rzecz niewidaną obecni, a ośmieliwszy się gdy mu chcieli onego listu pociągnąć, aby gładko, y prosto w ręce trzymał: żadną miarą ruszyć nie mogli, tak że kto listu wzwyż pociągnął, ręka listu nie puszczaiąc za pociągnieniem wzgorę szła. Doznawał tego ktokolwiek chciał przez kilka niedziel, doznawali samiż iedności Ś. nieprzyiaciele, opatruiąc zewsząd ieśli nie przyszyty list był do ręki vmarłego, ieśli nie przykleiony, a widząc iawny cud Boży, z dumieniem odchodzili. Zdanie to iest ludzi zacnych, Szlachetnych, żeby było y ciało z truny wyciągniono za onym listem, ktorego nikomu wydrzeć sobie nie dał iakoby iuż nie vsty, ale ręką wołał *Fidem seruaui*. Dochowałem wiary kościołowi powszechnemu, y Rządcy iego Nawyższemu."

6. After eight days according to Ruc'kyj's official report to Rome of 2 August 1634 (see Velykyj 1956a, 305).

7. Kortycki 1634, G1^r: "Ale mało dziw ieden na dowod tak wielkiey, cnoty Oyca tak świętobliwego. Patrzcie proszę, co nastąpiło. Sprawiony o śmierci nieboszczykowskiey Iaśnie przewiel. Ociec Metropolita, ktorego y sam nieboszczyk, w tey iuż chorobie, iako mi powiadał, do siebie, gdyby rzecz można, pokornym pisaniem zapraszał, przyiachał do Dermania. Tu z żalem na Brata vmarłego, a z podziwieniem na rzecz onę prawie cudowną patrząc, roskazał, aby mu on list z ręki wzięto. Rzecz dziwna! ręka okrzepła, iakby rozkazanie, y wolą starszego zrozumiała, list zarazem wziąć sobie dopuściła."

8. Kortycki 1634, G2^r: "Puszczam to mimo się, co w tey sprawie godno też było vważenia, że gdy mu w ten czas po śmierci prędko list Patryarchy Hierozolimskiego w rękę drugą dawano, y iednym go palcem nie przyiął. ale to vważeniu waszemu słuchacze łaskawi zostawuię."

9. Kortycki 1634, G2^r: "To znowu dziwna, a iakoby powtorzonym cudem potwierdzona rzecz, że gdy z roskazania Iego M. Oyca Metropolity onże list w też rękę włożono: tak go powtore ścisnęła, że żadnym ciągnieniem, żadnym podnoszeniem wyruszyć go nie możono."

10. Kortycki 1634, G2ᵛ: "Ieszcze y temu się wielce zadziwić godzi, że kilką dni przed pogrzebem ręka ta strupiała tak się czerstwą, y wolną stała, że się da y każdy z osobna palec tak właśnie obracać, prostować, y nachylać, iakoby ręka śpiącego była, na com sam wieczora wczorayszego z kilką kapłanow patrzał."

11. See Rucʹkyj's letter of 16 January/26 January 1634 (Golubev 1877, 66) and his official report to Rome of 2 August 1634 (see Velykyj 1956a, 305).

12. Kortycki 1634, G1ᵛ: "Acz mnie się zda, że w tey ręce Bog wszechmocny ponowić raczył cud, ktorym przy śmierci sługi swego Alexiusa Rzymskie Miasto ku zdumieniu przywiodł, Iako bowiem Alexius vmarły, maiąc w ręku kartę na ktorey spisany był żywot iego, nikomu iey ani rodzicom swoim puścić nie chciał, samemu ią tylko Innocentemu Papieżowi przy obecności Honoriusza Cesarza oddał: tymże sposobem Meletyus Przywiley godności, y świadectwo iedności, y wiary swoiey nikomu inszemu iedno Nawyższemu, y powszechnemu Biskupowi Namiestnika iego oddał."

13. Kortycki 1634, A2ʳ: "Cokolwiek w tym kazaniu mowi się o cudownym tego Przewieleb: Oyca Meletiusa Smotryskiego, po śmierci przyięciu, y trzymaniu listu Papieskiego, także y puszczeniu tegoż listu przy obecności moiey y powtorzonym ściśnieniu, nakoniec o dziwney czerstwości tey ręki przed tym skrzepłey, y skościałey: to wszytko za niepochybną prawdę zeznawam, iako ten, ktorym y pilnością dozoru Pasterskiego z powinności moiey, y własnym moim doświadczeniem nieomylney o tym wiadomość doszedł, A iako żadna o tym wątpliwość nie zostaie, tak moim zdaniem rzecz tak dziwna ku chwale Bożey w milczeniu zostawać nie ma."

14. One of the dates given in this letter is marked as old style (Golubev 1877, 67: "першаго Августа по старому . . ."). If the date in the signature to the letter was also old style (and the date given by Kortycki was presumably new style), then Rucʹkyj's testimony was written on 26 January, three days before Kortycki delivered his sermon.

15. Golubev 1877, 65: "одное речи запомнели вложить въ руки листу папежского . . ."

16. Golubev 1877, 65: "потомъ вложили листъ патриаршии. . . . ни однимъ пальцомъ не принялъ его."

17. Golubev 1877, 66–67: "Хороба его такая была: одинъ зацъный сенаторъ всѣмъ добре знаемый, едучи презъ Межиречъ, который под Острогомъ, вступилъ до отцовъ францѣшкановъ, тамже ксенъдцу Квардданови поведилъ, ижъ слышалъ отъ стороны противное, же отецъ Смотрицкій въ короткомъ часе знесеный будетъ презъ трутизну и просилъ его отца францѣшкана, жебы доехалъ до небощика и перестереглъ его."

18. Golubev 1877, 67: "Кгды пришолъ до него дякъ одинъ с Кіева, который добрый характеръ въ писаню мелъ, а онъ такого писаря потребовалъ, принялъ его . . ."

19. Golubev 1877, 67: "затымъ ускаржатися почалъ на слезену першаго Августа по старому, ходилъ еднакъ и все отправовалъ яко и первей, хотяжъ отъ часу слазелъ; хотечи поратовати здорове свое до Острога поехалъ, а такъ тамъ слаземъ будучи бралъ лекарство презъ две недели; тымъ часомъ тотъ дякъ зникнолъ и не ведаютъ где есть. По лекарствахъ далеко слабшихъ вернулъ се до монастыря . . . "

20. Suša 1666, 134–35: "Sed iam vltimam Meletij dissolutionem aggredienti memorari ea visum, quae partim Iosephus Rutscius Russiae Archiepiscopus, in litteris de obitu eius, ad Religiosos vnitos in Lithuaniam datis, breuiter perstringit, partim Cortiscius in concione sua describit. Ante ipsam Smotriscij lethalem inualetudinem, amplissimus quidam Regni Poloniae Senator, cuius nomen siluit Rutscius, per Oppidum Miedzyrzecz Ostrogio proximum iterfaciens, ad Patres Ordinis Seraphici illic degentes deflexit, et loci Praeposito retulit: ad aduersa parte certo se accepisse, breui Meletium veneno tollendum: orauitque, moneret eum, qui sibi caueret. Monuit ille, sed cupiens dissolui, et esse cum Christo, neglexit iste. . . . Intereae cantorem quendam, et scriptorem bonum Kijouia venientem, vt eo indigus seruicijs adscripsit suis. Nihilque mali suspicatus, in intima admisit penetralia, eoque ad scribendas suas vsus lucubrationes. Modicum fluxit temporis, ecce Augusti 11. 1633. anni, liene caepit laborare, et grauiter querulari. Neque tamen a consuetis tam priuatis, quam publicis, quae sanus egit, destitit operibus. Licet sensim sine sensu consumi, et deficere visus. Cui consulens aegritudini, Ostrogium accessit: duasque illi septimanas curandae insumpsit. Sed vires tantum abfuit, vt resumpserit, vt etiam longe debilior, et magis fractus, ad monasterium redierit. Sub moram autem istam in medicamentis absumptam, cantor ille nil moratus, vt aquae disperijt. Increbuitque ab eo id malum Meletio factum."

21. Suša 1666, 135: "Meletius aeger probabiliter ex veneno." Suša had introduced the suspicion of poison in Smotryc'kyj's death more directly one year earlier in his life of Josafat (Suša 1665, 111): "Anno enim 1633. circa finem Decembris non sine suspicione propinati ab aduersarijs aconiti, pedetentim aestuantibus confestus visceribus."

22. Suša 1666, 138: "Decembris vigesima septima, vt colligere mihi licuit, diuini munitus viatici praesidio, non sine caelesti instillatione, et praescia miraculorum futurorum mente, vocatos nonnullos monuit Religiosos, morienti sibi Breue Sanctissimi Vrbani VIII. quo a censuris vt fieri solet soluebatur, ac Throno Hierapolitano donabatur, ad manus traderent. Corpus autem suum post mortem illis quae parari mandaueret, vestimentis induerent."

23. Suša 1666, 138: "Elapsis quinque ab exitu animae Sanctae horis, arrepente noctis medio, exanguibus, iam penitus rigescentibus artubus, tandem recordati Breuis, manui illud dextrae, pollicem inter et indicem inseruerunt. Rem miram digiti reuiuiscentes, atque ad volam manus, et pollicem inflexi, Breue Apostolicum, vsque adeo constrinxerunt, vt membrana contorta, corrugataque fuerit!"

24. Suša 1666, 139: "Itaque consilij inopes, Litterarum quarundam Patriarchae Constantinopolitani memorati, non sine Numine diuino, eas quantocyus attulerunt, manuique alteri accipiendas porrexerunt. Verum emortua sinistra, dexterrime cuius illae essent litterae discernens, digitos retraxit, ad volam contraxit, inhabilesque ad complectendum reddidit."

25. Suša 1666, 139: "Affluere hinc et inde, plebs, Ciues, nobiles, idque diebus singulis frequentiores. Intueri compressam vtramque manum, hanc tenentem Romani Pontificis, illam reijcientem Constantinopolitani litteras! Extrahere ab illa Breue, imponere isti Epistolium! sed neque illud ab illa eripi, neque istud ab ista suscipi!"

26. One Latin version from the Vatican archives is published in Velykyj 1972, 130–45. A somewhat different Latin version was published by Suša (1666, 71–81).

27. See Smotryc′kyj 1629b, 8^{r-v}/708–709.

28. Velykyj 1956a, 305–306: "Unius rei, ordinatae a defuncto, obliti sunt tres, qui assignati erant, ut curam haberent corporis, hoc est non dederunt in manus Breve Apostolicum pro Archiepiscopatu Hieropolitano, ipsi a moderno Summo Pontifice collato, quod ipse defunctus, ut facerent, demandavit. Accepit igitur unus illorum dictum Breve et quia manus iam obriguerat, quae erat supra pectus extensa, imponunt dictum Breve inter policem et palmam. Postea in aliam manum hoc est sinistram posuerunt literas Chirotoniae coniurationis a Theophane Patriarcha Hierosolymitano; et ecce digiti manus dextrae, qui erant extensi, strinxerunt hoc Breve ita fortiter, ut membrana huius Brevis contraheretur, quod ipsi, advertentes, volebant melius reponere hoc Breve ut esset sine rugis. Interim vident manum contractam, quae erat extensa, quaerunt unus ex altero, quis contraxisset; negat omnes, conantur deducere digitos, et iam non possunt; conantur extrahere Breve, tam a police, quam ab auriculari et non possunt, apprehensam membranam trahunt sursum, et ecce tota manus attollitur; obstupuerunt; alia autem manus prouti erat deducta, in quam membrana Patriarchae erat reposita, decidit ad latus sinistrum, et illae literae remanserunt supra pectus, quas manus illa sinistra non tangebat."

29. Velykyj 1953a, 139: "Referente eodem Emin.mo D. Card. S. Sixti partem litterarum ex Russia ad Episcopum Pinscensem scriptarum, in quibus de Meletio, Archiepiscopo Hieropolitano, Rutheno unito, veneno a Schismaticis propinato vita functo, et de miraculo, quod in eius morte occasione Brevis Pontificii accidit, Sac. Congregatio censuit super praedictis morte, et miraculo conficiendum esse Processum, et ut canonice per Apostolicae Sedis Nuncium, in Polonia residentem, fieri possit, cum R.mis DD. Cerro, Promotore fidei, et Ruspilioso, Sac. Congregationis Rituum Secretario, agi iussit."
See also Šeptyc′kyj 1974, 108.

30. Velykyj 1953a, 155: "In ea, primo, actum fuit iuxta Decretum Sac. Congregationis de Prop. Fide de Remissioriali expedienda a Sac. Rituum

Congregatione pro miraculis, quae contingere in morte Meletii, Archiepiscopi Hieropolitani rutheni uniti probandis, et cum lectae fuissent litterae Nuntii Poloniae super eiusdem miraculis Congregatio dixit agendum esse de huiusmodi negotio in dicta Sac. Congregatione Rituum, quod ut fieri quamquam possit, iussit copiam dictarum litterarum cum prima relatione de eisdem miraculis tradi eidem R. P. D. Fachinetto, et aliam copiam dictarum litterarum R. P. D. Cerro, ut possint in dicta Sac. Congregatione Rituum de eis referri."

31. Velykyj 1961, 175: "Con la morte dell'Arcivescovo Meletio io sentii narrar alcuni casi straordinarii . . . ma non havendo havuto fin hora cosa autentica, ne altro, che quello scrivevano alcuni particolari, non ho premuto di communicarlo a Vostra Emminenza."

32. Velykyj 1961, 187–88: "Il P. Vicario, Isaia Rodovicz, sentito per interprete il Padre Giovanni Dubowicz, asserisce nella sequente forma: l'Arcivescovo Meletio, poco prima della sua agonia, mi ordinò in presentia del Padre Metrofane Ferenczowicz, e Stefano Neubescki e Stefano Glossosotti, ch'io l'imponessi, non mi ricordo bene, se o dopo che fosse morto, o mentre agonizzava, nella mano destra le Littere Pontificie, nelle quali era stato da S. B. creato Arcivescovo, e nella sinistra le Patriarhali del Patriarcha di Gerusaleme."

Šeptyc'kyj's transcription of the same letter (1974, 134) gave "Glossoscki" for "Glossosotti." Ruc'kyj's Ruthenian letter of 16 January/26 January 1634 gave the name Isaja Radevyč, identified Mytrofan as a deacon, and mentioned a certain *Pan* Nehrebec'kyj (presumably "Stefano Neubescki"), whom he identified as a layman and a servant and relative of Smotryc'kyj. See Golubev 1877, 65.

33. Šeptyc'kyj 1974, 177: " . . . ordinò, che dopo il suo transito se li ponesse nella mano destra il breve sudetto, e la chirotonia del detto patriarca nella man sinistra. Fu esequita l'ordine, e il morto lasciando la chirotonia, strinse di maniera colla man destra il breve sudetto . . . "

34. Golubev 1877, 66: "которое цудо такъ се розславило увезде вколо, же еще отъ княжати его мил. Радивила, канцлера Вел. князства Литовского слышалемъ, будучи у него."

35. Golubev 1877, 64: "людъ княжати его мил. Жаславского и ездный и пѣший въ моцъ свою взялъ такъ самъ монастыръ, яко и фолварки того монастыра з всѣмъ што въ нихъ было, а ижъ никого не пущаютъ до монастыра такъ свецкихъ яко и духовнихъ."

36. Published in Velykyj 1972, 204–211.

37. Kortycki 1634, D1ᵛ: "W tey samey chorobie gdym tak osłabionego widział, że zaledwie tchnął, wmowiłem to weń, żeby dla zawzięcia iakiego posiłku kieliszeczek wina wpołudnie y wieczor brał, posłuchałci mię wprawdzie ale na czas barzo krotki."

38. On two early images of Smotryc'kyj holding the papal breve in his right hand, see Popov 1928.

CHAPTER 10

1. Velykyj 1972, 127: "Cum id unicum jam in votis mihi sit, ne ad latum quidem unguem discedere a voluntate Sanctissimi D.N. et Dominationis Vestrae."

2. See the third-person summary of Smotryckyj's petition to the Holy Office (Velykyj 1972, 128): "Denique petit, ut in Missae sacrificio mentionem faciat patriarchae Constantinopolitani, mutata intentione, scilicet, ut eum non tanquam pastorem agnoscat, sed ut pro illius conversione Deum precetur."

3. See Velykyj 1972, 129: "Denique si aliqua ratio urgeret in Meletio apertum catholicismum haec esset, ne scandalum sit aliis ipsius schisma. Et hoc non: omnes enim sciunt, illum hucusque fuisse schismaticum, nullus (exceptis aliquot, qui ad hoc negotium spectarunt) nunc redisse ad gremium Ecclesiae. Unde ac si Patres Societatis Iesu et alii Religiosi in India cum gentilibus habitu saeculari conversantes, neminem scandalisaret, praesertim cum multo maior, Deo auxiliante, speretur fructus sanctae Unionis ex occultato ad tempus catholicismo, quam si ex nunc omnibus innotesceret."

4. Cited according to Golubev 1898, 68: Radziwiłł—"nie miey W.K.M. tey intencyi"; Władysław IV—"komu przysięgam usty, temu przysięgam y intencją."

5. Suša 1666, 55: "Quia tamen respicio, ne scripta V. Reuerendissimae Dominationis, minus accepta sint schismaticis, ideo malim et desiderarim, vt cum se merum et sincerum probauerit vnitum, schismatis seipsum veste obuelare velit. Non enim obfuit Nicodemo occultus discipulatus Christi. Neque Apostolis, non statim post Ascensionem Domini praedicauisse; sed propter metum Iudaeorum sese occlusos tenuisse; vsque dum S. super eos descendisset Spiritus. Vestra porro Dominatio non metu id faceret, sed quia eiusmodi ratione, plures in viam salutis deducere posset."

Out of fear, the Pharisee Nicodemus would come to hear Jesus only in secret and by night (cf. John 3:1–2). On sixteenth-century "Nicodemism," see Zagorin 1990 and Ginzburg 1970.

6. Smotryckyj 1628b, Diii^v/641: "Gdyżem Bogu memu daną, y iemu *per obedientiam* szlubioną wiarę moię y pod ten samy czas cało zachował: y serce moie na tę ich, na ten moy script nieprawowiernym sercem rzuconą Anathemę nigdy nie zezwalało, y zbożnie zezwolić nie mogło. Zkąd było, że oni klęli moy prawosławny Katholicki script, ktory im ia z wielkim vważeniem pisał, y każdą rzecz moię w nim pismem Ś. y Dokotorow Cerkiewnych Wschodnych y Zachodnych nauką dowodnie y poważnie sparł, obiaśnił, y zmocnił. A iam klął ich kąkolosiewcow Zyzaniow, refutowane przez mię w tym moim scripcie, bluźnierstwa błędy y Hęrezye: te darłem, na te świecę zgasiłem, te y pod nogi moie rzuciłem."

7. Smotryckyj 1621b, 42^v/367: "Ale troiakie mowią kłamstwo, (bo tak się

strofowani z tey złości Teologowie Apostatscy obmawiaią) *Officiosum, Iocosum, Perniciosum*. Zaż na vczciwe y na krew Bliźniego kłamać ktore z tych trzech pozwala? Zaż Żartowne y Sprzyiaźliwe kłamstwo tey są własności, aby szkodziły?"

8. Smotryc̆kyj 1621b, 42ᵛ/367: "... im Teologia ich tego pozwala: My y Cerkiew Boża tego zwyczaiu nie mamy."

9. Suárez 1859, 682: "Mendacium igitur triplex est: perniciosum, jocosum et officiosum."

10. Smotryc̆kyj 1610, 82ᵛ/99: "Turczyn w świetskiey Politiey, A Papież w Cerkwi Bożey tyran."

11. Smotryc̆kyj 1628a, 81/564: "Zaczym poszło to iuż nam ze zwyczaiu w nałog że, by niewiedzieć kto on był, y by niewiedzieć co nie nasze, za nasze vdawał, byle tylko Papieża lżył, wiarę tego y Kościoł ganił: dobry to nam człowiek, poczestny mąż y święty, mądry y sławny."

12. Smotryc̆kyj 1628a, 95/571: "Poswar tedy ten, złego tego naszego iest przyczyną, w ktory my z nierownią zawziąwszy sie, a niezdolnością swoią sprostać mu nie mogszy, do nieprzyiacioł iego o poradę y o ratunek vdaliśmy sie: ktorego od nich nabywszy, sobieśmy go za czasem przyswoili, wstąpiwszy, mowię, dla przyiętey od starszych naszych Duchownych z Rzymskim Kościołem iedności, tak z Rzymiany, iak y z swoimi, za ktorymi iść nie chcieliśmy, w poswar, a zdołać ich nie mogszy, vdaliśmy sie o pomoc y o ratunek do Luteran y do Kalwinistow, od ktorych błędow ich y Haereziy pożyczka wziąwszy, przeciwney stronie w przeciw zastawialiśmy sie, a potymeśmy samych siebie tymiż ich błędami y Haerezyami zarazili. Za ktorymi iużeśmy teraz y swey przyrodzoney wiary zapomnieli, y to co z nich wyczerpnione nam iest podano, wiarę bydź ś. Wschodniey Cerkwie rozumiemy."

13. Smotryc̆kyj 1629a, 44/667: "Co wszytko [i.e., the rejection of Roman beliefs] iest przeciw iawney, iasney, y wyraźney pisma ś. y pism Doktorow śś. nauce, na to samo przez was y waszych sporządzone, y negowane, abyście się w czym zgodnymi z Rzymiany naydować nie zdali: Bo im się od nich dalszymi w wiary Dogmat wyznaniu odsądzacie, tym się Prawosławnieyszymi bydź mniemacie."

14. Smotryc̆kyj 1629b, 96ʳ/798: "Iest to w zwyczaiu wszytkim Chrześciańskim Sektam Apostatami, abo odstępnikami zwać tych, ktorzy ich Sektę opuściwszy, do Drugiey sie przyłączaią. Y Żydzi tych, Ktorzy sie z miedzy nich wyłączaią, a przez Krzest do społeczności z Chrześciany wstępuią, odstępcami też nazywaią."

15. Smotryc̆kyj 1628a, 112/579: "Acz my mamy gotową zwykłą swoię y w tym vcieczkę, że nie my iesteśmy Schismatykami, ale Rzymianie: A że ich zwierzchność świetska, tą oni bespieczni, sobie właśnie należną hańbą nas hańbią, y swoią sromotą nas sromocą. Sami odszczepieńcami od Cerkwie

Wschodniey będąc, nas tym nazwiskiem z potęgi swey, a nie z własności naszey lżą y hańbią."

16. This letter has been reprinted in *Arxiv* 1887, 193–231.

17. Smotryc'kyj 1610, 67^v/84: "Teraz iawnie każdy obaczyć może, iaką chytrością y kiedy nieszczęsny ten niezmierney hardości Instrument był sklecony, ktory iako niesłuszny y ze wszech miar niepodobny odrzuciwszy, otworzą na potym serdeczne swe oczy, że snadniey miedzy inszemi kłamstwy, y owę twoię piekielnego dymu zarazę obaczą, ktorąś ty pod twym imieniem w Roku 1605 z Wilna, na oszukanie y zmamienie biednego narodu Rosieyskiego wydać się nie wstydził, z takim napisem. Poselstwo do Papieża Rzymskiego Syxta 4. od Duchowieństwa, y od Książąt y Panow Ruskich w roku 1476. o ktorym ty w Przedmowie twoiey Ruskiey to zeznawasz, że wszystkie pisma Doktorow starych y nowych Rzymskiego nabożeństwa zbiegawszy, v żadnego naleść nie możesz tak wielkiey y przedziwney Rzymskiego Papieża pochwały, iaka mu się w tym liście przypisuie."

18. Smotryc'kyj 1628a, 83/565: "Ktorego przepis, po nalezionym w Krewie, naleziony był w Cerkwi sioła Wielboyna pod Ostrogiem, pisma starego, molem iuż niemal wpoł obiadły."

19. Smotryc'kyj 1629b, 93^v/796: "nasz w Cerkwi Krewskiey, w Domu Bożym między Cerkiewnymi Księgami naleziony, na świat przez druk znamienito iest puszczony."

20. Smotryc'kyj 1621c, 22–23/410: " . . . w ktorych y o to się na Verificatora obraża, że lepszą wiarę daie pewnym, znamienitym, y wiary godnym, zacnego imienia, y dobrey sławy Kronikarzom, niż s podławia wydartym, bezimennym nieiakimś Latopiscom."

21. Smotryc'kyj 1628a, 82/564: "Mnie zaś przeciwnym sposobem vkazać należy, z swych Przodkow Rusi, z Graekow, z Rzymian, y z postronnych świadectwa . . . "

22. Smotryc'kyj 1629b, 91^v/794: "Ba to dziw wielki Antidotysto, że przez tak wiele dziesiąt lat, ta syta Owca między głodnymi wilkami scalała. że mowię, ten powszechney vchwały Dekret od was Schismatykow ze wszytkich po wszey Rusi Ksiąg wyszarpany nie został. . . . W Twey Bibliotheki Księgach by dobrze y beł, dałbyś go ty po Zyzaniowsku swym rękom na strawienie." Smotryc'kyj 1628a, 88/567: "My więcey iako sie z samego doświadczenia wiedzieć daie, nie umiemy nic, tylko zagabnąć: a zagabnąć nie poważną iaką, iaka sie w sprawach zbawiennych zachowywać zwykła, materią, ale lżeniem, łaianiem, sromoceniem, vszczypowaniem, fałszami, kłamstwy, potwarzą, błędami, bluźnierstwy, Hęrezyami, złym na koniec wykładem y wywrotami świadectw pisma Bożego y pism Oycow ŚŚ. wymazowaniem tego z ksiąg Cerkiewnych, co sie nam nie podoba: a przydawaniem tego, co sie podoba."

CHAPTER 11

1. Of course there are some studies of Ukrainianisms in Polish and of Polonisms in Ukrainian. These investigations presuppose the closed nature of each linguistic system within which it is possible to find "foreign" elements. For a perceptive treatment of lexical Polonisms in literary Ukrainian and for bibliography on Ukrainianisms in Polish, see Shevelov 1975.

2. Smotryc̈kyj 1618, Щ7ᵛ: "О СОЧИНЕНІЙ междометія: Правило / а. оле, и / о, Сѣтованія: и / о, Оудивленія: Родителному сочиняются: яко, о мене окояннаго ч[е]л[о]в[ѣ]ка: о премудрых судебъ твоихъ х[ристо]се: и проч."

3. The term "Orthodox" here includes both Uniates and Orthodox. It makes a distinction between the Latin orientation of "normal" Polish usage and Smotryc̈kyj's attempts to introduce Greek, Slavonic, or "Orthodox" elements. This remained part of Smotryc̈kyj's rhetoric after his conversion to the Uniate Church.

4. See Smotryc̈kyj 1621a, F2ᵛ/258: "O wiary serca pobożnego" and Smotryc̈kyj 1620, D3ʳ: "о вѣры Бл[а]гочестивого срдца"; Smotryc̈kyj 1621a, F3ʳ/258: "O głosu świętego! O głosu pasterskiego! O wieczney pamięci godnych słow!" and Smotryc̈kyj 1620, D3ʳ: "о голоса с[вя]того: о голоса пастырского: о словъ вѣчнои памяти годных"; Smotryc̈kyj 1621a, F4ʳ/259: "O godnych słow wielkiego tego Nauczyciela pobożności!" and Smotryc̈kyj 1620, D4ʳ: "о Великого сего Учителя Побожности годныхъ словъ."

The genitive of remorse may have been more "normal" in Ruthenian than in Polish. Cf. Zaxarija Kopystens̈kyj's funeral oration of 1620 for Jelisej Pletenec̈kyj (cited according to Titov 1924, 170): "о зыску! о Пожитку з Памяти смерти!"

5. The presence of this rhetorical feature throughout Smotryc̈kyj's work makes what would otherwise seem obvious cases of the vocative of i-stem nouns possible genitives of exclamation. How are we to interpret the following: "O złości" (Smotryc̈kyj 1621b, 28ᵛ/353, 42ᵛ/367), "O niewstydliwości" (Smotryc̈kyj 1621b, 42ʳ/366), "O zbożności" (Smotryc̈kyj 1621b, 46ᵛ/371), especially since the vocative is not impossible—"O przezacna krwi Ruska" (Smotryc̈kyj 1621b, 60ᵛ/385)? Here as elsewhere, only the context can provide an answer.

6. Szymon Budny, who himself used the *accusativus cum infinitivo* construction in his Polish (Budny 1989, 166: " . . . jako jednego Boga, tak też jednego Pana być powiada . . . "), considered it nonetheless "non-Polish": in citing Acts 8:36 (Budny 1989, 154), he wrote " 'Wierzę Synem Bożym być Jezusa Chrysta' albo (po polsku mowiąc): 'Wierzę, że Synem Bożym jest Jezus Chrystus'."

7. Or rather, this observation applied for some users of the Ruthenian language. Actually, people meant many things by the term руский языкъ in this period. One type of Ruthenian was characterized by its close relationship with Polish.

8. Well known is the story recounted by Kasijan Sakovyč in his *Epanorthōsis* (Cracow, 1642) of the Orthodox priest who prefaced his homily saying "Listen, Christians, to the sermon of St. Rej." (Cited in Wiszniewski 1851, 368: "Posłuchayte Chrestyane kazania światoho Reia.")

9. He drew material from the Bible (1572) and the New Testament (1574) of the radical Antitrinatarian Szymon Budny when he offered Ruthenian Gospel pericopes in his *Homiliary Gospel* of 1616. See Frick 1988.

10. Smotryc̆kyj 1628b, Aiv^v/630: " . . . posłałem ią dla wydrukowania iȩzykiem Polskim."

11. *Apolleia* 1628, A1^r/302: "ΑΠΟΛΛΕΙΑ Апологіи Книжки Діалектомъ Роускимъ написанои, Полскимъ зась ве Львовѣ друкованои . . . "

12. Smotryc̆kyj 1621a, G1^v/261: "na początku tey Biesiady mey . . . "

13. Here, too, we know that Smotryc̆kyj was aware of the "normal" usage. See Smotryc̆kyj 1629a, 86/688: " . . . gdyby to cudo [the fire that descends upon Christ's sepulcher at Easter] v nas tymi czasy siȩ działo, wszyscy by Turcy w Chrystusa Pana dawno iuż byli *vwierzyli*." (Emphasis added.)

14. And Smotryc̆kyj made other jokes. I do not think that the following figures would have been chosen (to make serious points) by a man who had no sense of humor: "Iam twemu chłopcu wczora wierzył, że ciȩ doma nie było, a ty dziś mnie samemu wiary nie daiesz, że miȩ, doma nie masz, chociem sam z domu swego przez okno odpowiedział" (Smotryc̆kyj 1622a, 9/471); "boiȩ sie aby sie my z tego nie tak właśnie chlubili y cieszyli, iak gdyby kto spadszy z woza w błoto, cieszył sie z tego, że siedział na wozie" (Smotryc̆kyj 1628a, 191/618).

The first anecdote cited above was a reworking of a well-known story about the Roman military leader Cornelius Scipio Africanus Major and the poet Quintus Ennius. Smotryc̆kyj could have known it from a variety of sources, including Cicero's *De oratore* (II, 276), Mikołaj Rej's *Figliki,* Łukasz Górnicki's *Dworzanin polski* (or the model for that work, Baldesar Castiglione's *Il libro del Cortegiano*), as well as sixteenth- and seventeenth-century collections of Polish *facetiae.* See Krzyżanowski 1960, 102 and Górnicki 1954, 250–51.

The following example (Smotryc̆kyj 1618, Ш7^r), on the other hand, is probably inadvertently humorous, and a glimpse of pedagogical methods in an age when, as Smotryc̆kyj wrote in the preface to his grammar "The Slavonic dialect is to be maintained among the pupils in normal school conversation by threat of punishment" (Smotryc̆kyj 1618,)(3^r: "Діалектъ в звыклой школной розмовѣ Славенскїй, межи тщателми под каранемъ захованъ.")—"бїю оуч[е]н[и]ка; бїяй оуч[е]н[и]ка; бїюся оучителем или от оучителя"

15. On the practice of sacred philology among the humanists and in the Age of Reform, see Berger 1879; Lagrange 1934–1935; Garofalo 1946; Harbison 1956; Hall 1970; Hall 1978; Jarrott 1970; Trinkaus 1970, 563–614; Holeczek 1975; Bentley 1976; Bentley 1977; Bentley 1978; Bentley 1979; Bentley 1983.

On the Renaissance revival of textual criticism and the advances in its theory and practice, see Timpanaro 1981; Kenney 1974; Grafton 1977; Prete 1965; Prete 1969; Pfeiffer 1976; Reynolds and Wilson 1974; Grafton 1975; Grafton 1983; D'Amico 1988; Waszink 1975; Grafton 1991.

16. On the debate over the status of the Vulgate, see Höpfl 1913, 1–43; Vosté 1946; Sutcliff 1948; Emmi 1953a; Emmi 1953b; Emmi 1953c; Pelikan 1984, 209, 309, 320, 344–47. The decree stated (*Concilium* 1911, 91–92) that "of all the Latin editions of the sacred books now in circulation, . . . the Holy Synod ordains and declares that the old Latin Vulgate Edition, which, in use for so many hundred years, has been approved by the Church, be held as authentic in public lectures, disputations, sermons, and expositions" ("sacrosancta synodus . . . ex omnibus latinis editionibus, quae circumferuntur . . . statuit et declarat, ut haec ipsa vetus et vulgata editio, quae longo tot saeculorum usu in ipsa ecclesia probata est, in publicis lectionibus, disputationibus, praedicationibus et expositionibus pro authentica habeatur").

17. On the Catholic debate over the translation of Holy Scripture, see Crehan 1978, 202–203; Ehses 1908; Cavallera 1945; Schmidt 1950, 81–95; and especially Lentner 1964, 228–64. For a discussion of sixteenth-century Catholic attitudes toward St. Jerome and his Latin version of the Bible, see Rice 1985, 173–99.

18. Luther 1911, 424: "Si enim solus essem in toto orbe terrarum, qui retinerem verbum, solus essem Ecclesia."

19. On the establishment of the principle of *sola Scriptura* and its various applications, see Preus 1955, 1–12, 103–130, and passim; Bainton 1963, 1–6; Sykes 1978, 175–78; Pelikan 1984, 128, 174, 181–83, 207–211.

20. On the Catholic rejection of *sola Scriptura* and the balancing of scriptural and ecclesiastical authorities, see Pelikan 1984, 262–77; Beumer 1950, 54–57; Crehan 1978, 199–202; Oberman 1963, 365–92.

21. See *Concilium* 1901, 519: "Expediret igitur magis unamquamque nationem in suis institutis circa hoc relinquere, ut ubi bonum esset concederetur, ubi malum, prohiberetur."

22. *Corpus* 1891, 197: "ego uero euangelio non crederem, nisi me catholicae ecclesiae conmoueret auctoritas."

23. On the Polish debates over the translation and interpretation of the Bible in the Reformation and the Counter-Reformation, see Frick 1989.

24. See Szczucki 1964, 98–102; Frick 1989, 116–24.

25. On Wujek's translation and the controversies currounding them, see Poplatek 1950; Drzymała 1948; Drzymała 1951; Frick 1989, 133–219. The ban on the reading of other versions found in the Bible of 1599 is printed in Frick 1989, 219.

26. The best study of the importance of the Polish language in Rus′ remains Martel 1938.

27. Czechowic 1577, ttiiii′: "A imo to wszytko y Ruskich rozdziałow, ktore oni zaczałami zowią, vżywamy, kładąc ie też na kraiach, iż nas o to z osobna

bracia Ruskich kraiow żądali. Gdyż oni w swych pisanych księgach, kapituł naszych nie maią."

28. Smotryc'kyj 1610, 158ᵛ–159ʳ/175: "Przywodzicie na świadectwo błogosławionego Augustyna, albo inszego kogo z Rzymskich tego wieku Doktorow, ktorzy inaczey te Pawłowe słowa rozumieli, a mieysca tego, miasto fundamentu Czyścowego ognia vżywali. Ktorym, tak odpowiadamy, Ieśli słuszna rzecz iest, aby Graeckie pisma Graekowie wykładali, gdyż przeciw temu nie masz co rzec, iż Graekowie lepiey pospolity swoy ięzyk vmieią z przyrodzenia, aniż ludzie inszey nacyey z nauki, ponieważ tedy to po Graecku Apostoł pisał, nikt zaiste z Łacinnikow tego mieysca właśniey wyrozumieć y przystoyniey wyłożyć nie mogł nad Chryzostoma świętego, dla czego słuszniey na owych, ktorych iest więcey, *sententią* przyzwolić, aniżli na Łacińskich Doktorow zdanie, ktorzy taki wykład vczynili, albo prze niedostatek ięzyka Łacińskiego w wyrażeniu własności słow Graeckich, albo się też więtszemu złemu opponuiąc, mnieyszemu złemu mieysce podali."

29. Smotryc'kyj 1610, 125ʳ⁻ᵛ/141–42: "ieśliby teraz w swoie pisma przez Rzymskiego Kościoła naśladowce, a zwłaszcza nowo wydane weyźrzeć, a z nami rozmowić, można rzecz była, wiele by, przewrotnych ludzi, chytrych przysad w nich naleźli, o ktorych im ani się kiedy śniło, ani też o nich kiedy pisać zamyślali."

30. Subbotin 1876, 86–87; Subbotin 1878a, 15; Subbotin 1878b, 257; Subbotin 1881, 157.

31. See Podskalsky 1988, 46–47 and the literature cited there.

32. On Smotryc'kyj's library, see Losievskij 1986.

33. Skarga 1610, 53: "Nie na Rzymski ani Łaciński kościoł, ale na Grecki stara iest przymowka: *Graeca fides.* y dawne ich obwinienie, iż księgi fałszuią nie tylo Doktorow, ale samego pisma ś. słowa, a miasto nich heretyckie podmiataią, a Katholickie wyrzucaią. Co się o dobrych nie mowi. Biblia na ich ięzyk naprzod przełożona, ktorą 70. zowiem, dziwnie od Grekow pofałszowana iest. vymą y przydatkiem, y fałszem. co twierdzi ś. Ieronym. Poprawował tey Bibliey Origenes, Lucianus, Esichius, y nasz Ieronym Żydowskiego się textu dokładaiąc: ale zaś pogmatwana iest tak barzo y pofałszowana od Grekow, iż prawie zniszczała, y ledwie się o iey płatkach dopytać. y musiał się kościoł Rzymski do textu Żydowskiego, Grecki opuściwszy, vdać. z ktorego nasza Wulgata vrosła, okrom Psałterza, ktory się iuż był po wszech kościołach wkorzenił. ktorey Wulgaty z dziwną pilnością postrzegał kościoł Łaciński, y Grekowie prawdę miłuiący, muszą się do naszey Łacińskiey Bibliey vciekać. Toż się sstało z nowym Testamentem, ktory także Grekowie pofałszowali, heretycy zwłaszcza, ktorych ten ięzyk zawżdy matką był nieszczęśliwą. Grekowie z Ewangeliey wyrzucili historyą o cudzołożnicy, y ostatni rozdział ś. Marka. y przydali do pacierza: Twoie iest krolestwo y moc, y chwała na wieki. Co się v żadnego Ewangelisty nie nayduie. Iako znać v Tertuliana, Cypryana, Ambrożego, Ieronyma, ktorzy tę modlitwę Pańską wykładali bez tego przydatku. To więtszy przykład, niż on: *y od syna.*"

34. See, for example, the discussion of Mt. 6:13 and John 7:35–8:11 in Jakub Wujek's New Testament of 1593. See also Frick 1989, 147.

35. Smotryc̆kyj 1610, ()i^r/1: ΘΡΗΝΟΣ *To iest Lament iedyney ś. Powszechney Apostolskiey Wschodniey Cerkwie . . . Pierwey z Graeckiego na Słowieński, a teraz z Słowieńskiego na Polski przełożony.*

36. Smotryc̆kyj 1616, ˮ/15: Ев[ан]г[е]ліе учителное: албо Казаня, на кождую нед[ѣ]лю И Свята урочистыи, презъ С[вя]т[о]го Отца нашего Калиста, Архіеп[и]скопа Константинопол҂кого, и Вселенского Патріарха, пред[ъ] двѣма сты лѣт[ъ] По кгрецку написаныи, а теперъ ново з Кгрецкого и Словенского языка на Руский переложеныи.

37. The Orthodox Smotryc̆kyj responded to Uniate charges that the Orthodox had neglected education, stating (Smotryc̆kyj 1622a, 28^v/491): "Szkoły dla ćwiczenia dziatek w ięzyku Graeckim, Łacińskim, Słowieńskim, Ruskim y Polskim są nam sporządzone."

38. Smotryc̆kyj 1618,)(2^r–v: "Пожитокъ грамматіки в языку грецком[ъ] и Латінском[ъ] самым[ъ] досвѣдченем[ъ] оказале значный, абы и в Славенском[ъ] дознанъ, а за часом[ъ] подобнымъ досвѣдченем[ъ] и значне оказанъ был[ъ], на повинной вашей Люботщателныи Оучителе пилности залежати будетъ. Вѣдаете абовѣмъ, которыистеся грецкои, любъ Латінскои Грамматіки художству учили, што она есть ку понятю як[ъ] языка чистости, такъ и правого а сочинного, ведлугъ власности діалектовъ и мовеня, и писаня, и писмъ вырозуменя. Вшелякій пожитокъ, который колвекъ преречоныхъ языковъ Грамматіки чинити звыклы, без вонтпеня и Славенская в своемъ языцѣ Славенскомъ оучинити можетъ."

39. On the history of the Greek text of the New Testament, see Metzger 1968.

40. Smotryc̆kyj 1629b, 45^r/745: "Choć to y po Haebreysku z Kalepina Rabinie, niepospolicie vmiesz, iednak a to y z Lechemchomecami swymi prostotę swoię, y Zakonu Bożego niewiadomość, przed tymi, od ktorych prokuruiesz obnażasz; że w rzeczach zbawiennych vfać ci, *si sapiunt,* nie maią komu."

41. See Frick 1989, 248–49. Czechowic wrote (1577, tiii^r): "wiedz żem się nigdziey nie ważył naprawiać textu pospolitego greckiego . . . iuż z dawna od wszytkich przyiętego y pochwalonego."

42. See Diplic 1633, 33: "Z tey pierwszey, aby sie iako naybarziey vtaić mogł przed drugimi, o co Pana Boga pod ten czas w modlitwach swych prosił. Z drugiey zasie owey, żeby sie w czym w Greckim ięzyku ni potknął, gdyby mu co głośno, y bez księgi przyszło wymowić, iako temu, co sie nie nazwyczaił był ięzykiem tym taki obrząd odprawować."

43. See, for example, Ruc̆kyj's argument for the authority of Krevza's *Defense of Unity (Sowita* 1621, 52/480): "Wszytko się to dowodnie vkazało w Książecce naszey o obronie iedności, wszytko z Ksiąg słowieńskich, mało co z Łacińskich."

44. For Wujek's position and his debt to Bellarmine, see Frick 1989, 149–50.

45. See Smotryc'kyj 1628a, 200/623: "Może też na koniec kogo z nas, abo y wszytkich od Iedności Cerkiewney odstraszać, obchodzony iuż po Synodzie Florencskim Synod Tridenski. Ale y to byłby nam strach tam gdzie go nie masz. y owszem Cerkiew nasza Wschodna Cerkwi Zachodney wielce za to ma bydź powinna, y nieśmiertelne iey za to dzięki czynić, że ona swego czystego wiary wyznania od Luterskich y Kalwińskich świeżo wynikłych bluźnierstw przez ten Synod broniąc, y Wschodney Cerkwie Prawosławne wiary wyznanie obroniła: w owych mianowicie wiary Dogmatach. *De libero Arbitrio, de peccato Originali, et Actuali, de Originali Iustitia, de Prouidentia, de praescientia, de praedestinatione, de Gratia, de Fide, de Iustificatione, de Ecclesia, de Sacramentis, de Scriptura S. et de eius Canone, de Traditionibus . . .*"

46. See Mużylovs'kyj 1629, 23[r]: "a ieżeli do Łacińskich Xiąg odzowiesz się, ochyliwszy własne Graeckie, niechayże miedzy nim y tobą *Index expurgatorius* sądzi." Diplic 1633, 71: "Ieśli mi rzecze Apologiuiący, że gdy Apostoł ś. mowi, iż Christus Pan oczyścia Cerkiew, omyciem wody w słowie *żywota*, iako on z Wulgaty przydaie . . . " (Cf. Eph. 5:26.)

47. On Wujek's translations and the internal conflicts among the Polish Jesuits, see Frick 1989, 167–80, 212–16.

48. Wujek 1593, 16: "Tak iż tu masz, Czytelniku miły, wszytek Nowy testament Polski, zarazem z Graeckiego y z Łacińskiego tak przełożony, że iednym poźrzeniem wnet obaczysz, kędy w Graeckim iest co inaczey, abo kędy iest co więcey, abo mniey, niżli w Łacińskim. Iedno ta iest rożność: iż Łaciński, iako pewnieyszy, kładziemy w samym texcie: a Graecki gdzie się kolwiek z Łacińskim nie zgadza, na brzegu znaczymy."

49. Wujek 1599, ***iiii[r]: "bo się w pierwszey editiey w niektórych rzeczach Greckiego textu, dla tych którzy tego pragnęli naszladowało: co teraz wszytko odrzuciwszy, masz tu szczerze text łaciński iako sam w sobie iest."

CHAPTER 12

1. Smotryc'kyj 1629a, 78/684: "w tych wszystkich wyższey pomienionych wiary Artykułach, z Rzymiany lub z Ewangelikami nam iest zgoda, lub też co trzeciego śrzedniego my trzymamy y wyznawamy."

2. Smotryc'kyj 1629a, 77/683: "czego się mam trzymać, y iako mam nie tylko o tych pomienionych, ale y o inszych wiary Artykułach rozumieć, iako te są: *De Arbitrio seruum, ne illud sit an liberum: de Peccato, tum Originali, tum Actuali; de Gratia, de Fide, de Iustificatione, de bonorum operum Iustitia, de Prouidentia, de Praescientia, de Praedestinatione, de Ecclesia, de Sacramentis, de Scriptura Sacra, de Traditionibus, et de statu animarum, etc. etc.*"

3.   According to the *acta* of *Propaganda Fide* for 5 November 1627 (two and a half months after the letter addressed to Lukaris), Smotryćkyj had requested a copy of Zacharias Gerganos' Greek catechism printed in Wittenberg, which he would use in convincing Rus′ that their leaders in Constantinople were heretics. The Congregation sent directions to the Swiss nuncio, asking for two copies, one to be sent to Rome, and another to the nuncio in Warsaw that he might forward it to Rućkyj (see Velykyj 1953, 58–59). On 25 November 1628, *Propaganda Fide* expressed its awareness of Smotryćkyj's letter to Lukaris (Velykyj 1953, 65–66). On the long-term preoccupation of *Propaganda Fide* with attempts to declare Lukaris a Calvinist, see Hering 1968, 110.

4.   Smotryćkyj 1610, ()()()i^r/9: "Tymi y tym podobnymi słowy Cerkiew ś. *Orientalna* każdemu w niewiadomości błądzącemu o sobie sprawę daie, ktore to danie sprawy, tu w tych pod titułem iey pisanych Ksiąszkach, ile według czasu y innych circumstantiy być mogło, dosyć się za pomocą Bożą dostatecznie y dowodnie tractuie." Smotryćkyj 1610, 26^v–27^r/43: "Izalim ieszcze mało lat nie dawno przeszłych vcierpiała potwarzy y calumnij od iawnych aduersarzow, ktoremi oni świętą, y niepodeyrzaną w Boga w Troycy iedynego wiarę moię y prawdziwych moich synow sławnego narodu Rosieyskiego ku ohydzie wszystkiemu światu podać vsiłuiąc Miasto Kanonow lub Prawidł, albo Artykułow Religiey Cerkwie Rosieyskiey wszystkiemu światu do czytania podaią."

5.   See the list of distinctions between the "Eastern" and the "Roman" Churches in *Thrēnos* (Smotryćkyj 1610, 186^v–87^r/203).

6.   See Smotryćkyj 1628a, Cc1^v/624: "bliższa nam zgoda z Rzymiany, niżli z Hęretykami."

7.   Smotryćkyj 1610, 31^{r-v}/47–48: "y że z siebie to tak cięszkie Papieskiey nauki iarzmo zrzucili, vstawicznie się cieszą. Aczkolwiek y oni na drogę zbawienney prawdy nie trafili."

8.   Smotryćkyj cited St. Basil in the preface to *Thrēnos* (()()i^v/6): "Pismo . . . Bogiem natchnione sędzią od nas niechay będzie postanowione, y v kogo się naydzie nauka z słowem Bożym zgodna, tego zdanie za prawdziwe vznane być ma."

9.   Smotryćkyj 1610, 186^v–87^r/203: "Wschodnia Cerkiew z Chrystusem Panem naucza, iż pisma Boskiego rozum żadnym sposobem nad własne swe ktorym rzeczone iest wyrozumienie odmienić się nie może. Zachodni Kościoł z Papieżem, gdy się Rzymskiey Cerkwie wyrozumienie odmieni, *necessario* y Duch ś. swoy rozum w piśmie odmienia. Wschodnia z Chrystusem, Pisma świętego czytanie wszystkim ludziom, dla nauki świetskim y Duchownym iest wolne, Zachodni z Papieżem, Pisma Bożego świetscy ludzie czytać niech się nie ważą. Wschodnia z Chrystusem, Pisma Bożego wykład wszelkiemu komu Duch święty w ktoreykolwiek Prouincialney Cerkwi odkryie, iest wolny. Zachodnia z Papieżem, żadna Prouincialna Cerkiew pisma Bożego wykładać władzy nie ma, tylko sam Rzymski Kościoł."

10. Smotryc̆kyj 1610, 92ʳ/108: "... z szczerego pisma Bożego, zebraną powieść przekładam."

11. Smotryc̆kyj 1610, 86ᵛ/103: "Nie Papieskich nowo zmyślonych Tradiciy, ale Chrystusowey y iego Zwolennikow świętych nauki zbawienney słucha."

12. Smotryc̆kyj 1610, 167ʳ/183: "prędzey swemu rozumowi tudzież ludzkim baykom, aniżli pismu Bożemu, y prawdziwemu niepokalaney Cerkwie wyrozumieniu wiary dodawaią."

13. Smotryc̆kyj 1628a, 105/576: "im daley, tym rzadszy byłem w następowaniu na dogmata prawdziwe, szerszy w rzeczach potocznych, pod te czasy nagle przypadłych."

14. Smotryc̆kyj 1628a, 118/582: "Że pisma ś. wykładaczem, iest toż same pismo. . . . Że Traditie są niepotrzebne."

15. The Uniates wrote concerning these events in 1621 (*Examen* 1621, 43/590): "... [Smotryc̆kyj] może pomnieć, bo czterech lat temu nie masz . . . "

16. *Examen* 1621, 46/591: "A w tym czasie poddano mu Xięgi ze Zboru Marka Antoniego, Arcybiskupa Spalateńskiego Apostaty, za ktorą się chwyciwszy, został tym czym teraz iest. Taki statek tego człowieka, że iedna Xiążka iednego Apostaty, ktory nową sektę w Chrześciaństwie dotąd niebywałą, wprowadzał, y ktorey sekty Krolestwo Angielskie (do ktorego się był vdał) przyiąć nie chciało, tak go we wszytkim odmieniła, że *ab equis descendit ad asinos.*"

17. Of the more recent studies devoted to the career of Marcantonio de Dominis, see Cantimori 1958; Cantimori 1960; Clark 1968; Patterson 1978; Malcolm 1984. On the importance of de Dominis for the Ruthenian debates of the early sixteenth century, I am aware only of Petrov 1879, which, in the light of the material I will present here, will require some revision and amplification. De Dominis' life, death, and especially his posthumous heresy trial, are described briefly, but with great drama, in Redondi 1987, 107–118.

18. See Malcolm 1984, 23, 105–106. De Dominis wrote in Book VII of *De Republica Ecclesiastica*: "Laetor plurimum quod nostra natio Illyrica, etiamsi Romanae ecclesiae addictissima, vulgari tamen lingua Slaua omnia divina officia habere voluit."

19. English translation from Malcolm 1984, 39. De Dominis 1618, a4ʳ: "Fouebam a primis mei Clericatus annis in me innatum pene desiderium videndae vnionis omnium Christi Ecclesiarum: separationem Occidentis ab Oriente, in rebus fidei; Austri ab Aquilone, aequo animo ferre nunquam poteram: cupiebam anxie tot, tantorumque schismatum causam agnoscere: ac perspicere num posset aliqua excogitari via, omnes Christi Ecclesias ad veram antiquam vnionem componendi: Idque videndi ardebam desiderio."

20. English translation from Malcolm 1984, 64–65. This text from Book VII of the *De Republica Ecclesiastica* cited according to Malcolm 1984, 130: "Rideo

illos ego qui ingenti incommodo et periculo ab vna ad aliam partem, solius conscientiae causa, transfugiunt. Illi soli prudenter id faciunt, qui de abusibus, superfluitatibus et erroribus alterutrius partis libere disserere, et scribere ibi volunt, vbi impedimentum nullum inueniant."

21. Smotryc̆kyj 1621c, 77–78/437–38: "Zaż Cerkiew Boża, nie iest imię Cerkwie Chrześciańskiey y Katholickiey? Przeć nie możesz. Lecz Krol Iego M. Pan nasz M. w Vniwersale Oycu Patriarsze Ieremiaszowi (o ktorym tu wzmiankę czyniliśmy) danym, Cerkwi nasze Ruskie pod posłuszeństwem Patriarszym będące, Cerkwiami Bożymi nazywa: Coż ci za dziw że y w tym swoim nam danym Przywileiu, ludźmi nas Relligiey Chrześciańskiey Katholickiey mianować raczy? Bo by tak, mowisz, siebie samego odsądzał wiary Katholickiey. Mylisz się Panie *Redargutorze.* Rzekłbym, lepiey Krol Iego M. vmie, co iest iedyna Ś. Katholicka y Apostolska Cerkiew *definiować,* niżli ty: ale tępości twey tak wysokiemu rozumowi *comparować* nie ważę się. Wiedzieć Krol Iego M. raczy, że nas oboią stronę, y Wschodnią, mowiemy, Cerkiew pomiestną y Zachodnią, Cerkiew Ś. Katholicka, ktora iest iedyna w wnętrznościach swoich, w ktorych się one zaczęły, nosi: do ktorey iedno y toż prawo obie maią: a iednością miłości wzaiemnie będąc ziednoczone, Pana Boga o to z oboiey strony prosząc, aby on to, co ie dzieli, to iest, co się kolwiek *non per defectum,* ale *per excessum* w rożnicę miedzy nie podało, oycowsko vprzątnął, y zniosł. A iż *defectus,* iako mowią, *fide non vtitur, excessu fide abutitur:* Nie nayduie przeto Krol Iego M. *defectu* w świętey wierze naszey Graeckiey, nie nayduie y w swey Rzymskiey: zaczym gdy nas ludźmi Relligiey Chrześciańskiey Katholickiey Graeckiey nazywać raczy: siebie samego tegoż tytułu Chrześciańskiego Katholickiego nie odsądza: w czym się *Redargutor,* rzecz przeciwną stanowiąc, bardzo myli, nie chcąc wiedzieć, że *neque in excessu, neque in defectu* (ieśli y o swey toż rzec może) Ś. Cerkiew Wschodnia z Katholickiey nie wystąpiła."

22. But did Smotryc̆kyj already know this definition in 1617? In the same *Defense of the Verification* of 1621 he defended the Orthodoxy of his overtures toward the Uniates in that earlier period, saying (Smotryc̆kyj 1621c, 106/452): "A co się Zbawienia dotyczę wyznawcow wiary Rzymskiey, mogł to bespieczne rzec, że *defectus fidei non excessus condemnat:* a zatym, kto to od niego słyszał, to co się iemu podobało, według swego pożądania inferować mogł." I suspect, however, that in 1621 Smotryc̆kyj was recasting his conversations of 1617 in the light of his later reading. After all, in *Twofold Guilt,* Ruc̆kyj had not accused Smotryc̆kyj of using this precise definition; he had simply alleged in general terms that in 1617 the future archbishop of Polack had discussed matters of faith with the Uniates, and that he had said that he believed what they believed and that the Romans could achieve salvation in their Church (*Sowita* 1621, 69–71/492–93). This inclusive definition of correct faith was useful not only in defending the Orthodox against the Catholics, but also in defending the Smotryc̆kyj of 1617 to the Orthodox against the Uniate allegations of 1621.

However this may be, I have been unable to find this definition in any form in Part 1 (Books I, II, and III) of de Dominis' work. It is worth considering whether Smotryc'kyj may first have found this way of thinking and arguing in de Dominis' answer to Suárez. This suggests two observations. First, Smotryc'kyj would seem an avid reader of de Dominis if he drew on part 2 the year after it appeared, and if he had already been citing de Dominis to the Uniates in 1617 (the same year part 1 had appeared, and the year after the *Profectionis consilium*, de Dominis' apology for abandoning Rome for London, had first appeared in a separate edition). Second, it would not have been in any way out of character for Smotryc'kyj to look to a defense of the Church of England against the Church of Rome for ammunition in his defense of Ruthenian Orthodoxy against the Union of Brest.

23. De Dominis 1620, 267: "Fides enim est omnia credenda credere. Infidelitas vero est nihil illorum credere: at haeresis est aliqua credendorum credere, aliqua vero negare seu non credere, aut discredere, siue positiua illa sint, siue negatiua. Credere tamen omnia, et aliquid amplius, quod tamen a Deo credendum non proponitur, etiam si id falsum sit, et vt verum, ac de re fide credatur, non puto aut infidelitatem, aut haeresim in se continere: sed errorem; nisi virtute, vt dixi, adsit alicuius veritatis a Deo reuelatae reiectio. Et consequenter reijcere, et non credere fide diuina, illa additamenta, quae Deus credenda non reuelauit, sed homines addiderunt, etiam si alioquin vera sint, et non falsa, nullum facit verae fidei detrimentum, neque haeresim continet, neque peccatum ex eo duntaxat, quod tanquam res de fide non credatur."

24. De Dominis 1620, 269: "Teneamus tamen iam datam distinctionem, quod fides Catholica potest pati detrimentum, vel in defectu vel in excessu. Ex defectu ipsa vere vel perit, vel mutilatur, ex excessu non perit, sed inquinatur et deturpatur."

25. De Dominis 1620, 269: "Hic ego rursus superfluas cupio praecidere disputationes: et aliam appono communissimam et tritam distinctionem; aliquid esse loqui de Ecclesia vniuersali, aliud de Ecclesiis particularibus. . . . vniuersalem autem Ecclesiam intelligo illam, quae omnes penitus Ecclesiae particulares, nulla dempta, imo vero potius quae omnes fideles, nullo dempto, complectitur."

26. Smotryc'kyj had first couched his argument in terms that implicitly included both East and West in the Universal Church; later in the polemic he stated that the Romans were mistaken in assuming they suffered no "defect" in faith. This change may reflect Smotryc'kyj's growing frustration with the other side; it was as if he had first said, "Let us tolerate one another." When the other side refused, he then said, "Well, then, we will not tolerate you, either." But it could also be the case that the shift reflected his attempts to quell growing suspicions among the Orthodox about the reliability of their leader.

27. *Examen* 1621, 26/579: "Y swoie *axiomata* iakoby *ex communi sensu Theologorum*, nam podał. *Defectus fide non vitutur, Excessus fide abutitur.* . . . Nowe v Theologow y niesłychane, tak *axiomata*, iako y *distinctio fidei*. Od nowego też Theologa a od dawnego Grammatyka wymyślone."

28. *Examen* 1621, 27/579: "Niechże się nie wstyda nauczyć v dawnieyszego Philosopha y Theologa: W każdey Cnocie trzy rzeczy kładzie Philosophia *moralis*, albo raczey rozum przyrodzony każdego vważnego człowieka: *Medium*, to iest śrzodek, a dwoie *extremum* koło niego, ktore po polsku możemy zwać kraiami abo stronami. Ieden kray możemy zwać *defectem*, drugi *excessem*, a oboie to są *vitia*. Cnota zawsze zawiera się *in medio*, to iest we śrzodku, z ktorego na ktorą się kolwiek stronę do *defectu* abo do *excessu* wychyli, tym samym siłę y imię swe traci, a występkiem zostaie."

29. See de Dominis 1620, 266: "Sic Ariana Ecclesia non erat vera Ecclesia, quia in Christum diminutum credebat, diuinitatem Christo nimirum detrahens: sic Nestoriana, quae vnionem hypostaticam duarum in Christo naturarum negabat: Sic aliae haereses, quae omnes per defectum et ellypsim fidem destruunt."

30. *Antelenchus* 1622, 35–36/705–706: "te rzeczy ktore Pan Bog obiawił, y ktore wierzyć powinniśmy, są w pewney liczbie. Położmysz dla łacnieyszego zrozumienia pewną tych rzeczy liczbę, to iest 100. zaczym tak mowimy: kto wierzy z rzeczy 100. od Pana Boga obiawionych 99. a iedney ostatniey nie wierzy, grzeszy przeciwko wierze przez defekt, bo mu iednego nie dostaie do sta. Kto zasię wierzy sto y nadto iescze iedno, grzeszy przeciwko wierze, nie iuż przez vymę, gdyż wierzy spełna sto, ale przez przydatek, że nad liczbę rzeczy obiawionych zawierzoną, wierzy iednę."

31. Šmurlo 1928, 35: " . . . eodem modo etiam se credere purgatorium et fruitionem sanctorum, solum ergo remanet punctum difficultatis primatus Papae, non habent enim hoc pro articulo fidei in quo insigniter corrupti sunt per librum Marci Anton. 'De dominis,' quos pseudoepiscopus Polocensis assiduo legit et fere memoriter recitat."

32. Smotryckyj 1629b, 88ᵛ/791: "wyssałeś to *absurdum* z Spalatensa: łykayże ie z nim wespoł."

33. Smotryckyj 1629, 88ᵛ/791: "W dowodzeniu tego Absurdum zażył Schismatyk Antidotista Schismatyka Spalatensa."

34. Also published in English translation as *A Manifestation of the Motives, Whereupon . . . Marcus Antonius de Dominis, Archbishop of Spalato . . . Undertooke his departure thence* (London, 1616) and in Polish. According to Myc'ko (1990, 112), Smotryckyj himself "translated" this work (from the Polish version) into Ruthenian.

35. The first was also published in English translation as *M. Antonius de Dominis Archbishop of Spalato Declares the cause of his Returne, out of England* (Rome, 1623) and reprinted in facsimile in de Dominis 1978; it was also published in Polish translation as *Marcus Antonius de Dominis Arcybiskup Spalateński swego zwrocenia się z Angliey, radę przekłada* (Vilnius). A second apology was published in English translation as *The Second Manifesto of Marcus Antonius de Dominis . . .* (Liège, 1623) and reprinted in facsimile in de Dominis 1973.

36. The "scale" of deviations from the confessional "norm" was implicit in many passages in Smotryc'kyj's writings. See Smotryc'kyj 1629a, 29ʳ/659: "Niech postawi przed sobą wszelkiey Sekty człowieka, Katholika, Schizmatyka, Heretyka, Żyda, Machometana, Bałwochwalcę, a pyta o wierze ich: ieśli nie każdy z nich rzecze: day Boże w tey wierze mnie vmrzeć, w ktoreyem się narodził." Also Smotryc'kyj 1629a, 52/671: " . . . Klerykowym powieściom, iak fałszywym y potwarnym, wiarę odiąwszy, z tą Bracią, ktorzy prawdę Bożą wyklinaią, pod nogi ią swoie rzucaią y depcą, y iuż nie tylo w Schizmie, ale y w Herezyach są, y z ich zheretyczałym Pasterzem daley przestawać nie chcę . . . " Also Smotryc'kyj 1628a, 111/579: " . . . Schizma bez Hęrezyey bydź może, ale Hęrezya bez Schismy nie bywa." And Smotryc'kyj 1629b, 1ᵛ–2ʳ/702: "nie tylko schismatyckie, ale y hęretyckie piętno . . . "

37. Golubev 1877, 68: "Все тое што колвекъ мелъ геретицкаго, схизматицкаго на писме въ скриняхъ двохъ, казавъши принести до себе, самъ руками своими перебралъ и сторожа свего, который для нагреваня келіи его уставичне былъ, упевнилъ, жебы попалилъ, и на томъ три дни стравилъ, иншихъ не пущаючи до себе, и презъ тые три дня тыми тылко скриптами палилъ въ печи тотъ сторожъ дровъ не носечи, и десетъ золотыхъ ему за то обецалъ, якожъ и въ тестаменъте написалъ."

38. Hofmann 1929, 88: " . . . mitto ill.mis ac Rev.mis Dominationibus D. Vestris, itemque aliud exemplar litterarum pseudopatriarchae praesentis Constp. scriptarum ante aliquos annos ab illo ipso ad Marcum Antonium Spalatensem propria manu ipsius descriptum et cum libris eiusdem M. Antonii ad confraternitatem Vilnensem schismaticorum missum."

39. Šeptyc'kyj 1965, 119: "Instructio pro faciendo processu super recognitione fragmenti literarum Cyrilli ad Marcum Antonium, olim archiepiscopum Spalatensem. In primis curandum, ut inveniantur testes, qui viderint Cyrillum illud fragmentum scribere, vel saltem, si tales habere non possunt, alii qui eius manum notam habeant, ut quia alias viderint eum scribere, vel propter aliam rationem concludentem de scientia et notitia characteris illius."

40. Smotryc'kyj 1629b, 89ʳ⁻ᵛ/791–92: "a do tych Ktorzy go za Antichrysta *calumniose* tradukuią, [de Dominis] mowi, *Antichristus esse non potest, qui Christum praedicat, exaltat, verum Deum, verumque Hominem agnoscit, seque eius famulum Confitetur, qui totam suam dignitatem ex sola Christi suprema excellentia et diuinitate agnoscit, Confitetur et profitetur.* . . . y z tey tedy tego twego poradźcy rady, do Iedności Ś. brać byś sie miał Antidotysto: a nie w głębszą przepaść przemierzłey Schismy siebie y insze zawodzić."

41. Smotryc'kyj 1629b, 89ʳ/791: "Ieśliś w opisaniu tego *Absurdum* zażył rady Spalatensowey: czemu też w tym iego rady nie naśladuiesz, że on tego Rzymskiego wyznania Haerezyą, iak wy bluźnicie, nie nazywa; ale ie ma za Prawosławne. że on Wiarę Katholicką Rzymskiemu Kościołowi przyznawa, choć mu excessy w tych Wiary Dogmatach, ktore są iemu z Cerkwią Wschodnią pospolite, obłudnie przypisuie. Iakie są *Sacrificium incruentum, Propitiatorium,*

Transubstantiatio in Sacramento Eucharistiae panis et vini. Adoratio Sacramenti Eucharistiae, Numerus septenarius Sacramentorum, Ieiunia ab Ecclesia instituta, Imaginum adoratio: Sanctorum inuocatio: Sacrarum reliquiarum veneratio: y tym podobne. . . . W czym ieśli Rzymski Kościoł *excedit*: we wszytkim tym tęż przyganę nosi y Cerkiew Wschodna."

42. De Dominis 1666: "Protestantes sane . . . non posse secessionis causam legitimam allegare quod Ecclesia Romana sit Schismatica; Illa enim Schisma non fecit, sed passa est."

43. Smotryćkyj 1628a, 113/580: "W rozerwaniu sie abowiem iedney Cerkwie od Cerkwie, ta pomiestna Cerkiew grzech y hańbę Schismy ponosi, ktora nie maiąc słuszney przyczyny, z rozerwaną drugą pomiestną Cerkwią, y wzywana bywszy, ziednoczyć sie nie chce. A słuszna przyczyna tego insza bydź nie może, tylko sama Hęresis."

44. Smotryćkyj 1629a, 23/656: " . . . wiedząc ia to dobrze, że pożyteczneysza iest rzecz bydź w Cerkwi Katholickiey Laikiem, niż w Cerkwi Schizmatyckiey Archiepiskopem, namniey o to nie trwam. Laicy abowiem w Cerkwi Bożey, *legitimi* iey są synowie, y krolestwa niebieskiego przyrodni dziedzice: a Episkopowie w Schizmie y *legitimi* nie są, y dziedzictwa do krolestwa niebieskiego nie maią: *Non potest Deum habere Patrem, qui Ecclesiam non habet Matrem*; mowi Cyprian ś. . . . Przetoż wiedząc ia o tym, na to co mi przekładacie, namniey się nie oglądam, dosyć maiąc na owym powyższeniu, że się w Cerkwi Bożey nayduię; a przez to, mam Cerkiew Pana Chrystusową za matkę, a Boga za oyca: czego w Schizmie y Archiepiskopem będąc, mieć nie mogłem."

45. Typical is Smotryćkyj's reference to "Orthodox blasphemies" and "Roman non-blasphemy" (Smotryćkyj 1629a, 100/573): "Co oboie, to iest, Rzymskie niebluźnierstwo, a swoie bluźnierstwa vważaiąc . . . " Again, I suspect this formulation may owe something to a way of viewing correct faith that Smotryćkyj shared with de Dominis.

46. To cite one example: see Smotryćkyj 1629a, 11/528: "To mię dolegało . . . że ia Episzkop, ba y Archiepiszkop w Cerkwi narodu mego Ruskiego nie wiedziałem com wierzył."

47. See Zasławski's letter to Smotryćkyj of 16 February 1627, cited according to Suša 1666, 45: "Verum meminisse suorum velit verborum, se non a sexennio, sed plusquam a decennio agnouisse errorem, non spiritum Dei in se operatum, cum pestilens scripsisset lamentum; Sed spiritu, pace eius dixerim, ambitionis, spiritu haereseos, quem in scholis attraxisset haereticis. Ecquid ergo Vestra Reuerendissima Paternitas, alios procudit libros? in quibus ea quae in lamento continebantur, confirmabat, collaudabat, et reuoluere cuique suadebat."

48. See Smotryćkyj 1629a, 102–104/574–75: "Vważenie o Cerkwi powszechney y pomiestney."

49. On de Dominis' view of Church order, see Cantimori 1960, 109. Smotryc̄kyj's calls for episcopal councils were constant in his Uniate period. He argued in favor of establishing a local Kievan patriarchate in the *Paraenesis* (51 ff/670 ff) of 1629.

CHAPTER 13

1. Smotryc̄kyj 1629a, 59/674: "Bo ieśli bliźniego swego z roskazania Bożego tak lubić powinni, iak lubią siebie samych, nie wykonawszy tego, winni będą wszytkiemu zakonowi: Aby życząc sobie z Panem Bogiem wiecznego pomieszkania, życzyli tego y nam nie słowy tylo, ale y samą rzeczą; owego zbawicielowego pamiętni, *Compelle intrare*, przymuś wniść; wszelaką nas z sobą tąż y iedną Krolewską drogą do wiecznego żywota wiodącą, iść, ktorą idą sami, aby vbiedził: bocieśmy się po przecznicach y rozdrożu błędow y Hereziy, aż nazbyt porozbłąkiwali."

2. Velykyj 1972, 209–210: "En modum tuae Beatitudini, suggero, eumque planum et pium, facillimum et efficacissimum. Pro auctoritate tua, qua ex Dei instituto polles, nil cunctando, dic caput brachiis tuis quae tibi in hoc praeclarissimo Regno Poloniae sunt, alteri spirituali, alteri saeculari: Fiat in regno Poloniae Unio; et verbo ocius facta conspicietur. Quid enim tu non potes, qui cooperatorem tuum Omnipotentem habes? Qui cum sis fidelis ejus servus et prudens dispensator, super familiam ejus constitutus, ut des illis cibum in tempore, in unum omnes colligere studeas. . . . si ex commissione et mandato brachii spiritualis sacerdotes tum saeculares, tum regulares, qui per singulas Rossiae provincias, paroecias conventus et collegia habent, praecipue vero Societatis Jesu patres: si, inquam, hi dictum tuum hoc unum Fiat ad exsequendum fideliter susceperint, dictum Fiet illico factum: hac ratione. Demandetur sub conscientia sanctae obedientiae singuilis, qui sunt a confessione, neminem istorum absolvant, aut ad SS. Altaris Sacramenti communionem admittant, qui vel verbo vel opere Unionem opprimit, schisma vero promovet. Quales sunt isti schismaticorum intrusorum ultranei patroni, nutritores, defensores, ac proinde schismatis maledicti fautores, et quantum in illis est, promotores."

3. See Bantyš-Kamenskij 1805, 73; Żychiewicz 1986, 162: "zwłaszcza w naszej Rzplitey, gdzie nie służy ono z Euangelii: *compelle intrare.*"

4. See Smotryc̄kyj 1621c, 54/426: " . . . aby nie byli od was przez gwałt zaciągani y przymuszani do posłuszeństwa Biskupa Rzymskiego . . . " and Smotryc̄kyj 1621c, 126/462: "Gwałt y mus, Vniey nierzkąc nie sprawi, ale ani pomnoży."

5. Smotryc̄kyj 1629a, 60/675: "Był tego zdania Augustyn ś. aby nikt do iedności Cerkwie Pana Chrystusowey nie był przymuszany, ale aby się to sprawowało słowy; dysputacyami aby się dowodziło, y racyami aby się

zwyciężało: żebyśmy mowi, zmyślonych Katholikow nie mieli z tych, ktorycheśmy iawnemi znali Heretykami."

6. Smotryc'kyj 1629a, 60–61/675: "Wszakże zdanie to swoie ten ś. Doktor odmienił, y mowi: że to moie zdanie nie słowom tych, ktorzy się mnie w tym sprzeciwiali, ale samym rzeczywisto vkazanym przykładom vstąpić musiało. Napierwey abowiem pokładano było naprzeciwko mnie Miasto moie, ktore wszystko z części Donatowey bywszy, do iedności Katholickiey boiaźnią Praw Cesarskich nawrociło się; ktore teraz tą Donatystow zginienia śmiałością, tak brzydzące się widzimy, że nikt temu wierzyć nie chce, aby kiedy ono w tym zginienia błędzie było. Przypominane też mi były tymże sposobem imienno insze Masta, żem też z samych rzeczy wyrozumiał, iż y do tey sprawy owo słusznie ściągać się może; co iest napisano; *Da sapienti occasionem, et addetur ei sapientia*; day mądremu przyczynę, a przydana mu będzie mądrość." Perhaps Smotryc'kyj also had in mind here section 24 of St. Augustine's *Letter* 185, known as *On the Correction of the Donatists* (*De Correctione Donatistarum Liber seu Epitola CLXXXV*, Migne 1845, 803–804), where just this sort of argument was made based on Lk. 14:22–23. See Schaff 1956, 642: "Wherefore, if the power which the Church has received by divine appointment in its due season, through the religious character and the faith of kings, be the instrument by which those who are found in the highways and hedges—that is, in heresies and schisms—are compelled to come in, then let them not find fault with being compelled."

7. See the report in the *acta* of *Propaganda Fide* dated 29 July 1631 (Velykyj 1953a, 104): "Referente eodem Emin.mo Domino Card. Sancti Sixti, quae Rex Poloniae respondit ad media a Meletio, Archiepiscopo Polocensi rutheno unito, nunc vero Archiepiscopo Hieropolitano, proposita pro Sanctae Unionis Ruthenorum propagatione, Sac. Congregatio, auditis difficultatibus a praefato Rege allegatis, ob quas non est facile eiicere Episcopos, et popos schismaticos ab Episcopatibus et Parochiis, auditaque simul sententia Regis perseverantis in oppugnando Decreto de prohibito transitu Ruthenorum unitorum ad latinum ritum, Sac. Congregatio quoad difficultates circa eiectionem schismaticorum Episcoporum, et poporum nihil rescripsit."

8. Smotryc'kyj 1629a, 58/674: "A w głowach iakom rzekł, obrońcę y promotora ma [i.e., the Union] samego Pana Boga, v ktorego iey na tym samym stanęło, aby się od niego w ten, ktory on sam postanowił czas, przez nawyższą Cerkiewną zwierzchność rzekło, sstań sie; y natychmiast słowo sstanie sie dziełem."

9. Velykyj 1972, 209: "dic caput brachiis tuis quae tibi in hoc praeclarissimo Regno Poloniae sunt, alteri spirituali, alteri saeculari: Fiat in regno Poloniae Unio; et verbo ocius facta conspicietur."

10. Velykyj 1972, 207: "Quid enim aliud est compelle intrare, quam noli permittere opiniosos et obstinatos perire?"

11. For investigations on the formation of Polish national consciousness in the early modern period, see Kot 1938, Tazbir 1971, Tazbir 1978.

12. For investigations on the formation of Ruthenian national consciousness in the early modern period, see Sysyn 1980, Sysyn 1981, Sysyn 1984, Sysyn 1986a, Sysyn 1986b, Sysyn 1990. See also Chynczewska-Hennel 1985, Chynczewska-Hennel 1986, Korduba 1933, Kryp'jakevyč 1966.

13. On the communities of *Slavia Orthodoxa* and *Slavia Romana*, see Picchio 1962; Picchio 1963a; Picchio 1963b.

14. See, for example, the preface to the *Homiliary Gospel* (Smotryc'kyj 1616, '''$^{r-v}$/25–26); Smotryc'kyj 1621c, 90/444. See also the texts cited in Korduba 1933, 54–56 for statements by Smotryc'kyj's contemporaries.

15. Smotryc'kyj 1628a, 196/621: "Ta to Cerkiew nas do swey iedności wzywa, ktora Słowackim narodom ięzykiem Słowieńskim Ś. Liturgię odprawować, y wszytkiego nabożeństwa nim zażywać pozwoliła."

16. Smotryc'kyj 1628a, 6–7/526: "A przynosiłem na tym zbawienia naszego mieyscu y na inszych bezkrewną ofiarę ięzykiem Słowieńskiem, mogszy zwyczaynym tam ięzykiem ofiarować Graeckim, w samy koniec ow, żem za ciebie przenamilszy moy narodzie Ruski y za wszytkie te narody, ktore ięzykiem Słowieńskiem Stworzyciela swego chwalą, wysławiaią, y wielbią, vbłagalnią y grzech oczyszczącą bezkrewną ofiarę z osobliwey mey intentiey przynosił. W ten dobry koniec z umysłu to czyniłem abym wszytkie Słowieńskie narody oraz P. Bogu memu w święty iego Oycowski Przemysł z części mey Kapłańskiey podał y poruczył, prosząc iego świętey dobroci, aby wszytkim nam iakiemi on wie sądami proszone przez niego v Boga Oyca swego IEDNO być, y iak iednymi vstami y iednem sercem wewnątrz Cerkwie iego świętey Przechwalebne y Przeuwielbione Imię Oyca y Syna, y Ś. Ducha chwalić, y wysławić, darować raczył."

17. This was a unicum in Smotryc'kyj's usage, probably a neologism created by analogy with *Żydostwo*, i.e., Judaism. In this passage (Smotryc'kyj 1628a, 103/575), the archbishop was adapting Gal. 1:13–14: as St. Paul had "profited in Judea," so Smotryc'kyj had "profited in Rhossianism."

18. Smotryc'kyj 1629b, 100^{r-v}/802–803: "Były dostatki w Narodzie naszym Ruskim; Są y teraz w Moskiewskim; Szkołom iednak podniesionym być, ni tu v nas, ni tam w Moskwie, P. Bog nie zezwolił." Cf. also the texts cited in Korduba 1933, 42–50.

19. Cf. Smotryc'kyj's words to Lukaris in the Latin and Polish versions: Velykyj 1972, 144–45: "Ipse in perpetua tui memoria hoc tibi ascriptum referes, quod pacis Ecclesiae Christi qui es illi in hoc clarissimo Poloniae regno restitutor et pene iam amissae libertatis gentis Rossiacae restaurator audies"; and Smotryc'kyj 1629a, 94/692: "Sam na wieczną twoię pamiątkę to tobie przypisano być sprawisz, że pokoiu Cerkwie P. Chrystusowey, ktora mu iest w tym Przezacnym Krolestwie Polskim, *restitutor,* y iuż prawie vtraconey wolności w narodzie Ruskim *restaurator,* słynąć będziesz."

20. Smotryc̆kyj 1621b, 59ᵛ/384: "Kogoż to, prze Bog żywy z narodu naszego Ruskiego boleć nie ma? kogo y z społobywatelow iego do *commiseraciey* nie poruszy? Swobodnieyszemi są w tey mierze wszyscy y nieChrześciańscy *sectarze*, ktorzy z wolności Państw tych cieszyć się żadnego przystępu nie maią, niżeli my Naród, iakośmy rzekli wolny, Narod swobodny, Naród w iedney Oyczyźnie z drugiemi dwiema vrodzony, y wszytkie ciężary zarowno z niemi noszący: Naród Pomazańcom Bożym Krolom Panom swoim M. szczyrze wierny, krew swoię na wszelakie ich roskazanie ochotnie rozlewaiący."

21. Smotryc̆kyj 1628a, 9/527: "w Cerkwi naszey w narodzie (mowię) naszym Ruskim . . ."

22. Smotryc̆kyj 1622b, 3ᵛ–4ʳ/513: "Za te pomienione zacnego narodu naszego Ruskiego ku wielkim Xiążętom, Panom swoim, Krolom Ich M. Polskim, uczciwe zadziały y przeważne odwagi dana iest iego od nich wolność, obok Ich M. zarowno z dwiema narodami Polskim y Litewskim w senatorskiey poważności siadać, o dobrym państw ich a oyczyzny swey radzić, y ze wszytkich krolestwa Polskiego dostoieństw, praerogatiw, urzędow zawołania, swobod, praw, y wolności cieszyć się."

23. Smotryc̆kyj 1629a, 31–32/660–61: "Coż na tym Cerkwi Ruskiey zbyło, że tych Metropolitow, nie tylo nie od Patryarchy, ale y nad wolą Patryarchow, sobie poświęcała, y od Papieża poświęconego słuchała? Co to narodowi Ruskiemu, y Prawosławney iego Wierze, prawom iego y świebodom (co wy sobie teraz pretenduiecie) zaszkodziło? Nic. Co zaszkodzić może y teraz, gdy sie dla wielu, wielce słusznych y ważnych, przyczyn, z posłuszeństwa tamtego vchyli: a przykładem tych oto pomienionych narodow, swego sobie Archiepiskopa, abo y Patryarchę vdzielnego vczyni? Nie tylo nic mu to nie zaszkodzi, ale mu wielkie a zbawienne pożytki z sobą poda, oto te: Ziednoczy go z narodem Katholickim, Polskim y Litewskim, w wierze, y w miłości, a przez to oczyści go od tych błędow y Hereziy, Zyzaniow twoich."

24. Smotryc̆kyj 1621b, 63ʳ/387: "zgoda y miłość tych dwu albo trzech Narodow, to iest, Wschodniey y Zachodniey Cerkwie w Państwach Oyczyzny naszey."

25. On the rights and privileges of the Ruthenian nation, see Smotryc̆kyj 1621b, 59ᵛ/384, 61ʳ⁻ᵛ/385–86; Smotryc̆kyj 1622a, 14–15/476–78; Smotryc̆kyj 1622b, 3ᵛ–7ʳ/512–17; Smotryc̆kyj 1629a, 50/670.

26. See, for example, Smotryc̆kyj 1621b, 59ᵛ–61ʳ/384–85.

27. See, for example, Smotryc̆kyj 1610, 15ʳ⁻ᵛ/31–32; Smotryc̆kyj 1621b, 52ᵛ/ 377; Smotryc̆kyj 1628a, 94/570; Smotryc̆kyj 1629a, 49/669, 53–54/671–72; 66/678, 92/691; Smotryc̆kyj 1629b, 100ʳ/802.

28. See, for example, the title page to *Verification of Innocence: Verificatia Niewinności: Y omylnych po wszytkiey Litwie y Białey Rusi rozsianych, żywot y vczciwe cnego Narodu Ruskiego o vpad przyprawić zrządzonych Nowin . . . Chrześciańskie Vprzątnienie.*

29. See Smotryćkyj 1610, ()()()()i^r/13: "Ktora bowiem Religio tak często y gęsto te Apostolskie słowa [1 Tim. 2] wykonywa iako Cerkiew ś. Wschodnia, gdzie żadne nabożeństwo, żadna porządku Cerkiewnego Caeremonia, ani się zacznie ani dokończy, bez oddania prośby do Boga wszechmogącego, za dobre zdrowie y szczęśliwe (z zwycięstwem nad nieprzyiacioły) pomnożenie, panowania Krola I.M." Also Smotryćkyj 1610, 8^v/25: "A do pospolitego narodu w te słowa napomnienie y naukę czynimy: Wszelka Dusza mocam wyższym niechay będzie poddana . . . " Also Smotryćkyj 1622b, 2^v–3^r/512: "Od czasu szczęśliwie przed sześciąset lat zawitałego do krain Ruskich zbawiennego imienia Pana Chrystusowego, gdy przy nim zaraz, za zdarzeniem Boskim, ze Wschodu y taiemnicą krztu św. narod nasz Rusky stał się oświecony, y oboiego zakonu Bogiem natchnionemi pismy stądże, zkąd y krztem św. był nadarzony: od tego samego czasu y tey przełożoney nami Apostolskiey Ewanielskiego zwiastowania nauki stał się nauczony, na ustawiczney to pamięci y w codziennym używaniu maiąc: władzy, ktorą nad sobą od p. Boga postanowioną znał, niwczym się nie zastanawiać, niwczym się nie sprzeciwiać, ale we wszem być iey powolnym, posłusznym, y to co iest dobrego czyniącym,— wszytko to, cokolwiek iey w użytek powinien, ochotnie oddaiącym, tribut y cło, a przy tym boiaźń y cześć."

30. *Sowita* 1621, 80/499: "Szkoły są ieno wy o nich wiedzieć nie chcecie, y o dalszych iest przemysł. Co się tknie ięzyka Słowieńskiego nigdyśmy im nie pogardzali, Ktoś wam omylną sprawę dał y owszem z Ksiąg Słowieńskich przeciwko wam dowodzimy y pilno ie chowamy, kochamy się w nich y owszem z waszey gromady był Ktoś, ktory im wiary dawać nie kazał Ruskiego ięzyka y *publice* na Kazaniach zażywamy y *priuatim* im mawiamy, potwarz żeby u nas był naśmiany."

This seems to have been one of those overreactions that might betray a sense of guilt: Smotryćkyj had not alleged that the Ruthenian language was derided by the Uniates; he said it was derided because of the situation in which the nation found itself. (See Smotryćkyj 1621b, 51^v/376.) Someone else could have done the "deriding." (The Poles, for example.)

31. Smotryćkyj 1621b, 60^{r-v}/384–85: "Ieśliż są prawdziwa Ruś, iakoż maią być y muszą (bo nie iuż zaraz y ze krwie się ten wyradza, kto się w Wierze odmienia: nie iuż kto z Ruskiego Narodu Rzymskiey wiary zostaie, zaraz y z vrodzenia Hiszpanem albo Włochem zostawa, Rusin Szlachetny po staremu. Nie wiara abowiem Rusina Rusinem, Polaka Polakiem, Litwina Litwinem czyni: ale vrodzenie y krew Ruska, Polska, y Litewska:) Ieśli tedy są prawdziwa Ruś, iakoż są: (ktorego narodu y krwie, y przy boku Pomazańca Bożego Kr. P. naszego M. Senatorskim Dostoieństwem vczczoney, z łaski Boga wszechmogącego nie podleysza niż inszych, bo tego należnych dwu Narodow liczba. Ruska przezacna krew temi czasy w Senacie Litewskim Duchownym y Świetskim przodkuie. Ruska przezacna krew, o tych czasiech w powierzeniu swym nieocenione Rzeczyposp. Litewskiey kleynoty ma, Pieczęć, y Buławę.) Ieśli tedy są prawdziwa Ruś, że y po trzecie rzeczemy, iakoż są: iakim prze Bog sercem na zawżdy wiernym, czystym y nigdy niwczym Krolom Ich M. Polskim,

y Wielkim Xiążętom Lit. Panom swoim M. niepodeyźrzanym narodzie swoim tę tak szkaradą zmazę ponosić mogą: Iakiemi vszyma tę przeraźliwą, zdrowie oraz y vczciwe Narodu swego zacnego, na vpad kanceruiącą hańbę słyszeć znoszą?"

32. See, for example, Smotryc̆kyj 1621b, 59^{r-v}/383–84.

33. Smotryc̆kyj 1610, ()()()()iii^r/15: "Świadectwa też tak naszych Graeckich Oycow śś. iako y rożnych Łacińskich Authorow przy boku naznaczyć, a niektorych y samy text ięzykiem Łacińskim (dla tego y z Łacinnikami spor iest) przytoczyć się zdało."

34. Most of Smotryc̆kyj's references to works of the Church Slavonic tradition came from the Uniate period. The theoretical motivation of this program was given by Lev Krevza (1617, A2^v/4): "czego wszystkiego za pomocą Bożą księgami samymi Słowieńskimi dowodzić chcemy, a księgami starożytnymi, niepodeyźrzanemi, iakie y strona przeciwna ma v siebie, albo mieć może, gdy ich po swoich Cerkwiach y Manastyrach poszuka."

35. *Justification of Innocence* was based in its entirety on this argument. See, for example, Smotryc̆kyj 1622b, 3^v–4^r/513: "Za te pomienione zacnego narodu Ruskiego ku wielkim Xiążętom, Panom swoim, Krolom Ich M. Polskim, uczciwe zadziały y przeważne odwagi dana iest iego od nich wolność, obok Ich M. zarowno z dwiema narodami Polskim y Litewskim w senatorskiey poważności siadać, o dobrym państw ich a oyczyzny swey radzić, y ze wszytkich krolestwa Polskiego dostoieństw, praerogatiw, urzędow zawołania, swobod, praw, y wolności cieszyć się. Dano to iest iemu iako rownemu do rownego, iako wolnemu do wolnego narodu Polskiego w społeczność czci y w iedność ciała złączonemu y wcielonemu narodowi: xiążętom, paniętom, szlachcie y rycerstwu, duchownym stanom y świetskim. Dane są tegdyż zaraz y ludziom tegoż narodu condiciey mieyskiey za tegoż poddaństwa wierność, y życzliwości uprzeymość, swoie im prawa y wolności. Ktorą to nieocenioną naszę wolność pospolicie krwią kupionym kleynotem naszym raczymy."

36. See Smotryc̆kyj 1629a, 51/670: "Vnia wszytkie nasze Duchowne y świeckie prawa, świebody y wolności zatrzymać może, ktore teraz nowo Constitucyami renowowane (iak te, ktore Vniey, a nie Nieuniey nalężą) y warowane bywszy, przysięgą następuiących Krolow Polskich stwierdzone będą: a bez Vniey wszytko to nam snadno vpadnie, prze to, iż ta wasza Nieunia Szlachtę nam pewnie y w rychle zwiedzie. Za ktorych z naszey stroney zeszciem, każdy Rzymskiey Religiey Xiążę, Pan, Szlachcic, po maiętnościach swoich, z Cerkwiami, y z nabożeństwem naszym, w poddanych swych to vczni, co ku pomnożeniu Kościoła Rzymskiego, z vciechą sumnienia, będzie lubo. Vczyni toż y Zwierzchność nawyższa, po tytułu iey Miastach, żadnym prawem ludzkim, aby tego nie czyniła, nie będąc zatrzymywana: a prawem Bożym aby to czyniła, pod dusze swey zbawieniem, obowiązana bywszy." See also Smotryc̆kyj 1629a, 54/672.

37. From the Orthodox Smotryc̆kyj (1610, 24ᵛ/41): "Gdzie moie duchowne pokarmy z Ewanielskiey roley zebrane, y powierzoney trzodzie podane? aby wszytkie owieczki iednym pokarmem się karmiły, y iednym się napoiem posiłały, a po cudzych rożnych pastwiskach nie chodzili." From the Uniate Smotryc̆kyj (1629b, 6ᵛ/707): "By nie Rzymskie Postille, nie pokwapił byś sie Krasomowco na Kazalnicę: y gęby Mędrelo rozdziewać nie umiał byś. Cału Besseusza, ktory cię z kazalnicy twey mowić vczy: czegom dobrze świadom." From the Orthodox Smotryc̆kyj (1621c, 125/461): "Mielibyśmy swoy własny Kathechism: mielibyśmy swoie własne y Postille." From the Uniate Smotryc̆kyj (1629b, 101ʳ/803): "Nuż Postille, nuż Żywoty Świętych, y insze tym podobne Cerkiewne dobra?"

38. Smotryc̆kyj 1629a, 31/660: "Co zaszkodzić może y teraz, gdy się dla wielu, wielce słusznych y ważnych, przyczyn, z posłuszeństwa tamtego vchyli: a przykładem tych oto pomienionych narodow, swego sobie Archiepiskopa, abo y Patryarchę vdzielnego vczyni?"

39. Smotryc̆kyj 1629a, 31–32/660–61: "Pożytki zbawienne, ktore Iedność ś. narodowi Ruskiemu z sobą przynosi."

40. Smotryc̆kyj 1629a, 33/661: "Nie tylko tedy to narodowi Ruskiemu, gdyby sobie przykładem inszych naciy Archiepiskopa, abo Patryarchę vdzielnego podniosł, nie szkodziłoby, ale wiele by mu to, y według dusze, y według ciała, pożyteczno było: bo by za tym takim domowym, Cerkiewnym sprawcą, Sobory odprawowały się poważnie, niedostatki Cerkiewne vdostatczyłyby się: y to cobykolwiek Cerkwi było pożyteczno y zbawienno, bez żadnych przeszkod byłoby namawiano, y do skutku przywodzono: y w rychle, da Bog, do tego by przyszło, że z Duchownych Cerkwie Ruskiey obfitości, y inszy tegoż ięzyka y nabożeństwa narodowie, vdostatczyliby się."

41. Smotryc̆kyj 1629a, 56/673: "Patryarcha Alexandriyski tymi czasy w Kairze rezyduie, a iednak Alexandriyski. Y ieśli to prawda, że *ibi Roma, vbi Papa*: zstanie się y to prawda, że *ibi Constantinopolis, vbi oecumenicus Patriarcha*: a Bog nam będzie błogosławił." Smotryc̆kyj 1629a, 51–52/670–71: "Patryarchią Konstantynopolską do ziemie Ruskiey przenieśmy: do czego czas, y pogodę, y przyczynę, a wszytko troie według Boga, y prawdy iego, słuszne mamy. . . . Nowy to zaprawdę śrzodek ku pokoiowi Cerkiewnemu, ale narodowi naszemu Ruskiemu wysoce poczesny: a wszytkiey Cerkwi wschodniey . . . wielce duszezbawienny."

42. Smotryc̆kyj 1628a, *2ᵛ–3ʳ/519: "Widzi abowiem W.X.M. Religiey Graeckiey narody Boskimi niepoiętymi sądami, na trzy stany bydź rozdzielone. Na stan niewolniczy: na stan wolny, a nieuki na stan wolny y vczony. Dobra tego zbawiennego nie spodziewa się W.X.M. ni z niewolnikow, ni z nieukow, tylo z samey nauki, a tey na świebodzie będącey. W ktorym Trzecim postanowieniu W.X.M. Narod nasz Ruski Za łaską Bożą bydź sądzi. . . . narod Moskiewski, acz bądź to świebodny, nieuki iednak, rzeczy tey wszelako niewiadomy, y w tey o Rzymianach opiniey zatwardziały."

43. Smotryćkyj 1629a, 94/692: "Sam na wieczną twoię pamiątkę to tobie przypisano być sprawisz, że pokoiu Cerkwie P. Chrystusowey, ktora mu iest w tym Przezacnym Krolestwie Polskim, *restitutor*, y iuż prawie vtraconey wolności w narodzie Ruskim *restaurator*, słynąć będziesz."

44. Smotryćkyj 1629a, 92/691: "gdzie o nas pieczołowicie przemyślać Wieleb: twoia nie będziesz, w rychle nas od posłuszeństwa swego odstradasz. A to z tey przyczyny, że co przednieysza nasza Ruskiey Religiey Szlachta, to abo prosto do Rzymian, abo do Vnitow, a przy nas iuż rzadki: y to tak, że rodzice z nami, a syny ich y corki, abo z Vnitami, abo z Rzymiany."

45. Smotryćkyj 1629a, 91/690: "Racz pytać o tym y tych, ktorzy tam z naszych zaieżdżaią, iako tych wiele przy posłuszeństwie Wieleb: twey, ktorym prawa, świebody, y wolności, przezacnego tego Krolestwa służą, nad lud pospolity rzeczoną będzie, *Compelle intrare*: a mało y nie słusznie się sstanie."

46. In 1629, in his last work, Smotryćkyj still wrote of the loss of the "Ruthenian nation" to the Roman Catholic Church, among others (Smotryćkyj 1629b, 100ʳ/802): "Te Narody Chrześciańskie, ktore są w niewoli Tureckiey, po więtszey części iuż zTurczały: naszego też Narodu po niemałey części wziął Kościoł Rzymski, po niemałey pourywały go Haeretyctwa, Kalwiństwo, y Aryaństwo, ba y Machometaństwo. Domow Xiążęcych odpadliśmy: Szlachty mało: Paniąt mniey." That is, Smotryćkyj, who insisted on adherence to the decree *De non transitu*, represented the Union as an antidote to creeping Latinization. See also the Orthodox *Defense of the Verification* (Smotryćkyj 1621c, 104–106/451–52).

47. Smotryćkyj 1628a, 112/579: "Acz my mamy gotową zwykłą swoię y w tym vcieczkę, że nie my iesteśmy Schismatykami, ale Rzymianie: A że ich zwierzchność świetska, tą oni bespieczni, sobie właśnie należną hańbą nas hańbią, y swoią sromotą nas sromocą. Sami odszczepieńcami od Cerkwie Wschodniey będąc, nas tym nazwiskiem z potęgi swey, a nie z własności naszey lżą y hańbią."

48. Smotryćkyj 1628a, 127/587: "A ieśli przy tym przykre na nas, y owo słowo, że M. W. społobywatele wasi y witaią y żegnaią Schismatykami, abo odszczepieńcami. Moia rada, a rada, moim zdaniem, zdrowa, nie cierpcie y tey hańby. Heretykiem słynąć w prawie Duchownym, iest w prawie świetskim słynąć wywołańcem. A odszczepieńcem słynąć, iest słynąć *perduellem*: y pokoiu pospolitego turbatorem. Oboie bezecne."

49. Smotryćkyj 1628a, 95/571: "Poswar tedy ten, złego tego naszego iest przyczyną, w ktory my z nierownią zawziąwszy sie, a niezdolnością swoią sprostać mu nie mogszy, do nieprzyiacioł iego o poradę y o ratunek vdaliśmy sie."

50. Smotryćkyj 1628a, 183/614: "Przykład weźmimy z Vniey świetskiey, Korony Polskiey y Wiel: X. Litewskiego, a obaczymy co to za stworzenie iest, Vnia. To Fundament tych dwu państw Vniey, obudwu tym Państwom znać

iednego Pana, w Radzie y w przemyśle o nich, społkować: a każdemu swych iemu własnych Praw świebod y wolności zażywać. Duchowney zaś Vniey Fundament, iednego Cerkwie Pana Chrystusowey znać zwierzchnieyszego Pasterza, z nim w wierze y w miłości społkować: a swoich każdey pomiestney Cerkwi zwyczaiow, Praw, Ceremoniy, y obrządkow, ile do porządku Cerkiewnego zażywać." See also Smotryc̄kyj 1629a, 49–50/669–70.

51. According to the Polish historian Tadeusz Grabowski (1916, 320), after his conversion Smotryc̄kyj came to the conclusion that the state could not exist without religious unity, and that he thus shared the views of Hosius, Powodowski, Sokołowski, and Skarga. If the picture that I have been developing is accurate, then Grabowski has made Smotryc̄kyj's point of departure into his goal: Smotryc̄kyj came to the conclusion that, since the existing Ruthenian Orthodox nation would not be permitted to survive (due to the success of people like Skarga in effecting their view of the Commonwealth), therefore it would be necessary to create a new Rus' that was acceptable to the authorities.

52. *Akty* 1848, 158: "dobrze by, ojcowie, żebyście wy my, a my wy byli, i drogą nami utorowaną chodzili."

53. Smotryc̄kyj 1629a, 60/675: "Nie gwałt czyni lekarz gdy pacyentowi swemu wywinioną z stawu rękę abo nogę, z niemałym iego bolem naciąga: toż się będzie dziać y z nami."

54. Smotryc̄kyj 1628b, Aiiiᵛ/629: "Szkodliwy wrzod niegdy wyrzynan bywa, niegdy wypalon, a patient cierpieć to musi. A ieśli ktory cierpieć nie chce, ale raczey vmrzeć od tego wrzodu zezwala, wiązan takowy od tych, ktorzy o nim pieczołuią, bywa, y poniewolnie krotko trapiony, aby przez niedługą cierpliwość, w dalszy swoy żywot vleczony stawszy sie, bolu iuż więcey nie cierpiał."

55. On Lipsius' contacts with Poles, see Borowski 1977, 247–50.

56. On Lipsius, see Saunders 1955 and Bireley 1990, 72–100.

57. Smotryc̄kyj 1621b, 313: "*Nihil quidquam tam probe aut provide dici potest, quod non vellicare malignitas possit.* Nic nigdy tak ostrożnie y cale wyrzec się nie może, czego by złość sczypać nie mogła."

58. Lipsius 1610, 79–80: "Ergo firmiter haec nostra sententia est, Vnam religionem in vno regno servari. Quaeri tamen duo possunt: Semperne puniendi qui dissentiunt, et An omnes? Qua de re vt disseram, non Curiositas me impellit, sed publica Vtilitas, et praesens hic Europae status, quem nego me sine lacrimis intueri. O melior mundi pars, quas dissidiorum faces religio tibi accendit! Colliduntur inter se Christianae reipub. capita, et milleni aliquot homines perierunt ac pereunt per speciem Pietatis. Quis hic silebit? non ego. . . . Nec quidquam tam probe aut prouide hic dici, *quod non vellicare malignitas possit.*"

59. See Smotryc̄kyj 1629b, 94ᵛ/797: "Wzięło pospolstwo gorę: tak pląsać

muszą dziś Popi, iako im graią chłopi. Nie zachceszli; vkazuią obuchi: straszą niebespieczeństwy: grożą śmiercią."

60. Šmurlo 1928, 35: "vellent subesse immediate Patriarchae Constantinopolitano, mediate autem Summo Pontifici . . . "

CONCLUSIONS

1. Kortycki 1634, C4ᵛ: "Sam s sobą Meletius, Sam z sobą srogą woynę co dzień, co godzina, co moment toczył."

2. See, for example, Golubev 1883a, 145–46.

3. Smotryc'kyj 1628a, 139/592: "czterdziestą niemal laty przed Soborem Florentskim, wiele Philosophow Graeckich . . . okrucieństwa Tureckiego boiąc sie, a Oyczyzny swey Gręckiego Państwa zniewolenie, iakoby iuż przytomne widząc, do ziemi Włoskiey vdali sie, y tam, (podczas Schismy miedzy Graekami y Rzymiany,) iedność z Cerkwią Rzymską przyiąwszy, żywota swego dokończyli. . . . Po ktorych Mędrcow z Gręciey vstąpieniu, vstąpiły zaraz y Atheny Graeckie, a do Włoch sie za niemi przeniosły, y tam sie vfundowały. Ci abowiem Grękowie, po wszytkich zachodnych K[r]ainach nauki Gręckie, ktore y do dziś dzień kwitną, vkorzenili."

4. Smotryc'kyj 1629a, 3/646: " . . . abym vprzątnął tę o sobie suspicyą . . . że mię owi vdaią za Vnita; a drudzy, że coś nowego zamyślam: y tak na trzecią część Ruś rozerwać pokuszam się."

5. Smotryc'kyj 1629a, 78/684: " . . . z Rzymiany lub z Ewangelikami nam iest zgoda, lub też co trzeciego średniego my trzymamy y wyznawamy."

6. Smotryc'kyj 1629b, 7ᵛ–8ʳ/708: "Gdyżem Cognitione speciali nie wiedział, ktora by Wiara, tą czystą y niepokalaną wiarą była. Ta, ktorą ia, y Ci naszy przede mną scriptorowie opisaliśmy: lub ta, na ktorą nam vkazowały rescripta Unitskie: Abo też ktora insza, trzecia."

7. Smotryc'kyj 1628a, *2ᵛ/519: " . . . zażywaiąc sposobow, ktore by y Kościoła Rzymskiego ku W.X.M. nie obrażały, y Wschodney Cerkwie molestne być nie zdały sie: idąc medio tutissimus."

8. Smotryc'kyj 1629a, 77/683: "Trydentskiegoli Synodu o tych Boskich rzeczach vchwała ma mi bydź w naśladowaniu, lub też ta strona, naprzeciwko ktorey ten Synod w tych wiary Artykułach pracował."

9. Smotryc'kyj 1618, Ъ1ʳ: "Братїе мои измроша, Іаков[ъ] в[ъ] Вилни, Стефан[ъ] в Краковѣ, Ніколай в Кіевѣ."
Smotryc'kyj, of course, differed from the Romantic poet in that Mickiewicz's view of the Federation was party-line Uniate-Roman Catholic. Cf. the "Modlitwa Pielgrzyma" at the end of the Księgi pielgrzymstwa polskiego (Mickiewicz

1955, 59): "Matko Boska, którą ojcowie nasi nazwali królową Polski i Litwy,/ Zbaw Polskę i Litwę./Święty Stanisławie, opiekunie Polski,/Módl się za nami./ Święty Kazimierzu, opiekunie Litwy,/Módl się za nami./Święty Jozafacie, opiekunie Rusi, módl się za nami."

10. See the works of Cantimori (1958 and 1960), as well as Clark 1968; Patterson 1978; Malcolm 1984.

11. Smotryc′kyj cited from Cassander's *Consultatio de Articulis Religionis inter Catholicos et Protestantes Controversis* (1577) in *Thrēnos* (()()iv^v/9). On attempts of Cassander (to whom Smotryc′kyj referred as a "Roman doctor") to mediate between Protestants and Catholics, see Bröder 1931; Kantzenbach 1957.

12. See Podskalsky 1988, 229–36 and the literature cited there on Mohyla's doctrinal writings.

Smotryc'kyj's Letters

1. Mižhirrja, 29 August/8 September 1626. To the abbess and nuns of the Vilnius convent. In Ruthenian. Golubev 1883b, 285–87.

2. Dubno, 6 July 1627. To Urban VIII. In Latin. Velykyj 1972, 125–26.

3. Dubno, 6 July 1627. To Cardinal Ottavio Bandini. In Latin. Velykyj 1972, 126–27.

4. Dubno, 6 July 1627. To the Holy Office. In Latin. Velykyj 1972, 127–29 (third-person summary).

5. Derman', 21 August 1627. To Cyril Lukaris. In Latin. Velykyj 1972, 130–45. (Polish version: Smotryc'kyj 1628c, 63–96.)

6. Derman', after 20 October/30 October 1627. To the Vilnius Brotherhood. In Ruthenian. *Arxiv* 1883, 605–607.

7. Before 5 November 1627. To *Propaganda Fide*. In Latin. Šeptyc'kyj 1971, 632.

8. Derman', 2 March/12 March 1628. To Josyf Ruc'kyj. In Ruthenian. Kojalovič 1861, 366–73.

9. Derman' (?), April(?) 1628. To Jov Borec'kyj. In Polish. Smotryc'kyj 1628b, Aiii^r–iv^r/628–29.

10. Derman' (?), April(?) 1628. To Peter Mohyla. In Polish. Smotryc'kyj 1628b, Aiv^{r-v}/629–30.

11. Kiev, 14 August/24 August 1628. To Jov Borec'kyj. In Polish. Smotryc'kyj 1628b, Bii^{r-v}/631–32.

12. Kiev, 14 August/24 August 1628. To Jov Borec'kyj. In Ruthenian. *Akty* 1865, 76–77. (Polish version: Smotryc'kyj 1628b, Bii^(r-v)/632–33.)

13. Derman', 28 September/8 October 1628. To Lavrentij Drevyns'kyj. In Ruthenian. Golubev 1883b, 317–22.

14. Before 10 November 1628. To *Propaganda Fide*. In Latin. Velykyj 1972, 172–73.

15. Derman', 25 July/4 August 1629. To Oleksander Puzyna. In Polish. Diplic 1633, 434–35.

16. Mižhirrja, 28 August/7 September 1629. To the Mahilëŭ Brotherhood. In Ruthenian. *Akty* 1865, 77–78.

17. Derman', 30 October 1629. To Cyril Lukaris. In Latin. Velykyj 1972, 186–97.

18. Derman', 16 February 1630. To Urban VIII. In Latin. Velykyj 1972, 204–211.

19. Derman', 12 July 1631. To Ludovico Ludovisi. In Latin. Velykyj 1972, 222–24.

20. Volodymyr, 16 June 1631. To *Propaganda Fide*. In Latin. Velykyj 1972, 224–25.

Smotryc'kyj's Critical Use of Biblical Citations

1. Sources for Smotryc'kyj's Polish Biblical Citations (see p. 197):

   a. Leviticus 23:10

   Smotryc'kyj 1610, 142ᵛ/159: Gdy wnidziecie do ziemie ktorą ia wam dam, a będziecie żąć zboże, przyniesiecie snopy z kłosami do Kapłana, pierwiasnki żniwa waszego.

   Leopolita 1577: Gdy wnidziecie do ziemie ktorą ia wam dam, a będziecie żąć zboże, przyniesiecie snopy z kłosami do Kapłana, pierwiasnki żniwa waszego.

   Leopolita 1561: Gdy iuż wnidziecie do tey ziemie ktorą ia wam dam, a będziecie żąć zboże, przyniesiecie snopy wasse s kłosami do kapłana, iakoby pierwiasnki żniwa wassego.

   Wujek 1599: Gdy wnidziecie do ziemie, ktorą ia wam dam, y pożniecie zboże: przyniesiecie snopy kłosow pierwociny żniwa waszego do kapłana.

   b. Exodus 13:7

   Smotryc'kyj 1629b, 44ᵛ/745: Praśniki ieść będziecie przez siedm dni. Nie vkaże sie v ciebie nic kwaśnego: ani we wszytkich granicach twoich.

   Wujek 1599: Praśniki ieść będziecie przez siedm dni: nie vkaże się v ciebie nic kwaszonego, ani we wszytkich granicach twoich.

   Leopolita 1577: Przasny chleb będziecie ieść siedm dni, nie będzie naleziono v ciebie nic kwaszonego, ani po wszyskich granicach twoich.

c. Matthew 22:12

Smotryc'kyj 1629b, 16ʳ/716: Przyiacielu iakoś tu wszedł nie maiąc odzienia wesela?

Wujek 1593: Przyiacielu, iakoś tu wszedł nie maiąc odzienia wesela?

Leopolita 1577: Przyiacielu, iakoś ty tu wszedł nie maiąc odzienia godownego?

2. The Orthodox Smotryc'kyj's Corrections of the Polish New Testament according to Greek Scripture (see p. 200):

a. Luke 22:7

Smotryc'kyj 1610, 146ᵛ/163: w ktory było potrzeba ofiarować Baranka Wielkonocnego.

Leopolita 1577: w ktory było trzeba zabić BAranka Wielkonocnego.

The Greek text: ᾗ δεῖ ἐθύεσθαι τὸ πάσχα

The Latin text: in qua necesse erat occidi pascha.

The Leopolita correctly rendered the Latin *occidi* with *zabić*; Smotryc'kyj rendered the Greek ἐθύεσθαι with *ofiarować*.

b. 2 Peter 3:10

Smotryc'kyj 1610, 160ʳ/176: Przyidzieć Pański dzień, iako złodziey w nocy.

Leopolita 1577: Przyidzieć Pański dzień iako złodziey.

The Greek text: ἥξει δὲ ἡμέρα κυρίου ὡς κλέπτης ἐν νυκτί

The Latin text: Adveniet autem dies Domini ut fur.

Smotryc'kyj added *w nocy*, which had an equivalent in the Greek edition of Estienne, but which is lacking in the Clementina and in most other Latin editions.

3. Smotryc'kyj's Corrections of Old Testament Scripture (see p. 201):

a. Proverbs 12:19

Smotryc'kyj 1622a, Aiᵛ/424: Labium veritatis firmum erit in perpetuum.

Prawdziwe wargi trwałe będą na wieki.

Wujek 1599: Warga prawdy trwała będzie na wieki.

The Greek text: χείλη ἀληθινὰ κατορθοῖ μαρτυρίαν

Wujek rendered the singular genitival construction *labium veritatis* with *warga prawdy*; Smotryc'kyj rendered the plural adjectival construction χείλη ἀληθινὰ with *prawdziwe wargi.*

4. The Uniate Smotryc'kyj's Corrections of the Polish Bible According to Greek Scripture (see p. 203):

   a. Matthew 8:31

   Smotryc'kyj1628a, 39/543: ieśli wyrzucasz nas ztąd, poślisz nas w stado wieprzow.

   Wujek 1599: Ieśli nas wyrzucasz ztąd, puść nas w stado wieprzśw.

   The Greek text: εἰ ἐκβάλλεις ἡμᾶς, ἀπόστειλον εἰς ἡμᾶς τὴν ἀγέλην τῶν χοίρων.

   The Latin text: Si eicis nos hinc, mitte nos in gregem porcorum.

   Smotryc'kyj corrected *puść* to *pośli* in accordance with *mitte/* ἀπόστειλον.

   b. Exodus 12:19 and 13:7

   Smotryc'kyj 1629b, 44ᵛ/745: Ktoby iadł kwaśne *w te dni*, zginie dusza iego.

   Wujek 1599: ktoby iadł kwaszone, zginie dusza iego.

   The Greek text: πᾶς, ὃς ἂν φάγῃ ζυμωτόν, ἐξολεθρευθήσεται ἡ ψυχὴ ἐκείνη.

   The Latin text: qui commederit fermentatum, peribit anima eius.

   Smotryc'kyj 1629b, 44ᵛ/745: Nie vkaże sie v ciebie nic kwaśnego.

   Wujek 1599: nie vkaże sie v ciebie nic kwaszonego.

   The Greek text: οὐκ ὀφθήσεταί σοι ζυμωτόν.

   The Latin text: non apparebit apud te aliquid fermentatum.

Wujek rendered the Latin passive participle *fermentatum* with the equivalent *kwaszone*. Smotryc'kyj rendered the Greek adjective ζυμωτόν with the equivalent *kwaśne*. (The words *w te dni* in the first example were an addition to aid the sense and appeared in italics.)

5. Smotryc'kyj Citation of Greek Scripture in Favor of Purgatory (see p. 204):

   a. Luke 16:23

   Smotryc'kyj 1629b, 41ᵛ/742: Et in inferno (iak w Graeckim texcie stoi) eleuans oculos suos, Cum esset in tormentis. A w adzie podniozszy Oczy swoie, gdy był w mękach.

   The Greek text: . . . καὶ ἐτάφη. καὶ ἐν τῷ ᾅδη ἐπάρας τοὺς ὀφθαλμοὺς αὐτοῦ, ὑπάρχων ἐν βασάνοις.

   The Latin text: . . . et sepultus est in inferno. Elevans autem oculos suos, cum esset in tormentis.

6. Smotryc'kyj's Corrections of Church Slavonic Scripture (Relative to the Ostroh Bible; see p. 204):

   a. Psalms 101:3

   Smotryc'kyj 1618, Ҁ3ᵣ: Вонже аще день скорблю . . . вонже аще день призову тя.

   Ostroh 1581: воньже днь аще скорблю . . . воньже днь аще призову тя.

   The Greek text: ἐν ᾗ ἂν ἡμέρᾳ θλίβωμαι . . . ἐν ᾗ ἂν ἡμέρᾳ ἐπικαλέσωμαί σε.

   The Latin text: in quacumque die tribulor . . . In quacumque die invocavero te.

   Smotryc'kyj brought the the word order more or less in line with the Greek and the Latin.

   b. Matthew 24:3

   Smotryc'kyj 1618, Б8ᵣ: и что [есть] знаменіе твоего пришествіа и кончины вѣка;

   Ostroh 1581: и что есть знаменіе твоего пришествіа и кончина вѣка;

The Greek text: καὶ τί τὸ σημεῖον τῆς σῆς παρουσίας καὶ συντελείας τοῦ αἰῶνος;

The Latin text: et quod signum adventus tui, et consummationis saeculi?

Smotryc'kyj used brackets (following the rule given in the grammar) to show that [есть] was an addition to aid the sense. The word did not appear in either the Greek or the Latin text. In addition, Smotryc'kyj corrected the nominative кончина to the genitive кончины in accordance with *consummationis*/συντελείας.

c. Romans 4:16

Smotryc'kyj 1618, Ц4ᵛ: Не еже точію сущему от закона.

Ostroh 1581: не еже точію сущим от закона.

The Greek text: οὐ τῷ ἐκ τοῦ νόμου μόνον.

The Latin text: non ei, qui ex lege est solum.

Smotryc'kyj rendered the masculine dative singular *ei*/τῷ correctly with *сущему*.

Works Cited

Akty istoričeskie, otnosjaščiesja k Rossii sobrany v inostrannyx arxivax i bibliotekax i izdany Arxeografičeskoju komissieju. 1848. *Dopolnenija.* St. Petersburg.

Akty, izdavaemye Vilenskoj arxeografičeskoj komissieju. 1875. 1900. Vol. 8. Vol. 27. Vilnius.

Akty, otnosjaščiesja k istorii južnoj i zapadnoj Rossii. 1865. Vol. 2, *1599–1637*. St. Petersburg.

Aničenko, V.V. 1973. "Moskovskoe izdanie grammatiki M. Smotrickogo." *Russkaja reč'* 5:104–110.

Antelenchus, To iest odpis na skrypt vszczypliwy zakonnikow Cerkwie odstępney Ś. Ducha, Elenchus nazwany. 1622. Vilnius. [Reprint: *Arxiv* 1914:674–731. (The edition I consulted had a pagination different from that indicated by the editors of the *Arxiv*; apparently there was more than one edition that bore the date 1622.)]

Anuškin, A.I. 1962. *Vo slavnom meste Vilenskom. Očerki iz istorii knigopečatanija.* Moscow.

—————. 1970. *Na zare knigopečatanija v Litve.* Vilnius.

Apolleia Apolohii Knyžky. 1628. Kiev. [Reprint: Golubev 1883b:302–317.]

Arxeografičeskij sbornik dokumentov otnosjaščixsja k istorii severozapadnoj Rusi. 1867. 1869. 1870. Vol. 2. Vol. 6. Vol. 9. Vilnius.

Arxiv jugozapadnoj Rossii. 1883. 1887. 1893. 1914. Part 1, vol. 6. Part 1, vol. 7. Part 1, vol. 9. Part 1, vol. 8. Kiev.

Askočenskij, V.I. 1856. *Kiev s drevnejšim ego učiliščem akademieju.* Kiev.

Bainton, Roland H. 1963. "The Bible in the Reformation." In *The West from the Reformation to the Present Day,* ed. S.L. Greenslade, pp. 1–37. Cambridge. [=*The Cambridge History of the Bible.* Vol. 3.]

Bantyš-Kamenskij [Bantyš-Kamins'kyj], N. 1805. *Istoričeskoe izvestie o voznikšej v Pol'še Unii.* Vilnius.

Baumann, H. 1956–1957. "Slavica in der Universitätsbibliothek Jena: Die 'Slavische Grammatik' des Meletij Smotrickij vom Jahre 1619." *Wissenschaftliche Zeitschrift der Friedrich-Schiller-Universität Jena* 6:63–68.

—————. 1958. "Das Erscheinungsjahr der 'Slawischen Grammatik' Meletij Smotrickijs." *Zeitschrift für Slawistik* 3:682–85.

Bentley, Jerry H. 1976. "Erasmus' *Annotationes in Novum Testamentum* and the Textual Criticism of the Gospels." *Archiv für Reformationsgeschichte* 67:33–53.

————. 1977. "Biblical Philology and Christian Humanism: Lorenzo Valla and Erasmus as Scholars of the Gospels." *Sixteenth-Century Journal* 8 (2): 9–28.

————. 1978. "Erasmus, Jean Le Clerc, and the Principle of the Harder Reading." *Renaissance Quarterly* 31:309–321.

————. 1979. "New Testament Scholarship at Louvain in the Early Sixteenth Century." *Studies in Medieval and Renaissance History,* n. s. 2:51–79.

————. 1983. *Humanists and Holy Writ: New Testament Scholarship in the Renaissance.* Princeton.

Berger, Samuel. 1879. *La Bible au seizième siècle. Étude sur les origines de la critique biblique.* Paris.

Berynda, Pamvo. 1961. *Leksykon slovenoros'kyj.* Ed. V.V. Nimčuk. Kiev.

Beumer, J. 1950. "Heilige Schrift und kirchliche Lehrautorität." *Scholastik* 25:40–72.

Bireley, Robert. 1990. *The Counter-Reformation Prince: Anti-Machiavellianism or Catholic Statecraft in Early Modern Europe.* Chapel Hill, North Carolina.

Birkowski, Fabian. 1629. *Głos krwie B. Iozaphata Kuncewicza, Archiepiskopa Połockiego.* Cracow.

Borowski, Andrzej. 1977. "Polska a Niderlandy. Związki i analogie kulturalne i literackie w dobie humanizmu, renesansu oraz baroku." In *Literatura staropolska w kontekście europejskim (związki i analogie). Materiały konferencji naukowej poświęconej zagadnieniom komparatystyki (27–29 X 1975),* ed. Teresa Michałowska and Jan Ślaski, pp. 233–52. Wrocław.

Bröder, Paula. 1931. *Georg Cassanders Vermittlungsversuche zwischen Protestanten und Katholiken.* Marburg.

Bystroń, J.S. 1930. *Polacy w Ziemi Świętej, Syrji i Egipcie.* Cracow.

Cantimori, Delio. 1958. "Su M.A. De Dominis." *Archiv für Reformationsgeschichte* 49:245–58.

————. 1960. "L'utopia ecclesiologica di M.A. De Dominis." In *Problemi di vita religiosa in Italia nel Cinquecento. Atti del Convegno di storia della chiesa in Italia (Bologna, 2–6 sett. 1958).* Padua. [=Italia sacra: Studi e documenti di storia ecclesiastica. Vol. 2.]

Čexovyč, Konstantyn. 1934. "Meletij Smotryc'kyj jak hramatyk." In *Zbirnyk prysvjačenyj svitlij pamjati Meletija Smotryc'koho z nahody trysotnix rokovyn smerty.* Ed. Mykola Čubatyj, pp. 49–63. L'viv. [=Arxiv Seminara Istoriji Cerkvy pry Hrekokatolyc'kij Bohoslovs'kij Akademiji u L'vovi. Vol. 1.]

Chynczewska-Hennel, Teresa. 1985. *Świadomość narodowa szlachty ukraińskiej i kozaczyzny od schyłku XVI do połowy XVII w.* Warsaw.

————. 1986. "The National Consciousness of Ukrainian Nobles and Cossacks from the End of the Sixteenth to the Mid-Seventeenth Century." *Harvard Ukrainian Studies* 10:377–92.

Clark, David L. 1968. "Marco Antonio de Dominis and James I: The Influence of a Venetian Reformer on the Church of England." In *Papers of the Michigan Academy of Science, Arts, and Letters.* Vol. 53. Ann Arbor, pp. 219–30.

Concilium Tridentinum, diariorum, actorum, epistularum, tractatuum nova collectio. 1901. 1911. Freiburg im Breisgau. Vol. 1. Vol. 5.

Corpus scriptorum ecclesiasticorum latinorum. 1891. Vol. 25. Vienna.

Crehan, F. J. 1978. "The Bible in the Roman Catholic Church from Trent to the Present Day." In *The West from the Reformation to the Present Day,* ed. S. L. Greenslade, pp. 199–237. Cambridge. [=*The Cambridge History of the Bible.* Vol. 3.]

Čubatyj, Mykola. 1934. "Slovo pro Meletija Smotryc'koho." In *Zbirnyk prysvjačenyj svitlij pamjati Meletija Smotryc'koho z nahody trysotnix rokovyn smerty,* ed. Mykola Čubatyj, pp. 3–8. L'viv. [=Arxiv Seminara Istoriji Cerkvy pry Hrekokatolyc'kij Bohoslovs'kij Akademiji u L'vovi. Vol. 1.]

Czechowic, Marcin, transl. 1577. *Nowy Testament. To iest Wszytkie pisma nowego Przymierza, z Greckiego ięzyka na rzecz Polską wiernie y szczerze przełożone. Przydane iest rożne czytanie na brzegach, ktore się w inszych księgach nayduie: y Reiestr na końcu.* Cracow.

D'Amico, John F. 1988. *Theory and Practice in Renaissance Textual Criticism: Beatus Rhenanus between Conjecture and History.* Berkeley.

De Dominis, Marcantonio. 1618. 1620. *De Republica Ecclesiastica.* Pt. 1, bks. 1, 2, and 3. Heidelberg. Pt. 2, bks. 4 and 5. Frankfurt.

————. 1973. *The Second Manifesto* (Liège, 1623). Facsimile reprint: English Recusant Literature. Selected and edited by D.M. Rogers. Vol. 128. Yorkshire.

————. 1978. *M. Antonius de Dominis Archbishop of Spalato Declares the Cause of His Returne, Out of England* (Rome, 1623). Facsimile reprint: English Recusant Literature. Selected and edited by D.M. Rogers. Vol. 363. Yorkshire.

Demjanovič, A. 1871. "Iezuity v Zapadnoj Rossii." *Žurnal Ministerstva narodnogo prosveščenija* 156:181–236; 157:1–46, 250–79; 158:40–86, 181–231.

Dietze, J. 1974. "Eine gekürzte bearbeitete Faßung der Grammatik von Smotrickij aus dem Jahre 1638." *Zeitschrift für Slawistik* 19:364–76.

Diplic, Gelazjusz. 1633. *Antapologia.* Raków(?).

Dobrjanskij, F. 1882. *Opisanie rukopisej Vilenskoj publičnoj biblioteki.* Vilnius.

Drzymała, Kazimierz. 1948. "Ks. Stanisław Grodzicki T.J. jako teolog i kaznodzieja 1541–1613." *Polonia Sacra* 1:267–88.

—————. 1951. "Wpływ ks. Stanisława Grodzickiego T.J. na tłumaczenie Biblii ks. Jakuba Wujka T.J." *Polonia Sacra* 4: 71–80.

Dylevskij, N.M. 1958. "Grammatika Meletija Smotrickogo u bolgar v èpoxu ix vozroždenija." *Trudy Otdela drevnerusskoj literatury* 14:461–73.

Elenevskij, K.S. 1861. "Meletij Smotrickij, arxiepiskop polockij." *Pravoslavnoe obozrenie* 5 (6): 111–50; 5 (7): 172–98; 5 (8): 422–54.

Emmi, B. 1953a. "Il Decreto Tridentino sulla Vulgata nei commenti della prima polemica protestanto-cattolica." *Angelicum* 30:107–130.

—————. 1953b. "Il Decreto Tridentino sulla Volgata nei commenti della seconda polemica protestantico-cattolica." *Angelicum* 30:228–72.

—————. 1953c. "Senso e portato del decreto tridentino sulla Volgata nelle due polemiche protestantico-cattoliche." *Angelicum* 30:347–74.

Evgenij [Bolxovitinov]. 1827. *Slovar' istoričeskij o byvšix v Rossii pisateljax duxovnogo čina Greko-Rossijskoj cerkvi.* Vol. 2. St. Petersburg.

Examen Obrony, To iest Odpis na Script Obrony Werificatij nazwany. 1621. Vilnius. [Reprint: *Arxiv* 1914:562–96.]

Fedoriv, Jurij. 1974. "Kobryns'kyj Synod 1626 r. (Krytyčnyj ohljad doby i sytuaciji)." *Bohoslovija* 38:5–91.

Fedyšyn, Ivan. 1934. "Meletij Smotryc'kyj ta joho unijna dijal'nist'." In *Zbirnyk prysvjačenyj svitlij pamjati Meletija Smotryc'koho z nahody trysotnix rokovyn smerty,* ed. Mykola Čubatyj, pp. 8–37. L'viv. [=Arxiv Seminara Istoriji Cerkvy pry Hrekokatolyc'kij Bohoslovs'kij Akademiji u L'vovi. Vol. 1.]

Finocchiaro, Maurice A., ed. 1989. *The Galileo Affair: A Documentary History.* Berkeley.

Frick, David A. 1984. "Meletij Smotryc'kyj and the Ruthenian Question in the Early Seventeenth Century." *Harvard Ukrainian Studies* 8:351–75.

—————. 1985. "Meletij Smotryc'kyj and the Ruthenian Language Question." *Harvard Ukrainian Studies* 9:25–52.

—————. 1986. "The Beinecke Copy of Smotricky's *Grammatiki Slavenskije Pravilnoe Suntagma.*" In *Studia Slavica Mediaevalia et Humanistica Riccardo Picchio Dicata,* ed. M. Colucci, G. Dell'Agata, and H. Goldblatt, pp. 273–77. Rome.

—————. 1987. "Meletij Smotryc'kyj's *Thrēnos* of 1610 and Its Rhetorical Models." *Harvard Ukrainian Studies* 11:462–86.

————. 1988. "Petro Mohyla's Revised Version of Meletij Smotryc'kyj's Ruthenian *Homilary Gospel*." In *American Contributions to the Tenth International Congress of Slavists*. Vol. 1, *Linguistics*, ed. Alexander M. Schenker, pp. 107–120. Columbus.

————. 1989. *Polish Sacred Philology in the Reformation and the Counter-Reformation: Chapters in the History of the Controversies (1551–1632)*. University of California Publications in Modern Philology. Vol. 123. Berkeley.

————. 1991. "*Fides Meletiana*: Marc.ntonio de Dominis and Meletij Smotryc'kyj." *Harvard Ukrainian Studies* 15:383–414.

Garofalo, S. 1946. "Gli umanisti italiani del secolo XV e la Bibbia." *Biblica* 27:338–75.

Gil'tebrandt, Petr, ed. 1878. 1882. 1903. *Pamjatniki polemičeskoj literatury v Zapadnoj Rusi*. Vol. 1. Vol. 2. Vol. 3. St. Petersburg. [=Russkaja istoričeskaja biblioteka. Vol. 4. Vol. 7. Vol. 19.]

Ginzburg, Carlo. 1970. *Il Nicodemismo. Simulazione e dissimulazione religiosa nell'Europa del '500*. Turin.

————. 1982. *The Cheese and the Worms. The Cosmos of a Sixteenth-Century Miller*. New York.

————. 1985. *Night Battles. Witchcraft and Agrarian Cults in the Sixteenth and Seventeenth Centuries*. New York.

Golubev, Stefan Timofeevič. 1876. "Bibliografičeskie zamečanija o nekotoryx staropečatnyx cerkovno-slavjanskix knigax, preimuščestvenno konca XVI i XVII stoletij." *Trudy Kievskoj duxovnoj akademii* 1:121–61; 2:359–98.

————. 1877. "Okružnoe poslanie uniatskogo mitropolita Veliamina Rutskogo s izveščeniem ob obstojatel'stvax, predšestvovavšix i soprovoždavšix smert' Meletija Smotrickogo." *Kievskie eparxial'nye vedomosti* 3:62–70.

————. 1883a. 1883b. 1889. *Kievskij Mitropolit Petr Mogila i ego spodvižniki. (Opyt istoričeskago issledovanija.)* Vol. 1. Vol. 1, *Priloženija (=Materialy dlja istorii Zapadnorusskoj cerkvi)*. Vol. 2. Kiev.

Górnicki, Łukasz. 1954. *Dworzanin polski*. Ed. Roman Pollak. Wrocław. [=Biblioteka narodowa, series 1, vol. 109.]

Grabowski, T. 1916. "Ostatnie lata Melecjusza Smotryckiego: Szkic z dziejów literatury unicko-prawosławnej wieku XVII." In *Księga pamiątkowa ku czci Bolesława Orzechowicza*. Vol. 1, pp. 297–327. L'viv.

Grafton, Anthony. 1975. "Joseph Scaliger's Edition of Catullus (1577) and the Traditions of Textual Criticism in the Renaissance." *Journal of the Warburg and Courtauld Institutes* 38:155–81.

————. 1977. "On the Scholarship of Politian and its Context." *Journal of the Warburg and Courtauld Institutes* 40:150–88.

————. 1983. *Joseph Scaliger: A Study in the History of Classical Scholarship.* Vol. 1. Oxford.

————. 1991. *Defenders of the Text. The Traditions of Scholarship in an Age of Science, 1450–1800.* Cambridge, Massachusetts.

Hall, Basil. 1970. "Erasmus: Biblical Scholar and Reformer." In *Erasmus,* ed. Th. Dorey, pp. 81–114. London.

————. 1978. "Biblical Scholarship: Editions and Commentaries." In *The West from the Reformation to the Present Day,* ed. S.L. Greenslade, pp. 38–93. Cambridge. [=*The Cambridge History of the Bible.* Vol. 3.]

Harbison, E. Harris. 1956. *The Christian Scholar in the Age of the Reformation.* New York.

Hering, Gunnar. 1968. *Ökumenisches Patriarchat und europäische Politik 1620–1638.* Wiesbaden.

Hofmann, Georg. 1929. *Griechische Patriarchen und römische Päpste. Untersuchungen und Texte.* II. *Patriarch Kyrillos Lukaris und die römische Kirche.* Orientalia Christiana 15:1, num. 52. Rome.

Holeczek, Heinz. 1975. *Humanistische Bibelphilologie als Reformproblem bei Erasmus von Rotterdam, Thomas More und William Tyndale.* Leiden.

Höpfl, Hildebrand. 1908. *Kardinal Wilhelm Sirlets Annotationen zum Neuen Testament. Eine Verteidigung der Vulgata gegen Valla und Erasmus.* Biblische Studien 13. Freiburg im Breisgau.

Horbatsch, Olexa. 1964. *Die Vier Ausgaben der kirchenslavischen Grammatik von M. Smotryćkyj.* Wiesbaden.

Indicium, to iest, pokazanie Cerkwie prawdziwey. 1638. Vinnycja. [Reprint: *Arxiv* 1914:762–98. I cite from the reprint.]

Isaievych [Isajevič], Jaroslav. 1981. *Preemniki pervopečatnika.* Moscow.

Jaremenko, P.K. 1984. "Do pytannja pro evoljuciju svitohljadu Meletija Smotryc'koho." In *Ukrajins'ka literatura XVI–XVIII st. ta inši slov'janski literatury,* ed. O.V. Myšanyč, pp. 96–116. Kiev.

————. 1986. *Meletij Smotryc'kyj. Žyttja i tvorčist'.* Kiev.

Jarrott, C. A. L. 1970. "Erasmus' Biblical Humanism." *Studies in the Renaissance* 17:119–52.

Kantzenbach, Friedrich Wilhelm. 1957. *Das Ringen um die Einheit der Kirche im Jahrhundert der Reformation. Vertreter, Quellen und Motive des "ökumenischen" Gedankens von Erasmus von Rotterdam bis Georg Calixt.* Stuttgart.

Kenney, E. J. 1974. *The Classical Text: Aspects of Editing in the Age of the Printed Book.* Berkeley.

Kniha Belarusi 1517–1917. Zvodny kataloh. 1986. Minsk.

Kociuba, Ostap. 1975. "The Grammatical Sources of Meletij Smotryc̆kyj's Church Slavonic Grammar of 1619." Ph.D. diss. Columbia University.

Kojalovič, M.I. 1859. 1861. *Litovskaja cerkovnaja unija*. Vol. 1. Vol. 2. St. Petersburg.

————, ed. 1865. *Documents servant a éclaircir l'histoire des provinces occidentales de la Russie ainsi que leurs rapports avec la Russie et la Pologne*. St. Petersburg.

Kolosova, V.P. 1985. "Ideologičeskie predposylki dejatel'nosti Ostrožskogo kružka (Gerasim Smotrickij kak redaktor-polemist)." In *Fedorovskie čtenija 1981*, ed. E.L. Nemirovskij. Moscow.

Kolosova, V.P. and Krekoten', V.I., eds. 1978. *Ukrajins'ka poezija. Kinec' XVI–počatok XVII st*. Kiev.

Korduba, Miron. 1933. "Die Entstehung der ukrainischen Nation." In *Contributions a l'histoire de l'Ukraïne au VIIe Congrès International des Sciences Historiques*, pp. 19–67. L'viv.

Korotkyj, V. H. [Korotkij, V. G.] 1987. *Tvorčeskij put' Meletija Smotrickogo*. Minsk.

————. 1984. "Literaturna polemika Meletija Smotryc̆kogo v 20-ti roki XVII st." In *Ukrajins'ka literatura XVI–XVIII st. ta inši slov'jans'ki literatury*, ed. O.V. Myšanyč, pp. 117–36. Kiev.

Korowicki, I. 1935. Review of *Zbirnyk* (see Čubatyj above). *Elpis* 9.

Kortycki, Wojciech. 1634. *Widok Potyczki Wygraney, Zawodu dopędzonego, Wiary dotrzymaney. Od przewielebnego w Chrystusie Iego Mości Oyca Meletiusa Smotryskie[g]o, Archiepiskopa Hierapolitańskiego Archimandryty Dermańskiego, na iegoż pogrzebie*. Vilnius.

Kosman, Marceli. 1973. *Reformacja i kontrreformacja w Wielkim Księstwie Litewskim w świetle propagandy wyznaniowej*. Wrocław.

Kosov, Syl'vestr. 1635. *Exegesis, to iest danie sprawy o szkołach kiiowskich y winickich, w ktorych uczą zakonnicy Religiey Graeckiey*. Kiev. [Reprint: *Arxiv* 1914:422–47. I cite from the reprint.]

Kot, Stanisław. 1938. "Świadomość narodowa w Polsce XV–XVII." *Kwartalnik Historyczny* 52:15–33.

————. 1953. *La Réforme dans le Grand-Duché de Lithuanie. Facteur d'occidentalisation culturelle*. Brussels.

Krajcar, J. 1964. "The Ruthenian Patriarchate. Some Remarks on the Project for Its Establishment in the 17th Century." *Orientalia Christiana Periodica* 30:65–84.

Krevza, Lev. 1617. *Obrona iedności cerkiewney, Abo Dowody ktorymi się pokazuie, iż Grecka Cerkiew z Łacińską ma być ziednoczona*. Vilnius. [Reprint: *Lev Krevza's* Obrona iedności cerkiewney *and Zaxarija*

Kopystens'kyj's Palinodija, Omeljan Pritsak and Bohdan Struminsky, eds., Harvard Library of Early Ukrainian Literature, Texts, vol. 3, Cambridge, 1987.]

Kryp'jakevyč, Ivan P. 1913. "Novi materijaly do istoriji soboriv 1629 r." *Zapysky Naukovoho Tovarystva im. Ševčenka* 116. L'viv.

—————. 1966. "Do pytannja pro nacional'nu samosvidomist' ukrajins'koho narodu v kinci XVI ta počatku XVII st." *Ukrajins'kyj istoryčnyj žurnal* 2:82–84.

Krzyżanowski, Julian and Żukowska-Billip, Kazimiera, eds. 1960. *Dawna facecja polska (XVI–XVIII w.)* Warsaw.

Kułak, Kazimierz. 1984. *Psychologia nawrócenia z prawosławia na katolicyzm Melecjusza Smotryckiego, arcybiskupa ruskiego w Połocku na początku XVII w.* Białystok.

Lagrange, M.-J. 1934–1935. "La critique textuelle avant le Concile de Trente." *Revue Thomiste*, n.s. 17:400–409.

Lavrov, P.A. 1966. *Materialy po istorii vozniknovenija drevnejšej slavjanskoj pis'mennosti.* The Hague.

Legrand, Emile. 1896. *Bibliographie Hellénique ou description raisonnée des ouvrages publiés par des Grecs au dix-septième siècle.* Vol. 4. Paris.

Lentner, Leopold. 1964. *Volkssprache und Sakralsprache: Geschichte einer Lebensfrage bis zum Ende des Konzils von Trient.* Vienna. [=Wiener Beiträge zur Theologie. Vol. 5.]

Leopolita, Jan, transl. 1561. *Biblia To iest Księgi Stharego y Nowego Zakonu na Polski ięzyk, z pilnością według Łacińskiey Bibliey od Kościoła Krześciańskiego powszechnego przyięthey, nowo wyłożona.* Cracow.

—————, transl. 1988. *Biblia.* Paderborn [facsimile edition of Leopolita 1561].

Levi, Giovanni. 1991. "On Microhistory." In *New Perspectives on Historical Writing*, ed. Peter Burke, pp. 93–113. University Park, Pennsylvania.

Linde, M. Samuel Bogumił. 1854–1860. *Słownik języka polskiego.* 6 vols. L'viv. [1855=vol. 2; 1859=vol. 5; 1860=vol. 6 and addenda.]

Lipsius, Justus. 1610. *Politicorum, sive civilis doctrinae libri sex.* Antwerp.

List do zakonnikow monastera cerkwie ś. Ducha Wileńskiego, na ich przedmowę, w Werificatiey iakoby niewinności ich powtore wydaney położoną, odpisany. 1621. Vilnius. [Reprint: *Arxiv* 1914:732–61. I cite from the reprint. In-text reference, *Letter*.]

Lithos abo kamień z procy prawdy Cerkwie Świętey Prawosławney Ruskiey. 1644. Kiev. [Reprint: *Arxiv* 1893.]

Losievskij, I.Ja. 1986. "Biblioteka Meletija Smotrickogo." In *Pamjatniki kul'tury. Novye otkrytija. Pis'mennost', iskusstvo, arxeologija. Ežegodnik 1984*, pp. 87–96. Leningrad.

Lukaris, Cyril. 1974. *Sermons, 1598–1602.* Ed. Keetje Rozemond. Leiden. [=Byzantina Neerlandica. Vol. 4.]

Luther, Martin. 1911. *Werke. Kritische Gesamtausgabe.* Vol. 42. Weimar.

Makaruška, Ostap. 1908. *Hramatyka Meletija Smotryc'koho. Krytyčno-istoryčna studija.* L'viv.

Malcolm, Noel. 1984. *De Dominis (1560–1624): Venetian, Anglican, Ecumenist and Relapsed Heretic.* London.

Martel, Antoine. 1938. *La langue polonaise dans les pays Ruthènes: Ukraine et Russie Blanche, 1569–1657.* Lille. [=Travaux et mémoires de l'Université de Lille, nouvelle série, Droit et lettres, no. 20.]

Masini, Eliseo. 1665. *Sacro Arsenale ouero Prattica dell'Officio Della Santa Inquisitione. Nuouamente corretto, et ampliato.* Bologna.

Maslov, S. 1908. "Kazan'e M. Smotrickogo na čestnyj pogreb o. Leontija Karpoviča." *Čtenija v Istoričeskom obščestve Nestora-letopisca* 20 (3), pts. 2–3: 101–155.

Mathiesen, Robert C. 1981. "Two Contributions to the Bibliography of Meletij Smotryc'kyj." *Harvard Ukrainian Studies* 5:230–44.

Metzler, Joseph. 1971. "Foundation of the Congregation 'de Propaganda Fide' by Gregory XV." In *Sacrae Congregationis de Propaganda Fide Memoria Rerum.* Vol. I/1, *1622–1700*, pp. 79–111. Freiburg im Breisgau.

Mickiewicz, Adam. 1955. *Dzieła.* Vol. 6. *Pisma prozą, part II. Księgi narodu polskiego i pielgrzymstwa polskiego. Pisma polityczne z lat 1832–1835.* Warsaw.

Migne, J.P., ed. 1845. *Patrologiae cursus completus. Series Latina.* Vol. 33. Paris.

Moroxovs'kyj, Illja (Morochowski, Eliasz). 1612. ΠΑΡΗΓΟΡΙΑ *Albo Vtulenie vszczypliwego Lamentu mniemaney Cerkwie Świętey wschodniey zmyślonego Theophila Orthologa.* Vilnius.

Muir, Edward. 1991. "Introduction: Observing Trifles." In *Microhistory and the Lost Peoples of Europe,* ed. Edward Muir and Guido Ruggiero, pp. vii–xxviii. Baltimore, Maryland.

Mužylovs'kyj, Andrij (Mużyłowski, Andrzej). 1629. *Antidotum, Przezacnemv Narodowi Rvskiemv. Albo, Warvnek Przeciw Apologiey Iadem Napełnioney; ktorą wydał Melety Smotrzysky, niesłusznie Cerkiew Ruską prawosławną w niey pomawiaiąc Haeresią y Schismą, dla niektorych Scribentow. W porywczą przygotowany y podany.* Vilnius.

Myc'ko, I. Z. 1984. "Smotryc'kyj i misto Ostroh." *Zorja komunizmu* 83.

————. 1990. *Ostroz'ka slov'jano-hreko-latyns'ka akademija (1576–1636).* Kiev.

Nimčuk, V.V., ed. 1979. *Hramatyka M. Smotryc'koho.* Kiev.

————, ed. 1982. _Sxidn'o-slov'jans'ki hramatyky XVI–XVII st._ Kiev.

Oberman, Heiko. 1963. _The Harvest of Medieval Theology: Gabriel Biel and Late Medieval Nominalism._ Cambridge, Massachusetts.

Osinskij, A. 1911. "Meletij Smotrickij, arxiepiskop polockij." _Trudy Kievskoj duxovnoj akademii_, no. 7–8, pp. 425–66; no. 9, pp. 40–86; no. 10, pp. 275–300; no. 11, pp. 405–432; no. 12, pp. 605–619.

"Pamflet na Meletija Smotrickago". 1875. Ed. S. Golubev. _Kievskie eparxial'nye vedomosti_ 17 (2): 556–67.

Patterson, W.B. 1978. "The Peregrinations of Marco Antonio De Dominis." In _Religious Motivation: Biographical and Sociological Problems for the Church Historian_, ed. Derek Baker, pp. 241–57. Oxford. [=Studies in Church History. Vol. 15.]

Pelikan, Jaroslav. 1984. _The Christian Tradition. A History of the Development of Doctrine._ Vol. 4, _Reformation of Church and Dogma (1300–1700)._ Chicago.

Petrov, N. I. 1879. "Spletskij arxiepiskop Mark Antonij de Dominis i ego značenie v južno-russkoj polemičeskoj literature XVII veka." _Trudy Kievskoj duxovnoj akademii_ 20 (2): 204–227; (3): 332–55.

Petruševič, A. 1874. _Svodnaja galicko-russkaja letopis' 1600–1700 gg._ L'viv.

Pfeiffer, Rudolf. 1976. _History of Classical Scholarship from 1300–1850._ Oxford.

Picchio, Riccardo. 1962a. "Die historisch-philologische Bedeutung der kirchenslavische Tradition." _Die Welt der Slaven_ 7:1–27.

————. 1962b. "O cerkiewnosłowiańskiej wspólnocie kulturalno-językowej." _Sprawozdania z Posiedzeń Komisji Oddziału Polskiej Akademii Nauk w Krakowie_, pp. 449–54. Cracow.

————. 1963. "A proposita della Slavia ortodossa e della comunità linguistica slava ecclesiastica." _Ricerche Slavistiche_ 11:105–127.

————. 1982. "VC and VM's Pauline Connotations of Cyril and Methodius' Apostleship." _Palaeobulgarica_ 6 (3): 112–18.

Pobihuščyj, Bohdan. 1934. "Meletij Smotryc'kyj jak polemist." In _Zbirnyk prysvjačenyj svitlij pamjati Meletija Smotryc'koho z nahody trysotnix rokovyn smerty_, ed. Mykola Čubatyj, pp. 38–48. L'viv. [=Arxiv Seminara Istoriji Cerkvy pry Hrekokatolyc'kij Bohoslovs'kij Akademiji u L'vovi. Vol. 1.]

Podskalsky, Gerhard. 1982. _Christentum und theologische literatur in der Kiever Rus' (988–1237)._ Munich.

————. 1988. _Griechische Theologie in der Zeit der Türkenherrschaft (1453–1821). Die Orthodoxie im Spannungsfeld der nachreformatorischen Konfessionen des Westens._ Munich.

Polnoe sobranie russkix letopisej. 1975. Vol. 32. Moscow.

Poplatek, Jan. 1950. "Obecny stan badań nad życiem ks. Jakuba Wujka i program dalszej pracy." *Polonia Sacra* 3:20–65.

Popov, P. 1928. "Do ikonohrafiji pys'mennykiv XVII v. Meletija Smotryc'koho ta Josypa Veljamyna-Ruts'koho." In *Juvilejnyj zbirnyk na pošanu akademyka Myxajla Serhijevyča Hruševs'koho,* vol. 1. Kiev.

Prete, Sesto. 1965. "Die Leistungen der Humanisten auf dem Gebiete der lateinischen Philologie." *Philologus* 109:259–69.

—————. 1969. *Observations on the History of Textual Criticism in the Medieval and Renaissance Periods.* Collegeville, Minnesota.

Preus, R. 1955. *The Inspiration of Scripture.* Edinburgh.

Prochaska, Antoni. 1927. *Hetman Stanisław Żółkiewski.* Warsaw.

Prokošina, E.S. 1966. *Meletij Smotrickij.* Minsk.

Pugh, Stefan M. 1985. "The Ruthenian Language of Meletij Smotryc'kyj: Phonology." *Harvard Ukrainian Studies* 9:53–60.

—————. 1987. "Omega in the East Slavonic Orthographic Tradition." *Slavonic and East European Review* 65:1–12.

Redondi, Pietro. 1987. *Galileo Heretic.* Princeton.

Reynolds, L. D. and N. G. Wilson. 1974. *Scribes and Scholars: A Guide to the Transmission of Greek and Latin Literature.* Oxford.

Rice, Eugene F., Jr. 1985. *Saint Jerome in the Renaissance.* Baltimore, Maryland.

Sabol, S. S. 1951. *Meletij Smotryckyj Polemista Anticatholico.* Rome.

Sakovyč, Kasijan (Sakowicz, Kasjan). 1641. *Sobor Kiiowski schismaticki.* Warsaw. [Reprint: Gil'tebrandt 1878:21–48.]

Saunders, Jason Lewis. 1955. *Justus Lipsius: The Philosophy of Renaissance Stoicism.* New York.

Scepuro, D. 1898–1899, "Vilenskoe sv.-duxovskoe bratstvo v XVII i XVIII stoletijax." *Trudy Kievskoj duxovnoj akademii* 1898 (9): 75–96, (11): 345–73; 1899 (4): 546–77, (6): 225–62, (8): 523–63, (9): 38–52.

Schaff, Philip. 1877. *The Creeds of Christendom.* Vol. 3. New York.

—————, ed. 1956. *A Select Library of the Nicene and Post-Nicene Fathers of the Christian Church.* Vol. 4. Grand Rapids, Michigan.

Schütte, Josef Franz. 1980. *Valignano's Mission Principles for Japan.* St. Louis, Missouri.

Šeptyc'kyj, A., ed. 1965. 1971. 1974. *Monumenta Ucrainae historica.* Vol. 2. Vols. 9–10. Vol. 11. Rome.

Shevelov, George, Y. 1975. "On Lexical Polonisms in Literary Ukrainian." In *For Wiktor Weintraub. Essays in Polish Literature, Language, and History Presented on the Occasion of his 65th Birthday*, ed. Victor Erlich, Roman Jakobson, Czesław Miłosz, Riccardo Picchio, Alexander M. Schenker, Edward Stankiewicz, pp. 449–64. The Hague.

Siarczyński, F. 1828. *Obraz wieku panowania Zygmunta III*. Vol. 2. L'viv.

Sjöberg, Anders. 1966. "Two Unknown Translations of Smotrickij's Slavonic Grammar." *Scando-Slavica* 12:123–31.

Skarga, Piotr. 1610. *Na Treny y Lament Theophila Orthologa, Do Rusi Greckiego Nabożeństwa, Przestroga*. Cracow. [In-text reference, *Admonition*.]

Smotryc'kyj, Meletij. 1610. ΘΡΗΝΟΣ *To iest Lament iedyney ś. Powszechney Apostolskiey Wschodniey Cerkwie*. Vilnius. [Facsimile edition: Smotryc'kyj 1987a:1–235; in-text reference, *Thrēnos*.]

———. 1616. *Єѵангеліє учителноє*. Vievis. [Facsimile edition: Smotryc'kyj 1987b; in-text reference, *Homiliary Gospel*.]

———. 1618. *ГРАММАТІКН Славенскиѧ правилноє Сѵнтаґма*. Vievis. [Facsimile edition: Nimčuk 1979; in-text reference, *Church Slavonic grammar*.]

———. 1620. *Казанье: На честный Погреб пречестного и превелебного Мужа Г[о]с[по]д[и]на и Отца: Г[о]с[по]д[и]на Отца Леонтія Карповича*. Vilnius. [Reprint: Maslov 1907; in-text references, *Kazan'e*, *Sermon*.]

———. 1621a. *Kazanie: Na znamienity Pogrzeb przezacnego y przewielebnego Męża, Pana y Oyca: Leontego Karpowicza*. Vilnius. [Facsimile edition: Smotryc'kyj 1987a:236–64.]

———. 1621b. *Verificatia niewinności*. Vilnius. [Facsimile edition: Smotryc'kyj 1987a:313–98; in-text reference, *Verification of Innocence*.]

———. 1621c. *Obrona verificaciey*. Vilnius. [Facsimile edition: Smotryc'kyj 1987a:399–462; in-text reference, *Defense of the Verification*.]

———. 1622. *Elenchvs pism vszczypliwych*. Vilnius. [Facsimile edition: Smotryc'kyj 1987a:463–513; in-text reference, *Elenchus*.]

———. 1623. *Ivstificacia niewinności*. Vilnius (?). [Reprint: *Arxiv* 1887:511–32; in-text reference, *Justification of Innocence*. I cite from the reprint.]

———. 1628a. *Apologia peregrinatiey do Kraiow Wschodnych*. L'viv. [Facsimile edition: Smotryc'kyj 1987a:514–625; in-text reference, *Apology*.]

———. 1628b. *Protestatia Przeciwo Soborowi w tym Roku 1628. we dni Augusta Miesiąca, w Kiiowie Monasteru Pieczerskim obchodzonemu, vczyniona przez vkrzywdzonego na nim*. L'viv. [Facsimile edition: Smotryc'kyj 1987a:627–42; in-text reference, *Protestation*.]

―――――. 1629a. *Paraenesis abo Napomnienie*. Cracow. [Facsimile edition: Smotryc'kyj 1987a:643–94; in-text reference, *Paraenesis*.]

―――――. 1629b. *Exęthesis abo Expostvlatia*. L'viv. [Facsimile edition: Smotryc'kyj 1987a:695–805; in-text reference, *Exaethesis*.]

―――――. 1974. *Грамматики Славенския правилное Синтагма*. Ed. Olexa Horbatsch. Munich. [=Specimena Philologiae Slavicae 4.]

―――――. 1987a. *Collected Works of Meletij Smotryc'kyj*. Cambridge, Massachusetts. [=Harvard Library of Early Ukrainian Literature, Texts, vol. 1.]

―――――. 1987b. *The 'Jevanhelije učytelnoje' of Meletij Smotryc'kyj*. Cambridge, Massachusetts. [=Harvard Library of Early Ukrainian Literature, Texts, vol. 2.]

Šmurlo, E. 1928. *Le Saint-Siège et l'Orient Orthodoxe Russe 1609–1654*. Prague.

―――――. 1932. "Meletij Smotrickij v ego snošenijax s Rimom." In *Trudy V-go S''ezda russkix akademičeskix organizacij za granicej v Sofii 14–21 sentjabrja 1930 goda*. Part 1, pp. 501–529. Sofia.

Solovij, Meletij M. 1977. 1978. *Meletij Smotryc'kyj jak pys'mennyk*. 2 vols. Rome-Toronto.

Sowita Wina. To iest Odpis na script, Maiestat Krola Iego Mości honor y reputatią Ludzi Zacnych Duchownych y Świeckich obrażaiący, nazwany, Verificatia Niewinności. 1621. Vilnius. [Reprint: *Arxiv* 1887:443–510.]

Stebel's'kyj (Stebelski), I. 1782. *Dwa wielkie światła na horyzoncie Połockim z cieniów zakonnych powstające*. Vilnius.

Studyns'kyj, Kyrylo. 1906. *Pam'jatky polemičnoho pys'menstva kincja XVI i poč. XVII v.* Vol. 1. *Pam'jatky ukrajins'ko-rus'koji movy i literatury*. Arxeohrafična komisija Naukovoho Tovarystva im. Ševčenka. Vol. 5. L'viv.

―――――. "*Αντιγραφή*, polemičnyj tvir Maksyma (Meletija) Smotryc'koho z 1608 r." *Zapysky Naukovoho Tovarystva im. Ševčenka* 141–43:1–40.

Suárez, Francisco. 1859. *Opera omnia*. Vol. 14. Paris.

Subbotin, N. 1876. 1878a. 1878b. 1881. 1885. *Materijaly dlja istorii raskola za pervoe vremja ego suščestvovanija*. Vol. 2. Vol. 3. Vol. 4. Vol. 6. Vol. 7. Moscow.

Suša, Jakiv (Susza, Jakub). 1665. *Cursus vitae et certamen martyrii, B. Iosaphat Kuncevicii, Archiepiscopi Polocensis Episcopi Vitepscensis et Miscislauien*sis. Rome.

―――――. 1666. *Saulus et Paulus Ruthenae unionis sanguine B. Josaphat transformatus. Sive Meletius Smotriscius archiepiscopus polocensis*. Rome.

Sutcliff, E. F. 1948. "The Council of Trent on the *Authentia* of the Vulgate."
Journal of Theological Studies 49:35–42.

Sykes, Norman. 1978. "The Religion of Protestants." In *The West from the
Reformation to the Present Day*, ed. S.L. Greenslade, pp. 175–98.
Cambridge. [=*The Cambridge History of the Bible.* Vol. 3.]

Symanowicz, Tymoteusz. 1621. *Proba Verificatiey Omylnej. Y Dowod
swowoleństwa małosłychanego Czerńcow, y Iednomyślnych Bratctwa
Wileńskiego. Chrześciańskiem Katholickiem vwaźeniem.* Zamość.

*Synopsis, albo krotkie spisanie praw, przywileiow, świebod y wolności od
naiaśnieyszych św. pamięci Krolow Ich Miłości Polskich, y Wielkich Xiążąt
W.X.L. y Ruskiego, et caet., et caet. Przezacnemu starowiecznemu narodowi
Ruskiemu, pod posłuszeństwem św. Oyca Patriarchy Konstantinopolskiego
stale y nieodmiennie od okrzczenia się swoiego trwaiącemu nadanych y
poprzysiężonych.* 1632. Vilnius. [Reprint: *Arxiv* 1887:533–76. I cite from
the reprint.]

Sysyn, Frank E. 1980. "Ukrainian-Polish Relations in the Seventeenth Century:
The Role of National Consciousness and National Conflict in the
Khmelnytsky Movement." In *Poland and Ukraine: Past and Present*, ed.
Peter Potichnyj, pp. 58–82. Toronto.

————. 1981. "Seventeenth-Century Views on the Causes of the
Khmel'nyts'kyi Uprising: An Examination of the 'Discourse on the Present
Cossack or Peasant War'." *Harvard Ukrainian Studies* 5:430–66.

————. 1985. *Between Poland and the Ukraine: The Dilemma of Adam
Kysil, 1600–1653.* Cambridge, Massachusetts.

————. 1986a. "The Cultural, Social and Political Context of Ukrainian
History-Writing: 1620–1690." *Europa Orientalis* 5:285–310.

————. 1986b. "Concepts of Nationhood in Ukrainian History Writing,
1620–1690." *Harvard Ukrainian Studies* 10:393–423.

————. 1990. "The Cossack Chronicles and the Development of Modern
Ukrainian Culture and National Identity." *Harvard Ukrainian Studies*
14:593–607.

Szczucki, Lech. 1964. *Marcin Czechowic (1532–1613). Studium z dziejów
antytrynityzmu polskiego XVI wieku.* Warsaw.

Tazbir, Janusz. 1971. "Świadomość narodowa." In *Rzeczpospolita i świat.
Studia z dziejów kultury XVII wieku.* Wrocław, pp. 23–43.

————. 1978. "Świadomość narodowa szlachty." In his *Kultura szlachecka
w Polsce. Rozkwit—upadek—relikty*, pp. 89–108. Warsaw.

————. "Polish National Consciousness in the Sixteenth to the Eighteenth
Century." *Harvard Ukrainian Studies* 10:316–335.

Timpanaro, Sebastiano. 1981. *La genesi del metodo del Lachmann.* Padua.

Titov, Xv. 1924. *Materijaly dlja istoriji knyžnoji spravy na Vkrajini v XVI–XVIII vv. Vsezbirka peredmov do ukrajins'kyx starodrukiv.* Ukrajins'ka Akademija Nauk. Zbirnyk Istoryčno-Filolohičnoho Viddilu, No. 17. Kiev. [Facsimile edition, with an introduction by Hans Rothe, Bausteine zur Geschichte der Literatur bei den Slaven, vol. 16, Cologne, 1982.]

Trevor-Roper, Hugh. 1978. "The Church of England and the Greek Church in the Time of Charles I." In *Religious Motivation: Biographical and Sociological Problems for the Church Historian,* ed. Derek Baker, pp. 213–40. Oxford. [=Studies in Church History. Vol. 15.]

Trinkaus, Charles. 1970. "Italian Humanism and the Scriptures." In *In Our Image and Likeness.* Vol. 2, 563–614. Chicago.

Urban, Wincenty. 1957. "Konwersja Melecjusza Smotrzyskiego, polemisty i dyzunickiego arcybiskupa połockiego w latach 1620–27." *Nasza Przeszłość* 5:133–216.

Urbańczyk, Stanisław. 1983. "Uwagi o polszczyźnie Melecjusza Smotryckiego." In *Studien zu Literatur und Kultur in Osteuropa. Bonner Beiträge zum 9. Internationalen Slawistenkongreß in Kiew,* ed. Hans-Bernd Harder and Hans Rothe, pp. 371–80. Cologne. [=Bausteine zur Geschichte der Literatur bei den Slaven. Vol. 18.]

Velykyj, Athanasius, ed. 1952. 1955. 1967. *S. Josaphat Hieromartyr documenta Romana beatificationis et canonizationis.* Vol. 1, *1623–1628.* Vol. 2, *1628–1637.* Vol. 3, *1637–1867.* Rome. [=Analecta Ordinis Sancti Basilii Magni, Series II, Sectio III, Documenta Romana Ecclesiae Catholicae in Terris Ucrainae et Bielarusjae.]

————, ed. 1953a. *Acta Sanctae Congregationis de Propaganda Fide Ecclesiam Catholicam Ucrainae et Bielarusjae spectantia.* Vol. 1, *1622–1667.* Rome. [=Analecta Ordinis Sancti Basilii Magni, Series II, Sectio III, Documenta Romana Ecclesiae Catholicae in Terris Ucrainae et Bielarusjae.]

————, ed. 1953b. *Documenta Pontificum Romanorum historiam Ucrainae illustrantia (1075–1953).* Vol. 1, *1075–1700.* Rome. [=Analecta Ordinis Sancti Basilii Magni, Series II, Sectio III, Documenta Romana Ecclesiae Catholicae in Terris Ucrainae et Bielarusjae.]

————, ed. 1956a. *Epistolae Josephi Velamin Rutskyj Metropolitae Kioviensis Catholici (1613–1637).* Rome. [=Analecta Ordinis Sancti Basilii Magni, Series II, Sectio III, Documenta Romana Ecclesiae Catholicae in Terris Ucrainae et Bielarusjae.]

————, ed. 1956b. *Epistolae metropolitarum Kioviensium Catholicorum: Raphaelis Korsak, Antonii Sielava, Gabrielis Kolenda (1637–1674).* Rome. [=Analecta Ordinis Sancti Basilii Magni, Series II, Sectio III, Documenta Romana Ecclesiae Catholicae in Terris Ucrainae et Bielarusjae.]

————, ed. 1959. 1960. 1961. *Litterae nuntiorum apostolicorum historiam Ucrainae illustrantes (1550–1850).* Vol. III, *1609–1620.* Vol. IV, *1621–1628.* Vol. V, *1629–38.* Rome. [=Analecta Ordinis Sancti Basilii Magni,

Series II, Sectio III, Documenta Romana Ecclesiae Catholicae in Terris Ucrainae et Bielarusjae.]

————, ed. 1972. *Litterae episcoporum historiam Ucrainae illustrantes (1600–1900)*. Vol. I, *1600–1640*. Rome. [=Analecta Ordinis Sancti Basilii Magni, Series II, Sectio III, Documenta Romana Ecclesiae Catholicae in Terris Ucrainae et Bielarusjae.]

Vosté, G.-M. 1946. "La Volgata al Concilio di Trento." *Biblica* 27:301–319.

Waczyński, Bogusław. 1937. "Codex autographus Maximi Smotrycki." *Orientalia Christiana Periodica* 3:665–669.

————. 1949. "Czy Antigrafe jest dziełem Maksyma (Melecjusza) Smotryckiego?" *Roczniki Teologiczne-Kanoniczne*.

Waszink, J. H. 1975. "Osservazioni sui fondamenti della critica testuale." *Quaderni urbinati di cultura classica* 19:7–21.

Węgierski, Andrzej. 1679. *Libri Quattuor Slavoniae Reformatae*. Amsterdam. [Facsimile edition, with an introduction by Janusz Tazbir: *Biblioteka Pisarzy Reformacyjnych*, no. 11, Warsaw, 1973.]

Weingart, M. 1923. "Dobrovského *Institutiones*. Part 1. Církevněslovanské mluvnice před Dobrovským." *Sborník filosofické fakulty University Komenského v Bratislavě* 1, no. 16:637–95.

Wiszniewski, Michał. 1851. *Historya literatury polskiej*. Vol. 8. Cracow.

Woysznarowicz, Kazimierz Jan. 1647. *Krwawa Chrystusowa winnica Abo Kazanie O Błogosławionym Iozaphacie Kvncewiczu, Archiepiskopie Połockim, Władyce Witepskim, Mścisławskim, etc. etc.* Cracow.

Wujek, Jakub, transl. 1593. *Nowy Testament Pana naszego Iesvsa Christvsa. Znowu z Łacińskiego y z Greckiego na Polskie wiernie a szczyrze przełożony: y Argumentami abo Summariuszami każdych Ksiąg, y Rozdziałow, y Annotacyami po brzegach obiaśniony. Przydane są Nauki y Przestrogi mało nie za każdym Rozdziałem: Porownanie Ewangelistow ŚŚ. Dzieie y drogi rozmaite Piotra y Pawła Ś. y Regestr rzeczy głownieyszych na końcu. Przez D. Iakuba Wujka*. Cracow.

————, transl. 1599. *Biblia To iest Księgi Starego y Nowego Testamentv, według Łacińskiego przekładu starego, w kościele powszechnym przyiętego, na Polski ięzyk znowu z pilnością przełożone z dokładaniem textu Żydowskiego y Greckiego, y z wykładem Katholickim, trudnieyszych mieysc, do obrony Wiary świętey powszechney przeciw kacerztwom tych czasów należących*. Cracow.

Xarlampovič, K. V. 1914. *Malorossijskoe vlijanie na velikorusskuju cerkovnuju žizn'*. Vol. 1. Kazan'.

Xoma, Ivan. 1973. "Ideja spiľnoho synodu 1629 r." *Bohoslovija* 37:20–64.

————. 1974. "Dejaki z peršyx instrukcij Kongregaciji Pošyrennja Viry vidnosno Cerkvy na Rusi-Ukrajini." *Bohoslavija* 38:93–121.

Zagorin, Perez. 1990. *Ways of Lying: Dissimulation, Persecution, and Conformity in Early Modern Europe*. Cambridge, Massachusetts.

Zapasko, Jakym and Isajevyč, Jaroslav. 1981. *Pamjatky knyžkovoho mystectva. Kataloh starodrukiv, vydanyx na Ukrajini. Knyha perša (1574–1700)*. Kiev.

Zasadkevič, N. 1883. *Meletij Smotrickij kak filolog*. Odessa.

Žukovič, P. 1905. "Pervyj poľskij sejm posle vozstanovlenija pat. Feofanom pravoslavonoj cerkovnoj ierarxii." *Xristianskoe čtenie* 85 (Nov.): 580–97, (Dec.): 723–47.

————. 1906. "Arxiepiskop Meletij Smotrickij v Vilne v pervye mesjacy posle svoej xirotonii." *Xristianskoe čtenie* 86 (April): 533–51, (May): 697–715, (June): 858–77.

————. 1907. "Ubijstvo Iosafata Kunceviča." *Xristianskoe čtenie* 87 (Sept.): 277–312.

————. 1908a. "Pervyj poľskij sejm posle ubijstva Iosafata Kunceviča." *Xristianskoe čtenie* 88 (Jan.): 27–41, (March): 385–401.

————. 1908b. "Novye materialy dlja načaľnoj istorii sejmovoj borby s cerkvonoj uniej." *Xristianskoe čtenie* 88 (June–July): 852–79.

————. 1910. "Vopros o primirenii pravoslavnyx s uniatami na Varšavskom sejme 1629 goda." *Xristianskoe čtenie* 110 (Sept.): 1122–35, (Oct.): 1233–48.

————. 1911a. "Kievskij sobor 1629 goda (po novym materialam)." *Xristianskoe čtenie* 111 (Jan.): 74–92, (March): 353–69.

————. 1911b. "Ľvovskij sobor 1629 goda v svjazi s političeskimi obstojateľstvami vremeni." *Xristianskoe čtenie* 111 (May–June): 661–84.

Žuraŭski, A. I. 1958. "Da pytannja ab roli carkoŭnaslavjanskaj movy ŭ razvicci belaruskaj literaturnaj movy XVI st." *Matèryjaly da IV Mižnarodnaha z'ezda slavistaŭ*, 51–66. Minsk.

Żychiewicz, Tadeusz. 1986. *Jozafat Kuncewicz*. Kalwaria Zebrzydowska.

Index

Note on usage. The following italicized abbreviations are used to indicate variant language spellings or forms of names where they might be helpful: *B* Belarusian, *I* Italian, *L* Latin, *P* Polish, *R* Russian, *U* Ukrainian. Both the respective church and position within that church (relative to the period under discussion in the text) have been included for ecclesiastical figures.

Smotryc'kyj, Meletij (con't)
and Council of Trent 202–203, 210
and Cyril Lukaris. *See* Lukaris, Cyril
and Cyrillo-Methodian tradition
113–15
and de Dominis. *See* de Dominis,
Marcantonio
death 6, 107, 158, 160, 162–69
passim, 260
and death of Josafat Kuncevyč 7, 79,
86, 88, 89–90, 93–94, 95, 98,
102–103, 104–108, 109, 147, 167,
248
and Derman' Monastery 5, 7, 10, 11,
46, 71, 87, 100, 104, 109, 110,
112, 116, 118, 124, 125, 126, 130,
131, 140, 141, 145, 149, 155, 160,
163
and dissimulation. *See ars
dissimulandi*
in the East and the Holy Land xii,
88, 89–101 passim, 103, 112, 231,
248
editorial activity 59, 61
education xii, 9, 22–23, 28, 31–37
passim, 50, 51, 53, 63, 64, 105,
153, 154, 200, 202, 244, 247,
249–50
ecumenicism 65, 156, 213–17, 220–
21, 224–26, 250, 255–57
faith and confession 61–63, 65–66,
98, 108, 109, 110, 111, 116, 117,
118, 119, 120, 123, 126, 130,
137–40 passim, 143, 144, 145,
154, 155, 159, 161, 169, 174,
175–76, 177, 178–79, 202, 204,
206–207, 209, 210, 216–17, 218,
220–23, 224, 225–26, 227–29,
244–45, 247. *See also above*
catechism and confession of Rus'
family xi, 23–24, 31
and the *Filioque* 62, 65-66, 73, 209,
214, 217–18
and the fire of Purgatory 197, 198
in Germany xii, 30–31, 32, 33, 34,
35, 36–37, 56, 57, 60, 63, 89, 108,
248, 249
Hierapolis, Uniate Archbishop of 5,
124, 147, 150–52, 155, 158, 160,
164, 165, 166

and the Holy Office 119, 120, 121,
148, 151, 153, 154, 173, 174, 202
humor 189–91
and the Jesuits xii, 30–31, 32, 33,
34, 35, 37, 173, 203, 224, 225,
247, 249
as Judas figure 102, 110, 155
language use and literary style xii,
xiii–xiv, 45, 47–48, 50, 53–54,
120, 121, 154, 156, 181–205,
231–34, 238, 252
legal actions against 26, 77–79, 80
and L'viv Brotherhood. *See* L'viv
(brotherhood)
miracles. *See below* posthumous
miracles
monastic life 23, 25, 35, 56, 57, 58,
60, 61, 64, 68, 69, 71, 73, 75, 81,
83, 87, 111, 116, 158, 160, 163,
248, 255
names 24–25, 58, 77
and Orthodox brotherhoods. *See* city
of specific brotherhood
and Orthodoxy 61, 63, 117, 119,
120, 121, 122, 124, 126, 130, 131,
134, 137–38, 139, 145, 149, 156,
177, 202, 204, 206–208, 220,
221–23, 239
patriarchal exarch 99–100
personal characteristics 1, 4–5, 7, 8,
9, 10, 12–13, 14, 15–16, 30, 72,
78, 80, 82–83, 84, 99, 109–110,
140–41, 211, 247–48
Polack (*P* Połock, *U* Poloc'k),
Orthodox Archbishop of xii, 1, 8,
10, 11, 17, 25, 26, 37, 39, 56, 61,
71, 75–88, 90, 96, 98, 103, 104,
105, 106, 107, 111, 112–13, 134,
140, 141, 142, 145, 147–48, 150,
151, 152, 157, 165, 167, 239, 248,
255, 260
posthumous miracles 108, 109, 158–
169 passim
preacher 54, 58, 61, 88
and procession of the Holy Spirit 45,
62, 63, 71–72, 73, 217
and *Propaganda Fide* xii, 54, 119,
120, 142–46 passim, 148, 149–50,
151, 152–53, 164, 165, 167, 173,
206

 Ukrainian Research Institute
Harvard University
Publications Office

Titles Relating to the Union of Brest and Other Studies of that Period

Gudziak, Borys. *Crisis and Reform: The Kievan Metropolitanate, the Patriarchate of Constantinople, and the Genesis of the Union of Brest.* Harvard Series in Ukrainian Studies. Forthcoming. Hardcover, ISBN 0-916458-74-1; Paperback, ISBN 0-916458-80-6.

Pugh, Stefan. *Testament to Ruthenian: A Linguistic Analysis of the Smotryc'kyj Variant.* Harvard Series in Ukrainian Studies. Forthcoming. Hardcover, ISBN 0-916458-75-X; Softcover, ISBN 0-916458-46-6.

Lev Krevza's Defense of Church Unity *(1617) and Zaxarija Kopystens'kyj's* Palinodija or Book of Defense of the Holy Apostolic Eastern Catholic Church and Holy Patriarchs *(1620–1623).* Translated and with an Introduction by Bohdan Strumiński. Edited by Roman R. Koropeckyj, Dana R. Miller, with William R. Veder. Harvard Library of Early Ukrainian Literature, English Translation Series, vol. 3, parts 1 and 2. Forthcoming. Hardcover, ISBN 0-916458-29-6.

The Collected Works of Meletij Smotryc'kyj. Introduction by David A. Frick. Harvard Library of Early Ukrainian Literature, Texts and Facsimiles, vol. I. Hardcover, ISBN 0-916458-20-2.

The Jevanhelije učytelnoje *of Meletij Smotryc'kyj.* Introduction by David A. Frick. Harvard Library of Early Ukrainian Literature, Texts and Facsimiles, vol. II. Hardcover, ISBN 0-916458-21-0.

Lev Krevza's Obrona iednosci cerkiewney *and Zaxarija Kopystens'kyj's* Palinodija. Introduction by Omeljan Pritsak and Bohdan Struminsky. Harvard Library of Early Ukrainian Literature, Texts and Facsimiles, vol. III. Hardcover, ISBN 0-916458-22-9.

Sysyn, Frank. *Between Poland and the Ukraine: The Dilemma of Adam Kysil, 1600–1653.* Harvard Series in Ukrainian Studies. Hardcover, ISBN 0-916458-08-3.

Struminsky, Bohdan. *Pseudo-Meleško: A Ukrainian Apocryphal Speech of 1615–1618.* Harvard Series in Ukrainian Studies. Hardcover, ISBN 0-916458-11-3.

For further information on ordering or for Institute publications catalogues:

Ukrainian Research Institute, Harvard University
Publications Office, Rm. 209
1583 Massachusetts Ave.
Cambridge, MA 02138
tel. 617-495-3692 / fax 617-495-8097